Ron Magagu
January 1989

THE
CAKE
BIBLE

ALSO BY ROSE LEVY BERANBAUM

Romantic and Classic Cakes
(Irena Chalmers, 1981)

THE
CAKE
BIBLE

ROSE LEVY
BERANBAUM

Edited by Maria D. Guarnaschelli
Photographs by Vincent Lee
Book design by Richard Oriolo
Food styling by Rose Levy Beranbaum
Line drawings by Dean Bornstein
Foreword by Maida Heatter

WILLIAM MORROW
AND COMPANY, INC.
NEW YORK

PHOTO CREDITS

Over the years, both Vincent Lee and I have been collecting the many beautiful plates, serving pieces, and linen shown in these photographs. I'd like to express special gratitude to my friends for generously offering me some of their treasures with which to enhance my cakes.

NANCY BLITZER
Georgian sterling-silver plate (Black Forest Cake)
Victorian tablecloth (Swan Lake)
antique tablecloth (Perfect All-American Chocolate Butter Cake with Burnt Orange Silk Meringue Buttercream)
Crown Derby dessert plate (Orange Chocolate Crown)
cut-crystal sauce bowl (Scarlet Empress)

CHELSEA PASSAGE AT BARNEYS
antique lace cloth (White Lilac Nostalgia Cake)

DEAN & DELUCA
porcelain Pillivuyt cake plate (Guilt-Free Chocolate Chiffon Cake and Cordon Rose Banana Cake with Sour Cream Ganache)

JUDI ELKINS
glass cake stand (Golden Cage)
lace tablecloth (La Porcelaine)
purple cake plate and vase (White Lilac Nostalgia)
Art Deco plate (Art Deco Cake)

FORTUNOFF
sterling-silver oval platter with gadroon edge (Swan Lake)

ROYAL COPENHAGEN PORCELAIN CORP., N.Y.
Georg Jensen blossom pattern pastry fork (A Taste of Heaven)

MCNULTY'S TEA AND COFFEE COMPANY, NYC
coffee beans (All-Occasion Downy Yellow Butter Cake with Classic Coffee Buttercream)

MUMM
Cordon Rosé champagne (Rose Trellis)

ROMANOFF CAVIAR
beluga caviar (Best Buckwheat Blini La Tulipe)

DAVID SHAMAH
Andrée Putman demitasse cup and saucer (Art Deco Cake)

WILLIAM EMANUEL SONNENREICH
special effects (Star-Spangled Rhapsody Cake)

TYSON OF LES FLEURS
exotic pineapple crown (Baked Hawaii)

Library of Congress Cataloging-in-Publication Data

Beranbaum, Rose Levy.
The Cake Bible / Rose Levy Beranbaum; edited by Maria D. Guarnaschelli; photographs by Vincent Lee; line drawings by Dean Bornstein; food styling by Rose Levy Beranbaum; foreword by Maida Heatter.
p. cm.
Includes index.
ISBN 0-688-04402-6
1. Cake. I. Guarnaschelli, Maria. II. Lee, Vincent. III. Oriolo, Richard. IV. Title.
TX771.B458   1988
641.8′653—dc19   88-1369
                                                      CIP

Printed in the United States of America

4 5 6 7 8 9 10

BOOK DESIGN BY RICHARD ORIOLO

Foreword

*R*ose Levy Beranbaum has an amazing ability to learn everything there is to know about a recipe, and then to teach it carefully to her readers. She was born to teach. Her patience is extraordinary. She writes with loving care and attention. She tells you not only "how," but "why." If you ever bake a cake, or if you always bake cakes—professionally or not—this book will become your partner in the kitchen.

Although many of the cakes have names that you will recognize, all through the book you will come across new ways of doing things. I am intrigued by the technique for putting together a butter cake. The dry ingredients are mixed in a bowl, then the butter and the liquids are added (just the reverse of starting by beating or creaming the butter). It is quick and easy—and the results are delicious.

The first cakes I made from this book were simple little butter cakes made in loaf pans. They were Lemon Poppy Seed Pound Cake and White Spice Pound Cake. I simply followed the meticulously complete instructions—and had great fun while doing it. When I served the cakes to two European-trained pastry chefs who are friends of ours, they liked them so much they wanted the recipes.

Then (using the same technique) I made the Chocolate Domingo Cake, about which Rose says, "The most intense, round, full, chocolate flavor of any. . . ." How could I resist? It is wonderful—and it is quick and easy. It is a round cake that does not have any icing—it doesn't need any.

Making yeast doughs can be one of the most absorbing and gratifying—and addictive—techniques of all baking. When I read the recipe for Rose's Holiday Hallelujah Streusel Brioche I knew it would not be long before I tried it. Actually, I waited only a few minutes. As with the other recipes I made, I felt Rose guiding me every step of the way. And then, "hallelujah" to be sure. It is as pretty as a picture. It can be made ahead and frozen. As Rose says, "It is guaranteed to become one of your favorites."

Many of us have pet peeves in the kitchen; things we would rather not have to do. I have only a few. One procedure I have always disliked is sifting or straining cocoa. I usually have to spend more time cleaning up after it than actually doing it. In this book I read a tip about processing it in the food processor to get the same results as straining. I tried it. It is a pleasure. I'll never do it any other way from now on.

Rose developed a trick for making real old-fashioned whipping cream that has enough fat content when the only kind you can buy has a low fat content. And she lets you in on a secret for making whipped cream that will hold up for six hours without separating, even at room temperature.

It was difficult not to spend all my time making one after another of these cakes. They all cry out, "Make me." It is seldom that I really want to make every single recipe from cover to cover in a book. I do in this book.

This is a grand, encyclopedic collection of cakes and everything related to them—crystallized flowers, fondant, thirty-eight different buttercreams, white or dark chocolate roses, lifelike bees made of marzipan, spun sugar, chocolate ribbons, caramel cages, chocolate writing, 22K gold-leaf letters and decorations, enough piped flowers to fill a florist's shop, and still more. Throughout it all I have the feeling that Rose really shines the brightest when she is talking about cakes for special occasions. Show-off cakes. Wedding cakes. Celebration cakes. Cakes to serve a hundred and fifty people. They are splendid, breathtaking, dramatic, exquisite, memorable works of art.

Frankly, I am in awe of Rose's scientific and scholarly mind. She approaches a recipe like a chemist in a laboratory. But mainly, Rose is a wonderful cook and baker—and her book is, to be sure, a bible.

—MAIDA HEATTER

Acknowledgments

I must begin by thanking my parents: my mother for passing on the specter of perseverance (my favorite and most vital attribute), my father for his hands of gold, and both my parents for their example of love of their craft. I cannot think of a more precious gift, except perhaps for another one, that of kindness.

This book could not have been written without the total support and consideration of my husband, Elliott. I also want to thank my stepchildren, Beth and Michael, who offered so much enthusiasm and advice over the years while they and these recipes were growing up.

Much credit goes to my generous and brilliant friend Shirley Corriher, who cares more than anyone else I know what really happens inside a cake and has offered me unending conversation and information to this effect.

There is simply no way to do justice to Maria Guarnaschelli. I feel that I am among the luckiest authors in the world to have her as my editor. Never have I felt more encouraged or better understood. Not only did we share the same vision, we both were always open to possibilities and ready to put aside our own egos for the sake of what was "best for the book." I am especially grateful to Maria for offering me total creative freedom and all the time that I needed in which to accomplish my best work. Her brilliantly unswerving wisdom and personal touches made the book come alive.

Vincent Lee is an artist with a camera. Without his exquisite color photographs, this book would be a mere shadow of what it is. I am thankful for his untiring patience, his infinite inventiveness and his friendship. Working with him has been a special joy.

No one has contributed more to this book than my assistant, David Shamah. When I first started this book, he was still in high school. In the interim he graduated from the Culinary Institute of America. Despite distance, long and early hours in the kitchen, and final exams, hardly a night went by that we did not have long conversations about cake concepts and what is new in the culinary world. David is well acquainted with every theory, every recipe, and every word in this book. In fact, it is often hard to separate the ideas that originated from his brilliantly inquiring young mind. He has worked on this book with as much love as if it were his own. I am blessed with his friendship.

I want to express my undying gratitude to all the people who involved themselves with the production of this book, taking a personal interest and making it a part of their lives. It has been a privilege to be part of a team, a network of such extraordinary dedication and creativity.

Chief copy editor: Deborah Weiss
Book design director: Maria Epes
Designer: Richard Oriolo
Managing editor: Andrew Ambraziejus
Assistant to the editor: John Guarnaschelli
Production: Harvey Hoffman
My chief proofreader: Heidi Trachtenberg. *Other proofreaders:* Shirley Corriher, Dr. Lillian Wager Levy, David Shamah, Madeline Shamah.
Testers: Nancy Blitzer, Marion Bush, Judi Elkins, Ruth Margolies, David Shamah
Chief technical consultant: Shirley Corriher, Research Biochemist of Confident Cooking, Atlanta, Georgia
Technical advisers: ALBERT USTER IMPORTS: Albert Uster and Ben Reed, Claude Burke; CHOCOLATE GALLERY: Joan Mansour; CPC INTERNATIONAL: Sherry McGoldrick; CUISINARTS, INC.: Carl Sontheimer; HAUSER CHOCOLATIER: Rüdi Hauser; LINDT: Rudolph Sprüngli and Arthur Oberholzer; Deanne Miller; SUGAR ASSOCIATION: Jack O'Connell; THOMAS J. LIPTON, INC., KNOX GELATIN: Anna Marie Coccia; TOBLER/SUCHARD: Dr. Buser and Marcus Gerber; TUSCAN DAIRIES: Helen Shull; WILTON ENTERPRISES: Zella Junkin; Richard Walker; WOLF RANGE COMPANY: Laxminarasimhan Vasan.

Special thanks to:

Bert Greene for naming this book.

Terron Hecht for her contribution to the artwork.

Bernard and Florence Wager, my chemist uncle who devoted his Saturday mornings to tutor me through high school chemistry and my aunt who made delicious lunches for afterward.

Eleanor Lynch and Cecily Brownstone for encouraging me to continue my studies.

Dr. Jed H. Irvine, Dr. Stephen L. Gumport, and Dr. Harold H. Sage for enabling me to finish college.

James Beard and Julia Child, my first teachers, for setting a wonderful example of passion and professionalism.

John Clancy, for his generosity, humor and unforgettable pastry lessons.

Maida Heatter, my sweets guru, whose wonderful writing and recipes showed me just how sensational a dessert could be and who graces this book with her wonderful presence.

Sue Hoffman, former food editor of the *Ladies' Home Journal,* who had faith in me.

Linda Foster Gomé, former head of the *Ladies' Home Journal* test kitchen, who took me under her wing and taught me the principles of food styling, recipe testing, and development—I know no hands more skilled than hers.

Lydie Marshall for encouraging me to specialize in cakes.

Mimi Sheraton for first telling me about LeNôtre.

Irena Chalmers, my first publisher, for showing me the way to be a food writer.

Barbara Langley and Gus Belverio of Pinehill Farms for their never-ending supply of fresh farm eggs.

Paula Perlis for her never-ending supply of friendship.

Contents

Special Categories

* For kosher chocolate, see Maestrani (page 445)

Introduction

*F*riends and students often regard my commitment to the confectionery as treasonous since my mother was a dentist. That is not, however, entirely the case—although I was aware of the pitfalls of sweets at a very young age. My father remembers that I confiscated his candy, stating matter-of-factly that it would give him "tavities!"

It was when I wrote my masters dissertation on whether sifting affects the quality of a yellow cake that I discovered my calling. My conclusions were so thorough I received not only an A+ but also an invitation to read my paper to the next class the following year. Feeling proud, after seven years of night school as a food major, I presented my paper to a boyfriend who was a physician.

To my amazement, he actually snickered, saying: "Is this what you consider a suitable topic for a dissertation?"

It only required a week's interval to recover sufficiently to hazard showing the paper on a first date to Elliott Beranbaum, also a physician whose specialty was radiology of the gastrointestinal tract. By then the paper had taken on the aspect of a test of sorts. I watched as he leafed through the twenty-four pages, gravely nodding his head. Finally, I couldn't resist asking: "You don't find this topic a little funny?"

"Not at all," he replied, "I have encountered the same problem with dry ingredients for my digestion studies and my conclusion is the same as yours: Sifting does not uniformly mix dry ingredients—it merely aerates them, helping them absorb the liquid more uniformly. In fact," he continued, "I bought a blender to mix the dry ingredients after sifting." This was so remarkably similar to my solution of beating dry ingredients together in a mixer that with a burst of intuition I thought to myself: "Ah hah! This is the man I'm going to marry. We have the same approach to life."

It was never the flavor of desserts alone that beguiled me. It was also my fascination with the variety of textures derived from so few ingredients. When reading through cookbooks I encountered endless variations of cakes and buttercreams and descriptions of how delicious they were. But nowhere was there an explanation of how they compared to each other or a clue as to how they looked and tasted. When faced with three chocolate buttercream recipes—(one with yolks, one with whites, and one with cream—how could one decide which to make?

It became increasingly apparent to me that there were certain basic formulas from which all these seemingly disparate recipes evolved. I began to long for a book which would demystify and reveal all the basic and classic cakes, buttercreams, icings, fillings, and toppings in their simplest form and then show how to combine them to create just about any cake imaginable. While I would have preferred to be mixing a cake batter or shaping a chocolate rose, I finally realized that in order to have the ideal cake book I was going to have to write it!

This book is dedicated to my husband who, among other wonderful qualities, unquestioningly supports my commitment to my profession, and to the many students and readers who want to understand the basics of baking in order to be free to create new and wondrous desserts of their own.

SPECIAL NOTE ON THE WEIGHTS AND MEASURING SYSTEM

Three systems have been used throughout this book: Volume, avoirdupois, and metric. Each of these methods will yield perfect results. Personally, I prefer weighing to measuring because it is much faster and more precise, but measuring is fine if you measure with care.

Do not expect the mathematics of the metric system to correlate exactly with the avoirdupois system. The grams have been rounded off to the nearest whole number without decimal points (except for leavening, which needs to be more precise) whereas the ounces have been rounded off to the nearest quarter ounce.

Chocolate Bread (page 28)

All-Occasion Downy
Yellow Butter Cake
(page 39)
with Classic
Coffee Buttercream
(page 232)

White Spice Pound Cake (page 30)

Orange Glow Chiffon Cake (page 155)

Less Fruity Fruitcake (page 66)

Cordon Rose Cream Cheesecake (page 81)
with Fresh Cherry Topping (page 344)

Schoggi S (Chocolate S) (page 300)

Sour Cream Coffee Cake (page 90)

Chocolate Domingo Cake (page 58)

Buttermilk Country Cake
(page 41)
with Crème Fraîche Topping
(page 259)
and Fresh Peaches

Golden Grand
Marnier Cakelettes
(page 46)
with Chocolate Cream
Glaze (page 271)

Perfect All-American Chocolate Butter Cake (page 54)
with Burnt Orange Silk Meringue Buttercream (page 242)

Less Fruity Fruitcake
(page 66)

Cordon Rose Banana Cake (page 69) with
Sour Cream Ganache (page 275)

Pumpkin-Walnut Ring with Chocolate
Walnut Drizzle Glaze (page 249)

Zucchini Cupcakes
(page 73)

Golden Wheat Carrot Ring (page 75)

Pineapple Upside-down
Cake (page 92)

Chocolate Oblivion Truffle Torte (page 84)
with Raspberry Sauce (page 337)

Holiday Hallelujah
Streusel Brioche (page 94)
and Sticky Buns (page 98)

Blueberry
Buttermilk Pancakes
(page 100)

Marion Cunningham's
Raised Waffles (page 105)

Best Buckwheat
Blini La Tulipe (page 106)

Swedish Pancakes
(page 108)

Chantilly Crêpes
Suzette (page 112)

Golden Génoise (page 125)
with Lemon Mousseline Buttercream (page 249)

Almond Biscuit Roulade (page 144)
with Raspberry Cloud Cream (page 265)

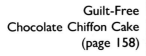

Bert Greene's
Special Sponge Cake
(page 152)

Guilt-Free
Chocolate Chiffon Cake
(page 158)

Blueberry Swan Lake
(page 165)

A Taste of Heaven
(page 166)

White Lilac
Nostaliga
(page 167)

Baked Hawaii
(page 168)

Star-Spangled
Rhapsody (page 169)

Praline Brioche
Cake (page 171)

Ethereal Pear
Charlotte (page 175)

Golden Cage (*Zaüber Torte*) (page 172)

Scarlet Empress
(page 177)

Chocolate Chip
Charlotte (page 179)

Orange Chocolate
Crown (page 181)

Strawberry Maria
(page 184)

Queen Bee
(page 185)

Barquettes Chez
L'Ami Louis (page 186)

Chestnut Chocolate
Embrace (*La Châtaigne*)
(page 189)

The Enchanted Forest
(*Le Fôrét Enchanté*) (page 195)

Swiss Black Forest
Cake (*Schwarzwalder
Kirschtorte*)
(page 190)

Chocolate Pine Cone
(page 196)

Chocolate Spike (page 198)

Cordon Rose
Christmas Log
(*Bûche de Noël*)
(page 197)

La Porcelaine (page 199)

Triple Chocolate Cake (page 201)

Rose Trellis (page 207)

White Lily Cake (page 203)

Bleeding Heart Wedding Cake
(Designed for Trish Fleming) (page 214)

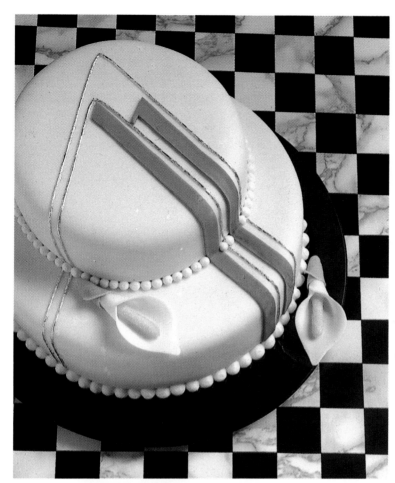

Art Deco Cake
(page 204)

Chocolate
Praline Wedding Cake
(Designed for *Chocolatier*
magazine) (page 216)

Golden Glory
Wedding Cheesecake
(Designed for the
Joan Beranbaum/Judge John
Stackhouse Wedding)
(page 217)

Pistachio and
Rose Wedding Cake
(Designed for Michael Levy)
(page 219)

Dotted Swiss Dream
(Designed for *Bon Appétit* magazine) (page 222)

PART I

CAKES

Simply Delicious Foolproof Cakes

ew pleasures are greater than turning out a perfect cake. And perfect cakes can be achieved by any cook who is careful and who is willing to follow recipe directions. Cake-making is an exact process; the ingredients and their relation to each other are balanced like a chemical formula; in fact, during the baking, a chemical process takes place transforming the raw ingredients into a delicious new entity. . . . However inspired, no written definition of the word "cake" could approximate the glories of sweetened dough, baked, filled, frosted, and made ravishing with edible decorations. Such creations can bring happiness to both our childhood and mature years, for few, if any, people are im- mune to their charm, and memories of them will lighten the dark corners of life.

This chapter contains my favorite foolproof renditions of most basic cakes, including cheesecakes, breakfast cakes, vegetable cakes, and even a brioche cake (which is really a bread). Not only are Amendola and Lundberg absolutely correct in stating that work- ing from a well-balanced recipe will yield perfect cakes, I know that they also agree about how fascinating it is to have a peek behind the scenes and understand what goes into the creation of a cake formula and how one type of cake differs from another. It is fascinating, and also puts you in control. If something goes wrong, for example, it is possible to figure out the problem and correct it. If you want to alter a component, you must understand what it consists of and how it contributes to the cake. I have organized this chapter so that you can start baking with as little interference and as much basic guidance as possible. Separate from each recipe are pointers that highlight key factors and also, for those who are interested, a little about the science of each cake and how it compares to others.

I am beginning with pound cake because it is from this basic formula that all other butter cakes evolve. For a fuller under-

* Joseph Amendola and Donald E. Lundberg, *Understanding Baking* (Boston: CBI Publishing Company, 1970), p. 98.

standing of cake formulation, ingredients and baking, there is an in-depth section called Understanding Cakes at the back of the book (page 469).

Rapid heat penetration gives superior cake texture, so ideally cake pans are manufactured from highly conductive metals such as aluminum, that have a dull, heat-absorbing finish. Stainless steel pans, with their shiny, heat-reflective finish, are poor heat conductors and should not be used for baking cakes. (They make pretty planters if you already happen to have them.) Black metal is also a poor choice because it absorbs heat too quickly and overbrowns the crust.

What is best for the inside of a cake is not, unfortunately, best for the outside. The sides of the cake, touching the hot metal, bake and set faster than the center, which continues to rise resulting in a peaked surface. The solution is to slow down the baking at the sides while promoting rapid and even penetration at the bottom of the pan. Magi-Cake Strips (pages 20 and 456) are made of aluminized fabric which, when moistened and wrapped around a pan, keep the sides cooler. This slows down the baking at the perimeter so that it rises at the same rate as the center and results in a level top.

The size of the pan in relation to the amount of batter also influences how the cake bakes. Ideally, the pan should be the same height as the cake will be at its highest point during baking. Pans should be filled no less than one-half full. If the pan is too big, the sides shield the batter and slow down the baking. The resulting cake will be drier with a paler surface. If the pan is too small, the batter will run over the sides and the cake will collapse from inadequate support.

PREPARING THE PANS: I like to use a round of parchment to line the bottom to ensure that the bottom crust releases completely. While this is not essential for yellow or white cakes, chocolate cakes are notorious for sticking, so lining the pan is important insurance.

A pan for a cake that will rise must never be greased without flouring because a slippery surface will prevent the cake from adhering and rising to its full volume.

Baker's Joy, a shortening spray mixed with flour, is ideal for creating a smooth, tightly sealed crust. Alternately, solid vegetable shortening is preferable to butter and can be applied with a piece of plastic wrap. Butter, unless it is clarified, will leave gaps where the flour will not adhere but the cake unfailingly will. After greasing the pan, add some flour, tilt the pan and rotate it, tapping the sides to spread the flour evenly. Invert the pan and tap lightly.

Return the excess flour to the bin. If desired, wrap the pan with Magi-Cake Strips.

Most cakes (with the exception of very low sheet cakes, which bake in the lower third of the oven) should be baked as close to the center of the oven as possible, with room for air circulation between the pans. I find 350°F. the ideal temperature for baking most cakes. Lower than 350°F., the texture will be coarse for layer cakes and lacking volume for sponge-type cakes. Higher than 375°F., layer cake tops will peak and sponge-type cakes will overbrown.

When a cake is at the end of its baking period, the walls surrounding the air bubbles rupture, releasing their leavening gases and causing the cell walls to shrink very slightly. There is a visible lowering in the pan at this point—a clue to doneness.

To test for doneness, insert a wire cake tester or toothpick as close to the center as possible. It should come out clean, with no crumbs clinging to it. Cakes should also spring back when pressed lightly in the center. Layer cakes under ten inches should not start shrinking from the sides of the pan before being removed from the oven or they will be slightly dry.

Cakes that require more than forty minutes baking time usually need to be covered loosely with lightly greased foil after forty minutes to prevent overbrowning.

Problems with cake baking usually begin at over three thousand feet. Lower air pressure causes water to boil at a lower temperature so that more evaporation takes place during baking and cakes may be dry. If too much evaporation takes place, there will not be adequate moisture to fully gelatinize the starch and set the structure. Structure is further weakened by the tendency for cakes to rise too much at decreased air pressure and subsequently collapse.

Decreasing the sugar to make more liquid available for gelatinizing the starch is one of the standard approaches to this problem. Since my butter cake formulas have less sugar than most (equal weights of sugar and flour) and are more velvety than those made by the creaming method (where one creams the butter and sugar before adding the other ingredients), they will be less affected by high altitude. Also, decreasing the sugar would adversely affect the flavor balance, so I recommend slightly decreasing the leavening and slightly increasing the liquid. The next possibility would be to increase the number of eggs to add more structure.

At elevations above thirty-five hundred feet, increasing the oven temperature by 25°F. will help to set the structure faster.

For a butter cake which uses very little baking powder and a high level of butter, such as a pound cake, it may help to strengthen the cake's structure by decreasing the butter. As each cake formula varies, guidelines can be given but experimentation is the only sure way.

The USDA lists the following recommendations for high-altitude adjustment:

Adjustment	3,000 feet	5,000 feet	7,000 feet
decrease baking powder per teaspoon used	⅛ teaspoon	⅛ to ¼ teaspoon	¼ teaspoon
increase liquid per cup used	1 to 2 tablespoons	2 to 4 tablespoons	3 to 4 tablespoons

In studies performed by General Mills over twenty years ago, the recommended increase in flour was 2.5 percent at thirty-five hundred feet, gradually increasing to 10 percent at eight thousand feet.

Sponge-type cakes are affected by high altitude in a way similar to butter cakes. In a sponge-type cake that does not contain baking powder, it is advisable to decrease the sugar. This will speed coagulation of the egg proteins which stabilize or set the cake and interfere less with gelatinization of the starch. Alternately, slightly more flour can be added to strengthen the structure and, over thirty-five hundred feet, the temperature can be increased to 375°F.

UNMOLDING THE
CAKE

Génoise and *biscuit* must be unmolded as soon as they are baked to prevent steam from softening the cake and collapsing it. Sponge-type cakes that are usually baked in ungreased two-piece tube pans—such as chiffon, sponge, and angel food—need to cool upside down in the pan to prevent collapsing.

Small butter cakes can be unmolded immediately, but butter cakes larger than nine inches risk breaking if unmolded too soon. To be on the safe side, it's fine to wait ten to twenty minutes before turning the cakes out onto lightly greased racks. Always run a small metal spatula around the sides first to be sure they are completely dislodged. Be careful to press the spatula against the sides of the pan, not the sides of the cake.

It is usually best to reinvert unmolded cakes so that top side is up. This prevents splitting if the top is rounded, and the firm top crust helps to maintain maximum volume.

Allow cakes to cool fully before storing or frosting or residual heat will make them soggy and melt the frosting.

STORING THE CAKE

Refrigerated or frozen cakes must be stored airtight to prevent drying out or absorbing odors. Wrap them first in plastic wrap, then in heavy-duty foil.

To freeze a frosted cake, place it uncovered in the freezer just until the frosting is very firm and it should not be damaged by wrapping. Wrap first in plastic wrap, then in heavy-duty foil, trying to eliminate as much air space as possible without pressing on decorations. The most airtight wrap is known as the drugstore wrap: Place the cake in the center of the foil and bring the two long sides together so that the edges meet. Fold the edges over several times until close to the cake. Proceed in the same way for the short ends. Delicate decorations can be protected further by placing the wrapped cake in a rigid box.

TO DEFROST CAKE

For unfrosted cake, remove from the freezer and thaw without unwrapping. If desired, freshen the thawed cake by placing it in a 350°F. oven for five minutes or in a microwave oven on low power for a few seconds.

To thaw frosted cake, unwrap it and place it in the refrigerator overnight. It is best to keep the cake in a large airtight container such as a cake carrier or glass dome (page 461) to avoid absorbing any odors. Iced cakes should be defrosted gradually to prevent moisture condensation or beading.

BUTTER CAKES

The pound cake, according to *Larousse Gastronomique,* originated in England and was the first "butter cake." France adopted it, calling it *quatres-quarts* because traditionally it was prepared using one-fourth flour, one-fourth butter, one-fourth eggs, and one-fourth sugar.

In America the pound cake is often thought of as the "mother" cake from which all other butter cakes (usually referred to as layer cakes) evolved. The American butter cake contains 6 to 12 percent solid butter (not including the liquid and milk solids in the butter) or other shortening, 18 to 36 percent liquid (usually milk or water), 27 percent flour or a combination of flour and cocoa, 27 to 40 percent sugar, 5 to 10 percent egg, a small amount of salt and flavoring, and leavening such as baking powder and/or baking soda.

The butter cake derives its light texture from the air bubbles produced by creaming the sugar and fat and by the leavening—which enlarges these bubbles during baking. In the traditional method, the butter and sugar are creamed before adding the other ingredients. The method I have chosen for my butter cakes is faster, easier, and virtually eliminates any possibility of toughening the cake by overbeating. Creaming still takes place but in a different way: All the dry ingredients are first combined with the butter and a minimum amount of liquid, which coats the flour before adding the remaining liquid ingredients.

The American butter cake is flavorful yet not overly sweet, soft and light in texture, and moist enough to stand on its own or to accommodate a variety of frostings and toppings. It is one of the world's great cakes.

NOTE: All butter cake recipes can be doubled if you have extra pans. Be sure to place them in the oven so air can circulate freely around the sides of all the pans. If you lack room, pour the batter into the pans and refrigerate them until the first set of cake layers has baked. (Do not refrigerate batter in a bowl as it will lose leavening power if not transferred to pans soon after mixing.)

HIGHLIGHTS FOR
SUCCESSFUL
BUTTER
CAKES

For fuller details, see the suggested page number.
• Have all ingredients near room temperature (65°F. to 75°F., page 475).
• Use *cake* flour that does *not* already contain leavening (page 471). Do not use self-rising cake flour.
• Use superfine sugar for finest texture (page 472).
• Use unsalted butter (pages 425 and 472).
• Use fresh baking powder (pages 420 and 473).
• Measure or weigh ingredients carefully (page 438).
• If using a hand-held mixer, beat at high speed.
• Use the correct pan size (page 20).
• For very even layers and maximum height use Magi-Cake Strips (pages 20 and 456).
• Check for accurate oven temperature (page 448).
• Use correct baking time; do not overbake (page 21).
• Wrap cake layers well or frost them when cool (page 23).

This cake not only has a silky-smooth dissolving texture similar to famous Sara Lee pound cake but also the incomparable moist, buttery flavor of a home-baked cake. Its excellent keeping qualities make it ideal for slicing ahead and bringing on picnics.

Perfect Pound Cake

INGREDIENTS	MEASURE	WEIGHT	
room temperature	*volume*	*ounces*	*grams*
milk	3 tablespoons	1.5 ounces	45 grams
3 large eggs	scant 5 fluid ounces	5.25 ounces	150 grams (weighed without shells)
vanilla	1½ teaspoons	•	6 grams
sifted cake flour	1½ cups	5.25 ounces	150 grams
sugar	¾ cup	5.25 ounces	150 grams
baking powder	¾ teaspoon	•	3.7 grams
salt	¼ teaspoon	•	•
unsalted butter (must be softened)	13 tablespoons	6.5 ounces	184 grams

Preheat the oven to 350°F.

In a medium bowl lightly combine the milk, eggs, and vanilla.

In a large mixing bowl combine the dry ingredients and mix on low speed for 30 seconds to blend. Add the butter and half the egg mixture. Mix on low speed until the dry ingredients are moistened. Increase to medium speed (high speed if using a hand mixer) and beat for 1 minute to aerate and develop the cake's structure.

Scrape down the sides. Gradually add the remaining egg mixture in 2 batches, beating for 20 seconds after each addition to incorporate the ingredients and strengthen the structure. Scrape down the sides.

Scrape the batter into the prepared pan and smooth the surface with a spatula. The batter will be almost ½ inch from the top of the 4-cup loaf pan. (If your pan is slightly smaller, use any excess batter for cupcakes.) Bake 55 to 65 minutes (35 to 45 minutes in a fluted tube pan) or until a wooden toothpick inserted in the center comes

One 8-inch by 4-inch by 2½-inch loaf pan (4 cups)—most attractive size—or any 6-cup loaf or fluted tube pan, greased and floured. If using a loaf pan, grease it, line the bottom with parchment or wax paper, and then grease again and flour.

FINISHED HEIGHT:
In a 4-cup loaf: 2¼ inches at the sides and 3½ inches

in the middle. In a 6-cup loaf: 1¾ inches at the sides and 2½ inches in the middle. In a 6-cup fluted tube: 2¼ inches in the middle.

STORE:
Airtight: 3 days room temperature, 1 week refrigerated, 2 months frozen. Texture is most evenly moist when prepared at least 8 hours ahead of serving.

COMPLEMENTARY ADORNMENT:
A simple dusting of powdered sugar.

SERVE:
Room temperature.

POINTERS FOR SUCCESS:
See page 24. Be sure to use a wooden toothpick to test for doneness. The cake will spring back when pressed lightly in the center even before it is done. If the cake is underbaked, it will have tough, gummy spots instead of a fine, tender crumb.

out clean. Cover loosely with buttered foil after 30 minutes to prevent overbrowning. *The cake should start to shrink from the sides of the pan only after removal from the oven.*

To get an attractive split down the middle of the crust, wait until the natural split is about to develop (about 20 minutes) and then with a lightly greased sharp knife or single-edged razor blade make a shallow mark about 6 inches long down the middle of the cake. This must be done quickly so that the oven door does not remain open very long or the cake will fall. When cake splits, it will open along the mark.

Let the cake cool in the pan on a rack for 10 minutes and invert it onto a greased wire rack. If baked in a loaf pan, to keep the bottom from splitting, reinvert so that the top is up and cool completely before wrapping airtight.

UNDERSTANDING

In creating this recipe I started out with the classic pound cake proportions: equal weights of flour, sugar, eggs, and butter and no leavening. But I soon discovered that the traditional balance of ingredients benefits from a few minor alterations: A small amount of milk adds marvelous moisture and also strengthens the cake's structure by gelatinizing the flour and joining the gluten-forming proteins enough to be able to hold some extra butter. More butter adds flavor and tenderizes the crumb, producing that "melt-in-the-mouth" quality. A very small amount of baking powder opens the crumb slightly, contributing more tenderness and less of that heavy chewiness characteristic of the original pound cake.

Over forty trials have led me to believe that there is no way to get this melting texture in a pound cake that is larger so it is best to keep the cake small. If you happen to prefer a denser, chewier cake, however, replace the regular sugar with equal weight powdered sugar (1¼ cups unsifted) and reduce the butter to 10½ tablespoons (5.25 ounces/150 grams) and the baking powder to ½ teaspoon. (The smooth grains of the powdered sugar do not trap air the way the sharp-edged grains of granulated sugar do. The cornstarch added to powdered sugar to prevent lumping also increases the chewy quality of the cake.)

VARIATIONS

DELUXE DOUBLE-VANILLA POUND CAKE: Tiny black grains from the vanilla bean offer a round, full flavor and a barely perceptible crunch. Using a vanilla bean along with vanilla extract is a technique that can be applied to any cake or custard sauce. The vanilla bean imparts a deeper, sweeter, more aromatic flavor, but not in a sugary sense. By contrast increasing the extract would add a hint of bitterness. *To make Deluxe Double-Vanilla Pound Cake:* You will need 1 vanilla bean (½ bean if it is Tahitian, exceptionally aromatic and delicious). With a small, sharp knife split it in half lengthwise. Place it in a small saucepan with the 3 tablespoons of milk and scald the milk (small bubbles will start to form around edges). Cover immediately, remove from the heat, and allow to cool to room temperature. Remove the vanilla bean and scrape the black grains from its center into the milk. (Vanilla beans may be saved for future use, see page 436). Add the vanilla-infused milk to the vanilla extract and eggs and proceed as usual with the recipe.

LEMON POPPY SEED POUND CAKE: This is perhaps my favorite way to eat pound cake! The fresh light flavor of lemon blends beautifully with the buttery flavor of pound cake. The lemon syrup tenderizes, adds tartness, and helps to keep the cake fresh for a few days longer than usual. Poppy seeds add a delightful crunch. Lemon blossoms and lemon leaves make a lovely and appropriate garnish.

To make Lemon Poppy Seed Pound Cake: You will need

1 tablespoon (6 grams) loosely packed grated lemon zest	¼ cup + 2 tablespoons sugar (2.75 ounces/75 grams)
3 tablespoons (1 ounce/ 28 grams) poppy seeds	¼ cup freshly squeezed lemon juice (2 ounces/63 grams)

Add the lemon zest and poppy seeds to the dry ingredients and proceed as above. Shortly before the cake is done, prepare the Lemon Syrup: In a small pan over medium heat, stir the sugar and lemon juice until dissolved. As soon as the cake comes out of the oven, place the pan on a rack, poke the cake all over with a wire tester, and brush it with ½ the syrup. Cool in the pan for 10 minutes. Loosen the sides with a spatula and invert onto a greased wire rack. Poke the bottom of the cake with the wire tester, brush it with some syrup, and reinvert onto a greased wire rack. Brush the sides with the remaining syrup and allow to cool before wrapping airtight. Store 24 hours before eating to give the syrup a chance to distribute evenly. The syrup will keep the cake fresh a few days longer than a cake without syrup.

NOTE:
This cake is very attractive made in individual portions. A 6-cake Bundt-lette pan (page 453) is the perfect size. This recipe will make 6 individual cakelettes, which require about 20 minutes to bake.

Chocolate Bread

SERVES 8

*T*he individual slices of this cake resemble pieces of dark bread, so it is a delightful surprise to discover instead a moist, exceptionally full-flavored chocolate pound cake! This is, in fact, a chocolate cake quite unlike any other butter cake and deserves a category of its own. This is perfect to take to the beach because it requires no frosting.

INGREDIENTS	MEASURE	WEIGHT	
room temperature	*volume*	*ounces*	*grams*
unsweetened cocoa (Dutch-processed)	3 tablespoons + 1½ teaspoons	0.75 ounce	21 grams
boiling water	3 tablespoons	1.5 ounces	44 grams
vanilla	1½ teaspoons	•	6 grams
3 large eggs	scant 5 fluid ounces	5.25 ounces	150 grams (weighed without shells)
sifted cake flour	1¼ cups	4.5 ounces	125 grams
sugar	¾ cup + 2 tablespoons	6 ounces	175 grams
baking powder	¾ teaspoon	•	3.7 grams
salt	¼ teaspoon	•	•
unsalted butter (must be softened)	13 tablespoons	6.5 ounces	184 grams

One 8-inch by 4-inch by 2½-inch loaf pan (4 cups)— most attractive size—or any 6-cup loaf or fluted tube pan, greased and floured. If using a loaf pan, grease it,

Preheat the oven to 350°F.

In a medium mixing bowl whisk together the cocoa and water until smooth. Allow to cool to room temperature and lightly whisk in the vanilla and eggs.

In a large mixing bowl combine the remaining dry ingredients and mix on low speed for 30 seconds to blend. Add ½ the chocolate mixture and the butter. Mix on low speed until the dry ingredients are moistened. Increase to medium speed (high speed if using a hand mixer) and beat for 1 minute to aerate and develop the cake's structure. Scrape down the sides. Gradually add the remaining chocolate mixture in 2 batches, beating for 20 seconds after each addition to incorporate the ingredients and strengthen the structure. Scrape down the sides.

Scrape the batter into the prepared pan and smooth the surface with a spatula. The batter will be almost ½ inch from the top of the 4-cup pan. (If your pan is slightly smaller, use any excess batter for cupcakes.) Bake 50 to 60 minutes (40 to 50 minutes in fluted tube pan) or until a wooden toothpick inserted in the center comes out clean. Cover loosely with buttered foil after 25 minutes to prevent overbrowning. *The cake should start to shrink from the sides of the pan only after removal from the oven.*

To get an attractive split down the middle of the crust, wait until the natural split is about to develop (about 20 minutes) and then with a lightly greased sharp knife or single-edged razor blade make a shallow mark 6 inches long down the middle of the cake. This must be done quickly so that the oven door does not remain open very long or the cake will fall. When cake splits, it will open along mark.

Let the cake cool in the pan on a rack for 10 minutes. Loosen the sides with a small metal spatula and invert onto a greased wire rack. If baked in a loaf pan, to keep the bottom from splitting, reinvert so that the top is up and cool completely before wrapping airtight.

UNDERSTANDING

This is a variation on the basic formula for Perfect Pound Cake. Some of the flour is replaced by Dutch-processed cocoa and the sugar increased slightly to balance the bitterness. The result is a dense, velvety cake.

NOTE: For extra moistness and a subtle coffee accent, brush cake with syrup. *To make syrup:* In a small pan, stir together ¼ cup water and 2 tablespoons sugar. Bring to a full rolling boil. Cover and remove from heat. When cool, add 1 tablespoon Kahlúa.

When the cake is baked, brush half the syrup onto the top. Cool the cake 10 minutes and invert it onto a lightly greased rack. Brush the bottom and sides with the remaining syrup. Reinvert onto a rack, top side up, to finish cooling. The coffee flavor stays in the background, accentuating the chocolate.

line the bottom with parchment or wax paper, and then grease again and flour.

FINISHED HEIGHT:
In a 4-cup loaf: 2½ inches at the sides, and 3 inches in the middle. In a 6-cup loaf: 1¾ inches at the sides, and 2½ inches in the middle.

STORE:
Airtight: 3 days room temperature, 1 week refrigerated, 2 months frozen. Texture is most evenly moist when prepared at least 8 hours ahead of serving.

COMPLEMENTARY ADORNMENT:
A simple dusting of powdered sugar.

SERVE:
Room temperature.

POINTERS FOR SUCCESS:
See page 24. Be sure to use a wooden toothpick to test for doneness. The cake will spring back when pressed lightly in the center even before it is done. If the cake is underbaked, it will have tough, gummy spots instead of a fine, tender crumb.

White Spice Pound Cake

This variation on basic pound cake eliminates some of the cholesterol by using egg whites instead of egg yolks. The cake, however, seems just as rich because of the fragrant addition of cinnamon, cloves, and cocoa. The inspiration for this special blend is a gift from my wonderful friend Nancy Blitzer. When making her spice cake, she also replaces the usual vanilla with brandy—an interesting subtlety that I have adopted for mine as well.

This cake is exceptionally moist and velvety with a positively addictive flavor. It is great to have on hand in the freezer for unexpected company.

INGREDIENTS	MEASURE	WEIGHT	
room temperature	*volume*	*ounces*	*grams*
milk	¼ liquid cup	2 ounces	60 grams
4 large egg whites	½ liquid cup	4.25 ounces	120 grams
brandy	2 teaspoons	•	8 grams
sifted cake flour	2 cups	7 ounces	200 grams
sugar	1 cup	7 ounces	200 grams
baking powder	1 teaspoon	•	5 grams
salt	½ teaspoon	•	3.5 grams
cinnamon	½ teaspoon	•	•
cloves	½ teaspoon	•	•
unsweetened cocoa	1½ teaspoons	•	•
unsalted butter (must be softened)	16 tablespoons	8 ounces	227 grams

One 6-cup loaf pan or fluted tube pan, greased and floured. If using a loaf pan, grease it, line the bottom

Preheat the oven to 350°F.

In a medium bowl lightly combine the milk, egg whites, and brandy.

In a large mixing bowl combine the dry ingredients and mix on low speed for 30 seconds to blend. Add the butter and ½ the egg mixture. Mix on low speed until the dry ingredients are moistened. Increase to medium speed (high speed if using a hand mixer) and beat for 1 minute to aerate and develop the cake's structure. Scrape down the sides. Gradually add the remaining egg mixture in 2 batches, beating for 20 seconds after each addition to incorporate the ingredients and strengthen the structure. Scrape down the sides.

Scrape the batter into the prepared pan and smooth the surface with a spatula. The batter will almost fill the pan. Bake 45 to 55 minutes (40 to 50 minutes in a fluted tube pan) or until a wire cake tester inserted in the center comes out clean and the cake springs back when pressed lightly in the center. *The cake should start to shrink from the sides of the pan only after removal from the oven.*

To get an attractive split down the middle of the crust when using a loaf pan, wait until the natural split is about to develop (about 20 minutes) and then with a lightly greased sharp knife or single-edged razor blade make a shallow mark 6 inches long down the middle of the cake. This must be done quickly so that the oven door does not remain open very long or the cake will fall. When cake splits, it will open along the mark.

Let the cake cool in the pan on a rack for 10 minutes and invert onto greased wire rack. If baked in a loaf pan, to keep the bottom from splitting, reinvert so that the top is up and cool completely before wrapping airtight.

UNDERSTANDING

Aside from the flavoring and the substitution of egg whites for whole eggs, the formula for this cake is identical to the one for Perfect Pound Cake but is one third larger. In this version it is still possible to have a melting, tender quality despite the larger size because there are no yolks to toughen it.

with parchment or wax paper, and then grease again and flour.

FINISHED HEIGHT:
In a loaf pan: 2 inches at the sides and 2½ inches in the middle. In a 6-cup fluted tube: 4 inches in the middle.

STORE:
Airtight: 3 days room temperature, 1 week refrigerated, 2 months frozen.

COMPLEMENTARY ADORNMENT:
A simple dusting of powdered sugar.

SERVE:
Room temperature.

POINTERS FOR SUCCESS:
See page 24.

Chocolate Cherry Almond Pound Cake

SERVES 10

*T*he uniquely flavorful base for this moist cake is the creation of one of my favorite of all pastry chefs: Peter Roggensinger. His grandmother made it for him when he was a child in Switzerland. He normally uses an apricot and a lemon glaze, which is wonderful, but as I adore the flavors of chocolate, almond, and cherry, I am offering this cherry version.

INGREDIENTS	MEASURE	WEIGHT	
room temperature	*volume*	*ounces*	*grams*
Brandied Burgundy Cherries (page 346)	1 cup, drained	•	•
hazelnuts with skins	¾ cup	4 ounces	113 grams
chocolate (preferably extra-bittersweet or bittersweet)	1½ (3-ounce) bars	4.5 ounces	128 grams
cornstarch	1 tablespoon	0.25 ounce	7.5 grams
sifted cake flour	1 cup	3.5 ounces	100 grams
2 large eggs	3 fluid ounces	3.5 ounces	100 grams (weighed without shells)
2 large egg whites	¼ liquid cup	2 ounces	60 grams
cream of tartar	⅜ teaspoon	•	•
sugar	1 cup	7 ounces	200 grams
softened unsalted butter	8 tablespoons	4 ounces	113 grams
almond paste (domestic)	2½ tablespoons	1.5 ounces	43 grams
vanilla	¾ teaspoon	•	•
hot water	¼ liquid cup	2 ounces	60 grams
cherry jelly, melted	¼ cup	2.75 ounces	77 grams

One 8-cup loaf pan (9-inch by 5-inch by 3-inch) greased, bottom lined with

Preheat oven to 350°F.

Place cherries in a single layer in the bottom of the prepared pan. Toast hazelnuts for 10 to 15 minutes or until skins split and nuts are lightly brown. Cool completely, grate finely, and mix with cornstarch. Place in a medium bowl.

Using a sharp knife, chop chocolate into coarse little pieces and add to the nuts. Mix in cake flour and set aside.

Divide the eggs between two bowls, placing three egg whites in a large bowl and one whole egg plus one yolk in a smaller bowl. Add vanilla to egg yolks and mix lightly to blend.

In a mixing bowl, at medium speed, cream butter, almond paste, and all but ⅓ cup sugar until fluffy. Gradually beat in egg yolk mixture until incorporated. Add flour mixture and beat just until mixed into the batter. Beat in the hot water and set aside. On low speed, beat egg whites until foamy. Add cream of tartar, raise speed to medium, and beat until soft peaks form when beater is raised. Gradually add the remaining ⅓ cup sugar. Raise speed to high and beat until stiff peaks form when the beater is raised slowly. With a large rubber spatula, stir about one quarter of the egg whites into the batter until blended. Gently but rapidly fold in the remaining whites. Scrape the batter into the prepared pan.

Bake for one hour and check for doneness. Cake tests done when a small sharp knife inserted in the center comes out clean.

Let the cake cool in the pan on a rack for 10 minutes. Loosen the sides with a small metal spatula and invert onto a serving plate or greased rack. Remove parchment and brush with heated cherry jelly. Cool completely before wrapping airtight.

NOTE: To make the apricot version, use a 6-cup loaf pan to bake the cake; omit the Brandied Burgundy Cherries and replace the cherry jelly with sieved apricot preserves. After spreading the glaze on the cake, allow it to set for about 10 minutes. Stir together ¼ cup powdered sugar and 2 teaspoons lemon juice and spread on top of apricot glaze.

UNDERSTANDING

This cake contains about half the butter of other pound cakes. Less butter is required to tenderize it because nuts replace some of the flour, affording less structure. Because baking powder is not needed to tenderize the cake, the egg whites, beaten into a meringue, are used instead for extra volume. Hot water is added to the batter to make it less stiff and easier to fold in the egg whites.

parchment or wax paper, then greased again and floured.

FINISHED HEIGHT OF CAKE:
2½ inches.

STORE:
Airtight: 3 days at room temperature, 5 days refrigerated, 3 months frozen.

SERVE:
Room temperature.

POINTERS FOR SUCCESS:
See page 24. To get nice tiny chunks of chocolate, use a sharp knife. To keep nuts from becoming oily while grating, use the fine shredding disc of the food processor and then the metal blades. See almond paste (page 430). If imported almond paste is used, the cake will be much sweeter.

Golden Butter Cream Cake

SERVES 8

*I*f you love butter, this will be your favorite cake. There is, quite simply, no cake with more mellow, buttery flavor or golden color. It needs no buttercream but marries well with one if you should choose to frost it. The high proportion of butter makes it seem dense at first bite, but this cake instantly dissolves in the mouth, leaving behind a heavenly flavor and the illusion of lightness.

INGREDIENTS	MEASURE	WEIGHT	
room temperature	*volume*	*ounces*	*grams*
3 large egg yolks	scant 2 fluid ounces	2 ounces	56 grams
heavy cream	½ liquid cup	4 ounces	116 grams
vanilla	¾ teaspoon	•	3 grams
sifted cake flour	1½ cups	5.25 ounces	150 grams
sugar	¾ cup	5.25 ounces	150 grams
baking powder	1¼ teaspoons	•	6 grams
salt	¼ teaspoon	•	•
unsalted butter (must be softened)	10.5 tablespoons	5.25 ounces	150 grams

One 9-inch by 2-inch cake or quiche pan or 9-inch springform pan, greased, bottom lined with parchment or wax paper, and then greased again and floured.

FINISHED HEIGHT:
1⅜ inches; 1⅛ inches in quiche pan

STORE:
Airtight: 3 days room tem-

Preheat the oven to 350°F.

In a medium bowl lightly combine the yolks, 2 tablespoons cream, and vanilla.

In a large mixing bowl combine the dry ingredients and mix on low speed for 30 seconds to blend. Add the butter and remaining 6 tablespoons cream. Mix on low speed until the dry ingredients are moistened. Increase to medium speed (high speed if using a hand mixer) and beat for 1½ minutes to aerate and develop the cake's structure. Scrape down the sides. Gradually add the egg mixture in 3 batches, beating for 20 seconds after each addition to incorporate the ingredients and strengthen the structure. Scrape down the sides.

Scrape the batter into the prepared pan and smooth the surface with a spatula. Bake 25 to 35 minutes or until a wire cake tester inserted in the center comes out clean and the cake springs back when pressed lightly in the center. The *cake should be just starting to shrink from the sides of the pan.* It will shrink quite a bit while cooling.

Let the cake cool in the pan on a rack for 10 minutes. It will have a level top. Loosen the sides with a small metal spatula and invert onto a greased wire rack. For an attractive top crust, reinvert so that the top is up and cool completely before wrapping airtight.

UNDERSTANDING

This cake is a cross between Perfect Pound Cake and All-Occasion Downy Yellow Butter Cake, with the incomparable, flowery flavor of cream replacing the milk. The butter content is about the same as in Perfect Pound Cake when one takes into account the butterfat in the cream. Compared to Perfect Pound Cake, Butter Cream Cake has egg yolks instead of whole eggs, to add color and fineness of crumb. It also has more baking powder for a more tender, lighter texture.

This cake is used to make Rose Trellis (page 207).

perature, 1 week refrigerated, 2 months frozen. Moisture distributes most evenly the day after baking.

COMPLEMENTARY ADORNMENTS:
A simple dusting of powdered sugar. Royal Honey Buttercream (page 235). Perfect Whipped Cream (page 253) and fresh strawberries.

SERVE:
Room temperature.

POINTERS FOR SUCCESS:
See page 24.

𝒯his moist, tender yellow cake has a light, soft crumb. The sour cream imparts a mellow undertone which blends perfectly with the buttery flavor. This is one of my favorite cakes to make in summer, and I serve it with *crème fraîche* and fresh berries, peaches, or nectarines.

Sour Cream Butter Cake

**S E R V E S   8
T O   1 0**

INGREDIENTS	MEASURE	WEIGHT	
room temperature	*volume*	*ounces*	*grams*
4 large egg yolks	2 full fluid ounces	2.5 ounces	74 grams
sour cream	⅔ cup	5.5 ounces	160 grams
vanilla	1½ teaspoons	•	6 grams
sifted cake flour	2 cups	7 ounces	200 grams
sugar	1 cup	7 ounces	200 grams
baking powder	½ teaspoon	•	2.5 grams
baking soda	½ teaspoon	•	2.5 grams
salt	½ teaspoon	•	3.5 grams
unsalted butter (must be softened)	12 tablespoons	6 ounces	170 grams

One 9-inch springform pan, greased, bottom lined with parchment or wax paper, and then greased again and floured.

FINISHED HEIGHT:
1¾ inches.

STORE:
Airtight: 2 days room temperature, 5 days refrigerated, 2 months frozen. Moisture distributes evenly and any pastiness disappears the day after baking.

COMPLEMENTARY ADORNMENTS:
A simple dusting of powdered sugar. *One recipe:* Apricot Buttercream (page 233 or 243). Sour Cream Ganache (page 275). *Crème fraîche* (page 259) topped with fresh peaches.

SERVE:
Room temperature.

POINTERS FOR SUCCESS:
See page 24.

Preheat the oven to 350°F.

In a medium bowl lightly combine the yolks, ¼ of the sour cream, and the vanilla.

In a large mixing bowl combine the dry ingredients and mix on low speed for 30 seconds to blend. Add the butter and the remaining sour cream. Mix on low speed until the dry ingredients are moistened. Increase to medium speed (high speed if using a hand mixer) and beat for 1½ minutes to aerate and develop the cake's structure. Scrape down the sides. Gradually add the egg mixture in 3 batches, beating for 20 seconds after each addition to incorporate the ingredients and strengthen the structure. Scrape down the sides. Scrape the batter into the prepared pan and smooth the surface with a spatula.

Bake 35 to 45 minutes or until a wire cake tester inserted in the center comes out clean and the cake springs back when pressed lightly in the center. *The cake should start to shrink from the sides of the pan only after removal from the oven.*

Let the cake cool in the pan on a rack for 10 minutes. It will have a level top. Loosen the sides with a small metal spatula and remove the sides of the pan. Invert onto a lightly greased cake rack and cool completely before wrapping airtight. If you wish to remove the pan bottom, slide a cardboard round at least 9 inches in diameter between the parchment and metal bottom when the cake is completely cool.

UNDERSTANDING

The ratio of ingredients is similar to Butter Cream Cake except for a decrease in butter which makes the cake lighter and more suitable with fillings and toppings. Baking soda is used to temper the acidity of the sour cream. The combined leavening is higher in this cake to compensate for the lower amount of butter. (Both butter and leavening agents tenderize cake. Butter, however, produces a denser texture while leavening creates a lighter texture.)

This butter cake has the lovely flavor of almond. It also has a soft and dissolving texture, with a beautiful golden crust. The cake takes no time at all to make. When the mood strikes I can assemble and mix the batter in the time it takes to preheat the oven (using the microwave to soften the butter). I bake it for 45 minutes and, ignoring the safety precaution of cooling the cake in the pan for 10 minutes before unmolding, unmold it onto a rack, place it in the freezer for 10 minutes and then cut a piece to eat. Still slightly warm, it is at its most tender.

Golden Almond Cake

SERVES 8 TO 10

INGREDIENTS	MEASURE	WEIGHT	
room temperature	*volume*	*ounces*	*grams*
2 large eggs	3 fluid ounces	3.5 ounces	100 grams
		(weighed without shells)	
sour cream	⅔ cup	5.5 ounces	160 grams
almond extract	1 teaspoon	•	4 grams
vanilla	¼ teaspoon	•	•
sifted cake flour	1⅔ cups	5.75 ounces	166 grams
unblanched sliced almonds, toasted and finely ground	⅓ cup (ground)	1.25 ounces	35 grams
sugar	1 cup	7 ounces	200 grams
baking powder	½ teaspoon	•	2.5 grams
baking soda	½ teaspoon	•	2.5 grams
salt	½ teaspoon	•	3.5 grams
unsalted butter (must be softened)	12 tablespoons	6 ounces	170 grams

Preheat the oven to 350°F.

In a medium bowl lightly combine the eggs, ¼ of the sour cream, and the extract.

In a large mixing bowl combine the dry ingredients and mix on low speed for 30 seconds to blend. Add the butter and remaining sour cream. Mix on low speed until the dry ingredients are moistened. Increase to medium speed (high speed if using a hand mixer) and beat for 1½ minutes to aerate and develop the cake's structure. Scrape down the

One 9-inch by 2-inch cake pan or 9-inch springform pan, greased, bottom lined

with parchment or wax paper, and then greased again and floured.

FINISHED HEIGHT:
1½ inches at the sides and 1¾ inches in the middle.

STORE:
Airtight: 2 days room temperature, 5 days refrigerated, 2 months frozen.

COMPLEMENTARY ADORNMENTS:
A simple dusting of powdered sugar. Raspberries, peaches and chocolate all have a natural affinity for almonds. *One recipe:* Raspberry Buttercream (page 233, 243, or 245). Sour Cream Ganache (page 275). *Crème fraîche* (page 259) topped with fresh peaches or raspberries.

SERVE:
Room temperature.

POINTERS FOR SUCCESS:
See page 24.

sides. Gradually add the egg mixture in 3 batches, beating for 20 seconds after each addition to incorporate the ingredients and strengthen the structure. Scrape down the sides.

Scrape the batter into the prepared pan and smooth the surface with a spatula. Bake 35 to 45 minutes or until a wire cake tester inserted in the center comes out clean and the cake springs back when pressed lightly in the center. The *cake should start to shrink from the sides of the pan only after removal from the oven.*

Let the cake cool in the pan on a rack for 10 minutes. Loosen the sides with a small metal spatula and unmold or remove the sides of the springform pan. Allow to cool completely before wrapping airtight.

UNDERSTANDING
The formula for this cake is the same as that for Sour Cream Butter Cake except that ⅓ cup flour is replaced by ⅓ cup finely grated almonds. The almonds add flavor and bulk but do not contribute structure so whole eggs are needed and leavening must be decreased. The small amount of vanilla is added to enhance the almond flavor.

*I*f I had to choose among all my cakes, this one would win first place because it is delicious by itself yet versatile enough to accommodate a wide range of buttercreams. The cake combines the soft texture of white cake with the buttery flavor of yellow cake. Using all yolks instead of whole eggs produces a rich yellow color, fine texture, and delicious flavor.

All-Occasion Downy Yellow Butter Cake

SERVES 12

INGREDIENTS	MEASURE	WEIGHT	
room temperature	*volume*	*ounces*	*grams*
6 large egg yolks	3.5 fluid ounces	4 ounces	112 grams
milk	1 liquid cup	8.5 ounces	242 grams
vanilla	2¼ teaspoons	•	9 grams
sifted cake flour	3 cups	10.5 ounces	300 grams
sugar	1½ cups	10.5 ounces	300 grams
baking powder	1 tablespoon + 1 teaspoon	•	19.5 grams
salt	¾ teaspoon	•	5 grams
unsalted butter (must be softened)	12 tablespoons	6 ounces	170 grams

Preheat the oven to 350°F.

In a medium bowl lightly combine the yolks, ¼ cup milk, and vanilla.

In a large mixing bowl combine the dry ingredients and mix on low speed for 30 seconds to blend. Add the butter and remaining ¾ cup milk. Mix on low speed until the dry ingredients are moistened. Increase to medium speed (high speed if using a hand mixer) and beat for 1½ minutes to aerate and develop the cake's structure. Scrape down the sides. Gradually add the egg mixture in 3 batches, beating for 20 seconds after each addition to incorporate the ingredients and strengthen the structure. Scrape down the sides.

Scrape the batter into the prepared pans and smooth the surface with a spatula. The pans will be about ½ full. Bake 25 to 35 minutes or until a tester inserted near the center comes out clean and the cake springs back when pressed lightly in the center. *The cakes should start to shrink from the sides of the pans only after removal from the oven.*

Two 9-inch by 1½-inch cake pans greased, bottoms lined with parchment or wax paper, and then greased again and floured.

FINISHED HEIGHT:
Each layer is 1¼ inches.

STORE:
Airtight: 2 days room temperature, 5 days refrigerated, 2 months frozen.

Texture is most perfectly
moist the same day as
baking.

COMPLEMENTARY
ADORNMENTS:
A simple dusting of pow-
dered sugar. *One recipe:*
Any buttercream, glaze, or
fondant.

SERVE:
Room temperature.

POINTERS FOR SUCCESS:
See page 24.

Let the cakes cool in the pans on racks for 10 minutes.
Loosen the sides with a small metal spatula and invert onto
greased wire racks. To prevent splitting, reinvert so that the
tops are up and cool completely before wrapping airtight.

VARIATION

MAPLE BUTTER CAKE: This cake has a deep golden color
and a real New England flavor. It is superb frosted with
Neoclassic Maple Buttercream (page 233) and encrusted with
toasted walnuts, coarsely chopped (page 324).

To make this cake, simply replace the sugar with an
equal weight of maple sugar (or 2 cups). Decrease the vanilla to ¾ teaspoon and add 1 teaspoon of maple flavoring.

NOTE: Maple sugar is available in specialty stores such as
Dean & DeLuca (page 445). It is expensive, but the resulting cake, frosted with Maple Buttercream, is uniquely delicious.

UNDERSTANDING

Compared to Perfect Pound Cake, this cake has more than
double the baking powder, less than half the butter, and no
egg whites. The decrease in butter is responsible for the
lighter and softer texture. The increased baking powder
further lightens the cake and also makes it more tender.

Buttermilk
Country Cake

S E R V E S   8

*B*uttermilk imparts a slightly tangy and rich flavor to butter cake, although it is actually lower in cholesterol than whole milk. This cake is delicious with softly whipped *crème fraîche* and ripe peaches. I also like to bring it plain to picnics and serve it with windfalls of fresh wild berries.

INGREDIENTS	MEASURE	WEIGHT	
room temperature	*volume*	*ounces*	*grams*
4 large egg yolks	2 full fluid ounces	2.5 ounces	74 grams
buttermilk	⅔ liquid cup	5.5 ounces	160 grams
vanilla	1½ teaspoons	•	6 grams
sifted cake flour	2 cups	7 ounces	200 grams
sugar	1 cup	7 ounces	200 grams
baking powder	1 tablespoon	•	15 grams
salt	½ teaspoon	•	3.5 grams
unsalted butter (must be softened)	8 tablespoons	4 ounces	113 grams

Preheat the oven to 350°F.

In a medium bowl lightly combine the yolks, ¼ of the buttermilk, and vanilla.

In a large mixing bowl combine the dry ingredients and mix on low speed for 30 seconds to blend. Add the butter and remaining buttermilk. Mix on low speed until the dry ingredients are moistened. Increase to medium speed (high speed if using a hand mixer) and beat for 1½ minutes to aerate and develop the cake's structure. Scrape down the sides. Gradually add the egg mixture in 3 batches, beating for 20 seconds after each addition to incorporate the ingredients and strengthen the structure. Scrape down the sides.

Scrape the batter into the prepared pan and smooth the surface with a spatula. The pan will be about ½ full. Bake 30 to 40 minutes or until a tester inserted near the center comes out clean and the cake springs back when pressed lightly in the center. *The cake should start to shrink from the sides of the pan only after removal from the oven.*

Let the cake cool in the pan on a rack for 10 minutes. Loosen the sides with a small metal spatula and invert onto

One 9-inch by 2-inch cake pan or 9-inch springform pan, greased, bottom lined with parchment or wax paper, and then greased again and floured.

FINISHED HEIGHT:
1½ inches at the sides and 2 inches in the middle.

STORE:
Airtight: 3 days room temperature, 5 days refriger-

ated, 2 months frozen. Texture is most perfectly moist the same day as baking.

COMPLEMENTARY ADORNMENTS:
A simple dusting of powdered sugar. *One recipe:* Lemon Buttercream (page 234 or 245). *Crème fraîche* (page 259) topped with peach slices.

SERVE:
Room temperature.

POINTERS FOR SUCCESS:
See page 24.

Chestnut Sand Cake

SERVES 12

a greased wire rack. To prevent splitting, reinvert so that the top is up and cool completely before wrapping airtight.

UNDERSTANDING

This cake is similar to All-Occasion Downy Yellow Butter Cake, except that buttermilk replaces the whole milk. Although buttermilk has a tangy taste and most recipes using buttermilk call for baking soda to temper it, it is not necessary to use the baking soda. Actually, when buttermilk is added to a batter, it does not lower the pH (make it more acid). Instead, the buttermilk acts as a buffer, neutralizing any extremes of acid or base already in the batter. Using baking powder instead of baking soda allows the subtle, delicious tanginess of the buttermilk to come through and results in a cake with a much finer texture.

*C*hestnut flour gives this cake its lovely hue and fine, moist texture. In combination with bread flour, it produces a tender layer cake with unusual, subtle chestnut flavor and a suggestion of spiciness. I fill and frost this cake with Chestnut Buttercream (page 233, 243, or 353) and call it Le Marron, which in French, means "chestnut."

INGREDIENTS	MEASURE	WEIGHT	
room temperature	*volume*	*ounces*	*grams*
3 large eggs	scant 5 fluid ounces	5.25 ounces	150 grams (weighed without shells)
milk	1 liquid cup	8.5 ounces	242 grams
vanilla	2¼ teaspoons	•	9 grams
sifted bread flour	1½ cups + 1 tablespoon	6.75 ounces	190 grams
sifted chestnut flour	1 cup	3.75 ounces	110 grams
sugar	1½ cups	10.5 ounces	300 grams
baking powder	1 tablespoon	•	14.5 grams
salt	½ teaspoon	•	3.5 grams
unsalted butter (must be softened)	12 tablespoons	6 ounces	170 grams

Preheat the oven to 350°F.

In a medium bowl lightly combine the eggs, ¼ cup milk, and vanilla.

In a large mixing bowl combine the dry ingredients and mix on low speed for 30 seconds to blend. Add the butter and remaining ¾ cup milk. Mix on low speed until the dry ingredients are moistened. Increase to medium speed (high speed if using a hand mixer) and beat for 1½ minutes to aerate and develop the cake's structure. Scrape down the sides. Gradually add the egg mixture in 3 batches, beating for 20 seconds after each addition to incorporate the ingredients and strengthen the structure. Scrape down the sides.

Scrape the batter into the prepared pans and smooth the surface with a spatula. The pans will be about ½ full. Bake 25 to 35 minutes or until a tester inserted near the center comes out clean and the cake springs back when pressed lightly in the center. *(The cakes should start to shrink from the sides of the pans only after removal from the oven.)*

Let the cakes cool in the pans on racks for 10 minutes. Loosen the sides with a small metal spatula and invert onto greased wire racks. To prevent splitting, reinvert so that the tops are up and cool completely before wrapping airtight.

UNDERSTANDING

Chestnut flour, available in specialty or health food stores (see page 421), contains mainly starch and has no gluten to support a cake's structure—so I added sufficient bread flour to provide the necessary gluten. This cake also contains whole eggs instead of yolks and less baking powder than All-Occasion Downy Yellow Butter Cake to further strengthen its structure.

Two 9-inch by 1½-inch cake pans greased, bottoms lined with parchment or wax paper, and then greased again and floured.

FINISHED HEIGHT:
Each layer is 1⅛ inches.

STORE:
Airtight: 2 days room temperature, 5 days refrigerated, 2 months frozen. Moisture distributes most evenly the day after baking.

COMPLEMENTARY ADORNMENTS:
A simple dusting of powdered sugar. *One recipe:* Chestnut Buttercream or any dark chocolate frosting or glaze such as ganache (page 267 or 271).

SERVE:
Room temperature.

POINTERS FOR SUCCESS:
See page 24.

Golden Grand Marnier Cake

*T*he divine flavors of orange, Grand Marnier, chocolate, and almond—supported by a mellow sour cream butter cake base—combine to produce a sensational cake. The orange flower water enhances the flavor. The Grand Marnier syrup makes the cake soft and moist (though not at all wet) and helps to preserve it so well that I used to ship this cake to the University of Michigan for my daughter Beth's birth-

INGREDIENTS	MEASURE	WEIGHT	
room temperature	*volume*	*ounces*	*grams*
chocolate mini-chips or bittersweet chocolate chopped into ¼-inch pieces	½ cup	3 ounces	85 grams
Grand Marnier	¼ teaspoon	•	•
cake flour	1½ teaspoons	•	•
3 large eggs	scant 5 fluid ounces	5.25 ounces (weighed without shells)	150 grams
sour cream	1 cup	8.5 ounces	242 grams
orange flower water or vanilla	2 teaspoons 1½ teaspoons	• •	8 grams 6 grams
sifted cake flour	2½ cups	8.75 ounces	250 grams
unblanched sliced almonds, toasted and finely ground	½ cup + 1 tablespoon (ground)	2 ounces	60 grams
sugar	1 cup	7 ounces	200 grams
baking powder	1½ teaspoons	•	7.5 grams
baking soda	1 teaspoon	•	5 grams
salt	¾ teaspoon	•	5 grams
grated orange zest	2 tablespoons	•	12 grams
unsalted butter (must be softened)	1 cup	8 ounces	227 grams
GRAND MARNIER SYRUP			
sugar	½ cup	3.5 ounces	100 grams
orange juice, freshly squeezed	¼ liquid cup	2 ounces	60 grams
Grand Marnier	⅓ liquid cup	2.75 ounces	80 grams

day. I once added a little extra Grand Marnier and sent it airmail to a friend in France!

Preheat the oven to 350°F.

In a small bowl toss the chocolate chips and Grand Marnier until the chips are moistened and shiny. Add the 1½ teaspoons flour and toss until evenly coated.

In a medium bowl lightly combine the eggs, ¼ cup sour cream, and orange flower water or vanilla.

In a large mixing bowl combine the dry ingredients and orange zest and mix on low speed for 30 seconds to blend. Add the butter and remaining ¾ cup sour cream. Mix on low speed until the dry ingredients are moistened. Increase to medium speed (high speed if using a hand mixer) and beat for 1½ minutes to aerate and develop the cake's structure. Scrape down the sides. Gradually add the egg mixture in 3 batches, beating for 20 seconds after each addition to incorporate the ingredients and strengthen the structure. Scrape down the sides. Stir in the chocolate chips.

Scrape the batter into the prepared pan and smooth the surface with a spatula. Bake 55 to 65 minutes or until a wire cake tester inserted in the center comes out clean and the cake springs back when pressed lightly in the center. *The cake should start to shrink from the sides of the pan only after removal from the oven.*

Shortly before the cake is done, prepare the syrup: Heat the sugar, orange juice, and Grand Marnier until the sugar is dissolved. Do not boil. As soon as the cake comes out of the oven, place the pan on a rack, poke the top all over with a wire tester, and brush on ½ the syrup. Cool in the pan on the rack for 10 minutes, then invert onto a lightly greased wire rack. Brush with the remaining syrup and cool completely before glazing with chocolate or wrapping airtight.

One 9-cup fluted tube pan, greased and floured.

FINISHED HEIGHT:
Depends on design of pan.

STORE:
Airtight, 3 days room temperature, 7 days refrigerated, 2 months frozen. Moisture distributes most evenly one day after baking.

COMPLEMENTARY ADORNMENTS:
A light dusting of powdered sugar. ½ recipe Chocolate Cream Glaze (page 271).

SERVE:
Room temperature.

POINTERS FOR SUCCESS:
See page 24.

UNDERSTANDING

This cake is similar to Buttermilk Country Cake with the less tangy sour cream replacing the buttermilk. A more significant difference, however, is that ½ cup flour is replaced by ground almonds and that ½ cup sugar, dissolved in orange juice and Grand Marnier, is added to the cake after baking.

To compensate for the missing ½ cup of sugar during baking, the leavening is increased to aerate and tenderize the texture. I like to add tiny chocolate chips to the batter because dark chocolate blends so beautifully with the orange flavor. This cake can support the chips because of both the decrease in sugar and the acid provided by the sour cream. An old baker's trick to suspend ingredients in a batter is to make the batter more acid. The acid coagulates the egg faster, in effect setting the cake's structure before the heavier particles can fall to the bottom. A decrease in sugar also enables the egg to coagulate faster and for the starch in the flour to gelatinize better, also strengthening the structure. Another trick is coating the chips with flour, giving them a rougher surface with which to cling to the batter.

NOTE: This cake is very attractive made in individual portions. A 6-cake Bundt-lette pan (page 453) is the perfect size. This recipe will make 9 individual cakelettes, so you will need either to make only ⅔ recipe, using 1¼ teaspoons baking powder, or bake the cakelettes in 2 batches. Be sure to fill any unused sections of the pan with water to promote even baking. The cakelettes require 30 to 40 minutes baking time.

White Velvet Butter Cake

SERVES 12

*T*his is the softest and most delicate of all butter cakes. The butter and vanilla give the cake an off-white color but also contribute delicious flavor. This versatile cake blends well with just about any buttercream except for chocolate—which tends to overwhelm the delicate flavor.

INGREDIENTS	MEASURE	WEIGHT	
room temperature	*volume*	*ounces*	*grams*
4½ large egg whites	4 full liquid ounces	4.75 ounces	135 grams
milk	1 liquid cup	8.5 ounces	242 grams
vanilla	2¼ teaspoons	•	9 grams
sifted cake flour	3 cups	10.5 ounces	300 grams
sugar	1½ cups	10.5 ounces	300 grams
baking powder	1 tablespoon + 1 teaspoon	•	19.5 grams
salt	¾ teaspoon	•	5 grams
unsalted butter (must be softened)	12 tablespoons	6 ounces	170 grams

Preheat the oven to 350°F.

In a medium bowl lightly combine the egg whites, ¼ cup milk and vanilla.

In a large mixing bowl combine the dry ingredients and mix on low speed for 30 seconds to blend. Add the butter and remaining ¾ cup milk. Mix on low speed until the dry ingredients are moistened. Increase to medium speed (high speed if using a hand mixer) and beat for 1½ minutes to aerate and develop the cake's structure. Scrape down the sides. Gradually add the egg mixture in 3 batches, beating for 20 seconds after each addition to incorporate the ingredients and strengthen the structure. Scrape down the sides.

Scrape the batter into the prepared pans and smooth the surface with a spatula. The pans will be about ½ full. Bake 25 to 35 minutes or until a tester inserted near the center comes out clean and the cake springs back when pressed lightly in the center. The *cakes should start to shrink from the sides of the pans only after removal from the oven.*

Let the cakes cool in the pans on racks for 10 minutes. Loosen the sides with a small metal spatula and invert onto greased wire racks. To prevent splitting, reinvert so that the tops are up and cool completely before wrapping airtight.

UNDERSTANDING
This cake is identical to All-Occasion Downy Yellow Butter Cake except that each egg yolk is replaced by 1½ whites. Egg whites produce a softer cake than yolks or whole eggs.

This cake is used to make White Lilac Nostalgia (page 167).

Two 9-inch by 1½-inch cake pans greased, bottoms lined with parchment or wax paper, and then greased again and floured.

FINISHED HEIGHT:
Each layer is 1⅛ inches.

STORE:
Airtight: 2 days room temperature, 5 days refrigerated, 2 months frozen. Texture is most perfectly moist the same day as baking.

COMPLEMENTARY ADORNMENTS:
A simple dusting of powdered sugar. Any nonchocolate buttercream, glaze, or fondant.

SERVE:
Room temperature.

POINTERS FOR SUCCESS:
See page 24.

Golden Luxury Butter Cake

SERVES 12

*N*o one would ever guess that white chocolate is one of the ingredients in this cake. The addition of *real* white chocolate (the kind which contains cocoa butter) to a cake adds a velvety texture, deepens the yellow color, and heightens the "melt-in-the-mouth" quality. This is because cocoa butter is very firm at room temperature but melts faster than butter at body temperature. Cocoa butter is also a splendid emulsifier and is responsible for the extra smoothness of the batter and the velvety grain of the baked cake. The slight acidity of the cocoa butter, together with the milk solids in the chocolate, perfumes the cake with an almost lemony edge. Accentuate this flavor with a lemon buttercream.

INGREDIENTS	MEASURE	WEIGHT	
room temperature	*volume*	*ounces*	*grams*
white chocolate	•	6 ounces	170 grams
6 large egg yolks	3.5 fluid ounces	4 ounces	112 grams
milk	1 liquid cup	8.5 ounces	242 grams
vanilla	1½ teaspoons	•	6 grams
sifted cake flour	3 cups	10.5 ounces	300 grams
sugar	1 cup + 3 tablespoons	8.5 ounces	240 grams
baking powder	1 tablespoon + 1½ teaspoons	•	22 grams
salt	¾ teaspoon	•	5 grams
unsalted butter (must be softened)	9 tablespoons	4.5 ounces	128 grams

Two 9-inch by 1½-inch cake pans greased, bottoms lined with parchment or wax paper, and then greased again and floured.

Preheat the oven to 350°F.

In a double boiler melt the chocolate over hot (not simmering) water, stirring frequently. Remove from the water.

In a medium bowl lightly combine the yolks, ¼ cup milk, and vanilla.

In a large mixing bowl combine the dry ingredients and mix on low speed for 30 seconds to blend. Add the butter and remaining ¾ cup milk. Mix on low speed until the dry ingredients are moistened. Increase to medium speed (high speed if using a hand mixer) and beat for 1½ minutes to aerate and develop the cake's structure. Scrape down the sides. Gradually add the egg mixture in 3 batches, beating for 20 seconds after each addition to incorporate the ingredients and strengthen the structure. Scrape down the sides. Add the melted chocolate and beat to incorporate.

Scrape the batter into the prepared pans and smooth the surface with a spatula. The pans will be a little more than ½ full. Bake 25 to 35 minutes or until a tester inserted near the center comes out clean and the cake springs back when pressed lightly in the center. *The cakes should start to shrink from the sides of the pans only after removal from the oven.*

Let the cakes cool in the pans on racks for 10 minutes. Loosen the sides with a small metal spatula and invert onto greased wire racks. To prevent splitting, reinvert so that the tops are up and cool completely before wrapping airtight.

UNDERSTANDING

The formula for this cake is, beneath the surface, practically identical to All-Occasion Downy Yellow Butter Cake. The added fat from the cocoa butter is balanced by removing the equivalent butter from the basic recipe. The added sugar in the chocolate has also been subtracted. The milk solids are the only extra and, as they tend to toughen a cake's structure, a slight increase in baking powder was used.

FINISHED HEIGHT:
Each layer is 1¼ inches.

STORE:
Airtight: 2 days room temperature, 5 days refrigerated, 2 months frozen. Texture is most perfectly moist the same day as baking.

COMPLEMENTARY ADORNMENTS:
A simple dusting of powdered sugar. *One recipe:* Lemon Buttercream (page 234 or 245). White Chocolate Buttercream or Glaze (page 246 or 248).

SERVE:
Room temperature.

POINTERS FOR SUCCESS:
See page 24 and Melting White Chocolate (page 379).

White Chocolate Whisper Cake

SERVES 12

*W*hite chocolate offers the double advantage of velvety, melt-in-the-mouth texture and, because of white cake's gentle flavor, a definite whisper of cocoa butter. This special flavor blends well with a lemon buttercream or, of course, a white chocolate buttercream or glaze.

INGREDIENTS	MEASURE	WEIGHT	
room temperature	*volume*	*ounces*	*grams*
white chocolate	•	6 ounces	170 grams
4½ large egg whites	4 full liquid ounces	4.75 ounces	135 grams
milk	1 liquid cup	8.5 ounces	242 grams
vanilla	1½ teaspoons	•	6 grams
sifted cake flour	3 cups	10.5 ounces	300 grams
sugar	1 cup + 3 tablespoons	8.5 ounces	240 grams
baking powder	1 tablespoon + 1½ teaspoons	•	22 grams
salt	¾ teaspoon	•	7 grams
unsalted butter (must be softened)	9 tablespoons	4.5 ounces	128 grams

Two 9-inch by 1½-inch cake pans greased, bottoms lined with parchment or wax paper, and then greased again and floured.

FINISHED HEIGHT:
Each layer is 1¼ inches (1¾ inches when baked in oval pans).

Preheat the oven to 350°F.

In a double boiler melt the chocolate over hot (not simmering) water, stirring frequently. Remove from the water.

In a medium bowl lightly combine the egg whites, ¼ cup milk, and vanilla.

In a large mixing bowl combine the dry ingredients and mix on low speed for 30 seconds to blend. Add the butter and remaining ¾ cup milk. Mix on low speed until the dry ingredients are moistened. Increase to medium speed (high speed if using a hand mixer) and beat for 1½ minutes to aerate and develop the cake's structure. Scrape down the sides. Gradually add the egg mixture in 3 batches, beating for 20 seconds after each addition to incorporate the ingredients and strengthen the structure. Scrape down the sides. Add the melted chocolate and beat to incorporate.

Scrape the batter into the prepared pans and smooth the surface with a spatula. The pans will be about ½ full. Bake 25 to 35 minutes or until a tester inserted near the center comes out clean and the cake springs back when pressed lightly in the center. *The cakes should start to shrink from the sides of the pans only after removal from the oven.*

Let the cakes cool in the pans on racks for 10 minutes. Loosen the sides with a small metal spatula and invert onto greased wire racks. To prevent splitting, reinvert so that the tops are up and cool completely before wrapping airtight.

UNDERSTANDING

Real white chocolate is made up of one-third cocoa butter, one-third sugar, one-third milk solids, and a tiny amount of vanilla and lecithin, a natural emulsifier found in soybeans. In this cake a small amount of white chocolate is added and comparable amounts of fat (butter) and sugar are subtracted. The result, compared to White Velvet Cake, is a more velvety crumb and fuller flavor. Because of the extra milk solids and the lecithin, the cake is also higher, lighter, and more golden in color.

The cocoa butter, which is firmer than butter yet melts in the mouth, makes this cake easy to cut.

This cake is used to make Blueberry Swan Lake (page 165).

STORE:
Airtight: 2 days room temperature, 5 days refrigerated, 2 months frozen. Texture is most perfectly moist the same day as baking.

COMPLEMENTARY ADORNMENTS:
A simple dusting of powdered sugar. *One recipe:* Lemon Buttercream (page 234 or 245). White Chocolate Buttercream or Glaze (page 246 or 248).

SERVE:
Room temperature.

POINTERS FOR SUCCESS:
See page 24.

Checkerboard Fantasy Cake

SERVES 12

𝒜 delightful trompe l'oeil of yellow and chocolate checkerboard with the same exquisite texture and well-balanced flavor of All-Occasion Downy Yellow Butter Cake (page 39). A great party cake, especially for children. Chicago Metallic and Rowoco, two major pan producers, like this recipe so much they both offer it with their checkerboard cake pans!

INGREDIENTS	MEASURE	WEIGHT	
room temperature	*volume*	*ounces*	*grams*
extra bittersweet or semisweet chocolate		3 ounces	85 grams
4 large eggs	6 full fluid ounces	7 ounces (weighed without shells)	200 grams
milk	1⅓ liquid cups	11.25 ounces	320 grams
vanilla	1 tablespoon	•	12 grams
sifted cake flour	4 cups	14 ounces	400 grams
sugar	2 cups	14 ounces	400 grams
baking powder	2 tablespoons	•	29.5 grams
salt	1 teaspoon	•	7 grams
unsalted butter (must be softened)	1 cup	8 ounces	227 grams

A set of three 9-inch by 1-inch checkerboard cake pans, greased, bottoms lined with parchment or wax paper, and then greased again and floured.

Preheat the oven to 350°F.

In a double boiler melt the chocolate over hot (not simmering) water, stirring frequently. Remove from the water.

In a medium bowl lightly combine the eggs, ¼ of the milk, and vanilla.

In a large mixing bowl combine the dry ingredients and mix on low speed for 30 seconds to blend. Add the butter and remaining milk. Mix on low speed until the dry ingredients are moistened. Increase to medium speed (high speed if using a hand mixer) and beat for 1½ minutes to aerate and develop the cake's structure. Scrape down the sides. Gradually add the egg mixture in 3 batches, beating for 20 seconds after each addition to incorporate the ingredients and strengthen the structure. Scrape down the sides.

Divide the batter approximately in half (1¾ pounds/ 793 grams in one bowl, 1½ pounds/680 grams in another bowl). Stir the melted chocolate into the smaller batch of batter until uniform in color. Fill 2 large pastry bags fitted with large round tubes ¾ inches in diameter (a large number 9 tube) with the 2 batters.*

Place the divider rings in 1 of the prepared pans and pipe batter into each section, alternating batter colors. The batter should fill the pan about ½ full. Using a small metal spatula or the back of a spoon, smooth any seams or divisions in the batter. Now carefully lift out the divider and rinse it off. When piping batter for the second layer, alternate the colors, i.e. if you started with yellow for the outside ring, start with chocolate. Pipe batter for the third layer exactly like the first.

Bake 25 minutes or until a tester inserted near the center comes out clean and the cakes spring back when pressed lightly in the centers. *The cakes should start to shrink from the sides of the pans only after removal from the oven.*

Let the cakes cool in the pans on racks for 10 minutes. Loosen the sides with a small metal spatula and invert onto greased wire racks. To prevent splitting, reinvert so that the tops are up and cool completely before wrapping airtight.

When stacking the layers, use a very thin coating of yellow or chocolate frosting to adhere the layers without disturbing the checkerboard effect.

UNDERSTANDING

A slightly higher level of baking powder is used for this cake because the pans are only 1-inch high. Whole eggs provide the structure to accommodate the melted chocolate, which is stirred into half the batter at the very end of mixing. The batter is thick enough to pipe through a pastry bag, making filling the special sections of these pans quick and easy.

I use melted chocolate instead of cocoa because it is convenient to add to the batter and also because its less intense chocolate flavor blends better with the more subtle yellow cake.

FINISHED HEIGHT:
Each layer is 1⅛ inches.

STORE:
Airtight: 2 days room temperature, 5 days refrigerated, 2 months frozen. Texture is most perfectly moist the same day as baking.

COMPLEMENTARY ADORNMENTS:
One recipe: Any dark chocolate frosting or glaze such as Chocolate Cream Glaze (page 271) or Classic Buttercream (page 228 or 230).

SERVE:
Room temperature.

POINTERS FOR SUCCESS:
See page 24.

---

* You may also use glass measuring cups to pour the batter into the pans, but pastry bags are faster and easier to use.

Perfect All-American Chocolate Butter Cake

SERVES 12

*T*his cake has a full chocolate flavor and exceptionally soft, fine texture for a chocolate butter cake. Dutch-processed cocoa makes the neutralizing effect of baking soda unnecessary, eliminating the slightly bitter edge often associated with baking soda chocolate cakes. Ross Horowitz, after photographing this cake for *Chocolatier* magazine, came up with a marvelous description: "When you bite into this cake," he rhapsodized, "it seems light; then it becomes fudgy and chocolaty; then, just when you begin to think you have something, it simply vanishes so you want to take another bite!" My mother was more succinct: "It tastes just like a chocolate bar but softer." (And that was my goal.)

INGREDIENTS	MEASURE	WEIGHT	
room temperature	*volume*	*ounces*	*grams*
unsweetened cocoa (Dutch-processed)	½ cup + 3 tablespoons (lightly spooned into cup)	2.25 ounces	63 grams
boiling water	1 liquid cup	8.25 ounces	236 grams
3 large eggs	scant 5 fluid ounces	5.25 ounces (weighed without shells)	150 grams
vanilla	2¼ teaspoons	•	9 grams
sifted cake flour	2¼ cups + 2 tablespoons	8.25 ounces	235 grams
sugar	1½ cups	10.5 ounces	300 grams
baking powder	1 tablespoon	•	15 grams
salt	¾ teaspoon	•	5 grams
unsalted butter (must be softened)	12 tablespoons	8 ounces	227 grams

Preheat the oven to 350°F.

In a medium bowl whisk together the cocoa and boiling water until smooth. Cool to room temperature.

In another bowl lightly combine the eggs, ¼ of the cocoa mixture, and vanilla.

In a large mixing bowl combine the remaining dry ingredients and mix on low speed for 30 seconds to blend. Add the butter and remaining cocoa mixture. Mix on low speed until the dry ingredients are moistened. Increase to medium speed (high speed if using a hand mixer) and beat for 1½ minutes to aerate and develop the cake's structure. Scrape down the sides. Gradually add the egg mixture in 3 batches, beating for 20 seconds after each addition to incorporate the ingredients and strengthen the structure. Scrape down the sides.

Scrape the batter into the prepared pans and smooth the surface with a spatula. The pans will be about ½ full. Bake 25 to 35 minutes or until a tester inserted near the center comes out clean and the cake springs back when pressed lightly in the center. *The cakes should start to shrink from the sides of the pans only after removal from the oven.*

Let the cakes cool in the pans on racks for 10 minutes. Loosen the sides with a small metal spatula and invert onto greased wire racks. To prevent splitting, reinvert so that the tops are up and cool completely before wrapping airtight.

UNDERSTANDING

The formula for this cake is similar to All-Occasion Downy Yellow Butter Cake with just a few minor concessions to the special nature of chocolate. Some of the flour is replaced with equal weight of cocoa. (Cocoa gives a fuller chocolate flavor than bitter chocolate in a cake. See page 422.) The butter is increased because cocoa creates a stronger and drier structure. Water replaces the milk because, in a chocolate layer cake, milk protein brings out the bitterness in chocolate and ties up flavor—whereas water allows for quick release of full chocolate flavor. Whole eggs are used instead of yolks for practicality, because the flavor improvement offered by yolks alone is not as noticeable in a chocolate cake as it is in a yellow cake.

This cake is used to make La Porcelaine (page 199).

Two 9-inch by 1½-inch cake pans greased, bottoms lined with parchment or wax paper, and then greased and floured.

FINISHED HEIGHT:
Each layer is about 1⅛ inches.

STORE:
Airtight: 2 days room temperature, 5 days refrigerated, 2 months frozen. Texture is most perfectly moist the same day as baking.

COMPLEMENTARY ADORNMENTS:
A simple dusting of powdered sugar. *One recipe:* Any buttercream except for lemon. Any glaze or fondant.

SERVE:
Room temperature.

POINTERS FOR SUCCESS:
See page 24.

Perfect All-American Chocolate Torte

SERVES 8

*T*o my taste, there is no more appealing presentation than an elegant torte glazed with a shiny coating of dark or white chocolate. (Especially if one suspects that there is more chocolate within!)

This richly chocolate butter cake is 1¾ inches high—just right for a torte. It is easy to serve and, with a single long-stemmed red rose on top, fancy enough for a black-tie dinner party.

INGREDIENTS	MEASURE	WEIGHT	
room temperature	*volume*	*ounces*	*grams*
unsweetened cocoa (Dutch-processed)	¼ cup + 3 tablespoons	1.5 ounces	42 grams
boiling water	⅔ liquid cup	5.5 ounces	156 grams
4 large egg yolks	2 full fluid ounces	2.5 ounces	74 grams
vanilla	¾ teaspoon	•	3 grams
sifted cake flour	1½ cups + 1 tablespoon	5.5 ounces	156 grams
sugar	1 cup	7 ounces	200 grams
baking powder	2 teaspoons	•	10 grams
salt	½ teaspoon	•	3.5 grams
unsalted butter (must be softened)	8 tablespoons	5 ounces	142 grams

One 9-inch by 2-inch cake pan or 9-inch springform pan, greased, bottom lined with parchment or wax paper, and then greased again and floured.

FINISHED HEIGHT: 1¾ inches.

Preheat the oven to 350°F.

In a medium bowl whisk together the cocoa and boiling water until smooth. Cool to room temperature.

In another bowl lightly combine the eggs, ¼ of the cocoa mixture, and vanilla.

In a large mixing bowl combine the remaining dry ingredients and mix on low speed for 30 seconds to blend. Add the butter and remaining cocoa mixture. Mix on low speed until the dry ingredients are moistened. Increase to medium speed (high speed if using a hand mixer) and beat for 1½ minutes to aerate and develop the cake's structure. Scrape down the sides. Gradually add the egg mixture in 3 batches, beating for 20 seconds after each addition to incorporate the ingredients and strengthen the structure. Scrape down the sides.

Scrape the batter into the prepared pan and smooth the surface with a spatula. The pan will be about ½ full. Bake 30 to 40 minutes or until a tester inserted near the center comes out clean and the cake springs back when pressed lightly in the center. *The cake should start to shrink from the sides of the pan only after removal from the oven.*

Let the cake cool in the pan on a rack for 10 minutes. Loosen the sides with a small metal spatula, invert onto a greased wire rack, and cool completely before wrapping airtight.

UNDERSTANDING

The formula for this cake is almost identical to the preceding one with two exceptions: Egg yolks are used in place of whole eggs (which weakens the structure enough to result in a perfectly level top), and only two-thirds of the batter is prepared.

This cake is used to make Bittersweet Royale Torte (page 198).

STORE:
Airtight: 2 days room temperature, 5 days refrigerated, 2 months frozen. Texture is most perfectly moist the same day as baking.

COMPLEMENTARY ADORNMENTS:
A simple dusting of powdered sugar. *One recipe:* Any chocolate glaze (white chocolate is especially attractive) or fondant.

SERVE:
Room temperature.

POINTERS FOR SUCCESS:
See page 24. Magi-Cake Strips (pages 20 and 456) gives the best shape for glazing.

Chocolate Domingo Cake

SERVES 10 TO 12

*T*his is quite simply the tenor of chocolate butter cakes. It has the most intense, round, full chocolate flavor notes of any I have experienced, mainly due to the almost double amount of butter it contains. In effect, I have taken the butter usually used in the buttercream and put it in the cake, making it unnecessary and almost undesirable to frost the cake. This cake literally melts in the mouth. The extra butter in this cake also makes it slightly fudgy and easy to slice without crumbs.

In the ancient tradition of creating a fabulous recipe for a favorite opera star, this cake is named for mine: Placido Domingo, in gratitude for the pleasure of his incomparable performances.

INGREDIENTS	MEASURE	WEIGHT	
room temperature	*volume*	*ounces*	*grams*
unsweetened cocoa (Dutch processed) *or* ½ cup nonalkalized cocoa such as Hershey's	¼ cup + 3 tablespoons	1.5 ounces	42 grams
sour cream	⅔ cup	5.5 ounces	160 grams
2 large eggs	3 fluid ounces	3.5 ounces (weighed without shells)	100 grams
vanilla	1½ teaspoons	•	6 grams
sifted cake flour	1½ cups + 1 tablespoon	5.5 ounces	156 grams
sugar	1 cup	7 ounces	200 grams
baking powder	¾ teaspoon	•	4 grams
baking soda	¼ teaspoon	•	1.5 grams
salt	½ teaspoon	•	3.5 grams
unsalted butter (must be softened)	14 tablespoons	7 ounces	200 grams

Preheat the oven to 350°F.

In a medium bowl whisk together the cocoa, sour cream, eggs, and vanilla until smooth.

In a large mixing bowl combine all the remaining dry ingredients and mix on low speed for 30 seconds to blend. Add the butter and ½ the cocoa mixture. Mix on low speed until the dry ingredients are moistened. Increase to medium speed (high speed if using a hand mixer) and beat for 1½ minutes to aerate and develop the cake's structure. Scrape down the sides. Gradually add the remaining cocoa mixture in 2 batches, beating for 20 seconds after each addition to incorporate the ingredients and strengthen the structure. Scrape down the sides.

Scrape the batter into the prepared pan and smooth the surface with a spatula. The pan will be about half full. Bake 30 to 40 minutes or until a tester inserted near the center comes out clean and the cake springs back when pressed lightly in the center. *The cake should start to shrink from the sides of the pan only after removal from the oven.*

Let the cake cool in the pan on a rack for 10 minutes. Loosen the sides with a small metal spatula and invert onto a greased wire rack. Reinvert so that the top is up and cool completely before wrapping airtight.

UNDERSTANDING

This formula is similar to Perfect All-American Chocolate Torte, but sour cream replaces the water to add a lovely, mellow flavor to the chocolate. Although the protein in sour cream normally acts as a flavor inhibitor in chocolate cakes, the close to double amount of butter (this includes the butterfat in the sour cream) corrects this tendency because it is a superb releaser of other flavors. Butter tenderizes cake, so I decreased the leavening to equal half the leavening power of the Perfect All-American Chocolate Torte (page 56).

NOTE: This cake was created at the insistence of my incomparable assistant, David Shamah. He loves the quality that sour cream gives to yellow cake and felt certain it would do something equally wonderful for chocolate unlike milk or buttermilk. He was right; sour cream, it seems, is an exception, and this has become his favorite chocolate cake.

One 9-inch by 2-inch cake pan or a 9-inch springform pan, greased, bottom lined with parchment or wax paper, and then greased again and floured.

FINISHED HEIGHT:
1½ inches (the top of the cake will be rounded when done and will become perfectly flat on cooling).

STORE:
Airtight: 2 days room temperature, 5 days refrigerated, 2 months frozen. Texture is most perfectly moist the same day as baking.

COMPLEMENTARY ADORNMENTS:
A dusting of powdered sugar and a red chocolate rose (page 390) or real red rose. Or the special Chocolate Fossil technique (page 386).

SERVE:
Room temperature.

POINTERS FOR SUCCESS:
See page 24.

Chocolate Fudge Cake

SERVES 12

*T*he molasses in the brown sugar gives this cake a distinctive and pleasantly bitter edge. The texture is soft and light yet moist with good chocolate flavor impact and a lingering bittersweet aftertaste. The particular bittersweet chocolate flavor of this cake goes splendidly with Milk Chocolate Buttercream (page 250).

INGREDIENTS	MEASURE	WEIGHT	
room temperature	*volume*	*ounces*	*grams*
unsweetened cocoa (Dutch-processed) *or* 1 cup nonalkalized cocoa such as Hershey's *	¾ cup + 3 tablespoons (lightly spooned into a cup)	3 ounces	85 grams
boiling water	1½ liquid cups	12.5 ounces	354 grams
3 large eggs	scant 5 fluid ounces	5.25 ounces (weighed without shells)	150 grams
vanilla	1½ teaspoons	•	6 grams
sifted cake flour	3 cups	10.5 ounces	300 grams
light brown sugar	2 cups (firmly packed)	15.25 ounces	434 grams
baking powder	2¼ teaspoons	•	11 grams
baking soda	¾ teaspoon	•	4 grams
salt	¾ teaspoon	•	5 grams
unsalted butter (must be softened)	1 cup	8 ounces	227 grams

Two 9-inch by 1½-inch cake pans greased, bottoms lined with parchment or wax paper, and then greased again and floured.

Preheat the oven to 350°F.

In a medium bowl whisk together the cocoa and boiling water until smooth. Cool to room temperature.

In another bowl lightly combine the eggs, ¼ of the cocoa mixture, and vanilla.

In a large mixing bowl combine the remaining dry ingredients and mix on low speed for 30 seconds. Add the butter and remaining cocoa mixture. Mix on low speed until the dry ingredients are moistened. Increase to medium speed (high speed if using a hand mixer) and beat for 1½

* If using nonalkalized cocoa, eliminate the baking powder and use a total of 1¼ teaspoons of baking soda.

minutes to aerate and develop the cake's structure. Scrape down the sides. Gradually add the egg mixture in 3 batches, beating for 20 seconds after each addition to incorporate the ingredients and strengthen the structure. Scrape down the sides.

Scrape the batter into the prepared pans and smooth the surface with a spatula. The pans will be about ½ full. Bake 20 to 30 minutes or until a tester inserted near the center comes out clean and the cake springs back when pressed lightly in the center. *The cakes should start to shrink from the sides of the pans only after removal from the oven.*

Let the cakes cool in the pans on racks for 10 minutes. Loosen the sides with a small metal spatula and invert onto greased wire racks. To prevent splitting, reinvert so that tops are up and cool completely before wrapping airtight.

UNDERSTANDING

The formula for this cake is similar to Perfect All-American Chocolate Butter Cake. The most significant differences are brown sugar instead of granulated and extra liquid (from the water and the molasses in the brown sugar) replacing one of the eggs. Baking soda is used to neutralize some of the molasses' acidity. The baking soda and baking powder provide equivalent leavening to 2 tablespoons of baking powder. Less vanilla is necessary because the brown sugar contributes so much flavor. This cake has less structure (egg) and more liquid, therefore it is moister, softer, and more tender.

This cake is used to make Chocolate Spike (page 203).

FINISHED HEIGHT:
Each layer is 1⅛ inches.

STORE:
Airtight: 2 days room temperature, 5 days refrigerated, 2 months frozen. Texture is most perfectly moist same day as baking.

COMPLEMENTARY ADORNMENTS:
A simple dusting of powdered sugar. *One recipe:* Milk Chocolate Buttercream (page 250). Ganache Frosting (page 267).

SERVE:
Room temperature.

POINTERS FOR SUCCESS:
See page 24.

Triple Layer Devil's Food Cake

SERVES 18

*T*his is a moist, fine-textured, intensely chocolate cake, with a flavor strongly reminiscent of the beloved deeply cocoa cake of childhood.

INGREDIENTS	MEASURE	WEIGHT	
room temperature	*volume*	*ounces*	*grams*
unsweetened cocoa (nonalkalized, such as Hershey's)	1 cup (lightly spooned into cup)	3 ounces	82 grams
boiling water	1½ liquid cups	12.5 ounces	354 grams
4 large eggs	6 full fluid ounces	7 ounces (weighed without shells)	200 grams
vanilla	1 tablespoon	•	12 grams
sifted cake flour	3½ cups	12.25 ounces	350 grams
sugar	2¼ cups	15.75 ounces	450 grams
baking soda	1 teaspoon	•	5 grams
salt	1 teaspoon	•	7 grams
unsalted butter (must be softened)	1½ cups	12 ounces	340 grams

Three 9-inch by 1½-inch cake pans greased, bottoms lined with parchment or wax paper, then greased again and floured.

Preheat oven to 350°F.

In a medium bowl whisk together cocoa and boiling water until smooth and cool to room temperature.

In a second medium bowl lightly combine eggs, about ¼ of the cocoa mixture, and the vanilla.

In a large mixing bowl combine the remaining dry ingredients and mix on low speed for 30 seconds. Add butter and remaining ¾ of the cocoa mixture. Mix on low speed until dry ingredients are moistened. Increase to medium speed (high speed if using hand mixer) and beat for 1½ minutes to aerate and develop cake's structure. Scrape down the sides.

Gradually add the egg mixture to batter in three batches, beating for 20 seconds after each addition to incorporate ingredients and strengthen structure. Scrape down the sides.

Scrape batter into prepared pans and smooth surface

with a spatula. Pans will be about half full. Bake 20 to 30 minutes or until a tester inserted near center comes out clean and the cake springs back when pressed lightly in center. *The cakes should start to shrink from sides of pans only after removal from the oven.* Let the cakes cool in the pans on racks for 10 minutes. Loosen the sides with a small metal spatula and invert onto greased wire racks. To prevent splitting, reinvert so that tops are up and cool completely before wrapping airtight.

UNDERSTANDING

This cake is essentially the same formula as Perfect All-American Chocolate Butter Cake, one and a half times the quantity. The difference is the use of nonalkalized cocoa and baking soda to neutralize its acidity. The texture is quite similar, due to having maintained the acid balance. It is perhaps a shade less moist due to a slight decrease in cocoa butter contained in the nonalkalized cocoa. The flavor, however, packs a strong, less subtle chocolate punch.

FINISHED HEIGHT:
Each layer about 1⅛ inch.

STORE:
Airtight: 2 days room temperature, 5 days refrigerated, 2 months frozen. Texture is most perfectly moist the same day as baking.

COMPLEMENTARY ADORNMENTS:
One recipe: Milk Chocolate Buttercream (page 250); Burnt Almond Milk Chocolate Ganache Frosting (page 277) or Classic Coffee Buttercream (page 232).

SERVE:
Room temperature.

POINTERS FOR SUCCESS:
See page 24.

Down-Home Chocolate Mayonnaise Cake

SERVES 10

*T*his recipe was given to me by Pauline Howard, of Wardsboro, Vermont, when I was a very young bride who didn't know how to cook or bake. It was invented by the wife of a Hellmann's mayonnaise salesman who was trying to help her husband. It's a homey-looking cake with a glossy dark-brown crust that dips in the center. Coarse yet tender and utterly moist, it's the kind of cake that your mother may have made for you if you were a child in the fifties. Like my mother, yours probably misplaced the recipe, and you have longed for its strangely satisfying, unique flavor ever since. There are a few people, I am sure, who will be as overjoyed as I that I found the original recipe, written on a 4¢ postcard, over twenty-five years later. This book would not be complete without it—my first chocolate cake recipe!

INGREDIENTS	MEASURE	WEIGHT	
room temperature	*volume*	*ounces*	*grams*
unsweetened cocoa (nonalkalized, such as Hershey's)	⅓ cup (lightly spooned into cup)	1 ounce	28 grams
boiling water	1 liquid cup	8.25 ounces	236 grams
vanilla	1 teaspoon	•	4 grams
mayonnaise	¾ cup	5.5 ounces	160 grams
sifted cake flour	2 cups	7 ounces	200 grams
sugar	1 cup	7 ounces	200 grams
baking soda	2 teaspoons		10 grams
salt	½ teaspoon	•	•

Two 8-inch by 1½-inch cake pans greased, bottoms lined with parchment or wax paper, then greased again and floured.

Preheat oven to 350°F.

In a medium bowl whisk together cocoa and boiling water until smooth and cool to room temperature. Whisk in vanilla and mayonnaise.

In a large mixing bowl combine the remaining ingredients and mix on low speed for 30 seconds to blend. Add chocolate mixture. Mix on low speed until dry ingredients are moistened. Increase to medium (high speed if using hand mixer) and beat for 1 minute to aerate and develop cake's structure. Scrape batter into prepared pans (it will be very liquid) and fill the pans only about one third full.

Bake 20 to 25 minutes or until tester inserted near center comes out clean and cake springs back when pressed lightly in center. *Cakes should start to shrink from sides of pans only after removal from oven.* Allow cakes to cool in pans on racks for 10 minutes. Loosen the sides with a small metal spatula and invert onto greased wire racks. Cool completely before wrapping airtight.

UNDERSTANDING

No one will ever divine the mystery ingredient, but mayonnaise is simply an emulsification of egg yolk and oil with a tiny bit of vinegar. The large amounts of oil (in the mayonnaise) and baking soda account for the tenderness of this cake. The extra baking soda also creates the slightly dipped center and the coarse, dark, reddish crumb with a deliciously bitter edge.

FINISHED HEIGHT:
Each layer is 1¼ inches (1⅛ inches in center).

STORE:
Airtight: 3 days room temperature, 5 days refrigerated, 2 months frozen.

COMPLEMENTARY ADORNMENTS:
A simple dusting of powdered sugar. *One recipe:* Any buttercream except for lemon.

SERVE:
Room temperature.

POINTERS FOR SUCCESS:
See page 24.

The cakes in this section are all (with the exception of brioche) variations of basic butter cake, with fruit or vegetable purees supplying most of the liquid. Banana Cake, one of my personal favorites, is the most similar in texture to butter cake. The other cakes are denser, moister and chewier and for the most part speedy to make. Because of their moistness and complexity of flavors and textures, they require no frosting and have a longer shelf life than most other cakes. These qualities also make them suitable for gift-giving. To offer as a more lavish gift, wrap and present the cake in the pan in which it was baked. (Be sure to spray the pan with nonstick vegetable spray before returning the cake to the pan.)

NOTE: Recipes can be doubled if you have extra pans.

FRUIT, VEGETABLE, AND BREAD CAKES

Less Fruity Fruitcake

SERVES 10
TO 12

Fruitcake is one of the most personal cakes. Either you love it or hate it; prefer all fruit to a more cakelike type; prefer the cake saturated with spirits or the spirits in the background.

Robert Farrar Capon stated his case with eloquent and zany humor in a Christmas article called "Fruitcakes: Solid Evidence of Christmas," written some years ago for *The New York Times*. He begins with the question "Whatever happened to the cake in these concoctions?" and proceeds with the following possible explanation as to its disappearance:

Since the public would be unwilling to purchase fruitcakes of a size large enough to contain all of these ingredients (the usual assortment of dried fruits and nuts)—and since making them smaller (the fruitcakes) would raise the probability that a given fruit or nut might not find its way into a given cake—the purveyors of fruitcakes found themselves forced to choose between the two basic components of their product. The cake, of course, lost, giving rise to the now omnipresent and unavoidable holiday gift: the fruit brick. In recent studies by the physics departments of major universities, the atomic weight of this remarkable confection has been calculated to be just below that of uranium.

This extreme density, it was discovered, is due to the method by which modern fruitcakes are made. After the manufacturers abandoned the use of agglutinating agents such as flour and eggs, they developed a special bonding technique by which the fruits and nuts were compacted by a hydraulic press. This special piece of "bakery" equipment, seventy times more powerful than the ram that reduces used cars to crumpled blocks, creates in the "cake" an internal pressure so great that the fruits and nuts adhere to each other by their own molecular attraction.

My fruited offering to posterity is an answer to Capon's opening question "Whatever happened to the cake . . . ?" It's back. In fact, it is the sort of fruitcake that has more batter than fruit and is so moist it can almost be described as a pudding. Molasses provides the slightly bitter edge to temper the sweetness of the glacéed fruit. The rum flavor comes through as aromatic but subdued. It took years to perfect this recipe because each version had to ripen for three months before tasting, and many months would pass between tasting and subsequent rebaking. A taste of this triumphant final fruitcake calls up images of dark Victorian houses filled with secret corners and haunting old memories.

The texture and flavor of this cake are at their best when baked in small pans, which also makes serving the small, rich portions easier. Decorative baking molds such as the Turk's head provide attractive shapes for gift-giving.

As a special note I must add that my friend Blair Brown offered her six-month-old daughter, Julia, a taste of this cake and she wanted more. (We call her Julia child.) It was the first cake she'd ever eaten and, I would say, a dramatic initiation into the world of sweets!

INGREDIENTS	MEASURE	WEIGHT	
room temperature	*volume*	*ounces*	*grams*
small mixed candied fruit	½ cup	2.25 ounces	64 grams
candied citron	2 tablespoons	1.25 ounces	35 grams
dried currants	¼ cup	1.25 ounces	35 grams
broken pecans	¼ cup	1 ounce	28 grams
Myers's dark rum	½ liquid cup	3.75 ounces	110 grams
unsifted cake flour	½ cup (dip and sweep method)	2.25 ounces	65 grams
cinnamon	¼ teaspoon	•	•
baking soda	⅛ teaspoon	•	•
salt	¼ teaspoon	•	3.5 grams
unsalted butter (must be softened)	8 tablespoons	4 ounces	113 grams
dark brown sugar	¼ cup (firmly packed)	2 ounces	60 grams
1 large egg	3 tablespoons	1.75 ounces (weighed without shell)	50 grams
unsulfured molasses (preferably Grandma's)	¼ liquid cup	2.75 ounces	80 grams
milk	2 tablespoons	1 ounce	30 grams

One 3½- to 4-cup baking mold or a 6-inch by 2-inch cake pan, greased and floured. My favorite mold is a 3-cup Turk's head (page 453). If using the Turks' head, fill it only three-fourths full and bake the remaining batter in a small greased and floured custard cup.

FINISHED HEIGHT:
Baked in a 3-cup Turk's head mold: 2½ inches.

STORE:
Keep at cool room temperature for 3 months without opening the container. This will allow the rum to mellow. If you plan to store it longer, unwrap the cake and sprinkle it with an additional tablespoon of rum or else the aromatic edge of the rum will dull and the cake will become dry. Repeat this procedure every 3 months. Fruitcakes have been known to keep for years. (I usually eat the little one baked in the custard cup as soon as it's baked—still warm from the oven!)

COMPLEMENTARY ADORNMENTS:
If baked in a decorative mold, the cake is beautiful unadorned or with a simple wreath of holly or boxwood. Baked in a plain cake pan, the cake can be cov-

Preheat the oven to 325°F.

At least 24 hours ahead mince the candied fruit and citron (a food processor sprayed lightly with nonstick vegetable spray works beautifully for this sticky task) and soak with the currants and nuts in ¼ cup rum. Cover tightly and store at room temperature.

In a small bowl whisk the flour, cinnamon, baking soda, and salt to combine. In a large mixing bowl cream the butter and sugar until light and fluffy. Beat in the egg and then the flour mixture in 3 batches, alternating with the molasses and milk. Add the candied fruit mixture with the soaking rum and beat until blended. The batter will be slightly curdled because of the small amount of flour but this will not affect the cake's texture.

Scrape the batter into the prepared mold and bake 40 to 45 minutes or until the cake springs back when lightly touched and just begins to shrink from the sides of the pan and a tester comes out clean.

Let the cake cool in the pan for 10 minutes and then sprinkle with 2 tablespoons rum. Place a piece of plastic wrap large enough to wrap the cake on the counter. Moisten a piece of cheesecloth also large enough to wrap the cake with 1 tablespoon rum. Place the cheesecloth on the plastic wrap, unmold cake onto it, and sprinkle the top with the remaining 1 tablespoon rum. Drape the top and sides of the hot cake with the cheesecloth and plastic wrap, pressing closely to the cake.

Let the cake cool to room temperature before covering tightly with heavy-duty foil. Place the cake in an airtight container such as a small tin or heavy-duty plastic container. If using the tin, run a piece of masking tape around the rim to create a better seal.

VARIATION

FRUIT CUPCAKES: For some mystical reason, these little gems require no mellowing. They are delicious warm from the oven and remain moist for up to 6 weeks! Fill 8 greased and floured muffin tins ¾ full and bake 20 minutes or until a cake tester inserted in the center comes out clean. Sprinkle each with 1 teaspoon rum, unmold after 5 minutes and store airtight at room temperature. For a more decorative shape, use a Bundt-style muffin pan (see Maid of Scandinavia, page 465). The batter makes 11 little cakes. Bake for 20 minutes.

For those who prefer a sweeter cake without the bitter edge: Replace 2 tablespoons of the molasses with Lyle's refiner's syrup or light corn syrup. Cake will not be as dark brown.

ered with rolled fondant and decorated. The contrast of the pristine white fondant against the almost black color of the fruitcake is breathtaking.

SERVE:
Room temperature, cut into thin slivers with a serrated knife.

POINTERS FOR SUCCESS:
See page 24.

*T*his moist, light, exquisitely tender cake with the rich taste of banana is accented by the lively tang of sour cream and lemon. The 2-inch layer is perfect as a European-style torte. Unfrosted, it makes a great picnic cake. Because chocolate and banana are such a perfect combination, Sour Cream Ganache (page 275) is sublime with this cake. For a more subtle combination, pick up the lemon accent instead and frost with Lemon Buttercream (page 234 or 245).

Cordon Rose Banana Cake

SERVES 8

INGREDIENTS	MEASURE	WEIGHT	
room temperature	volume	ounces	grams
2 large ripe bananas	1 cup	8 ounces	227 grams
sour cream *	2 tablespoons	1 ounce	30 grams
2 large eggs	3 fluid ounces	3.5 ounces	100 grams (weighed without shells)
grated lemon zest	2 teaspoons	•	4 grams
vanilla	1½ teaspoons	•	6 grams
sifted cake flour	2 cups	7 ounces	200 grams
sugar	¾ cup + 2 tablespoons	6 ounces	170 grams
baking soda	1 teaspoon	•	5 grams
baking powder	¾ teaspoon	•	3.7 grams
salt	½ teaspoon	•	3.5 grams
unsalted butter (must be softened)	10 tablespoons	5 ounces	142 grams

* For extra moistness you can use up to ½ cup (4¼ ounces/121 grams) sour cream

One 9-inch by 2-inch cake pan or 9-inch springform pan, greased, bottom lined with parchment or wax paper, and then greased again and floured.

FINISHED HEIGHT:
2 inches to within 1 inch of the side; 1½ inches at the side.

STORE:
Airtight: 2 days room temperature, 5 days refrigerated, 2 months frozen.

COMPLEMENTARY ADORNMENTS:
A simple dusting of powdered sugar. *One recipe:* Sour Cream Ganache (page 275). A half recipe: Lemon Buttercream (page 234 or 245) or Passion Buttercream (page 245) and chopped macadamia nuts.

SERVE:
Room temperature.

POINTERS FOR SUCCESS:
See page 24.

Preheat the oven to 350°F.

In a food processor process the banana and sour cream until smooth. Add the eggs, lemon zest, and vanilla and process briefly just to blend.

In a large mixing bowl combine the dry ingredients and mix on low speed for 30 seconds to blend. Add the butter and ½ the banana mixture. Mix on low speed until the dry ingredients are moistened. Increase to medium speed (high speed if using a hand mixer) and beat for 1½ minutes to aerate and strengthen the cake's structure. Scrape down the sides. Gradually add the remaining banana mixture in 2 batches, beating for 20 seconds after each addition to incorporate the ingredients and develop the structure. Scrape down the sides.

Scrape the batter into the prepared pan and smooth the surface with a spatula. Bake 30 to 40 minutes or until a wire cake tester inserted in the center comes out clean and the cake springs back when pressed lightly in the center. *The cake should start to shrink from the sides of the pan only after removal from the oven.*

Let the cake cool in the pan on a rack for 10 minutes. Loosen the sides with a small metal spatula and unmold or remove the sides of the springform pan. Allow the cake to cool completely before wrapping airtight.

UNDERSTANDING

This banana cake is based on a basic butter cake (page 470). Banana, which is about 75 percent water, supplies the liquid. Because it also adds sweetness, the sugar is reduced by 15 percent. The reduction of sugar and the addition of fiber from the banana toughen the cake so an extra ounce of butter is added to compensate for this. Baking soda is used to temper the acidity of the banana and the sour cream. The fiber makes it possible to add extra sour cream without weakening the structure. (With ½ cup sour cream, the cake will keep 5 days at room temperature)

This firm, moist cake, fragrant with spices, is perfect for holiday entertaining. A snap to prepare, it freezes beautifully and the flavor and texture actually benefit from preparation a day or two ahead. The subtlety of walnut oil echoes and complements the walnuts in the cake; pumpkin adds the illusion of richness. Actually, it is hard to believe that this delicious cake has low cholesterol (64.5 mg. per serving). To make it cholesterol-free, substitute 3 large egg whites (3 liquid ounces) for the 2 whole eggs.

Pumpkin-Walnut Ring

SERVES 6 TO 8

INGREDIENTS	MEASURE	WEIGHT	
room temperature	*volume*	*ounces*	*grams*
sifted cake flour	1¼ cups	4.5 ounces	125 grams
baking soda	1 teaspoon	•	5 grams
cinnamon	1 teaspoon	•	•
nutmeg	½ teaspoon	•	•
ground cloves	¼ teaspoon	•	•
salt	¼ teaspoon	•	•
coarsely chopped toasted walnuts	½ cup	2 ounces	57 grams
2 large eggs	3 fluid ounces	3.5 ounces	100 grams (weighed without shells)
light brown sugar	¾ cup (firmly packed)	5.75 ounces	163 grams
safflower oil	3 liquid ounces	2.75 ounces	80 grams
walnut oil	2 tablespoons	1 ounce	28 grams
fresh *or* canned unsweetened pumpkin puree	1 cup	8.25 ounces	238 grams

Preheat the oven to 350°F.

In a small bowl combine the flour, soda, spices, and walnuts and whisk to blend.

In a large mixing bowl, beat the eggs, sugar, and oils for 2 to 3 minutes or until very smooth. Add the pumpkin and beat just until smooth. Add the flour mixture and beat until completely moistened.

One 6-cup baby Bundt pan or loaf pan, greased and floured.

FINISHED HEIGHT:
Baked in a 6-cup Bundt: 3 inches high in the middle.

STORE:
When completely cool, wrap well in plastic wrap and foil and store at room temperature overnight. Keeps 5 days refrigerated or 3 months frozen. Flavors blend best when prepared 1 day ahead.

COMPLEMENTARY ADORNMENTS:
One Recipe: Chocolate Walnut Drizzle Glaze (page 249).

SERVE:
Room temperature.

POINTERS FOR SUCCESS:
See page 24. Do not double this recipe to bake in a larger pan as the side crust gets too brown.

Scrape the batter into the prepared pan and bake 30 to 35 minutes or until a cake tester inserted in the thickest part of the cake comes out clean. Cool in the pan on a rack for 10 minutes and then unmold onto the rack.

UNDERSTANDING

Compared to a butter cake, the addition of nuts and the fiber from the pumpkin are compensated for by using less flour. Oil replaces the butter (a little less is used because oil is 100 percent fat, whereas butter is only 81 percent fat). The liquid is provided by the pumpkin, which is 90 percent water. Baking soda is used to temper the acidity of the pumpkin and the molasses in the brown sugar, and ¼ cup extra sugar is added to balance the pumpkin and spice flavors.

These cupcakes are miniature versions of zucchini bread, which, to my mind, has always seemed more like a cake than a bread. Perhaps it was dubbed "bread" because it is traditionally baked in a loaf pan. The cupcakes are less sweet than most cakes in this book and far less sweet than commercial muffins.

These healthy, easy-to-make gems are delicious treats to pack in lunch boxes or to serve for breakfast. The optional raisins make the cupcakes even moister and more nutritious. To make them cholesterol free, substitute 3 large egg whites (3 liquid ounces) for the 2 whole eggs.

Although zucchini "breads" are usually made with white sugar, I prefer the richer color and flavor of brown sugar.

Zucchini Cupcakes

MAKES
14 TO 16
CUPCAKES

INGREDIENTS	MEASURE	WEIGHT	
room temperature	volume	ounces	grams
sifted cake flour	1½ cups (lightly spooned into cup)	6 ounces	170 grams
baking soda	1 teaspoon	•	5 grams
cinnamon	1 teaspoon	•	•
powdered ginger	½ teaspoon	•	•
ground cloves	¼ teaspoon	•	•
salt	¼ teaspoon	•	•
coarsely chopped toasted walnuts (page 324)	⅔ cup	2.5 ounces	75 grams
2 large eggs	3 fluid ounces	3.5 ounces (weighed without shells)	100 grams
light brown sugar	¾ cup (firmly packed)	5.75 ounces	163 grams
safflower oil	½ cup	3.75 ounces	107 grams
grated zucchini	2 cups (firmly packed)	8 ounces	227 grams
optional: raisins	½ cup	2.5 ounces	72 grams

Preheat the oven to 350°F.

In a small bowl combine the flour, baking soda, spices, and walnuts and whisk to blend.

In a mixing bowl beat the eggs, sugar, and oil for 2 to

Greased and floured muffin tins.

STORE:
Airtight: 3 days room temperature, 5 days refrigerated, or 3 months frozen. The flavor is even more delicious the day after baking.

SERVE:
Room temperature.

POINTERS FOR SUCCESS:
See page 24. Use a food processor with the shredding disc or the largest holes on a hand grater to grate the zucchini. To promote even baking, add a few tablespoons of water to any unfilled muffin cups.

3 minutes or until very smooth. Add the zucchini and beat just until smooth. Add the dry ingredients and optional raisins and beat until completely moistened.

Scrape the batter into the prepared muffin tins, filling each cup ¾ full, and bake 20 to 25 minutes or until a cake tester inserted in the center comes out clean. Cool in the pan on a rack for 5 minutes. Unmold onto the rack. Cool and wrap airtight.

UNDERSTANDING

This formula is almost identical to Pumpkin Walnut Cake. Since pumpkin supplies a little more structure than zucchini, extra flour is added to compensate.

If using all whites instead of whole egg, the cakes will be slightly more chewy.

NOTE: If you prefer a paler version with a more delicate flavor, replace the brown sugar with ¾ cup (5.25 ounces/ 150 grams) granulated sugar, reduce the baking soda to ½ teaspoon, and add ½ teaspoon baking powder.

This cake, inspired by Jean Hewitt's Carrot Cake,* is moist without being heavy. It is wheat colored with flecks of golden carrot throughout, and has a fresh, wheaty, delicious flavor with the sweet perfume of honey coming through only as a wonderful lingering aftertaste. Of course, it is lovely with White Chocolate Cream Cheese Frosting, but I'd just as soon eat this cake *au nature*. I'm sure it is an illusion, but eating this cake makes me feel pure and healthy!

Golden Wheat Carrot Ring

SERVES 10 TO 12

INGREDIENTS	MEASURE	WEIGHT	
room temperature	*volume*	*ounces*	*grams*
finely shredded carrots	2 cups	7 ounces	200 grams
lemon juice, freshly squeezed	¼ liquid cup	2 ounces	62 grams
sifted whole wheat flour	1 cup	4.5 ounces	125 grams
sifted cake flour	1 cup	3.5 ounces	100 grams
salt	½ teaspoon	•	3.5 grams
baking powder	½ teaspoon	•	2.5 grams
baking soda	1 teaspoon	•	5 grams
cinnamon	1 teaspoon	•	•
2 large eggs	3 fluid ounces	3.5 ounces (weighed without shells)	100 grams
unsalted butter, melted	10 tablespoons	5 ounces	142 grams
honey	¾ liquid cup	8.75 ounces	250 grams

Preheat the oven to 350°F.

In a small bowl combine the carrots and lemon juice.

In a large mixing bowl combine the dry ingredients and mix for 30 seconds to blend. Add the eggs, butter, honey, and carrot mixture. Mix on low speed until the dry ingredients are moistened. Increase to medium speed (high speed if using a hand mixer) and beat for 30 seconds or until well mixed.

Scrape the batter into the prepared mold and bake 30 minutes or until the cake springs back when lightly pressed in the center and a tester comes out clean.

* Jean Hewitt, *The New York Times Natural Foods Cookbook* (New York: Quadrangle Books, 1971).

One 5-cup savarin ring mold, well-buttered. (No flour necessary. The butter gives a lovely flavor to the outside of the cake.)

FINISHED HEIGHT: 2¼ inches.

La Brioche Cake

SERVES 14 TO 16
(frosted)

Let the cake cool 10 minutes in the pan on a rack. Unmold onto a lightly greased rack and cool completely.

UNDERSTANDING

Compared to basic butter cake (page 470), the ¾ cup of honey replaces the sweetness of 1 cup of sugar, and the carrots, which are 88 percent water, provide the liquid. To compensate for the extra water provided by the honey and carrots, ¼ cup flour has been added. Because more flour and water tend to toughen and strengthen a cake's structure, an extra ounce of butter and extra leavening have been added. To temper the acidity of the honey and lemon juice, part of the leavening is baking soda. The butter is melted to increase its tenderizing capability. The extra leavening also helps to lighten the texture.

A fine bread such as brioche makes a glorious base for a cake. It offers a satiny-soft, resilient texture, yeasty flavor, and the advantage of very little sugar (only enough to feed the yeast). This means that the cake can be refreshingly saturated with syrup without becoming cloyingly sweet.

My favorite buttercream for this cake is Praline Silk Meringue Buttercream (page 241) or Crème Ivoire Praliné (page 249). Both blend beautifully with the faint edge of molasses and burnt sugar in the dark rum syrup.

Although this brioche takes two days to make, the total working time only adds up to about 15 minutes!

DAY BEFORE
MAKE THE SPONGE

When using yeast always begin by proofing it to make sure it is alive. If using fresh yeast, smell it to be sure it doesn't have a sour odor. To proof the yeast, use warm water (hot water would kill it). In a small bowl combine the water (ideally a tepid 100°F. if using fresh yeast; a little warmer, 110°F., if using dry), ½ teaspoon sugar, and the yeast. If using fresh yeast, crumble it slightly while adding. Set aside in a draft-free spot for 10 to 20 minutes. By this time, the mixture should be full of bubbles. If not, the yeast is too old to be useful.

Place ⅓ cup of the flour and 1 egg in a food processor (preferably with the dough blade) and process a few seconds until mixed. Add the yeast mixture and stir

INGREDIENTS	MEASURE	WEIGHT	
room temperature	*volume*	*ounces*	*grams*
water	2½ tablespoons	1.25 ounces	37 grams
sugar	2 tablespoons	1 ounce	25 grams
fresh yeast* *or*	2 packed teaspoons	0.5 ounce	14 grams
dry yeast (*not* rapid-rise)	1½ teaspoons	•	4.5 grams
unsifted bread flour	about 1½ cups (dip and sweep method)	8 ounces	227 grams
salt	½ teaspoon	•	3.5 grams
1 large egg 2 large eggs, cold	•	6 ounces 170 grams (weighed in the shells)	
unsalted butter	10 tablespoons	5 ounces†	142 grams†
1¾ CUPS SYRUP (18 OUNCES/510 GRAMS)			
sugar	¾ cup	5.25 ounces	150 grams
water	1¼ liquid cups	10.5 ounces	295 grams
dark rum	6 tablespoons	3 ounces	82 grams

* Fresh yeast causes dough to rise faster.
† 4 to 6 ounces of butter may be used. The lesser amount offers a lighter texture, the higher amount a richer flavor. (Brioche Mousseline is made with equal weight of butter and flour, but it must be prepared by hand. Madeleine Kamman tells me that in France the dough for this brioche is mixed using only the fingertips so as not to develop much gluten. This keeps the butter from oozing out during baking.)

with a rubber scraper until smooth. Sprinkle the remaining flour over the mixture but do not mix it in. Cover and let stand for 1½ to 2 hours.

KNEADING THE DOUGH

Add the remaining sugar, salt, and remaining 2 cold eggs and process 1½ minutes or until the dough is smooth, shiny, and cleans the bowl. Let rest 5 minutes with the feed tube open. Add the butter in 2 batches and process for 20 seconds after each addition or until incorporated. (The butter must be soft so as not to overtax the motor of the processor. If the processor should stall, let rest 5 minutes.)*

* To prepare brioche dough in a heavy-duty mixer such as the KitchenAid, use the flat beater and, when the dough starts to climb up the beater, change to the dough hook. Beat about 5 minutes on medium speed or until the dough is smooth, shiny, very elastic, and begins to clean the bowl. Beat in the butter by the tablespoon until incorporated.

One 8-inch by 2-inch cake pan or 8-inch springform pan, buttered.

FINISHED HEIGHT:
1½ inches.

STORE:
Syrup: 1 month refrigerated in an airtight container.
Brioche: Wrapped airtight, 2 days room temperature and 3 months frozen. It is

best not to refrigerate brioche as it hardens.

COMPLEMENTARY ADORNMENTS:
Half recipe Praline Silk Meringue Buttercream (page 241) or *one recipe* Crème Ivoire Praliné (page 249) and toasted chopped hazelnuts (page 324).

SERVE:
Room temperature or lightly chilled.

POINTERS FOR SUCCESS:
Use bread flour. *Do not* use rapid-rise yeast. Be sure the yeast is active. Do not allow rising dough to be in an area over 80°–85°F. Do not allow the dough to rise more than the recommended amounts or it will weaken the structure. Do not deflate the dough before chilling or the butter will leak out. If this should happen inadvertently, chill the dough for 1 hour and knead the butter back into the dough.

FIRST RISE

Scrape the dough into a lightly buttered bowl. It will be very soft and elastic. Sprinkle lightly with flour to prevent a crust from forming. Cover the bowl tightly with plastic wrap and let rise in a warm place (80°F. but not above or the yeast will develop a sour taste) until double in bulk, about 2 hours. Refrigerate for at least 30 minutes to 1 hour. Deflate dough by gently stirring it and refrigerate for another hour.

REDISTRIBUTING THE YEAST

Turn dough onto a lightly floured surface and gently press it into a rectangle. Fold the dough into thirds (as in folding a business letter) and again press it out into a rectangle, lightly flouring the surface as needed to prevent stickiness. Fold it again into thirds and dust it lightly with flour on all sides. Wrap it loosely but securely in plastic wrap and then foil and refrigerate it for 6 hours or up to 2 days to allow dough to ripen and harden.

Gently deflate the dough by kneading lightly with floured hands, and press it into the prepared pan.

Cover the dough loosely with buttered plastic wrap and let rise in a warm, preferably humid, area away from drafts for 1½ to 3 hours or until it has almost tripled in bulk. It will reach the top of a 2-inch-high cake pan.

Place a baking sheet in the oven and preheat to 425°F. (The hot baking sheet will boost the "oven spring"—the sudden expansion of the dough during the first few minutes of baking.)

Place the cake pan on the hot baking sheet and bake for 5 minutes. Lower the temperature to 375°F. and bake for 20 minutes or until a skewer comes out clean. Unmold the brioche and cool on a rack. When ready to complete the cake, trim the top, bottom, and sides with a serrated knife so that the brioche measures 7 inches by 1½ to 1¾ inches (about 1 pound in weight).

Place in a 9-inch pan and pour the syrup on top. Let stand for 10 minutes or until the syrup is absorbed, turning the cake over to help absorption.

TO MAKE SYRUP

In a small saucepan with a tight-fitting lid combine the sugar and water and bring to a rolling boil, stirring constantly. Cover immediately, remove from the heat, and cool completely. Transfer to a liquid measuring cup and stir in the rum. If syrup has evaporated slightly, add enough water to equal 1¾ cups syrup.

UNDERSTANDING
Unlike a cake, which is primarily a starch structure, bread depends on protein in the form of gluten to create its framework. The higher the protein content of the flour, the stronger the structure will be and the finer the grain of the bread (directly the opposite of cake). This dough is exceptionally wet. Just enough extra flour is added to handle it for shaping, resulting in a very light, soft brioche.

I do not use rapid-rise yeast because the flavor development and texture are superior with slower rising. During extended periods of rising, the yeast produces a desirable acidic quality, and it is for this reason that dough is refrigerated overnight before baking. A brilliant technique, discovered by Shirley Corriher, to stimulate this acidity when time does not allow to let the dough rest overnight is to add ½ teaspoon cider vinegar or mild-flavored fruit vinegar for every 1½ cups of flour. Add it to the flour and salt before blending. Do not add any more vinegar or it will weaken the gluten.

Paula Wolfert (in her superb articles on brioche in *The Pleasures of Cooking,* which greatly influenced the development of this recipe) recommends melting and browning one fifth (2 tablespoons) of the butter for extra-rich flavor. Be sure to let the butter cool before adding it along with the rest of the butter. I add the browned particles as well.

Paula's sponge method and technique for redistributing the yeast result in the lightest, finest grained brioche possible. The dough actually surges upward, practically leaping from the pan, when baked!

Brioche made in a food processor is a speedy and simple operation. If you wish to double this recipe, it is safer to use the heavy-duty mixer method because a larger amount of dough might overheat some food processors, causing them to stall. (I have successfully made a double batch using the Cuisinart DLC-7 by melting the butter and allowing it to cool to barely tepid before adding it with the motor running.)

This cake is used to make Praline Brioche (page 171).

VARIATION
STRAWBERRY SAVARIN: A Savarin is actually a brioche dough baked in the shape of a ring. Use a well-buttered 6-

cup ring mold. Baking time is the same as for brioche baked in a cake pan. For the syrup, replace the dark rum with 2 tablespoons of freshly squeezed lemon juice, ¼ cup kirsch and 1 tablespoon finely grated lemon zest.

For an attractive and delicious accompaniment, fill center of ring with 2 pints of strawberries, washed and hulled and brush savarin and berries with ¼ cup red current jelly, heated and strained. Garnish with rosettes of lightly sweetened Perfect Whipped Cream (page 253) and Crystallized Violets (page 326).

CUSTARD CAKES

The two basic cakes in this section, Cheesecake and Chocolate Mousse or Truffle Cake, contain no flour, rise little, and are cooked in water baths to keep them creamy. They are actually custard fillings in the shape of cakes—rich, delicious, and lush in texture.

These cakes are probably the two most beloved and timeless of American cakes, so I have included all of my favorite permutations. A bonus: These cakes are quick and easy to make.

NOTE: Recipes can be doubled if you have extra pans.

CHEESECAKES

I am passionate on the subject of cheesecake. While many ethnic groups have versions of cheesecake, my favorite is my own culture's claim to fame: New York Jewish. It is one of the things displaced New Yorkers seem to miss most. (Why else would menus as far away as California boast "New York Cheesecake"?) It is a thoroughly creamy cheesecake, smooth and dense yet easy to eat because of the refreshing tartness of lemon and sour cream.

Cheesecake could really be classified more as a custard than as a cake. When this realization first hit me I decided to treat cheesecake as a custard and bake it in a water bath. To my delight, the result was perfectly creamy from stem to stern (without the usual dry outer edge).

It has been reported to me that this cheesecake converts people who think they don't like cheesecake and that it spoils those who are already devotees. A friend told me that after making this cake for every major family event during the past three years, one of her nephews turned down the cheesecake at a renowned restaurant stating: "I don't eat cheesecake out!" This same friend, Shirley Corriher, once featured this cake on her local radio program. The station informed her several weeks later that the program brought in more letters requesting the recipe than did any other in the history of the station. The gem of the collection was from the Atlanta Federal Penitentiary which read (and you have to supply the southern drawl): "We simple must have the recipe for that Cordon Rose Cheesecake!"

Cordon Rose Cream Cheesecake

SERVES 8 TO 12

INGREDIENTS	MEASURE	WEIGHT	
room temperature	*volume*	*pounds/ounces*	*grams*
cream cheese*	2 (8-ounce) packages	1 pound	454 grams
sugar	1 cup	7 ounces	200 grams
optional: cornstarch†	1 tablespoon	•	8 grams
3 large eggs	scant 5 fluid ounces	5.25 ounces	150 grams (weighed without shells)
freshly squeezed lemon juice	3 tablespoons	1.5 ounces	47 grams
vanilla	1½ teaspoons	•	6 grams
salt	¼ teaspoon	•	•
sour cream	3 cups	1 pound 9.5 ounces	726 grams

* Don't be tempted to use the more expensive "natural" cream cheese. Philadelphia brand, available even in Japan, offers the best and most consistent flavor for this cake.
† If cornstarch is omitted, a small amount of liquid will seep out after unmolding. If the cake has a sponge base, this is no problem. Otherwise, liquid can be absorbed with a paper towel. I prefer not using the cornstarch as the cake is a shade more creamy. Also, it makes it suitable to serve as a Passover dessert.

Preheat the oven to 350°F.

In a large mixing bowl beat the cream cheese and sugar until very smooth (about 3 minutes), preferably with a whisk beater. Beat in the cornstarch if desired. Add the eggs, 1 at a time, beating after each addition until smooth and scraping down the sides. Add the lemon juice, vanilla, and salt and beat until incorporated. Beat in the sour cream just until blended.

Pour the batter into the prepared pan. Set the pan in the larger pan and surround it with 1 inch of very hot water. Bake 45 minutes. Turn off the oven without opening the door and let the cake cool for 1 hour. Remove to a rack

One 8-inch by 2½-inch or higher springform pan, greased and bottom lined with greased parchment or wax paper; outside of the pan wrapped with a double layer of heavy-duty foil to prevent seepage.

One 10-inch cake pan or roasting pan to serve as a water bath.

FINISHED HEIGHT:
2½ inches.

STORE:
1 week refrigerated. Do not freeze because the texture will become less smooth.

COMPLEMENTARY ADORNMENTS:
¾ cup Lemon Curd (page 340). *One recipe*: White Chocolate Cream Cheese Buttercream (page 237). Cherry Topping (page 344 or 345). Blueberry Topping (page 348 or 349). Cran-Raspberry Glaze (page 330). Jewel Glaze (page 329).

POINTERS FOR SUCCESS:
Wrapping the pan with foil keeps it watertight. Grease the sides of the pan so the surface will not crack when the cake starts to shrink on cooling. Chill thoroughly before unmolding.
The water bath pan must not be higher than the springform pan or it will slow down baking.

and cool to room temperature (about 1 hour). Cover with plastic wrap and refrigerate overnight.

To Unmold: Have ready a serving plate and a flat plate at least 8 inches in diameter, covered with plastic wrap. Place pan on heated burner and move it around for 15 seconds. Wipe sides of pan with a hot, damp towel.

Run a thin metal spatula around the sides of the cake and release the sides of the springform pan. Place the plastic-wrapped plate on top and invert. Remove the bottom of the pan and the parchment. Reinvert onto the serving plate and use a small metal spatula to smooth the sides. Refrigerate until shortly before serving.

NOTES: An 8- by 3-inch solid cake pan can be used instead of a springform. To unmold the cake, run a thin spatula around the sides, place the pan on heated burner for 10 to 20 seconds, moving the pan back and forth, and then invert. If the cake does not release, return to the hot burner for a few more seconds.

For a richer, denser cheesecake that completely holds its moisture without cornstarch, replace the 3 whole eggs with 6 egg yolks.

PROCESSOR METHOD
A food processor also works well to mix this batter. Process the cream cheese and sugar for 30 seconds or until smooth. Add the cornstarch if desired and pulse to blend. Add the eggs, 1 at a time, with the motor running. Add the lemon juice, vanilla, salt, and sour cream and pulse to combine.

BOTTOMS FOR CHEESECAKE

AU NATUREL: This cheesecake is firm enough to be unmolded and served without a base if desired.

BISCUIT ROULADE: A very elegant presentation is to "sandwich" the cheesecake between soft layers of sponge-type cake. Almond Biscuit blends particularly well with the lemon and cheese flavors. Bake Almond Biscuit (page 144) and cut it into two 8-inch rounds. Use 1 round to line the bottom of the parchment-lined springform pan before pouring in the batter. After baking the cheesecake, top it with the second round. Chill and unmold as usual. Sprinkle with powdered sugar if desired. Cake scraps can be cut into shapes to decorate the sides.

BISCUIT À LA CUILLIÈRE: Homemade or packaged ladyfingers can be used to line the bottom and sides of the cake pan. Use a 9- by 3-inch pan and butter to grease the sides of the pan; this holds the ladyfingers in position. After baking 25 minutes, cover the top of the cheesecake loosely with foil to prevent over-browning. Before unmolding, wipe the outside of the pan with a hot, wet towel.

COOKIE CRUMB CRUST: Chocolate cookies blend well with cherry topping. Ginger, graham, and lemon-nut cookies go well with fruit-flavored fillings or toppings. As crumb crusts become soggy if placed in the pan before baking, I prefer to pat the crumbs onto the cake after baking and unmolding. You will need about ¾ cup if you wish to do the bottom as well as the sides. Use the same technique as for applying chopped nuts (page 324).

FILLINGS AND RECIPE VARIATIONS
There are so many possible ways to flavor a cheesecake that entire books have been devoted to the subject. Herewith are some of my own personal favorites.

WHITE CHOCOLATE CHEESECAKE: Fine-quality white chocolate, such as Tobler Narcisse (which contains cocoa butter), adds a luscious flavor to the cream cheese base. The cake is mildly reminiscent of white chocolate and slightly tangy. It is not cloyingly sweet because the amount of sugar contained in the white chocolate is removed from the amount of sugar in the batter. The texture of this cake is slightly firmer because of the cocoa butter but is still creamy with a special melt-in-the-mouth quality.
To make White Chocolate Cheesecake: Reduce the sugar to ¼ cup (1.75 ounces/50 grams) and the lemon juice to 2 tablespoons. Melt 9 ounces/255 grams white chocolate and cool. Blend into the batter after the sour cream is incorporated.

BANANA CHEESECAKE: Anyone who has ever eaten bananas and sour cream and loved it will know before even tasting this cake just how mellow and delicious it's going to be. The bananas seem to have some preserving quality as well because this cake stays fresh tasting for at least 12 days! Bananas and sour cream have about the same moisture content so all you do is replace 1 cup of the sour cream with 1 cup of mashed banana. Blueberry Topping (page 348 or 349) is a perfect complement.
To make Banana Cheesecake: Replace 1 cup (8.5 ounces/ 242 grams) sour cream with 1 cup (8 ounces/227 grams) mashed banana. (You will need 2 very ripe bananas.) To keep the banana from discoloring, stir the 3 tablespoons of lemon juice into the mashed banana. Blend into the batter after the sour cream is incorporated.

FRUIT SWIRL CHEESECAKE: Tart, assertive fruit purees such as apricot, raspberry, and strawberry are splendid additions to a cheesecake base.

To make Fruit Swirl Cheesecake: Add ⅔ cup lightly sweetened fruit puree (page 335, 337 or 338) in the following way: Pour ⅓ of the cheesecake batter into the prepared pan. Drizzle ½ the puree over it. Add another ⅓ of the batter and repeat with the remaining puree. Top with the remaining batter. Using a small spatula or knife, cut through the batter and swirl to marble the puree throughout the filling (including the top).

TIP: Do not use peach puree as it curdles the filling.

NOTE: If you like apricots, please try the apricot version. My assistant and collaborator, David Shamah, did not like cheesecake before he tried this cake. Now it is one of his favorite cakes in this book, and he insisted that I sing its praises. (I don't disagree!)

Chocolate Oblivion Truffle Torte

SERVES 16

*T*his cake is my favorite way to eat chocolate. It is easy to make and contains only three essential ingredients: the very best chocolate,* for a full, rich flavor and smooth, creamy texture; unsalted butter to soften the chocolate and release the flavor; and eggs to lighten it. The result is like the creamiest truffle wedded to the purest chocolate mousse. It is chocolate at its most intense flavor and perfect consistency. I prefer to serve this cake at room temperature because, when served chilled, the texture metamorphoses into dense fudge. But as my friend Susan Wyler says: "Who on earth is going to complain about that?"

INGREDIENTS	MEASURE	WEIGHT	
room temperature	*volume*	*pounds/ounces*	*grams*
bittersweet chocolate	5⅓ (3-ounce) bars	1 pound	454 grams
unsalted butter	1 cup	½ pound	227 grams
6 large eggs	1¼ scant liquid cups	10.5 ounces (weighed without shells)	300 grams

* Two of my favorites are Lindt Courante (page 421) and Tobler extra bittersweet. If using Courante chocolate, add ⅓ cup (2.25 ounces/66 grams) sugar to the eggs while beating. If using the extra bittersweet, add 3 tablespoons (1.5 ounces/37 grams) sugar. Lindt and Tobler bittersweet are also excellent.

Preheat the oven to 425°F.

In large metal bowl set over a pan of hot, not simmering, water (the bottom of the bowl should not touch the water) combine the chocolate and butter and let stand, stirring occasionally, until smooth and melted. (The mixture can be melted in the microwave on high power, stirring every 15 seconds. Remove when there are still a few lumps of chocolate and stir until fully melted.)

In a large bowl set over a pan of simmering water heat the eggs, stirring constantly to prevent curdling, until just warm to the touch. Remove from the heat and beat, using the whisk beater, until triple in volume and soft peaks form when the beater is raised, about 5 minutes. (To insure maximum volume if using a hand mixer, beat the eggs over simmering water until they are hot to the touch, about 5 minutes. Remove from the heat and beat until cool.)

Using a large wire whisk or rubber spatula, fold ½ the eggs into the chocolate mixture until almost incorporated. Fold in the remaining eggs until just blended and no streaks remain. Finish by using a rubber spatula to ensure that the heavier mixture at the bottom is incorporated. Scrape into the prepared pan and smooth with the spatula. Set the pan in the larger pan and surround it with 1 inch very hot water. Bake 5 minutes. Cover loosely with a piece of buttered foil and bake 10 minutes. (The cake will look soft, but this is as it should be.)

Let the cake cool on a rack 45 minutes. Cover with plastic wrap and refrigerate until very firm, about 3 hours.

TO UNMOLD

Have ready a serving plate and a flat plate at least 8 inches in diameter, covered with plastic wrap. Wipe the sides of the pan with a hot, damp towel.

Run a thin metal spatula around the sides of the cake and release the sides of the springform pan. Place the plastic-wrapped plate on top and invert. Wipe the bottom of the pan with a hot, damp towel. Remove the bottom of the pan and the parchment. Reinvert onto the serving plate.

TIP: If you have an oven with a pilot light, it can save you a lot of time. The night before baking, place the chocolate and butter in the oven along with the eggs *still in their shells* in another mixing bowl. (Eggs should weigh about 12 ounces/340 grams.) The next morning, the chocolate and butter will be fully melted and the eggs the perfect temperature. Stir the chocolate and butter until smooth and be sure to remove it and the eggs from the oven before preheating oven!

One 8-inch springform pan at least 2½ inches high, buttered and bottom lined with buttered parchment or wax paper; outside of pan wrapped with a double layer of heavy-duty foil to prevent seepage.
One 10-inch cake pan or roasting pan to serve as a water bath.

FINISHED HEIGHT:
1½ inches.

STORE:
2 weeks refrigerated. Do not freeze because freezing changes the texture.

COMPLEMENTARY ADORNMENTS:
A chocolate band or encasement of chocolate rose leaves (page 385 or 387) filled with Brandied Burgundy Cherries (page 346) or ruffles of whipped cream (either piped shortly before serving or stabilized, pages 253 to 255), served with Raspberry Sauce (page 337). Frost with: *One recipe:* White Chocolate Buttercream (page 246 or 248), White Ganache (page 278), or Chocolate Cream Glaze (page 271) or top with Jewel Glaze (page 329). Serve with whipped cream and Raspberry Sauce (page 337) or *crème anglaise* flavored with any liqueur of your choice (pages 280 to 284).

SERVE:
Room temperature. Cut into narrow wedges with a thin sharp knife that has been dipped in hot water.

POINTERS FOR SUCCESS:
For a moist airy texture, be sure to add beaten eggs to chocolate mixture and not the chocolate to the eggs. Wrapping the pan with foil keeps it watertight. Chill thoroughly before unmolding. Use the plastic-wrapped plate when unmolding to protect the surface of cake if you're not planning to use a topping.

NOTE: An 8- by 2-inch solid cake pan can be used instead of a springform—or an 8- by 3-inch pan if adding other ingredients from the variation section (pages 86 and 87). Once in San Francisco I made this cake for my newly married brother and his wife using a straight-sided Calphalon saucepan because they had no cake pans. The handle worked well to unmold the cake! To unmold, run a thin spatula around the sides, place the pan on a heated burner for 10 to 20 seconds, moving it back and forth, and then invert. If the cake does not release, return it to the hot burner for a few more seconds.

A triple recipe of this cake is used to make the Art Deco Cake (page 204).

UNDERSTANDING

Just as for cheesecake, baking the Oblivion in a water bath keeps the texture creamy throughout. When this cake is served at room temperature, you get a rush of chocolate from the moment it enters your mouth. The full flavor of chocolate can best be appreciated only in a softened state. (A chocolate bar, for example, has to start melting in the mouth before the flavor comes through.) The butter and eggs do not distract. Instead they contribute structure and the desired creamy texture.

VARIATIONS

These variations are so special that over the years I have given each its own special name.

MINI-MOUSSE TORTE: A darling size, just right for 6 to 8 servings.
To make Mini-Mousse Torte: Use ½ the recipe (½ pound chocolate, 4 ounces butter, and 3 large eggs) in a 6-inch by 2-inch pan. Bake for the same amount of time.

CHOCOLATE INDULGENCE: Smooth praline paste (page 430), commercially made with hazelnuts and 50 percent sugar, stays in the background but does wonders to intensify the chocolate flavor. It is important to use a chocolate that is not too sweet as the praline paste adds about 2.75 ounces of sugar.
To make Chocolate Indulgence: Use Lindt Courante or Tobler extra bittersweet chocolate. Add ½ cup (5.5 ounces/ 156 grams) praline paste to the chocolate before melting. (If using Courante, add 1 tablespoon sugar to the eggs while beating.)

CHOCOLATE DEPENDENCE: Liqueur heightens the flavor of chocolate. Stir 2 tablespoons of your favorite into the melted chocolate mixture and serve with *crème anglaise* flavored with the same liqueur. A few of my favorites are Grand Marnier, Cointreau, Mandarine Napoléon, William's pear, Cognac, bourbon, and Pistasha.

CHOCOLATE FLAME: Raspberry Puree (page 337) blends magnificently with the chocolate, brightening the flavor and deepening the color. Add ruby Raspberry Jewel Glaze and serve with *crème anglaise* flavored with Chambord (black raspberry liqueur).

To make Chocolate Flame: Stir ⅔ cup slightly sweetened Raspberry Sauce or ¾ cup sieved Cordon Rose Raspberry Conserve into the melted chocolate mixture and add ¼ cup sugar when beating the eggs. You may also use ¾ cup commercial seedless raspberry jam, but, to cut the sweetness, use extra bittersweet chocolate for the cake.

CHOCOLATE TORTURE: My friend Paula Perlis, an enchanting resourceress, once creatively mispronounced Chocolat Teuscher (TOYsher), a renowned Swiss chocolate boutique. I saved this best name of all for the best version of this cake, which incorporates both coffee and hot fudge. It is divine accompanied by Brandied Burgundy Cherries (page 346) and creamy Vanilla Ice Cream (page 285)—a deluxe hot fudge sundae cake. If desired, warm the cherries and flambé them by heating a little cognac in a ladle over the flame and tipping it slightly to ignite or using a long match.

To make Chocolate Torture: Make Hot Fudge (recipe follows). For the batter, Tobler extra bittersweet chocolate is preferable. Add 2 tablespoons instant expresso powder to the melted chocolate mixture. Before beating the eggs, warm the Hot Fudge until just pourable. Scrape ½ the batter into the prepared pan. Pour on ½ the Hot Fudge and top with the remaining batter. Pour on the remaining Hot Fudge and bake.

Hot Fudge

*T*his sticky, intense hot fudge is as fabulous over Vanilla Ice Cream (page 285) as it is in Chocolate Torture (page 87). The chocolate contributes the irresistible edge of burnt sugar; the cocoa offers a deep chocolate flavor and rich, dark color.

INGREDIENTS	MEASURE	WEIGHT	
room temperature	*volume*	*ounces*	*grams*
chocolate, preferably Tobler extra bittersweet or bittersweet	½ (3-ounce) bar	1.5 ounces	43 grams
unsweetened cocoa (Dutch-processed)	2 tablespoons	0.5 ounce	12 grams
water	⅓ liquid cup	2.75 ounces	80 grams
unsalted butter	3 tablespoons	1.5 ounces	43 grams
sugar	⅓ cup	2.25 ounces	66 grams
corn syrup	2 tablespoons	1.5 ounces	41 grams
pinch of salt	•	•	•
vanilla	½ teaspoon	•	•

STORE:
1 month refrigerated.

In a small heavy saucepan (ideally with a nonstick lining) melt the chocolate and cocoa with the water, stirring constantly. Add the butter, sugar, corn syrup, and salt. Simmer, stirring until the sugar has completely melted. Stop stirring and cook at a moderate boil 5 to 10 minutes or until the mixture thickens and reduces to just under ⅔ cup (grease a heatproof glass cup before measuring). Swirl the mixture in the pan occasionally but do not stir.

Cool slightly and add the vanilla. Keep warm or reheat in a water bath or microwave, stirring gently.

NOTE: The microwave is great for making hot fudge because the chocolate does not come into contact with direct heat so there is less risk of scorching. Use a 4-cup heatproof glass measure or bowl as the fudge will bubble while reducing.

I never have time on weekdays for more than a hurried cup of coffee for breakfast, so indulging in pancakes or waffles on weekends is a special treat.

A pancake or waffle is similar to a butter cake except it has about half the flour and no sugar. A cake baked without sugar is usually rubbery and tough, but a pancake, if not overmixed, manages to be even more tender than a butter cake. This contradiction is because of the low amount of flour and because, during the mixing stage, almost no gluten is activated. The structure relies on the intense heat of frying to set the outside and support the incredibly soft, light interior. Also, unlike cakes, pancakes are eaten hot while still at their most tender. The absence of sugar makes it possible to add lots of maple syrup!

A pancake or waffle batter is much more forgiving than a regular cake batter. The size of the eggs or the type of flour is far less important. All-purpose flour works almost as well as cake flour (although cake flour makes more tender pancakes), and it's fine to dip the measuring cup into the flour bin and level it off; it really isn't necessary to sift.

I am presenting these recipes in the usual precise way for consistency of style, but weekends are the time to relax and it's great to know that you can have your cake and eat it too!

Often, I mix all the dry ingredients and take out the eggs and butter the night before. Raised Waffles are ideal for slow risers as most of the batter must be prepared the night before.

I don't mind waking up a little early on the weekends at our country house in Hope, New Jersey, just to be able to have the pleasure of an old-fashioned breakfast. I always accompany my pancakes or waffles with corncob-smoked bacon or sausage from Harrington's in Vermont (page 445) or slices of scrapple (from a stand down the road), fried crisp and sprinkled with freshly ground pepper and thyme from my garden. In the fall I can't resist adding Stayman-Winesap apple rings, fried in a little butter with chopped walnuts and a drizzle of Vermont maple syrup.

Leftover pancakes and waffles freeze beautifully for future carefree yet indulgent weekend breakfasts.

Two marvelous old-fashioned cakes, Sour Cream Coffee Cake and Pineapple Upside-Down Cake, are terrific for brunch.

This chapter also includes crêpes, the world's most delicate pancakes, and buckwheat blini, the ultimate vehicle for caviar, both eminently suitable for special brunches.

You will also find two of my favorite breakfast treats—Streusel Brioche and Sticky Buns—glorious yeast breads, perfect for pampering weekend guests.

Sour Cream Coffee Cake

This is the most delicious streusel coffee cake I have ever tasted and is one of my favorite cakes. The combination of ingredients was inspired by a recipe my old friend Elaine Marie Kohut once entered in a contest. (She won first prize: a set of silverware.) The buttery flavor has the mellow undertone of sour cream. The combination of cake, optional melting layer of thin apple or peach slices, and crunchy sprinkling of cinnamon-scented nuts is close to perfection. The apple adds a moist tartness, the peach mellowness.

INGREDIENTS	MEASURE	WEIGHT	
room temperature	*volume*	*ounces*	*grams*
STREUSEL TOPPING AND FILLING			
light brown sugar	⅓ cup (firmly packed)	2.5 ounces	72 grams
granulated sugar	2 tablespoons	1 ounce	26 grams
walnuts or pecans	1 cup	4 ounces	113 grams
cinnamon	1½ teaspoons	•	•
unsifted cake flour	½ cup (dip and sweep method)	2.25 ounces	65 grams
unsalted butter (must be softened)	4 tablespoons	2 ounces	57 grams
vanilla	½ teaspoon	•	•
BATTER			
4 large egg yolks	2 full fluid ounces	2.5 ounces	74 grams
sour cream	⅔ cup	5.5 ounces	160 grams
vanilla	1½ teaspoons	•	6 grams
sifted cake flour	2 cups	7 ounces	200 grams
sugar	1 cup	7 ounces	200 grams
baking powder	½ teaspoon	•	2.5 grams
baking soda	½ teaspoon	•	2.5 grams
salt	¼ teaspoon	•	•
unsalted butter	12 tablespoons	6 ounces	170 grams

OPTIONAL: 1 Greening or Granny Smith apple, peeled, cored, sliced ¼-inch thick (1 heaping cup of slices), and sprinkled with 2 teaspoons fresh lemon juice. *Or* 1 heaping cup frozen peaches, thawed on paper towels and sliced ¼-inch thick while still partially frozen.
Preheat the oven to 350°F.

TO MAKE STREUSEL TOPPING AND FILLING

In a food processor fitted with the metal blade, pulse the sugars, nuts, and cinnamon until the nuts are coarsely chopped. Reserve ¾ cup to use as a filling. To the remainder add the flour, butter, and vanilla and pulse briefly to form a coarse, crumbly mixture for the topping.

TO MAKE BATTER

In a medium bowl lightly combine the yolks, about ¼ of the sour cream, and vanilla.

In a large mixing bowl combine the dry ingredients and mix on low speed for 30 seconds to blend. Add the butter and remaining sour cream. Mix on low speed until the dry ingredients are moistened. Increase to medium speed (high speed if using a hand mixer) and beat for 1½ minutes to aerate and develop the cake's structure. Scrape down the sides. Gradually add the egg mixture in 3 batches, beating for 20 seconds after each addition to incorporate the ingredients and strengthen the structure. Scrape down the sides.

Reserve about ⅓ of the batter and scrape the remainder into the prepared pan. Smooth the surface, preferably with a small angled spatula. Sprinkle with the streusel filling and top with the apple or peach slices if desired. Drop the reserved batter in large blobs over the fruit and spread evenly with the spatula. Sprinkle with the streusel topping and bake 55 to 65 minutes or until a wire cake tester inserted in the center comes out clean and the cake springs back when pressed lightly in the center. (Move aside a small patch of the streusel before testing.) *The cake should start to shrink from the sides of the pan only after removal from the oven.* Cover loosely with buttered foil after 45 minutes to prevent overbrowning.

Let the cake cool in the pan on a rack for 10 minutes. The cake will have a level top. Loosen the sides with a small metal spatula and remove the sides of the springform pan. Cool completely before wrapping airtight. If you wish to remove the bottom of the pan, slide a cardboard round at least 9 inches in diameter between the parchment and the bottom when the cake is completely cool.

One 9-inch springform pan, greased, bottom lined with parchment or wax paper, and then greased again and floured. Magi-Cake Strips (pages 20 and 456) are especially useful for this cake because the side crust tends to brown more than with other cakes due to the use of all yolks and the long baking period.

FINISHED HEIGHT:
2 inches.

STORE:
Airtight: 2 days room temperature, 5 days refrigerated, 2 months frozen. Moisture distributes most evenly the day after baking.

SERVE:
Room temperature.

POINTERS FOR SUCCESS:
See page 24.

Pineapple Upside-Down Cake

SERVES 8 TO 10

*T*his is a true American classic, traditionally baked in a cast-iron skillet. When inverted, the pineapple slices lining the pan encase the cake, moistening its buttery, soft crumb with delicious caramelized juices. The sour cream batter provides the perfect flavor balance for any fruit. Try an apple, pear, plum, peach, apricot, or even banana variation.

INGREDIENTS	MEASURE	WEIGHT	
room temperature	*volume*	*ounces*	*grams*
FRUIT TOPPING			
14 pineapple slices, fresh or canned—packed in unsweetened pineapple juice	1½ (20-ounce) cans	•	•
14 pitted sweet cherries		•	•
unsalted butter	4 tablespoons	2 ounces	57 grams
light brown sugar	½ cup (firmly packed)	3.75 ounces	108 grams
pecan halves	¼ cup	1 ounce	28 grams
3 large egg yolks	2 scant fluid ounces	2 ounces	56 grams
sour cream	½ cup	4.25 ounces	121 grams
vanilla	1 teaspoon	•	4 grams
sifted cake flour	1½ cups	5.25 ounces	150 grams
sugar	¾ cup	5.25 ounces	150 grams
baking powder	¾ teaspoon	•	3.7 grams
baking soda	¼ teaspoon	•	•
salt	¼ teaspoon	•	•
unsalted butter (must be softened)	9 tablespoons	4.5 ounces	128 grams

One 10-inch cast iron skillet (measured at bottom; top measures 11 inches).

FINISHED HEIGHT: 1½ inches.

Preheat oven to 350°F.
Place oven rack in lower third of oven.

TO MAKE FRUIT TOPPING
Drain pineapple slices and cherries and place on paper towels to absorb excess moisture. You will need 8 whole pine-

apple slices and 8 whole cherries. Halve 6 of both the remaining slices and remaining cherries.

In the skillet, melt the butter over medium heat. Stir in the brown sugar until moistened and remove from the heat.

Place 1 whole pineapple slice in the center of the pan and 7 whole slices surrounding it. Place the half slices side by side against the sides of the pan, the two cut edges down, touching the brown sugar. Place the whole cherries in the center of the whole pineapple slices; the halved cherries in the center of the half slices. Tuck the pecans into any gaps between the fruit.

TO MAKE CAKE BATTER

In a medium bowl, lightly combine yolks, about ¼ of the sour cream, and the vanilla.

In a large mixing bowl, combine the dry ingredients and mix on low speed for 30 seconds to blend. Add butter and the remaining sour cream. Mix on low speed until dry ingredients are moistened. Increase to medium (high speed if using hand mixer) and beat for 1½ minutes to aerate and develop cake's structure. Scrape down the sides.

Gradually add egg mixture to batter in 3 batches, beating for 20 seconds after each addition to incorporate ingredients and strengthen structure. Scrape down the sides. Scrape batter into fruit-lined skillet, smoothing evenly with a spatula. Bake for 40 to 50 minutes or until golden brown and the wire cake tester inserted in center comes out clean and the cake springs back when pressed lightly in center. Run a small metal spatula around sides and invert at once onto a serving plate. Leave the skillet in place one or two minutes before lifting it. If any fruit has stuck to the skillet, simply use a small spatula to place it back on the cake.

UNDERSTANDING

A cast-iron skillet is ideal for preparing this cake not only because the butter and brown sugar for the topping can be heated directly in it on top of the stove, but because it helps the brown-sugar topping to caramelize while baking. If you prefer to use a 10-inch springform pan, it is advisable to wrap the outside in heavy-duty foil to prevent leakage. Preheat an aluminum baking sheet and place the springform directly on it to help caramelize the sugar.

STORE:
Airtight: 1 day room temperature, 3 days refrigerated, 2 months frozen.

SERVE:
Warm or room temperature.

POINTERS FOR SUCCESS:
See page 24.

Holiday Hallelujah Streusel Brioche

SERVES 12

*T*here is simply nothing more soul-satisfying with which to start the day than this cinnamon-imbued brioche. Everyone adores its springy crumb and the delectable yeasty buttery flavor.

Streusel brioche is easy to make. And since it freezes well, it can be baked several weeks ahead and frozen. Thawed overnight at room temperature and warmed briefly before serving, it tastes as fresh as if it had just come out of the oven.

I created this recipe for *Family Circle*'s December 1987 holiday baking issue. The name I gave it expresses my unbridled enthusiasm for it. It is guaranteed to become part of your heirloom repertoire.

INGREDIENTS	MEASURE	WEIGHT	
room temperature	volume	ounces	grams
BRIOCHE DOUGH			
water	2½ tablespoons	1.25 ounces	38 grams
sugar	3 tablespoons	1.25 ounces	40 grams
fresh yeast* *or*	2 packed teaspoons	0.5 ounce	11 grams
dry yeast (*not* rapid-rise)	1½ teaspoons	•	4.5 grams
unsifted bread flour	about 1½ cups (dip and sweep method)	8 ounces	227 grams
salt	½ teaspoon	•	3.5 grams
1 large egg 2 large eggs cold	•	6 ounces (weighed in the shells)	170 grams
unsalted butter (must be very soft)	10 tablespoons	5 ounces†	142 grams *
STREUSEL FILLING			
golden raisins	½ cup	2.5 ounces	72 grams
light rum	2 tablespoons	1 ounce	28 grams
boiling water	¼ cup	2 ounces	60 grams
brown sugar	¼ cup (firmly packed)	2 ounces	56 grams
granulated sugar	1 tablespoon	0.5 ounce	13 grams
cinnamon	2 teaspoons	•	•

INGREDIENTS	MEASURE	WEIGHT	
room temperature	*volume*	*ounces*	*grams*
pecans, finely chopped	½ cup	2 ounces	56 grams
unsalted butter, melted	2 tablespoons	1 ounce	28 grams
milk	about 2 tablespoons	•	•
EGG GLAZE			
1 large egg yolk lightly beaten with 1½ teaspoons heavy cream	•	•	•
OPTIONAL: APRICOT GLAZE			
¼ cup melted, strained apricot preserves	•	•	•

* Fresh yeast causes dough to rise faster.
† 4 to 6 ounces of butter may be used. The lesser amount offers a lighter texture, the higher amount a richer flavor.

DAY BEFORE
MAKE THE SPONGE

When using yeast always begin by proofing it to make sure it is alive. If using fresh yeast, smell it to be sure it doesn't have a sour odor. To proof the yeast, use warm water (hot water would kill it). In a small bowl combine the 2½ tablespoons water (ideally a tepid 100°F. if using fresh yeast; a little warmer, 110°F., if using dry), ½ teaspoon of the sugar and the yeast. If using fresh yeast, crumble it slightly while adding. Set aside in a draft-free spot for 10 to 20 minutes. By this time, the mixture should be full of bubbles. If not, the yeast is too old to be useful.

Place ⅓ cup of the flour and 1 egg in a food processor (preferably with the dough blade) and process a few seconds until mixed. Add the yeast mixture and stir with a rubber scraper until smooth. Sprinkle the remaining flour over the mixture but do not mix it in. Cover and let stand for 1½ to 2 hours.

KNEADING THE DOUGH

Add the remaining sugar, salt, and remaining 2 cold eggs and process 1½ minutes or until the dough is smooth, shiny, and cleans the bowl. Let rest 5 minutes with the feed tube

One large brioche pan (9 inches at the widest point by 3 inches high) or an 8-inch by 2-inch cake pan or springform pan, well buttered.

STORE:
Airtight: 2 days refrigerated, 3 months frozen. To reheat, wrap loosely in foil and bake for 10 minutes at 350°F.

COMPLEMENTARY ADORNMENTS:
Buttery enough to serve plain, the Streusel Brioche is also delicious with softened, unsweetened butter. Serve along with a cup of steaming hot coffee or a glass of milk.

POINTERS FOR SUCCESS:
Use bread flour. *Do not* use
rapid-rise yeast. Be sure the
yeast is active. Do not allow
rising dough to be in an
area over 80° to 85°F. Do
not allow the dough to rise
more than recommended
amounts or it will weaken
the structure. Do not deflate
the dough before chilling or
the butter will leak out. If
this should happen inadvertently, chill the dough for 1
hour and knead the butter
back into the dough.

open. Add the butter in 2 batches and process for 20 seconds after each addition or until incorporated. (The butter
must be soft so as not to overtax the motor of the processor. If the processor should stall, let rest 5 minutes.) *

FIRST RISE

Scrape the dough into a lightly buttered bowl. It will be
very soft and elastic. Sprinkle lightly with flour to prevent
a crust from forming. Cover the bowl tightly with plastic
wrap and let rise in a warm place (80°F. but not above or
the yeast will develop a sour taste) until double in bulk,
about 2 hours. Refrigerate for at least 30 minutes to 1 hour.
Deflate dough by gently stirring it and refrigerate for another hour.

REDISTRIBUTING THE YEAST

Turn dough onto a lightly floured surface and gently press
it into a rectangle. Fold the dough into thirds (as in folding
a business letter) and again press it out into a rectangle,
lightly flouring the surface as needed to prevent stickiness.
Fold it again into thirds and dust it lightly with flour on all
sides. Wrap it loosely but securely in plastic wrap and then
foil and refrigerate it for 6 hours or up to 2 days to allow
dough to ripen and harden.

TO MAKE STREUSEL FILLING

In a small heatproof bowl place the raisins and light rum.
Add the boiling water, cover, and let stand for at least 1
hour. When ready to fill the dough, drain the raisins. Use
your fingers or a fork to blend all the ingredients except
the butter and milk.

The dough will have expanded. Gently deflate it by
kneading lightly with floured hands. Roll it out on a heavily floured surface into an 18-inch by 8-inch rectangle. Brush
with the melted butter, sprinkle with the streusel and raisins, and roll up from a short end, brushing off the excess
flour as you go.

Use a sharp knife to cut the roll into 4 pieces if using
a large brioche mold, 8 pieces if using a cake pan. Stand
the slices on end, wedging them into the pan and brushing
between them with the milk so they will adhere well during
baking.

---

* To prepare brioche dough in a heavy-duty mixer such as the KitchenAid,
use flat beater and, when the dough starts to climb up the beater, change to
the dough hook. Beat about 5 minutes on medium speed or until the dough
is smooth, shiny, very elastic, and begins to clean the bowl. Beat in the butter
by the tablespoon until incorporated.

Let rise 1 to 2 hours (fresh yeast rises faster) or until the dough comes to the top of the mold and is very light.

Place a foiled-lined baking sheet in the oven and preheat to 425°F. (The hot baking sheet will boost the "oven spring" of the brioche; the foil will catch any bubbling caramelized sugar.)

Brush the brioche with the egg glaze, being careful not to drip any on the side of the pan or it will impede rising (although little can stop this energetic dough).

Place the brioche on the hot baking sheet and bake 5 minutes. Lower the heat to 375°F. and bake 20 to 25 minutes or until a wooden skewer inserted in the center comes out clean. Cover loosely with foil after 10 to 15 minutes or when the crust starts to darken.

Unmold onto a wire rack and reinvert to cool top side up. For a glistening surface, brush with Apricot Glaze.

UNDERSTANDING
See page 79.

Sticky Buns

SERVES 12

$\mathscr{T}$he same dough used to make Streusel Brioche makes the most glorious sticky buns imaginable. They are everything you'd want a sticky bun to be: gooey with buttery caramel and crunchy pecan topping; airy, soft, moist, buttery, yeasty dough beneath coiled around a spiral filling of rum-plumped raisins, brown sugar, and cinnamon. Make this recipe 1 day ahead and reheat to serve warm at breakfast.

INGREDIENTS	MEASURE	WEIGHT	
room temperature	*volume*	*ounces*	*grams*
1 recipe Holiday Hallelujah Streusel Brioche dough (page 94)	•	•	•
STICKY BUN FILLING			
raisins	½ cup	2.5 ounces	72 grams
dark rum	2 tablespoons	1 ounce	28 grams
boiling water	¼ cup	2 ounces	60 grams
light brown sugar	¼ cup (firmly packed)	2 ounces	56 grams
granulated sugar	1 tablespoon	0.5 ounce	13 grams
cinnamon	2 teaspoons	•	•
unsalted butter, melted	2 tablespoons	1 ounce	28 grams
STICKY BUN TOPPING			
unsalted butter, softened	¼ cup	2 ounces	56 grams
light brown sugar	½ cup (firmly packed)	4 ounces	112 grams
pecan halves	½ cup	2 ounces	56 grams
STICKY BUN GLAZE			
reserved raisin-soaking liquid			
unsalted butter	1 tablespoon	0.5 ounce	14 grams

TO MAKE THE STICKY BUN FILLING

In a small heatproof bowl place the raisins and rum. Add the boiling water, cover, and let stand for at least 1 hour. When ready to fill the dough, drain the raisins, reserving the soaking liquid.

In another bowl combine the sugars and cinnamon.

TO MAKE THE STICKY BUN TOPPING

In a small bowl stir together the butter and sugar until well mixed. Spread evenly in the prepared pan with a small spatula or rubber scraper. Top with the pecan halves top sides down.

FILLING THE DOUGH

Roll out the dough on a well-floured surface into a 14-inch by 12-inch rectangle. Brush with the 2 tablespoons of melted butter and sprinkle with the sugar mixture and raisins. Roll up from a short end, brushing off the excess flour as you go. The dough will have that lively, silky, "soft as a baby's bottom" feel.

Using a very sharp knife, cut the roll into 4 pieces and then cut each piece into thirds. Place each piece cut side down in the prepared pan, pressing tops so that the sides touch. Cover with well-buttered plastic wrap and let rise until the dough reaches the top of the pan (about 1 hour if using fresh yeast, up to 2 hours if using dry).

TO MAKE THE STICKY BUN GLAZE

In a small saucepan over high heat or in a 2-cup heatproof measuring cup in a microwave on high power reduce the raisin soaking syrup to 1 tablespoon. Add the butter and stir until melted. The glaze should be lukewarm when used. Set a foil-lined baking sheet on lowest shelf and preheat the oven to 425°F. (The hot baking sheet will boost the "oven spring" of the brioche; the foil will catch any bubbling caramelized syrup.)

Brush the buns with the glaze. Place the pan on the hot baking sheet and bake 10 minutes. Lower the heat to 375°F. and bake 15 minutes or until a skewer inserted in the center comes out clean. If becoming too brown, cover loosely with foil after 5 or 10 minutes.

Let the buns cool in the pan for 3 minutes before unmolding onto a serving plate or foil-lined counter. Sticky buns may be eaten at once or reheated in a 350°F. oven for 10 minutes, loosely wrapped in foil.

NOTES: The butter and raisin syrup glaze keeps the tops of the buns soft. My friend Shirley Corriher swears by the plumping raisins method. She says she hates finding a hard, dried-up raisin in an otherwise soft dough.

Paula Wolfert (in her superb articles on brioche in *Pleasures of Cooking,* which greatly influenced the development of this recipe) recommends melting and browning about one fifth of the butter (2 tablespoons) for an extra rich, delicious flavor. Be sure to let the butter cool before

One 8-inch by 2-inch square pan, lightly greased.

Day ahead, prepare the Brioche Dough. The Sticky Bun Topping and Filling can also be prepared the day ahead.

STORE:
Airtight: 2 days room temperature, 3 months frozen.

COMPLEMENTARY ADORNMENTS:
The textural variation and moisture from the caramel makes any addition to the Sticky Buns unnecessary. However, they cry out for a cup of hot coffee or a glass of cold milk.

SERVE:
Preferably warm.

POINTERS FOR SUCCESS:
Use bread flour. *Do not* use rapid-rise yeast. Be sure the yeast is active. Do not allow rising dough to be in an area over 80° to 85°F. Do not allow the dough to rise more than the recommended amounts or it will weaken the structure. Do not deflate the dough before chilling or the butter will leak out. If this should happen inadvertently, chill the dough for 1 hour and knead the butter back into it.

adding it along with the rest of the butter. Add the browned particles as well.

Brioche made in a food processor is a speedy and simple operation. If you wish to double this recipe, it is safer to use the heavy-duty mixer method as a larger amount of dough might overheat some food processors, causing them to stall. (I have successfully made a double batch using the Cuisinart DLC-7 by melting the butter and allowing it to cool to barely tepid before adding it, with motor running.)

Blueberry Buttermilk Pancakes

SERVES 4 TO 6

*B*uttermilk makes the most delicious pancakes, especially if no baking soda is used to dull the slightly tangy flavor. Baking powder and beaten egg whites contribute the leavening. In fact, these are the lightest pancakes I have ever tasted.

Blueberry buttermilk pancakes are my favorite version, and the secret for having plump, juicy, evenly distributed berries is to add them fresh or still frozen to the pancakes after they're on the griddle.

INGREDIENTS	MEASURE	WEIGHT	
room temperature	*volume*	*ounces*	*grams*
unsifted cake flour *or* all-purpose flour	1¾ cups 1⅔ cups (dip and sweep method)	8 ounces 8 ounces	227 grams 227 grams
baking powder	4 teaspoons	•	19.5 grams
salt	½ teaspoon	•	3.5 grams
4 large eggs, separated yolks whites	2 full fluid ounces ½ liquid cup	2.5 ounces 4.25 ounces	68 grams 120 grams
buttermilk	2 liquid cups	17 ounces	484 grams
cream of tartar	½ teaspoon	•	•
unsalted butter, melted and cooled	4 tablespoons	2 ounces	57 grams
blueberries, fresh or frozen and unthawed	2 cups	8 ounces	227 grams

Preheat a griddle or frying pan.

In a large bowl whisk the flour, baking powder, and salt until blended.

In a small bowl beat the yolks and buttermilk to blend slightly.

In a mixing bowl beat the egg whites until foamy. Add the cream of tartar and beat until stiff peaks form when the beater is raised slowly.

Add the yolk mixture to the flour mixture and mix lightly with a fork until the flour is moistened. Stir in the butter. The batter should be lumpy as overmixing will produce tough pancakes. Add the whites and fold in with a slotted skimmer or rubber spatula.

The griddle or frying pan should be hot enough to sizzle a drop of water. Lightly butter it and pour on the batter in 4-inch rounds. Quickly drop 6 berries onto each pancake. Test for doneness by lifting a corner of each pancake with a metal spatula. When golden brown, turn over and cook 30 seconds on the other side.

Remove the pancakes to warm plates and keep warm in a low oven while cooking the remaining batter.

Makes about 22 pancakes.

VARIATION

BUTTERMILK PUFFS: Frying the batter in a Danish Ebleskiver pan (page 460), which has 8 round recesses, produces pancake puffs with a delightfully airy and moist texture. You will need 1½ tablespoons clarified butter for brushing on the preheated pan before frying. Fill each recess ½ full with batter. Use a small metal spatula to turn the puffs. Blueberries tend to stick slightly, making it necessary to wash the pan between batches, so, if you add them, use only 2 per puff and push them in slightly so they are covered with batter. The batter makes 54 puffs.

UNDERSTANDING

Cake flour makes a more tender pancake because it contains less gluten-forming protein than does all purpose.

STORE:
3 days refrigerated, 2 months frozen. Best served fresh.

COMPLEMENTARY ADORNMENTS:
Warm maple syrup, crisp corncob-smoked bacon, sausages, or scrapple with fried sage or thyme. No extra butter is necessary as there's plenty in the pancakes!

SERVE:
Hot on warmed plates.

POINTERS FOR SUCCESS:
Do not overmix batter. If using frozen blueberries, be sure they remain frozen when added to the batter. To coat griddle with a thin film of butter, run a frozen piece of butter lightly across it.

Blueberry Buckwheat Pancakes

𝒯hese pancakes have a light, tender texture with the earthy flavor of buckwheat.

INGREDIENTS	MEASURE	WEIGHT	
room temperature	*volume*	*ounces*	*grams*
unsifted buckwheat flour	1½ cups	6.75 ounces	188 grams
unsifted cake flour *or* all-purpose flour	¼ cup ¼ cup (dip and sweep method)	1 ounce 1.25 ounces	33 grams 36 grams
baking soda	1 teaspoon	•	5 grams
salt	½ teaspoon	•	3.5 grams
4 large eggs, separated yolks whites	 2 full fluid ounces ½ liquid cup	 2.5 ounces 4.25 ounces	 68 grams 120 grams
milk	1 liquid cup	8.5 ounces	242 grams
sour cream	1 cup	8.5 ounces	242 grams
cream of tartar	½ teaspoon	•	•
unsalted butter, melted and cooled	4 tablespoons	2 ounces	57 grams
blueberries, fresh or frozen and unthawed	2 cups	8 ounces	227 grams

STORE:
3 days refrigerated, 2 months frozen. Best served fresh.

COMPLEMENTARY ADORNMENTS:
Warm maple syrup, crisp corncob-smoked bacon, sausages, or scrapple with fried sage or thyme. No extra butter is necessary as there's plenty in the pancakes!

SERVE:
Hot on warmed plates.

Preheat a griddle or frying pan.

In a large bowl, whisk the flours, baking soda, and salt until blended.

In a small bowl, beat the yolks, milk, and sour cream to blend slightly.

In a mixing bowl, beat the egg whites until foamy. Add the cream of tartar and beat until stiff peaks form when the beater is raised slowly.

Add the yolk mixture to the flour mixture and mix lightly with a fork until the flour is moistened. Stir in the butter. The batter should be lumpy because overmixing will produce tough pancakes. Add the whites and fold in with a slotted skimmer or rubber spatula.

The griddle or frying pan should be hot enough to sizzle a drop of water. Lightly butter it and pour on batter in 4-inch rounds. Quickly drop 6 berries onto each pancake. Test for doneness by lifting a corner of each pancake with a metal spatula. When golden brown, turn over and cook 30 seconds on the other side.

Remove the pancakes to warm plates and keep warm in a low oven while cooking the remaining batter. Makes about 22 pancakes.

UNDERSTANDING

Cake flour makes a more tender pancake because it contains less gluten-forming protein than does all purpose. Baking soda is used instead of baking powder to temper the acidity of the sour cream. The sour cream is thinned with milk to produce a lighter, more tender texture.

*T*he ingredients for this waffle batter are exactly the same as for the buttermilk pancake batter except for the butter. Because of the different cooking technique, the waffle batter is able to incorporate 4 times the amount of butter without becoming too tender and falling apart (as would a cake). Also, the egg whites are not beaten separately because the heavy pressure of the waffle iron lid would defeat the purpose.

I like to use a 7-inch diameter, heart-shaped waffle iron to make 5 waffle hearts at a time. With a nonstick coating no extra butter is necessary. Electric waffle irons are the easiest to use because both top and bottom heat evenly.

POINTERS FOR SUCCESS:
Do not overmix batter. If using frozen blueberries, be sure they remain frozen when added to the batter. To coat griddle with a thin film of butter, run a frozen piece of butter lightly across it.

Buttermilk Waffles

SERVES 6 TO 8

INGREDIENTS	MEASURE	WEIGHT	
room temperature	*volume*	*ounces*	*grams*
unsifted cake flour *or* all-purpose flour	1¾ cups 1⅔ cups (dip and sweep method)	8 ounces 8 ounces	227 grams 227 grams
baking powder	4 teaspoons	•	19.5 grams
salt	½ teaspoon	•	3.5 grams
4 large eggs	6 full fluid ounces	7 ounces	200 grams (weighed without shells)
buttermilk	2 liquid cups	17 ounces	484 grams
unsalted butter, melted and cooled	16 tablespoons	8 ounces	227 grams

Preheat a waffle iron. (For crispy waffles, be sure to preheat both sides until very hot before adding the batter.)

In a large bowl whisk the flour, baking powder, and salt until blended.

In a small bowl beat the eggs and buttermilk until well mixed. Add to the flour mixture and mix lightly with a fork until the flour is moistened. Stir in the butter. The batter should be lumpy as overmixing will produce tough waffles.

The waffle iron should be hot enough to sizzle a drop of water. Pour the batter onto center of the waffle iron, using a light hand because the batter will spread when the lid is lowered. If using a 7-inch heart-shaped iron, use a scant ½ cup batter and a spoon or small metal spatula to spread it around the outer edges. Lower the lid and cook until the bottom is golden brown. Flip the waffle iron over and briefly cook the other side until just golden brown. (If using an electric waffle iron, follow the manufacturer's directions.)

Keep the waffles warm and crisp by placing them in a single layer on racks in a warm oven with the door slightly ajar to allow any moisture to escape. Makes about twelve 7-inch heart-shaped waffles or about six 9-inch square waffles.

UNDERSTANDING

Cake flour makes a more tender waffle because it contains less gluten-forming protein than does all purpose.

When I visited my cousin Joan in Berkeley, California, we went to breakfast at a charming spot, the Bridge Creek Restaurant, where I enjoyed the most ethereal waffles I had ever experienced. When my feet touched ground again, I discovered Marion Cunningham sitting nearby and learned that she was part owner and chief menu consultant. To my delight she not only promised to send me the recipe but also allowed me to offer it in this book.

Marion Cunningham's Raised Waffles

INGREDIENTS	MEASURE	WEIGHT	
room temperature	*volume*	*ounces*	*grams*
warm water	½ liquid cup	4.25 ounces	120 grams
sugar	1 teaspoon	•	4 grams
fresh yeast *or*	1 packed tablespoon	0.75 ounce	21 grams
dry yeast	2¼ teaspoons	0.25 ounce	7 grams
warm milk	2 liquid cups	17 ounces	484 grams
unsalted butter, melted	8 tablespoons	4 ounces	113 grams
salt	¾ teaspoon	•	5 grams
unsifted all-purpose flour	2 cups (dip and sweep method)	10 ounces	284 grams
2 large eggs	3 fluid ounces	3.5 ounces (weighed without shells)	100 grams
baking soda	¼ teaspoon	•	•

NIGHT BEFORE

In a large mixing bowl (at least 3-quarts in capacity) combine the warm water (100°F. if using fresh yeast, 110°F. if using dry yeast), sugar, and yeast. Stir and let stand 10 to 20 minutes proof. If the yeast is active, it will produce many bubbles.

Add the milk, butter, salt, and flour and beat until smooth and blended. (Marion likes to use a hand-rotary beater to get rid of the lumps.) Cover the bowl with plastic wrap and let stand overnight at room temperature. (The batter will rise from 4 cups to 12 cups and then collapse.)

The batter keeps well for several days refrigerated or frozen for up to 2 months. To use frozen batter, thaw in the refrigerator overnight.

COMPLEMENTARY ADORNMENTS:
Warm maple syrup, and crisp corncob-smoked bacon, sausage, or scrapple with fried sage or thyme.

SERVE:
Hot on warmed plates.

POINTERS FOR SUCCESS:
Do not overheat the yeast. Use a large bowl as the batter will rise to 3 times its original volume. Use a sizzling hot waffle iron. Do not use rapid-rise yeast.

MORNING

Preheat the waffle iron until it is hot enough to sizzle a drop of water. (For crispy waffles, be sure to preheat both sides until very hot before adding the batter.)

Beat in the eggs. Add the baking soda and stir until well mixed. The batter will be very thin.

Pour the batter onto center of the waffle iron, using a light hand because the batter will spread when the lid is lowered. If using a 7-inch heart-shaped iron, use a scant ⅓ cup batter. Tilt the waffle iron to spread the batter around the edges. Lower the lid and cook until the bottom is golden brown. Flip the waffle iron over and briefly cook the other side until just golden brown. (If using an electric waffle iron, follow the manufacturer's directions.)

Keep the waffles warm and crisp by placing them in a single layer on racks in a warm oven with the door slightly ajar to allow any moisture to escape. Makes about eight 9-inch-square waffles or about sixteen 7-inch heart-shaped waffles.

UNDERSTANDING

The formula for these waffles is quite similar to Buttermilk Waffles except that they have half the eggs and butter. This is part of the reason for their lightness, but the real secret is that they are leavened with yeast. The tiny amount of baking soda does not add leavening—instead it rounds out the slightly acidic flavor produced by the yeast. The yeast also contributes a richness and depth of flavor.

Best Buckwheat Blini La Tulipe

SERVES 8 TO 10

A good recipe for buckwheat blini is very hard to find. The combination of assertive buckwheat flavor and light tender texture is elusive.

I fell in love with these blini at a New York Women's Culinary Alliance caviar tasting given several years ago by Sara Moulton, the group's founder. She was then *chef tournant* at La Tulipe, one of my favorite Village restaurants, and was honor-bound not to divulge the recipe.

It was almost as this book went to press that it suddenly occurred to me to ask Sally Darr, chef-owner of La Tulipe, if I could include her blini recipe. She said yes. I lived in fear for one week that she might change her mind. These blini are that wonderful.

INGREDIENTS	MEASURE	WEIGHT	
room temperature	volume	pounds/ounces	grams
fresh yeast * or	2 packed teaspoons	0.5 ounce	11 grams
dry yeast (not rapid-rise)	1½ teaspoons	•	4 grams
warm milk	2½ cups	1 pound 5.25 ounces	605 grams
sugar	1 tablespoon + ½ teaspoon	0.5 ounce	15 grams
stone-ground buckwheat flour	½ cup (lightly spooned into cup)	2 ounces	57 grams
sifted all-purpose flour	2¼ cups	10 ounces	284 grams
3 large egg yolks	3½ tablespoons	2 ounces	56 grams
1 large egg white	2 tablespoons	1 ounce	30 grams
salt	½ teaspoon	•	•
heavy cream	1 cup	8 ounces	232 grams
clarified butter *	2 tablespoons	1 ounce	25 grams

* If you do not have clarified butter on hand, you will need to clarify 3 tablespoons (1.5 ounces/43 grams) unsalted butter. In a heavy saucepan melt the butter over medium heat, partially covered to prevent splattering. When it looks clear, cook, uncovered, watching carefully until the solids drop and begin to brown. Pour immediately through a fine strainer or a strainer lined with cheesecloth.

The batter requires 3½ hours rising time, so you must start it at least 4 hours before serving the blini. I suggest starting the batter the day before.

DAY BEFORE

When using yeast always begin by proofing it to make sure it is alive. To proof the yeast, use warm liquid (hot liquid would kill it). In a small bowl combine ½ cup warm milk (ideally a tepid 100°F. if using fresh yeast; a little warmer, 110°F., if using dry yeast), ½ teaspoon of the sugar, and the yeast. If using fresh yeast, crumble it slightly while adding. Set aside in a draft-free spot for 10 to 20 minutes. By this time, the mixture should be full of bubbles. If not, the yeast is too old to be useful.

Transfer the mixture to a large bowl (at least 10-cup capacity) and stir in the buckwheat flour and 1½ cups warm milk. Cover and allow to stand in a warm place for 2 hours.

STORE:
Blini are best fresh but can be refrigerated 3 days and reheated, covered, in a 300°F. oven for 10 to 15 minutes or for a few seconds in a microwave oven, uncovered.

COMPLEMENTARY ADORNMENTS:
Sour cream or crème fraîche (page 259) and caviar. Or thin slivers of smoked salmon and sprigs of fresh dill.

POINTERS FOR SUCCESS:
Sally swears by Kenyon's Buckwheat Flour, available at Dean & DeLuca (page 445). She says that stone-ground buckwheat flour produces the best texture.

Stir in the all-purpose flour and the remaining ½ cup milk until smooth. Add the egg yolks, remaining sugar, and salt. Mix well, cover, and allow to stand in a warm place for 1 hour. (The recipe may be prepared to this point 1 day ahead.) Refrigerate overnight. The batter will be thick and have bubbles all over the surface.

Whip the cream until soft peaks form when the beater is raised and fold into the batter.

Beat the egg white until soft peaks form when the beater is raised and fold into the batter. You will have about 8 cups batter.

SERVING DAY
Preheat the oven to 300°F.

Pour 2½-inch rounds of batter (2 scant tablespoons) onto a hot griddle, lightly greased with the clarified butter between each batch. Cook until puffed and golden, about 1½ minutes. Turn and cook the other side for 30 seconds or until lightly brown. Place in the oven for 10 minutes to finish cooking the inside of the blini. Makes 70 blini.

NOTE: A Swedish pancake or "Plett" pan (page 460) with 2½-inch round individual recesses is very convenient to use. Fill each section to the top.

Swedish Pancakes

Plättar

SERVES 8
TO 10

*M*y assistant, David Shamah, a recent graduate of the Culinary Institute of America, raved about these pancakes, which he learned from chef-instructor John Jensen. The original recipe used part light cream and milk, but I have converted it to heavy cream and milk (maintaining the same percentage of butterfat) due to the scarcity of light cream on the market.

Swedish pancakes are a cross between American pancakes and crêpes. Sprinkled with powdered sugar and topped with lingonberries, they are traditionally eaten with the fingers as a lovely brunch dish or as an unusual dessert for an informal dinner.

INGREDIENTS	MEASURE	WEIGHT	
room temperature	volume	ounces	grams
4 large eggs	¾ liquid cup	7 ounces (weighed without shells)	200 grams
heavy cream	½ cup	4 ounces	116 grams
cake flour or	1 cup + 2 tablespoons	5 ounces	145 grams
all-purpose flour	1 cup (measured by dip and sweep method)	5 ounces	145 grams
milk	1½ cups	12.75 ounces	363 grams
unsalted butter, melted	3 tablespoons	1.5 ounces	43 grams
salt	½ teaspoon	•	•
grated lemon zest	½ teaspoon	•	•
clarified butter *	2 tablespoons	1 ounce	25 grams

* If you do not have clarified butter on hand, you will need to clarify 3 tablespoons (1.5 ounces/43 grams) unsalted butter. In a heavy saucepan melt the butter over medium heat, partially covered to prevent splattering. When it looks clear, cook, uncovered, watching carefully until the solids drop and begin to brown. Pour immediately through a fine strainer or a strainer lined with cheesecloth.

In a large bowl beat the eggs and cream. Add the flour and beat until smooth. Beat in the remaining ingredients. The batter is quite thin.

Pour 2½-inch rounds of batter (1 tablespoon) onto a hot griddle, lightly greased with clarified butter between each batch. Cook over medium-high heat 1½ minutes or until golden brown. Turn and cook the other side for 30 seconds or until lightly brown. The pancakes will be ⅛-inch thick.

Remove the pancakes to warm plates and keep warm in a low oven while cooking the remaining batter. Makes 4 dozen pancakes.

NOTE: A Swedish pancake or "Plett" pan (page 460) with 2½-inch round individual recesses is very convenient to use. Fill each section almost to the top.

UNDERSTANDING
Cake flour makes a more tender pancake because it contains less gluten-forming protein than does all purpose.

STORE:
3 days refrigerated. Reheat, loosely covered, in a 300°F. oven for 10 to 15 minutes or for a few seconds in a microwave oven, uncovered. Best served fresh.

COMPLEMENTARY ADORNMENTS:
Powdered sugar and lingonberries in syrup (available at specialty food stores).

Chantilly Crêpes

(Pronunciation: crep as in yep, not crayp)

S E R V E S 6 T O 8

*T*hese are the lightest, laciest, most tender crêpes imaginable. I discovered the idea of using cornstarch instead of the usual flour when I did a free-lance project at CPC International (Corn Products) many years ago. In addition to producing more tender crêpes, you can also cook the crêpes immediately after mixing the batter, unlike the hour-long wait when using flour.

I discovered that using half the recommended amount of cornstarch produces crêpes that are as delicate as handkerchiefs.

INGREDIENTS	MEASURE	WEIGHT	
room temperature	*volume*	*ounces*	*grams*
3 large eggs	scant ⅔ cup	5.25 ounces	150 grams (weighed without shells)
milk	1 cup	8.5 ounces	242 grams
vanilla	1 teaspoon	•	4 grams
unsalted butter, melted	3 tablespoons	1.5 ounces	43 grams
Grand Marnier	1 tablespoon	0.5 ounce	15 grams
cornstarch *	¾ cup	3 ounces	90 grams
salt	⅛ teaspoon	•	•
sugar	1 tablespoon	0.5 ounce	12 grams
clarified butter †	1 tablespoon	0.5 ounce	12 grams

One 6-inch crêpe pan.

STORE:
2 days refrigerated, 3 months frozen.

* You can use up to 1 cup cornstarch if you prefer a thicker crêpe with more bite.
† If you do not have clarified butter on hand, you will need to clarify 3 tablespoons (1.5 ounces/43 grams) unsalted butter. In a heavy saucepan melt the butter over medium heat, partially covered to prevent splattering. When it looks clear, cook, uncovered, watching carefully until the solids drop and begin to brown. Pour immediately through a fine strainer or a strainer lined with cheesecloth.

The easiest and fastest way to mix the batter is in a blender. Place the ingredients in the order given in a blender and blend at high speed for 10 seconds.

Heat the crêpe pan on medium-high heat until hot enough to sizzle a drop of water. Brush lightly with clarified butter and pour a scant 2 tablespoons batter into the center. Immediately tilt the pan to the left and then down and around to the right so that the batter moves in a counterclockwise direction, covering the entire pan.

Cook until the top starts to dull and the edges begin to brown, about 15 to 20 seconds. I like to use a small metal spatula to lift the upper edge and check to see if the creêpe is golden brown. Then, grasping the edge of the crêpe with my fingers, I flip it over and cook for 10 seconds, or just until lightly browned. Invert the pan over the counter and the crêpe will release.

It is fine to place 1 crêpe on top of another if serving the same day. If refrigerating or freezing the crêpes, however, separate them with pieces of wax paper or they may stick to each other. Makes 21 to 24 crêpes (the larger amount if using 1 cup cornstarch).

Crêpes Suzette

*T*his is one of the world's most glorious and dramatic desserts. There was a time, when I first discovered Crêpes Suzette in a class with James Beard, that everyone I loved had to experience them. I made them for my parents when they invited me for dinner, for my mentor Cecily Brownstone and her sister when I graduated from college, for a sophisticated Parisian girl friend who picked up her plate and licked it (prompting me to do the same); for a cellist who broke our date and never knew what he missed. (I never forgave him.) Then for years I stopped making them only to rediscover them with renewed interest. My favorite sauce version was inspired by Julia Child and Simone Beck in *Mastering the Art of French Cooking*. Although it is traditional to rub sugar cubes on the orange rind to absorb the oils, it has become difficult to find large sugar cubes, so I candy the rind instead and use it to garnish the crêpes. It is delicious to eat.

INGREDIENTS	MEASURE	WEIGHT	
room temperature	volume	ounces	grams
1 recipe Chantilly Crêpes (page 110)			
FOR CANDYING THE RIND			
1 large orange			
sugar	⅓ cup	2.25 ounces	67 grams
water	⅓ cup	2.75 ounces	79 grams
corn syrup	1 teaspoon	•	•
ORANGE/BUTTER SAUCE			
1 large orange	•	•	•
lemon juice, freshly squeezed	1½ teaspoons	•	•
unsalted butter	1 cup	8 ounces	227 grams
sugar	¼ cup	1.75 ounces	50 grams
Grand Marnier	3 tablespoons	1.5 ounces	46 grams
FOR FLAMBÉING			
powdered sugar	3 tablespoons	1.25 ounces	38 grams
Grand Marnier or Curaçao	⅓ cup	2.75 ounces	80 grams
brandy	⅓ cup	2.5 ounces	74 grams

TO CANDY THE ORANGE RIND

Use a stripper (page 458) or vegetable peeler to peel 1 of the oranges. Be sure to remove only the orange portion and not the bitter white pith beneath. If using the vegetable peeler, cut the strips with a knife to make them narrower (about ¼-inch wide).

Place the strips in a saucepan of boiling water and simmer 15 minutes. Drain and rinse under cold water.

In a small saucepan combine the ⅓ cup sugar, ⅓ cup water and 1 teaspoon corn syrup and bring to a boil, stirring constantly. Stop stirring, add the orange strips, and cover tightly. Simmer on low heat for 15 minutes without stirring or uncovering. Cool covered.

TO MAKE THE ORANGE BUTTER SAUCE

Remove the rind of the second orange with a zester or vegetable peeler and chop into fine zest.

Squeeze both oranges and strain the juice. You should have ⅔ cup. Add the lemon juice.

In mixing bowl, with whisk beater cream the butter and sugar for 1 minute or until very soft. Very gradually beat in the juice, chopped zest, and the 3 tablespoons of Grand Marnier. (Makes 2¾ cups orange butter sauce.) Set aside at room temperature for 1 day, refrigerate up to 5 days, or freeze up to 3 months.

TO SERVE: Lay a crêpe with its most attractive side down and spread lightly with the orange butter. Fold in half and spread with more orange butter. Fold into triangles by folding in half or thirds. (To fold in thirds, the center of the flat edge will become the point of the triangle. Fold each side down so that they meet in the center, spread with a little more orange butter, and fold in half.) Use a total of 1 tablespoon orange butter for each crêpe. Place the remaining orange butter in a large crêpe or sauté pan and heat until melted and bubbling. Place the crêpes and candied orange rind in the pan. Heat for 1½ minutes, spooning the orange butter over the crêpes. Remove from the heat and sprinkle with the powdered sugar.

Place the liqueur in a large ladle or saucepan with a long handle. Heat until very hot and starting to flame. If necessary, tilt the ladle slightly so that the gas burner flame will ignite it or use a very long match. Pour over the crêpes and allow to flame until it goes out.

Serve the crêpes garnished with the orange rind.

NOTE: The butter-spread, folded crêpes and remaining orange butter can be frozen for 3 months. Reheat covered in a 350°F. oven 20 to 30 minutes or until bubbling hot.

Lemon Crêpes Suzette

SERVES 6 TO 8

*L*overs of lemon may prefer this lilting butter sauce to the traditional orange one. Light rum accents the refreshing lemon flavor. Fresh blueberries are a colorful addition.

INGREDIENTS	MEASURE	WEIGHT	
room temperature	*volume*	*ounces*	*grams*
1 recipe Chantilly Crêpes (page 110)			
LEMON BUTTER SAUCE			
unsalted butter	¾ cup	6 ounces	170 grams
sugar	1 cup	7 ounces	200 grams
grated lemon zest	2 teaspoons	•	4 grams
lemon juice, freshly squeezed	½ cup	4.25 ounces	125 grams
optional: fresh blueberries	1 cup	4 ounces	114 grams
FOR FLAMBÉING			
powdered sugar	3 tablespoons	1.25 ounces	38 grams
light rum	½ cup	2 ounces	56 grams

In a mixing bowl with whisk beater, cream the butter and sugar for 1 minute or until very soft. Very gradually beat in the lemon zest and juice. (Makes 2¼ cups lemon butter sauce.) Set aside at room temperature for 1 day, refrigerate up to 5 days, or freeze up to 3 months.

TO SERVE: Lay a crêpe with its most attractive side down and spread lightly with the lemon butter. Fold in half and spread with more lemon butter. Fold into triangles by folding in half or thirds. (To fold in thirds, the center of the flat edge will become the point of the triangle. Fold each side down so that they meet in the center, spread with a little more lemon butter, and fold in half.) Use a total of 1 tablespoon lemon butter for each crêpe. Place the remaining lemon butter in a large crêpe or sauté pan and heat until melted and bubbling. Place the crêpes and optional blueberries in the pan. Heat for 1½ minutes, spooning the lemon butter over the crêpes. Remove from the heat and sprinkle with the powdered sugar.

Place the rum in a large ladle or saucepan with a long handle. Heat until very hot and starting to flame. If necessary, tilt the ladle slightly so that the gas burner flame will ignite it or use a very long match. Pour over the crêpes and allow to flame until it goes out.

NOTE: The butter-spread, folded crêpes and remaining lemon butter can be frozen for 3 months.

Lemon Cream Illusion Crêpes

SERVES 6 TO 8

1 large sheet cake or jelly-roll pan, lightly buttered

*T*hese individual little lemon souffléed crêpes are absolutely divine. They were inspired by the invention of Lemon Cream Illusion. This lemon curd and Italian meringue mixture is layered into each crêpe. During baking, it puffs up slightly to form an airy but creamy filling. This elegant presentation, unbelievably, can be assembled 1 day ahead and briefly baked just before serving.

INGREDIENTS
1 recipe Lemon Cream Illusion *without* gelatin (page 266)
1 recipe Chantilly Crêpes (page 110)

Lay a crêpe with its most attractive side down on a work surface and spread one half with 2 tablespoons Lemon Cream Illusion. Fold, spread 1 tablespoon of cream on half, and fold again.

Place the crêpes in the prepared pan. If not baking same day, cover with plastic wrap and refrigerate.

When ready to bake, *preheat the oven to 350°F.*

TO SERVE: Bake for 10 minutes or until slightly puffed. (Bake 15 minutes if the crêpes were refrigerated.) Sprinkle with powdered sugar, if desired.

Chocolate Velour Crêpes with Orange-Apricot Sauce

*T*he flavor combination of velvety bittersweet chocolate and tangy, golden honeyed apricot is a marriage made in heaven. A scoop of Vanilla Ice Cream (page 285), slowly melting in the hot apricot sauce, is not entirely unwelcome.

INGREDIENTS	MEASURE	WEIGHT	
room temperature	volume	ounces	grams
BATTER			
1 large egg	3 tablespoons + ½ teaspoon	1.75 ounces (weighed without shell)	50 grams
1 large egg yolk	1 tablespoon + ½ teaspoon	0.6 ounce	19 grams
milk	⅔ cup	5.5 ounces	160 grams
vanilla	¾ teaspoon	•	3 grams
unsalted butter, melted	2½ tablespoons	1.25 ounces	35 grams
cognac	2 teaspoons	•	9 grams
cornstarch	⅓ cup	1.5 ounces	40 grams
unsweetened cocoa (Dutch-processed) or ¼ cup nonalkalized cocoa such as Hershey's	3 tablespoons	0.75 ounce	18 grams
sugar	3 tablespoons	1.25 ounces	38 grams
salt	pinch	•	•
clarified butter *	1 tablespoon	0.5 ounce	12 grams

*If you do not have clarified butter on hand, you will need to clarify 2 tablespoons (1 ounce/25 grams) unsalted butter. In a heavy saucepan melt the butter over medium heat, partially covered to prevent splattering. When the butter looks clear, cook uncovered, watching carefully until the solids drop and begin to brown. Pour immediately through a fine strainer or a strainer lined with cheesecloth.

INGREDIENTS	MEASURE	WEIGHT	
room temperature	*volume*	*ounces*	*grams*
ORANGE-APRICOT SAUCE			
grated orange zest	2 teaspoons	•	4 grams
orange juice, freshly squeezed	½ liquid cup	4.25 ounces	121 grams
unsalted butter	2 tablespoons	1 ounce	28 grams
apricot lekvar or preserves	½ cup	•	•
FOR FLAMBÉING			
powdered sugar	2 tablespoons	0.5 ounce	13 grams
Barack Palinka or apricot brandy	¼ cup	2 ounces	56 grams

TO MAKE BATTER

The easiest and fastest way to mix the batter is in a blender. Place the ingredients in the order given into a blender and blend at high speed for 10 seconds.

Heat the crêpe pan on medium heat until hot enough to sizzle a drop of water. Brush lightly with clarified butter and pour a scant 2 tablespoons batter (1 tablespoon if using a 4-inch pan) in the center. Immediately tilt the pan to the left and then down and around to the right so that the batter moves in a counter-clockwise direction, covering the entire pan.

Cook until the top starts to dull and the edges begin to brown, about 15 to 20 seconds. I like to use a small metal spatula to lift the upper edge and check to see if the crêpe is golden brown. Then, grasping the edge of the crêpe with my fingers, I flip it over and cook for 10 seconds, or just until lightly browned. Do not use too high a heat as chocolate crêpes are more prone to burning. Invert the pan over the counter and the crêpe will release.

It is fine to place 1 crêpe on top of another if serving the same day. If refrigerating or freezing the crêpes, however, separate them with pieces of wax paper or they may stick to each other. Makes fourteen 6-inch crêpes or twenty-four 4-inch crêpes.

TO MAKE ORANGE-APRICOT SAUCE

In a bowl stir together the orange zest, juice, butter, and preserves until smooth.

One 6-inch or 4-inch crêpe pan.

STORE:
2 days refrigerated, 3 months frozen.

TO SERVE: Lay crêpe with its most attractive side down and spread very lightly with the orange-apricot butter. Fold in half and spread with more butter. Fold into triangles by folding in half or thirds. (To fold in thirds, the center of the flat edge will become the point of the triangle. Fold each side down so that they meet in the center, spread with a little more orange-apricot butter, and fold in half.) Use ½ tablespoon orange-apricot butter for each crêpe.

Place the remaining orange-apricot butter in a large, attractive crêpe or sauté pan and heat until melted and bubbling. Place the crêpes in the pan. Heat for 1½ minutes, spooning the orange-apricot sauce over the crêpes. Remove from the heat and sprinkle with the powdered sugar.

Place the liqueur in a large ladle or saucepan with a long handle. Heat until very hot and starting to flame. If necessary tilt the ladle slightly so that the gas burner flame will ignite it or use a very long match. Pour over the crêpes and allow to flame until it goes out.

NOTE: The butter-spread, folded crêpes and remaining orange-apricot butter can be frozen for 3 months.

SPONGE-TYPE CAKES

Sponge-type (also known as foam) cakes, depend on a large amount of beaten egg for their light, airy texture. These are the cakes to consider if you are trying to cut cholesterol, as most do not use butter and the angel food cake uses no egg yolks, making it cholesterol free.

Some of these cakes, such as sponge cake and chiffon cake, are moist enough to be eaten without a soaking syrup and therefore maintain their springy, lighter-than-air quality. The texture and flavors are so delightful that these cakes are usually eaten without frosting.

Other sponge-type cakes, such as classic *génoise* and Biscuit de Savoie, would seem dry and even rubbery without a soaking syrup and rather plain without whipped cream or buttercream. Liqueur-flavored syrup transforms the resilient quality of *génoise* or *biscuit* into a delightfully tender and soft crumb.

Génoise is a European sponge-type cake which differs from American sponge in that it contains butter to partially tenderize and flavor it and much less sugar. Even when syrup has been added to *génoise,* it is still less sweet than sponge cake, though a lot more moist. With a judicious amount of syrup, *génoise* is moist without being wet. Europeans, however, tend to favor a greater amount of syrup than do Americans. This is a question of personal preference.

Biscuit de Savoie is also a European sponge-type cake which, like American sponge, contains no butter or oil but a lot more egg, making it lighter, drier, and tougher until well soaked with syrup. Because it contains no added fat, it is lighter and can absorb more syrup than a *génoise* without losing its delicate texture. This makes it an especially refreshing cake.

For a detailed explanation of sponge-type cakes and a chart comparing the percentage of components in all cakes, see page 470.

NOTE: It is best not to double most recipes in this chapter as standard mixing bowls are too small to accommodate their volume.

For fuller details see the suggested page number.
- Use *cake* flour that does not contain leavening (page 476). (Do not use self-rising cake flour.)
- Use superfine sugar for finest texture (page 476).
- Measure or weigh ingredients carefully (page 438).
- Heat eggs (or allow to warm) to temperature indicated in recipe.
- If a recipe indicates heating the egg/sugar mixture and you are using a hand-held mixer, beat the mixture over hot water until thickened. Then remove and continue beating until cool.
- When beating egg whites, use cream of tartar or beat just until stiff peaks form when the beater is raised slowly.
- Work quickly once the eggs are beaten so that they do not deflate.
- Fold flour gently but *thoroughly* into the batter.
- Bake immediately after mixing.
- Use the correct pan size (page 20).
- For very even layers and maximum height use Magi-Cake Strips (pages 20 and 456).
- Check for accurate oven temperature (page 448).
- Use correct baking time; do not underbake (page 21).
- Wrap cake layers well or glaze and frost them when cool (page 23).

HIGHLIGHTS FOR SUCCESSFUL GÉNOISE, BISCUIT, AND SPONGE CAKES

Génoise Classique

(JenWAHZ ClassEEK)

SERVES 8

A *génoise* that is gossamer and perfectly moistened and perfumed with syrup is pure poetry. The flavor and texture come to life only with the right amount of syrup. Too little will make the cake seem dry and tasteless; too much causes it to become heavy and sodden. I find the perfect amount of syrup to be 3 to 4 tablespoons for every egg used in the batter. If the cake is several days old and on the dry side, I add the extra tablespoon.

This *génoise* is the best I have ever experienced. It is very light yet perfectly fine-grained. The *beurre noisette* makes it seem rich without having to add so much butter that the texture loses its airy quality.

Since this recipe first appeared in print in 1981, I have received more calls about it from readers than for any other recipe. Many say that for the first time in their lives they have succeeded in making a perfect *génoise*.

INGREDIENTS	MEASURE	WEIGHT	
room temperature	*volume*	*ounces*	*grams*
clarified *beurre noisette* *	3 tablespoons	1.25 ounces	37 grams
vanilla	1 teaspoon	•	4 grams
4 large eggs	6 full fluid ounces	7 ounces (weighed without shells)	200 grams
sugar	½ cup	3.5 ounces	100 grams
sifted cake flour	½ cup	1.75 ounces	50 grams
cornstarch, lightly spooned ¾ CUP SYRUP (7 OUNCES/200 GRAMS):	½ cup − 1 tablespoon	1.75 ounces	50 grams
sugar	¼ cup + 1½ teaspoons	2 ounces	56 grams
water	½ liquid cup	4 ounces	118 grams
liqueur of your choice	2 tablespoons	1 ounce	28 grams

* If you do not have clarified butter on hand, you will need to clarify 2 tablespoons (1 ounce/25 grams) unsalted butter. In a heavy saucepan melt the butter over medium heat, partially covered to prevent splattering. When the butter looks clear, cook uncovered, watching carefully until the solids drop and begin to brown. Pour immediately through a fine strainer or a strainer lined with cheesecloth.

Preheat the oven to 350°F.

Warm the *beurre noisette* until almost hot (110°F. to 120°F.). Add the vanilla and keep warm.

In a large mixing bowl set over a pan of simmering water heat the eggs and sugar until just lukewarm, stirring constantly to prevent curdling. (The eggs may also be heated by placing them *still in their shells* in a large mixing bowl in an oven with a pilot light for 3 hours or up to overnight. The weight of the unshelled eggs should be 8 ounces.) Using the whisk beater, beat the mixture on high speed for 5 minutes or until triple in volume. (A hand beater may be used but it will be necessary to beat for at least 10 minutes.)

While the eggs are beating, sift together the flour and cornstarch.

Remove 1 scant cup of the egg mixture and thoroughly whisk it into the *beurre noisette*.

Sift ½ the flour mixture over the remaining egg mixture and fold it in gently but rapidly with a large balloon whisk, slotted skimmer, or rubber spatula until almost all the flour has disappeared. Repeat with the remaining flour mixture until the flour has disappeared completely. Fold in the butter mixture until just incorporated.

Pour immediately into the prepared pan (it will be about ⅔ full) and bake 25 to 35 minutes or until the cake is golden brown and starts to shrink slightly from the sides of the pan. (No need for a cake tester. Once the sides shrink the cake is done.) Avoid opening the oven door before the minimum time or the cake could fall. Test toward the end of baking by opening the door slightly and, if at a quick glance it does not appear done, close door at once and check again in 5 minutes.

Loosen the sides of the cake with a small metal spatula and unmold at once onto a lightly greased rack. Reinvert to cool. Trim the bottom and top crust when ready to complete the cake and sprinkle the syrup evenly on both sides (page 357).*

TO MAKE SYRUP

In a small saucepan with a tight-fitting lid bring the sugar and water to a rolling boil, stirring constantly. Cover immediately, remove from the heat, and allow to cool completely. Transfer to a liquid measuring cup and stir in the liqueur. If the syrup has slightly evaporated, add enough water to equal ¾ cup syrup.

UNDERSTANDING

It is fascinating to compare *génoise* to basic butter cake. For the same size cake, the *génoise* uses double the egg,

* After being sprinkled with syrup, *génoise* becomes fragile and more prone to splitting when moved. Use a cardboard round or a removable pan bottom for support.

One 9-inch by 2-inch pan or 9-inch springform pan or 9-inch by 2-inch heart-shaped pan or 8-inch by 2-inch square pan, greased, bottom lined with parchment, and then greased again and floured.

FINISHED HEIGHT:
After trimming bottom and top crusts: 1½ inches.

STORE:
Syrup: 1 month refrigerated in an airtight container. *Génoise:* Without syrup, 2 days room temperature, 5 days refrigerated, 2 months frozen. After adding the syrup the flavors ripen and the moisture is more evenly distributed 1 day later. The completed cake can be refrigerated up to 5 days and frozen up to 2 months.

COMPLEMENTARY ADORNMENTS:
One recipe: Any buttercream, whipped cream, glaze, or fondant.

SERVE:
Room temperature or lightly chilled.

POINTERS FOR SUCCESS:
See page 119. A large balloon whisk or a slotted skimmer is ideal for folding in the flour with the least amount of air loss. If using the whisk, periodically shake out the batter which collects on the inside.

half the sugar, flour/cornstarch, and butter, and no chemical leavening or added liquid. This explains why the *génoise* is "lighter than air!" With the addition of syrup, however, the sugar level is almost as high as in the butter cake.

I once spent an entire week playing with *génoise* variations, proportions, and techniques. I discovered by accidentally burning the butter that brown butter *(beurre noisette)* transforms the flavor of a *génoise,* adding richness and dimension. (This was published in *Cook's* magazine, May/June 1981.) Butter is warmed before folding into the batter so that it stays liquid and does not weigh down the batter.

Replacing some of the flour with cornstarch (a European technique) tightens the grain and holds the moisture supplied by the eggs and sugar. Although using part cake flour produces the best texture, other flours will work, even flours that are all starch such as potato flour (although the higher the starch content, the lower the *génoise*). I have demonstrated this cake in England, France, and even Japan with "native" flours and always with success.

VARIATION

GÉNOISE RICHE (JenWAHZ Reesh): For a more buttery *génoise* that is denser and moister, use ⅓ cup (2.5 ounces/71 grams) *beurre noisette.* This *génoise* will require only half the syrup for moisture and flavor so it will be richer but less sweet!

This cake is used to make A Taste of Heaven (page 166), Star-Spangled Rhapsody (page 169), and Chocolate Chip Charlotte (page 179).

Chestnut Génoise

SERVES 8

*C*hestnut flour has almost the same starch content as cornstarch, so it occurred to me one day to try substituting it for the cornstarch portion of a *génoise.* The result was exciting: The incredible lightness of *génoise* remained, augmented by the mild spiciness of chestnut. This particular *génoise* tastes exquisite with rum syrup and filled and frosted with Chestnut Whipped Cream. I call the finished cake La Châtaigne (lah shaTAIN), a lovely French word for "chestnut." This cake makes an elegant and unusual Thanksgiving dessert.

INGREDIENTS	MEASURE	WEIGHT	
room temperature	*volume*	*ounces*	*grams*
clarified *beurre noisette**	¼ cup	1.75 ounces	50 grams
vanilla	1½ teaspoons	•	6 grams
6 large eggs	10 scant fluid ounces (scant 1¼ liquid cups)	10.5 ounces 300 grams (weighed without shells)	
sugar	¾ cup	5.25 ounces	150 grams
sifted cake flour	¾ cup	2.63 ounces†	75 grams
sifted chestnut flour	⅔ cup	2.63 ounces†	75 grams
I CUP + 2 TABLE-SPOONS RUM SYRUP (10.5 OUNCES/300 GRAMS):			
sugar	¼ cup + 3 tablespoons	3 ounces	88 grams
water	¾ liquid cup	6 ounces	177 grams
dark rum	3 tablespoons	1.5 ounces	40 grams

* If you do not have clarified *beurre noisette* on hand, you will need to clarify 5½ tablespoons (2.75 ounces/78 grams) unsalted butter. In a heavy saucepan melt the butter over medium heat, partially covered to prevent splattering. When the butter looks clear, cook uncovered, watching carefully until the solids drop and begin to brown. When they become deep brown, pour immediately through a fine strainer or a strainer lined with cheesecloth.
†If you don't have an electronic scale, don't worry about getting the ounces for the cake flour and chestnut flour exact as long as their combined total is 5.25 ounces.

Preheat the oven to 350°F.

Warm the *beurre noisette* until almost hot (110°F. to 120°F.). Add the vanilla and keep warm.

In a large mixing bowl set over a pan of simmering water heat the eggs and sugar until just lukewarm, stirring constantly to prevent curdling. (The eggs may also be heated by placing them *still in their shells* in a large mixing bowl in an oven with a pilot light for 3 hours or up to overnight. The weight of the unshelled eggs should be 12 ounces.) Using the whisk beater, beat the mixture on high speed for 5 minutes or until triple in volume. (A hand beater may be used but it will be necessary to beat for at least 10 minutes.)

While the eggs are beating, sift together the flours.

Two 9-inch by 1½-inch pans, greased, bottoms lined with parchment, and then greased again and floured.

FINISHED HEIGHT:
After trimming the bottom and top crusts each layer is 1 inch.

STORE:
Syrup: 1 month refrigerated in airtight container. Génoise: Without syrup, 2 days at room temperature, 5 days refrigerated, 2 months

frozen. After adding the syrup the flavors ripen and the moisture is more evenly distributed 1 day later. The completed cake can be refrigerated up to 5 days and frozen up to 2 months.

COMPLEMENTARY ADORNMENTS:
Chestnut Mousse Cream (page 262).

SERVE:
Lightly chilled.

POINTERS FOR SUCCESS:
See page 119. A large balloon whisk or a slotted skimmer is ideal for folding in the flour with the least amount of air loss. If using the whisk, periodically shake out the batter which collects on the inside.

Remove 1 scant cup of the egg mixture and thoroughly whisk it into the *beurre noisette*.

Sift ½ the flour mixture over the remaining egg mixture and fold it in gently but rapidly with a large balloon whisk, slotted skimmer, or rubber spatula until almost all the flour has disappeared. Repeat with the remaining flour mixture until the flour has disappeared completely. Fold in the butter mixture until just incorporated.

Pour immediately into the prepared pans (they will be almost ⅔ full) and bake 25 to 30 minutes or until the cakes are golden brown and start to shrink slightly from the sides of the pans. (No need for a cake tester. Once the sides shrink the cakes are done.) Avoid opening the oven door before the minimum time or the cakes could fall. Test toward the end of baking by opening the door slightly and, if at a quick glance they do not appear done, close the door at once and check again in 5 minutes.

Loosen the sides of the cakes with a small metal spatula and unmold at once onto lightly greased racks. Reinvert to cool. Trim the bottom and top crusts when ready to complete the cakes and sprinkle the syrup evenly on all sides (page 357).*

TO MAKE SYRUP

In a small saucepan with a tight-fitting lid bring the sugar and water to a rolling boil, stirring constantly. Cover immediately, remove from the heat, and allow to cool completely. Transfer to a liquid measuring cup and stir in the rum. If the syrup has evaporated slightly, add enough water to equal 1 cup + 2 tablespoons syrup.

This cake is used to make Chestnut Chocolate Embrace (page 189).

---

* After being sprinkled with syrup, *génoise* become fragile and more prone to splitting when moved. Use a cardboard round or a removable pan bottom for support.

Golden Génoise

*T*his unique *génoise* has the most velvety, tender texture and rich golden color of any cake in this book. The batter, by the way, also makes the loveliest of *madeleines* (shell-shaped cookies).

Golden Génoise is so moist no syrup is necessary, but a sprinkling of liqueur is a fine enhancement. The fine, dense texture of this cake can support any buttercream, from classic to mousseline. This is a superb party cake—a real favorite.

SERVES 12

INGREDIENTS	MEASURE	WEIGHT	
room temperature	*volume*	*ounces*	*grams*
clarified *beurre noisette* *	3.5 fluid ounces (a scant ½ cup)	3 ounces	85 grams
vanilla	1 teaspoon	•	4 grams
12 large egg yolks	7 fluid ounces	7.75 ounces	223 grams
sugar	¾ cup + 2 tablespoons	6 ounces	175 grams
sifted cake flour	1 cup	3.5 ounces	100 grams
unsifted cornstarch	3 tablespoons	0.75 ounce	24 grams
water	¼ liquid cup	2 ounces	60 grams

* If you do not have clarified *beurre noisette* on hand, you will need to clarify 9 tablespoons (4.5 ounces/128 grams) unsalted butter. In a heavy saucepan melt the butter over medium heat, partially covered to prevent splattering. When the butter looks clear, cook uncovered, watching carefully until the solids drop and begin to brown. When they become deep brown, pour immediately through a fine strainer or a strainer lined with cheesecloth.

Preheat the oven to 350°F.

Warm the *beurre noisette* until almost hot (110°F. to 120°F.). Add the vanilla and keep warm.

In a large mixing bowl set over a pan of simmering water heat the yolks and sugar until almost hot to the touch, stirring constantly to prevent curdling. Using a whisk beater, beat the mixture on high speed for 5 minutes or until triple in volume. (A hand beater may be used but it will be necessary to beat for at least 10 minutes.)

While the eggs are beating, sift together the flour and cornstarch. Decrease the speed and beat in the water. Sift ½ the flour mixture over the egg mixture and fold it in gently but rapidly with a large balloon whisk, slotted skimmer, or rubber spatula until almost all the flour has disap-

One 9-inch by 2-inch heart-shaped pan or a 9-inch springform pan, greased, bottom lined with parchment, and then greased again and floured. Or a 9-cup Kugelhopf pan, greased and floured.

FINISHED HEIGHT:
2 inches including crust. Kugelhopf is 3 inches.

2 days room temperature, 5 days refrigerated, 2 months frozen.

COMPLEMENTARY ADORNMENTS:
The texture of this cake is firm enough to support any nonchocolate buttercream (chocolate would overwhelm the flavor) but interesting enough to stand up beautifully under just a light sprinkling of powdered sugar. Suggested buttercreams: *One recipe:* Any fruit-flavored buttercream such as Apricot Buttercream (page 233 or 243) or Orange Blossom Buttercream (page 234) or Praline Buttercream (page 239 or 249).

SERVE:
Room temperature.

POINTERS FOR SUCCESS:
See page 119. A large balloon whisk or a slotted skimmer is ideal for folding in the flour with the least amount of air loss. If using the whisk, periodically shake out the batter which collects on the inside.

peared. Repeat with the remaining flour mixture until the flour has disappeared completely. Fold in the *beurre noisette* in 2 batches until just incorporated.

Pour immediately into the prepared pan (no more than ¾ full) and bake 30 to 40 minutes or until the cake is golden brown and springs back when pressed lightly in the center.

(In the Kugelhopf pan the cake should start to shrink slightly from the sides. In the heart-shaped pan it will rise about ½ inch above the top during baking and will start to sink slightly when done. No need for a cake tester. Once the sides shrink the cake is done.) Avoid opening the oven door before the minimum time or the cake could fall. Test towards the end of baking by opening the door slightly and, if at a quick glance it does not appear done, close the door at once and check again in 5 minutes.

Unmold at once onto a lightly greased rack. Reinvert to cool. If sprinkling with liqueur, trim the top and bottom crusts to prevent pastiness. The cake may be split horizontally to make 2 layers. I love the texture of this cake so much I prefer 1 uninterrupted layer with frosting on the top.

UNDERSTANDING

In contrast to classic *Génoise*, this recipe uses all yolks instead of whole eggs, more butter, and less flour. A small amount of water is added because the yolks alone make such a thick batter.

This cake is used to make Golden Cage (page 172).

This is another unusual *génoise* with less cholesterol than the classic formula. It is a cross between an angel food cake and a *génoise:* less airy than the angel food but buttery and more tender. Syrup makes the cake's texture pasty, so for flavor orange zest is added to the batter instead. For a delightful orange blossom flavor, replace 1 tablespoon of the water with orange flower water. Any fruit-flavored buttercream, especially orange, is a fine complement.

White Génoise

**SERVES
10 TO 12**

INGREDIENTS	MEASURE	WEIGHT	
room temperature	*volume*	*ounces*	*grams*
clarified *beurre noisette* *	3 full fluid ounces (6.5 tablespoons)	2.75 ounces	80 grams
vanilla	1½ teaspoons	•	6 grams
grated orange zest	2 tablespoons	0.5 ounce	12 grams
cake flour	1½ cups (lightly spooned into cup)	6 ounces	170 grams
cornstarch	¾ cup minus 2 teaspoons (lightly spooned into cup)	3 ounces	85 grams
9 large egg whites	9 fluid ounces (1 liquid cup + 2 tablespoons)	9.5 ounces	270 grams
sugar	1¼ cups	9 ounces	255 grams
water	¾ liquid cup	6.25 ounces	177 grams
optional: Cointreau	½ cup	4.25 ounces	122 grams

* If you do not have clarified *beurre noisette* on hand, you will need to clarify 9 tablespoons (4.5 ounces/128 grams) unsalted butter. In a heavy saucepan melt the butter over medium heat, partially covered to prevent splattering. When the butter looks clear, cook uncovered, watching carefully until the solids drop and begin to brown. When they become deep brown, pour immediately through a fine strainer or a strainer lined with cheesecloth.

Preheat the oven to 350°F.

Warm the *beurre noisette* until almost hot (110°F to 120°F.). Add the vanilla and orange zest and keep warm.

Sift together the flour and cornstarch.

In a large mixing bowl beat the egg whites until soft peaks form when the beater is raised. Gradually beat in the

Two 9-inch by 1½-inch pans, greased, bottoms lined with parchment, and then greased again and floured.

After trimming the bottom and top crusts each layer is 1¼ inches.

STORE:
1 day room temperature, 3 days refrigerated, 2 months frozen.

COMPLEMENTARY
ADORNMENTS:
One recipe: **Orange, Lemon, or Raspberry Buttercream (pages 233 to 234). Any flavored whipped cream, especially Chocolate Chip (page 258). Rolled Fondant (page 306).**

SERVE:
Room temperature.

POINTERS FOR SUCCESS:
See page 119. A large balloon whisk or slotted skimmer is ideal for folding in the flour with the least amount of air loss. If using the whisk, periodically shake out the batter that collects on the inside.

sugar, beating just until stiff peaks form when the beater is raised slowly. Gradually beat in the water until incorporated. Remove 1 scant cup of the mixture and thoroughly whisk it into the butter.

Sift ½ the flour mixture over the remaining egg mixture and fold it in gently but rapidly with a large balloon whisk, slotted skimmer, or rubber spatula until the flour has disappeared. Repeat with the remaining flour mixture. Fold in the butter mixture until just incorporated.

Pour immediately into the prepared pans and bake 20 to 25 minutes or until the cake is golden brown and a tester inserted in the center comes out clean. Avoid opening the oven door before the minimum time or the cakes could fall. Test towards the end of baking by opening the door slightly and, if at a quick glance glance they do not appear done, close the door at once and check again in 5 minutes.

Unmold at once onto lightly greased racks. Reinvert to cool.

Trim bottom and top crusts when ready to complete cake. For extra moistness and flavor, sprinkle evenly on all sides with Cointreau (page 357).

UNDERSTANDING

The proportions of this cake are similar to classic *génoise* (equal weight sugar and flour/cornstarch: one quarter their combined weight in butter, before it has been clarified) but the yolks are replaced by water. The water enables the whites to stretch and expand in the oven resulting in a fine-textured, tender cake.

This cake is used to make White Lily Cake (page 203).

This *génoise* variation is as light and airy as a classic *génoise* but with the magic seduction of rich chocolate flavor! A syrup maintains a moist, tender quality. Be sure to flavor the syrup with a complementary liqueur. Coffee, hazelnut, raspberry, and orange are all delicious with chocolate. An airy frosting (flavored to correspond with the syrup) such as a Fruit Cloud Cream (page 264) or Fruit Mousseline (page 245) adds just the right touch.

This elegant cake is light enough to serve at the end of an elaborate dinner party. Conveniently, it benefits from advance preparation.

Génoise au Chocolat

(JenWAHZ au-ChocoLA)

SERVES 8

INGREDIENTS	MEASURE	WEIGHT	
room temperature	*volume*	*ounces*	*grams*
clarified *beurre noisette**	3 tablespoons	1.25 ounces	37 grams
unsweetened cocoa (Dutch-processed) or ¼ cup + 2 tablespoons nonalkalized cocoa such as Hershey's	⅓ cup (lightly spooned into cup)	1 ounce	28 grams
boiling water	¼ liquid cup	2 ounces	60 grams
vanilla	1 teaspoon	•	4 grams
5 large eggs	1 liquid cup	8.75 ounces	250 grams (weighed without shells)
sugar	½ cup	3.5 ounces	100 grams
sifted cake flour	¾ cup	2.5 ounces	75 grams
¾ CUP SYRUP (7 OUNCES/200 GRAMS):			
sugar	¼ cup + 1½ teaspoons	2 ounces	56 grams
water	½ liquid cup	4 ounces	118 grams
liqueur of your choice	2 tablespoons	1 ounce	28 grams

* If you do not have clarified *beurre noisette* on hand, you will need to clarify 4 tablespoons (2 ounces/57 grams) unsalted butter. In a heavy saucepan melt the butter over medium heat, partially covered to prevent splattering. When the butter looks clear, cook uncovered, watching carefully until the solids drop and begin to brown. When they become deep brown, pour immediately through a fine strainer or a strainer lined with cheesecloth.

One 9-inch by 2-inch pan,
9-inch springform pan, or a
9-inch by 2-inch heart-
shaped pan, greased, bottom
lined with parchment or
wax paper, and then greased
again and floured.

FINISHED HEIGHT:
After trimming the bottom
and top crusts: 1½ inches.

STORE:
Syrup: 1 month refrigerated
in an airtight container.
Génoise: Without syrup, 2
days at room temperature, 5
days refrigerated, 2 months
frozen. After adding the
syrup the flavors ripen and
the moisture is more evenly
distributed 1 day later. The
completed cake can be re-
frigerated up to 5 days and
frozen up to 2 months.

**COMPLEMENTARY
ADORNMENTS:**
One recipe: Any glaze, fondant, buttercream, or
whipped cream—especially
coffee, praline, chestnut, orange, apricot, and raspberry.

SERVE:
Room temperature or lightly
chilled.

Preheat the oven to 350°F.

Warm the *beurre noisette* until almost hot (110°F. to 120°F.) and keep warm.

In a small bowl whisk together the cocoa and boiling water until the cocoa is completely dissolved. Stir in the vanilla and set aside, leaving whisk in bowl and cover with plastic wrap.

In a large mixing bowl set over a pan of simmering water heat the eggs and sugar until just lukewarm, stirring constantly to prevent curdling. (The eggs may also be heated by placing them *still in their shells* in a large bowl in an oven with a pilot light for at least 3 hours. The weight of the unshelled eggs should be 10 ounces.) Using the whisk beater, beat the mixture on high speed for 5 minutes or until triple in volume. (A hand beater may be used but it will be necessary to beat for at least 10 minutes.)

Remove 2 cups of the egg mixture and whisk it into the cocoa mixture until smooth.

Sift the flour over the remaining egg mixture and fold it in gently but rapidly with a slotted skimmer or large rub-ber spatula until the flour has disappeared. Fold in the co-coa mixture until almost incorporated. Fold in the *beurre noisette* in 2 batches with a large whisk or rubber spatula until just incorporated.*

Pour immediately into the prepared pan (it will be about ¾ full) and bake 30 to 35 minutes or until the cake starts to shrink from the sides of the pan. (No need for a cake tester. Once the sides shrink the cake is done.) Avoid open-ing the oven door before the minimum time or the cake could fall. Test toward the end of baking by opening the oven door slightly and, if at a quick glance it does not ap-pear done, close door at once and check again in 5 min-utes.

Loosen the sides of the cake with a small metal spatula and unmold at once onto a lightly greased rack. Reinvert to cool. The firm upper crust prevents falling. Trim the bot-tom and top crusts when ready to complete the cake and sprinkle the syrup evenly on both sides (page 357).†

TO MAKE SYRUP

In a small saucepan with a tight-fitting lid bring the sugar and water to a rolling boil, stirring constantly. Cover im-

---

* Using your fingers is actually the best way to feel for lumps of flour. Dis-solve them by pressing them between thumb and forefinger.
† After being sprinkled with syrup, *génoise* becomes fragile and more prone to splitting when moved. Use a cardboard round or a removable pan bottom for support.

mediately, remove from the heat, and allow to cool completely. Transfer to a liquid measuring cup and stir in the liqueur. If the syrup has evaporated slightly, add enough water to equal ¾ cup syrup.

UNDERSTANDING

I have never before liked chocolate *génoise* as much as classic *génoise* because I feel a mere shadow of chocolate is not enough to justify the loss of delicate texture. The problem is that cocoa is very difficult to incorporate into an egg mixture as it tends to lump and drop to the bottom. Also, it does not release its full flavor unless it has been dissolved in water before being added to the batter (page 474). Although water is not conventionally used in *génoise,* to solve these problems I combined the cocoa with just enough water to dissolve it and softened the resulting "cream" by whisking in 2 cups of the beaten egg/sugar mixture before folding it into the remainder. An extra egg has been added to make up for deflating some of the batter with the cocoa. For further lightness, the cornstarch has been eliminated. The cocoa/flour mixture is equal in weight to the cornstarch/flour mixture of classic *génoise.*

This cake is used to make Strawberry Maria (page 184).

VARIATION

NUT-FLAVORED CHOCOLATE GÉNOISE: This interesting variation substitutes nut oil for the butter, giving it nut flavor without affecting the lovely, light texture of the *génoise.* It also lowers the cholesterol content. The nut motif can be enhanced by using Frangelico as the liqueur in the syrup.
To make Nut-Flavored Chocolate Génoise: Substitute 3 tablespoons (40 grams/1.5 ounces) walnut or hazelnut oil for the butter. There is no need to warm the oil as it remains liquid at room temperature and does not harden when added to the batter.

NOTES: The ideal amount of syrup to use for the finished *génoise* is equal in volume to the flour.

The upper crust of a chocolate *génoise* is usually easy to remove in one piece. It has a wonderful texture and very chocolaty flavor so I usually spread it with a layer of lightly sweetened whipped cream, roll and slice it, and serve the slices as petits fours.

POINTERS FOR SUCCESS: See page 119. The cocoa mixture must be thoroughly mixed into the batter to keep from dropping to the bottom. The cake must start shrinking from the sides of the pan before removal from the oven or it will fall slightly on cooling.

Moist Chocolate Génoise

*T*his cake has the light texture of a *génoise* but is more velvety and moist. An equivalent amount of chocolate is used instead of cocoa, but a special technique is employed to intensify the flavor. Before being added to the batter, the chocolate is cooked with water which releases its flavor (page 474). This enables you to have a *génoise* the flavor of your favorite bittersweet chocolate bar!

INGREDIENTS	MEASURE	WEIGHT	
room temperature	*volume*	*ounces*	*grams*
bittersweet chocolate	•	8 ounces	227 grams
boiling water	1 liquid cup	8.25 ounces	236 grams
8 large eggs	1½ liquid cups	14 ounces (weighed without shells)	400 grams
sugar	1 cup	7 ounces	200 grams
sifted cake flour	1½ cups	5.25 ounces	150 grams
I CUP + 2 TABLE-SPOONS SYRUP (10.5 ounces/300 grams)			
sugar	¼ cup + 3 tablespoons	3 ounces	88 grams
water	¾ liquid cup	6 ounces	182 grams
liqueur of your choice	3 tablespoons	1.5 ounces	40 grams

Two 9-inch by 2-inch cake pans or 9-inch springform pans, greased, bottoms lined with parchment, and then greased again and floured.

Preheat the oven to 350°F.

In a heavy saucepan bring the chocolate and water to a boil over low heat, stirring constantly. Simmer, stirring, for 5 minutes or until the chocolate thickens to a pudding-like consistency. (It will fall from the spoon and pool slightly before disappearing.) Cool completely.

In a large mixing bowl, beat the eggs and sugar with the whisk beater on high speed for 5 minutes or until triple in volume. (A hand beater may be used but it will be necessary to beat for at least 10 minutes.)

Sift ½ the flour over the egg mixture and fold it in gently but rapidly with a slotted skimmer or large rubber spatula until some of the flour has disappeared. Repeat with the remaining flour until all flour has disappeared. Fold in the chocolate mixture until incorporated.

Pour immediately into the prepared pans (they will be about ⅔ full) and bake 30 to 35 minutes or until a tester inserted in the centers enters as easily as it does when inserted closer to the sides. The cakes rise to the tops of the pans during baking and will lower slightly when done, pulling slightly away from the sides. Avoid opening the oven door before the minimum time or the cakes could fall.

Loosen the sides of the cakes with a small metal spatula and unmold at once onto lightly greased racks. Reinvert to cool. The firm upper crusts prevent falling. Trim the bottom and top crusts when ready to complete the cake and sprinkle syrup evenly on all sides.*

TO MAKE SYRUP

In a small saucepan with a tight-fitting lid bring the sugar and water to a rolling boil, stirring constantly. Cover immediately, remove from the heat and allow to cool completely. Transfer to a liquid measuring cup and stir in the liqueur. If the syrup has evaporated slightly, add enough water to equal 1 cup plus 2 tablespoons syrup.

UNDERSTANDING

The ratio of ingredients in this cake is similar to Génoise au Chocolat. The Moist Chocolate Génoise has the same amount of sugar and flour as the same size Génoise Au Chocolat (the 4 ounces of sugar provided by the bittersweet chocolate are exactly equal to the 4 ounces of sugar provided by the syrup used for two layers of the Génoise au Chocolat). Moist Chocolate Génoise, however, contains a little less egg, more than double the water, and, instead of butter, 2.5 ounces of cocoa butter contained by the chocolate. All of these variables are responsible for making this cake's texture more moist and dense than classic Génoise au Chocolat. Because this cake is not as light and airy, two layers are necessary for sufficient height. Since the chocolate contains vanilla, no extra vanilla is added.

This cake is used to make Swiss Black Forest Cake (page 190) and Triple Chocolate Cake (page 201).

FINISHED HEIGHT:
After trimming the bottom and top crusts each layer is 1¼ inches.

STORE:
Syrup: 1 month refrigerated in an airtight container. *Genoise* without syrup: 2 days room temperature, 5 days refrigerated, 2 months frozen. After adding the syrup the flavors ripen and the moisture is more evenly distributed 1 day later. The completed cake can be refrigerated up to 5 days and frozen up to 2 months.

COMPLEMENTARY ADORNMENTS:
A light sprinkling of liqueur. Any ganache (pages 267 to 278). This cake is not too sweet so it is perfect as a base for some of the sweeter decorative toppings such as Chocolate Praline Leaves (page 386). It also makes an excellent base for the Swiss Black Forest Cake (page 190).

SERVE:
Room temperature or lightly chilled.

POINTERS FOR SUCCESS:
See page 119.

---

* After being sprinkled with syrup, a *génoise* becomes fragile and more prone to splitting when moved. Use a cardboard round or removable bottom of a pan to support it.

Bittersweet
Cocoa Almond Génoise

SERVES 8

The perfect cake for the cocoa lover, this recipe was inspired by Maida Heatter's glorious Queen Mother's Cake, which has become a classic. It is so chocolaty and moist without being sweet that I like to serve it unfrosted without even a sprinkling of powdered sugar. But if you insist on gilding the lily, the ideal way to do it is with lightly sweetened whipped cream (page 253) on the side.

It is not necessary to grease and flour the sides of the cake pan (making it a totally flourless cake, ideal for Passover, but omit the cream of tartar) because it is easy to dislodge the cake using a small metal spatula.

INGREDIENTS	MEASURE	WEIGHT	
room temperature	*volume*	*ounces*	*grams*
unsweetened cocoa (Dutch-processed)	½ cup + 1 tablespoon (lightly spooned into cup)	1.75 ounces	50 grams
boiling water	scant ½ liquid cup (3.5 fluid ounces)	3.5 ounces	100 grams
vanilla	1 teaspoon	•	4 grams
unsalted butter (must be softened)	16 tablespoons	8 ounces	227 grams
sugar	1 cup + 2 tablespoons	8 ounces	227 grams
6 large eggs, separated yolks white	3.5 fluid ounces ¾ liquid cup	4 ounces 6.25 ounces	112 grams 180 grams
unblanched sliced almonds, toasted and finely ground	scant 1⅔ cups (ground)	6 ounces	170 grams
salt	⅛ teaspoon	•	•
cream of tartar	¾ teaspoon	•	•

Preheat the oven to 350°F.

In a small bowl stir together the cocoa and boiling water until the cocoa is dissolved and mixture is the consistency of smooth buttercream. Stir in the vanilla and cool.

In a mixing bowl beat the butter and 1 cup sugar for 3 minutes or until light and fluffy. Add the egg yolks and beat until incorporated, scraping down the sides. Add the cocoa mixture and almonds and beat until blended, scraping down the sides.

In a large mixing bowl beat the egg whites and salt until foamy. Add the cream of tartar and beat until soft peaks form when the beater is raised. Gradually beat in the remaining 2 tablespoons sugar, beating until stiff peaks form when the beater is raised slowly. Stir ¼ of the whites into the chocolate mixture to lighten it. Then gently fold in the remaining whites with a large rubber spatula.

Pour into the prepared pan (it will be about ½ full) and bake 70 minutes. After 30 minutes, cover the top loosely with foil to prevent overbrowning. Cool the cake in the pan for 45 minutes. Run a small metal spatula around the sides of the cake and remove the sides of the pan. Invert onto a lightly greased rack and reinvert to cool. The cake sinks very slightly in the center which adds interest to its shape!

UNDERSTANDING

The formula for Chocolate Nut Génoise is almost identical to Maida Heatter's Queen Mother's Cake,* with the chocolate replaced by Dutch-processed cocoa, which contains less cocoa butter and no sugar. Therefore the sugar has been increased and butter replaces the cocoa butter. A small amount of water releases and intensifies the flavor of the cocoa. The result is a cake with assertive flavor but lighter texture than the original, particularly because butter is softer at room temperature and cocoa butter is firm. Cream of tartar is used to stabilize the egg whites as the chocolate mixture is quite heavy and tends to break them down.

One 9-inch springform pan ungreased, bottom lined with parchment or wax paper, sides wrapped with Magi-Cake Strips (pages 20 and 456). With this cake it is particularly wise to use Magi-Cake Strips to prevent the sides from overbrowning during the long baking time.

FINISHED HEIGHT:
1½ inches at the sides, 1¼ inches in the center.

STORE:
3 days room temperature, 5 days refrigerated, 2 months frozen.

COMPLEMENTARY ADORNMENTS:
A light dusting of powdered sugar. Perfect Whipped Cream (page 253).

SERVE:
Room temperature or very lightly chilled.

POINTERS FOR SUCCESS:
See page 119.

* Maida Heatter, *Maida Heatter's Book of Great Desserts* (New York: Alfred A. Knopf, 1974).

Fudgy
Génoise Jeffrey

SERVES 8

*his unusual *génoise* is delicate yet moist and fudgy with a crisp meringuelike crust. It was offered to me by a brilliant young podiatrist who turned his scientific talents to creating a cake which uses less than half the flour of ordinary chocolate *génoise* and no butter. Dr. Elterman prefers to use Lindt Excellence chocolate to make this cake. (I have no complaint!)

INGREDIENTS	MEASURE	WEIGHT	
room temperature	*volume*	*ounces*	*grams*
bittersweet chocolate	•	10 ounces	284 grams
8 large eggs, separated			
yolks	4.5 fluid ounces	5.25 ounces	150 grams
whites	1 liquid cup	8.5 ounces	240 grams
cream of tartar	1 teaspoon	•	3 grams
sugar	1¼ cups	8.75 ounces	250 grams
sifted cake flour	⅔ cup	2.25 ounces	65 grams

Two 9-inch by 1½-inch pans, greased, bottoms lined with parchment or wax paper, and then greased again and floured.

FINISHED HEIGHT:
After trimming the bottom and top crusts, each layer is almost 1 inch.

STORE:
2 days room temperature, 5 days refrigerated. Freezing is not recommended as the texture becomes heavy after thawing and the flavor alters.

Preheat the oven to 350°F.

In a double boiler set over hot (not simmering) water, on low heat, melt the chocolate.

In a large mixing bowl set over a pan of simmering water heat the yolks and ¼ cup sugar until almost hot to the touch, stirring constantly to prevent curdling. Using the whisk beater, beat the mixture on high speed for 5 minutes or until triple in volume. (A hand beater may be used but it will be necessary to beat for at least 10 minutes.) Add the chocolate and immediately beat until incorporated.

In another large mixing bowl beat the egg whites until foamy, add the cream of tartar, and beat until soft peaks form when the beater is raised. Gradually beat in the remaining 1 cup sugar, beating until stiff peaks form when the beater is raised slowly.

Stir ¼ of the whites into the chocolate batter to lighten it. Sift ⅓ of the flour over the batter and fold it in with a large rubber spatula gently but rapidly until partially blended. Add ⅓ of the remaining whites and fold until partially blended. Repeat 2 more times, starting with the flour and ending with the egg whites. After the final batch of flour, make sure all of it has disappeared before adding the whites.

Pour immediately into the prepared pans and bake for 35 minutes.

Loosen the sides with a small metal spatula and unmold at once onto lightly greased racks. Reinvert to cool.

UNDERSTANDING

Aside from the unusually small quantity of flour, this cake is similar in formula to Moist Chocolate Génoise. The chocolate, however, is not cooked in water (which would release more flavor). Instead, an extra ounce is used to intensify flavor. Also, more sugar is added to produce a chocolaty flavor without a bittersweet edge. As in Moist Chocolate Génoise, the only fat here comes from the cocoa butter in the chocolate.

COMPLEMENTARY ADORNMENTS:
Cake can be served plain in small wedges or with a dollop of Perfect Whipped Cream (page 253) or Light Whipped Ganache (page 268) spooned on top.

SERVE:
Room temperature.

POINTERS FOR SUCCESS:
See page 119.

Chocolate Cloud Roll

SERVES 8

*T*his is more a flourless soufflé than a cake. It is so light and delicate (both in texture and flavor) it has to be baked in a low sheet pan or it will fall. I have discovered since including it in my first cookbook *(Romantic and Classic Cakes)* that severely cutting back the sugar not only intensifies the chocolate flavor but also improves the texture and helps to prevent cracking when the cake is rolled! Attractive as a cake roll, it also may be cut into squares, rounds, or ovals and used as a layer cake.

Optional nuts add a subtle texture and flavor. Omit the nuts for an uninterrupted silken smooth texture. Filled with whipped cream and fresh berries, this cake is the perfect light summer dessert for chocolate lovers.

INGREDIENTS	MEASURE	WEIGHT	
room temperature	*volume*	*ounces*	*grams*
sugar	¼ cup + 2 tablespoons	2.75 ounces	78 grams
6 large eggs, separated yolks whites	3.5 fluid ounces ¾ liquid cup	4 ounces 6.25 ounces	112 grams 180 grams
bittersweet chocolate, melted	•	4 ounces	113 grams
optional: unblanched sliced almonds, toasted and finely ground	⅓ cup (finely ground)	1.25 ounces	35 grams
cream of tartar	¾ teaspoon	•	•
unsweetened cocoa	1 tablespoon	0.25 ounce	6 grams

One 17-inch by 12-inch jelly-roll pan, greased, bottom lined with a nonstick liner or foil (extending slightly over the sides), and then greased again and floured. (For Passover, it's fine to omit the flour as

Position the oven rack in the lower third of the oven.
Preheat the oven to 350°F.

In a mixing bowl beat ¼ cup sugar and the egg yolks for 5 minutes or until light and fluffy. Add the chocolate, and almonds if desired, and beat until incorporated, scraping down the sides.

In a large mixing bowl beat the egg whites until foamy, add the cream of tartar, and beat until soft peaks form when the beater is raised. Gradually beat in the remaining 2 tablespoons sugar, beating until stiff peaks form when the beater is raised slowly.

With large balloon whisk, slotted skimmer, or rubber spatula fold ¼ of the whites into the chocolate mixture to lighten it. Then gently fold in remaining egg whites.

Pour into the prepared pan, spreading evenly with a spatula, and bake 16 minutes. The cake will have puffed and lost its shine and will spring back when lightly pressed with a finger.

Wet a clean dish towel and wring it out well. Remove the cake from oven and leave it in the pan. Dust with the cocoa and cover immediately with the damp towel. (Use a dry towel if planning to cut the cake into shapes.) Allow the cake to cool. Remove the towel and, lifting by a long edge of the liner or foil overhang, gently slide the cake from the pan onto a flat surface. To use as a roll, spread at once with 2 cups filling and roll up, using the liner or foil for support and gently peeling it away as you go. To use as layers, cut in half for 2 rectangles or use an 8-inch cardboard round to cut out 2 rounds or a 9-inch oval cardboard to cut out 2 ovals.

UNDERSTANDING

A larger amount of sugar causes chocolate rolls to crack because it absorbs some of the batter's moisture, making the cake more brittle.

This cake is used to make Chocolate Pine Cone (page 196) and Cordon Rose Chocolate Christmas Log (page 197).

cake will release almost as smoothly without it. Also omit the cream of tartar.)

FINISHED HEIGHT:
½ inch before rolling.

STORE:
3 days room temperature, 5 days refrigerated, 2 months frozen.

COMPLEMENTARY FILLINGS:
One recipe: **Perfect Whipped Cream or Raspberry Jam Cream (page 253 or 263). Perfect Mocha Whipped Cream (page 253). Light Whipped Ganache (page 268).**

SERVE:
Lightly chilled. If used as a roll, cut on the diagonal to form oval slices.

POINTERS FOR SUCCESS:
See page 119. A large balloon whisk or slotted skimmer is ideal for folding in the flour with the least amount of air loss. If using the whisk, periodically shake out the batter which collects inside.

Cocoa Soufflé Roll

*T*his chocolate roll is airy yet exceptionally moist and intensely chocolate. The high moisture makes it virtually incapable of cracking! It is perfect with any whipped cream filling.

INGREDIENTS	MEASURE	WEIGHT	
room temperature	*volume*	*ounces*	*grams*
unsifted cocoa (Dutch-processed) or ¼ cup + 3 tablespoons nonalkalized cocoa such as Hershey's	⅓ cup + 1 tablespoon	1.25 ounces	37 grams
boiling water	¼ liquid cup	2 ounces	60 grams
vanilla	1 teaspoon	•	4 grams
unsalted butter (must be softened)	2 tablespoons	1 ounce	28 grams
sugar	⅔ cup	4.5 ounces	132 grams
6 large eggs, separated yolks whites	3.5 fluid ounces ¾ liquid cup	4 ounces 6.25 ounces	112 grams 180 grams
optional: unblanched sliced almonds, toasted and finely ground	⅓ cup (finely ground)	1.25 ounces	35 grams
cream of tartar	¾ teaspoon	•	•

One 17-inch by 12-inch jelly-roll pan, greased, bottom lined with a nonstick liner or foil (extending slightly over the sides), and then greased again and floured. (For Passover, it's

Position the oven rack in the lower third of the oven.
Preheat the oven to 350°F.

In a small bowl stir together all but 1 tablespoon cocoa and the boiling water until the cocoa is completely dissolved. Stir in the vanilla and butter and cool.

In a mixing bowl beat ½ cup sugar and the egg yolks for 5 minutes or until light and fluffy. Add the chocolate mixture and almonds if desired and beat until incorporated, scraping down the sides.

In a large bowl beat the egg whites until foamy, add the cream of tartar, and beat until soft peaks form when the beater is raised. Gradually beat in the remaining sugar, beating until stiff peaks form when the beater is raised slowly. With large balloon whisk, slotted skimmer, or rubber spatula fold ¼ of the whites into the chocolate mixture to lighten it. Then gently fold in the remaining egg whites.

Pour into the prepared pan, spreading evenly with a spatula, and bake 18 minutes. The cake will have puffed and lost its shine and will spring back when lightly pressed with a finger.

Wet a clean dish towel and wring it out well. Remove the cake from oven and leave it in the pan. Dust with the remaining 1 tablespoon cocoa and cover immediately with the damp towel. (Use a dry towel if planning to cut the cake into shapes.) Allow the cake to cool. Remove the towel and, lifting by a long edge of the liner or foil overhang, gently slide the cake from the pan onto a flat surface. To use as a roll, spread at once with 2 cups filling and roll up, using the liner or foil for support and gently peeling it away as you go. To use as layers, cut in half for 2 rectangles or use an 8-inch cardboard round to cut out 2 rounds, or a 9-inch cardboard to cut out 2 ovals.

UNDERSTANDING

Cocoa replaces the cocoa solids previously provided by the chocolate. In the same way butter compensates for the cocoa butter and extra sugar for the sugar originally contained in the bittersweet chocolate. Water is used to dissolve the cocoa, releasing fuller chocolate flavor and providing moisture.

This cake is used to make The Enchanted Forest (page 195).

fine to omit the flour because the cake will release almost as smoothly without it. Also omit the cream of tartar.)

FINISHED HEIGHT:
½ inch before rolling.

STORE:
3 days room temperature, 5 days refrigerated, 2 months frozen.

COMPLEMENTARY ADORNMENTS:
One recipe: Perfect Whipped Cream (page 253) or Raspberry Jam Cream (page 263). Perfect Mocha Whipped Cream (page 253). Light Whipped Ganache (page 268).

SERVE:
Lightly chilled. If used as a roll, cut on the diagonal to form oval slices.

POINTERS FOR SUCCESS:
See page 119. A large balloon whisk or slotted skimmer is ideal for folding in the flour with the least amount of air loss. If using the whisk, periodically shake out the batter which collects inside.

Biscuit Roulade

(BeeskWee RueLAHD)

SERVES 8

When moistened with syrup, Biscuit Roulade is one of the most tender and ethereal of cakes. A sheet of *biscuit* has many possibilities. It can be filled with whipped cream and loosely rolled. It can be spread with jam, tightly rolled, and sliced to line a mold (as for Scarlett Empress, page 177). It can be cut with scissors into rounds to serve as a base and top for cheesecake or even cut with a cookie cutter to decorate the sides of a cheesecake.

If this roulade is used with moist fillings such as whipped cream, Bavarian cream, or cheesecake, a syrup would make the cake too wet. With a less moist filling, such as Lemon Curd, I sprinkle the cake roll with about 4 teaspoons of syrup for each whole egg used in the batter.

INGREDIENTS	MEASURE	WEIGHT	
room temperature	*volume*	*ounces*	*grams*
sifted cake flour	⅓ cup	1.25 ounces	33 grams
unsifted cornstarch	3 tablespoons	0.75 ounce	23 grams
4 large eggs	•	8 ounces	227 grams (weighed in the shell)
1 large egg yolk	3½ teaspoons	0.5 ounce	18 grams
sugar	½ cups + 1 tablespoon	4 ounces	113 grams
vanilla	¾ teaspoon	•	3 grams
cream of tartar	¼ teaspoon	•	•
OPTIONAL: ⅓ CUP SYRUP (3.5 OUNCES/100 GRAMS)			
sugar	2 tablespoons + a pinch	1 ounce	28 grams
water	¼ liquid cup	2 ounces	59 grams
liqueur of your choice	1 tablespoon	0.5 ounce	14 grams

Position the oven rack in the lower third of the oven.
Preheat the oven to 450°F.

In a small bowl whisk together the cake flour and cornstarch.

Separate 2 of the eggs, placing the yolks in 1 large mixing bowl and the whites in another. To the yolks, add the additional yolk, the 2 remaining eggs, and ½ cup sugar. Beat on high speed 5 minutes or until thick, fluffy, and triple in volume. Beat in the vanilla.

Sift ½ the flour mixture over the egg mixture and fold it in gently but rapidly with a large balloon whisk, slotted skimmer, or rubber spatula until the flour has disappeared. Repeat with the remaining flour mixture.

Beat the egg whites until foamy, add the cream of tartar, and beat until soft peaks form when the beater is raised. Beat in the remaining 1 tablespoon sugar and beat until stiff peaks form when the beater is raised slowly. Fold the whites into the batter and pour into the prepared pan, using an angled metal spatula to level it.

Bake for 7 minutes or until golden brown, a cake tester comes out clean, and the cake is springy to the touch.

Loosen the edges with a small metal spatula or sharp knife and, lifting by a long edge of the liner or parchment overhang, gently slide the cake from the pan onto a flat surface. To use the *biscuit* for a round cake base or cutouts, allow to cool flat, covered with a clean dish towel. To use it for a roll, roll it up while still hot. If using a liner, tightly roll up the *biscuit* with the liner. (This keeps the *biscuit* especially moist.) If using parchment, flip the *biscuit* onto a clean dish towel, carefully remove the parchment, and roll it up tightly, towel and all. Cool on a rack. When ready to fill, unroll the *biscuit*. (If a liner was used, first detach the cake from liner and then replace it on the liner.) If using the syrup, sprinkle it on the cake before spreading it with 2 cups filling.

TO MAKE SYRUP

In a small saucepan with a tight-fitting lid bring the sugar and water to a rolling boil, stirring constantly. Cover immediately, remove from the heat, and cool. Transfer to a liquid measuring cup and stir in the liqueur. If the syrup has evaporated slightly, add enough water to equal ⅓ cup syrup.

UNDERSTANDING

This *biscuit* is even lighter than a *génoise* because it contains no butter and because some of the whites are beaten separately and folded into the batter.

When baking the *biscuit* as a thin sheet, less structural support is necessary, so the flour/cornstarch mixture can be reduced to about half of what is used for classic *génoise* (instead of equal weight flour mixture and sugar, the Biscuit Roulade uses only half the weight in flour mixture). A high oven temperature, however, is necessary to set the cake's structure before it can fall. And an extra yolk is added to increase flexibility for rolling the sheet if desired.

One 17-inch by 12-inch jelly-roll pan, greased, bottom lined with a nonstick liner or parchment, and then greased again and floured. (Liner extends slightly over the sides.)

FINISHED SIZE:
16¾ inches by 11¾ inches by ½ inch. When the cake is rolled or assembled, it compresses to ⅜ inch high.

STORE:
Syrup: 1 month refrigerated in an airtight container. *Biscuit:* 3 days room temperature, 5 days refrigerated, 2 months frozen.

COMPLEMENTARY FILLINGS:
One recipe: Perfect Whipped Cream (page 253) or Raspberry Jam Cream (page 263). Lemon Curd Cream (page 264). Bavarian Cream if making Charlotte (page 287).

SERVE:
Lightly chilled. If used as a roll, cut on the diagonal to form oval slices.

POINTERS FOR SUCCESS:
See page 119. A large balloon whisk or slotted skimmer is ideal for folding in the flour with the least amount of air loss. If using the whisk, periodically shake out the batter which collects on the inside.

This cake is used to make: Ethereal Pear Charlotte (page 175), Scarlett Empress (page 177), and Barquettes Chez L'Ami Louis (page 186).

VARIATIONS

GINGER BISCUIT: 1 tablespoon ginger juice added to the yolk mixture cuts the sweetness and adds a unique, subtle flavor. (To make ginger juice, grate fresh ginger on a fine grater and press with your fingers to squeeze out as much juice as possible.)

COMPLEMENTARY FILLING: Perfect Whipped Cream and poached pears.

CHOCOLATE BISCUIT: Ideal for use as a chocolate version of the Scarlett Empress (page 177) because it is firmer than the Cloud Roll. It also has an excellent texture to use as ice-cream roll. Replace the cornstarch with equal weight or ¼ cup cocoa. Dissolve the cocoa in 3 tablespoons boiling water and cool. Stir in the vanilla and add to the beaten yolk mixture, beating a few seconds or until incorporated. If not using the syrup, increase the sugar to ⅔ cup plus 1 tablespoon (5 ounces/145 grams).

COMPLEMENTARY FILLINGS: Perfect Whipped Cream. Light Whipped Ganache. Bavarian Cream, especially orange or raspberry.

ALMOND BISCUIT: My favorite of all *biscuits*—moist, tender, and flavorful because there are more almonds than flour.

In place of the flour/cornstarch mixture, use ⅓ cup (1.25 ounces/35 grams) blanched, toasted, and finely ground almonds and 3 tablespoons unsifted cake flour (.75 ounces/ 21 grams).

COMPLEMENTARY FILLINGS: Perfect Whipped Cream, Raspberry Jam Cream, or any Cloud Cream. This is wonderful as a bottom for cheesecake.

GREEN TEA BISCUIT: The moss-green tea of the Japanese tea ceremony adds a lovely color and exquisitely haunting flavor to the delicacy of *biscuit*. Filled with Green Tea Mousse Cream (page 261), it is an unforgettable dessert. It must be served the day it is baked or the elusive flavor is lost. To make this *biscuit*, replace 1 tablespoon of the cornstarch with equal measure or weight of powdered green tea (available in stores where Japanese and Oriental products are sold, page 445).

COMPLEMENTARY FILLINGS: Perfect Whipped Cream (page 253) or Green Tea Whipped Cream (page 261).

*T*his lovely cake bears the name of the Savoy region in the French Alps, where it is said to have originated. Biscuit de Savoie makes an excellent cake layer and, after dousing with syrup, is exceptionally light, soft and moist without ever becoming soggy. It can be used interchangeably with a *génoise* and is an especially refreshing alternative for summertime cakes.

For a tender texture, it is essential to moisten the baked Biscuit de Savoie with at least ¼ cup syrup (page 357) for every egg used in the batter. Another rule of thumb is to use syrup equal in weight to the baked and trimmed *biscuit*. This will transform the *biscuit* from dry and rubbery to moist and dissolving!

I tip my *toque* to my friends and colleagues Bruce Healy and Paul Bugat (*Mastering the Art of French Pastry*) for their superb method of folding the whites together with the flour mixture. This achieves the highest, lightest possible result!

Biscuit de Savoie

(*BeeskWEE duh SavWAH*)

SERVES 12 TO 14
(3 round layers)

INGREDIENTS	MEASURE	WEIGHT	
room temperature	*volume*	*ounces*	*grams*
8 large eggs, separated			
yolks	4.5 fluid ounces	5.25 ounces	150 grams
whites	1 liquid cup	8.5 ounces	240 grams
sugar	1 cup	7 ounces	200 grams
vanilla	2½ teaspoons	•	10 grams
warm water	1 tablespoon	0.5 ounce	15 grams
sifted cake flour	1 cup + 2 tablespoons	4 ounces	113 grams
cornstarch	½ cup + 1 tablespoon (lightly spooned into cup)	2.25 ounce	66 grams
cream of tartar	1 teaspoon	•	3 grams
2 CUPS SYRUP (21 OUNCES/590 GRAMS)			
sugar	¾ cup + 2 tablespoons	6 ounces	175 grams
water	1½ liquid cups	12.5 ounces	355 grams
liqueur of your choice	6 tablespoons	3 ounces	90 grams

Three 9-inch by 1½-inch cake pans, bottoms greased and lined with parchment or wax paper. Do *not* grease or flour sides.

FINISHED HEIGHT:
After trimming the bottom and top crusts, each layer is 1 inch.

STORE:
Syrup: 1 month refrigerated in an airtight container. *Biscuit:* Without syrup, 2 days room temperature, 5 days refrigerated, 2 months frozen. After sprinkling with the syrup the flavors ripen and the moisture is more evenly distributed 1 day later. The completed cake can be refrigerated up to 5 days or frozen up to 2 months.

COMPLEMENTARY ADORNMENTS:
One recipe: Any buttercream, whipped cream, or glaze.

SERVE:
Room temperature or lightly chilled.

POINTERS FOR SUCCESS:
See page 119. A large balloon whisk or slotted skimmer is ideal for folding in

Preheat the oven to 325°F.

In a large mixing bowl beat the yolks and ⅔ cup sugar on high speed for 5 minutes or until the mixture is very thick and ribbons when dropped from the beater. Lower the speed and beat in the vanilla and water. Increase to high speed and beat for 30 seconds or until it thickens again.

Stir together the flour and cornstarch. Sift over the yolk mixture without mixing in and set aside.

In another large mixing bowl beat the whites until foamy, add the cream of tartar, and beat until soft peaks form when the beater is raised. Gradually beat in the remaining ⅓ cup sugar, beating until stiff peaks form when the beater is raised slowly. Add ⅓ of the whites to the yolk mixture and with a large balloon whisk, skimmer, or rubber spatula fold until incorporated. Gently fold in the remaining whites.

Pour into the prepared pans. (They will be almost ½ full.) Bake 25 minutes or until a cake tester inserted in the center comes out clean. Loosen the sides with a small metal spatula and unmold at once onto lightly greased racks and reinvert to cool. The firm upper crust prevents falling and results in a light texture.

Trim the crust when ready to complete the cake and sprinkle the syrup evenly on all sides (page 357).*

TO MAKE SYRUP

In a small saucepan with a tight-fitting lid bring the sugar and water to a rolling boil, stirring constantly. Cover immediately, remove from the heat, and cool. Transfer to a liquid measuring cup and stir in the liqueur. If the syrup has evaporated slightly, add enough water to equal 2 cups.

UNDERSTANDING

When *biscuit* is baked as a round layer cake, it requires much more structure than a low sheet cake, so proportionally more flour/cornstarch mixture is used and all of the whites are beaten separately.

The absence of butter is what makes Biscuit de Savoie lighter than a *génoise*. Since butter has a tenderizing effect, its absence will make the *biscuit* rubbery unless it is adequately moistened with a syrup.

Since the *biscuit* can be saturated with syrup without becoming soggy, there is no danger of dryness so the cake

---

* After syruping a *biscuit* layer becomes fragile and more prone to splitting when moved. Use a cardboard round or removable bottom of a pan to support it.

can be made as light and high-rising as possible. By not greasing and flouring the sides of the pans, the batter can rise better, attaining maximum height.

This cake is used to make Queen Bee (page 185).

This is the same recipe as the preceding one, but it yields about two thirds of the amount. It makes 2 oval layers that are perfect in cakes such as Baked Hawaii (page 168).

the flour with the least amount of air loss. If using the whisk, periodically shake out the batter which collects inside.

Oval Biscuit

INGREDIENTS	MEASURE	WEIGHT	
room temperature	*volume*	*ounces*	*grams*
6 large eggs, separated			
yolks	3.5 fluid ounces	4 ounces	112 grams
whites	¾ liquid cup	6.25 ounces	180 grams
sugar	⅔ cup	4.5 ounces	132 grams
vanilla	1¾ teaspoons	•	7 grams
warm water	2 teaspoons	•	10 grams
sifted cake flour	¾ cup	2.5 ounces	75 grams
cornstarch	⅓ cup + 2 teaspoons (lightly spooned into cup)	1.5 ounces	45 grams
cream of tartar	¾ teaspoon	•	•

Beat ¼ cup (1.75 ounces/50 grams) sugar instead of ⅓ cup with the whites and beat the remainder with the yolk mixture. Proceed as for full-size recipe (page 146).

    Divide the batter between 2 oval cake pans and bake 25 minutes or until the cakes test done. Loosen the sides with a small metal spatula; unmold at once onto lightly greased racks and reinvert to cool.

Two 9¼-inch by 6⅝-inch oval pans (page 453) bottoms greased and lined with parchment or wax paper. Do not grease or flour sides.

FINISHED HEIGHT:
After trimming the bottom and top crusts, each layer is 1¾ inches.

Biscuit à la Cuillière

(BeeskWEE ah lah KweeAIR)

MAKES ABOUT 2 DOZEN
3-inch by 1½-inch ladyfingers and an 8-inch circular cake base or about 3½ dozen fingers

The name *cuillière*, the French word for "spoon," was given to these traditional ladyfingers because they were originally shaped with a spoon. Using a pastry bag, however, results in a more uniform shape and much greater speed.

This *biscuit* is so light that it stales quickly. It is best to eat it the day it is baked. For less fresh *biscuit*, sprinkle lightly with liqueur.

Ladyfingers have the perfect, ethereal but firm texture to encase and support a Bavarian cream filling such as Orange Chocolate Crown (page 181).

INGREDIENTS	MEASURE	WEIGHT	
room temperature	*volume*	*ounces*	*grams*
6 large eggs, separated			
yolks	3.5 fluid ounces	4 ounces	112 grams
whites	¾ liquid cup	6.25 ounces	180 grams
sugar	¾ cup	5.25 ounces	150 grams
vanilla	2½ teaspoons	•	10 grams
warm water	1 tablespoon	0.5 ounce	15 grams
sifted cake flour	1½ cups	5.25 ounces	150 grams
cream of tartar	¾ teaspoon	•	•
powdered sugar for dusting	about 1 cup	•	•

Two large baking sheets, lined with a nonstick liner, parchment, or foil and outlined with piping guides (parallel lines 3 inches apart and an 8-inch to 9-inch circle, page 373). A large pastry bag fitted with a ¾-inch diameter pastry tube (no. 9).

FINISHED SIZE:
Ladyfingers: 3 strips, each 12 inches long, or 2 strips, each 18 inches long. Cake base: 7 to 8 inches (for an 8-inch or 9-inch charlotte).

Preheat the oven to 400°F.

In a large mixing bowl beat the yolks and ½ cup sugar on high speed for 5 minutes or until the mixture is very thick and ribbons when dropped from the beater. Lower the speed and beat in the vanilla and water. Increase to high speed and beat for 30 seconds or until thick again. Sift the flour over the yolk mixture without mixing in and set aside.

In another large mixing bowl beat the whites until foamy, add the cream of tartar, and beat until soft peaks form when the beater is raised. Gradually beat in the remaining ¼ cup sugar, beating until very stiff peaks form when the beater is raised slowly. Add ⅓ of the whites to the yolk mixture and with a skimmer or rubber spatula fold until all the flour is incorporated. Gently fold in the remaining whites.

Working quickly so that the batter does not lose volume, scoop 4 cups into the pastry bag and pipe out the disc for the base (page 373). An 8-inch charlotte requires about 17 ladyfingers to go around the sides, a 7-inch base to fit inside the fingers, and an 8-inch top if desired. A 9-inch charlotte requires about 19 ladyfingers to go around the sides, an 8-inch base to fit inside the fingers, and a 9-inch top if desired. (To make a decorative top you will need to make another ½ batch of batter.)

Scoop the remaining batter into the pastry bag and pipe out 3-inch by 1½-inch side-by-side "fingers." Be sure to hold the pastry tube high enough above the surface of the sheet so that the batter can fall freely from the tube and not get flattened by the edge of the tube (page 373). There should be a ¼-inch space between the "fingers" as they spread sideways as they are piped. (After baking, the ladyfingers will be attached to one another in continuous strips. Each finger will be about 1½ inches wide.) Sift the powdered sugar completely over the fingers. After a few seconds the batter will dissolve and absorb some of the sugar. For a pearled effect, sprinkle with a second coat. Bake 8 to 10 minutes or until light golden brown and springy to the touch. Remove the sheets to racks and cool slightly. To prevent cracking, remove from the sheets while still warm with a long, thin spatula or pancake turner. For discs, invert onto a rack covered with a paper towel, peel off the liner, and reinvert onto a second rack. Cool on racks and then wrap airtight.

UNDERSTANDING

This *biscuit* recipe has the same weight flour and sugar and double the egg as Génoise Classique but no butter. Biscuit à la Cuillère has more flour than Biscuit de Savoie in order to hold its shape when piped. (It is also baked at a higher temperature to set the shape faster.)

To achieve a lighter texture no cornstarch is used and all of the egg whites are beaten separately and *very stiffly*.

This cake is used to make Orange Chocolate Crown (page 181).

STORE:
Use same day or freeze 1 month.

COMPLEMENTARY FILLINGS:
Ladyfinger-lined molds can be filled with *one recipe:* Bavarian Cream (pages 287 to 289), Fruit Cloud Cream (page 264), or Lemon Cream Illusion (page 266).

SERVE:
Room temperature if served plain, lightly chilled if used as a Charlotte (page 181).

POINTERS FOR SUCCESS:
See page 119. Egg whites must be beaten stiffly enough for the batter to hold its shape and form attractive designs. If the proper amount of cream of tartar is used it is virtually impossible to overbeat the whites. A slotted skimmer is ideal for folding in the flour with the least amount of air loss.

Nancy Blitzer's Classic American Sponge Cake

SERVES 10

$\mathcal{M}$y friend Nancy has been baking for family and friends for over forty years. This perfect sponge cake is her creation and is so pure and simple it needs no adornment. Nancy serves it plain with tea or sometimes even lightly toasted for breakfast. This cake contains no sodium and only about 226 mg. cholesterol per serving.

INGREDIENTS	MEASURE	WEIGHT	
room temperature	*volume*	*ounces*	*grams*
water	2 tablespoons	1 ounce	30 grams
vanilla	½ teaspoon	•	•
grated lemon zest	1½ teaspoons	•	•
sifted cake flour	1⅓ cups	4.75 ounces	133 grams
sugar	1 cup	7 ounces	200 grams

6 large eggs, separated
    yolks
    whites
	
	3.5 fluid ounces
	¾ liquid cup
		
		4 ounces
		6.25 ounces
			
			112 grams
			180 grams

cream of tartar	¾ teaspoon	•	•

One ungreased two-piece 10-inch tube pan.

FINISHED HEIGHT:
3⅛ inches high overall, 2¾ inches at the sides.

Preheat the oven to 350°F.

In a small bowl combine the water, vanilla, and lemon zest.

Remove 1 tablespoon of the sugar and reserve to beat with the whites.

In another small bowl whisk together the flour and 3 tablespoons of the sugar.

In a large mixing bowl beat the yolks and the remaining ¾ cup sugar on high speed for 5 minutes or until the mixture is very thick and ribbons when dropped from the beater. Lower the speed and gradually add the water mixture. Increase to high speed and beat for 30 seconds. Sift the flour mixture over the yolk mixture without mixing in and set aside.

Beat the whites until foamy, add the cream of tartar, and beat until soft peaks form when the beater is raised.

Beat in reserved 1 tablespoon sugar and beat until very stiff peaks form when the beater is raised slowly. Add ⅓ of the whites to the yolk mixture and with a large skimmer or rubber spatula fold until incorporated. Gently fold in the remaining whites in 2 batches.

Pour into the pan. (It will be a little more than ½ full.) Bake 30 to 35 minutes or until golden brown and a cake tester comes out clean when inserted in the center. Invert the pan, placing the tube opening over the neck of a soda or wine bottle to suspend it well above counter, and cool the cake completely in the pan (this takes about 1 hour).

Loosen the sides with a long metal spatula and remove the center core of the pan. (To keep the sides attractive, press the spatula against the sides of the pan and avoid any up-and-down motion.) Dislodge the bottom and center core with a metal spatula or thin, sharp knife. (A wire cake tester works well around the core.) Invert onto a greased wire rack and reinvert onto a serving plate. Wrap airtight.

UNDERSTANDING

This sponge cake contains the same basic ingredients as Biscuit de Savoie except that the *biscuit* has half the weight of sugar to eggs and this sponge has almost as much sugar as eggs. The high quantity of sugar produces a sponge cake so moist and tender that no syrup or frosting is necessary. Some of the sugar is added to the flour to separate the grains and help keep it from clumping when folded into the batter.

The addition of lemon zest tempers the sweetness. Baking at 350°F. rather than 325°F. ensures a more tender and moist cake (page 476).

STORE:
3 days room temperature, 5 days refrigerated, 2 months frozen.

COMPLEMENTARY ADORNMENTS:
A light sprinkling of powdered sugar. Or decorate the base and center with fresh flowers.

SERVE:
Room temperature or lightly chilled.

POINTERS FOR SUCCESS:
See page 119. A slotted skimmer is ideal for folding in the flour with the least amount of air loss.

Bert Greene's Special Sponge Cake

SERVES 8

I am so pleased to be able to present this extraordinary recipe, offered by one of my dearest friends and most esteemed colleagues. Bert has come up with some truly original and inventive tricks to create one of the most moist and tender sponge cakes I've ever tasted.

As a special touch, some of the sugar is sprinkled on top of the raw batter to produce a delightfully crunchy crust. This cake is perfect for the person with a real sweet tooth, although extra lemon zest helps temper the sweetness and makes salt unnecessary. As an added bonus, it has only 161 mg. cholesterol per serving.

INGREDIENTS	MEASURE	WEIGHT	
room temperature	*volume*	*ounces*	*grams*
orange juice	2 tablespoons	1 ounce	30 grams
grated lemon zest	2 teaspoons	•	4 grams
vanilla	½ teaspoon	•	6 grams
superfine sugar	1 cup + 7 tablespoons	10 ounces	288 grams
sifted cake flour	1 cup	3.5 ounces	100 grams
5 large eggs, separated, + 3 additional whites			
yolks	full ⅓ liquid cup	3.25 ounces	93 grams
whites	1 liquid cup	8.5 ounces	240 grams
cream of tartar	1 teaspoon	•	3 grams

One ungreased 10-inch two-piece tube pan, preheated for at least 5 minutes.

FINISHED HEIGHT: 3 inches.

Preheat the oven to 350°F.

In a small bowl combine the orange juice, lemon zest, and vanilla.

Remove 2 tablespoons of the sugar and reserve to beat with the whites. Remove another 2 tablespoons of the sugar and reserve to sprinkle on top of raw batter.

Remove 3 more tablespoons of the sugar and whisk together with the flour.

Rinse a large mixing bowl with hot water and wrap the sides with a hot towel. (If using a hand mixer, place the bowl in a sink partially filled with hot water.)

Beat the yolks, gradually adding the remaining 1 cup sugar, on high speed for 5 minutes or until the mixture is very thick and ribbons when dropped from the beater. Lower the speed and gradually add the orange juice mixture. Increase to high speed and beat for 30 seconds. Sift the flour mixture over the yolk mixture without mixing in and set aside.

Beat the whites until foamy, add the cream of tartar, and continue to beat until soft peaks form when the beater is raised. Gradually beat in the 2 tablespoons of reserved sugar, beating until very stiff peaks form when the beater is raised slowly. Add ⅓ of the whites to the yolk mixture and with a large skimmer or rubber spatula fold until incorporated. Gently fold in the remaining whites in 2 batches.

Pour the batter into the hot pan. (It will be a little more than ½ full.) Sprinkle the top evenly with the remaining 2 tablespoons sugar. Bake 35 to 40 minutes or until golden brown and a cake tester comes out clean when inserted in the center. Invert the pan, placing the tube opening over the neck of a soda or wine bottle to suspend it well above the counter, and cool the cake completely in the pan (this takes about 1 hour).

Loosen the sides with a long metal spatula and remove the center core of the pan from the sides. (To keep the sides attractive, press the spatula against the sides of the pan and avoid any up-and-down motion.) Dislodge the bottom and center core with a spatula or thin, sharp knife. (A wire cake tester works well around the core.) Invert onto a greased wire rack and reinvert onto a serving plate. Wrap airtight.

UNDERSTANDING

One of the secrets of this cake's exceptional moistness and tenderness is using ⅓ cup less flour than classic sponge cake and a very high proportion of sugar (almost ½ cup more). For additional volume, Bert applies heat while beating the yolks and uses 3, sometimes even 4, extra egg whites to compensate for structure usually provided by a higher quantity of flour. To ensure that the cake will not collapse during baking, he preheats the empty pan so that the batter starts to expand and set immediately.

NOTE: Bert eliminates the cream of tartar and uses a copper bowl to whisk the egg whites by hand. This results in extra-high volume for those of you who have the strength (not to mention the will) to do it.

STORE:
3 days room temperature, 5 days refrigerated, 2 months frozen.

COMPLEMENTARY ADORNMENTS:
Decorate base and center with fresh flowers.

SERVE:
Room temperature or lightly chilled.

POINTERS FOR SUCCESS:
See page 119. Superfine sugar is important to attain maximum volume and for sprinkling on top of the cake. Heating the yolks also improves volume. A slotted skimmer is ideal for folding in the flour with the least amount of air loss.

When Harry Baker, a Los Angeles insurance salesman who baked for private Hollywood parties, invented the chiffon cake, it was the first major new type of cake since the angel food cake, invented about one hundred years before it. He kept the recipe a secret for twenty years and finally, deciding to share it with the world, approached Betty Crocker, owned by General Mills. They purchased the recipe in 1947 and billed it as "glamorous as an angel food cake but easier to make."

The chiffon cake combines the moist richness of a butter cake with the lightness of a sponge cake. Because oil, which remains liquid at room temperature, is used instead of butter, the texture is much softer than a layer cake. Even refrigerated, the oil in the cake remains soft (unlike butter). Oil also tenderizes and provides moisture, making the chiffon cake much more tender than a *biscuit*. Safflower oil is my preference (except for the chocolate chiffon, which is much more delicious with walnut oil) because it contains no silicates (which inhibit foaming).

A chiffon cake has many virtues. It is easy to make, keeps exceptionally well, and slices easily even when frozen. It has about half the fat of a butter cake and less cholesterol and saturated fat than any other cake except for angel food. But, unlike angel food, it does not have the disadvantage of excessive sweetness. On top of all these wonderful qualities, it also provides a use for your extra-egg-white collection.

Chiffon cakes are best baked at 325°F. because the tops crack more at higher temperatures.

I don't like to ice chiffon cakes because that defeats the lightness and the low cholesterol advantage. (The icings of my preference all have either butter or cream.)

Any of the following chiffon recipes can be halved and baked in a 9-inch tube pan (page 447) for a 3-inch-high cake that serves 6 to 8. Bake for only 35 minutes or until the cake tests done.

For fuller details see the suggested page number.
- Use *cake* flour that does not contain leavening (page 476). (Do not use self-rising cake flour.)
- Use superfine sugar for finest texture and maximum volume (page 476).
- Measure or weigh ingredients carefully (page 438).
- Do not use oil that contains silicates—it will be listed on the label (page 431).
- Egg whites must be free of even a trace of yolk and the bowl must be spotless.
- When beating egg whites, use cream of tartar or be careful to beat just until stiff peaks form when the beater is raised slowly.

- Fold flour gently but *thoroughly* into the batter.
- Use the correct pan size (page 20).
- Bake immediately after mixing.
- Check for accurate oven temperature (page 448).
- Use correct baking time; do not underbake (page 21).
- Cool cakes upside down, well elevated from the countertop, in a draft-free area (page 476).
- Wrap cakes well when cool (page 23).

Orange Glow Chiffon Cake

SERVES 14

*M*oist, billowy, light as a feather, and perfumed with fresh orange juice and zest, this is an incomparably refreshing cake. If you live in a part of the world where oranges grow, you could not ask for a more appropriate and aromatic adornment than orange blossoms, but fresh daisies also convey the lighthearted spirit of this lovely cake. A serving contains only 129 mg. of cholesterol.

INGREDIENTS	MEASURE	WEIGHT	
room temperature	*volume*	*ounces*	*grams*
sifted cake flour	2¼ cups	8 ounces	225 grams
sugar	1½ cups	10.5 ounces	300 grams
baking powder	2 teaspoons	•	10 grams
salt	½ teaspoon	•	3.5 grams
safflower oil	½ liquid cup	3.75 ounces	108 grams
7 large eggs, separated, + 3 additional whites			
yolks	½ liquid cup	4.5 ounces	130 grams
whites	1¼ liquid cups	10.5 ounces	300 grams
orange juice, freshly squeezed	¾ liquid cup	6.25 ounces	182 grams
grated orange zest	2 tablespoons	•	12 grams
vanilla	1 teaspoon	•	4 grams
cream of tartar	1¼ teaspoons	•	4 grams

One ungreased 10-inch two-piece tube pan.

FINISHED HEIGHT:
4½ inches high in the middle.

STORE:
3 days room temperature, 10 days refrigerated, 2 months frozen.

COMPLEMENTARY ADORNMENTS:
A light sprinkling of powdered sugar and/or decorate the base and center with orange blossoms or fresh daisies. Candied Orange Zest (page 342) scattered on top also makes an attractive and flavorful addition.

SERVE:
Room temperature or lightly chilled. Cut with a serrated knife.

POINTERS FOR SUCCESS:
See page 154. An angel food cake folder, large balloon whisk, or slotted skimmer is ideal for folding in the flour with the least amount of air loss. If using the whisk, periodically shake out the batter which collects inside.

Preheat the oven to 325°F.

In a large mixing bowl combine the flour, all but 2 tablespoons of the sugar, baking powder, and salt and beat 1 minute to mix. Make a well in the center. Add the oil, egg yolks, orange juice, orange zest, and vanilla and beat 1 minute or until smooth.

In another large mixing bowl beat the egg whites until frothy, add the cream of tartar, and beat until soft peaks form when the beater is raised. Beat in the remaining 2 tablespoons sugar and beat until stiff peaks form when the beater is raised slowly. Gently fold the egg whites into the batter with a large balloon wire whisk, slotted skimmer, or angel food cake folder until just blended.

Pour into the tube pan (the batter will come to 1 inch from the top) and bake for 55 minutes or until a cake tester inserted in the center comes out clean and the cake springs back when lightly pressed in the center. Invert the pan, placing the tube opening over the neck of a soda or wine bottle to suspend it well above the counter, and cool the cake completely in the pan (this takes about 1½ hours).

Loosen the sides with a long metal spatula and remove the center core of the pan. Dislodge the bottom and center core with a metal spatula or thin, sharp knife. (A wire cake tester works well around the core. To keep the sides attractive, press the spatula against the sides of the pan and avoid any up-and-down motion.) Invert onto a greased wire rack and reinvert onto a serving plate. Wrap airtight.

$\mathcal{T}$his cake offers the lilting flavor of lemon, balanced by the moist, light texture found only in a chiffon cake. A serving contains only 129 mg. cholesterol.

INGREDIENTS	MEASURE	WEIGHT	
room temperature	volume	ounces	grams
sifted cake flour	2¼ cups	8 ounces	225 grams
sugar	1½ cups	10.5 ounces	300 grams
baking soda	½ teaspoon	•	2.5 grams
salt	½ teaspoon	•	3.5 grams
safflower oil	½ liquid cup	3.75 ounces	108 grams
7 large eggs, separated, + 3 additional whites			
yolks	½ liquid cup	4.5 ounces	130 grams
whites	1¼ liquid cups	10.5 ounces	300 grams
water	⅔ liquid cup	5.5 ounces	156 grams
lemon juice, freshly squeezed	2 tablespoons	1 ounce	30 grams
grated lemon zest	1 tablespoon	•	6 grams
vanilla	1 teaspoon	•	4 grams
cream of tartar	1¼ teaspoons	•	4 grams

Preheat the oven to 325°F.

In a large mixing bowl combine the flour, all but 2 tablespoons of the sugar, baking powder, and salt and beat 1 minute to mix. Make a well in the center. Add the oil, egg yolks, water, lemon juice, lemon zest, and vanilla and beat 1 minute or until smooth.

In another large mixing bowl beat the egg whites until frothy, add the cream of tartar, and beat until soft peaks form when the beater is raised. Beat in the 2 tablespoons sugar and beat until stiff peaks form when the beater is raised slowly. Gently fold the egg whites into the batter with a large balloon wire whisk, slotted skimmer, or angel food cake folder until just blended.

One ungreased 10-inch two-piece tube pan.

FINISHED HEIGHT:
4½ inches high in the middle.

3 days room temperature,
10 days refrigerated, 2
months frozen.

COMPLEMENTARY
ADORNMENTS:
A light sprinkling of powdered sugar and/or decorate
the base and center with
lemon blossoms or fresh
daisies.

SERVE:
Room temperature or lightly
chilled. Cut with a serrated
knife.

POINTERS FOR SUCCESS:
See page 154. An angel food
cake folder, large balloon
whisk, or slotted skimmer is
ideal for folding in the flour
with the least amount of air
loss. If using the whisk, periodically shake out the batter which collects inside.

Pour into the tube pan (the batter will come to 1 inch
from the top) and bake for 55 minutes or until a cake tester
inserted in the center comes out clean and the cake springs
back when lightly pressed in the center. Invert the pan,
placing the tube opening over the neck of a soda or wine
bottle to suspend it well above the counter, and cool the
cake completely in the pan (this takes about 1½ hours).

Loosen the sides with a long metal spatula and remove
the center core of pan. Dislodge the bottom and center core
with a metal spatula or thin, sharp knife. (A wire cake tester
works well around the core. To keep the sides attractive,
press the spatula against the sides of the pan and avoid any
up-and-down motion.) Invert onto a greased wire rack and
reinvert onto a serving plate. Wrap airtight.

UNDERSTANDING

Baking soda replaces baking powder to retain the lemon
flavor while neutralizing some of the acidity.

Guilt-Free
Chocolate
Chiffon
Cake

SERVES 14

*I*t is a rare thing indeed that so intensely chocolate a
cake can boast a minuscule cholesterol content. It happened behind my back.

I never liked chocolate chiffon cakes because the oil
did not seem to enhance the flavor of chocolate the way
butter does and because the lower part of the cake always
seemed heavy and gummy. But my mother so loudly sang
the praises of its possibilities ("It has delicate chocolate flavor and heavenly texture even eaten directly from the
freezer") that I decided to give it one last try. I took advantage of the synergistic effect of chocolate and walnut by
replacing some of the vegetable oil with walnut oil. Cocoa
offered richness, and extra whites and 1 less yolk perfected
the texture so beautifully that I now use a total of 10 whites
for the orange and lemon chiffon cakes as well. A serving
of this cake contains only 110.6 mg. cholesterol.

INGREDIENTS	MEASURE	WEIGHT	
room temperature	volume	ounces	grams
unsweetened cocoa (Dutch-processed) or ½ cup + 2 tablespoons nonalkalized cocoa such as Hershey's *	½ cup + 1 tablespoon (lightly spooned into cup)	1.75 ounces	50 grams
boiling water	¾ liquid cup	6.25 ounces	177 grams
sifted cake flour	1¾ cups	6 ounces	175 grams
sugar	1¾ cups	12.25 ounces	350 ounces
baking powder	2 teaspoons	•	10 grams
salt	½ teaspoon	•	3.5 grams
walnut oil	3 liquid ounces (6 tablespoons)	2.75 ounces	80.5 grams
safflower oil	2 tablespoons	1 ounce	27 grams

6 large eggs, separated + 4 additional whites
  yolks
  whites
	
	3.5 liquid ounces
	1¼ liquid cups
		
		4 ounces
		10.5 ounces
			
			300 grams

vanilla	2 teaspoons	•	8 grams
cream of tartar	1¼ teaspoons	•	4 grams

* If using nonalkalized cocoa, replace the baking powder with ½ teaspoon baking soda.

Preheat the oven to 325°F.

In a medium bowl combine the cocoa and boiling water and whisk until smooth. Cool.

In a large mixing bowl combine the flour, all but 2 tablespoons of the sugar, baking powder, and salt and beat 1 minute to mix. Make a well in center. Add the oils, egg yolks, chocolate mixture, and vanilla and beat 1 minute or until smooth.

In another large mixing bowl beat the egg whites until frothy, add the cream of tartar, and beat until soft peaks form when the beater is raised. Beat in the remaining 2 tablespoons of sugar and beat until stiff peaks form when the beater is raised slowly. Fold 1 heaping cup of egg whites into the chocolate mixture with a large balloon wire whisk, slotted skimmer, or angel food cake folder. Gently fold in the remaining egg whites until just blended.

Pour into the tube pan (the batter will come to 1¾

One ungreased 10-inch two-piece tube pan.

FINISHED HEIGHT:
4 inches high in the middle.

STORE:
3 days room temperature, 10 days refrigerated, 2 months frozen.

A light sprinkling of powdered sugar or cocoa. Or
decorate the base and center
with fresh flowers such as
fresia.

SERVE:
Room temperature or lightly
chilled. Cut with a serrated
knife.

POINTERS FOR SUCCESS:
See page 154. An angel food
cake folder, large balloon
whisk, or slotted skimmer is
ideal for folding in the flour
with the least amount of air
loss. If using the whisk, periodically shake out the batter which collects inside.

Chocolate Lover's Angel Food Cake

SERVES 14

inches from the top) and bake for 60 minutes or until a
cake tester inserted in the center comes out clean and the
cake springs back when lightly pressed in the center. Invert
the pan, placing the tube opening over the neck of a soda
or wine bottle to suspend it well above the counter, and
cool the cake completely in the pan (this takes about 1½
hours).

Loosen the sides with a long metal spatula and remove
the center core of the pan. Dislodge the bottom and center
core with a metal spatula or thin, sharp knife. (A wire cake
tester works well around the core. To keep the sides attractive, press the spatula against the sides of the pan and avoid
any up-and-down motion.) Invert onto a greased wire rack
and reinvert onto a serving plate. Wrap airtight.

*T*his cake has many special qualities, not least of which
is that it is the only cake I deem worth eating that has not
even a smidgen of "devil" cholesterol!* It is lovely on its
own, with fresh strawberries or raspberries, or for dipping
into chocolate fondue.

Angel food cake is one of the sweetest cakes because
it has virtually no fat to tenderize it and relies on an extra-
high proportion of sugar for this purpose. I find white angel food overpoweringly sweet but cocoa does wonders to
temper the sweetness in this version.

Interestingly, everyone who has tasted this cake, when
questioned individually about the sweetness level, has said:
"I don't usually like sweet things, but this cake is so moist,
light and wonderful, I don't find it too sweet at all." My
doorman went one step further: All smiles, eyes glowing,
and seemingly at a loss for words, he expressed himself
most eloquently by kissing my hand. Coincidentally, his
name is Angelo!

* The cocoa contains 7 grams or less of saturated fat.

INGREDIENTS	MEASURE	WEIGHT	
room temperature	*volume*	*ounces*	*grams*
unsweetened cocoa (Dutch-processed)	¼ cup + 1 tablespoon (lightly spooned into cup)	1 ounce	28 grams
boiling water	¼ liquid cup	2 ounces	60 grams
vanilla	2 teaspoons	•	8 grams
sugar	1¾ cups	12.25 ounces	350 grams
sifted cake flour	1 cup	3.5 ounces	100 grams
salt	¼ teaspoon	•	1.7 grams
16 large egg whites	2 liquid cups	17 ounces	480 grams
cream of tartar	2 teaspoons	•	6 grams

Preheat the oven to 350°F.

In a medium bowl combine the cocoa and boiling water and whisk until smooth. Whisk in vanilla.

In another medium bowl combine ¾ cup sugar, the flour, and salt and whisk to blend.

In a large mixing bowl beat the egg whites until frothy, add the cream of tartar, and beat until soft peaks form when the beater is raised. Gradually beat in the remaining 1 cup sugar, beating until very stiff peaks form when the beater is raised slowly. Remove 1 heaping cup of egg whites and place it onto the cocoa mixture.

Dust the flour mixture over the remaining whites, ¼ cup at a time, and fold in quickly but gently. It is not necessary to incorporate every speck until the last addition. The ideal implement was designed in England especially for this type of cake (page 458), but a large balloon wire whisk or slotted skimmer also works well.

Whisk together the egg white and cocoa mixture and fold into the batter until uniform. Pour into the tube pan (the batter will come to ¾ inch from the top), run a small metal spatula or knife through the batter to prevent air pockets, and bake for 40 minutes or until a cake tester inserted in the center comes out clean and the cake springs back when lightly pressed. (The center will rise above the pan while baking and sink slightly when done. The surface will have deep cracks like a soufflé.)

Invert the pan, placing the tube opening over the neck of a soda or wine bottle to suspend it well above the counter,

One ungreased 10-inch two-piece tube pan.

FINISHED HEIGHT:
4 inches high in the middle.

STORE:
3 days room temperature, 10 days refrigerated. Freezing toughens the texture.

COMPLEMENTARY ADORNMENTS:
A light sprinkling of cocoa. Lacy drizzles of Chocolate Lattice (page 388). Or fresh flowers.

SERVE:
Room temperature or lightly chilled. Lovely with ice

cream and/or chocolate sauce. Or, to keep totally free of cholesterol, Tofutti and/or Raspberry Sauce (page 337). Cut with a serrated knife.

POINTERS FOR SUCCESS: See page 154. An angel food cake folder, large balloon whisk, or slotted skimmer is ideal for folding in the flour with the least amount of air loss. If using the whisk, periodically shake out the batter which collects on the inside.

and cool the cake completely in the pan (this takes about 1½ hours).

Loosen the sides with a long metal spatula and remove the center core of the pan. Dislodge the bottom and center core with a metal spatula or thin, sharp knife. (A wire cake tester works well around the core. To keep the sides attractive, press the spatula against the sides of the pan and avoid any up-and-down motion.) Invert onto a serving plate. Wrap airtight.

UNDERSTANDING

In contrast to chocolate chiffon cake, an equal volume of egg whites replaces the whole eggs, and the oil and baking powder are eliminated. This produces a stronger structure so the flour can be cut back by ¾ cup, yielding a lighter texture. The sugar remains the same because it is needed to tenderize what would otherwise be a rubbery cake. This means that the sugar in relation to the other ingredients is higher than for the chiffon cake so the angel food cake is somewhat sweeter. Part of the sugar is beaten into the whites to add stability and the remainder is mixed with the flour to separate the grains, which helps it to incorporate evenly into the resulting meringue.

A small amount of cocoa tempers the excessive sweetness so often objectionable in an angel food. As in the Génoise au Chocolat, I have used my new technique of adding water (not traditionally called for in this type of cake) to the cocoa. The water adds moisture, tenderizes the cake, and dissolves the cocoa, thereby both facilitating its incorporation and intensifying the flavor. Also, a slightly higher baking temperature is used compared to chiffon cake to produce a lighter and more tender and moist cake (page 476).

Showcase Cakes

The cakes in this chapter illustrate how to achieve glorious creations from the basic recipes in the rest of the book. They are perfect for important occasions like weddings, anniversaries, birthdays, graduations, promotions, holidays, and dinner parties. Some have appeared already in magazines, others only at private gatherings. Each cake has its own story, and—for inspiration and amusement—I am including two of the most dramatic in this chapter.

To invoke romance and poetry, some of my cakes bear European titles but most are as American as I am. The handful of European classics have undergone contemporary American culinary evolution. They contain less sugar, are lighter in texture, and have more pronounced flavors.

For the sake of practicality and purity of flavor, I limit the number of components in each cake to three or four. Although narrow layers filled with many varying creams sound exciting and scrumptious, the taste tends to confuse the palate and diminish eating pleasure—the way mixing together too many colors in a painting results in loss of individual identity.

Cakes made for special occasions must dazzle the eye. But no matter how carried away I get with decorating, my chief concerns are always flavor and texture. If a cake isn't going to taste absolutely delicious, there is no point in making it!

Once you have learned some of the the techniques in this book, the special cakes in this chapter will showcase all your baking and decorating skills. Believe it or not, the cakes are easy to assemble. The components can be made in steps and, as much as possible, I have suggested timing and plans for preparation at the beginning of each cake. The recipes for the individual components (given in other chapters) also contain tips for advance preparation and storage.

Of course recipe components can be used interchangeably and the cakes decorated in any number of ways, including the simple frosting techniques on page 360. But for special occasions, here are some examples to inspire you to ever-greater flights of fantasy.

TIPS FOR SHOWCASE CAKES

EXTRA BUTTERCREAM

The buttercream recipes in this chapter are generous to ensure that there will be enough to complete the cake. Any leftover buttercream can be frozen for future use. In fact, when I have collected several different varieties, I make cupcakes using the All-Occasion Downy Yellow Butter Cake (page 39) or Perfect All-American Chocolate Butter Cake (page 54). Half recipe of either makes 9 cupcakes. Use 2¼ teaspoons baking powder for ½ recipe of yellow cake, 1¾ teaspoons of baking powder for ½ recipe of chocolate cake. Fill paper-lined or greased and floured muffin tins two thirds full and bake 20 to 25 minutes or until the cupcakes test done. I frost the cupcakes with thawed, rebeaten buttercream. Arranged on a serving plate, they are most attractive, often displaying a rainbow of colors.

STORING A COMPLETED CAKE

Cakes and buttercreams are prone to absorbing other flavors so, if cakes are frosted far ahead, precautions must be taken. A small cake can be stored in an airtight plastic cake carrier or glass cake dome (page 461). A large tiered cake can be placed in a heavy cardboard box and taped shut.

FREEZING A COMPLETED CAKE

If you are planning to freeze a frosted cake, place it uncovered in the freezer just until the frosting is very firm and it will not be damaged by wrapping. Wrap the cake first in plastic wrap, then in heavy-duty foil, trying to eliminate as much air as possible without pressing on the decorations. The most airtight wrap is known as the drugstore wrap: Place the cake in center of the foil and bring the two long sides together so that the edges meet. Fold the edges over several times until close to the cake. Proceed in the same way for the short ends. Delicate decorations can be protected further by placing the wrapped cake in a rigid box.

Be sure to defrost the cake overnight in the refrigerator and then allow it to come to room temperature before serving. Gradual defrosting prevents water droplets from forming on the frosting. When you remove the cake from the freezer, take off the wrapping while the frosting is still frozen solid—before refrigerating the cake in an airtight container.

STORING LEFTOVER CAKE

Begin by offering any leftover cake to your guests; it's rare to receive a refusal. Most cakes are still delicious the day after if wrapped airtight in plastic wrap and foil, even without refrigeration. I sometimes cut individual pieces of leftover cake, wrap them tightly in plastic wrap and foil, and freeze them for future desserts or afternoon tea.

CAVEAT: Butter cake must be eaten at room temperature to fully appreciate the flavors and soft, tender texture. Cakes cold from the refrigerator have muted flavors and much firmer textures.

The fanciful image of this cake reflects the flavor within: soft-as-swan's-down white butter cake, silky lemon buttercream, and a shimmering lake of dark blueberry topping.

The Victorian dessert spoons in the picture were found at an antiques fair held in a Moravian church in Hope, New Jersey. I spent a small fortune on them because they reminded me of swans' wings.

This cake is lovely to serve any time of year and satisfying yet light enough as the finale for a grand dinner.

SPECIAL EQUIPMENT NEEDED

- Plastic swans can be used in place of piped meringue swans. They are available at party supply stores and can be painted with a thin coating of Royal Icing (page 294).
- Two 9¼-inch x 6⅝-inch oval pans (page 453)
- Oval platter or board, flat portion at least 10 inches by 7 inches
- Pastry bag and number 22 star tube

CAKE COMPONENTS

- 2 meringue swans (pages 297 and 377) and ¼ cup Stabilized Whipped Cream (page 255)
- 1 recipe White Chocolate Whisper Cake (page 50), baked in two 9¼-inch by 6⅝-inch oval cake pans (page 453)
- 1 recipe Neoclassic or Classic Lemon Buttercream (page 234)
- 1 recipe Winter Blueberry Topping (page 349)

METHOD FOR ASSEMBLING CAKE

1. Frost directly on a serving plate, using strips of wax paper slid under the sides. Or make a cardboard base, using one of the cake pans as a template.
2. Spread a little buttercream on the base so that the cake will stick to it.
3. Fill and frost the layers with a ¼-inch-thick layer of buttercream. Use a small metal spatula to create vertical lines to represent waves on the sides.
4. With the remaining buttercream pipe a border of sideways shells (page 400—reverse shell technique without altering direction), using a number 22 star tube. Chill for 30 minutes.
5. Up to 2 hours before serving, carefully, so as not to damage the border, spoon room temperature Winter Blueberry Topping smoothly over the cake.
6. Complete the swans by piping the whipped cream and securing the heads and necks and set on the cake.

Blueberry Swan Lake

SERVES 12

TIMING:
The cake can be assembled 1 day ahead and refrigerated except for the blueberry topping and swans, which should be placed on the cake no more than 2 hours before serving. The frosted cake (without the swans or blueberry topping) can be frozen 2 months.

SERVE:
If the cake has been refrigerated, allow it to come to room temperature before serving (at least 2 hours). Cut into wedges radiating from the center.

A Taste of Heaven

TIMING:
The cake can be assembled 2 days ahead and refrigerated. It can be frozen 2 months.

SERVE:
Lightly chilled or room temperature. (Buttercream should be warm enough to be creamy.) Cut with a serrated knife into wedges radiating from the center.

*T*his is my personal translation of the classic Swiss Zuger Kirschtorte. In Swiss German the word *Zuger* sounds like the word *Zucker,* which means "sugar." Actually, *Zuger* refers to something that comes from the town of Zug, renowned for its kirsch (cherry liqueur).*

In Switzerland this cake ranks as the favorite non-chocolate cake. Truly, it is a miracle of textures—a small taste of heaven. My version consists of a *génoise* heart drenched in kirsch syrup, cloaked in pale pink buttercream, and embraced by a pair of crisp, heart-shaped *dacquoise.* Due to the nature of the components, this is one of the sweeter cakes in this book. It is, however, less sweet than the Swiss version because I have decreased the sugar in the syrup and opted for *dacquoise* rather than the sweeter meringue normally used.

Traditionally, Zuger Kirschtorte is round, but I think the heart shape emphasizes the romance of this exquisite dessert. And it provides the perfect centerpiece for a Valentine's Day celebration or engagement party.

SPECIAL EQUIPMENT NEEDED
- 9-inch by 2-inch heart-shaped pan (The cake also can be made in a 9-inch by 2-inch cake pan or a 9-inch springform pan.)

CAKE COMPONENTS
- 1 recipe Génoise Classique (page 120), baked in a 9-inch by 2-inch heart-shaped pan (page 453) and top and bottom crusts removed
- 1 recipe syrup flavored with kirsch (page 120)
- 1 recipe Dacquoise (page 302), piped in 2 heart-shaped discs slightly smaller than the outline of the pan to allow for spreading during baking (page 375)
- 1 recipe Neoclassic or Classic Buttercream (page 230 or 228), flavored with ⅓ cup kirsch and tinted pale pink with 6 drops of red food color
- 1 cup sliced blanched almonds (3 ounces/85 grams), toasted at 350°F. for a few minutes until lightly browned

METHOD FOR ASSEMBLING CAKE
1. Use the heart-shaped pan to trace a heart-shaped cardboard base.
2. Sprinkle each side of the cake with 3 tablespoons syrup.

---

* The best kirsch I have ever tasted is Etter Kirsch, manufactured in the town of Zug, Switzerland. If you visit Switzerland, be sure to bring back a bottle.

3. Spread a few small dabs of buttercream on the cardboard base and place 1 *dacquoise* disc flat side down on it.

4. Spread a thin layer of buttercream on the *dacquoise* and top with the *génoise* layer. Spread another thin layer of buttercream on the *génoise* and top with the second *dacquoise* flat side up.

5. Use the remaining buttercream to frost the top and sides.

6. Gently press the toasted almond slices on the sides, supporting the cake on the palm of 1 hand and tilting it slightly toward the other hand, cupped to hold the nuts.

7. Refrigerate up to 1 hour before serving.

*O*ne of my earliest memories is of the smell of lilacs, and sunshine glinting through their leaves as my stroller was pushed to and fro to encourage the ever-resisted afternoon nap. Individual lilac blossoms are exquisite. Crystallized with lavender sugar and embedded in white chocolate buttercream, they make magnificent cake decorations. The pale pink of Raspberry Mousseline Buttercream against the pale yellow cake provides a harmony of color and flavor.

This cake would make a lovely centerpiece for a Mother's Day party.

CAKE COMPONENTS
- 1 recipe White Velvet Butter Cake (page 46), layers split in half horizontally
- ½ recipe Raspberry Mousseline (page 245), tinted with 3 drops of red food color
- 1 recipe Crème Ivoire Deluxe (page 246)
- Crystallized Lilacs (page 326)

METHOD FOR ASSEMBLING CAKE
1. Spread a little mousseline on a 9-inch cardboard round so the cake layers adhere.

2. Stack the cake layers on top of each other, sandwiching each with ¾ cup mousseline (⅓ of the mousseline in between each layer).

3. Chill the cake for 10 minutes.

4. Frost with Crème Ivoire Deluxe.

5. Decorate the sides and top with the crystallized lilacs. If necessary, make a tiny hole in the frosting with a skewer before inserting a lilac. The cake can be held at cool room temperature until the following day.

White Lilac Nostalgia

SERVES 10 TO 12

TIMING:
The cake can be assembled 1 day ahead. It can be frozen without the lilacs for 2 months.

SERVE:
Room temperature. Cut with a thin, sharp knife.

Baked Hawaii

TIMING:
The cake should be assembled 1 to 2 days ahead. The meringue must be applied and baked for 5 minutes in a very hot oven just before serving.

SERVE:
Starting at the bottom, cut thin slices—making the first slice thicker as it will contain less of the ice cream—with a thin, sharp knife dipped in hot water. If the ice cream is very firm, allow the cut pieces to sit for 10 minutes or until it starts to soften slightly before serving.

STORE:
Leftovers will stay delicious for at least 2 days if wrapped airtight and kept frozen.

*M*any years ago, on my first trip to France, I was invited by Stella Standard, to eat at the legendary Left Bank bistro Chez Allard. It was renowned for its *canard aux navets* ("duck with turnips"), but it was a dessert, in all its perfect simplicity, which most intrigued me: ripe fresh pineapple, bathed in a fine-quality kirsch. That was all. And it was divine.

The combination of pineapple and kirsch experienced those twenty years ago is what inspired this special version of Baked Alaska. Every component contains either kirsch or pineapple and sometimes both. The kirsch keeps the ice cream and *biscuit* from freezing too hard, while fresh pineapple juice keeps the Italian meringue from being too sweet.

This is a real showstopper dessert. Although the meringue must be piped and browned just before serving, it's quick and easy to do, and guests enjoy the anticipation of watching the final preparations.

SPECIAL EQUIPMENT NEEDED
- Two 9¼-inch by 6⅝-inch oval pans (page 453)
- Ice-cream freezer
- Pastry bag and a large number 6 star tube

CAKE COMPONENTS
- 1 recipe Fresh Preserved Pineapple in syrup (page 351). Be sure to save the pineapple juice while cutting pineapple for the meringue. The preserved pineapple is used in the ice cream, the syrup for brushing on the cake.
- 4 cups Pineapple Ice Cream (pages 286 and 351), slightly softened
- 1 recipe Oval Biscuit (page 147)
- 2 tablespoons melted and strained apricot preserves
- 1 cup Pineapple Kirsch Syrup: Stir together ¾ cup reserved pineapple poaching syrup (page 351) and ¼ cup kirsch.
- 1½ recipes Light Italian Meringue (page 298), replacing the water with fresh pineapple juice

METHOD FOR ASSEMBLING CAKE
1. Cut 1 *biscuit* oval in half horizontally for the top and bottom of the cake.
2. Cut out the center of the second oval, leaving a ¾-inch ring. Reserve the center for another use.*

---

* I freeze this center oval until I am ready to use it. Then I sprinkle it with its weight in Pineapple Kirsch Syrup, frost it with Pineapple Buttercream, and adorn it with grated coconut.

3. Sprinkle 3 tablespoons syrup on each side of the 2 ovals and brush 2 tablespoons on each side of the ring.

4. Use an oval cake pan to make an oval cardboard base. Wrap the base in foil.

5. Place 1 *biscuit* oval on the base and carefully stack the ring on top, brushing the ring and the outside perimeter of the base with the apricot preserves to make them adhere. (Support the ring with a flat baking sheet when lifting.)

6. Spoon softened ice cream into the center of the ring, mounding it.

7. Top with the second oval.

8. Wrap with plastic wrap and then foil and freeze for at least 24 hours.

9. Just before serving, place a rack in the upper third of the oven and preheat the oven to 500°F. Spread the cake with the Italian Meringue to seal it. Pipe connecting stars of meringue with a large number 6 star tube.

10. Bake the cake 3 to 5 minutes or until the meringue begins to brown. Watch carefully to prevent burning.

*R*aspberry-scented buttercream encases a complexity of textures from soft moist *génoise* to crisp meringue. Fresh raspberries and blueberries interrupt the crunchy layers with bursts of juicy tartness.

This pretty and delectable cake works with other fruit themes as well (see Note). I designed the raspberry red, white, and blueberry theme for a 100th anniversary of the Statue of Liberty party. When I use blueberries alone, my husband calls the cake "Rhapsody in Blueberries." This is a fun cake to make for Fourth of July celebrations.

SPECIAL EQUIPMENT NEEDED
• Pastry bag and number 3 round tube and number 22 star tube

CAKE COMPONENTS
• 1 recipe Crisp French Meringue (pages 296 and 375), piped in two 8½-inch spiral discs
• 1 recipe Génoise Classique (page 120), top and bottom crusts removed and sliced in half horizontally
• 1 recipe Syrup flavored with *crème de myrtilles* (blueberry liqueur), framboise (eau-de-vie of raspberries), or amaretto (page 120)

Star-Spangled Rhapsody

SERVES 14 TO 16

TIMING:
The cake should be assembled 1 to 3 days ahead and refrigerated. The berries should not be placed on top until the day of serving. The completed cake freezes well without the fruit topping for 3 months.

SERVE:
Lightly chilled or room temperature. (Buttercream should be warm enough to be creamy.) Cut with a serrated knife.

- 1 recipe Mousseline Buttercream (page 244) flavored with framboise eau-de-vie (which is clear in color)
- ⅓ cup heavy cream softly whipped with ¼ teaspoon vanilla (page 253)
- 1 cup Fresh Blueberry Topping (use large blueberries) (page 348) and 2 cups small raspberries

METHOD FOR ASSEMBLING CAKE

1. Trim the meringue discs to the same diameter or slightly smaller than the *génoise*. Use a small serrated knife and support the discs on a cardboard round or removable pan bottom, allowing the part to be trimmed to extend slightly over the edge.
2. Sprinkle each side of the *génoise* with 3 tablespoons syrup.
3. Spread a little mousseline on the 9-inch cardboard round and attach a meringue disc, flat side down. Spread with a thin layer (about ⅛ inch) of mousseline and top with 1 layer of *génoise*.
4. Spread the whipped cream on the *génoise* and top with ¼ cup each Fresh Blueberry Topping and raspberries, saving the most attractive berries for decor.
5. Top with the second *génoise* layer. Spread curved top side of second meringue disc with another thin layer of mousseline and place on top of *génoise* layer.
6. Frost the sides and top with some of the remaining mousseline.
7. Pipe mousseline decorations with a number 3 round tube for the string work (page 404) and a number 22 star tip for the shell border (page 399). Refrigerate until firm.
8. Top with the remaining Fresh Blueberry Topping and raspberries in a decorative pattern. Use the number 22 star tip to pipe stars (page 398).

NOTE: Other fruit possibilities: Fresh or Winter Cherry Topping (page 344 or 345), fresh strawberries, or an 11-ounce can of mandarin orange slices, drained and marinated overnight in 2 tablespoons Mandarine Napoléon liqueur. Use liqueurs for the syrup and buttercream to complement the fruit (kirsch for the cherries, Grand Marnier for the strawberries, and Mandarine Napoléon for the oranges). Mandarine Napoléon is especially pretty because it gives the mousseline a pale apricot hue.

The first time I encountered brioche as a cake was at LeNôtre's school in Plaisir, France. It was my favorite of all the cakes we made during that intensive week of classes.

The original version of this cake was in my first book, *Romantic and Classic Cakes*. I have since made my praline buttercream much less sweet and sometimes vary the recipe by using white chocolate praline buttercream in its place.

The cake is a study in contrasts—gossamer-soft brioche saturated with a refreshingly light rum syrup and encased by a rich, light, smooth praline buttercream. The nutty richness makes it especially suitable for cool weather occasions.

SPECIAL EQUIPMENT NEEDED
- 2-inch high expandable flan ring and an 8-inch cardboard round. Or an 8-inch loose-bottom or springform pan fitted with cardboard rounds until the correct depth is obtained
- Pastry bag and number 22 star tube

CAKE COMPONENTS
- 1 recipe La Brioche Cake (page 76), trimmed to 7 inches by 1½ inches to 1¾ inches
- 1 recipe Rum Syrup (page 76)
- ½ recipe Praline Silk Meringue Buttercream (page 241) or 1 recipe Crème Ivoire Praliné (page 249)
- ½ cup (2 ounces/57 grams) skinned and toasted hazelnuts (page 324). Reserve 24 whole nuts for the garnish and coarsely chop the remainder.

METHOD FOR ASSEMBLING CAKE
1. Place the brioche cake in a large pan and pour the syrup over it. Allow it to sit for 10 minutes or until the syrup is absorbed. Turn the brioche occasionally or use a bulb baster to help it absorb as much syrup as possible.
2. Spread the cardboard round with a very thin layer of buttercream and place it in the bottom of the ring. If using a bottomless ring, set on a baking sheet for support.
3. Using a small metal spatula, spread a thin layer of buttercream inside the ring.
4. Slide the brioche into the ring and top with some buttercream. Use a long metal spatula to create a smooth top, allowing the blade to rest on the sides of the ring to create a very even surface.

Praline Brioche Cake

SERVES 14 TO 16

TIMING:
The cake can be assembled 1 to 4 days ahead and refrigerated. The completed cake can be frozen 3 months.

SERVE:
Lightly chilled or room temperature. (Buttercream should be warm enough to be creamy.)

5. Refrigerate for at least 30 minutes.

6. *To unmold:* Very briefly heat the sides of the ring or pan with a hairdryer on the hot setting or a hot, wet towel (page 358).

7. Place the cake on top of a firm object slightly smaller in diameter than the bottom, such as a canister. Pull the ring firmly down, away from the cake.

8. Gently press the chopped nuts on the sides, supporting the cake on the palm of 1 hand and tilting it slightly toward the other hand, cupped to hold the nuts.

9. Use the reserved whole hazelnuts to form a border, alternating with buttercream piped from a number 22 star tube to resemble hazelnuts.

10. Refrigerate up to 30 minutes before serving.

Golden Cage

Zauber Torte

SERVES 12 TO 16

TIMING:
The cake can be assembled 1 day ahead and refrigerated or frozen 2 months. The caramel cage, however, should not be refrigerated or frozen. Remove the frosted cake from the refrigerator at least 2 hours before serving and place the cage on top.

SERVE:
Room temperature. Light the candles or sparkler. Remove the cage before cutting. Break the cage into pieces and use for garnish.

*T*he German name of this cake was inspired by Mozart's joyful opera "Die Zauberflöte" ("The Magic Flute").

Beneath a shimmering golden caramel cage lies still more gold: buttery, dense golden *génoise* frosted with tart Apricot Silk Meringue Buttercream and sprinkled with Caramel Gold Dust. I serve this dessert for very special occasions (New Year's Eve, fiftieth birthday parties, golden anniversaries). For extra golden glitter, present it with a sparkler and serve it with Sauternes or an Eiswein (the most glorious of dessert wines).

SPECIAL EQUIPMENT
• one 9-cup Kugelhopf pan (page 447)

CAKE COMPONENTS
• 1 recipe Golden Génoise (page 125), baked in the 9-cup Kugelhopf pan
• 2 tablespoons Barack Palinka (apricot eau-de-vie) or apricot brandy
• ½ recipe Apricot Silk Meringue Buttercream (page 243)
• Gold Dust and Caramel Cage (page 313)

OPTIONAL DECOR
• Crystallized Violets (page 326)
• A sparkler or long, thin, dripless candles

METHOD FOR ASSEMBLING CAKE

1. Frost directly on a serving plate, using strips of wax paper slid under the sides. Or make a cardboard base, using the inverted cake pan as a guide.

2. Split the *génoise* in half horizontally with a serrated knife. Sprinkle each cut side with 1 tablespoon Barack Palinka.

3. Sandwich the layers together with ⅓ cup buttercream. Remove any loose crust and spread the remaining buttercream over the outside of the cake. If not serving the same day, refrigerate.

4. Using a small strainer, sift the Gold Dust over the buttercream, tilting the cake to get an even coating. Place the cake on a large flat platter or serving plate and cover it with the Caramel Cage. (If the cage should accidentally break, use the broken pieces as decoration right on the frosting.)

5. Attach the crystallized violets, if desired, with tiny dabs of caramel. (Leftover caramel from the cage can be remelted in the microwave on high power or in a small heavy saucepan over medium heat.)

6. If desired, insert candles through the cage so that they radiate from the center. If using a sparkler, insert it at an angle away from the cake so sparks do not fall on the cake.

CHARLOTTES

A charlotte is made by lining a mold with gossamer *biscuit* or *génoise* (sponge-type cakes) in varying geometrical shapes, and then filling the mold with an airy Bavarian or whipped cream. When surrounded by slices of multilayered sponge cake and jam it is called charlotte royale. When surrounded by ladyfingers, it is known as a charlotte russe. The charlotte is so popular in France it is constantly reappearing in new guises and names. In America the charlotte has appeared and disappeared over the years, usually under the prosaic name "icebox cake," probably in deference to the advance preparation and prolonged refrigeration necessary before unmolding and serving it.

When I think of an icebox cake, I picture an easy-to-prepare cake that uses packaged ladyfingers. These are not a bad product, but, when you make your own ladyfingers or cake sheets, icebox cake is transformed into a charlotte and becomes one of my favorite desserts. Both from a visual and gustatory standpoint, one can ask for no more elegant finale to a dinner party.

NOTE: A charlotte must be prepared at least four hours in advance but can be refrigerated for up to 3 days with no loss of texture or flavor. The cake-lined mold must be prepared in advance. In fact, it can be frozen 3 months, making it a simple matter to complete the dessert well in advance of a party.

*T*his dessert, inspired by LeNôtre, one of the world's great *patissiers,* is perhaps my favorite of all charlottes. The flavor is pure pear and the texture incomparably creamy and billowy.

SPECIAL EQUIPMENT NEEDED
- 9-inch springform or loose bottom pan or a flan ring at least 2½ inches high
- 17-inch by 12-inch jelly roll pan

CAKE COMPONENTS
- 1 recipe Biscuit Roulade for the sides of the mold (page 142)
- ¾ cup Cordon Rose Raspberry Conserve (page 331) or seedless raspberry jam
- An 8-inch-round disc of Biscuit Roulade as the base (page 142)
- 1 recipe Poached Pears (page 350)
- 1 recipe Pear Bavarian Cream (page 290)
- ¼ cup Apple Jewel Glaze (page 329), thinned with William's pear liqueur. Or Shiny Apple Jewel Glaze (page 330) if preparing the charlotte more than 1 day ahead.
- Optional:
  1 recipe Raspberry Sauce (page 337) to echo the filling and contrast with the pale green color

METHOD FOR ASSEMBLING CHARLOTTE
LINING THE 9-INCH BY 2-INCH MOLD
1. Bake the *biscuit* and allow it to cool flat.
2. To cut the *biscuit,* use a pizza wheel or a sharp knife and a ruler to score where the cuts should be and then use sharp shears to do the actual cutting. Trim the edges so that the *biscuit* measures exactly 10 inches by about 16 inches. Now cut the *biscuit* lengthwise into 4 equal rectangles, 2½ inches wide by 16 inches long.
3. Spread 3 of the rectangles with a smooth layer of the raspberry conserve or jam. If the jam is too thick to spread easily, thin it with 1 tablespoon Chambord (black raspberry liqueur) or warm water. If using commercial jam, heat and strain it and use warm.
4. Stack the rectangles carefully on top of one another, ending with the one that has no jam. The flat side of a long metal ruler, pressed against the side helps to even the layers.

Ethereal
Pear Charlotte

**S E R V E S
8 T O 1 0**

TIMING:
The charlotte must be assembled 4 hours to 3 days ahead. It can also be frozen 3 weeks. The mold must be lined with the *biscuit* before preparing the filling.

SERVE:
Chilled. For an elegant effect, pour raspberry sauce onto the center of each serving plate and tilt to coat evenly. Top with a slice of the charlotte.

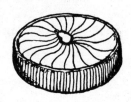

5. Cut the stacked rectangles in half to form 2 shorter rectangles (each 7½ inches long). You now have two 4-layer rectangles, each 2½ inches wide, 7½ inches long, and 2 inches high. (The only important measure is the width because when sliced and positioned in the pan, it will determine the height of the striped border.)

6. Wrap the rectangles in wax paper and put them in a large heavy-duty plastic freezer bag. Place them on a baking sheet to maintain their shape and freeze until firm.

7. Use a small serrated knife to cut the rectangles into ⅜-inch slices. If necessary, trim each slice so that it is exactly 2½ inches high when the stripes are up and down.

8. If molding the charlotte in a springform pan, remove the inner disc and place the outer ring directly on a serving plate. If using a loose-bottom pan, leave the inner disc in place but line it with a parchment round if planning to remove it before serving.

9. Lightly oil the inside of the ring. Place the striped slices around the ring so that the stripes are straight up and down. Brush 1 side of each slice with a light coating of conserve before placing the next slice firmly against it.

10. Measure the inside diameter of the lined ring for making the *biscuit* disc. Cover the ring tightly with plastic wrap and set aside while preparing the disc and filling.

11. Trim the *biscuit* base if necessary and fit it snugly into the bottom of the lined ring. Re-cover tightly with the plastic wrap.

12. Poach the pears, reserving the liquid for the filling.

13. Prepare the Pear Bavarian Cream and scoop it into the prepared mold. Level with a small angled spatula. Cover tightly and refrigerate for at least 30 minutes.

14. Use a thin, sharp knife to cut the poached pears lengthwise into thin slices. Place a fan of overlapping slices on top of the filling with the pointed ends at the center. To form a center pear-shaped decoration, place 2 small pear slices (slightly overlapping) and a small piece of stem at the top.

15. If serving the same day, brush the pears with a thin film of Apple Jewel Glaze. For a thicker glaze that keeps the pears moist and fresh for several days, brush with Shiny Apple Jewel Glaze instead. Allow the charlotte to set for 4 hours to 3 days before unmolding.

To unmold: For a springform, release the sides of the pan and lift away. For a loose-bottom pan, place on top of a sturdy canister smaller than the pan's bottom and press firmly downward. The pan sides will slip down to the counter and the charlotte can be lifted off the canister because it is supported by the pan base. Use a heavy-duty pancake turner to slide between the parchment and pan base and place the charlotte on a serving plate.

*S*piral slices of jam-filled tender Biscuit Roulade form a dome to encase a smooth vanilla Bavarian cream. This is a light, intensely flavorful cake with a dramatic design. It is especially delicious and attractive served with a tart raspberry sauce.

SPECIAL EQUIPMENT NEEDED
• 6-cup round-bottom bowl
• 17-inch by 12-inch jelly-roll pan

CAKE COMPONENTS
• ½ cup Cordon Rose Raspberry Conserve (page 331) or seedless raspberry jam
• 1 recipe Biscuit Roulade (page 142) for jam-filled roll and base
• 1 recipe Vanilla Bavarian Cream (page 287)
• *Optional:*
Shiny Apricot Glaze (page 178) for a transparent golden film which keeps the cake fresh and adds a pleasant tartness
1 recipe Raspberry Sauce (page 337)

METHOD FOR ASSEMBLING CHARLOTTE
Lining the 6-cup mold:
1. Lightly oil the 6-cup bowl and line it as smoothly as possible with a sheet of plastic wrap, leaving a small overhang. Measure the diameter of the bowl. You will need a round *biscuit* base that just fits inside.
2. As soon as the *biscuit* has finished baking, use lining to slip it out of the pan onto the counter and cut off a strip from 1 of the short ends just wide enough to serve as the top.
3. While still hot, roll the remaining *biscuit* as indicated in the recipe and allow it to cool.
4. When the cut strip has cooled, cut it with shears into

Scarlet Empress

TIMING:
The charlotte must be assembled 8 hours to 3 days ahead. It can also be frozen 3 weeks. The mold must be lined with the jelly-roll slices before preparing the filling.

SERVE:
Chilled. For an elegant effect, pour raspberry sauce onto the center of each serving plate and tilt it to coat evenly. Top with a slice of the charlotte.

a circle for the base. Wrap in plastic and set aside.

5. The jelly-roll slices used to line this charlotte must be tightly rolled for the most attractive appearance. To accomplish this, unroll the cooled *biscuit,* leaving it on the nonstick liner or towel, and spread the crust side with a very thin layer of raspberry conserve or jam. If the jam is too thick to spread easily, thin it with 2 teaspoons chambord (black raspberry liqueur) or warm water.

6. Roll up the *biscuit* tightly about ⅓ of the way and turn it so that the unrolled portion is facing you. Fold over the lining or towel to cover the rolled section and a little of the flat section. With the edge of a straight-sided baking sheet held at an angle on top of the towel just at the point where the rolled section ends, press firmly against the roll and tug the bottom of the towel toward you to compress the roll. Lift away the towel overlap, roll up another ⅓ of the way, and repeat process. Repeat 1 more time, again angling the baking sheet at the base of the roll. The completed roll will be 2 inches in diameter.

7. Wrap snugly with plastic wrap and then foil and freeze until firm enough to slice.

8. With a small serrated knife, cut the roll into ¼-inch slices.

9. To line the bowl, place 1 slice in the center and place other slices around it as tightly as possible to avoid gaps. It is usually necessary to cut the slices in half or smaller to fit the last row (Figs. 1 and 2).

10. Cover the lined bowl tightly to keep it from drying out until the filling is ready.

11. Make the Vanilla Bavarian Cream, spoon it into the mold, and place the round *biscuit* base in place. Cover tightly and refrigerate until set (at least 8 hours).

To unmold: Invert onto a serving plate and lift away the bowl, tugging gently on the plastic wrap to release it. To prevent drying out, glaze with Shiny Apricot Glaze or simply leave the plastic wrap in place until shortly before serving time.

TO MAKE SHINY APRICOT GLAZE

Sprinkle 1 teaspoon gelatin over ½ cup water and allow to sit for at least 3 minutes. Heat until the gelatin is dissolved. Heat ¼ cup apricot preserves and strain it. Stir in the gelatin mixture and allow to thicken slightly. Or stir briefly over ice water until syrupy before brushing onto cake.

*T*he dramatically complex shape of this charlotte is deceptively simple—merely cut and overlap rectangular strips of *génoise*. The easy-to-make Chocolate Chip Whipped Cream filling is light, crunchy and utterly delectable.

SPECIAL EQUIPMENT NEEDED
- 6-cup round bottom bowl
- 8-inch by 2-inch square metal pan
- Pastry bag and number 103 tube

CAKE COMPONENTS
- 1 recipe Génoise Classique (page 120), baked in an 8-inch by 2-inch square metal pan
- ½ cup Ganache Frosting (page 267), made with 2 ounces bittersweet chocolate and ¼ cup heavy cream
- ½ the Syrup recipe on page 120, made with Cognac or amaretto
- 1 recipe Chocolate Chip Whipped Cream (page 258)
- *Optional:*
  1 cup Ganache Sauce is a nice textural contrast to the soft cake and creamy filling. Simply make extra ganache when preparing it for frosting the *génoise*.

METHOD FOR ASSEMBLING CHARLOTTE
Lining the 6-cup mold:
1. Use a soft tape measure to measure the inside of the 6-cup bowl, measuring from the center to the edge and making sure that the tape follows the curve of the bowl. It should measure about 5½ inches. Using a long serrated knife, remove the top crust of the *génoise* and trim it so that it is perfectly square. Cut off 1 edge so that 1 side measures exactly 6 inches (one inch more than the curve of the bowl for a safety margin).

2. Prepare the Ganache Frosting and spread 2 tablespoons of the hot ganache on the top of the cake. Chill the cake for 15 minutes to set the ganache. Set aside the remaining ganache at room temperature.

3. Invert the cake, ganache side down, onto lightly greased foil and cut it into 6-inch by ¼-inch strips with a thin, sharp knife, wiping the blade between each slice. Cut 1 end of the unfrosted side of each strip on the diagonal so that it comes to a point (Fig. 1). This will prevent too much cake from building up in the center. Keep the slices covered with plastic wrap to prevent drying.

Chocolate Chip Charlotte

S E R V E S   6   T O   8

TIMING:
Génoise should be baked 1 day ahead to be firm enough for cutting. The charlotte must be assembled 2 hours to 3 days ahead. It can also be frozen 3 weeks. The cream filling is prepared just before lining the mold with the cake so that some of the whipped cream can be used to attach the cake strips.

SERVE:
Chilled. For an elegant effect, pour Ganache Sauce onto the center of each serving plate and tilt it to coat evenly. Top with a slice of the charlotte. If the ganache is too thick to pour, warm it gently in a double boiler. For extra flavor, add 1 tablespoon cognac or amaretto.

1

2

3

4. Prepare the Chocolate Chip Whipped Cream and set aside while lining the mold.

5. Lightly oil the 6-cup glass bowl and line it smoothly with buttered plastic wrap buttered side up, allowing a slight overhang. Starting at the bottom center of the bowl, place a strip of *génoise* from the center to the edge of the bowl, placing the pointed end at the center, the plain edge facing right, and the frosted edge facing left (Fig. 2).

6. Brush the strip with the syrup and a thin coating of the plain whipped cream reserved from the filling recipe. Place a second strip beside it in the same manner, slightly overlapping first strip at the rim. Brush it with the syrup and whipped cream. Continue working clockwise, from right to left, always having the frosted edge facing left so that it will show on the outside and create a striped motif when the charlotte is unmolded. When you come to the last strip, tuck the side under the first strip.

7. Trim the excess *génoise* flush with the edge of the bowl with sharp shears (Fig. 3). Cover tightly with plastic wrap while preparing filling.

8. Fill the lined mold with the Chocolate Chip Whipped Cream and chill until set (at least 2 hours).

9. Unmold onto a serving plate, tugging gently on the plastic wrap overhang to release the cake. Use the remaining ganache to pipe a fluted design on top to cover any imperfections.

crown of ladyfingers encases layers of Orange Bavarian Cream and Light Whipped Ganache. The contrasting flavors and textures are so pleasing that, even if time does not allow to make your own ladyfingers, the charlotte is still delicious with the packaged variety, freshened with a light sprinkling of Grand Marnier. The fingers can also be cut for the base and tapered to form a daisy top.

SPECIAL EQUIPMENT NEEDED

- Pastry bag and number 9 large tube (¾-inch diameter) for piping ladyfingers and discs
- 9-inch by 2-inch or 3-inch loose-bottom pan, springform pan, or flan ring

CAKE COMPONENTS

- 1 recipe Biscuit à la Cuillière (page 148), piped to make 2 dozen ladyfingers (you will need at least 19) and an 8½-inch base (page 373)
- ½ recipe Biscuit à la Cuillière, piped to make a 9-inch daisy top (page 182)
- If using packaged ladyfingers for the sides, base and top, purchase 2 packages (48 ladyfingers)
- 1 recipe Orange Bavarian (page 288)
- ¼ recipe Light Whipped Ganache (page 268)
- *Optional:*
  Orange Zest (page 342), a pretty garnish that adds a real sparkle of orange flavor and delightful chewy candied texture
  1 recipe Grand Marnier Crème Anglaise (page 280), fragrant with vanilla and a hint of orange, it ties together all the harmonious elements of this cake
  Brown and orange grosgrain or satin ribbons, to hint at the chocolate and orange flavors within

GUIDELINES FOR PIPING THE LADYFINGERS, BASE, AND DAISY TOP

A nonstick liner, parchment, or foil can be used to line the pans for piping the Biscuit à la Cuillière batter. If using parchment, lines can be drawn directly on it with pen or pencil. The parchment is inverted before piping so that the lines show through but the ink or pencil marks don't come into direct contact with the batter. Lines for foil can be marked with a skewer. A nonstick liner, however, is my favorite surface because the baked *biscuit* slides off it without hesitation. I use a bright felt-tip marker to make lines

Orange Chocolate Crown

S E R V E S 8 T O 1 0

TIMING:
The charlotte must be assembled 4 hours to 3 days ahead. It may also be frozen 3 weeks. The mold must be lined with the *biscuit* or ladyfingers before preparing the filling.

SERVE:
Remove from the refrigerator 1 hour before serving. For an elegant effect, pour the *crème anglaise* onto the center of each serving plate and tilt it to coat evenly. Top with a slice of the charlotte and garnish with the orange zest.

on a brown paper bag and cover it with the nonstick liner. It is also possible to grease and flour the pan and create lines in the surface of the flour. For piping ladyfingers, make parallel lines 3 inches apart. For discs, use a round cake pan to mark circles (8 inches for the base, 9 inches for the top).

PIPING METHOD TIPS: *Biscuit* batter flows fairly easily so it is unnecessary to squeeze the pastry bag. If the piped designs do not hold their shape, it means that the egg whites were not beaten stiffly enough. To stop the flow of batter, tilt the tube up just before you think it will be necessary. Work steadily so that batter can be baked soon after preparing it. This will enable it to retain as much air and lightness as possible.

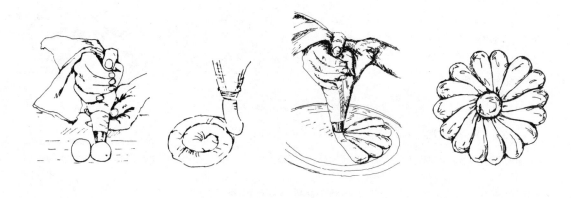

PIPED LADYFINGERS: Pipe the ladyfingers leaving ¼-inch space in between because the batter will spread sideways while piping the next finger. (After baking, the ladyfingers will be attached to each other in continuous strips. Each finger will be about 1½ inches wide.) Start piping just inside the top line and stop shortly before reaching the bottom line, moving the tip slightly forward and up to control the batter flow.

PIPED SPIRAL BASE: To pipe a spiral base, hold the pastry bag in a vertical (straight up-and-down) position, with the tube at least 1½ inches above the pan. To achieve full height and a rounded shape, the batter must be allowed to fall from the tube and not be pressed against the pan. Start in the center, moving the tip by turning the entire arm in smooth circles. To prevent gaps, allow the spirals of batter to fall against the sides—almost on top of—previous spirals. The weight of the batter will cause them to fall exactly in place.

PIPED DAISY TOP: Making this fancy design to top the charlotte involves piping a tear drop shape or shell design without ridges, radiating from the outline to center. Review piped shell borders (page 399). Finish the center with a round dot. *Pearled Sugar Effect:* After piping the fingers and daisy top, use a strainer and spoon to sift powdered sugar over them. After a few seconds, the batter will dissolve and absorb some of the sugar. For a pearled effect, sprinkle with a second coat.

Preheat the oven to 400°F.

BAKING BISCUIT:

Bake 8 to 10 minutes or until light golden brown and springy to the touch. Remove the pans to racks and cool slightly. To prevent cracking, remove from the pans while still warm with a long, thin spatula or pancake turner. For discs, invert onto a rack covered with a paper towel, peel off the backing, and reinvert onto a second rack. Finish cooling on racks and then wrap airtight.

METHOD FOR ASSEMBLING CHARLOTTE

Lining the 9-inch by 2-inch or 3-inch pan:

1. If molding the charlotte in a springform pan, you may remove the inner disc and place the outer ring directly on a serving plate. If using a loose-bottom pan, leave the inner disc in place but line with a parchment round if planning to remove the disc before serving. Lightly oil the inside of the ring.

2. If the ladyfingers have not been freshly baked, sprinkle them with a little Grand Marnier. Use the ladyfinger strips to line the inside of the ring.

3. Place the *biscuit* base in the bottom, trimming it if necessary for a snug fit.

4. Prepare the Orange Bavarian and scoop it into the lined mold. Level with a small angled spatula.

5. Add the Light Whipped Ganache and spread smoothly.

6. If not using the daisy top, garnish with the optional orange zest.

7. If using the daisy top, trim the tops of the ladyfingers encircling the mold so that they are flush with the filling and cover with the daisy top, sprinkled with Grand Marnier.

A TOUCH
OF CHOCOLATE

Strawberry Maria

SERVES 12

TIMING:
The torte should be assembled 4 hours to 1 day ahead.

SERVE:
Lightly chilled or room temperature. Break the chocolate lattice band and use the pieces for garnish.

$\mathcal{T}$he idea for this cake comes from one of my favorite things to do to a strawberry before eating it: Dip it in bittersweet chocolate and then inject it with Grand Marnier. This special creation exploits the same irresistible flavor combination and was designed with love and reverence for my editor, Maria Guarnaschelli.

SPECIAL EQUIPMENT NEEDED
- Parchment for cone to pipe the chocolate
- Pastry bag and large number 6 star tube

CAKE COMPONENTS
- 1 recipe Génoise au Chocolat (page 129), top and bottom crust removed and split horizontally
- 1 recipe Syrup flavored with Grand Marnier (page 129)
- 1 recipe Strawberry Cloud Cream (page 264)
- *Optional:*
  1 Chocolate Lattice Band (page 388), 29 inches long and 3 inches high
  Small strawberries dipped in quick-tempered chocolate

METHOD FOR ASSEMBLING CAKE
1. Spread a little Strawberry Cloud Cream on a 9-inch cardboard round to attach the cake.
2. Sprinkle each side of the cake layers with 3 tablespoons syrup.
3. Sandwich the cake layers with 1½ cups Strawberry Cloud Cream.
4. Spread ½ cup Strawberry Cloud Cream evenly on the top and ½ cup around the sides.
5. Use a large number 6 star tube and the remaining cream to pipe rows of shells on top of the cake. Start from a middle edge and reverse the direction of the shells for each row.
6. Pipe the Chocolate Lattice Band and when it just begins to dull, wrap it around the cake, peeling back one end slightly to overlap the ends.
7. Refrigerate for 10 minutes or until the chocolate is firm enough to allow easy removal of the wax paper.
8. Refrigerate the cake 30 minutes to 3 hours before serving time.
9. Garnish if desired with the chocolate-dipped strawberries.

The quintessential showoff cake. It was inspired by a Swiss candy bar containing honey and chocolate. Honey has been incorporated into almost every component but kept in the background as a subtle flavor that never becomes cloyingly sweet.

As optional décor, marzipan honey bees can be placed on the "hive" and suspended on angel hair pasta to give the illusion of bees hovering over the cake.

SPECIAL EQUIPMENT NEEDED
- A plastic squeeze dispenser is helpful for filling the hive openings with honey.

CAKE COMPONENTS
- 1 recipe Biscuit de Savoie (page 145), bottom and top crusts removed
- 1 recipe Rum Nectar: When making the syrup for the *biscuit* (page 145), use dark rum as the liqueur and add 1 teaspoon freshly squeezed lemon juice and 1 teaspoon honey.
- 1 recipe Royal Honey Buttercream (page 235).
- A 9-inch chocolate disc made with 3 ounces quick-tempered chocolate and 1-inch random holes cut in it (page 386).
- 1 recipe Nougatine Honey Crunch (page 319).
- 2 tablespoons honey in a plastic squeeze dispenser.
- *Optional:*
  Marzipan Bees (page 367)
  A few strands of dried uncooked angel hair pasta (capellini)

METHODS FOR ASSEMBLING CAKE
1. Spread a little buttercream on a 9-inch cardboard round to attach the cake.
2. Sprinkle each side of the cake layers with ⅓ cup Rum Nectar.
3. Sandwich the cake layers with ½ cup (⅛″) buttercream between each layer, ending with a layer of buttercream.
4. Use a sturdy pancake turner to lift the chocolate disc and place it on top of the buttercream.
5. Refrigerate 10 minutes or until the buttercream firms enough to hold the chocolate securely in place.
6. Frost the sides with the remaining buttercream.

Queen
Bee

**SERVES
14 TO 16**

TIMING:
The cake should be assembled 1 to 5 days ahead and refrigerated. The completed cake (without the bees) can be frozen 3 months.

SERVE:
Lightly chilled or at room temperature. (Buttercream should be warm enough to be creamy.) Score the chocolate disc with a knife that has been dipped in hot water and dried to facilitate cutting.

7. Gently press the Nougatine Honey Crunch on the sides, supporting the cake on the palm of 1 hand and tilting it slightly toward the other hand, cupped to hold the nougatine.

8. Using a plastic dispenser bottle or small teaspoon, fill the cut-outs in the chocolate with little pools of honey. For a casual look, allow some honey to drip randomly onto the chocolate or brush some on the surface in irregular patterns.

9. Refrigerate if preparing 1 day ahead. Remove from the refrigeratore at least 30 minutes before serving.

10. Garnish with the optional marzipan bees. To suspend the bees on pasta strands, use a heated metal cake tester to bore a small hole in the chocolate disc for inserting the pasta (for maximum support) or insert the pasta into the honey pools. Place a few bees near the honey pools so that they appear to be drinking the honey.

*T*hese multilayered little jewels are a treat of textures and flavors and are an adaptation of those served at my favorite Parisian two-star bistro, Chez l'Ami Louis. (I am grateful to my dear friend Heidi Trachtenberg for directing me there to taste and "figure out what's in it.") The barquette is a boat-shaped crunch of nougatine filled with soft, rum-saturated *biscuit,* topped with buttercream, and then glazed with bittersweet ganache.

Admittedly time-consuming to prepare, this recipe can be made well in advance—even frozen—and requires considerably less time and money than flying to Paris! Another advantage is that this version is a lot less sweet than the original French creation.

CAVEAT: Molding the nougatine barquettes requires advanced pastry skills.

SPECIAL EQUIPMENT NEEDED
- Lightly oiled barquette form, 3⅞ inches by 1⅝ inches (to use as a mold)
- Pastry bag and number 14 star tube (for optional piped decoration)

CAKE COMPONENTS
- 1 recipe Biscuit Roulade (page 142), cooled flat without rolling

A TOUCH
OF CHOCOLATE

Barquettes
Chez l'Ami
Louis

S E R V E S 1 2

TIMING:
All the components of these barquettes can be made several days ahead—even the nougatine if the weather is not humid. Barquettes may be assembled 1 day ahead and refrigerated or assembled 1 week ahead and frozen. (To prevent droplets of moisture and stickiness, defrost uncovered in the refrigerator for at least 6 hours

- 1 recipe Nougatine (page 318)

before removing to room
temperature.)

- Scant ¼ cup *Rum Syrup*: In a small saucepan with a tight-fitting lid, stir together 2 tablespoons water and 1 tablespoon sugar over high heat, until a full rolling boil. Cover immediately, turn off the heat, and allow to cool. Pour into a 1-cup glass measure and add 1 tablespoon dark rum. If syrup has evaporated, add enough water to equal a scant ¼ cup syrup.

- ¾ cup *Neoclassic Buttercream*: The following recipe will yield 1 cup, but the recipe requires only ¾ cup. Freeze the extra to use for cupcakes. In a bowl beat 2 large egg yolks with an electric mixer until light in color. In a small saucepan (preferably with a nonstick lining) combine ¼ cup sugar and 3 tablespoons corn syrup and cook over high heat, stirring constantly, until the sugar dissolves and the syrup comes to a rolling boil. (The entire surface will be covered by large bubbles.) Immediately transfer the syrup to a glass cup to stop the cooking. Beat the hot syrup into the yolks, avoiding pouring it on the beaters. When cool, beat in 5 ounces (10 tablespoons) softened unsalted butter until smooth and creamy.

- about ⅔ cup *Dark Ganache Frosting*: Stir ¼ cup heavy cream into 4 ounces melted bittersweet chocolate until smooth. Use at once while still soft, or reheat gently in a double boiler or for a few seconds in a microwave. (If planning to pipe the optional shell border, double the recipe and allow the remainder to cool until firm enough to pipe.)

- *Optional:*
  A small amount of whipped cream and Crystallized Lilacs or Violets (page 326).

METHOD FOR ASSEMBLING CAKE
Preheat the oven to 300°F. for warming the nougatine.

1. To cut ovals of nougatine for the barquettes, make a foil template by pressing foil into the barquette mold, then flattening it and cutting out the shape.

2. After the nougatine is cool enough to handle, cut it into 4 equal parts and roll 1 of them into a 7-inch by 4½-inch rectangle ⅛-inch thick. Keep the other 3 pieces warm in the oven with the door ajar. If the nougatine

SERVE:
Room temperature. Barquettes are most gracefully eaten by hand.

has cooled and hardened, warm it again until soft enough to mark easily.

3. Using a pizza cutter and the template as a guide, mark oval shapes on the nougatine rectangle. When cool enough to handle, cut out the ovals with scissors. Each rectangle will make 3 barquette ovals.

4. Press 1 oval into the barquette mold. The nougatine must still be warm enough to remain flexible. If necessary, return it briefly to a heat source until just flexible (not too long or it will lose its shape).

5. When cool, remove the hardened nougatine barquette from the mold and make more in the same manner. The barquettes keep for several weeks if stored airtight at room temperature away from direct sunlight, heat, and humidity.

6. Cut out ovals of *biscuit* with scissors, using the barquette mold as a guide.

7. Sprinkle ½ teaspoon rum syrup on each side of each *biscuit* oval and fit it into a nougatine shell.

8. With a small metal spatula spread 1 tablespoon buttercream in the center of each barquette, mounding it slightly in the center to create a ridge at the top. Freeze for 5 minutes to firm the buttercream.

9. Using the same size spatula spread a thin coat of ganache over the buttercream, also mounding it slightly in the center. To form an attractive center crest, hold the barquette in 1 hand and with the other hand hold the spatula against the side, angled slightly inward. Start at 1 end and bring the spatula smoothly to the other end. Repeat on reverse side.

10. Pipe a trimming of tiny ganache shells along the ridge and sides if desired. Or garnish with Crystallized Lilacs or Violets. (Use ice to chill your hand so the chocolate will stay firm enough to pipe.)

This fabulous cake is perfect for the holiday season, when fresh chestnuts abound. Although spicy and almost earthy in flavor, it is delicate enough to serve after a bountiful Thanksgiving or Christmas dinner. Chestnut Whipped Cream is a Swiss creation and so delicious it inspired my invention of the Chestnut Génoise to go with it. The band dramatically encases the cake while tying in the lovely combination of chocolate and chestnut.

SPECIAL EQUIPMENT NEEDED
• Pastry bag and large number 7 star tube

CAKE COMPONENTS
• 1 recipe Chestnut Génoise (page 122), top and bottom crusts removed
• 1 recipe Rum Syrup (page 122)
• 1 recipe Chestnut Mousse Cream (page 262)
• 1 Chocolate Band (page 387)
• *Marrons glacés* (candied chestnuts), brushed with chocolate

METHOD FOR ASSEMBLING CAKE
1. The cake can be frosted directly on a serving plate, using strips of wax paper slid under the sides. Or use a 9-inch cardboard round as a base.
2. Spread a little Chestnut Mousse Cream on the plate or cardboard round to attach the cake.
3. Sprinkle each side of the cake layers with 4½ tablespoons syrup.
4. Place the cake layers on the base and sandwich them with 2 cups chestnut mousse.
5. Reserve 1 cup chestnut mousse for piping the garnish and frost the cake with the remainder.
6. Make the Chocolate Band: The circumference of the cake is about 29 inches so cut a piece of wax paper 31 inches long. Fold the wax paper so that it is at least 1 inch higher than the finished height of the cake (about 2¾ inches). If planning to scallop the band, add an extra inch or 2. Temper 4 to 8 ounces dark chocolate, preferably *couverture,* using the classic or quick temper methods on pages 380 and 381. (If you don't temper the chocolate when melting it or if room temperature is too warm, the band may not be firm enough to wrap around the cake. Four ounces of chocolate will be enough

SERVES 12

TIMING:
The cake can be assembled 1 day ahead and refrigerated.

SERVE:
Lightly chilled or at room temperature. Break the chocolate band into pieces and use it for garnish.

for a band 3¾ inches high. Eight ounces will make a band 5 inches high.) Using an angled spatula, spread the chocolate evenly on the wax paper strip, making it a little longer than the desired length. Lift strip by the ends and transfer to clean section of counter for chocolate to set.

7. When the chocolate is firm but still malleable, use a small sharp knife to cut a straight line or a free-form scallop along 1 side. Attach the strip scallop side up around the cake. Gently pull away the ends of the wax paper and use a bit of melted chocolate to attach the overlapping ends. If the chocolate sticks to the paper, let it set longer or refrigerate for a few minutes until firm enough to release cleanly. Cut edge will break away easily on slight pressure.

8. Decorate the top of the cake with swirls of Chestnut Mousse Cream piped with a large number 7 star tube.

9. Garnish with the *marrons glacés.*

*M*y version of this classic was inspired by Confiserie Tschirren in Berne, Switzerland. They brought the recipe from Germany after World War II; and it has since become the national cake of Switzerland.

The Swiss rendition is far lighter and more delicate than the original German one, which also includes buttercream. A lofty layer of whipped cream studded with liqueur-soaked cherries is sandwiched between two thin, light layers of liqueur-moistened chocolate *génoise.* The chocolate flakes on top dissolve like snowflakes on the tongue.

In Switzerland, the Black Forest Cake is served in all *confiseries* and *konditorei* for afternoon tea, but the cake is elegant enough for fancy dinner parties as well.

SPECIAL EQUIPMENT:

- 8⅝-inch by 2⅜-inch (22-centimeter by 6-centimeter) French flan ring (page 453). Or a 9-inch springform or loose-bottom pan fitted with cardboard rounds until a depth of 2½ inches is achieved. Molding the cake this way makes it perfectly symmetrical. The French flan ring is the ideal size because the 9-inch cake layer shrinks to just that size after baking. The springform pan also works but the sides of the finished cake will not be quite as even.

- Pastry bag and a large number 6 star tube

VERY CHOCOLATE

Swiss Black Forest Cake

Schwarzwalder Kirschtorte

SERVES 10 TO 12

TIMING:
The cake should be assembled 4 to 12 hours ahead.

SERVE:
Chilled.

CAKE COMPONENTS

- 1 recipe Brandied Burgundy Cherries (page 346), well drained and the syrup reserved
- ¼ cup kirsch or brandy
- ½ recipe (1 layer) Moist Chocolate Génoise (page 132), top and bottom crusts removed and split in half horizontally to make (2) ½" layers
- 3 times the quantity of recipe for Super-Stabilized Whipped Cream (page 256) or Real Old-Fashioned Whipped Cream (page 254). The Real Old-Fashioned Whipped Cream is lighter in texture, but the cake cannot be held at room temperature for more than 15 to 30 minutes.
- ½ cup Chocolate Snowflakes (page 382)

METHOD FOR ASSEMBLING CAKE

1. Place the flan ring on a serving plate or cut out a cardboard round to fit the diameter of the ring. Or use a loose-bottom or springform pan fitted with cardboard rounds to a depth of 2½ inches.
2. Add the kirsch or brandy to the reserved cherry syrup to make ½ cup. Sprinkle each side of the cake layers with 2 tablespoons syrup.
3. Reserve 12 whole cherries for decor and cut the remaining cherries in half if they are large.
4. Reserve 2¼ cups whipped cream for the top of the cake and the rosettes. (This may be refrigerated for up to 6 hours).
5. Place 1 cake layer in the bottom of the flan ring and top with the remaining whipped cream.
6. Poke the cherries into the whipped cream, pressing some of the cut sides against the pan.
7. Use a small angled spatula to level the cream and top with the second cake layer.
8. Spread with 1 cup of the reserved whipped cream. Use a long metal spatula to create a smooth top, allowing the blade to rest on the sides of the ring to create a very even surface.
9. Cover with foil and refrigerate for at least 4 hours.
10. Wipe the sides of the ring with a warm, damp towel and lift away the ring or remove the sides of the pan.
11. Use the remaining whipped cream to decorate the top with rosettes using a large number 6 star tube. Top the rosettes with the reserved whole cherries. Spoon the chocolate snowflakes in the center.

VARIATION

Three times the quantity of recipe for White Ganache (page 278) or 1½ times the quantity of recipe for Light Whipped Ganache (page 268) may be used in place of the whipped cream for a more chocolaty effect.

*T*his summertime version of classic Black Forest Torte was inspired by Kleiner Konditorei in Zürich. It works as a frozen dessert because the liqueur keeps it from freezing too firmly. Chocolate Biscuit Roulade is an excellent base because it remains soft when frozen.

When the chocolate glaze is poured over the frozen ice cream, it sets immediately into an effortlessly even, shiny topping.

SPECIAL EQUIPMENT NEEDED
- Two 10-inch round cake pans
- 9-inch by 3-inch springform or loose-bottom pan, outside of pan wrapped with a double layer of heavy-duty foil
- Optional: pastry bag and large number 6 star tube

CAKE COMPONENTS
- 1 recipe Brandied Burgundy Cherries (page 346)
- 1 recipe Vanilla Ice Cream (page 285), using 2 table-spoons kirsch. Or 5 cups commercial vanilla ice cream
- 1 recipe Chocolate Biscuit Roulade (page 144), baked in two 10-inch round pans. When cool, trim with scissors to 9 inches (the exact diameter of the springform pan).
- Chocolate Cream Glaze: Process or chop 3 ounces bitter-sweet chocolate until very fine and place in a small bowl. Scald ⅓ cup heavy cream and add to the chocolate. Cover and allow to sit for 5 minutes. Add 1 teaspoon cognac and stir gently until the chocolate is fully melted and the mixture smooth. Cool until just tepid. When a small amount of glaze is dropped back onto the surface it should disappear smoothly.
- *Optional:*
  ¾ cup heavy cream whipped with 2 teaspoons sugar and ½ teaspoon vanilla (for rosettes)

METHOD FOR ASSEMBLING CAKE
1. Drain the cherries, reserving ¼ cup syrup. Dry the cherries well on paper towels. Refrigerate 12 whole cherries for the decor and slice the remaining cherries in half.

VERY CHOCOLATE

Black Forest Ice Cream Torte

SERVES 12

TIMING:
The cake should be assembled 1 to 5 days ahead.

2. Remove the ice cream from the freezer and allow to soften slightly until spreadable.

3. While assembling the cake, set the springform pan in a larger pan surrounded by ice to keep the ice cream from melting.

4. Sprinkle each side of the cake layers with 1 tablespoon syrup.

5. Place 1 cake layer in the bottom of the springform pan and spread with ½ the ice cream. Top with the cherries, pressing some against the sides of the pan, and top with the remaining ice cream. Arrange the second cake layer on top. Cover with foil and freeze for at least 24 hours.

6. Up to 4 hours ahead glaze the cake: Pour tepid Ganache Glaze onto the center of the cake and quickly tilt the pan to coat evenly. The glaze will set almost immediately.

7. Wipe the sides of the springform pan with a hot, damp towel and remove the sides. Refrigerate 1 hour to soften. Just before serving, pipe rosettes of whipped cream on top if desired and garnish with the reserved whole cherries.

*B*lack Forest Ice Cream Cake also makes a terrific ice-cream roll. The chocolate *biscuit* is the perfect cake to use because it stays flexible enough to roll, even when spread with ice cream. The attractive slices are even more delicious when topped with a hot ganache sauce and brandied cherries.

SPECIAL EQUIPMENT NEEDED
- 17-inch by 12-inch jelly roll pan
- Optional: pastry bag and large number 6 star tube

CAKE COMPONENTS
- 1 recipe Brandied Burgundy Cherries (page 346)
- ½ recipe Vanilla Ice Cream (page 285), using 1 tablespoon kirsch. Or 2 cups commercial vanilla ice cream
- 1 recipe Chocolate Biscuit Roulade (page 144), baked in a 17-inch by 12-inch jelly-roll pan. (Roll the cake while still hot.)

VERY CHOCOLATE

Black Forest Ice Cream Roll

SERVES 12

TIMING:
The cake should be assembled 1 to 5 days ahead.

- *Optional:*
  ¾ cup heavy cream whipped with 2 teaspoons sugar and ½ teaspoon vanilla (for rosettes)
- ½ cup Chocolate Snowflakes (page 382)
- Ganache Sauce: In a food processor grate finely 6 ounces bittersweet chocolate. Heat ¾ cup heavy cream to the boiling point and add to the chocolate. Process for a few seconds or until smooth.

METHOD FOR ASSEMBLING CAKE ROLL

1. Place a 17-inch by 12-inch jelly-roll pan in the freezer to chill.
2. Drain 1 cup of the cherries, reserving the syrup. Dry the cherries well on paper towels. Refrigerate 12 whole cherries for the decor and slice the remaining cherries in half.
3. Remove the ice cream from the freezer and allow to soften slightly until spreadable.
4. Unroll the chocolate *biscuit* onto back of chilled jelly-roll pan, leaving the towel underneath the *biscuit.*
5. Brush the cake evenly with ⅓ cup brandied cherry syrup.
6. Using an angled spatula, quickly spread the softened ice cream over the cake, leaving one inch uncovered along one long side. (Freeze any leftover ice cream.)
7. If the ice cream begins to melt, place the pan in the freezer for 5 to 10 minutes or until firm.
8. Scatter the halved cherries over the ice cream.
9. Starting with the long side that is covered with ice cream, use the towel to roll the cake. Set seam side down, cover lightly with plastic wrap, and return to the freezer.
10. When the roll is very firm, wrap airtight in foil and freeze for at least 12 hours before serving.
11. For an attractive presentation, use a large number 6 star tube to pipe 12 whipped cream rosettes on top of the roll. Place 1 whole cherry in the center of each. (Sprinkle with chocolate snowflakes. This may be done up to 3 hours ahead and the cake returned to the freezer.)
12. Gently heat the ganache sauce in a double boiler set over simmering water, stirring constantly, until hot. Or use a microwave on high power, stirring every 3 seconds. Heat the remaining cherries in any remaining syrup until just hot. Top each slice of ice cream roll with Ganache Sauce and Brandied Cherries or pass them separately.

When you cut into this fantasy cake, you will experience three distinctly different chocolates: velvety Light Whipped Ganache, moist flourless Cocoa Cloud Roll, and the lightest crisp Cocoa Meringue.

The meringue sticks keep their shape below the surface of the cake but turn mousse-like. Above the surface they stay perfectly crunchy.

I recently made this cake in a larger round shape and renamed it for the occasion: Mom's Chocolate Candle 75th Birthday Cake.

SPECIAL EQUIPMENT NEEDED
• Pastry bag and number 12 round tube

CAKE COMPONENTS
• 1 recipe Cocoa Soufflé Roll (page 140)
• 1 recipe Light Whipped Ganache (page 268)
• 1 recipe Cocoa Meringue (page 298) piped in sticks

METHOD FOR ASSEMBLING CAKE
1. Use an inverted oval pan as a template or draw a free-form 9¾-inch by 7-inch oval on cardboard. Use the cardboard oval and a sharp knife to cut 2 ovals from the cocoa roll. Carefully slide a long metal spatula under ovals to dislodge them. Remove all the cake surrounding the ovals.

2. Spread a little ganache on the cardboard oval so that cake will stick to it. Carefully slide a long pancake turner under 1 cake oval and transfer it to the cardboard.

3. Spread ⅔ of the ganache (a ½" layer) over the oval and top with the second oval. Spread the remaining ganache on the top and sides. Cake will be about 1½" high.

4. Surround the cake with some of the meringue sticks, using random lengths and pressing the flat sides against the ganache. This can be done 2 days ahead. Refrigerate uncovered.

5. Up to 1 hour before serving, insert the remaining meringue sticks into the cake so that they reach the base. All flat ends should face the same direction. For a pretty effect, dip the tops of the sticks in cocoa or powdered sugar. Allow the cake to sit at room temperature for 1 hour.

VERY CHOCOLATE

The Enchanted Forest

Le Fôret Enchanté
(le fawRAY AHNSCHAHNTAY)

SERVES 10

TIMING:
The cake can be assembled 2 days ahead and refrigerated or frozen 2 months, but it is best not to place the meringue sticks in the filling more than 1 hour before serving. If you must insert them earlier and they start to soften and tilt, simply push them slightly further into the cake.

SERVE:
Room temperature. Cut into wedges radiating from the center.

VERY CHOCOLATE

Chocolate Pine Cone

TIMING:
The cake may be assembled 2 days ahead and refrigerated.

SERVE:
Room temperature. Cut the cake into narrow curved strips, starting from the pointed end and working toward the back.

*S*mall petals of chocolate create the illusion of a pine cone. They are held in place by bittersweet ganache textured with chopped pine nuts. The ganache fills and frosts a moist light chocolate cake. Because it contains no flour this cake is marvelous for a Passover seder. The chocolate petals provide a lovely crunch against the soft and creamy textures within the cake. The petals look perky and adorable when the cake is cut, giving the individual pieces great visual distinction.

CAKE COMPONENTS
- 1 recipe Chocolate Cloud Roll (page 136).
- 1 recipe Dark Chocolate Ganache Frosting (page 269), with ⅔ cup (2.5 ounces/70 grams) chopped pine nuts added while still warm
- 6 ounces Chocolate Pine Cone Petals (page 383).
- 1 tablespoon pine nuts for garnish

METHOD FOR ASSEMBLING CAKE
1. Draw a free-form 11½-inch by 8-inch oval on a piece of cardboard, tapering 1 end slightly to resemble a pine cone. Use the oval and a sharp knife to cut 2 ovals from the Chocolate Cloud Roll. Remove the scraps and stir them into the ganache. Carefully slide a long metal spatula under the ovals to dislodge them.
2. Spread a little ganache on the cardboard oval so that cake will stick to it. Carefully slide a long pancake turner under 1 cake oval and transfer it to the cardboard.
3. Spread ½ of the ganache on the cake and top with the second cake oval. Spread the remaining ganache on the top and sides, mounding it slightly in the center.
4. Insert the Chocolate Pine Cone Petals, starting at the tapered end and, staggering each row. Place the whole pine nuts under some of the petals.

I made this traditional holiday cake for Christmas dinner in France some years ago in the home of my dear friends the Brossolets. (Something like bringing coals to Newcastle!) It quickly became a family project, with Martin, the youngest, running out to the corner store to purchase parchment for piping the meringue mushrooms and Nadège sneaking her husband's oldest rum for the ganache, saying he would have a fit if he knew it was being used for a cake. The best part, however, was when Max (Papa) contributed his antique toy buglers for the decoration.

My version uses a moist chocolate roll and whipped cream instead of the usual yellow cake roll and chocolate buttercream, which I always found too rich and heavy under the chocolate "bark."

CAKE COMPONENTS
- 1 recipe Chocolate Cloud Roll (page ~~136~~ *138*)
- 1 recipe Perfect Whipped Cream (page 253)
- 1 recipe Dark Ganache Frosting (page 269)

OPTIONAL DECOR
- Meringue Mushrooms (pages ~~298~~ *277* and 376)
- Pistachio Marzipan Ivy Leaves (page 363)
- Green Tea Pine Needles (pages 298 and 375)

METHOD FOR ASSEMBLING CAKE
1. Fill the Chocolate Cloud Roll with the Perfect Whipped Cream.
2. Chill for at least 1 hour.
3. Cut a diagonal slice from one end of the roll and place on top to form a knot.
4. Spread the ganache frosting over the log and use the tines of a fork to make lines resembling bark. Make a few round swirls with the fork on top of the knot.
5. Decorate with the meringue mushrooms, marzipan leaves, green tea pine needles, and any small appropriate figures such as porcelain elves or trumpeters.
6. Refrigerate until 1 hour before serving.

VERY CHOCOLATE

Cordon Rose Chocolate Christmas Log

Bûche de noël

SERVES 12

TIMING:
The cake can be assembled and refrigerated 2 days ahead. The meringue mushrooms should not be set on the log until serving day.

SERVE:
Lightly chilled or room temperature. Cut diagonal slices with a thin, sharp knife.

Chocolate Spike

TIMING:
The cake can be frosted 1 day ahead and does not require refrigeration. It can be frozen 2 months.

SERVE:
Room temperature.

*T*his casual, down-home cake is quick to make and elegant enough for special occasions as well. Perky little spikes of Milk Chocolate Frosting encase bittersweet Chocolate Fudge Cake.

CAKE COMPONENTS
- 1 recipe Chocolate Fudge Cake (page 60)
- 1 recipe Milk Chocolate Buttercream (page 250)

METHOD FOR ASSEMBLING CAKE

1. Frost the cake directly on a serving plate, using strips of wax paper slid under the sides. Or use a 9-inch cardboard round as a base.
2. Spread a little buttercream on the serving plate or cardboard to attach the cake.
3. Place the cake layers on the plate or cardboard and sandwich and frost with the buttercream.
4. For a decorative wave design on top, use a long serrated knife, moving it from left to right as you pull it forward.
5. For spikes, use a small metal spatula to lift the buttercream away from the sides in peaks.

Bittersweet Royale Torte

TIMING:
The cake should be filled, frosted, and refrigerated 4 hours to 1 day ahead. The glaze is most shiny when not refrigerated so it is best to glaze and decorate the cake same day as serving.

*T*his elegant torte has the flavor of a fine-quality Swiss chocolate bar but the soft, appealing texture of layer cake. An optional layer of Classic Chocolate Buttercream provides an interesting contrast in color and texture.

The chocolate roses are hand-modeled, but you can substitute real roses if you like.

SPECIAL EQUIPMENT NEEDED
- Fresh rose leaves without tears or holes
- Artist's paint brush or small metal spatula

CAKE COMPONENTS
- *Optional:*
  ½ recipe Neoclassic or Classic Chocolate Buttercream (page 228 or 230)
- 1 recipe Perfect All-American Chocolate Torte (page 56)
- 1 recipe Chocolate Cream Glaze (page 271)
- 20 chocolate rose leaves, each 2½ inches long, and 9 smaller chocolate rose leaves (page 385—use about 3 ounces of chocolate)
- 4 Red Chocolate Roses (pages 325 and 390), each slightly larger than the next

METHOD FOR ASSEMBLING CAKE

1. If using the optional Classic Chocolate Buttercream, make a 9-inch cardboard round for the base. If not using the buttercream, trim the cardboard round to 8½ inches or slightly smaller than the diameter of cake.

2. Spread a little buttercream or ganache on the cardboard round to attach the cake.

3. If using the buttercream, frost the cake and refrigerate it for at least 1 hour or until very firm.

4. Glaze the cake as per instructions in the Chocolate Cream Glaze recipe. (Use the extra glaze which falls onto the sheet to attach the rose leaves.)

5. Place the cake on a serving plate and attach the large chocolate rose leaves, using little dabs of room temperature Chocolate Cream. Angle each leaf a little to the right, overlapping slightly.

6. Use the back of a wooden spoon to make shallow depressions in the cake for the chocolate roses. Set the roses in place.

7. Insert the small chocolate rose leaves into the glaze, using little mounds of the Chocolate Cream to support them.

*R*ed "porcelainized" roses against a dark chocolate fondant-covered cake provide stunning visual appeal. This cake is at once elegant and richly, warmly inviting. The theme of long-stemmed chocolate roses was inspired by a cake I designed for *Good Housekeeping* magazine's one hundredth anniversary. The roses smell chocolaty and can even be eaten but are best saved as mementos.

This cake is a soft, full chocolate sensation; it is filled with my favorite ganache tinged with a scarlet edge of raspberry, and encased in fudgy chocolate fondant. Make this cake to celebrate the best events of your life.

NOTE: If making fondant stems for the roses, allow at least 30 minutes for them to dry before placing on the cake.

SPECIAL EQUIPMENT NEEDED

- Sheet of heavy-duty plastic, 31 inches by 6 inches (can be purchased in hardware or dime stores)

The cake can stay unrefrigerated for 1 day.

SERVE:
Room temperature.

INTENSELY CHOCOLATE

La Porcelaine

SERVES 10 TO 12

TIMING:
The cake can be assembled 1 day ahead without refrigeration or refrigerated 3 days.

SERVE:
Room temperature. Cut with a thin, sharp knife.

CAKE COMPONENTS
- 1 recipe Perfect All-American Chocolate Butter Cake (page 54)
- 1 recipe Raspberry Ganache (page 276)
- 1 recipe Chocolate Fondant (page 306)
- 8 Red Porcelain Roses (page 325) and chocolate fondant stems (see below), or fresh roses
- 20 Chocolate Rose Leaves (page 385), using about 3 ounces of chocolate and reserving the leftover melted chocolate to attach the roses and leaves

METHOD FOR ASSEMBLING CAKE
1. Spread a little ganache on a 9-inch cardboard round and center 1 cake layer on it.
2. Fill and lightly frost the cake layers with the remaining ganache. (Use 1 cup between the layers and the remaining 2 cups to frost the top and sides.) Chill until firm. Use a heavy-duty pancake turner to transfer the cake to serving plate.
3. Make the fondant disc and band: On a piece of plastic wrap, roll a piece of the chocolate fondant (about ¾ cup) into a ⅛-inch-thick disc. Transfer the plastic wrap and disc to a baking sheet and cut into a circle slightly larger than the diameter of the cake, using an inverted cake pan or lid as a guide and cutting with a pizza wheel or the tip of a sharp knife. Freeze for 10 minutes or until very firm. Invert onto another piece of plastic wrap, peel off the plastic from the bottom, and reinvert onto the cake while still firm enough to handle easily. Smooth the edges to follow the contour of the cake. Allow fondant to sit for 10 to 20 minutes or until no longer sticky. Use the palm of your hand to smooth it to a soft shine.

    For the band, you will need a piece of fondant 28¼ inches long and 4 inches high. Place the sheet of heavy-duty plastic on a flat surface. Roll the fondant into a long rope and lay it in the middle. Roll the fondant the length of the plastic into a thin band ⅛ inch thick. Using a long plastic ruler and a pizza wheel or sharp knife, even the edges, cutting the bottom edge flush with the bottom of the plastic. Use your finger to smooth the upper edge so that it thins slightly. Use the plastic to lift the fondant and curve it around the sides of the cake. Peel away the plastic, overlap the ends, and curve the upper edge gently toward the top of the cake to create a graceful free-form design.
4. Make the fondant rose stems: Roll a few small pieces of fondant into thin 4-inch ropes. Gently curve a few to

use around the base. Place on plastic wrap and allow to dry for at least 30 minutes or until stiff enough to transfer to the cake.

5. Sepals: Cut from little scraps of rolled fondant and press gently onto the roses.

6. Place the roses on top of the cake, securing them in place with dabs of melted chocolate.

7. Place the stems at the bases of the roses. Place the leaves on top, also securing with dabs of melted chocolate.

8. Store the cake uncovered or fondant will absorb moisture from the cake and become sticky.

*T*his intense chocolate cake resembles an abstract sculpture and consists of three distinct chocolate experiences: crunchy, creamy, and velvety soft.

Making it is always an exciting experience because it never looks the same way twice. Eating it is even more exciting. It seems to elicit dramatic responses. Over the years, I have received several marriage proposals at first bite and one thoroughly seduced victim suggested renaming it "The Triple Chocolate Orgasm." Why not?

CAKE COMPONENTS

- 1 recipe Light Whipped Ganache (page 268), preferably made with extra bittersweet chocolate
- 1 recipe Moist Chocolate Génoise (page 132), top and bottom crusts removed
- 1 recipe Syrup (page 132), flavored with Frangelico (hazelnut liqueur)
- 1 recipe Chocolate Praline Sheets (page 386)
- *Optional:*
  1 teaspoon powdered sugar

METHOD FOR ASSEMBLING CAKE

1. Frost the cake directly on a serving plate, using strips of wax paper slid under the sides. Or use a 9-inch cardboard round as a base. Place a dab of ganache on the base to attach the cake.

2. Sprinkle ¼ cup syrup on each side of the cake layers.

3. Place 1 layer on the plate or cardboard (support layer when lifting it with a spare cardboard round). Sandwich the layers with 1 cup ganache. Reserve ¼ cup ganache

INTENSELY CHOCOLATE

Triple Chocolate Cake

SERVES 14 TO 16

TIMING:
The cake can be assembled 1 day ahead and refrigerated. The completed cake can be frozen 4 months. Freeze until firm, wrap with plastic wrap, and then wrap in heavy-duty foil. Place in a cake container or box to protect it.

SERVE:
Room temperature. Cut with a thin, sharp knife. The chocolate praline sheets will shatter—which is part of the special effect.

to attach the praline sheets and frost top and sides of the cake with the remainder.

4. Applying the chocolate praline sheets: A warm room (80 to 85°F.) will make the sheets more flexible. (Any left-over can be remelted, retempered, and cut into decorative shapes.) Begin by laying each sheet on the counter and peeling off its top layer of paper. Lift up 1 sheet, using the bottom paper to support it, and press the long side against the cake, curving it gently to mold against the side. Carefully peel away the wax paper. Place a dab of frosting near the edge of the sheet and attach a second sheet, overlapping the first. Continue with the remaining sheets until the cake is completely surrounded. (Only 4 sheets are needed to encase a 9-inch cake so there are 2 extra in case of breakage.) If the room is warm enough, the sheets will begin to curve downward toward the center of the cake. Coax them gently into graceful, undulating shapes, allowing their natural inclination to be your guide. If the chocolate remains resolutely rigid, wave a hair drier (set on warm) briefly and evenly over the sheets. Stop before they appear to have softened and wait a few moments as it is easy to apply too much heat and melt the chocolate. To this day, this process feels slightly scary, slightly risky, and delightfully creative! A word of reassurance: Whatever happens, however it winds up looking, the sheets are always delicious.

5. A breath of powdered sugar contrasts nicely with the dark chocolate. For the finest possible dusting of sugar, place a few spoonfuls in a fine strainer and flick the side with your finger.

White Lily Cake

SERVES 8 TO 10

TIMING:
The cake can be assembled 2 days ahead. Refrigeration is unnecessary.

*T*his ethereal vision was designed as a bridal shower cake, but it would also be lovely for a special anniversary, sweet sixteen, or engagement party. The nosegay of lilies on top is contained by an antique handmade lace handkerchief given to me by my grandmother to carry at my wedding.

All the components are white or pale yellow in color, light in texture, and faintly scented with orange.

SPECIAL EQUIPMENT
• Narrow white satin ribbon to encircle cake

- 2 hatpins or pins with visible heads to hold ribbon while piping dots
- Pastry bag and numbers 1 and 8 round tubes
- Small artist's paint brush
- *Optional:*
  Lace handkerchief and nosegay of lilies of the valley

NOTE: Lilies of the valley have a short season. Your florist can order them from Holland any time of year, but they are expensive. As an alternative, you can use pale lavender cymbidiums or pale sweetheart roses.

CAKE COMPONENTS
- 1 recipe White Génoise (page 127), top and bottom crusts removed and layers split in half horizontally
- ½ cup Cointreau
- ½ recipe Orange Fruit Mousseline (page 245)
- 1 recipe Rolled Fondant with orange flower water (page 306)
- 1 recipe Royal Icing (page 294)

METHOD FOR ASSEMBLING CAKE
1. Sprinkle each side of the cake layers with 1 tablespoon Cointreau.
2. Spread a small amount of mousseline on a 9-inch cardboard round and place 1 cake layer on top.
3. Stack the remaining 3 layers on top of each other, sandwiching each with ¾ cup mousseline.
4. With a small serrated knife bevel the top edges of the cake (page 355).
5. Frost the top and sides with the thinnest possible layer of mousseline (just enough to make the fondant adhere).
6. The fondant should be rolled out on a lightly greased surface to 14 inches in diameter and ¼-inch thick. Rotate the fondant after every 2 or 3 rolls to ensure that it is not sticking. If necessary, apply more nonstick spray or shortening to the counter. With your hands palm sides down lift the rolled fondant onto the cake. Quickly smooth the top with a circular motion, starting from the center, to eliminate air bubbles. (Bubbles can be pierced with a needle and smoothed out if necessary.) Smooth the fondant against the sides, working from the top down with a semicircular motion. Oil from your hands will give the fondant a lustrous glow. Use a pizza cutter or

SERVE:
Be sure to remove the lily nosegay as the lilies are inedible. The cake should be served at room temperature. Cut with a thin, sharp knife.

small sharp knife to trim the fondant at the base of the cake. Transfer the cake to a serving plate and allow the fondant to dry overnight before decorating.

7. To attach a narrow band of satin ribbon around the cake, pin one end to the cake and then wrap the ribbon evenly around the cake's circumference, overlapping the ends and securing both ends with a second pin. Pipe tiny beads of Royal Icing with a number 1 round tube along both edges of the ribbon. When the cake has been completely encircled, the pins can be removed. For a pearl border around the base, use a number 8 round tube. If points form, flatten and smooth with a damp artist's paint brush.

8. To pipe lilies, see page 414.

9. If desired, fold the handkerchief and insert fresh lilies in the center. If cake will sit for several hours before serving, use a florist's flower sinker containing a moist sponge to keep them fresh.

Art
Deco Cake

SERVES 50

TIMING:
The cake layers must be chilled for at least 12 hours before covering with rolled fondant and another 12 hours before placing 1 tier on top of the other. Preparation should begin 4 days before serving to leave plenty of time for decorating. After tiering, the completed cake can be served the same day or refrigerated for an additional 2 days.

SERVE:
Room temperature. Remove the top tier and cut into narrow wedges. Use a thin, sharp knife dipped in hot

*T*he clean lines of the Art Deco look do not prepare you for the shock of bittersweet chocolate within this cake. The chocolate looks almost black against the pristine whiteness of the fondant. People actually gasp when the cake is cut and its velvet dark secret core revealed. The calla lilies are easy to make and in keeping with the Art Deco design.

This cake would be lovely for a small wedding or a black-tie affair. I designed it originally for Marcia Germanow, a New Jersey caterer, whose future son-in-law, an architect, had a special appreciation for the Art Deco period. She designed the entire wedding using the Art Deco motif.

Raspberry sauce and whipped cream are the perfect accompaniments for this cake, but it is also absolutely delicious on its own.

SPECIAL EQUIPMENT NEEDED
- 6-inch springform pan and 10-inch springform pan, both buttered, lined with parchment paper, and wrapped with a double layer of heavy-duty foil
- 2 larger pans to serve as water baths
- Pastry bag and numbers 3, 6, and 8 round tubes
- Artist's paint brush

STRUCTURAL SUPPORTS
- 2 cardboard rounds, 6 inches and 10 inches

- 14-inch-round black glass, silver foil-covered or mirrored serving board
- 5 inflexible plastic drinking straws

CAKE COMPONENTS

- 3 times the quantity of recipe for Chocolate Oblivion Truffle Torte (page 84), using 3 pounds chocolate, 1½ pounds unsalted butter, and 18 eggs (use a 10-quart Hobart mixer to beat eggs or beat eggs in two batches)
- 2 times the quantity of recipe for Classic Rolled Fondant (page 306)
- 1 recipe Royal Icing (page 294)
- Green liquid food color
- *Optional:*
  Silver Leaf (page 429) and 1 lightly beaten egg white or silver cord
  3 times the recipe for Raspberry Sauce (page 337)
  3 times the recipe for Perfect Whipped Cream (page 253)
- 3 Rolled Fondant Calla Lilies (page 366)

METHOD FOR ASSEMBLING CAKE

1. Prepare batter for Chocolate Oblivion Truffle Torte. Use a 10-quart or larger bowl to melt the chocolate and butter so there will be room to add the eggs. Fill the 6-inch springform pan 2 inches deep and scrape the remainder into the 10-inch pan. Bake in a pre-heated 425°F. oven in water baths 15 minutes for 6 inches, 20 minutes for 10 inches, covering loosely with foil after 5 minutes. Cool the cakes on a rack for 45 minutes and refrigerate for at least 4 hours.

2. Wipe outside of pans with a hot, damp towel. Run a thin metal spatula around the sides of the cakes and release the sides of the springform pans. Unmold the cakes onto the cardboard rounds and refrigerate for at least 12 hours. Use a hot, wet spatula to smooth surface of cakes so they are perfectly smooth. Smooth edges to bevel slightly. Return to refrigerator.

3. The fondant should be rolled out on a lightly greased surface in 2 parts: 10 inches in diameter for the smaller cake and 14 inches for the larger cake (both should be ¼-inch thick). Start with a 14-inch piece and knead any clean trimmings into remaining fondant. Rotate the fondant after every 2 or 3 rolls to ensure that it is not sticking. Apply more nonstick spray or shortening to the surface as necessary. With your hands palm sides down lift the rolled fondant onto the cakes. Quickly

water and wiped clean between cuts. If serving the raspberry sauce and whipped cream, spoon 2 tablespoons of whipped cream next to each slice of cake. Make a small hollow in it with the back of a spoon and pour 1 tablespoon raspberry sauce into it.

smooth the tops with a circular motion, starting from the center, to eliminate air bubbles. (Bubbles can be pierced with a needle and smoothed out if necessary.) Smooth the fondant gently against the sides, working from the top down with a semicircular motion. Oil from your hands will give the fondant a lustrous glow. Use a pizza cutter or small sharp knife to trim the fondant at the bases of the cakes. (Save scraps to tint green for decoration.)

4. Using a heavy-duty pancake turner, transfer the larger cake to the mirrored base, placing it off-center 1 inch from the edge. Use a loop of tape to adhere to it. Allow both tiers to dry overnight.

5. Place the bottom of the 6-inch pan off-center on the 10-inch tier 1 inch from the edge and mark a circle with a toothpick. Insert a straw into the center of the outline, straight through cake, until it reaches the cardboard bottom. Mark the straw at the surface of the cake, remove it, and cut 4 more of the same length. Insert 4 straws at even intervals *inside* the marked outline and the final one in the center.

6. Using a heavy-duty pancake turner, place the smaller tier off-center on top of the larger tier.

7. Use a toothpick and a ruler or string to mark lines on the cake for placement of the green fondant strips and Royal Icing lines. (You may instead use silver cord and pin it in place, but be sure to remove cord and all pins before serving.)

8. Using a number 3 round tip, pipe lines of Royal Icing to create 2 large V's, starting at the edge of the top tier and continuing down the sides.

9. Tint ¼ cup of the fondant scraps green, kneading well to incorporate the color. Roll out ⅛-inch thick and cut out two ½-inch strips, each 14 inches long. Work carefully when placing the strips on the cake as the fondant will stick to the fondant beneath it, making repositioning difficult.

10. If desired, apply silver leaf, using a bit of lightly beaten egg white brushed on the Royal Icing lines to make it adhere (page 412).

11. Using a number 8 tip, pipe a pearl border at the base of the bottom tier. Use a number 6 tip for the base of the 6-inch top tier. If points form, flatten and smooth them with a damp artist's paint brush.

12. Attach the calla lilies with dots of Royal Icing.

This cake was designed for my friends Connie and Marcel Desaulniers. Marcel is chef and part-owner of the Trellis Restaurant in Williamsburg, Virginia. Those fortunate enough to have dined there will understand immediately why it inspired this exquisitely detailed cake and why I intertwined our names in its décor and title.

The inside is also very special: Moist layers of Golden Butter Cream Cake are filled with an airy, fresh tasting strawberry buttercream. The intricacy of this cake makes it comparable to a tiered wedding cake but in miniature form. Make it for small family weddings, showers, anniversaries, or other very special occasions.

SPECIAL EQUIPMENT NEEDED

- 2 pastry bags and 2 number 2 round tubes
- Decorative foil or paper to cover the octagonal cardboard bases (page 463)

CAKE COMPONENTS

- 2 recipes Golden Butter Cream Cake (page 34), baked in two 9-inch by 2-inch pans or two 3-inch-high springform pans
- ½ recipe Strawberry Silk Meringue Buttercream (page 234), tinted with 3 drops of red food color
- 1 recipe Rolled Fondant (page 306), flavored with rose water
- 2 recipes Royal Icing (page 294) for the lattice. Tint ½ cup pink, using 1 drop of red food color.

METHOD FOR ASSEMBLING CAKE

1. Make the lattice panels, piping the rose with the pink icing. Pipe 1 pink rose without the rest of the panel to use for the top of the cake.

2. Make an octagonal cardboard template to place on top of the cake as a cutting guide. The baked cake will measure 8¼ inches in diameter, so first cut a circle of that size. (Plain cardboard is easier to cut than corrugated.) Then make eight 3⅛-inch connecting lines. Each line should begin and end at the edge of the circle. Cut exactly on the lines and the template is complete. Make a second octagon cardboard exactly the same to serve as the first base. (Cake will have 3 bases, each one larger than the one before.)

3. Make another larger octagon cardboard for the second base by placing the already-made template on a piece

Rose
Trellis

S E R V E S
16 TO 20

TIMING:
If the weather is not humid, the lattice panels can be piped months in advance. The cake can be assembled 1 day ahead if stored in a cool room. The lattice should not be refrigerated as humidity could soften it.

SERVE:
Room temperature. Remove the panels and set aside. Cut cake with a thin, sharp knife.

of cardboard and drawing lines in a 1½-inch border all around it. Cover with decorative foil.

4. For the third base, make another still larger octagon using the second base and the same method as for previous one (again with 1½-inch border). Use sturdy cardboard and cover it with decorative foil.*

5. Spread a small amount of buttercream on the first cardboard base.

6. Place 1 cake layer on a 9-inch cardboard round and frost with 1 cup buttercream.

7. Add a second layer and place the template on top. Cut 8 sides on the cake, cutting straight down. Remove the template.

8. Slightly bevel the edges with a serrated knife and lightly frost the top and sides with the thinnest possible layer of remaining buttercream (just enough to make the fondant adhere).

9. The fondant should be rolled out on a lightly greased surface to 15 inches in diameter and ¼-inch thick. Rotate the fondant after every 2 or 3 rolls to ensure that it is not sticking. Apply more nonstick spray or shortening to the counter as necessary. With your hands palm sides down lift the rolled fondant onto the cake. Quickly smooth the top with a circular motion, starting from the center, to eliminate air bubbles. (Bubbles can be pierced with a needle and smoothed out if necessary.) Smooth the fondant against the sides, working from the top down with a semicircular motion. Oil from your hands will give the fondant a lustrous glow. Use a pizza cutter or small sharp knife to trim the fondant at the base of the cake.

10. Using a heavy-duty pancake turner, center the cake on the second (foil-covered) cardboard base, using a loop of tape to afix it.

11. Use a second loop of tape to afix cake to third (foil-covered) cardboard base. Allow the cake to dry for at least 3 hours.

12. Attach the pink rose outline to the top of the cake with a few tiny dots of Royal Icing. Use pink Royal Icing to pipe a free-form stem and leaves.

13. Carefully attach the filligree panels to the sides with white Royal Icing. The tops of the panels should touch

*For the photograph, I used pink Plexiglas ordered from Canal Plastics in New York City. It is necessary to provide the template.

the top of the cake. The bottoms should touch the edge of the second base.

14. Using white Royal Icing, pipe tiny loops suspended from the bottom edge of the panels. Do not allow the loops to touch the base to prevent possible breakage when moving the cake if the base is at all flexible.

Valentine's Day, 1983, was the scheduled date for my only and beloved brother's San Francisco wedding. It was with great joy that several weeks before I began to prepare a most spectacular wedding cake in my New York kitchen as my present to Michael and Suzy. The cake was a triple-tiered fantasy, large enough to feed 150 guests (page 219). The tiers consisted of layers of soft white butter cake filled with silky buttercream and topped with pistachio marzipan. The frosting was a Swiss white chocolate buttercream invented especially for the occasion, and the decorations were a gold lamé ribbon from Paris, gold dragées, white chocolate rose leaves, and a dozen real pink sweetheart roses.

This was a very special cake not only because it was intended for my brother's wedding but also because it was destined to appear in the June 1983 issue of *Cook's* magazine and, subsequently, on the cover and inside thousands of recipe booklets. Its arrival in San Francisco, however, was thwarted by fate: the great snowstorm of February, 1983, which locked in the entire northeast coast—along with me and my cake.

Much planning had gone into the projected transportation of this perishable masterpiece. Because photography for the magazine had been scheduled a few weeks before the wedding, the cake needed to be frozen during the interim. An ordinary freezer was not large enough, but my butcher, Ottomanelli, upon learning that the cake was for a family wedding, sympathetically offered a safe corner in his spacious walk-in freezer.

My father, a cabinetmaker, fashioned a special protective crate to protect the cake from falling sides of beef in the freezer and from unknown hazards in the belly of the airplane.

My publicist had arranged special red-carpet treatment for me and the cake enroute, so the airline consented to store the crated cake in the plane's kitchen. Fresh roses were ordered from the florist. In short, everything was perfectly planned. The plans of mice and men . . .

The snow started falling early in the morning the day of the flight. My ninety-eight-year-old grandmother and my aunt Ruth were already on their way to California from their home in Pompano Beach, Florida. My parents had departed from Kennedy hours before. The airline suggested that I board an earlier flight than the one I had booked because the snow seemed to be coming faster than anticipated. So I picked up the cake from the butcher shop, optimistically leaving all the baggage for my husband, who was unable to leave work earlier than planned, and set out for Newark Airport.

No seats in tourist class were available on the earlier flight, so, when the airline offered me a first-class seat, I enthusiastically accepted.

Having made sure that The Cake was safely stored in the kitchen below, I sat looking out the window, watching the snow steadfastly falling, feeling relieved to have a seat on what might be the last flight leaving Newark that day. "Let's go! Let's go!" I thought, as the snow fell thicker and thicker. Then came the inevitable announcement: "We are now below minimal clearance . . . but this flight has not been officially canceled." A fellow passenger snickered at the word *officially*. The words *below minimal* and *canceled* were ignored by my brain as I desperately clung to the *not officially canceled* part. Gradually, the horrible truth hit me with full impact: Not only was my brother not to have this much planned and most extraordinary wedding cake, he was not going to have *me* at his wedding either!

When it was officially decided that the passengers were to disembark, I obtained permission to store my cake in the terminal's refrigerator. I then called my husband to ask him to pick me up—only to hear that the storm had become so severe that the streets in Manhattan were impassable. He suggested that I take the airport bus to the Port Authority bus terminal.

With some indignation I got on line for the bus and soon considered myself lucky to have been the last person to get a seat on the last bus. Four hours later I began to think I would have been luckier to have missed that bus and luckier still to get back to the airport! All traffic had stopped. The bus had no bathroom and no gas gauge. The driver was forced to open the door for ventilation, admitting exhaust fumes from countless other vehicles. The situation was unbelievable. Would we freeze to death, stranded between Newark and the Lincoln Tunnel? How could this civilized, familiar terrain have become a wilderness over which we had no control? Would people from nearby houses take us in, or would they panic like those in lifeboats fleeing the sinking *Titanic* and bar their doors?

Passengers started to take sides. The majority wanted to attempt a turnaround and go back to the airport. The unrealistic few who kept insisting that they wanted to go to Manhattan were transferred to a bus behind us. Several young male passengers forged into the snow-filled highway to direct traffic and give us space to turn around. Despite my distress, I could not help but notice what a splendid study of human nature this emergency was presenting. Already our small bus had become a mini-community.

With all remaining passengers in full agreement, we set out for the airport, but got stuck in a drift at the foot of a hill four miles from the first terminal. The snow was already several feet deep, and I started to wonder how long it takes to get frostbitten without boots. Luckily, a nearby taxi offered (after much arm-twisting and demands for fare) to take six of us up to the main terminal. The rest would have to walk.

The first terminal (where my cake was stored) was dark and locked for the night, but the second terminal, a quarter mile down the road, was filled with people who had already commandeered sleeping areas for themselves and their families. Hordes of people were stretched out on every available chair and all over the floor. Any food in the canteens had long since been consumed. I found a relatively cozy spot on the red-carpeted snail-shaped section of the baggage-unloading area and curled up to sleep. (Here, at last, was my red-carpet treatment!) I slept fitfully all night, awakened occasionally by the surrounding noise and the empty feeling in my stomach from not having eaten since the night before. Remembering that I was going to miss the wedding, I would cry against my better judgment and then go back to sleep. There was nothing else to do.

When dawn broke, we were informed that no planes would be able to take off until one or two days later. I managed to locate a manager and asked if the airline would hold my cake until I could come back by car to reclaim it. He looked at me in a puzzled way and said: "There is no more cake." When he smiled, I thought he was teasing me. "Well, what happened to the cake?" I asked, pretending to go along with the ill-fated joke. "Oh, we ate the cake," he said with imperturbable calm. "You what!" I practically screamed. He then explained, with total confidence that I would see the logic of his decision, that there had been no room in the terminal refrigerators for food from the stranded planes so the crew had removed my cake to make room for those incomparable airline delicacies. Then, evidently assuming (incorrectly) that the cake would spoil unrefrigerated, they ate it to keep it from going to waste. Not even the special crate remained. (Could they have been that hungry?)

Somehow, hours later, I got back to our Manhattan apartment. The streets were like ski trails, and it didn't seem at all like New York. My husband greeted me at the door and said there was no point crying. I had already reached that conclusion myself, and it didn't help.

I eventually got a full report on the wedding from my mother, which is about as close as I could get to having been there myself. (She always knows what I'm most interested in hearing.) For a wedding cake a few of my brother's friends had chipped in and purchased one of those hulking white baroque numbers, adorned with plastic Grecian columns and insipid cupids. A lot had been left over because, according to my mother, it was very, very sweet.

Months later I presented my brother and new sister-in-law with a framed photo of their intended wedding cake, clipped from *Cook's*, together with an article from *The New York Times* in which the cake had been immortalized by Marion Burros as one of the great mishaps of the snowstorm of '83. Eating the cake ourselves couldn't have been as unforgettable.

SEQUEL: Seven months later I baked and frosted one layer exactly like the original and dropped it off in San Francisco, enroute from teaching in Alaska to food-touring Japan. When I saw the first piece of cake enter my brother's mouth, I could finally lay to rest the whole sad episode. But it will be only with the greatest reluctance that I will ever attempt to fly a wedding cake anywhere again.

THE
ST. CLEMENT
WEDDING
CAKE OR THE
BLACKOUT
OF 1981

The events surrounding this wedding were so extraordinary it made *The New York Times* under the title "A Heaven Made in Marriage." Courtney was an artist from Texas marrying a sculptor from New York. The cake she had commissioned was enormous—large enough to feed at least 280 people, although the guest list was only 150, because "We Texans eat big." Courtney even presented me with a watercolor of her cake-to-be: chocolate covered with white fondant and adorned with long-stemmed roses on each tier. She was a dream to work with. She knew just what she wanted, but understood that certain compromises would be necessary due to the fact that the "medium" of the art material was to be nothing short of delicious to eat.

The theme of the wedding, "a marriage made in heaven," was to be executed in a friend's SoHo loft, decorated to look as though the event were actually taking place in—you guessed—heaven.

In addition to a ten thousand dollar budget, Courtney had a very talented and willing assortment of relatives and friends who were generous with their time and created some fantastic effects. Courtney herself, having worked as a set designer, devoted a year to creating eighteen-foot silver-sprayed facsimiles of her two favorite skyscraper tops: the Empire State and the Chrysler buildings. Her brother Tom, an inventor and art restorer for Sotheby's, strung tiny lights to resemble stars. Dry ice created billowing clouds underfoot and a taxidermist preserved the white pigeon wings worn by the angelic blonde ring bearer.

Courtney's friend Evelyn, a Broadway costume designer, created a white pearl-appliquéd silk chiffon dress, with petal-shaped layers inspired by the Chrysler building—and lovingly embroidered Courtney's name in white inside the white waistband. Another friend designed a sapphire wedding ring, again inspired by the Chrysler building's Art Deco peak. Even the groom's ex-wife contributed Texas chili!

Weeks before the wedding I started sculpting pink marzipan roses. Courtney's brother cast plaster of Paris leaf molds so I could create realistic marzipan leaves. The stems were to be piped on the cake after the roses were in place, using pale green royal icing.

Having never made a 15-inch chocolate cake before, I started baking a few days earlier than usual. Fortunately. I assumed (logically though incorrectly) that a larger cake would need extra baking powder in proportion to its other ingredients. Five minutes before the 15-inch layers were done I checked them by gently pressing the centers with my fingertip. Not quite.

Five minutes later, just as I opened the oven door, all the lights in the apartment went out and even the refrigerator motor came to an ominous halt. I could not see the cake, but I would feel it. I extended my index finger to where the center of one of the layers should be. Where minutes before there had been a cake, none was to be found. I carefully lowered my finger another inch and there was the cake. My aim had been impeccable—the center had sunk to the bottom of the pan.

It means only one thing when a cake falls five minutes before it has finished baking: The structure was not strong enough and the resulting cake will be heavy and somewhat fudgy. (Our son Michael was delighted because he knew he would get to eat the "failed" layers.) It turned out, after much analysis, research, and more baking the following day, that the larger the cake, the *less* baking powder is required.

The coincidence, though, was staggering. The cake had chosen to fall the exact moment of one of the two major New York City blackouts. Unfortunately, the reporter for the *Times* could not resist temptation. He dramatized the story by writing that my cake had fallen because of the blackout (my oven was gas, not electric) and blithely implied that I had sold a fallen thousand-dollar cake!

Actually, this cake was most instructive. I went on to develop precise formulas and techniques for achieving enormous, showpiece cakes with the same soft, downy texture and exquisite flavor as small cakes. If you use the same kind of cake flour (either Softasilk or Swan's Down) and carefully weigh or measure the other ingredients, you will be very happy with the results. As one little boy I overheard at a wedding put it: "But wedding cakes aren't suppose to taste this good!"

Bleeding Heart Wedding Cake

(Designed for Trish Fleming)

S E R V E S 1 5 0

TIMING:
All the components can be prepared ahead. It is fine to bake the cake 3 to 4 days ahead and refrigerate because the fondant will keep it fresh. The fondant must be applied at least 12 hours before tiering the cake.

SERVE:
Room temperature. For cutting instructions, see page 537.

When Trish Fleming ordered her wedding cake, she brought me a picture of bleeding hearts and asked if it was possible to design a cake around this theme. It was a delightful challenge and the blossoms and leaves were fun to pipe.

Because Trish is an industrial designer, she had strong feelings about the proportion of the tiers. She wanted them to be 5, 9 and 13 inches instead of the traditional 6, 9, and 12. As 5-inch pans are almost extinct, I have re-created the proportions back to the standard ones. If you prefer the original proportions and have 5-inch cake pans or soufflé dishes, refer to the chart on page 490 for batter quantities (use 1½ times the Rose factor for the 5-inch layers).

I chose Raspberry Buttercream as the filling to echo the pink blossoms on the rolled fondant.*

SPECIAL EQUIPMENT NEEDED
(see introduction to Master Cakes on page 481)
• 2 pastry bags, numbers 14 and 22 star tubes, and numbers 2 and 5 round tubes

STRUCTURAL SUPPORTS
• 3 cardboard rounds: 6 inches, 9 inches, and 12 inches
• Cake plate or foil-covered serving board at least 15 inches in diameter
• Inflexible plastic drinking straws

CAKE COMPONENTS
• 1 recipe for 3-Tier Yellow Butter Wedding Cake to Serve 150 (page 484)
• *Optional:*
  3 times the quantity of the recipe for Syrup flavored with framboise (page 505)
• 1 large scale recipe (8 cups) for Neoclassic or Classic Buttercream (page 516 or 517). Beat in 1 cup Raspberry Sauce (page 337) and add enough red food color to attain a pale pink color.
• 1 recipe (7.5 pounds/3 kilograms, 402 grams) lemon-flavored Classic Rolled Fondant for a 3-Tier Cake to Serve 150 (page 532)

* Review Frosting, Tiering, and Storing a Wedding Cake (page 533) and covering a cake with Rolled Fondant (page 360).

- 2 times the quantity of recipe for Royal Icing (page 294). Use red food color to tint the blossoms pink and some green paste food color for the leaves
- *Optional:*
  Gold monogram (page 412)

METHOD FOR ASSEMBLING CAKE

1. Level the cake layers and bevel the edges (page 355). Sprinkle with optional syrup for extra moistness.

2. Spread a small amount of buttercream on the 3 cardboard rounds and place a cake layer on each. Frost the tops with a generous layer of buttercream (about ⅜-inch thick) and add the second layers. There are now 3 tiers. Frost the top and sides of each tier with the thinnest possible layer of buttercream—just enough to make the fondant adhere.

3. Roll out ¾ of the fondant ¼-inch thick and 17 inches in diameter and cover the largest tier. Trim the bottom flush with the base of the cake and knead all the clean scraps into the remaining fondant.

4. Attach the tier to the serving board with several loops of tape. The fondant should be allowed to harden for at least 12 hours before tiering cake.

5. Cover the other 2 tiers with the remaining fondant, rolled out ¼-inch thick (14 inches in diameter for the 9-inch tier and 11 inches in diameter for the 6-inch tier). Allow all 3 tiers to sit uncovered at least 12 hours to firm.

6. Center a 9-inch cake pan on the 12-inch tier and use a toothpick or skewer to mark a circle. Use a 6-inch cake pan as a guide to mark a circle on the 9-inch cake. Working *inside* the marked circle on the 12-inch tier, insert a straw straight through the cake until it reaches the cardboard bottom. Mark the place on the straw where it reaches the top of the cake. Remove the straw and cut 6 more of the same length. Insert the 6 straws at even intervals *inside* the marked circle. Place the final straw in the center. Repeat the procedure for the 9-inch tier, using 5 straws.

7. Using 1 or 2 large spatulas, place the 9-inch tier on top of the 12-inch tier. Carefully center the 6-inch tier on the 9-inch tier.

8. Using a number 22 star tip and white Royal Icing, pipe a shell border at the base of each tier. Save a small amount of icing to pipe blossom tips and use the rest

to make the pink and green icing. Remember that the color will continue to deepen for several hours as it sits.

9. Pipe bleeding heart stems and leaves and then the blossoms (page 414).

10. Place optional monogram on top of cake.

*T*he warmth and elegance of chocolate and gold represents a sophisticated break with tradition. Dark chocolate cake blends with luscious praline buttercream and crunchy hazelnuts.*

SPECIAL EQUIPMENT NEEDED
(see introduction to Master Cakes on page 481)
- 3 pieces of gold lamé ribbon (page 463): 20 inches, 30 inches and 40 inches

CAKE COMPONENTS
- 1 recipe 3-Tier Chocolate Butter Wedding Cake to Serve 150 (page 486)
- *Optional:*
  3 times the quantity of recipe for Syrup flavored with Frangelico (page 505)
- 1 recipe (13 cups) for Silk Meringue Praline Buttercream for a 3-Tier Cake (page 526)
- 1⅔ cups (8 ounces/227 grams) hazelnuts, skinned, toasted, and coarsely chopped to equal 2 cups (page 324)
- Bittersweet Chocolate Curls (a 4-ounce block of chocolate) (page 382)
- Red Chocolate Rose (pages 325 and 390)
- Marzipan Stem and Leaves (page 363)

STRUCTURAL SUPPORTS
- 3 cardboard rounds: 6 inches, 9 inches, and 12 inches
- Cake plate or foil-covered serving board at least 15 inches in diameter (flat part must be at least 12 inches)
- Inflexible plastic drinking straws

METHOD FOR ASSEMBLING CAKE
1. Level the cake layers. Sprinkle with optional syrup for extra moistness.

2. Spread a small amount of buttercream on all 3 card-

* Review Frosting, Tiering, and Storing a Wedding Cake (page 533).

Chocolate Praline Wedding Cake

(Designed for Chocolatier magazine)

S E R V E S   1 5 0

TIMING:
All the components can be prepared ahead. It is best to bake the cake no more than 1 day before assembling it. The completed cake can be kept at room temperature for 1 day before serving or it can be frozen 2 months. Allow 24 hours to defrost in the refrigerator and at least 4 additional hours at room temperature.

SERVE:
Room temperature. For cutting instructions, see page 537.

board rounds and place a cake layer on each. Frost the tops with ¼ inch of buttercream and top with the second layers. There are now 3 tiers. Frost the top and sides of each tier with the remaining buttercream.

3. Apply the chopped nuts to the sides of each tier (page 324).

4. Attach the largest tier to the serving board with several pieces of double-faced tape or loops of tape.

5. Invert a 9-inch cake pan over the center of the 12-inch tier and lightly touch the frosting to mark a circle. Invert a 6-inch cake pan over the 9″ cake and mark a circle on the 9-inch cake. Working *inside* the marked circle on the 12-inch tier, insert a straw straight through the cake until it reaches the cardboard bottom. Mark the place on the straw where it reaches the top of the cake. Remove the straw and cut 6 more of the same length. Insert the 6 straws at even intervals *inside* the marked circle. Place the final straw in the center. Repeat the procedure for the 9-inch tier, using 5 straws.

6. Using 1 or 2 large spatulas, place the 9-inch tier on top of the 12-inch tier. Carefully center the 6-inch tier on the 9-inch tier. Using a spoon, distribute the chocolate curls over the exposed areas of each tier. Do not place chocolate curls on top of the cake.

7. Encircle the cake with the ribbon if desired.

8. Place the chocolate rose, marzipan stem, and leaves on top.

*C*reamy cheesecake, marbled with apricot and frosted with White Chocolate Cream Cheese Frosting. (Where is it written that the bride can't have her favorite cake as a tiered wedding cake?)

This cake was designed for my niece and her bridegroom and was featured in Martha Stewart's fabulous book *Weddings.* The layers do not require a base, but almond *biscuit* is a lovely option.*

SPECIAL EQUIPMENT NEEDED
(see introduction to Master Cakes on page 481)
- 3 pieces of gold lamé ribbon (page 463): 20 inches, 30 inches, and 40 inches
- Pastry bag and number 22 star tube

* Review Frosting, Tiering, and Storing a Wedding Cake (page 533).

Golden Glory Wedding Cheesecake

(Designed for the Joan Beranbaum/Judge John Stackhouse Wedding)

SERVES 150

TIMING:
All the components can be prepared ahead except for

the spun sugar, which will last for several hours if the weather is not humid. The cake should be assembled 1 day ahead and refrigerated.

SERVE:
Lightly chilled or room temperature. For cutting instructions, see page 537.

CAKE COMPONENTS
- 1 recipe 3-Tier Wedding Cheesecake to Serve 150 (page 507)
- 1 large-scale recipe Apricot Swirl Filling for Cheesecake (page 510)
- 1 recipe (13 cups) White Chocolate Cream Cheese Frosting for a 3-Tier Cake to Serve 150 (page 525)
- *Optional:*
Two recipes Almond Biscuit (page 144), cooled flat
- 1 cup Apricot Topaz Jewel Glaze (page 329)
- Fresh wild violets or Crystallized Violets (page 326)
- Spun Sugar (page 316)

STRUCTURAL SUPPORTS
- 3 cardboard rounds: 6 inches, 9 inches and 12 inches (preferably the sort that has been coated with glassine to waterproof them)
- Cake plate or foil-covered serving board at least 15 inches in diameter
- Inflexible plastic drinking straws

METHOD FOR ASSEMBLING CAKE
1. Spread a thin layer of frosting on all 3 cardboard rounds.
2. If using the optional *biscuit*, cut a 9-inch and a 6-inch disc from 1 sheet and a 12-inch disc from the other. (The baked *biscuit* is 11¾ inches by 16¾ inches so you will not get a full 12-inch circle). Place a *biscuit* disc on each cardboard round.
3. Unmold the cheesecake layers onto the *biscuit* or cardboard rounds and remove the parchment. There are now 3 tiers.
4. Frost the top and sides of each tier and chill thoroughly. Reserve any leftover icing at room temperature for piping the borders.
5. Attach the largest tier to the serving board with several pieces of double-faced tape or loops of tape.
6. Invert a 9-inch cake pan over the center of the 12-inch tier and lightly touch the frosting to mark a circle. Invert a 6-inch cake pan over the 9-inch cake and mark a circle on the 9-inch cake. Working *inside* the marked circle on the 12-inch tier, insert a straw straight through the cake until it reaches the cardboard bottom. Mark the place on the straw where it reaches the top of the cake. Remove the straw and cut 6 more of the same

length. Insert the 6 straws at even intervals *inside* the marked circle. Place the final straw in the center. Repeat the procedure for 9-inch tier using 5 straws.

7. Using 1 or 2 large spatulas, place the 9-inch tier on top of the 12-inch tier. Carefully center the 6-inch tier on the 9-inch tier.

8. Encircle the cake with the ribbons if desired.

9. With a small spoon or metal spatula, carefully spread the apricot glaze on each layer.

10. Using a number 22 star tube, pipe the remaining frosting in a shell border on the edge of each tier. (Chill your hand with ice from time to time to maintain the firm consistency of the frosting.)

11. Up to 4 hours ahead, make the spun sugar and wrap it around the base of the cake. Shortly before presenting the cake, place fresh violets on top and in the sugar strands. (If using crystallized violets, they can be placed as soon as the spun sugar is wrapped around the cake.)

*T*his is the cake that made history—the one that, while en route to my brother's San Francisco wedding, was eaten instead by airline employees during a snow layover! I shall always be grateful to Marion Burros and Alex Ward, who immortalized the cake in *The New York Times* and helped to assuage a good deal (but not all) of the pain!

The flavors and textures of this cake are unique. The soft white butter cake is frosted with Classic Buttercream. A thin layer of Pistachio Marzipan separates the buttercream from the firmer Crème Ivoire Deluxe (white chocolate buttercream).*

SPECIAL EQUIPMENT NEEDED
(see introduction to Master Cakes (on page 481)
- 3 pieces of gold lamé ribbon (page 463): 20 inches, 30 inches, and 40 inches
- Pastry bag and number 18 star tube

* Review Frosting, Tiering, and Storing a Wedding Cake (page 533).

Pistachio and Rose Wedding Cake

(Designed for Michael Levy)

S E R V E S   1 5 0

TIMING:
All the components can be prepared ahead. It is best to bake the cake no more than 1 day before assembling it. The completed cake can be

kept at room temperature for 1 day or it can be frozen 2 months.

SERVE:
Room temperature. For cutting instructions, see page 537. Be sure to remove the sweetpeas before serving.

STRUCTURAL SUPPORTS
- 3 cardboard rounds: 6 inches, 9 inches, and 12 inches
- Cake plate or foil-covered serving board at least 15 inches in diameter (flat part must be at least 12 inches)
- Inflexible plastic drinking straws

CAKE COMPONENTS
- 1 recipe 3-Tier White Butter Wedding Cake to Serve 150 (page 484)
- *Optional:*
  3 times the quantity of recipe for Syrup flavored with Pistasha or framboise (page 505)
- 1 large-scale recipe (8 cups) Neoclassic or Classic Buttercream (page 516 or 517)
- 1 large-scale recipe (1.25 pounds/567 grams) Pistachio Marzipan (page 530)
- 1 large-scale recipe (5.25 cups) Crème Ivoire Deluxe (page 522)
- 2 tablespoons (1 ounce/28 grams) gold dragées
- Rose and sweetpea corsage cake top (6 inches by 3 inches) purchased from a florist
- 18 pink sweetheart roses and lavender sweetpeas
- 36 white chocolate rose leaves (page 385)

METHOD FOR ASSEMBLING CAKE
1. Level the cake layers. Sprinkle with optional syrup for extra moistness.

2. Spread a small amount of buttercream on all 3 cardboard rounds and place a cake layer on each. Frost the tops with ¼ inch of the buttercream and top with the second layers. There are now 3 tiers. Frost the top and sides of each tier with the remaining buttercream.

3. Divide the marzipan in half. Roll ½ between 2 sheets of plastic wrap into a thin circle. Peel the top layer of plastic wrap off marzipan. Using a lightly greased 12-inch cake pan as a guide, cut a circle of marzipan with a sharp knife or pizza cutter. Knead the marzipan scraps into the remaining marzipan. Roll the remaining marzipan between 2 sheets of plastic wrap into a thin circle. Using a 9-inch cake pan as a guide, cut out a circle. Knead the marzipan scraps together and roll out between 2 sheets of plastic wrap into a thin circle. Using a 6-inch cake pan as a guide, cut out a circle. It is easiest to apply marzipan if it has been frozen for a few minutes to make it less flexible. Pick up the 12-

inch marzipan disc. Invert it (the marzipan will stick to the plastic) and position it over the 12-inch tier. Support it with your palm if necessary and lay it on the cake. It will be difficult to move once it is set down. Invert the 9-inch and 6-inch marzipan discs in the same manner.

4. Frost the top and sides of each tier with Crème Ivoire Deluxe.

5. Attach the largest tier to the serving board with strips of double-faced tape or several loops of tape. Allow the frosting to set until firm.

6. Center a 9-inch cake pan on the 12-inch tier and use a toothpick or skewer to mark a circle. Use a 6-inch cake pan to mark a circle on the 9-inch cake. Working *inside* the marked circle on the 12-inch tier, insert a straw straight through the cake until it reaches the cardboard bottom. Mark the place on the straw where it reaches the top of the cake. Remove the straw and cut 6 more of the same length. Insert the 6 straws at even intervals *inside* the marked circle. Place the final straw in the center. Repeat the procedure for the 9-inch tier using 5 straws.

7. Using 1 or 2 large spatulas, place the 9-inch tier on top of the 12-inch tier. Carefully center the 6-inch tier on the 9-inch tier.

8. Encircle the cake with the ribbons if desired and place gold dragées in free-form swirls, pressing them lightly into the sides. (A tweezer helps to pick them up.)

9. Using a number 18 star tube, pipe a shell border of Crème Ivoire Deluxe on the edge of each tier.

10. Place the corsage on top and the sweetheart roses and chocolate leaves around the tiers up to 4 hours ahead of serving. To keep sweetpeas from wilting, use small flower sinkers (page 463), camouflaged by the chocolate rose leaves, or place on cake no more than 30 minutes before serving.

Dotted
Swiss Dream

(Designed for Bon Appétit
magazine)

〰〰〰〰〰〰

T H R E E - T I E R
C A K E
S E R V E S I 5 0
F O U R - T I E R
C A K E †
S E R V E S 2 7 5

TIMING:
All the components can be prepared ahead, in fact, the marzipan roses can be prepared months ahead. (I recommend starting to make them the day the engagement is announced!) It is fine to bake the cake 3 to 4 days ahead as the fondant will keep it fresh even without refrigeration. (The decorated cake may be refrigerated if desired.) Fondant must be applied at least 12 hours before tiering the cake.

SERVE:
Room temperature. For cutting instructions, see page 537.

When I first designed this wedding cake, I had a vision of pearls on the top tier cascading down the alabaster fondant sides. But perhaps even more than the poetic image of pearls, this cake is reminiscent of the ethereal fabric called dotted Swiss. And many a bride who ordered this cake designed her entire wedding around the theme, from bridesmaids' dresses to tablecloths!

In the years following the cake's first appearance, the outside has remained essentially the same. But instead of a lemon curd filling, I now use my newest buttercream creation: Lemon Curd Mousseline. Either a white or yellow layer cake blends beautifully with the filling.*

SPECIAL EQUIPMENT NEEDED:
(See introduction to Master Cakes (on page 481.)
• Pastry bag and numbers 3, 4, 6, and 8 round tubes

STRUCTURAL SUPPORTS
• 3 cardboard rounds: 6 inches, 9 inches, and 12 inches
• Cake plate or foil-covered serving board at least 15 inches in diameter
• Inflexible plastic drinking straws

CAKE COMPONENTS
• 1 recipe 3-Tier White or Yellow Wedding Cake to Serve 150 (page 484).
• *Optional:*
3 times the quantity of recipe for Syrup flavored with Barack Palinka, apricot brandy, or framboise (page 505)
• 1½ times the quantity of recipe (6¾ cups) for Fruit Mousseline (page 245), using 1 recipe of Lemon Curd (page 340). With Lemon Curd it will be almost 8 cups.
• 1 recipe (7.5 pounds/3 kilograms, 402 grams) Classic Rolled Fondant for a 3-Tier Cake to Serve 150 (page 532), flavored with rosewater
• 3 times the quantity of recipe (2¼ cups) for Royal Icing (page 294).
• 13 pale pink marzipan roses (page 365) or fresh sweetheart roses. You will need 1 recipe of Marzipan for Modeling for the marzipan roses (page 322). Make a large

---

* Review Frosting, Tiering and Storing a Wedding Cake (page 533), covering a cake with Rolled Fondant (page 360), and piping Royal Icing pearls (page 402).
† See page 224 for four-tier instructions.

full-blown rose with 3 rows of petals for the top and smaller roses with 2 rows of petals for the tiers.

METHOD FOR ASSEMBLING CAKE

1. Level the cake layers and bevel the edges (page 355). Sprinkle with optional Syrup for extra moistness.

2. Spread a small amount of mousseline on all 3 cardboard rounds and place a cake layer on each. Frost the tops with a generous layer of mousseline (⅜-inch thick) and top with the second layers. There are now 3 tiers. Frost the top and sides of each tier with the thinnest possible layer of mousseline—just enough to make the fondant adhere.

3. Roll out ¾ of the fondant (5 pounds/2 kilograms, 268 grams) ¼-inch thick and 17 inches diameter and cover the 12-inch tier. Trim the bottom flush with the base of the cake and knead all the clean scraps into remaining fondant.

4. Attach the 12-inch tier to the serving board with strips of double-faced tape or several loops of tape. The fondant should be allowed to harden for at least 12 hours before tiering the cake.

5. Cover the remaining tiers with fondant, rolled ¼-inch thick (3½ pounds/1 kilogram, 587 grams, 14 inches in diameter for the 9-inch tier, 2 pounds/907 grams, 11 inches in diameter for the 6-inch tier). Allow all 3 tiers to sit uncovered at least 12 hours to firm.

6. Center a 9-inch cake pan on the 12-inch tier and use a toothpick or skewer to mark a circle. Use a 6-inch cake pan to mark a circle on the 9-inch cake. Working *inside* the marked circle on the 12-inch tier, insert a straw straight through the cake until it reaches the cardboard bottom. Mark the place on the straw where it reaches the top of the cake. Remove straw and cut 6 more of the same length. Insert the 6 straws at even intervals *inside* the marked circle. Place the final straw in the center. Repeat the procedure for the 9-inch tier using 5 straws.

7. Using 1 or 2 large spatulas, place the 9-inch tier on top of the 12-inch tier. Carefully center the 6-inch tier on the 9-inch tier.

8. Using a number 8 round tube and the Royal Icing, pipe a pearl border at the base of the 12-inch tier (page 402). If points form, flatten and smooth them with a damp artist's paint brush. Make a second row on top of the

first if desired, piping the pearls between those on the first row. Use a number 6 round tube for the 9-inch base border and number 4 round tube for the 6-inch base border. Use a number 3 round tube to pipe pearls on the sides of the tiers.

9. Place 4 roses around the base of the cake, 4 more on the 12-inch tier, 4 on the 9-inch tier, and the full-blown rose on top. Attach them with large dots of Royal Icing.

SPECIAL INSTRUCTIONS FOR A FOUR-TIER CAKE

ADDITIONAL EQUIPMENT NEEDED
- 15-inch cardboard round
- 18-inch serving board (instead of the 15-inch one)
- Lightweight wooden dowels for the bottom tier. (They are needed to support the weight of the 3 large layers. You will need a heavy-duty clipper or saw to cut them.)

ADDITIONAL CAKE COMPONENTS
- Two 15-inch cake layers (see chart on page 490)
- *Optional:*
  A total of 6 times the quantity of recipe for Syrup flavored with Barack Palinka, brandy, or framboise (page 505)
- A total of 1 large-scale recipe (11 cups) Lemon Mousseline (page 515), using 1¾ cups Lemon Curd (page 340). With Lemon Curd, it will be about 13 cups.
- A total of 5 recipes Rolled Fondant (12.5 pounds) (page 306)
- A total of 6 recipes Royal Icing (4.5 cups) (page 294)
- A total of 21 marzipan roses (8 for the base, 4 on each tier, and the full-blown rose on top) (pages 322 and 365)

NOTE: *Rolling Fondant for a 15-inch Bottom Tier:* Start by rolling 5½ to 6 pounds/2 kilograms, 600 grams, (about ½) of the fondant, into a round 20 inches in diameter and ¼-inch thick. Cover the 15-inch tier, trim, and knead the clean scraps into the remaining fondant.

When rolling fondant for the 15-inch and 12-inch tiers, use a piece of plastic wrap to cover the fondant and keep it from drying during the extended time needed to roll the larger diameters.

PART II

COMPLEMENTARY ADORNMENTS FOR ALL CAKES

Butter- cream Frostings and Fillings

*T*hese days it seems that rich buttercreams are suffering in favor of lighter counterparts made with whipped cream or fruit. Some people even prefer their cakes unfrosted. There are many cakes in this book—such as chiffon cakes, angel food cakes, fruitcakes, and my favorite coffee cake, to name just a few—which are more delicious unfrosted. But there is a time and a place for frostings and certain cakes simply cry out for them. One of the most satisfying cakes, Praline Brioche Cake, combines four basic textures: *soft* (La Brioche cake), *moist* (Rum Syrup), *creamy* (Praline Silk Meringue Buttercream), and *crunchy* (chopped hazelnuts).

Special occasion cakes become more festive and memorable with elaborately piped buttercream decorations. When you plan to make a major cake, however, it is important to remember that it is intended to be eaten. Large buttercream swirls and festoons mean large servings of buttercream in proportion to the cake.

My philosophy is that the cake is the main event and should be featured. Buttercream is lovely but should be kept to a minimum. I am not a proponent of seven-layer cakes which contain as much buttercream as cake.

Butter cakes which are velvety and firmer than sponge-type cakes lend themselves to buttercream frostings, whereas lighter whipped cream frostings are more suitable for *génoise* and *biscuit*. Buttercreams can be used for the lighter cakes too if not applied too thickly.

I think that many people object to buttercreams not because they are too rich but because they are often too sweet. When looking at a buttercream recipe, consider the ratio of butter to sugar and it will tell you more about the flavor than any other factor because if the sugar is too high it will dominate. I find a good balance to be at least double the weight of butter to sugar. Every buttercream recipe in this chapter, except for Crème Ivoire whose major ingredient is white chocolate, has 2.27 times butter to sugar. Crème Ivoire is a wonderful buttercream for wedding cakes because it is pale ivory and very creamy. To temper the sweet richness, I use only about half the thickness I would with another buttercream. And I add contrasting flavors such as Pistachio Marzipan between the outer Crème Ivoire and the inner, less sweet Classic Buttercream.

BUTTERCREAM THAT APPEARS IN ANOTHER CHAPTER:

Easy Chestnut Buttercream (page 353)

Consistency is important when working with buttercreams. If a completed buttercream looks curdled and you're not sure whether it needs heating or chilling, take a small amount and try first one method then the other. It's always a question of temperature. To frost a cake, the buttercream should be extremely soft to go on smoothly. Don't be afraid to heat it slightly if it seems too stiff.

I have given weights for the finished base buttercreams to facilitate making optional additions, because the final amounts may vary. If, for example, some of the sugar syrup used for the buttercream remains in the pan and some more spins onto the side of the bowl while mixing, there will be less buttercream at the end.

It may seem that there are a staggering amount of variations, but some buttercream bases blend better with certain additions than do others. These variations were worked out over years of baking and teaching. Although some variations are quite similar, I want to offer them all so that you have the convenience of being able to use whatever is in your pantry.

Classic Buttercream

MAKES 4 CUPS
1 pound 9.25 ounces
/720 grams
(enough to fill and frost two
9-inch by 1½-inch layers or
three 9-inch by
1-inch layers)

*T*his ultimate buttercream is so silky smooth, creamy, and buttery, it complements just about any cake.

INGREDIENTS	MEASURE	WEIGHT	
room temperature	*volume*	*pounds/ounces*	*kilograms/grams*
6 large egg yolks	3.5 fluid ounces	4 ounces	112 grams
sugar	1 cup	7 ounces	200 grams
water	½ cup	4 ounces	118 grams
unsalted butter (must be softened)	2 cups	1 pound	454 grams
optional: liqueur or eau-de-vie of your choice	2 to 4 tablespoons	1 to 2 ounces	28 to 56 grams

Have ready a greased 1-cup heatproof glass measure near the range.

In a bowl beat the yolks with an electric mixer until light in color. Meanwhile, combine the sugar and water in a small saucepan (preferably with a nonstick lining) and heat, stirring constantly, until the sugar dissolves and the syrup is boiling. Stop stirring and boil to the soft-ball stage (238°F.). *Immediately transfer the syrup to the glass measure to stop the cooking.*

If using an electric hand-held mixer, beat the syrup into the yolks in a steady stream. Don't allow syrup to fall on the beaters or they will spin it onto the sides of the bowl. If using a stand mixer, pour a small amount of syrup over the yolks with the mixer turned off. Immediately beat at high speed for 5 seconds. Stop the mixer and add a larger amount of syrup. Beat at high speed for 5 seconds. Continue with the remaining syrup. For the last addition, use a rubber scraper to remove the syrup clinging to the glass measure. Continue beating until completely cool.

Gradually beat in the butter and, if desired, any optional flavoring (page 231). Place in an airtight bowl. Bring to room temperature before using. Rebeat if necessary to restore texture.*

STORE:
6 hours room temperature, 1 week refrigerated, 8 months frozen.

POINTERS FOR SUCCESS:
See Sugar Syrups (page 435). To prevent crystallization, do not stir after the syrup comes to a boil. To keep the temperature from rising, remove the syrup from the pan as soon as it has reached 238°F. Don't allow the syrup to fall directly on the beaters as it will spin the syrup around the sides of the bowl. Using a hand-held beater makes this easier.

---

* Do not rebeat chilled buttercream until it has reached room temperature or it may curdle.

Neoclassic Buttercream

MAKES 4 CUPS
1¾ pounds/800 grams
(enough to fill and frost two
9-inch by 1½-inch layers or
three 9-inch by
1-inch layers)

*T*his is an easier technique than that for Classic Butter-cream and yields *identical* results. In fact, since I have come up with this method, I have never gone back to the classic way. I am also pleased to see that other bakers have adapted this technique in their work.

In the neoclassic method, some of the sugar and all of the water is replaced by corn syrup. (Corn syrup, by volume, is about half the sweetness of sugar so ½ cup is needed to replace the ¼ cup sugar.) The corn syrup provides just the right amount of water so that, when brought to a *full* boil, the temperature of the syrup is exactly 238°F. There is no need to use a thermometer. The corn syrup also prevents crystallization.

INGREDIENTS	MEASURE	WEIGHT	
room temperature	*volume*	*pounds/ounces*	*kilograms/grams*
6 large egg yolks	3.5 fluid ounces	4 ounces	112 grams
sugar	¾ cup	5.25 ounces	150 grams
corn syrup	½ liquid cup	5.75 ounces	164 grams
unsalted butter (must be softened)	2 cups	1 pound	454 grams
optional: liqueur or eau-de-vie of your choice	2 to 4 tablespoons	1 to 2 ounces	28 to 56 grams

STORE:
6 hours room temperature,
1 week refrigerated, 8
months frozen.

Have ready a greased 1-cup heatproof glass measure near the range.

In a bowl beat the yolks with an electric mixer until light in color. Meanwhile, combine the sugar and corn syrup in a small saucepan (preferably with a nonstick lining) and heat, stirring constantly, until the sugar dissolves and the syrup comes to a rolling boil. (The entire surface will be covered with large bubbles.) *Immediately transfer the syrup to the glass measure to stop the cooking.*

If using an electric hand-held mixer, beat the syrup into the yolks in a steady stream. Don't allow syrup to fall on the beaters or they will spin it onto the sides of the bowl. If using a stand mixer, pour a small amount of syrup over the yolks with the mixer turned off. Immediately beat at high speed for 5 seconds. Stop the mixer and add a larger amount of syrup. Beat at high speed for 5 seconds. Continue with the remaining syrup. For the last addition, use a rubber scraper to remove the syrup clinging to the glass measure. Continue beating until completely cool.

Gradually beat in the butter and, if desired, any optional flavoring (page 231). Place in an airtight bowl. Bring to room temperature before using. Rebeat to restore texture.*

POINTERS FOR SUCCESS: The syrup must come to a rolling boil or the buttercream will be too thin. Don't allow the syrup to fall directly onto the beaters as it will spin the syrup around the sides of the bowl. Using a hand-held beater makes this easier.

Classic Buttercream Variations

(One Recipe of Classic or Neoclassic Buttercream)

*C*lassic or Neoclassic Buttercream can be used plain or as a base for any number of flavors. One recipe can accommodate as much as ½ cup liquid without becoming too soft. Spirits can heighten the flavor of a buttercream, but do not add them to buttercreams containing fruit purees as they will become too liquid. Spirits are best kept in the background, so start with 2 tablespoons and add more only to taste.

Fresh fruit purees such as raspberry and strawberry blend beautifully with classic buttercreams and maintain their lovely hues. Apricot puree tends to curdle the buttercream slightly, however, so heated, strained apricot preserves or *lekvar* (page 429), cooled to room temperature, are preferable.

The sweetness level of the base buttercream is perfectly balanced so whatever is added must be neither too sweet nor too tart or adjustments to the base need to be made as indicated.

CLASSIC CHOCOLATE: Classic buttercreams can incorporate about 6 ounces of melted chocolate without becoming too stiff. This results in a light chocolate color and flavor which does not overpower yellow or white cake layers.
To make chocolate buttercream: Beat 6 ounces melted and cooled chocolate, preferably extra bittersweet or bittersweet, into Classic or Neoclassic Buttercream.

* Do not rebeat chilled buttercream until it has reached room temperature or it may curdle.

CLASSIC CHOCOLATE CARAMEL CRUNCH: The flavors of caramel and chocolate blend beautifully and the powdered caramel adds a slightly crunchy texture. Because caramel is sweet it is best to use extra bittersweet chocolate in the base.

To make chocolate caramel crunch buttercream: Beat ¼ cup powdered caramel (page 313) into Classic Chocolate.

CLASSIC COFFEE: This simple method makes a buttercream with the rich taste of good strong coffee.

To make coffee buttercream: Beat 2 tablespoons Medaglia d'Oro instant espresso powder dissolved in 1 teaspoon boiling water into Classic or Neoclassic Buttercream. For a more aromatic flavor, add 2 to 4 tablespoons Kahlúa.

CLASSIC MOCHA ESPRESSO: Chocolate and coffee always make a lovely combination.

To make mocha espresso buttercream: Beat 2 tablespoons Medaglia d'Oro instant espresso powder dissolved in 1 teaspoon boiling water into Classic Chocolate. For more intense coffee flavor, add 2 to 4 tablespoons Kahlúa.

CLASSIC PRALINE: The best praline paste (page 430), a smooth combination of hazelnuts and caramelized sugar, makes a fabulous addition to any buttercream. Because the paste contains about 50 percent sugar it is necessary to remove some of the sugar from the buttercream base.

To make praline buttercream: When making Classic Buttercream, decrease the sugar by 1½ tablespoons. Beat in ¼ cup praline paste.

CLASSIC CHOCOLATE PRALINE: Praline intensifies the delicious flavor of chocolate.

To make chocolate praline buttercream: Beat 6 ounces melted and cooled bittersweet chocolate into Classic Praline Buttercream. Alternately, beat ¼ cup praline paste into Classic Chocolate Buttercream made with extra bittersweet chocolate. (Each method is the same level of sweetness.)

CLASSIC PRALINE CRUNCH: Praline powder is made of ground hazelnuts and caramel but is not turned into a paste. This gives a crunchy texture to the buttercream.

To make praline crunch buttercream: When making Classic Buttercream, decrease the sugar by 1½ tablespoons. Beat in ⅓ cup praline powder (page 315).

CLASSIC CHOCOLATE PRALINE CRUNCH: This buttercream is exactly like classic Chocolate Praline except for the crunchy texture provided by the praline powder.

To make chocolate praline crunch buttercream: Beat 6 ounces melted and cooled bittersweet chocolate into Classic Praline Crunch Buttercream. Alternately, beat ⅓ cup praline powder into Classic Chocolate Buttercream made with extra bittersweet chocolate. (Each method results in the same level of sweetness.)

CLASSIC CHESTNUT: This buttercream is perfect with Chestnut Sand Cake or with the subtle spicy flavors of Chocolate Fudge Cake.

To make chestnut buttercream: Stir ½ recipe Classic or Neoclassic buttercream into 1 recipe of lightly sweetened, rum-flavored chestnut puree (page 353). (This will make 3 full cups buttercream.)

CLASSIC MAPLE: The essence of pure Vermont maple syrup, this buttercream is excellent with any white or yellow butter cake and is still more delicious encrusted with coarsely chopped walnuts.

To make maple buttercream: When making Neoclassic Buttercream, replace the corn syrup with an equal amount of pure maple syrup. Beat in 2 teaspoons of maple extract to the finished buttercream.

CLASSIC RASPBERRY: My Raspberry Sauce is so concentrated it scarcely affects the consistency of the buttercream base. This is the purest raspberry flavor of any frosting I know.

To make raspberry buttercream: Beat ½ cup lightly sweetened Raspberry Sauce (page 337) into finished buttercream. If not planning to use the same day, add a few drops of red food color to prevent fading.

CLASSIC STRAWBERRY: The strawberry flavor is surprisingly fresh and intense. It is also, of course, silky and creamy but has the added interest of tiny strawberry seeds. I find that strawberries frozen without sugar have more flavor than most commercially available fresh strawberries—even at the height of season.

To make strawberry buttercream: Beat ½ cup unsweetened Strawberry Puree (page 338) into finished buttercream and add a few optional drops of essence of wild strawberry (page 427) for further intensity. If not planning to use the same day, add a few drops of red food color to prevent fading.

CLASSIC APRICOT: This buttercream has a tart, honeyed flavor and a very pale golden color.

To make apricot buttercream: Beat ½ cup heated, strained,

and cooled apricot preserves or *lekvar* (page 429) into finished buttercream and add a few optional drops of essence of apricot (page 427) for further intensity.

CLASSIC PINEAPPLE: Home-preserved pineapple is a delicious, slightly tart addition to buttercream.
To make pineapple buttercream: Beat 1 cup pureed pineapple (page 351) into finished buttercream and add 1 to 2 tablespoons kirsch or rum.

CLASSIC LEMON: To achieve a truly lemon flavor it is necessary to use both fresh lemon juice and lemon extract (actually the pure oil of lemon). Lemon juice alone is not intense enough and the extract alone is too bitter.
To make lemon buttercream: When making Classic Buttercream, replace ¼ cup of the water with freshly squeezed lemon juice. After adding the butter, beat in ¼ teaspoon lemon extract.

CLASSIC ORANGE: An intense orange flavor is difficult to achieve using orange extract because it is quite bitter. Finely grated orange zest (the orange part of the rind only, as the pith is bitter) and an aromatic French orange essence (page 427), which includes the pulp, do produce an excellent orange flavor, however.
To make orange buttercream: Add 2 teaspoons orange pulp essence and 1 tablespoon grated orange zest.

CLASSIC ORANGE BLOSSOM: Orange flower water gives this buttercream the perfume of orange blossoms. Be sure to add the Tang, which is mainly orange oil. The small amount serves to add the lilting zip associated with fresh orange flavor. This buttercream perfectly complements Orange Chiffon Cake.
To make orange blossom buttercream: Add 1 teaspoon (13.5 grams) Tang dissolved in ⅓ cup orange flower water, 1 tablespoon (18 grams) grated orange zest, and 2 tablespoons Grand Marnier.

CLASSIC PASSION: This buttercream captures the slightly tart, utterly distinctive taste of fresh passion fruit.
To make passion buttercream: Beat up to ¾ cup passion curd (page 342) into finished buttercream and add 1 teaspoon of essence of passion fruit (page 427) for further intensity. This buttercream is fabulous with Cordon Rose Banana Cake (page 69).

Royal Honey Buttercream

$\mathcal{R}$eplacing both the sugar and the corn syrup of Neo-classic Buttercream with honey results in a mellifluous, subtly perfumed buttercream. Mild clover honey, available in supermarkets, produces the best flavor. (I find the more exotic varieties too assertive.) This buttercream is wonderful with any yellow cake but I created it especially for Queen Bee cake (page 185).

MAKES 3 ¾ CUPS
(enough to fill and frost two 9-inch by 1½-inch layers or three 9-inch by 1-inch layers)

INGREDIENTS	MEASURE	WEIGHT	
room temperature	volume	pounds/ounces	kilograms/grams
6 large egg yolks	3.5 fluid ounces	4 ounces	112 grams
clover honey	⅓ liquid cup	4 ounces	112 grams
unsalted butter (must be softened)	2 cups	1 pound	454 grams

Have ready a greased heatproof glass measure near the range.

In bowl beat the yolks with an electric mixer until light in color. Meanwhile heat the honey in a small saucepan (preferably with a nonstick lining), stirring constantly, until it come to a rolling boil. *Immediately transfer the honey to the glass measure to stop the cooking.*

If using an electric hand-held mixer, beat the honey into the yolks in a steady stream. Don't allow honey to fall on the beaters or they will spin it onto sides of bowl. If using a stand mixer, pour a small amount of honey over the yolks with the mixer turned off. Immediately beat at high speed for 5 seconds. Stop the mixer and add a larger amount of honey. Beat at high speed for 5 seconds. Continue with the remaining honey. For the last addition, use a rubber scraper to remove the honey clinging to the glass measure. Continue beating until completely cool.

Gradually beat in the butter. Place in an airtight bowl. Bring to room temperature before using. Rebeat to restore texture.*

* Do not rebeat chilled buttercream until it has reached room temperature or it may curdle.

STORE:
6 hours room temperature, 1 week refrigerated, 8 months frozen.

POINTERS FOR SUCCESS:
The honey must come to a rolling boil or the buttercream will be too thin. Don't allow the honey to fall directly onto the beaters as it will spin the honey around the sides of the bowl.

Classic Egg White Chocolate Buttercream

MAKES 4¾
CUPS
35 ounces/1 kilogram
(enough to fill and frost two
9-inch by 1½-inch layers or
three 9-inch by
1-inch layers)

*T*his special version of chocolate buttercream is the color of rich milk chocolate and has a more assertive chocolate flavor than the traditional one made with egg yolks. In fact, it is just as smooth and even easier and faster to prepare than Classic or Neoclassic Buttercream because a sugar syrup is not needed.

This buttercream is airy yet, because of the whites' structure, has more body than a buttercream made with all yolks. It is an excellent texture and flavor for both chocolate butter cakes and chocolate *génoise*.

INGREDIENTS	MEASURE	WEIGHT	
room temperature	*volume*	*pounds/ounces*	*kilograms/grams*
bittersweet chocolate	3⅓ (3-ounce) bars	10 ounces	284 grams
unsalted butter (must be softened)	2 cups	1 pound	454 grams
4 large egg whites	½ liquid cup	4.25 ounces	120 grams
sugar	1 cup	7 ounces	200 grams

STORE:
3 days room temperature, 2 weeks refrigerated, 6 months frozen.

POINTERS FOR SUCCESS:
Have egg whites at room temperature before beating. See Melting Chocolate (page 379).

Break the chocolate into squares and place in a double boiler over very hot water or low heat. The water must not exceed 160°F. or touch the bottom of the double boiler insert.

Remove double boiler from the heat and stir frequently until the chocolate begins to melt.

Return to the heat if the water cools, but be careful that it does not get too hot. Stir 8 to 10 minutes or until the chocolate is smooth. (Chocolate may be melted in a microwave oven on high power *if stirred every 15 seconds*. Remove before fully melted and stir, using residual heat to complete the melting.)

In a mixing bowl beat the butter until smooth and creamy.

In another mixing bowl beat the egg whites until soft peaks form when the beater is raised. Gradually beat in the sugar until stiff peaks form when the beater is raised slowly. Beat in the butter by the tablespoon. If the mixture looks slightly curdled, increase the speed a little and beat until smooth before continuing to add more butter. Add the melted and cooled chocolate all at once and beat until smooth and uniform in color. Place in an airtight bowl. Rebeat to restore texture.*

UNDERSTANDING

While it is necessary to cook egg yolks for a buttercream to prevent bacterial growth, raw egg whites are far less prone to this problem. Because the whites are not thickened by a hot syrup, the resulting buttercream is softer than the Classic or Neoclassic versions and can accommodate 4 more ounces of chocolate without becoming too stiff and unworkable.

White Chocolate Cream Cheese Buttercream

MAKES 4¾ CUPS
5.25 ounces/153 grams
(enough to fill and frost two
9-inch by 1½-inch layers or
three 9-inch by
1-inch layers)

*T*his ivory buttercream is mellow and creamy. Its luscious, slightly tangy flavor is a perfect complement for yellow cake, carrot cake, and especially cheesecake. It makes a spectacular presentation because it pipes wonderfully and is the identical color of cheesecake. White chocolate adds firmness of texture, sweetness, and an undefinable flavor.

INGREDIENTS	MEASURE	WEIGHT	
room temperature	volume	pounds/ounces	kilograms/grams
white chocolate (preferably Tobler Narcisse)	3 (3-ounce) bars	9 ounces	255 grams
cream cheese (must be softened)	4 small packages	12 ounces	340 grams
unsalted butter (must be softened)	¾ cup	6 ounces	170 grams
lemon juice, freshly squeezed	1½ tablespoons	•	23 grams

* Do not rebeat chilled buttercream until it has reached room temperature or it may curdle.

1 day room temperature, 2 weeks refrigerated, 2 months frozen.

POINTERS FOR SUCCESS: Do not overheat the white chocolate and be sure to stir constantly while melting. Be sure no moisture gets into the melted chocolate (see Melting Chocolate, page 379). Beat constantly while adding the cooled chocolate to prevent lumping. If lumping should occur, it can be remedied by pressing the buttercream through a fine strainer.

The buttercream may separate slightly if room temperature is very warm. This can be corrected by setting the bowl in ice water and whisking the mixture. Buttercream becomes spongy on standing. Rebeat to restore smooth creamy texture. Use ice to chill your hand during piping to maintain firm texture.

Break the chocolate into squares and place in the top of a double boiler set over very hot water (no hotter than 160°F.) on low heat. The water must not touch the bottom of the double boiler insert.

Remove the double boiler from the heat and stir until the chocolate begins to melt. Return to the heat if the water cools, but be careful that it does not get too hot. Stir 10 minutes or until smooth. (The chocolate may be melted in a microwave oven *if stirred every 15 seconds*. Remove before fully melted and stir, using residual heat to complete the melting.) Allow to cool.

In a mixing bowl beat the cream cheese (preferably with a flat beater) until smooth and creamy. Gradually beat in the cooled chocolate until smoothly incorporated. Beat in the butter and lemon juice. Rebeat at room temperature to ensure smoothness before frosting.*

NOTE: My friend Shirley Corriher reports that, when using this frosting for a wedding cake in the heat of an Atlanta summer, she tried decreasing the butter to 2 ounces and it held up quite well.

---

* Do not rebeat chilled buttercream until it has reached room temperature or it may curdle.

$\mathcal{T}$his is the buttercream to have on that proverbial dessert island. In fact, it is rather like a floating island buttercream with its combination of *crème anglaise* and Italian meringue!

Although more time-consuming and exacting to prepare than Classic Buttercream, it has the advantage of being equally smooth but more airy, stable, and resistant to warm temperatures. The greater stability makes it a dream for piping decorations. It's great to have a batch of this on hand in the freezer to flavor with any of the additions on page 241.

Silk Meringue Buttercream

MAKES 4 CUPS
almost 2 pounds/838 grams
(enough to fill and frost two
9-inch by 1½-inch layers or
three 9-inch by
1-inch layers)

INGREDIENTS	MEASURE	WEIGHT	
room temperature	*volume*	*pounds/ounces*	*kilograms/grams*
CRÈME ANGLAISE			
sugar	½ cup	3.5 ounces	100 grams
5 large egg yolks	3 fluid ounces	3.25 ounces	93 grams
milk	½ liquid cup	4.25 ounces	121 grams
1 large vanilla bean, split lengthwise * *or* ½ large Tahitian vanilla bean			
ITALIAN MERINGUE			
sugar	⅓ cup + 2 tablespoons	3.25 ounces	92 grams
water	2 tablespoons	1 ounce	30 grams
2 large egg whites	¼ liquid cup	2 ounces	60 grams
cream of tartar	¼ teaspoon	•	•
unsalted butter (must be softened)	2 cups	1 pound	454 grams

* A vanilla bean offers the most delicious flavor, but if you wish to avoid the little black specks, replace the bean with 1 teaspoon vanilla extract, added to the cooled *crème anglaise*.

TO MAKE CRÈME ANGLAISE

Have ready a sieve suspended over a bowl, near the range.

In a medium-size heavy noncorrodible saucepan combine the sugar and yolks.

In a small saucepan bring the milk and vanilla bean to a boil. Add 2 tablespoons of the milk to the yolk mixture, stirring constantly. Gradually add the remaining milk, stir-

STORE:
6 hours room temperature, 1 week refrigerated, 8 months frozen. If frozen or refrigerated, be sure to allow the buttercream to come to room temperature

before rebeating it or it will break down. Buttercream becomes almost liquid when it has reached room temperature but rebeating will make it as firm as before.

POINTERS FOR SUCCESS: Crème Anglaise: The temperature must reach at least 160°F. and must not exceed 180°F. or it will curdle.

Italian Meringue: For maximum stability, the syrup must reach 248°F. and not exceed 250°F. or the whites will break down. The whites must be free of any grease or trace of yolk. Do not overbeat.

Finished buttercream: Rebeat when it becomes spongy.

ring, and cook over medium-low heat, stirring constantly, until just below the boiling point. The mixture will start to steam slightly and an accurate thermometer will register 170°F. Strain immediately, scraping up any clinging to the bottom of the pan.

Scrape the seeds from the vanilla bean into the custard and cool to room temperature. (To speed cooling, put the bowl in another bowl or sink partially filled with ice water.) Cover and refrigerate up to 5 days or until ready to complete the buttercream.

TO MAKE ITALIAN MERINGUE

Have ready a heatproof glass measure near the range.

In a small heavy saucepan (preferably with a nonstick lining) combine 1/3 cup sugar and the 2 tablespoons of water. Heat, stirring constantly, until the sugar dissolves and the mixture is bubbling. Stop stirring and reduce the heat to low. (If using an electric range remove from the heat.)

In a mixing bowl beat the egg whites until foamy. Add the cream of tartar and beat until soft peaks form when the beater is raised. Gradually beat in the remaining 2 tablespoons sugar until stiff peaks form when the beater is raised slowly.

Increase the heat and boil the syrup until a thermometer registers 248°F. to 250°F. (the firm-ball stage). *Immediately transfer the syrup to the glass measure to stop the cooking.*

If using an electric hand-held mixer, beat the syrup into the egg whites in a steady stream. Don't allow syrup to fall on the beaters or they will spin it onto sides of bowl. If using a stand mixer, pour a small amount of syrup over the egg whites with the mixer off. Immediately beat at high speed for 5 seconds. Stop the mixer and add a larger amount of syrup. Beat at high speed for 5 seconds. Continue with the remaining syrup. For the last addition, use a rubber scraper to remove the syrup clinging to the glass measure. Lower speed to medium and continue beating until completely cool (about 2 minutes). (The Italian Meringue keeps for 2 days refrigerated. Rebeat briefly before using.)

TO COMPLETE BUTTERCREAM

Place the butter in a large mixing bowl and beat on medium speed for 30 seconds or until creamy. Gradually beat in the *crème anglaise* until smooth. Add the Italian Meringue and beat until just incorporated. If the mixture looks curdled instead of smooth it is too cold. Allow it to sit at room temperature to warm to 70°F. before continuing to beat. Or place the bowl in a hot water bath very briefly until the buttercream touching the bowl just starts to melt. Remove at once and beat until smooth. Beat in optional additions (page 241). Place in an airtight bowl. The buttercream becomes slightly spongy on standing. Rebeat before using.*

UNDERSTANDING

Crème anglaise must be heated to at least 160°F. to adequately thicken the egg yolks. Over 180°F. the yolks will start to curdle and the cream may not be smooth. (Commercial establishments sometimes bring it to a boil and quickly strain it, discarding the curdled part. This is done only to save time and ensure that the temperature is hot enough without bothering with other tests. I do not recommend this method.)

When stirring the hot milk into the yolk mixture, it is best to use a wooden spoon because a whisk will create air bubbles, making it difficult to judge when the mixture is done.

PRALINE SILK MERINGUE BUTTERCREAM: The nutty, burnt sugar flavor and smooth texture of fine-quality praline paste (page 431) make this a delicious buttercream. Because praline paste contains at least 50% sugar, it is necessary to use less sugar in the Silk Meringue base.

To make praline buttercream: Use only ¼ cup sugar instead of ½ cup when making the *crème anglaise.* Beat ½ cup (5.5 ounces/154 grams) praline paste into the buttercream before adding the meringue.

To make chocolate praline buttercream: Add 8 ounces melted and cooled extra bittersweet or bittersweet chocolate.

CARAMEL SILK MERINGUE BUTTERCREAM: This version offers the pure flavor of burnt sugar without any bitter overtones. When making the *crème anglaise,* the sugar is caramelized and dissolved in the milk. Double the milk is needed to compensate for evaporation when added to the hot caramel.

Silk Meringue Buttercream Variations

* Do not rebeat chilled buttercream until it has reached room temperature or it may curdle.

To make caramel buttercream: When making the *crème anglaise,* add the vanilla bean to 1 cup milk, bring to a boil, and keep warm. In a heavy pan combine the ½ cup sugar with 2 tablespoons water and bring to a boil, stirring constantly. Cook without stirring until deep amber (360°F.). Remove immediately from the heat and slowly pour in the hot milk, reserving the vanilla bean. Return to low heat and cook, stirring, until the caramel is totally dissolved. Proceed as for regular *crème anglaise* by gradually adding the caramel mixture to the yolks, cooking to 170°F., and adding the vanilla seeds.

BURNT ORANGE SILK MERINGUE BUTTERCREAM: This is an exciting combination of caramel with orange overtones.

To make burnt orange buttercream: Make caramel buttercream and beat in 1 tablespoon thawed orange juice concentrate and 1 tablespoon grated orange zest. (You can make your own concentrate by reducing ½ cup freshly squeezed orange juice.) If desired, use a tiny dab of orange paste food color to tint buttercream pale orange.

COFFEE CARAMEL SILK MERINGUE BUTTERCREAM: This subtle combination produces a harmonious melding of flavors.

To make coffee caramel buttercream: Make caramel buttercream and beat in 2½ teaspoons Medaglia d'Oro instant espresso powder dissolved in ½ teaspoon very hot water.

ESPRESSO SILK MERINGUE BUTTERCREAM: Although it is possible to steep ground coffee beans in the *crème anglaise* and then strain it through cheesecloth to give the buttercream a rich coffee flavor, instant espresso, such as Medaglia d'Oro, is a lot easier to use and also results in a deep rich coffee flavor.

To make espresso buttercream: Dissolve 2 tablespoons Medaglia d'Oro instant espresso powder in the hot *crème anglaise.* Beat up to ¼ cup Kahlua into the finished buttercream.

CHOCOLATE SILK MERINGUE BUTTERCREAM: Extra bittersweet chocolate adds a *café au lait* hue and thickens the buttercream, making it a dream for decorative piping.

To make chocolate buttercream: Beat 8 ounces melted and cooled extra bittersweet or bittersweet chocolate into the finished buttercream.

CHOCOLATE TRUFFLE SILK MERINGUE BUTTERCREAM: If you happen to have some leftover Light Whipped Ganache, it makes a terrific addition to silk meringue buttercream. The resulting buttercream is more creamy and stable than the airy ganache but lighter than the silk meringue buttercream. It is pale chocolate in color with a delicate flavor.

To make chocolate truffle buttercream: Beat together equal amounts of silk meringue buttercream base and Light Whipped Ganache (page 268).

CHESTNUT SILK MERINGUE BUTTERCREAM: The classic combination of chestnut and rum makes a buttercream with spicy, earthy overtones that blends beautifully with chocolate cakes.

To make chestnut buttercream: Use ½ recipe buttercream base and beat in 1 recipe of lightly sweetened chestnut puree (page 353) flavored with rum. (Makes 3 full cups.)

APRICOT SILK MERINGUE BUTTERCREAM: Bright orange, premium-quality dried apricots from California (purchased in a health food or specialty produce stores) make an intensely flavored buttercream. (Fruit puree buttercreams are slightly softer than the other versions but using this base they still pipe exceptionally well.)

To make apricot buttercream: Beat 1 cup unsweetened apricot puree (page 335) into the finished buttercream. Add 2 teaspoons apricot essence for further intensity if desired (page 427).

RASPBERRY SILK MERINGUE BUTTERCREAM: Raspberry Conserve or jam gives a better texture to this buttercream than raspberry sauce. This buttercream is slightly less intense in flavor than the classic one and has a lighter texture.

To make raspberry buttercream: Add ½ cup Cordon Rose Raspberry Conserve (page 331) or 1 cup commercial seedless raspberry jam plus 1 tablespoon freshly squeezed lemon juice to the finished buttercream. If the conserve or jam is very stiff, heat gently until softened. Add the lemon juice and allow to cool to room temperature before adding to the buttercream. To retain a nice pale pink color, stir in 6 drops of red food color.

STRAWBERRY SILK MERINGUE BUTTERCREAM: Avoid commercial strawberry jams, most are far too sweet to add to buttercream.

To make strawberry buttercream: Add ½ cup pureed Cordon Rose Strawberry Conserve (page 333) to the finished buttercream. To retain a pale pink color, stir in 6 drops of red food color. Add a few drops of essence of wild strawberry if desired for further intensity (page 247).

Mousseline Buttercream

(moosahLEAN)

MAKES 4½ CUPS
1 pound 14 ounces/
858 grams
(enough to fill and frost two
9-inch by 1½-inch layers or
three 9-inch by
1-inch layers)

*T*his buttercream is very light, smooth and incredibly easy to work with. It is soft enough for beautiful shell borders yet strong enough to pipe roses. Liqueur gently perfumes the buttercream, and if it is tinted it also enhances the color. Mandarine Napoléon, for example, lends the palest aura of apricot.

It is a thrilling buttercream to prepare because it starts out looking thin and lumpy and, about three-fourths of the way through, starts to emulsify and turn into a luxurious cream.

A word of caution: If the butter is too soft or the room too hot, what could have been a satin-smooth cream breaks down into a grainy hopeless puddle. Once the buttercream is made, however, it holds up better than any other.

Be sure to try the fruit variations (page 245). They are all superb and the orange is my favorite of all orange buttercreams. It is excellent with both chocolate and non-chocolate butter cakes and *génoise*.

INGREDIENTS	MEASURE	WEIGHT	
room temperature	*volume*	*pounds/ounces*	*kilograms/grams*
unsalted butter, softened but cool (65°F.)	2 cups	1 pound	454 grams
sugar	1 cup	7 ounces	200 grams
water	¼ liquid cup	2 ounces	60 grams
5 large egg whites	5 fluid ounces (use a glass measuring cup)	5.25 ounces	150 grams
cream of tartar	½ + ⅛ teaspoon	•	•
liqueur such as Mandarine Napoléon, Grand Marnier, or an eau-de-vie	3 fluid ounces (use a glass measuring cup)	3 ounces	90 grams

In a mixing bowl beat the butter until smooth and creamy and set aside in a cool place.

Have ready a heatproof glass measure near the range.

In a small heavy saucepan (preferably with a nonstick lining) heat ¾ cup sugar and the ¼ cup water, stirring constantly, until the sugar dissolves and the mixture is bubbling. Stop stirring and reduce the heat to low. (If using an electric range remove from the heat.)

In another mixing bowl beat the egg whites until foamy, add the cream of tartar, and beat until soft peaks form when the beater is raised. Gradually beat in the remaining ¼ cup sugar until stiff peaks form when the beater is raised slowly. Increase the heat and boil the syrup until a thermometer registers 248°F. to 250°F. (the firm-ball stage). *Immediately transfer the syrup to the glass measure to stop the cooking.*

If using a hand-held mixer beat the syrup into the whites in a steady stream. Don't allow the syrup to fall on the beaters or they will spin it onto the sides of the bowl. If using a stand mixer, pour a small amount of syrup over the whites with the mixer off. Immediately beat at high speed for 5 seconds. Stop the mixer and add a larger amount of syrup. Beat at high speed for 5 seconds. Continue with the remaining syrup. For the last addition, use a rubber scraper to remove the syrup clinging to the glass measure. Lower speed to medium and continue beating up to 2 minutes or until cool. If not *completely* cool, continue beating on lowest speed.

Beat in the butter at medium speed 1 tablespoon at a time. At first the mixture will seem thinner but will thicken beautifully by the time all the butter is added. If at any time the mixture looks slightly curdled, increase the speed slightly and beat until smooth before continuing to add more butter.

Lower the speed slightly and drizzle in the liqueur. Place in an airtight bowl. Rebeat lightly from time to time to maintain silky texture.* Buttercream becomes spongy on standing.

VARIATIONS

CHOCOLATE MOUSSELINE: Beat in 5 ounces of melted and cooled extra bittersweet or bittersweet chocolate.

WHITE CHOCOLATE MOUSSELINE: Beat in 6 ounces melted and cooled white chocolate, preferably Tobler Narcisse.

FRUIT MOUSSELINE: Add up to ¾ cup lightly sweetened strawberry or raspberry puree or orange, passion, lemon, or lime curd.

STORE:
2 days room temperature, 10 days refrigerated, 8 months frozen. Allow to come to room temperature before rebeating or it will break down irretrievably.

POINTERS FOR SUCCESS:
Correct butter temperature is crucial. If you suspect that the butter was too warm (or the kitchen is very hot) and the buttercream starts thinning out and curdling, check the temperature. If the mixture does not feel cool, refrigerate until it reaches 65°F. to 70°F. or is cool to the touch. If by chance you have used butter straight from the refrigerator and the mixture feels ice-cold, suspend the bowl over a pan of simmering water (don't let the bowl touch the water) and heat very briefly, stirring vigorously when the mixture just starts to melt slightly at the edges. Dip the bottom of the bowl in a larger bowl of ice water for a few seconds to cool it. Remove and beat by hand until smooth.

* Do not rebeat chilled buttercream until it has reached room temperature or it may curdle.

Crème
Ivoire Deluxe

(krem eveWAH duhLOUX)
Luxury White Chocolate
Buttercream and Glaze

MAKES 3 CUPS

---

*T*his glorious buttercream is for the white chocolate lover. The addition of extra cocoa butter, clarified butter, and a neutral oil softens the texture and provides a pale ivory color reminiscent of an antique satin wedding gown. It is excellent as frosting for a wedding cake and equally dramatic when used to frost or glaze a one-layer cake such as the Chocolate Oblivion Truffle Cake (page 84). This buttercream pipes with the most exquisite detail. The contrast of the bittersweet chocolate against the white chocolate buttercream is striking.

Crème Ivoire is like the finest bonbon or chocolate truffle. On first bite it seems firm, only to dissolve immediately in the mouth, releasing the buttery and faintly chocolate flavors. Because of its richness, this amount is enough to glaze or lightly frost and decorate a 9-inch by 3-inch cake.

INGREDIENTS	MEASURE	WEIGHT	
room temperature	*volume*	*pounds/ounces*	*kilograms/grams*
white chocolate (preferably Tobler Narcisse)	8 (3-ounce) bars	1.5 pounds	680 grams
cocoa butter, melted *	¼ liquid cup	2.25 ounces	64 grams
clarified unsalted butter†	¼ liquid cup	1.75 ounces	50 grams
flavorless oil such as mineral or safflower	¼ liquid cup	1.75 ounces	50 grams

* Melt cocoa butter in a double boiler, in an oven with the heat of the pilot light, or microwave the same way as chocolate (page 379).

†If you do not have clarified butter on hand, you will need to clarify 5½ tablespoons (2.75 ounces/78 grams) unsalted butter. In a heavy saucepan melt the butter over medium heat, partially covered to prevent splattering. When the butter looks clear, cook uncovered, watching carefully until the solids drop and just begin to brown. Pour immediately through a fine strainer or a strainer lined with cheesecloth.

STORE:
Mineral oil has an indefinite shelf life, but safflower oil will become rancid in a matter of weeks. Therefore, if prepared with mineral oil, the buttercream will keep at room temperature 1 month. (The clarified butter shortens the shelf life at room temperature.) If prepared with other oils, store at room temperature up to 1 week, in the refrigerator up to 3 months or freeze up to 1 year.

Break the chocolate into squares and place in the top of a double boiler. Add the cocoa butter, clarified butter, and oil and place over very hot water on low heat. The water must not exceed 160°F. or touch the bottom of the double boiler insert.

Remove the double boiler from the heat and stir until the chocolate begins to melt. Return to the heat if the water cools, but be careful that it does not get too hot. Stir 10 minutes or until smooth. (The chocolate may be melted with the oil and butters in a microwave oven on high power *if stirred every 15 seconds*. Remove before fully melted and stir, using residual heat to complete the melting.)

Because of the milk solids in the white chocolate, the buttercream must be chilled and stirred to prevent seeding (the formation of tiny lumps). Fill a large bowl with ice cubes and water and sprinkle the ice with 1 or 2 tablespoons salt. Fill a second bowl or the sink with very hot water. Set the top of the double boiler directly in the ice water.

TO MAKE A BUTTERCREAM
Stir constantly with whisk until you just see whisk marks on the surface. Immediately place over a bowl of hot water to take off the chill. This will take only seconds. The bottom of the pan should feel barely cool.

Allow the buttercream to sit for a few minutes, whisking occasionally. If it does not form peaks when the whisk is raised, chill again for a little longer.

TO MAKE A GLAZE
Stir the chocolate with a spoon to avoid air bubbles. Chill only until a small amount dropped from spoon just mounds before smoothly disappearing into the mixture. For glazing instructions, see page 272.

POINTERS FOR SUCCESS:
When clarifying butter, the solids must begin to brown to ensure that all the water in the butter has evaporated. Be sure that not even a drop of water gets into the melted chocolate. If seeding should occur, try beating with an immersion blender (page 457) or remelt the buttercream, pass through a fine strainer, and chill again, stirring constantly. Be sure to use fine-quality white chocolate which contains cocoa butter. I find Tobler Narcisse to have the best flavor and the least sweetness.

I like to frost the cake first with a thin layer of Classic Buttercream. This offers an interesting textural contrast and gives the Crème Ivoire Deluxe an ideal surface on which to adhere. Otherwise it has a tendency to separate from the cake when serving. (I also use the classic buttercream plain or flavored as a filling.) Keep piped decorations simple—such as a shell border (page 399).

The heat of your hand makes piping more than a few designs at a time difficult. To counteract this problem, use several parchment bags, placing just a small amount of buttercream in each, and switch bags at first sign of softening. Cooling your hand in ice water also helps.

Crème Ivoire

(Krem eveWAH)
White Chocolate Buttercream
and Glaze

MAKES 2 CUPS

*T*he delicious creamy flavor of this buttercream is similar to the preceding recipe but this version is simpler and less expensive to make. It consists of white chocolate softened with a neutral oil to frosting or glazing consistency. Its melt-in-the mouth quality comes from the cocoa butter in the white chocolate. (That is the only "butter" in the buttercream.)

This buttercream is suitable for glazing or frosting but is too soft to hold its shape for decorative piping. If you wish to make decorative borders on your cake, prepare the Crème Ivoire Deluxe instead (page 246) or the praliné version of this buttercream. A tart filling such as raspberry or lemon buttercream is an ideal contrast to the sweetness of the white chocolate. Because of its richness, 1¾ cups is enough to glaze or frost a 9-inch by 3-inch cake.

INGREDIENTS	MEASURE	WEIGHT	
room temperature	*volume*	*pounds/ounces*	*kilograms/grams*
white chocolate (preferably Tobler Narcisse)	5⅓ (3-ounce) bars	1 pound	454 grams
flavorless oil such as mineral or safflower	scant ½ liquid cup	3 ounces	87 grams

STORE:
Mineral oil has an indefinite shelf life, but safflower oil will become rancid in a matter of weeks. Therefore, if prepared with mineral oil, the buttercream will keep at room temperature 6 months. If prepared with other oils, store at room temperature 1 week, refrigerate up to 3 months, or freeze up to one year. (The praliné version keeps at room temperature 3 weeks if mineral oil was used instead of safflower oil.)

POINTERS FOR SUCCESS:
Be sure that not even a drop of water gets into the melted chocolate. If seeding should occur, try beating with an

Break the chocolate into squares and place in the top of a double boiler. Add the oil and place over very hot water on low heat. The water must not exceed 160°F. or touch the bottom of double boiler insert.

Remove the double boiler from the heat and stir frequently until the chocolate begins to melt. Return to the heat if the water cools, but be careful that it does not get too hot. Stir 8 to 10 minutes or until smooth. (The chocolate may be melted with the oil in a microwave oven on high power *if stirred every 15 seconds.* Remove before fully melted and stir, using residual heat to complete the melting.)

White chocolate buttercream must be chilled and stirred to prevent seeding (the formation of tiny lumps). Fill a large bowl with ice cubes and water and sprinkle the ice with 1 or 2 tablespoons salt. Fill a second bowl or the sink with very hot water. Set the top of the double boiler directly in the ice water. If making buttercream, whisk constantly until you just see whisk marks on the surface. Immediately place over a bowl of hot water to take off the chill. This will only take seconds. The bottom of the pan should feel barely cool.

Allow buttercream to sit for a few minutes, stirring occasionally with whisk. If it does not form peaks when the whisk is raised, chill again for a little longer.

If making a glaze instead of a buttercream, stir the chocolate with a spoon to avoid air bubbles. Chill only until a small amount dropped from the spoon mounds a bit before smoothly disappearing into the mixture. For glazing instructions see page 272.

VARIATION

CRÈME IVOIRE PRALINÉ: This is the most intense of all praline buttercreams and pipes like a dream. It is imperative to use 100 percent hazelnut paste *without* sugar. This product must be purchased (page 430) because homemade versions are not smooth enough. To prepare buttercream, whisk ½ cup (4.25 ounces/120 grams) pure hazelnut paste into the melted chocolate and oil. (You may use some of the oil which forms on top of the hazlenut paste to make up some of the oil needed for the buttercream.)

immersion blender (fitted with a disc blade) or remelt the buttercream, pass through a fine strainer, and chill again, stirring constantly. If the weather is 80°F. or above, reduce the oil to 6 tablespoons (3 liquid ounces).

*T*he assertive flavor of walnuts does wonders when used judiciously with chocolate. Using part milk chocolate tempers the slight bitterness of the walnut. The oil softens the chocolate and keeps it dark and shiny.

This glaze is particularly complementary to cakes containing walnuts or walnut oil—such as Pumpkin Walnut Ring (page 71) or Guilt-Free Chocolate Chiffon Cake (page 158).

Chocolate Walnut Drizzle Glaze

MAKES ¼ CUP

INGREDIENTS	MEASURE	WEIGHT	
room temperature	*volume*	*pounds/ounces*	*kilograms/grams*
bittersweet chocolate	⅓ of a 3-ounce bar	1 ounce	28 grams
milk chocolate	⅓ of a 3-ounce bar	1 ounce	28 grams
walnut oil	1 tablespoon	0.5 ounce	13 grams

Break the chocolates into squares and place in the top of a double boiler. Add the oil and place over very hot but not simmering water on low heat. The water must not touch the bottom of the double boiler insert.

Remove the double boiler from the heat and stir until the chocolate begins to melt. Return to the heat if the water cools, but be careful that it does not get too hot. Stir until smooth. (The chocolate may be melted with the oil in a microwave oven *if stirred every 15 seconds*. Remove before fully melted and stir, using residual heat to complete the melting.)

Using a parchment cone (page 394) or cup with a spout, drizzle over the top and sides of the cake. Allow to set for at least 3 hours at room temperature.

Milk Chocolate Buttercream

MAKES 3 CUPS
(enough to fill and frost two 8-inch by 1½-inch layers or two 9-inch by 1-inch layers)

*T*his is the quintessential easy-to-make buttercream for the milk chocolate lover. Since melted or softened milk chocolate seems much sweeter than the original bar, I have added half the milk chocolate's weight in bittersweet chocolate to compensate. The result is like eating a slightly softened bar of your favorite milk chocolate! This buttercream is especially good for filling and frosting Chocolate Fudge Cake (page 60) or Perfect All-American Chocolate Butter Cake (page 54).

INGREDIENTS	MEASURE	WEIGHT	
room temperature	*volume*	*pounds/ounces*	*kilograms/grams*
milk chocolate*	•	1 pound	454 grams
dark chocolate, preferably extra bittersweet or bittersweet	•	8 ounces	227 grams
unsalted butter (must be softened)	1½ cups	12 ounces	340 grams

Break the chocolate into squares and place in the top of a double boiler. Set over hot but not simmering water on low heat. The water must not touch the bottom of the double boiler insert. Remove the double boiler from the heat and stir until the chocolate begins to melt. Return to the heat if the water cools, but be careful that it does not get too hot. Stir until smooth, and cool until no longer warm to the touch. (The chocolate may be melted in a microwave oven *if stirred every 15 seconds*. Remove before fully melted and stir, using residual heat to complete the melting.)

In a bowl beat the butter with an electric mixer at medium speed and beat in the cooled chocolate until uniform in color.

* Lindt offers a smooth texture and caramel undertone.

*H*eavy cream is as good a medium as butter for blending flavors, but, because it has lighter texture and less pronounced flavor, it lets other flavors come through more clearly. Fruit purees lightened with whipped cream have the intense, fresh flavor of the fruit and make heavenly fillings and piped toppings. Chocolate, blended with heavy cream to become the most divine of all chocolate frostings, ganache, can be whipped full of air or left alone to become dense and creamy.

Plain lightly sweetened whipped cream complements any cake because of its soft, cloudlike texture and rich, faintly flowery flavor. It is particularly suited to sponge-type cakes such as *génoise, biscuit,* chiffon, and angel food cakes.

When used to fill a cake roll or accompany a slice of cake, whipped cream is loveliest when beaten only until it softly mounds when dropped from a spoon—not until stiff peaks form when the beater is lifted. To avoid overbeating, I usually finish the beating by hand with the detached whisk beater from the machine. When I raise the whisk and small but straight peaks form the cream is perfect.

When beaten conventionally, heavy cream at least doubles in volume. The food processor, however, produces a whipped cream that does not increase in volume. Its dense and velvety texture makes it ideal for piping decorative borders.

I like to sweeten whipped cream with 1 tablespoon granulated sugar per cup of cream. Powdered sugar adds an undesirable, slightly powdery texture because of the cornstarch it contains to keep it from lumping. (I use powdered sugar only when it is dissolved in liquid and heated to boiling to swell the starch and make its presence undetectable.)

Whipped cream usually must be refrigerated to preserve its texture. So when frosting and decorating a cake with whipped cream, select a sponge-type cake, not a butter cake which would harden if chilled.

The high heat required for ultrapasteurizing destroys some of the butterfat in cream; many areas of the country have cream with a low butterfat content to begin with. The combination of ultrapasteurization and low butterfat content make whipping cream more difficult and causes the finished cream to lack stability, losing 2 or more tablespoons of water per cup of cream if allowed

Cream Frostings and Fillings

to sit, even in the refrigerator. Consequently ultrapasteurized cream has many stabilizers added to it to enable it to whip. I have recently worked out a simple method for increasing the butterfat content of cream (page 254) and another easy method using cornstarch that locks in the moisture without increasing the butterfat. Both result in a more stable cream that holds up beautifully when piped.

Chilling the mixing bowl, beater, heavy cream, and even the sugar before beating helps to make the most of what butterfat the cream does contain. Whipped creams flavored with firm ingredients such as chocolate, cocoa, chestnut, powdered green tea, or fruit jams do not require any additional stabilizer. Except for chocolate or chestnut whipped cream, however, they will not hold for prolonged periods at room temperature.

To make plain whipped cream ahead without stabilizers, place the whipped cream in a cheesecloth-lined sieve to allow the liquid to drain off and then refrigerate lightly covered with plastic wrap. Or refrigerate the whipped cream and when ready to use whip lightly to reincorporate the liquid.

For icing a cake or making decorations, it is best to use whipped cream as soon as it is made, when its texture is smoothest. Decorated cakes may be kept one or two days in the refrigerator. Place them in an airtight cake carrier or glass dome (page 461) as cream absorbs other odors.

I have always been amazed and impressed by the whipped cream in Black Forest cakes in Switzerland. The taste is of rich cream and the texture is exceptionally light and soft, yet with a seemingly magical, invisible veil maintaining its form. I have only recently discovered the secret: A liquid product from Germany called Cobasan (page 425). It consists of sorbitol and glucose and stabilizes whipped cream and buttercreams. A minute quantity added to cream before whipping enables the whipped cream to hold up for as long as 6 hours at room temperature. It has no discernible color or odor and does not change the whipped cream's texture. This makes it possible to use whipped cream to frost and decorate cakes that are served at room temperature such as butter cakes and Chocolate Oblivion Truffle Torte.

Cobasan doesn't do a thing for ultrapasteurized cream (which is the soul of mediocrity and should be banned). If cream is ultrapasteurized, it will be indicated on the container. Cobasan stabilizes low butterfat cream but for a filling (as in the Black Forest Cake), a minimum of 35 percent butterfat cream is needed for it to work its wonders without the additional help of gelatin. The presence of gelatin in whipped cream is slightly detectable, but it does offer a firm texture for attractive slices of cake and whipped cream flowers.

*C*obasan (page 425) is easy to use and is the ideal method for stabilizing cream without changing flavor or texture. This frosting will hold up at room temperature for as long as 6 hours.

Whipped Cream

MAKES 2 CUPS
(enough to fill a cake roll)

INGREDIENTS	MEASURE	WEIGHT	
	volume	*pounds/ounces*	*kilograms/grams*
heavy cream	1 liquid cup	8 ounces	232 grams
sugar	1 tablespoon	0.5 ounce	13 grams
vanilla	½ teaspoon	•	•
optional: Cobasan, only if cream is not ultrapasteurized	full ¼ teaspoon	•	•

In a large mixing bowl place all the ingredients and refrigerate for at least 15 minutes. (Chill beater alongside bowl.)

Beat until stiff peaks form when the beater is raised. (For filling a cake roll or accompanying a slice of Chocolate Oblivion Truffle Torte, use softly whipped cream. To make softly whipped cream, beat only until soft peaks form or cream mounds softly when dropped from a spoon.)

Frost and decorate the cake and chill for at least 1 hour.

VARIATIONS

MOCHA WHIPPED CREAM: Increase sugar to 2 tablespoons and stir in 1 tablespoon cocoa (preferably Dutch-processed) and 1 teaspoon Medaglia d'Oro instant espresso powder.

COCOA WHIPPED CREAM: Increase sugar to 2½ tablespoons and stir in 2 tablespoons cocoa. Refrigerate for at least 1 hour to dissolve cocoa before beating.

POINTERS FOR SUCCESS:
Everything should be well chilled before beating. Do not overbeat. Chill the frosted cake for at least 1 hour before allowing it to stand at room temperature.

Real Old-Fashioned Whipped Cream

MAKES 2 CUPS
(enough to fill a cake roll)

*A*fter years of groaning about the deterioration of the quality of heavy cream (ultrapasteurization and a decrease in butterfat were the culprits) and envying those with access to 40 percent butterfat cream, I have finally found a way to get the butterfat back into the cream. I am both abashed and delighted to announce that it is the very soul of simplicity.

If the cream is low in butterfat (20 percent) this method will bring it to exactly 40 percent. If the cream is higher in butterfat (36 percent—whips readily), use only 3 tablespoons butter and the cream will end up with 52.5 percent butterfat and greatly increased stability.

This cream has the stability to use as a filling for Swiss Black Forest Cake (page 190), yet it has an extraordinarily light texture.

INGREDIENTS	MEASURE	WEIGHT	
	volume	*pounds/ounces*	*kilograms/grams*
heavy cream	1 liquid cup	8 ounces	232 grams
unsalted butter, softened	¼ cup	2 ounces	57 grams
vanilla	½ teaspoon	•	•
sugar	1 tablespoon	0.5 ounce	13 grams

STORE:
2 to 3 days refrigerated.

Refrigerate the mixing bowl and beater for at least 15 minutes.

In a small saucepan melt together ¼ cup cream and the butter, stirring constantly until the butter is fully melted. Pour into a small heatproof measuring cup and cool to room temperature. Add vanilla.

In the chilled mixing bowl beat the remaining ¾ cup cream and sugar just until traces of beater marks begin to show distinctly. Add the butter mixture on low speed in a steady stream, beating constantly. Beat until stiff peaks just form when the beater is raised.

NOTE: Whipped cream is smoothest when the butter mixture is added gradually. If the completed cake will have to sit at room temperature for more than 30 minutes, use whipped cream stabilized with gelatin as Real Old-Fashioned Whipped Cream will begin to soften.

UNDERSTANDING

According to the law of the land, heavy cream must be 20 to 40 percent butterfat. The average fat content is 37.5 percent, but alas, to date no law requires that the fat content be listed. You will know if your area of the country offers the 20 percent variety because you will encounter difficulty whipping it stiffly and, once whipped, it will separate or seem to curdle slightly at the edges if a fruit sauce is spooned onto it.

Butter contains 81 percent butterfat. The rest is milk solids and water. Using the method in the above recipe re-homogenizes the butter into the cream.

Cornstarch and powdered sugar (which contains 2 percent cornstarch) are cooked with a little cream until the starch swells and thickens it. The mixture is then beaten into the softly whipped cream. This whipped cream will not water out for up to 24 hours. While using this method does not affect the consistency, it will not stabilize the cream enough to keep at room temperature. It is excellent for frosting a cake that will remain refrigerated until serving time or for making whipped cream several hours ahead to serve on the side.

Stabilized Whipped Cream

MAKES 2 CUPS

INGREDIENTS	MEASURE	WEIGHT	
	volume	*pounds/ounces*	*kilograms/grams*
powdered sugar	2 tablespoons	0.5 ounce	13 grams
cornstarch *	1 teaspoon	•	•
heavy cream	1 liquid cup	8 ounces	232 grams
vanilla	½ teaspoon	•	•

* If your cream is very low in butterfat (page 427), 1¼ teaspoons cornstarch.

Refrigerate the mixing bowl and beater for at least 15 minutes.

In a small saucepan place powdered sugar and cornstarch and gradually stir in ¼ cup of the cream. Bring to a boil, stirring constantly, and simmer for just a few seconds (until the liquid is thickened). Scrape into a small bowl and cool to room temperature. Add vanilla.

STORE:
Up to 24 hours refrigerated; it will not water out.

POINTERS FOR SUCCESS:
The cornstarch mixture must not be warm when added to the cream. The cream must be cold when beaten. Do not overbeat.

Beat the remaining ¾ cup cream just until traces of beater marks begin to show distinctly.

Add the cornstarch mixture in a steady stream, beating constantly. Beat just until stiff peaks form when the beater is raised.

Super- Stabilized Whipped Cream

MAKES 2 CUPS

𝒢elatin stiffens whipped cream enough to make it suitable for a deep layer of filling or for piping roses. The gelatin makes the texture seem fuller and slightly spongy.

INGREDIENTS	MEASURE	WEIGHT	
	volume	pounds/ounces	kilograms/grams
powdered gelatin	½ to 1 teaspoon *	•	•
water	4 teaspoons	•	•
heavy cream	1 liquid cup	8 ounces	232 grams
sugar	1 tablespoon	½ ounce	13 grams
vanilla	½ teaspoon	•	•

* Use ½ teaspoon for roses, 1 teaspoon for deep fillings.

STORE:
2 days refrigerated. Frozen flowers keep 1 month.

POINTERS FOR SUCCESS:
The gelatin mixture must not be warm when added to the cream. The cream must be cold when beaten. Do not overbeat. Even a few extra seconds past stiff peaks and the consistency will no longer be velvety smooth.

Refrigerate the mixing bowl and beater for at least 15 minutes.

In a small heatproof measuring cup place gelatin and water. Allow to soften for 5 minutes. Set cup in a pan of simmering water and stir occasionally until gelatin is dissolved. (This can also be done in a microwave on high power, stirring once or twice.) Remove cup and cool to room temperature (about 7 minutes). Gelatin must be liquid but not warm when added to cream.

In the chilled bowl beat the cream and sugar just until traces of beater marks begin to show distinctly. Add the gelatin mixture in a steady stream, beating constantly. Add vanilla and beat just until stiff peaks form when beater is raised. Use at once to pipe roses. To keep their shape, freeze the roses before placing them on the cake. Whipped cream can be refrigerated for a few hours before piping rosettes.

*U*sing a food processor to "whip" the cream means that it will not be as light and airy as beaten whipped cream because it does not increase in volume. The added density makes this velvety whipped cream pipe like a dream.

INGREDIENTS	MEASURE	WEIGHT	
room temperature	*volume*	*pounds/ounces*	*kilograms/grams*
heavy cream	2 liquid cups	1 pound	464 grams
sugar	2 tablespoons	1 ounce	25 grams
vanilla	1 teaspoon	•	•
optional: Cobasan, only if cream is not ultrapasteurized	full ½ teaspoon	•	•

Place all the ingredients in the bowl of food processor fitted with the metal blade. Process, checking every few seconds by lifting a small amount of cream with a small metal spatula or spoon. The mixture should look thick and creamy and form a slight peak when lifted. It will not be fluffy. Use at once.

STORE:
Refrigerated up to 24 hours; cream will not water out.

POINTERS FOR SUCCESS:
The cream must be cold when processed. Do not overprocess. Even a few extra seconds past the peaking stage and the consistency will no longer be smooth.

For stability at prolonged room temperature, use Cobasan (page 425).

Chocolate Chip Whipped Cream

*T*his delectable filling has the lightness of whipped cream with the crunchy texture and wonderful flavor of chopped chocolate and almonds. It is the perfect consistency for filling Chocolate Chip Charlotte (page 179).

INGREDIENTS	MEASURE	WEIGHT	
room temperature	volume	pounds/ounces	kilograms/grams
powdered gelatin	2 teaspoons	•	6.2 grams
water	3 tablespoons	1.5 ounces	45 grams
heavy cream	2 liquid cups	1 pound	464 grams
sugar	2 tablespoons	1 ounce	25 grams
vanilla	1 teaspoon	•	4 grams
finely grated bittersweet chocolate	1 cup	5 ounces	142 grams
finely ground almonds	½ cup	2 ounces	54 grams

STORE:
3 days refrigerated.

POINTERS FOR SUCCESS:
The gelatin mixture must not be warm when added to the cream. The cream must be cold when beaten. Do not overbeat the cream as whipped cream will continue to stiffen after folding in chocolate and nuts.

Refrigerate the mixing bowl and beater for at least 15 minutes.

In a small heatproof glass measuring cup place gelatin and water. Allow to soften for 5 minutes. Set cup in a pan of simmering water and stir occasionally until gelatin is dissolved. (This can also be done in a microwave on high power, stirring once or twice.) Remove cup and cool to room temperature (about 7 minutes). Gelatin must be liquid but not warm when added to cream.

In the chilled bowl beat the cream and sugar just until traces of beater marks begin to show distinctly. Add the gelatin mixture in a steady stream, beating constantly. Add vanilla and beat just until soft peaks form when beater is raised. If preparing this filling for Chocolate Chip Charlotte (page 179), remove ½ cup whipped cream to use for attaching *génoise* strips. Cover with plastic wrap and place in refrigerator. To the remaining whipped cream, add chocolate and nuts and fold until evenly incorporated. Briefly set aside.

This recipe produces a *crème fraîche* reminiscent of the enchanting varieties found in France. I prefer it to any of the available commercial products. The proportion of 1 tablespoon buttermilk to 1 cup heavy cream results in a fresh, creamy taste with a gentle tang. I could eat it by the spoonful.

Sweetened with 1 tablespoon sugar and lightly beaten, it's a delightful topping for cheesecake, especially if crowned with fresh peach or banana slices.

Crème Fraîche Topping

(krem fresh)

MAKES 1 CUP

INGREDIENTS	MEASURE	WEIGHT	
	volume	*pounds/ounces*	*kilograms/grams*
heavy cream	1 liquid cup	8 ounces	232 grams
buttermilk	1 tablespoon	0.5 ounce	15 grams
sugar	1 tablespoon	0.5 ounce	13 grams

Combine the cream and buttermilk in a jar with a tight-fitting lid and place in a warm spot such as the top of the refrigerator or near the stove. Allow to sit undisturbed for 12 to 14 hours or until thickened but still pourable. (Ultra-pasteurized cream may take as long as 36 hours.)

NOTE: *Crème fraîche* is wonderful for finishing sauces not only because of its delicious flavor, but also because it does not curdle like sour cream.

STORE:
3 weeks refrigerated. *Crème fraîche* will continue to thicken on chilling. When ready to use, add the sugar and whisk lightly until soft mounds form when dropped from the spoon.

Quick Crème Fraîche

MAKES 3¾ CUPS

*T*his is an excellent substitute for the preceding recipe when time does not allow waiting for the *crème fraîche* to thicken. The taste is perhaps a bit less tangy.

The yield is perfect for filling 3 crispy rounds of meringue or dacquoise (pages 296 and 302) for a Fresh Berry Meringue Torte. Simply add a handful of fresh berries to each layer and top with a single decorative layer of berries. If you want the torte to stay crispy, assemble it 1 hour before eating. If made several hours ahead, the crisp rounds soften, and the torte becomes so light it seems to levitate.

INGREDIENTS	MEASURE	WEIGHT	
	volume	*pounds/ounces*	*kilograms/grams*
heavy cream	1½ liquid cups	12 ounces	348 grams
sour cream	½ cup	4.25 ounces	121 grams
sugar	2 tablespoons	1 ounce	25 grams

STORE:
24 hours refrigerated. Re-beat lightly before using.

In a large mixing bowl place all the ingredients and refrigerate for at least 15 minutes. Beat just until soft peaks form when the beater is raised or until it mounds when dropped from a spoon.

Mascarpone Frosting and Filling

MAKES 3 CUPS

I once saw a sign in Balducci's, a renowned New York food store, announcing: "Mascarpone Has Arrived from Italy!" My first thought was Marcel Mascarpone? Who is this? When I asked the cheese buyer, he offered me a taste of what turned out to be a creamy, delicious cheese. We both agreed that while similar to *crème fraîche*, it was more flavorful. I decided that I had to find a way to transform this slightly tangy, almost yeasty, utterly luscious cheese into a cake frosting.

On the first try, the frosting curdled drastically. Disappointed, I kept beating it relentlessly thinking: "What's the use?" Suddenly it emulsified and gained the perfect consistency for frosting or piping. It is especially delicious with fresh strawberries and Golden Butter Cream Cake (page 34).

INGREDIENTS	MEASURE	WEIGHT	
	volume	*pounds/ounces*	*kilograms/grams*
mascarpone	2 cups	1 pound	454 grams
sugar	2 tablespoons + 2 teaspoons	1.25 ounces	33 grams
heavy cream	⅔ liquid cup	5.5 ounces	160 grams

In a mixing bowl place the mascarpone and sugar and start beating at medium speed, preferably using a whisk beater. Gradually beat in the cream. The mixture will curdle at first but continue beating and it will become a smooth cream.

NOTE: Mascarpone varies in flavor. If it is more tangy it will require a bit more sugar.

STORE:
5 days refrigerated; 2 months frozen.

Green Tea Mousse Cream

MAKES 2 CUPS
(enough to fill a cake roll)

*T*he bitter moss green tea of the Japanese tea ceremony lends an exquisite color and flavor to whipped cream. Used to fill Green Tea Biscuit Roulade (page 144) it creates an extraordinary dessert, especially suitable for a Chinese or Japanese dinner when most Western desserts seem inappropriate. For further drama, make Green Tea Marzipan (page 321) and wrap the individual slices sushi-style by draping each with a thin free-form leaf shape. Oriental vegetable cutters in varying shapes also make dramatic marzipan decorations. Powdered green tea is available in Oriental food shops. For a mail-order source, see Katagiri (page 445).

INGREDIENTS	MEASURE	WEIGHT	
	volume	*pounds/ounces*	*kilograms/grams*
powdered green tea	2 teaspoons	•	•
sugar	1 tablespoon + 1 teaspoon	0.5 ounce	16 grams
heavy cream	1 liquid cup	8 ounces	242 grams

Refrigerate the mixing bowl and beater at least 15 minutes.
In the chilled mixing bowl place the green tea and sugar and gradually whisk in the cream. Beat until cream gently mounds when dropped from a spoon or until small peaks form when the beater is raised. Use at once.

STORE:
8 hours refrigerated.

POINTERS FOR SUCCESS:
Make Green Tea Mousse Cream the same day as serving because the flavor diminishes overnight.

Chestnut Mousse Cream

MAKES 5 CUPS
(enough to fill and frost two
9-inch by 1½-inch cake
layers)

*C*hestnut puree added to whipped cream makes one of my favorite cake fillings and toppings. The texture remains light and airy but the flavor, enhanced with rum, is assertive and earthy. This frosting and filling goes beautifully with Chestnut Génoise but also blends and contrasts well with any chocolate *génoise* or roll.

INGREDIENTS	MEASURE	WEIGHT	
	volume	*pounds/ounces*	*kilograms/grams*
unsweetened chestnut puree (see below)	1 cup	9.25 ounces	264 grams
powdered sugar	⅔ cup (lightly spooned into cup)	2.5 ounces	75 grams
dark rum	2 tablespoons	1 ounce	25 grams
heavy cream	2 liquid cups	1 pound	464 grams

STORE:
4 hours room temperature, 24 hours refrigerated.

POINTERS FOR SUCCESS:
The type of chestnut puree used will make or break this frosting. Crème de Marrons is cloyingly sweet and should not be used. French chestnut puree *(purée de marrons)*, available in fancy food stores (page 421), is softer than homemade but is acceptable. It is best to make your own from fresh or canned chestnuts (page 352) or use 1¼ cups (11.5 ounces/327 grams) Carma's chestnut puree (page 420), which has 25 to 30 percent sugar, and omit the powdered sugar.

Refrigerate the mixing bowl and beater for at least 15 minutes.

In a food processor fitted with the metal blade process the puree, sugar, and rum until smooth.

In the chilled bowl beat the cream until beater marks just start to appear. Add the chestnut mixture and beat just until stiff peaks form when the beater is raised.

NOTE: Whipped cream and chestnut puree are two of the components which make up my favorite winter dessert—discovered in Switzerland—Vermicelli. As the third component, *dacquoise,* is also in this book (page 302), I can't resist offering my version.

TO MAKE VERMICELLI
You will need a *dacquoise* disc (page 302), lightly whipped cream (page 253), about 1½ cups sweetened chestnut puree, and optional Chocolate Snowflakes (page 382). (The chocolate flakes are my contribution to this classic dessert.) For the chestnut puree, use the same proportion of unsweetened puree, powdered sugar, and rum as in the preceding recipe. Do not use canned puree as it will be too soft. An hour before serving, spoon the whipped cream over the

dacquoise. With a potato ricer or food mill fitted with the fine disc press the chestnut puree, allowing it to drop directly onto the whipped cream in vermicelli-like strands. If desired sprinkle with a flurry of chocolate flakes. This dessert can be made in a large 9- to 10-inch disc or individual 3- to 4-inch discs. At Confiserie Sprüngli in Zürich, individual portions are served in 3-inch decorative bonbon cups. (I could never pass the Paradeplatz without feeling the pull to go in and consume one.)

*R*aspberry whipped cream has the fresh tang of the berry with the billowy texture of whipped cream. The natural pectin in the berries acts as a stabilizer for the cream, preventing it from watering out and making it just firm enough for filling cake rolls.

Cordon Rose Raspberry Conserve is more than double the flavor concentration and less than two thirds the sugar of most jams. If using a commercial seedless raspberry jam in its place, double the amount will be required for equal flavor intensity and the sugar in the recipe should be eliminated.

Raspberry Jam Cream makes a lovely filling for Chocolate Cloud Roll (page 136) or Almond Biscuit Roulade (page 144).

Raspberry Jam Cream

MAKES 4½
CUPS
(enough for 2 cake rolls)

INGREDIENTS	MEASURE	WEIGHT	
	volume	*pounds/ounces*	*kilograms/grams*
Cordon Rose Raspberry Conserve (page 331)	½ cup	5 ounces	145 grams
Chambord liqueur or water	1 tablespoon	.	16 grams
heavy cream	2 liquid cups	1 pound	464 grams
sugar	2 tablespoons	1 ounce	26 grams

Refrigerate the mixing bowl and beater for at least 15 minutes. In a small bowl place the raspberry conserve or seedless jam and whisk in the chambord or water to soften it.

In the chilled bowl beat the cream and sugar just until beater marks begin to show distinctly. Add the conserve and beat just until stiff peaks form when the beater is raised. Use at once.

STORE:
Filled cake holds 2 hours at room temperature or 2 days refrigerated.

POINTERS FOR SUCCESS:
Cream must be cold when beaten. Do not overbeat.

VARIATIONS

Cordon Rose Strawberry Conserve also makes a delicious Jam Cream using the same proportions. Puree the conserve in a food processor before adding to the cream. (Do not use commercial strawberry jam; it is much too sweet.) Strawberry Jam Cream makes an exquisite filling and topping for Strawberry Shortcake. Use layers of Golden Butter Cream Cake (page 34) as the base. Or for a lighter, more elegant version, try layers of Génoise Classique moistened with Grand Marnier syrup. (Grand Marnier and strawberry is a classic and lovely combination.)

FRUIT CURD CREAM: Replace the conserve with 1 cup of Lemon, Lime, Passion, or Orange Curd (pages 340 to 342). Omit the Chambord and use water or a compatible fruit liqueur.

Fruit Cloud Cream

MAKES 5 CUPS
(enough for an 8-inch charlotte, page 369)

*F*ruit purees lightened with whipped cream are wonderful charlotte fillings because of their pure flavor and light texture. A small amount of gelatin makes the cloud cream just firm enough to unmold and to hold its form when sliced. This cream is also excellent for frosting and decorating *génoise*.

INGREDIENTS	MEASURE	WEIGHT	
	volume	*pounds/ounces*	*kilograms/grams*
powdered gelatin	2.5 teaspoons	•	7.75 grams
fruit puree, unsweetened and at room temperature	about 1 cup (see specific variations, page 265)	•	•
heavy cream	2 liquid cups	1 pound	464 grams
sugar	7 tablespoons to ⅔ cup (see specific variations, page 265)	•	•

Refrigerate the mixing bowl and beater for at least 15 minutes.

In a small heatproof measuring cup place the gelatin and ¼ cup fruit puree and allow to sit for 5 minutes. Set cup in a pan of simmering water for a few minutes, stirring occasionally until the gelatin is dissolved. (This can also be done in a few seconds in a microwave on high power, stirring once or twice.)

Remove the cup and stir the gelatin mixture into the remaining puree. The mixture should now be cool to the touch (not warm or ice cold).

In the chilled bowl beat the cream just until it mounds softly when dropped from a spoon. Add the puree and beat just until stiff peaks form when the beater is raised. Taste and fold in more sugar if you prefer a sweeter flavor. Use as soon as possible.

VARIATIONS

The strawberry and raspberry creams are rose colored, the apricot pale gold, and the peach pale yellow. All highlight the flavor of the fruit. The peach cream has the most delicate flavor.

STRAWBERRY CLOUD CREAM: 1 cup unsweetened Strawberry Puree (8.25 ounces/238 grams) (page 338) and 7 tablespoons sugar (3.25 ounces/92 grams). Serve with optional Grand Marnier Crème Anglaise (page 280).

RASPBERRY CLOUD CREAM: 1 cup unsweetened Raspberry Puree (8 ounces/227 grams) (page 337) and ⅔ cup sugar (4.5 ounces/132 grams). Serve with optional Chambord liqueur or Pistachio Crème Anglaise (page 282).

APRICOT CLOUD CREAM: 1 cup unsweetened Apricot Puree (9.5 ounces/270 grams) (page 335) and ½ cup sugar (3.5 ounces/100 grams). Use only 2 teaspoons gelatin with 1 tablespoon of water when softening in the ¼ cup puree. Serve with optional Barack Palinka (apricot eau-de-vie), apricot brandy, or Pistachio Crème Anglaise (page 282).

PEACH CLOUD CREAM: 2¼ cups unsweetened Peach Puree (18 ounces/510 grams) (page 336) and ⅔ cup sugar (4.5 ounces/132 grams). Use only 1½ cups cream. Serve with optional peach brandy, Pêcher Mignon, or Poire William Crème Anglaise (page 282).

NOTE: When serving the charlotte, if desired, use a complementary eau-de-vie or liqueur to flavor *crème anglaise* (page 280) to serve on the side and to flavor the soaking syrup for the *biscuit*. For a lighter touch serve raspberry sauce instead of *crème anglaise*.

STORE:
4 hours to 3 days refrigerated before unmolding filled cake; remove to room temperature 1 to 2 hours before serving.

POINTERS FOR SUCCESS:
The cream must be cold when beaten. The puree should be cool (not warm or ice cold) when added to the cream. For velvety smooth texture, do not overbeat.

Lemon Cream Illusion

MAKES 5 CUPS
(enough for an 8-inch
charlotte, page 369)

*T*his tart, intensely lemony cream is not technically a "cream" at all. Italian meringue replaces the whipped cream and the result is spectacular: lighter texture than Lemon Curd Cream (page 264), more intense lemon flavor, and far fewer calories! It is firm enough to use as filling for a cake roll but it needs the small amount of gelatin for a molded dessert such as a charlotte. Raspberry sauce is a perfect complement.

INGREDIENTS	MEASURE	WEIGHT	
room temperature	*volume*	*pounds/ounces*	*kilograms/grams*
optional: gelatin	1¼ teaspoons	•	•
water	2 tablespoons	1 ounce	30 grams
1 recipe Light Italian Meringue (page 298)	•	•	•
1 recipe Lemon Curd (page 340) prepared with ¼ cup sugar	•	•	•

STORE:
4 hours to 3 days refrigerated before unmolding a filled cake; remove to room temperature 1 to 2 hours before serving.

If using the gelatin: In a small heatproof glass measuring cup place the gelatin and water and allow to sit for 5 minutes. Set cup in a pan of simmering water for a few minutes, stirring occasionally until the gelatin is dissolved. (This can also be done in a few seconds in a microwave on high power, stirring once or twice.)

Prepare the Light Italian Meringue. When mixer is on medium speed to cool the meringue, beat in the optional gelatin. When completely cool, add cold Lemon Curd and beat *just* to incorporate. Taste and fold in more sugar if desired. Use as soon as possible.

Ganache, a wondrous combination of chocolate and heavy cream, has many permutations and possibilities. It is said to have originated in Switzerland, where it is used mainly as the base for chocolate truffles. Because of its dark, gleaming color and rich flavor it is my favorite of all chocolate frostings. (Of course, this is dependent on using the finest chocolate!)

Ganache is more chocolaty but less rich and buttery than a buttercream. It is so flavorful, however, that I use only about three quarters as much ganache frosting as buttercream.

The proportion of chocolate to cream can vary widely for a ganache, starting from less than ½ ounce of cream per ounce of chocolate (for a ganache so fudgy it cannot frost a cake without separating from the crumb) all the way up to 2 ounces of cream for every ounce of chocolate (for a light-colored, airy ganache).

When I use a higher proportion of cream I use a more bitter chocolate because the natural sugar in the cream adds sweetness. In general, I prefer whipped ganache with airy cakes such as *génoise* and denser ganache for chocolate butter cakes.

Any ganache should be smooth and creamy. Overbeating will curdle it and ruin its texture, but it is possible to remelt the mixture in a double boiler or microwave and start again. In the dark ages BC (Before Cuisinarts), ganache was tricky because the chocolate had to be heated with the cream and sometimes the cocoa butter in the chocolate would separate and come to the surface. In that case, I'd let the mixture cool and stir it back to a smooth emulsion.

The food processor has made this magnificent chocolate frosting into the easiest and most foolproof of all frostings to prepare! It also ensures the best possible flavor because the chocolate gets heated only enough to melt it. This places me in permanent debt to Carl Sontheimer, who brought the food processor to this country, enormously improved the design, and, in the old days, used to nudge me with occasional phone calls daring me to make the big transition from knife to processor. Actually this was a mental block that took years for the American cooking culture to overcome. As recently as five years ago I remember hearing at least two chocolate celebrities unequivocally state that "No! Ganache cannot be made in a food processor!" So much for that.

GANACHE FROSTING, FILLING, GLAZE, AND SAUCE

Light Whipped Ganache Filling and Frosting

MAKES 4 CUPS
(enough to fill and frost two 9-inch by 1½-inch layers)

*T*his ganache has double the weight of cream to chocolate. It is so light and airy it seems to disappear in the mouth. The pale brown color makes it ideal as a filling rather than a frosting, although it pipes well at room temperature. Light ganache is a less conventional filling for Swiss Black Forest Cake (page 190) or any light chocolate cake such as *génoise* and *biscuit*. It also works well as a filling for a charlotte (page 369) and is divine in Triple Chocolate Cake (page 201) encased in sheets of chocolate praline.

INGREDIENTS	MEASURE	WEIGHT	
	volume	*pounds/ounces*	*kilograms/grams*
bittersweet chocolate *	2⅔ (3-ounce) bars	8 ounces	227 grams
heavy cream	2 liquid cups	1 pound	464 grams
vanilla	½ teaspoon	•	•

* My favorite sweetness balance is 4 ounces semisweet chocolate and 4 ounces extra bittersweet. If I am planning a very sweet topping such as Chocolate Praline Sheets (page 315), I use all extra bittersweet.

STORE:
1 day room temperature, 1 week refrigerated, 3 months frozen.

POINTERS FOR SUCCESS:
The temperature of the mixture is critical when beating. If not cold it will not stiffen; if too cold it will not aerate well. Overbeating causes curdling.

Break the chocolate into pieces and process in a food processor until very fine. Heat the cream to the boiling point and, with motor running, pour it through the feed tube in a steady stream. Process a few seconds until smooth.

Transfer to a large bowl of electric mixer and refrigerate until cold, stirring once or twice (about 2 hours). You may speed chilling by setting the bowl in an ice water bath and stirring frequently. Do not allow the mixture to get too cold or it will be too stiff to incorporate air.

Add the vanilla and beat the mixture just until very soft peaks form when the beater is raised. It will continue to thicken after a few minutes at room temperature. The safest way not to overbeat is to use an electric mixture until the ganache starts to thicken and then continue with a hand-held whisk.

If the mixture gets overbeaten and grainy, it can be restored by remelting, chilling, and rebeating.

VARIATION

QUICK LIGHT WHIPPED GANACHE: If you need the whipped ganache sooner and cannot wait for the mixture to chill, the following method gives equal results but involves a little more work.

Refrigerate the mixing bowl and beaters.

Using a double boiler or a microwave on high power (stirring every 10 seconds if a microwave is used), melt the chocolate pieces with ⅔ cup cream. Remove from the heat before the chocolate is fully melted and finish melting by stirring constantly. Set aside until no longer warm.

In the chilled bowl beat the cream until traces of beater marks just begin to show distinctly. Add the chocolate mixture and beat just until soft peaks form when the beater is raised.

*C*lassic ganache frosting usually has equal weights of chocolate and cream. Since I find this consistency is just a shade too stiff to adhere well to cakes, I have very slightly increased the amount of cream so that the frosting is fudgy and thick while still able to cling to the cake. This ganache also makes a superb sauce for a chocolate charlotte, ice cream, or poached pears (Poires Belle Hélène).

Because dark ganache is so rich and chocolaty, 3 cups is sufficient to fill and frost two 9-inch round cake layers. The fudgy texture blends best with butter cake, preferably chocolate, as the ganache will overwhelm a more gently flavored cake. It also happens to blend wonderfully with a chestnut butter cake (page 42).

My preference is a dense unbeaten ganache, but, if you would like to try a slightly airier version with the same intensity, use the optional butter (about 1 teaspoon per ounce of chocolate) and beat the ganache slightly. The optional Cognac heightens the elegance of the chocolate without imparting any bitterness.

Dark Chocolate Ganache Filling, Frosting, and Sauce

MAKES 2¾ TO 3 CUPS
(enough to fill and frost two 8-inch by 1½-inch layers or two 9-inch by 1-inch layers)

INGREDIENTS	MEASURE	WEIGHT	
	volume	*pounds/ounces*	*kilograms/grams*
bittersweet chocolate	4 (3-ounce) bars	12 ounces	340 grams
heavy cream	1⅔ liquid cups	13.5 ounces	385 grams
optional: unsalted butter, softened	¼ cup	2 ounces	57 grams
Cognac	2 tablespoons	1 ounce	28 grams

days room temperature, 2
weeks refrigerated, 6
months frozen. To soften
ganache after chilling, allow
to warm to room tempera-
ture and, if necessary, warm
just to soften using a hot
water bath or a few seconds
in the microwave. Stir gently
if you do not wish to aerate.

POINTERS FOR SUCCESS:
Your favorite semisweet or
bittersweet eating chocolate
will result in the best flavored ganache. If the chocolate is not smooth-textured
in bar form it will not be
entirely smooth in the ganache either.

Break the chocolate into pieces and process in a food processor until very fine. Heat the cream to the boiling point
and, with the motor running, pour it through the feed tube
in a steady stream. Process a few seconds until smooth.
Transfer to a bowl and cool completely. Gently stir in the
optional butter and/or Cognac. Allow to cool for several
hours until of frosting consistency. If using butter, whisk
for a few seconds to aerate. The color will lighten.

To use ganache as sauce, reheat until pourable if made
ahead, using a double boiler or a microwave on low power,
stirring every 15 seconds.

VARIATION
PRALINE GANACHE: Add ⅓ cup praline paste (page 430)
to the chocolate before processing.

UNDERSTANDING
Students have often asked me why it isn't advisable to add
unheated cream to melted chocolate. If the cream is added
cold, the chocolate hardens unevenly, forming little specks
that melt on the tongue but are not visually attractive. The
reason that the cream is brought to the boiling point is not
only to melt the chocolate but also to give a longer shelf
life to the ganache. In commercial establishments in France,
the cream is brought to a full boil three times to destroy
any bacteria. This may be because their cream is not pasteurized to the same temperature as ours. It may also be to
improve shelf life in a commercial situation. If using ultra-
pasteurized cream, it is unnecessary to bring it to a boil
other than to melt the chocolate.

There are several ingredients that can be added to chocolate to create a dark, shiny glaze: butter, oil, jam, corn syrup, sugar syrup, even water. But cream seems to bring out the fullest chocolate flavor, so if I have cream on hand Chocolate Cream Glaze is the only one I use. A tablespoon of Cognac heightens the flavor of the chocolate, but if a fine-quality chocolate is used the Cognac is optional.

A chocolate glaze is an ideal adornment for a cake. It is easy to make and creates a flawless, shiny finish while sealing in freshness.

Chocolate Cream Glaze

MAKES 2
FULL CUPS
(enough to glaze a
9-inch cake)

INGREDIENTS	MEASURE	WEIGHT	
	volume	pounds/ounces	kilograms/grams
bittersweet chocolate	3 (3-ounce) bars	9 ounces	255 grams
heavy cream	1 liquid cup	8 ounces	232 grams
optional: Cognac	1 tablespoon	0.5 ounce	14 grams

TO PREPARE CAKE FOR GLAZING

Brush all crumbs from the surface and place on a cardboard round the same size as the cake. Suspend the cake on a rack set on a baking sheet to catch excess glaze.

It is best to have enough glaze to cover the cake with one application as touch-ups don't usually produce as flawless a finish. Excess glaze can be frozen and reheated at a later date.

TO PREPARE GLAZE

Break the chocolate into pieces and process in a food processor until very fine. Remove the chocolate to a small heavy saucepan.

Heat the cream to the boiling point and pour three quarters of it over the chocolate. Cover for 5 minutes to allow chocolate to melt. Gently stir together until smooth, trying not to create air bubbles. Pass through a fine strainer, stir in optional Cognac, and allow to cool until just tepid.

CHECK FOR CONSISTENCY

At a tepid temperature a small amount of glaze should mound a bit when dropped from a spoon before smoothly disappearing. If the glaze is too thick and the mound remains on surface or if the glaze seems curdled, add some

STORE:
3 days room temperature, 2 weeks refrigerated, 6 months frozen.

POINTERS FOR SUCCESS:
Your favorite semisweet or bittersweet eating chocolate will result in the best flavored glaze. If the chocolate is not smooth-textured in the bar it will not be entirely smooth in the glaze either.

The butterfat content of cream varies and will affect the glaze. Always check for consistency at a tepid temperature. If it is the correct consistency when tepid, even if it becomes too cool when applied to the cake and lumps, the cake can be placed in a warm oven for a few seconds and the glaze will smoothen. If glaze had been tested when hot and was the right consistency, the extra heat would not help if glaze lumps. On the other hand, if glaze had been the correct consistency when cool, it would never firm adequately on the cake.

To reheat glaze: Use a double boiler, stirring gently, or a microwave oven on high power, stirring and folding every 5 seconds.

of the warm remaining cream by the teaspoon. If the glaze is too thin, gently stir in a small amount of melted chocolate. When the consistency is correct, use at once or store and reheat.

The glaze should be poured onto the center of the cake, allowing the excess to flow down the sides. Smooth quickly and evenly with a large metal spatula, moving it lightly back and forth across the top until smooth. If any spots on the sides remain unglazed, use a small metal spatula to lift up some glaze which has fallen onto the baking sheet and apply to uncovered area.

Lift rack and tap lightly to settle glaze. Lift cake from rack using a broad spatula or pancake turner and set on a serving plate or on a clean rack if planning to apply a second coat of glaze.

If you want to cover the cake more thickly and evenly, two coats of glaze can be applied by the following technique: After the first coat is applied, refrigerate the cake for 20 minutes or until the glaze is firm. Apply a second coat of tepid glaze. (You will need 1½ times the glaze for a double coat.)

Allow cake to set for a least 2 hours at room temperature. Refrigerating the cake will dull the glaze slightly.

I use this recipe when I need a dark, shiny chocolate glaze and there is no cream in the house (there's always butter!). It is similar in makeup and flavor to Chocolate Cream Glaze (see Understanding below) but not quite as mellow.

INGREDIENTS	MEASURE		WEIGHT	
	volume	*pounds/ounces*	*kilograms/grams*	
bittersweet chocolate, chopped	4 (3-ounce) bars	12 ounces	340 grams	
unsalted butter, softened	¾ cup	6 ounces	170 grams	
water	½ liquid cup	4 ounces	118 grams	
corn syrup	1 tablespoon	0.75 ounce	20 grams	
vanilla	1 tablespoon	0.5 ounce	12 grams	

TO PREPARE CAKE FOR GLAZING

Brush all crumbs from the surface and place on a cardboard round the same size as the cake. Suspend the cake on a rack set on a baking sheet to catch excess glaze.

It is best to have enough glaze to cover the cake with one application as touch-ups don't usually produce as flawless a finish. Excess glaze can be frozen and reheated at a later date.

TO PREPARE GLAZE

Using a double boiler set over hot, not simmering, water on low heat or a microwave on high power (stirring every 10 seconds) melt the chocolate. Remove from the heat before the chocolate is fully melted and stir until melted. Stir in the butter, 1 tablespoon at a time, until blended. If necessary return briefly to the heat but do not allow to become too hot or the butter will separate.

Heat the water to 120°F. or use hot tap water. Add all at once to the chocolate mixture and stir until smooth. Stir in the corn syrup and vanilla until uniform in color.

CHECK FOR CONSISTENCY

Allow glaze to cool, stirring occasionally, until a small amount mounds a bit when dropped from a spoon before

STORE:
3 days room temperature, 2 weeks refrigerated, 6 months frozen.

POINTERS FOR SUCCESS:
Your favorite semisweet or bittersweet eating chocolate will result in the best flavored ganache. If the chocolate is not smooth-textured in bar form it will not be entirely smooth in the ganache either.

smoothly disappearing. The glaze will be cool when the proper consistency is attained but will harden on setting.

Use at once or store and reheat. For a glaze that is perfectly uniform in color, hold a fine strainer over the cake and pour the glaze through the strainer.

If you want to cover the cake more thickly and evenly, two coats of glaze can be applied by the following technique: Pour the glaze and smooth quickly with a spatula to create a thin, even coating. Refrigerate the cake for 20 minutes or until the glaze is firm. Apply a second coat of tepid glaze.

Allow the cake to set for at least 2 hours at room temperature. Refrigerating the cake will dull the glaze slightly.

UNDERSTANDING

For a glaze, 12 ounces chocolate require either 10.67 ounces cream or 6 ounces butter plus water to approximate the water contained by the cream.

Butter is 81 percent fat, 15.5 percent water, and 3.5 percent milk solids.

Cream is 37.6 percent fat, 56.5 percent water, and 5.8 percent milk solids.

Six ounces butter contain 4.86 ounces fat, 0.93 ounce water, and 0.21 ounce milk solids.

There are 4 ounces fat, 6 ounces water, and 0.62 ounce milk solids in 10.67 ounces cream.

This means that the butter has 0.86 ounce more fat, about 5 ounces less water, and almost ½ ounce less milk solids. The missing water for the glaze is supplied by the 4 ounces water, vanilla, and corn syrup. Corn syrup adds sweetness (the absent milk solids contain sugar) and extra shine.

Chocolate Butter Glaze is slightly thinner than Chocolate Cream Glaze (page 271) at a tepid temperature because of the missing milk solids and extra butterfat, but when set it is equally firm because the butter hardens.

Sour cream in place of heavy cream makes a smooth and lilting frosting with excellent piping consistency. This easy-to-make ganache has a unique tanginess which I find delicious with any chocolate layer cake. It is especially good with Cordon Rose Banana Cake (page 69).

INGREDIENTS	MEASURE	WEIGHT	
room temperature	volume	pounds/ounces	kilograms/grams
bittersweet chocolate	4 (3-ounce) bars	12 ounces	340 grams
sour cream	1⅔ cups	14 ounces	400 grams

In a double boiler set over hot water or in a microwave on high power, stirring every 10 seconds, melt the chocolate. Remove from the heat and add the sour cream. Stir with a rubber spatula until uniform in color. If the pan feels warm, transfer to a bowl.

Use at once or store, and when ready to use soften by placing the bowl in a water bath or a microwave for a few seconds, stirring gently.

STORE:
3 days room temperature, 3 weeks refrigerated, 6 months frozen.

POINTERS FOR SUCCESS:
The chocolate must still be warm and the sour cream room temperature when combined or the chocolate will lump.

Raspberry Ganache

MAKES 3 CUPS
(enough to fill and frost two
8-inch by 1½-inch layers
or two 9-inch by
1-inch layers)

*T*his most unique and glorious of ganache frostings is ideal for a special occasion. Be sure to use imported white chocolate that contains pure cocoa butter.

The intense puree adds a tangy undertone and lingering taste of raspberries to the chocolate, creating a subtle reddish brown gleam. A small amount of white chocolate tames the tartness of the raspberries.

INGREDIENTS	MEASURE	WEIGHT	
	volume	*pounds/ounces*	*kilograms/grams*
bittersweet chocolate	4 (3-ounce) bars	12 ounces	340 grams
white chocolate	1 (3-ounce) bar	3 ounces	85 grams
heavy cream	1 liquid cup	8 ounces	232 grams
Raspberry Sauce, lightly sweetened (page 337)	½ liquid cup	4.75 ounces	135 grams
optional: Chambord (black raspberry liqueur)	1½ tablespoons	•	24 grams

STORE:
1 day room temperature, 10 days refrigerated, 6 months frozen.

POINTERS FOR SUCCESS:
Use your favorite bittersweet chocolate and imported white chocolate, which contains cocoa butter. Tobler Narcisse is my personal preference.

Break the chocolate into pieces and process in food processor until very fine.

Heat the cream and raspberry puree in a saucepan or microwave on high power to the boiling point.

With the motor running, pour the cream mixture through the feed tube in a steady stream. Process a few seconds until smooth.

Transfer to a bowl and stir in the optional Chambord. Allow to cool for several hours until mixture reaches frosting consistency.

TIP: Raspberry Ganache makes an excellent glaze but needs to be slightly thinner. Add warm cream or more Chambord by the tablespoon until of glazing consistency (see techniques for Ganache Glaze, page 271). To avoid air bubbles, do not use the food processor.

Burnt Almond Milk Chocolate Ganache

This luscious frosting was inspired by Hershey's addictive Golden Almond bar. The cocoa is added to enrich the flavor and temper the sweetness of the melted milk chocolate. It is a wonderful frosting for just about any chocolate cake.

MAKES 3 CUPS
(enough to fill and frost two 8-inch by 1½-inch cake layers or two 9-inch by 1-inch layers)

INGREDIENTS	MEASURE	WEIGHT	
	volume	*pounds/ounces*	*kilograms/grams*
Hershey's Golden Almond bars	6 (3.2-ounce) bars	1 pound 3.2 ounces	544 grams
unsweetened cocoa	¼ cup (lightly spooned into cup)	0.75 ounce	23 grams
heavy cream	1¼ cups	10 ounces	290 grams
optional: amaretto	2 tablespoons	0.5 ounce	16 grams

In a food processor, break chocolate into large pieces and process together with the cocoa until the almonds are coarsely chopped. Transfer to a medium bowl.

In a saucepan or microwave on high power, heat cream to the boiling point. Pour into chocolate and stir until smooth. Stir in amaretto, if desired, and allow mixture to cool for several hours until it reaches frosting consistency.

STORE:
1 day at room temperature, 10 days refrigerated, 6 months frozen.

White Ganache

White chocolate is a superb stabilizer for whipped cream. It prevents watering out and enables it to hold its shape for several hours at room temperature. It pipes even from a small tube and also freezes well. If a judicious amount of white chocolate is used, there is no reason for White Ganache to be cloyingly sweet. In fact, the 3 ounces white chocolate in this recipe contain only 7 teaspoons sugar, making the ganache just a little sweeter than Perfect Whipped Cream (page 253).

In addition to stabilizing and sweetening the cream, the white chocolate also flavors it with vanilla and cocoa butter, lending it a chocolate quality so delicate as not to overwhelm other flavors.

White Ganache can be used in any number of ways. Serve it with fresh berries or fold in a stiffly beaten egg white and have an instant white chocolate mousse to serve with Raspberry (page 337) or Strawberry Sauce (page 338). Use the White Ganache to fill and frost Swiss Black Forest Cake (page 190) or to pipe elaborate festoons on Chocolate Oblivion Truffle Torte (page 84).

MAKES 2 CUPS
(enough to frost one 8-inch by 3-inch cake layer)

INGREDIENTS	MEASURE	WEIGHT	
	volume	*pounds/ounces*	*kilograms/grams*
white chocolate, chopped	1 (3-ounce) bar	3 ounces	85 grams
heavy cream	1 liquid cup	8 ounces	232 grams

STORE:
1 day room temperature, 3 days refrigerated, 2 months frozen.

POINTERS FOR SUCCESS:
Use imported white chocolate which contains cocoa butter. Tobler Narcisse is my personal preference. If leaving a decorated cake at room temperature, do not cover it or the ganache will soften.

Refrigerate the mixing bowl and beater for at least 15 minutes.

Using a double boiler or microwave on high power (stirring every 10 seconds if using microwave), melt the chocolate with ¼ cup cream. Remove from the heat before the chocolate is fully melted and stir until melted. Set aside until no longer warm.

In the chilled bowl beat the cream until traces of beater marks just begin to show distinctly. Add the white chocolate mixture and beat just until stiff peaks form when the beater is raised.

TIP: For a deliciously tart white ganache, great for serving with fresh fruit, replace the heavy cream with *crème fraîche*.

Custard Cream Fillings and Sauces

*C*ustard creams are the foundation for many desserts. The basic *crème anglaise* (or English custard sauce) consists of egg yolks, sugar, and milk or cream (or a combination of the two) and is a base for Silk Meringue Buttercream (page 239), an accompaniment to charlottes or fresh fruit, an ingredient in Bavarian creams, and the start of the richest, creamiest ice creams.

When making *crème anglaise,* I favor the lighter versions made with all milk to accompany a rich dessert and those with three-quarters cream to serve with fresh fruit. Ice cream has the smoothest texture when *crème anglaise* is made with at least three-quarters cream to one-quarter milk. More than that becomes too rich for my taste.

Three to four egg yolks per cup of cream or milk are ideal to thicken and enrich the sauce. If I am using praline paste, however, which adds more body, I use only two yolks.

I also prefer a rather low amount of sugar, two to three tablespoons per cup of milk or cream. Ice cream requires the higher amount because freezing makes it seem less sweet. In any event, it is a simple matter to stir in more sugar to taste even after making the sauce.

Bavarian cream is a molded *crème anglaise* with whipped cream added. It relies on gelatin to keep its shape, and, if prepared in a decorative mold, it may be served without cake. Encased by gossamer Biscuit Roulade (page 142) filled with a thin layer of tart jam and served with an intense raspberry sauce, it is (in my book) the most perfect of desserts. I call it the Scarlett Empress (page 177).

It is, of course, possible to flavor Bavarian cream with chocolate or fruit puree, but I find that most of these flavors become overwhelmed and dulled by the Bavarian base. I much prefer flavoring the Bavarian with vanilla and liqueur and making Light Whipped Ganache (page 268) or Fruit Cloud Cream (page 264) instead when I am in the mood for other flavors.

Two noteworthy exceptions are orange and pear Bavarians. For orange Bavarian, the *crème anglaise*'s milk base makes it possible to steep the orange zest, extracting more flavor. For pear Bavarian, using the poaching liquid instead of milk, combined with the Italian meringue, makes it lighter even than a cloud cream.

Liqueur such as kirsch or Grand Marnier is traditionally added to Bavarian cream not only for its lovely flavor and aroma but also because it effectively masks any gelatin flavor.

Most recipes beat the egg yolks with the sugar until very thick to make an airier Bavarian. But it is my belief that the air completely disappears during the subsequent cooking of the custard. If I want a denser, creamy Bavarian, I rely on whipped cream to lighten it slightly. For a moussier effect I add beaten egg whites and for a billowy, cloudlike Bavarian I use Italian meringue (egg whites stabilized with hot sugar syrup.)

I find that the gelatin in Bavarians continues to thicken over a 24-hour period and after that does not get any thicker even when frozen and defrosted. Therefore you can freeze any of the cakes filled with Bavarian cream for at least three weeks without loss of flavor or texture.

Crème Anglaise

(krem ahnGLEZ)

MAKES 1¼ CUPS

*T*his rich, smooth cream, served cold, is the perfect accompaniment for charlottes filled with Fruit Cloud Cream (page 264) or for seasonal fruit. Use the optional eau-de-vie or liqueur to complement the fruit. One of my favorites is Grand Marnier.

INGREDIENTS	MEASURE	WEIGHT	
	volume	*pounds/ounces*	*kilograms/grams*
sugar	2 tablespoons	1 ounce	25 grams
salt	pinch	•	•
4 large egg yolks	¼ liquid cup	2.5 ounces	74 grams
milk	1 liquid cup	8.5 ounces	242 grams
½ vanilla bean,* split lengthwise	•	•	•
optional: liqueur or eau-de-vie	2 to 3 tablespoons	0.75 to 1.25 ounces	21 to 35 grams

* You may substitute 1 teaspoon vanilla extract for the vanilla bean, but the bean offers a fuller, more aromatic flavor. If using extract, add it after the sauce is cool. If using a Tahitian bean, use only one quarter of the bean.

Have a fine strainer ready near the range, suspended over a small mixing bowl.

In a small heavy noncorrodible saucepan stir together the sugar, salt, and yolks until well blended, using a wooden spoon.

In another small saucepan (or heatproof glass measure if using a microwave on high power) heat the milk and vanilla bean to the boiling point. Stir a few tablespoons into the yolk mixture; then gradually add the remaining milk and vanilla bean, stirring constantly.

Heat the mixture to just before the boiling point (170°F. to 180°F.). Steam will begin to appear and the mixture will be slightly thicker than heavy cream. It will leave a well-defined track when a finger is run across the back of a spoon. Immediately remove from the heat and pour into the strainer, scraping up the thickened cream that settles on the bottom of the pan. Remove the vanilla bean and scrape the seeds into the sauce. Stir until seeds separate. For maximum flavor, return the pod to the sauce until serving time.

Cool in an ice-water bath or the refrigerator. Stir in the optional liqueur.

UNDERSTANDING

Commercial establishments sometimes bring the mixture to a boil and quickly strain it, discarding the curdled part. This is done only to save time and to ensure that the temperature is hot enough without bothering with other tests. (I do not recommend this method.)

STORE:
5 days refrigerated, 3 months frozen. Sauce thickens slightly overnight in refrigerator.

POINTERS FOR SUCCESS:
Don't use whisk to stir if not using accurate thermometer because the foam makes it difficult to see when mixture is getting close to the boiling point. Do not heat above 180°F. or the sauce will begin to curdle. If overheated and *slight* curdling does take place, pour instantly into a blender and blend until smooth before straining.

Pistachio Crème Anglaise

(Pistachio krem ahnGLEZ)

MAKES 1 FULL CUP

*T*his sauce is the palest of greens and beautifully perfumed by the pistachio nut. Pistasha liqueur intensifies the flavor and slightly deepens the color. This contrasts beautifully in color and flavor with the dark chocolate of Chocolate Oblivion Truffle Torte (page 84). Since I always have difficulty deciding whether I prefer pistachio or raspberry sauce with chocolate, I sometimes drop little pools of raspberry on top of the pistachio (using a squeeze bottle) and intermingle them.

INGREDIENTS	MEASURE	WEIGHT	
	volume	*pounds/ounces*	*kilograms/grams*
shelled unsalted pistachio nuts	¼ cup	1.25 ounces	38 grams
milk	1 liquid cup	8.5 ounces	242 grams
sugar	3 tablespoons	1.25 ounces	38 grams
salt	pinch	•	•
4 large egg yolks	¼ liquid cup	2.5 ounces	74 grams
optional: Pistasha (pistachio liqueur)	2 tablespoons	0.75 ounces	25 grams

POINTERS FOR SUCCESS:
Do not blanch the nuts to remove the skin as they will lose most of their flavor. If too much skin is left, the color will be slightly brown instead of green. Don't use a whisk to stir if not using an accurate thermometer because the foam makes it difficult to see when the mixture is getting close to boiling. Do not heat above 180°F. or the sauce will curdle. If overheated and *slight* curdling does take place, pour instantly into a blender and blend until smooth before straining.

Bake nuts in a 350°F. oven for 5 to 10 minutes or until skins separate from nuts when scratched lightly with a fingernail. Remove as much skin as possible. In a food processor or nut grinder grind nuts very fine.

In a small saucepan (or heatproof glass measure if using a microwave on high power) place nuts and milk and bring to the boiling point. Cover and allow to steep for at least 30 minutes. Strain through cheesecloth, pressing well to remove all milk, and discard nuts. Return milk to saucepan or glass measure.

Have a fine strainer ready near the range, suspended over a small mixing bowl.

In a small heavy, noncorrodible saucepan stir together the sugar, salt, and yolks until well blended, using a wooden spoon.

Heat the milk just to the boiling point. Stir a few tablespoons into the yolk mixture; then gradually add the remaining milk, stirring constantly.

Heat the mixture to just before the boiling point (170°F.

to 180°F.). Steam will begin to appear and the mixture will be slightly thicker than heavy cream. It will leave a well-defined track when a finger is run across the back of a spoon. Immediately remove from the heat and pour into the strainer, scraping up the thickened cream that settles on the bottom of the pan.

Cool in an ice-water bath or the refrigerator. Stir in the optional Pistasha liqueur.

*P*raline paste made with hazelnuts and caramelized sugar is a flavorful enrichment to *crème anglaise*. The praline paste adds body, so only half the usual number of egg yolks is needed. It also adds sweetness, making it unnecessary to add any sugar. Dark rum or cognac both highlight the praline flavor and cut the richness. This sauce is especially delicious with the praline version of Chocolate Oblivion Truffle Torte (page 86).

Crème Anglaise Praliné

(krem ahnGLEZ PRAHleanAY)

MAKES 1⅓ FULL CUPS

INGREDIENTS	MEASURE	WEIGHT	
	volume	*pounds/ounces*	*kilograms/grams*
praline paste (page 431)	¼ cup	2.75 ounces	77 grams
milk	1 liquid cup	8.5 ounces	242 grams
2 large egg yolks	2 tablespoons	1.25 ounces	37 grams
salt	speck	•	•
vanilla	1 teaspoon	•	4 grams
optional: rum or Cognac	1½ tablespoons	0.75 ounce	21 grams

In a food processor place the praline paste and, with the motor running, gradually add the milk. Process until smooth.

In a small, heavy, noncorrodible saucepan stir together the yolks and salt until well blended, using a wooden spoon.

In another small saucepan (or a heatproof glass measure if using a microwave on high power) heat the praline mixture to the boiling point. Stir a few tablespoons into the yolk mixture; then gradually add the remainder, stirring constantly.

Heat the mixture to just before the boiling point (170°F. to 180°F.). Steam will begin to appear and the mixture will

STORE:
5 days refrigerated, 3 months frozen.

POINTERS FOR SUCCESS:
Don't use a whisk to stir if not using an accurate thermometer because the foam makes it difficult to see when the mixture is getting close to boiling. Don't heat above 180°F. or the sauce will curdle. If overheated

and *slight* curdling does take place, pour instantly into a blender and blend until smooth.

Crème Anglaise Café

(krem ahnGLEZ kahFAY)

MAKES 1⅓
CUPS

be slightly thicker than heavy cream. It will leave a well-defined track when a finger is run across the back of a spoon. Immediately remove from the heat and pour into a bowl, scraping up the thickened cream that settles on the bottom of the pan.

Cool in an ice-water bath or the refrigerator. Stir in the vanilla and optional liqueur.

*T*his classic French method of extracting coffee essence provides intense flavor. Extra sugar is used to offset the bitterness of the coffee. This sauce is lovely served with Chocolate Torture (page 87) because it deepens the subtle coffee background flavor.

INGREDIENTS	MEASURE	WEIGHT	
	volume	*pounds/ounces*	*kilograms/grams*
4 large egg yolks	¼ liquid cup	2.5 ounces	74 grams
sugar *	¼ cup	1.75 ounces	50 grams
salt	pinch	•	•
milk	1 cup	8.5 ounces	242 grams
finely ground coffee beans	2.5 tablespoons	•	10 grams
½ vanilla bean, split lengthwise †	•	•	•
optional: Kahlúa (coffee liqueur)	1½ tablespoons	1 ounce	25 grams

* Use only 3 tablespoons sugar if adding Kahlúa.
† You may substitute 1 teaspoon vanilla extract for the vanilla bean, but the bean offers a fuller, more aromatic flavor. If using extract, add it after the sauce is cool.

STORE:
5 days refrigerated, 3 months frozen.

POINTERS FOR SUCCESS:
Don't use a whisk to stir if not using an accurate thermometer because the foam makes it difficult to see when the mixture is getting close to boiling. Do not heat

Have ready near the range a fine strainer lined with cheesecloth, suspended over a small mixing bowl.

In a small heavy noncorrodible saucepan stir together the yolks, sugar, and salt until well blended, using a wooden spoon.

In another small saucepan (or a heatproof glass measure if using a microwave on high power), heat the milk, coffee, and vanilla bean to the boiling point. Stir a few tablespoons into the yolk mixture; then gradually add the remaining milk, stirring constantly.

Heat the mixture to just before the boiling point (170°F. to 180°F.). Steam will begin to appear and the mixture will be slightly thicker than heavy cream. It will leave a well-defined track when a finger is run across the back of a spoon. Immediately remove from the heat and pour into the strainer, scraping up the thickened cream that settles on the bottom of the pan. Remove the vanilla bean and scrape the seeds into the sauce. Stir until the seeds separate. For maximum flavor return the pod to the sauce until serving time.

Cool in an ice-water bath or the refrigerator. Stir in the optional Kahlúa.

above 180°F. or the sauce will curdle. If overheated and *slight* curdling does take place, pour instantly into a blender and blend until smooth before straining.

*C*rème anglaise is the base for this glorious ice cream. It is dense, rich, and fragrant with the slightly flowery flavors of heavy cream and vanilla, yet it is not a drop too sweet. It will spoil you for even the best commercial brands. The secret ingredient for perfecting the texture is vodka—which does not impart a taste but keeps the ice cream from becoming too hard in the freezer.

Serve this ice cream alone or with Brandied Burgundy Cherries (page 346) and Hot Fudge (page 88) for a sophisticated sundae. Or use it for the summer version of Swiss Black Forest Cake (page 190).

Vanilla Ice Cream

MAKES 5 CUPS

INGREDIENTS	MEASURE	WEIGHT	
	volume	*pounds/ounces*	*kilograms/grams*
8 large egg yolks	4.5 fluid ounces	5.25 ounces	150 grams
sugar	¾ cup	5.25 ounces	150 grams
salt	pinch	•	•
heavy cream	3 liquid cups	1.5 pounds	696 grams
milk	1 liquid cup	8.5 ounces	242 grams
2 vanilla beans,* split lengthwise	•	•	•
optional: vodka	2 tablespoons	1 ounce	29 grams

* You may substitute 2 teaspoons vanilla extract for the vanilla bean, but the bean offers a fuller, more aromatic flavor. If using extract, add it after the sauce is cool. If using a Tahitian bean, use only 1 bean.

Ice cream has the best texture within 3 days of freezing.

POINTERS FOR SUCCESS:
Don't use a whisk to stir if not using an accurate thermometer because the foam makes it difficult to see when the mixture is getting close to boiling. Do not heat above 180°F. or the sauce will curdle. If overheated and *slight* curdling does take place, pour instantly into a blender and blend until smooth before straining. Do not add more than the recommended amount of vodka or ice cream will not freeze.

Have a fine strainer ready near the range, suspended over a medium mixing bowl.

In a small heavy noncorrodible saucepan stir together the yolks, sugar, and salt until well blended, using a wooden spoon.

In another small saucepan (or a heatproof glass measure if using a microwave on high power) heat the cream, milk, and vanilla beans to the boiling point. Stir a few tablespoons into the yolk mixture; then gradually add the remainder, stirring constantly.

Heat the mixture to just before the boiling point (170°F. to 180°F.). Steam will begin to appear and the mixture will be slightly thicker than heavy cream. It will leave a well-defined track when a finger is run across the back of a spoon. Immediately remove from the heat and pour into the strainer, scraping up the thickened cream that settles on the bottom of the pan. Remove the vanilla beans and scrape the seeds into the sauce. Stir until the seeds separate. Return the pod to the sauce until ready to freeze.

Cool in an ice-water bath or the refrigerator until cold. Stir in the optional vodka. Freeze in an ice-cream maker. Allow to ripen for 2 hours in the freezer before serving.

VARIATIONS

PINEAPPLE ICE CREAM: This is a sensational flavor. Do make your own pineapple puree (page 351). It is far superior to canned pineapple. For a generous quart of ice cream, prepare only two thirds of the recipe, using 5 egg yolks, a 2-inch long piece of vanilla bean, and 1 tablespoon plus 2 teaspoons of kirsch instead of vodka. Before freezing, stir ⅔ cup pineapple purée into the chilled cream mixture. This ice cream is delicious by itself but was created especially for Baked Hawaii (page 168).

FIRE AND ICE: For a slightly nutty, slightly fiery, utterly delicious flavor, add 2 teaspoons pink peppercorns, crushed, with the vanilla extract.

This sublime cream is an ideal filling for a dome-shaped charlotte such as the Scarlett Empress (page 177). It is silken smooth, fragrant with vanilla, and very creamy. It contains just enough gelatin to hold its shape while maintaining a soft, melt-in-the-mouth texture.

Vanilla Bavarian Cream

MAKES 5 CUPS
(enough for a 6-cup cake-lined mold)

INGREDIENTS	MEASURE	WEIGHT	
	volume	*pounds/ounces*	*kilograms/grams*
sugar	⅓ cup	2.25 ounces	66 grams
salt	pinch	•	•
gelatin *	1 tablespoon	•	9.3 grams
5 large egg yolks	3 fluid ounces	3.25 ounces	93 grams
milk	1⅔ liquid cups	14 ounces	402 grams
1 vanilla bean, split †	•	•	•
heavy cream	1 liquid cup	8 ounces	232 grams
optional: kirsch (cherry eau-de-vie)	1½ tablespoons	0.75 ounce	21 grams

* This is more than one envelope.
† You may substitute 1 teaspoon vanilla extract for the vanilla bean, but the bean offers a fuller, more aromatic flavor. If using extract, add it after the sauce is cool. If using a Tahitian bean, use only half the bean.

Refrigerate the mixing bowl for whipping the cream.

Have ready a fine strainer near the range, suspended over a small mixing bowl.

In a small, heavy, noncorrodible saucepan, stir together the sugar, salt, gelatin, and yolks until well blended, using a wooden spoon.

In another small saucepan (or a heatproof glass measure if using a microwave on high power) heat the milk and vanilla bean to the boiling point. Stir a few tablespoons into the yolk mixture; then gradually add the remaining milk and vanilla bean, stirring constantly.

Heat the mixture to just before the boiling point (170°F. to 180°F.). Steam will begin to appear and the mixture will be slightly thicker than heavy cream. It will leave a well-defined track when a finger is run across the back of a spoon. Immediately remove from the heat and pour into the strainer,

STORE:
Refrigerate 4 hours to 3 days before unmolding. Remove to room temperature 1 hour before serving. The Bavarian may be frozen for 2 weeks. Defrost for 24 hours in the refrigerator.

POINTERS FOR SUCCESS:
Don't use a whisk to stir when heating the custard if not using an accurate thermometer because the foam makes it difficult to see when the mixture is getting close to boiling. Do not heat above 180°F. or the sauce will curdle. If overheated and *slight* curdling does take place, pour instantly into a blender and blend until

smooth before straining. To prevent separation, the yolk mixture must start to thicken before adding the egg whites or whipped cream. If it starts to set prematurely, set the bowl briefly over hot water, and stir until smooth. Once the whipped cream has been added, avoid overmixing. Be sure to measure or weigh the gelatin. One envelope equals about 2.25 teaspoons.

scraping up the thickened cream that settles on the bottom of the pan. Remove the vanilla bean and scrape the seeds into the sauce. Stir until the seeds separate.

In the chilled bowl whip the cream until it mounds softly when dropped from a spoon. Refrigerate.

Cool the sauce in an ice-water bath, stirring with a large wire whisk until whisk marks barely begin to appear. The mixture will start to set around the edges but will still be very liquid. Whisk in the optional kirsch and continuing with whisk, fold in the whipped cream until just incorporated. The mixture will be soupy like melted ice cream. Remove at once from the water bath and pour into a 6-cup *biscuit*-lined bowl (page 370). Refrigerate for at least 4 hours before unmolding.

NOTE: If time allows, the Bavarian cream can be chilled in the refrigerator instead of stirred over ice water. It will take about 1½ hours to thicken and should be stirred occasionally. The advantage of refrigeration over ice water is that the thickening process is more gradual so there is less danger of the mixture becoming too thick before folding in the remaining ingredients.

UNDERSTANDING

Kirsch or other liqueurs are added to Bavarian creams not only for the lovely flavors but also to mask any gelatin flavor.

VARIATIONS

ORANGE BAVARIAN: Delicately perfumed with orange and Grand Marnier, flecked with tiny dots of orange zest, this Bavarian is delicious topped with a thin layer of Light Whipped Ganache (page 268) to create a stunning two-toned effect. If blood oranges are available, they provide a lovely pink color and more intense flavor. Preparation is similar to basic Bavarian cream with the following changes: Use ½ cup sugar. Replace the kirsch with Grand Marnier. Add 2 tablespoons fresh orange concentrate and 1 tablespoon grated orange zest. To make orange concentrate, start with ½ cup freshly squeezed orange juice (about 2 oranges) and reduce it to 2 tablespoons. (Using a microwave on high power gives the purest flavor.) Add the zest to the milk before heating and do not strain the custard. Add the orange concentrate when the mixture is cool. Pour into an 8-inch *biscuit*-lined mold (page 181) and refrigerate.

Make ¼ recipe Light Whipped Ganache (page 268) and immediately after whipping smooth over top of orange

Bavarian. Top with Chocolate Curls (page 382) and Candied Orange Zest (page 342) or a piped disc of Daisy Biscuit (page 183). Tie a brown and an orange ribbon around the finished mold. (See Orange Chocolate Crown, page 181.)

BAVARIAN CHIFFON: This Bavarian is also silky and creamy but has a lighter, faintly spongy texture from beaten egg whites. To make this version, beat 3 large egg whites (3 ounces/90 grams) until foamy, add ⅜ teaspoon cream of tartar, and beat until soft peaks form when the beater is raised. Gradually add 3 tablespoons sugar and beat until stiff peaks form when the beater is raised slowly. With a large whisk fold into the chilled yolk mixture. Then fold in the whipped cream. This will make 7 cups of Bavarian Chiffon Cream, enough for a 9-inch *biscuit*-lined mold (page 369).

Pear Bavarian Cream

MAKES 6 CUPS
(enough for one 9-inch by
2-inch charlotte)
(page 174)

I fell in love with charlottes and Bavarian cream fillings at the renowned Ecole LeNôtre in Plaisir, France, where I went to study seven years ago. This Bavarian cream for Ethereal Pear Charlotte (page 175) was my favorite. The flavor is purely pear and the texture incomparably creamy, billowy and light, yet, miraculously, it holds its shape for serving. The secrets are the use of pear juice instead of milk for the *crème anglaise* (LeNôtre jokingly called it *crème française*) and the addition of Italian meringue. The challenge in re-creating this recipe was to keep it from being too sweet because the meringue contains so much sugar. Instead of adding extra sugar to protect the eggs from curdling when adding the pear juice, I stole some sugar from the meringue and a little more from the poaching syrup. The result is a *succès fou*! It is one of my favorite recipes in this book.

INGREDIENTS	MEASURE	WEIGHT	
	volume	*pounds/ounces*	*kilograms/grams*
CUSTARD			
sugar	¼ cup	1.75 ounces	50 grams
salt	pinch	•	•
gelatin	1 tablespoon	•	9.3 grams
5 large egg yolks	3 fluid ounces	3.25 ounces	93 grams
pear poaching liquid (page 350)	1½ cups	14 ounces	400 grams
cold heavy cream	1 cup	8 ounces	232 grams
ITALIAN MERINGUE			
sugar	⅓ cup	2.25 ounces	66 grams
water	2 tablespoons	1 ounce	30 grams
2 large egg whites	¼ cup	2 ounces	60 grams
cream of tartar	¼ teaspoon	•	•
William's pear liqueur or eau-de-vie	2 tablespoons	1 ounce	28 grams

Refrigerate the mixing bowl for whipping the cream.

Have a fine strainer ready near the range, suspended over a small mixing bowl.

In a small, heavy, noncorrodible saucepan stir together ¼ cup of the sugar, salt, gelatin, and yolks until well blended, using a wooden spoon.

In another small saucepan (or a heatproof glass measure if using a microwave on high power) heat the pear poaching liquid to the boiling point. Stir a few tablespoons into the yolk mixture; then gradually add the remaining liquid, stirring constantly.

Heat the mixture to just before the boiling point (180°F. to 190°F). Steam will begin to appear and the mixture will be slightly thicker than heavy cream. It will leave a well-defined track when a finger is run across the back of a spoon. Immediately remove from the heat and pour into the strainer, scraping up the thickened cream that settles on the bottom of the pan.

In the chilled bowl whip the cream until it mounds softly when dropped from a spoon. Refrigerate and prepare the Italian meringue.

Have ready a 1-cup heatproof glass measure near the range.

In a small heavy saucepan (preferably with a nonstick lining) stir together the ⅓ cup sugar and water. Heat, stirring constantly, until the sugar dissolves and the syrup is bubbling. Stop stirring and turn down the heat to the lowest setting. (If using an electric range remove from the heat.)

In a mixing bowl beat the egg whites until foamy, add the cream of tartar and beat until stiff peaks form when the beater is raised slowly.

Raise the heat and boil the syrup until a thermometer registers 248°F. to 250°F. (firm-ball stage). Immediately remove from the heat and pour the syrup into the glass measure to stop the cooking.

If using an electric hand-held mixer, beat the syrup into the whites in a steady stream, avoiding the beaters, to keep syrup from spinning onto sides of bowl. If using a stand mixer, pour a small amount of syrup over the whites with the mixer off. Immediately beat at high speed for 5 seconds. Stop mixer and add a larger amount of syrup. Beat at high speed for 5 seconds. Continue with remaining syrup. With the last addition use a rubber scraper to remove the syrup clinging to the glass measure. Beat at medium speed until cool (about 2 minutes). Cover with plastic wrap and set aside.

STORE:
Refrigerate 4 hours to 3 days before unmolding. The Bavarian may be frozen for 2 weeks.

POINTERS FOR SUCCESS:
Custard: Don't use a whisk to stir if not using an accurate thermometer because the foam makes it difficult to see when the mixture is getting close to boiling. Do not heat above 190°F. or the sauce will curdle. If overheated and *slight* curdling does take place, pour instantly into a blender and blend until smooth before straining.

It is possible to heat this sauce 10 degrees higher than one made with milk because the acidity of the pear juice raises the boiling point.

Italian Meringue: For maximum stability, the syrup must reach 248°F. and not exceed 250°F. as higher temperatures will break down the whites. The whites must be free of any grease or trace of yolk. Don't overbeat.

Bavarian: To prevent separation, the yolk mixture must start to thicken before adding the Italian meringue and whipped cream. If it starts to set prematurely, set the bowl briefly over hot water and stir until smooth. Once the Italian meringue and whipped cream have been added, avoid overmixing. Be sure to measure or weigh the gelatin. One envelope equals about 2.25 teaspoons using Foley measuring spoons. It may measure 2.5 teaspoons with other brands of measuring spoons. The gelatin continues to thicken under refrigeration.

Cool the custard sauce in an ice-water bath, stirring with a large wire whisk just until traces of whisk marks begin to appear. The mixture will start to set around the edges but will still be very liquid. Whisk in the pear eau-de-vie and, continuing with whisk, fold in the Italian meringue and whipped cream until just incorporated. The mixture will be very billowy and soupy like melted ice cream. Remove at once from the water bath and pour into a 9-inch *biscuit*-lined mold (page 175).

NOTE: If time allows, the Bavarian cream can be chilled in the refrigerator instead of stirred over ice water. It will take about 1½ hours to thicken and should be stirred occasionally. The advantage of refrigeration over ice water is that the thickening process is more gradual so there is less danger of the mixture becoming too thick before folding in the remaining ingredients.

Meringue Icings, Fillings, and Decorations

Royal icing, meringue, and *dacquoise* all have two major ingredients in common: egg whites and sugar. Since their texture is dependent on properly beaten egg whites, this seems like a perfect place for a brief discussion on egg whites in general. First let's deal with the great baker's controversy: Which beat better, fresh egg whites or aged? It's six of one, half a dozen of the other. Fresh whites are thicker so they take longer to beat. The resulting foam has less volume but more stability and loses less volume when folded into other ingredients. Older whites are thinner so they beat more quickly and yield greater but less stable volume. When folded into other ingredients they lose the extra volume.

The flavor of fresh egg whites is slightly superior to that of older whites, so I tend to prefer them for recipes like mousses where the egg white does not get cooked.

Now for a simple demystification from my dear friend and brilliant colleague, Shirley Corriher:

Egg white is made up of water and protein. When exposed to air, heat, or acid, the proteins in the egg white change from their original form (denature). For the perfect egg white foam, the egg whites should be beaten so that the egg white proteins denature (change) just the right amount. They must remain moist and flexible and not dry out and become rigid. When the beaten egg white, filled with air bubbles, goes into a hot oven or is subjected to hot syrup, it should be soft, moist, flexible, and able to expand until it reaches the temperature that coagulates (sets) it. Overbeating produces dried out, rigid egg white foam that will not expand properly in the oven. The cook has several secret weapons to produce the perfect degree of egg white denaturization to result in beaten egg whites with the greatest volume and stability. These are the copper bowl, cream of tartar, and sugar. The copper bowl produces stable egg whites by combining with conalbumin, the protein in the egg white that lines each air bubble, to form a totally new protein, copper conalbumin. This copper conalbumin remains moist and flexible even when slightly overbeaten and provides a more stable foam.

Cream of tartar, an acid salt (byproduct of the wine industry), provides an even more stable foam in another way. The acid serves to denature the protein just enough to produce a moist stable foam. I have performed several experiments with cream of tartar and find that when the correct amount (1 teaspoon per cup of egg whites) is used, there is no danger at all of overbeating. Because of this, I recommend always using cream of tartar for egg whites that will be cooked. If the egg whites will remain uncooked, I prefer the copper bowl because it offers the least possibility of extraneous flavor.

Sugar is effective with either the copper bowl or cream of tartar to keep the proteins moist and flexible because sugar itself holds moisture. Superfine sugar is preferable because it dissolves faster. Sugar can be added at any time while beating the egg whites, however if added early it will require much longer beating and may not reach as great a volume. If added very late in the beating process, drying may have started to occur. Most recipes specify starting to add the sugar after the soft peak stage but before stiff peaks form.

Salt not only increases beating time, it decreases the foam's stability by drawing out water from the egg whites. I prefer adding salt to the other ingredients in the recipe.

Any fat substance or egg yolk is a foam inhibitor and even one drop will keep the egg whites from becoming stiff.

For the most stable foam, start beating the egg whites slowly, gradually increasing speed. Never decrease speed as the volume will permanently decrease. When it is necessary to stop the beater to check consistency, turn it off quickly and bring up speed quickly to prevent deflation.

When making a syrup to beat into egg whites, use a pan with a nonstick lining or a lot of the syrup will stick to the pan instead of getting into the whites.

Finally, because sugar is hygroscopic (readily absorbs water), *do not make royal icing, meringue, or dacquoise on humid days* as they will be soft and sticky and will not set well.

The recipes in this chapter appear as components throughout the book in many interesting and varied ways. Royal icing is used for fine decorative designs on some of the special occasion cakes. Delicious, crunchy *dacquoise* is an important part of A Taste of Heaven (page 166), while crisp French meringue is juxtaposed against soft *génoise* and buttercream in Star-Spangled Rhapsody (page 169). Italian meringue adds its billowy texture to mixtures from buttercream to Bavarian cream. And, of course, the various meringues, from chocolate to green tea, are perfect to eat by themselves.

Royal Icing

MAKES ¾ CUP

*T*he amount of sugar in royal icing is almost five times the weight of the egg white, resulting in a very stiff meringue used exclusively for cake decorating. Flowers made from royal icing and air dried will last almost indefinitely, so many bakers feel they are great to have on hand. However, it was a royal icing rose which remains in my memory as one of the great disappointments of childhood. I still remember the birthday party—holding my breath as the serving knife approached that special piece with the exquisite pink rose on it, hoping against hope that it would be mine and then, with dizzying ecstasy, there it was being lowered toward my plate. The joy of that moment ended when the rose crumbled between my baby molars like so much powdered cement.

To this day, I would never dream of putting royal icing flowers on a cake and disappointing some other unsuspecting child. Real flowers are preferable, and most people realize that they are merely there for décor. Once though, at a wedding, my husband nervously pointed out a certain ambassador's wife cheerfully munching on a pale lavender cymbidium from one of my wedding cakes! (See edible flowers, page 428.)

Royal icing is extremely well suited to small decorative touches: dots on Dotted Swiss Dream (page 222), lilies of the valley embroidery on White Lily Cake (page 203), monograms (page 412), string work (page 404). I tend to use it in conjunction with rolled fondant because the dead white of the royal icing stands out against the off-white of the fondant, giving the fondant an alabaster quality. An added advantage to the royal icing is that, since it contains no fat, it is easy to correct mistakes—unlike buttercream which leaves grease marks when removed.

There is no cake more elegant or breathtakingly beautiful than one covered with rolled fondant and decorated with royal icing. As they are both over 80 percent sugar, the main taste sensation is sweet. It is the one time I put beauty over flavor as long as the cake within is absolutely delicious.

INGREDIENTS	MEASURE	WEIGHT	
room temperature	*volume*	*pounds/ounces*	*kilograms/grams*
1 large egg white	2 tablespoons	1 ounce	30 grams
powdered sugar	1⅓ cups (lightly spooned into cup)	5.25 ounces	150 grams

In a large mixing bowl place the egg white and sugar and beat, preferably with the whisk beater, at low speed until the sugar is moistened. Beat at high speed until very glossy and stiff peaks form when the beater is lifted (5 to 7 minutes). Tips of peaks should curve slightly. If necessary, more powdered sugar can be added. Use at once to make decorations, keeping the bowl covered with a damp cloth.

For spider-web-fine string work piped with a 000 tube, Irene diBartollo, a great cake decorating artist and teacher, presses small amounts of icing through the toe of a nylon stocking to make sure that it is absolutely lump free!

Avoid preparing on humid days. If using a hand-held mixer, don't increase the size of the recipe because the icing is very stiff and may be hard on a weak motor. Keep the bowl and pastry tube covered with a damp cloth when not in use because the icing crusts and hardens very quickly when exposed to air.

NOTE: I don't know where the myth got started that royal icing made with fresh egg white cannot be rebeaten. It is true that it cannot be rebeaten as many times or for as many days as royal icing made with meringue powder, but it definitely holds up to 3 days.

STORE:
3 days tightly covered. The icing becomes slightly spongy on standing—rebeat lightly if necessary.

POINTERS FOR SUCCESS:
To avoid lint, don't sift powdered sugar and air dry all utensils. Utensils and egg whites must be absolutely grease free. Royal icing will break down if subjected to even a trace of grease, so all equipment should be washed well and rinsed in very hot water before using.

VARIATION

Royal icing made with fresh egg whites is strong and elastic, making it ideal for string work. Royal icing made with meringue powder is only slightly less elastic but can be stored and rebeaten up to 2 weeks. Meringue powder, available at cake decorating supply stores such as Maid of Scandinavia (page 445), contains mainly dried egg whites.

To make Meringue Powder Royal Icing: Replace the egg white with 1 tablespoon meringue powder and 2 tablespoons warm water (this is approximately the amount of water contained by the white). Proceed as for basic royal icing. Extra water or corn syrup may be added to the icing to soften it slightly for borders or string work (1 tablespoon per pound of powdered sugar). The addition of water will result in a harder, more brittle icing. If the weather is very dry and the icing crusts too quickly, 1 teaspoon glycerine per 2 pounds powdered sugar will keep it soft longer. To store the icing, place in an airtight container (not plastic, which is petrol-based and can break down the icing) at room temperature and rebeat before using.

CHOCOLATE ROYAL ICING: For a light chocolate royal icing which contrasts nicely with Chocolate Rolled Fondant (page 309), add 2 tablespoons cocoa to the powdered sugar.

Crisp French Meringue

MAKES
TWO 9-INCH
OR THREE
7-INCH DISCS

*T*he classic proportions for crisp meringue are approximately double the weight of sugar to egg white. But there is a special reason I have called this recipe French meringue. It is because of a French pastry chef named Didier who came to visit me one day when I had just baked a batch of meringue shells. He hefted one on his thumb and three fingers and muttered in a low voice *"C'est lourd."* ("It's heavy.") I waivered between insult and curiosity and then decided that I might have something to learn. It turns out that Didier's grandfather used mostly superfine sugar for the meringue in his pastry shop and always put in a *poignet* ("fistful") of powdered sugar. Since Didier could not recall the size of the batches prepared in his grandfather's bakery, I spent several days in my country kitchen experimenting with quantities ranging from 100 percent powdered sugar down to about 50 percent (which turned out to be the ideal). Didier was right. These are the lightest meringues I've ever experienced.

Crisp meringue shells provide delightful containers for ice cream and fresh fruit. Meringue discs make spectacular cake components when used to sandwich layers of *génoise* as in Star-Spangled Rhapsody Cake (page 169).

INGREDIENTS	MEASURE	WEIGHT	
room temperature	*volume*	*pounds/ounces*	*kilograms/grams*
4 large egg whites	½ liquid cup	4.25 ounces	120 grams
cream of tartar	½ teaspoon	•	•
superfine sugar	½ cup + 1 tablespoon	4 ounces	115 grams
powdered sugar	1 cup (lightly spooned into cup)	4 ounces	115 grams

Line a heavy baking sheet with a nonstick liner or foil. If making discs, trace shape onto foil or make template to slip under liner as a guide.

Preheat oven to 200°F.

In a mixing bowl beat the whites until frothy, add the cream of tartar, and beat at medium speed while gradually adding 2 tablespoons superfine sugar. When soft peaks form when the beater is raised, add 1 tablespoon superfine sugar and increase speed to high. When stiff peaks form when the beater is raised slowly, gradually beat in remaining superfine sugar and beat until very stiff and glossy.

Sift powdered sugar over meringue and fold in using a slotted skimmer or large rubber spatula. Use at once to pipe or spread on prepared baking sheet. (See piping instructions page 375.)

If your oven has a pilot light, the ideal way to dry the meringue is to bake it for 1 hour at 200°F. and then leave it overnight in the turned-off oven. Alternately, bake the discs for 2 to 2½ hours at 200°F. or until dry but not beginning to color. The most reliable way to test for doneness is to dig out a small amount of meringue from the center with the tip of a sharp knife. If only slightly sticky it will continue to dry at room temperature.

STORE:
Tightly covered at room temperature and low humidity, meringues will keep for more than 6 months.

POINTERS FOR SUCCESS:
Superfine sugar is as fine as sand. If you have trouble finding it, make your own by processing regular granulated sugar for a few minutes in a food processor. All utensils and egg whites must be free of grease. *Avoid preparing on humid days.* Do not use parchment or a greased and floured baking sheet because meringue often sticks to them. To prevent cracking, do not open the oven door during the first three quarters of cooking time.

VARIATIONS

FIGURE PIPING MERINGUE: When piping figures such as swans (page 376) for Blueberry Swan Lake (page 165) or mushrooms (page 376) for Cordon Rose Chocolate Christ-

for Mushrooms

mas Log (page 197), a less fragile meringue is preferable. Replace the 4 ounces powdered sugar with 4 additional ounces superfine sugar (using a total of 8 ounces/226 grams or 1 cup + 2 tablespoons). Beat all of the sugar into the meringue. For piping and baking instructions, see page 377.

PINE NEEDLE MERINGUE: Elizabeth Andoh and I worked out this Japanese-inspired pale green meringue, ideal for piping the most fragile of pine needles (page 00). Use 2 egg whites (¼ cup, 2 ounces/60 grams) and beat in ¼ cup (1.75 ounces/50 grams) superfine sugar which has been whisked with 2 teaspoons Japanese powdered green tea (page 429). For piping and baking instructions, see page 375.

COCOA MERINGUE: Whisk 2 tablespoons cocoa with the powdered sugar until uniformly blended. For piping and baking little puffs, round or heart-shaped discs, and meringue sticks see pages 374 and 375.

CHOCOLATE-SPANGLED MERINGUE: For a pale tan meringue with little speckles of chocolate throughout, place the powdered sugar and 2 ounces unsweetened chocolate in a food processor and process until chocolate is powdery. Fold into the beaten whites until uniformly blended. This meringue has a lovely chocolate flavor and dissolves in the mouth. The bitter chocolate makes it less sweet than other meringue recipes. Spangled meringue can be piped into little puffs, round or heart-shaped discs, and sticks (pages 374 and 375).

Light Italian Meringue

MAKES 5 CUPS

*C*lassic Italian meringue has double the weight of sugar to egg whites. This recipe has only a little more than 1½ times the sugar, giving it just enough body and sweetness to support the addition of lemon curd for Lemon Cream Illusion (page 266).

INGREDIENTS	MEASURE	WEIGHT	
room temperature	*volume*	*pounds/ounces*	*kilograms/grams*
sugar	¾ cup + 2 tablespoons	6 ounces	175 grams
water	¼ cup	2 ounces	60 grams
4 large egg whites	½ liquid cup	4.25 ounces	120 grams
cream of tartar	½ teaspoon	•	•

Have ready near the range a 1-cup heatproof glass measure.

In a small heavy saucepan (preferably with a nonstick lining) stir together ¾ cup sugar and the water. Heat, stirring constantly, until the sugar dissolves and the syrup is bubbling. Stop stirring and turn down the heat to the lowest setting. (If using an electric range remove from the heat.)

In a mixing bowl beat the egg whites until foamy, add the cream of tartar, and beat until soft peaks form when the beater is raised slowly. Gradually beat in the remaining 2 tablespoons sugar until stiff peaks form when the beater is raised slowly. Increase the heat and boil the syrup until a thermometer registers 248°F. to 250°F. (firm-ball stage). Immediately pour into the glass measure to stop the cooking.

If using an electric hand-held mixer, beat the syrup into the whites in a steady stream, avoiding the beaters to keep syrup from spinning onto sides of bowl. If using a stand mixer, pour a small amount of syrup over the whites with the mixer off.

Immediately beat at high speed for 5 seconds. Stop the mixer and add a larger amount of syrup. Beat at high speed for 5 seconds. Continue with remaining syrup. With the last addition use a rubber scraper to remove the syrup clinging to the measure. Beat at medium speed until cool (about 2 minutes).

STORE:
2 hours room temperature, 2 days refrigerated. Rebeat briefly before using.

POINTERS FOR SUCCESS:
For maximum stability, syrup must reach 248°F. and not exceed 250°F. as higher temperatures will break down the whites. The whites must be free of any grease or trace of yolk. Do not overbeat. *Avoid preparing on humid days.*

UNDERSTANDING

People have asked me if it is possible to use glucose (which has less water than corn syrup) to replace the water and some of the sugar the way I use corn syrup for Neoclassic Buttercream (page 230). Unfortunately, the resulting Italian meringue does not get firm enough even when the syrup is brought to 248°F.

Chocolate Italian Meringue

Neve Nero
(NEYveh NEYro)

MAKES 18
COOKIES

This fantastic recipe is a *lagniappe* (a Louisiana word defined as "an extra gift"). It is neither a cake nor a component of a cake but rather a romantically named cookie, crunchy on the outside, chocolaty-chewy inside. The recipe was a gift to me from a charming Swiss baker, Arthur Oberholzer. He enticed me by telling me that chocolate Italian meringue is called *neve nero* (black snow) in Italy. This mixture is used to make a famous Swiss cookie simply known as the Schoggi S (Chocolate S) because it is piped in that shape. He said it is so tricky and delicate "no one ever succeeds on the first try." The challenge was on. One cookie from my successful first batch was promptly mailed to Arthur Oberholzer, who now lives in Florida. Considering the humidity down there, I'll never know if he was adequately impressed!

INGREDIENTS	MEASURE	WEIGHT	
room temperature	*volume*	*pounds/ounces*	*kilograms/grams*
sugar	1¼ cups + 3 tablespoons	10 ounces	285 grams
water	⅓ liquid cup	2.75 ounces	80 grams
4 large egg whites	½ liquid cup	4.25 ounces	120 grams
cream of tartar	½ teaspoon	•	•
unsweetened chocolate, melted and slightly cooled	•	2 ounces	57 grams
* *optional:* 4 drops red food color	•	•	•

Have ready a large pastry bag fitted with a large number 8 star tube and a 17-inch by 14-inch baking sheet lined with a nonstick liner or foil.

STORE:
1 week to 10 days room temperature.

POINTERS FOR SUCCESS:
Avoid preparing on humid days. For maximum stability, the syrup must reach

Have ready a 2-cup heatproof glass measure near the range.

In a small heavy saucepan (preferably with a nonstick lining) stir together 1¼ cups sugar and the water. Heat, stirring constantly, until the sugar dissolves and the syrup is bubbling. Stop stirring and turn down the heat to the lowest setting. (If using an electric range remove from the heat.)

In a mixing bowl beat the egg whites until foamy, add the cream of tartar, and beat until soft peaks form when the beater is raised. Gradually beat in the remaining 3 ta-

* Four drops of red food color give the chocolate a richer appearance.

blespoons sugar until stiff peaks form when the beater is raised slowly.

Increase the heat and boil the syrup until a thermometer registers 248°F. to 250°F. (firm-ball stage). Immediately pour into the glass measure to stop the cooking.

If using an electric hand-held mixer, beat the syrup into the whites in a steady stream. Don't allow the syrup to fall on the beaters or they will spin the syrup onto the sides of the bowl. If using a stand mixer, pour a small amount of syrup over the whites with the mixer off. Immediately beat at high speed 5 seconds. Stop the mixer and add a larger amount of syrup. Beat at high speed for 5 seconds. Continue with remaining syrup. With the last addition use a rubber scraper to remove the syrup clinging to the measure. Beat 1 minute.

Now comes the critical moment. Stop beating, disengage the beater, and add the melted chocolate and optional food color. Holding the beater with your hand, immediately beat for a few seconds *only until incorporated.* Transfer at once to the pastry bag and pipe immediately while still hot. If overbeaten, the mixture will be soft and the ridges will not show.

Use a small spot of meringue at each corner of the pan to attach the liner. Pipe large, high S shapes, allowing the mixture to fall from the bag. Avoid flattening it by having the pastry tip too low. From end to end each S should measure 3½ inches. They will expand ½ inch when baked so leave at least 1½ inches between the cookies. Allow cookies to dry for 2 hours or until set. (When finger tip touches surface, meringue stays intact.)

Preheat oven to 350°F. Place cookies in preheated oven 10 minutes. Lower heat to 200°F. and bake without opening oven door just until they can easily be removed (using fingers) from the baking sheet. This will take 20 to 30 minutes. Do not overbake. The cookies should be wet inside as they continue to dry on removal from oven and should be soft and chewy inside even after cooling.

Put the cookies on a rack and as soon as they are cool store in airtight containers.

248°F. and not exceed 250°F. as higher temperatures will break down the whites. The whites must be free of any grease or trace of yolk.

The melted chocolate should be warm (ideally 100°F.) when added to the meringue. Beating must be minimal after adding the chocolate. Pipe the mixture while still hot. To prevent cracking, do not open the oven door during the early stage of baking. *Don't overbake cookies.* They should be chewy, not dry, inside.

VARIATION

Instead of S shapes, pipe hearts (page 375). Broken pieces of this meringue are an interesting addition when folded into Bavarian cream.

UNDERSTANDING

This recipe is based on classic Italian meringue because it needs the greatest stability to stand up to the fat in the chocolate. In fact, 2 extra ounces of sugar have been added for further stability. This is possible because the sweetness is tempered by the use of unsweetened chocolate.

Dacquoise

(daKWAHZ)

**MAKES
TWO 9-INCH
OR THREE
7-INCH DISCS**

A dacquoise is an exceptionally light and crisp meringue made with ground nuts. The nuts make it pale brown in color with a delicious nutty flavor. Crunchy, flavorful nuts are best. Use almonds, hazelnuts, or a combination of both. The mixture can be piped into discs or heart shapes and used to sandwich *génoise* and pink Classic Buttercream in A Taste of Heaven (page 166).

INGREDIENTS	MEASURE	WEIGHT	
room temperature	*volume*	*pounds/ounces*	*kilograms/grams*
toasted, peeled, and finely ground almonds or hazelnuts	¾ to 1 cup	4 ounces	113 grams
cornstarch	1½ tablespoons	•	12 grams
superfine sugar	½ cup + 1 tablespoon	4 ounces	113 grams
powdered sugar	¾ cup (lightly spooned into cup)	3 ounces	85 grams
4 large egg whites	½ cup	4.25 ounces	120 grams
cream of tartar	½ teaspoon	•	•

Line a heavy baking sheet with a nonstick liner or foil. If making discs, trace the shape onto the foil or make a template to slip under the liner as a guide.

Preheat the oven to 200°F.

In a food processor pulse the ground nuts, cornstarch, ½ the superfine sugar, and all the powdered sugar a few times to thoroughly combine. Set aside in a small bowl.

In a large mixing bowl beat the whites until frothy, add the cream of tartar, and beat at medium speed while gradually adding 1 tablespoon superfine sugar. When soft peaks form when the beater is raised, gradually add the remaining superfine sugar and beat at high speed until stiff peaks form when the beater is raised slowly.

Fold in reserved nut mixture with a slotted skimmer or large rubber spatula. Use at once to pipe or spread on the prepared baking sheet. (See piping instructions, page 375.) If the mixture is too soft to pipe well, pipe only an outline and fill in the center with a spoon.

If your oven has a pilot light, the ideal way to dry the *dacquoise* is to bake it for 1 hour and then leave it overnight in the turned-off oven. Alternately, bake the discs for 1½ to 2 hours or until dry but not beginning to color. The most reliable way to test for doneness is to dig out a small amount of *dacquoise* from the center with the tip of a sharp knife. If only slightly sticky it will continue to dry at room temperature.

UNDERSTANDING

Dacquoise varies in the proportion of nuts and sugar to egg white. It is possible to use as much as two thirds the combined weight of the egg whites and sugar in nuts but the *dacquoise* will be more fragile and have less body. The above recipe uses close to equal weight nuts and egg whites and, instead of double the sugar to egg whites, it has 1¾ the sugar. This decrease in sugar and the addition of nuts makes it far less sweet than a meringue. A small amount of cornstarch is used to help absorb any grease exuded by the nuts.

VARIATION

CHOCOLATE DACQUOISE: For a delicate chocolate flavor and color, whisk 2 tablespoons cocoa into the powdered sugar.

STORE:
Tightly covered at room temperature and low humidity, the *dacquoise* will keep for several weeks. The nuts will eventually become rancid.

POINTERS FOR SUCCESS:
Because grease breaks down meringue, it is important to grind the nuts in such a way that there is as little grease released as possible. If using a food processor, the best method is to use the shredding disc. Then add the cornstarch and use the steel blade to pulse until fine. Superfine sugar is as fine as sand. If you have trouble finding it, make your own by processing regular granulated sugar in a food processor. The *dacquoise* will not be as light and delicate if using fine granulated instead of superfine sugar. All utensils and egg whites must be free of grease. *Avoid preparing on humid days.* Do not use parchment or a greased and floured baking sheet as *dacquoise* often sticks to them. To prevent cracking, do not open the oven door during the first three-quarters of baking time.

Candy and Nut Embellishments

*A*ll of the recipes in this chapter, with the minor exception of chopped nuts, are on the sweet side of the dessert spectrum. Fondants, marzipans, caramel, and nougatine all have sugar as their major ingredient. Although I would not eat most of these components on their own, each can contribute something very special to the flavor and texture of a cake.

Rolled fondant is easy to prepare and fun to handle. It has a sensual, satiny texture that is lovely to smooth into place. It drapes and clings to a cake, sealing in freshness for several days and giving you time for the most painstaking and impressive piped decorations.

Chocolate rolled fondant, my newest creation, has the attributes of classic white rolled fondant with the flavor and texture of what one might fantasize a grown-up Tootsie Roll to possess.

Caramel is a component that has endless possibilities: It can be spun into angel's hair, threaded into a golden cage to adorn a cake (page 313), or grated into gold dust to sprinkle on top of a cake or to add to buttercream and melted chocolate for that special burnt sugar flavor and crunchy texture.

With the addition of nuts, caramel becomes nougatine, a crunchy confection that can be molded into forms and filled with cake and buttercream as in Barquettes Chez L'Ami Louis (page 186).

Marzipan, another confectionery component based on nuts and sugar, also adds superb flavor, texture, and color to cakes. The finest marzipan in the world is said to come from Lubek, Germany, and there is a recipe in this chapter that rivals its silky texture and almond-imbued flavor. Pistachio marzipan can be incorporated into a cake (Pistachio and Rose Wedding Cake, see color photograph) with its intense flavor and exquisite green color echoing the stems of the roses garnishing the cake. Orange marzipan, flecked with bits of golden zest, is especially delicious beneath a cake encased in or drizzled with dark chocolate glaze.

The recipes in this chapter truly deserve an honored place in this book as the most breathtaking and dramatic of all decorations. From the alabaster perfection of rolled fondant to the ethereal spun gold of angel's hair, these recipes offer joy in the making, a dramatic presentation, and magical eating.

$\mathcal{J}$his shiny fondant is the traditional topping for petits fours but can be used to glaze larger cakes as well. I sometimes add it to marzipan for a more refined texture. Professional bakers rarely make poured fondant because it is available ready made (see Maid of Scandinavia, page 445) and keeps for months refrigerated. Classic poured fondant has always been too slow and tedious for most people to bother with (even for me, who will spend hours embroidering a cake) until Helen Fletcher, in *The New Pastry Cook*, came up with this superb food processor method which makes it easier to prepare than to order!

Food Processor Poured Fondant

MAKES 1¾ CUPS
1⅓ pounds/600 grams/
(enough to glaze a
9-inch cake)

INGREDIENTS	MEASURE	WEIGHT	
	volume	pounds/ounces	kilograms/grams
sugar	2½ cups	17.5 ounces	500 grams
water	½ liquid cup	4 ounces	118 grams
corn syrup	¼ liquid cup	3 ounces	82 grams
optional: 1 teaspoon vanilla or ¼ teaspoon almond extract	•	•	•

Have ready near the range a food processor fitted with the steel blade.

In a medium-size, heavy saucepan (preferably with a nonstick lining) combine the sugar, water, and corn syrup and bring to a boil, stirring constantly. Stop stirring and allow the syrup to cook to the soft-ball stage (238°F.). Immediately pour into the food processor.

Wash the thermometer and reinsert into the syrup. Allow to cool, uncovered, to exactly 140°F. This will take 25 to 35 minutes. Add optional flavoring and process for 2 to 3 minutes or until fondant becomes opaque. (The fondant starts as a transparent syrup. As crystallization of the sugar starts, it becomes translucent and finally opaque or white.)

Pour the fondant into a heatproof container, such as a 2-cup glass measure, lined with a small heavy-duty plastic freezer bag. Close the bag without sealing. When completely cool and firm, expel the air, seal the bag, and lift out of the container. Store at room temperature for at least 24 hours.

STORE:
1 week at room temperature, 6 months refrigerated.

POINTERS FOR SUCCESS:
See sugar syrups (page 435). To prevent premature crystallization, do not stir after the syrup comes to a boil. To keep the temperature from rising too high, remove the pan from the heat slightly before the syrup reaches 238°F. and pour into the processor as soon as it reaches 238°F. It is essential to use an accurate thermometer (page 451). To prevent crystallization, the thermometer must be clean before reinsertion into syrup. When reheating fon-

dant, do not use an aluminum pan as it causes
discoloration. Fondant must
not be overheated or it will
lose its shine. Avoid vigor-
ous stirring to prevent air
bubbles.

TO GLAZE CAKES WITH FONDANT

Fondant must be thinned to make it pourable. Prepare a
stock syrup (30 percent syrup) by combining 1 part water
to 2 parts sugar (by volume) and bring it to a full boil,
stirring constantly. Cool until warm. The syrup will keep
for months at room temperature.

Heat the fondant in the top of a double boiler set over
hot water, stirring gently, until warm. To maintain its sheen,
fondant must not exceed 105°F. Stir in enough warm syrup
to make the fondant pourable.

UNDERSTANDING

This fondant is prepared by controlling crystallization of
the sugar syrup. The thermometer is washed after removing
it from the boiling syrup so that, on reinsertion, the syrup
clinging to the thermometer does not cause premature crystallization. Crystallization can also occur if sugar crystals
form on sides of saucepan, but they usually get washed down
by the steam of the boiling syrup. The syrup can be covered
for 1 minute after coming to a full boil to ensure that this
takes place.

Classic Rolled Fondant

MAKES
2½ POUNDS / 1
KILOGRAM
40 GRAMS
(enough to cover a 9-inch by
4-inch cake)

A cake covered with the alabaster perfection of rolled
fondant has the most exquisite background for decorating.
Rolled fondant is much less painstaking to make than poured
fondant (page 305). Instead of a shiny, glistening surface,
this fondant has a soft, matte glow.

Rolled fondant seals in the freshness of the cake for
several days, giving time for the most ethereal and elaborate of piped decorations. It also can be cut into decorative
shapes such as ribbons or figure appliqués (page 363).

This fondant originated in England, where it was used
to cover fruitcakes to keep them fresh. It is traditional for
even a home cook to wear only white when preparing fondant, because just a fleck of lint can cause an off color.

INGREDIENTS	MEASURE	WEIGHT	
room temperature	*volume*	*pounds/ounces*	*kilograms/grams*
gelatin	1 tablespoon	•	10 grams
water *	¼ liquid cup	2 ounces	60 grams
glucose †	½ cup	6 ounces	170 grams
glycerine	1 tablespoon	•	18 grams
solid white shortening	2 tablespoons	0.75 ounce	24 grams
powdered sugar	8 cups (lightly spooned into cup)	2 pounds	920 grams

* For a flavor variation replace 2 tablespoons water with rosewater, orange flower water, or freshly squeezed lemon juice.
† ½ cup (5.75 ounces/164 grams) corn syrup will give equal results if you use only 3 tablespoons water instead of ¼ cup.

STORE:
1 month room temperature.
Can be frozen indefinitely.

Sprinkle the gelatin over the water in a 2-cup heatproof glass measure or bowl and allow to sit for 5 minutes. Set in a small pan of simmering water and stir until the gelatin is dissolved. (This can also be done in a few seconds in a microwave on high power.) Blend in the glucose and glycerine, then add the shortening and stir until melted. Remove from the heat.

Place the sugar in a large bowl and make a well in the center. Add the gelatin mixture and stir with a lightly greased wooden spoon until blended. Mix with lightly greased hands and knead vigorously in the bowl until most of the sugar is incorporated. Turn out onto a smooth, lightly greased surface such as Formica or marble and knead until smooth and satiny. If the fondant seems dry, add several drops of water and knead well. If it seems too sticky, knead in more powdered sugar. The fondant will resemble a smooth, well-shaped stone. When dropped, it should spread very slightly but retain its shape. It should be malleable like clay, soft but not sticky.

Rolled fondant may be used at once but seems to work more easily when allowed to rest for several hours. It is important to cover the fondant to prevent it from drying. Wrap tightly with plastic wrap and place in an airtight container. It will firm slightly on standing.

When ready to roll out, spray the work surface and rolling pin with nonstick vegetable spray. For covering a cake or making ribbons and appliqués, see pages 360 and 363.

TIPS:

- If stored fondant seems very stiff, a few seconds in the microwave before kneading it makes it pliable and saves wear and tear on your hands!

- The easiest way to color rolled fondant evenly is to add a touch of paste food color to the finished fondant and blend it in with a food processor. At first it will separate into little pieces, but when it comes together to form a smooth ball the color is evenly dispersed. The friction of the processor blades may heat the fondant enough to soften it slightly, but if allowed to rest a few minutes it will firm up again. If the color is too bright, simply knead in some uncolored fondant.

- I use nonstick vegetable spray to grease the counter, rolling pin, cutters—even my hands.

- For large batches: I use my 10- or 20-quart Hobart mixer and the spade beater for the initial mixing. Kneading must always be done by hand or the texture suffers. A KitchenAid mixer can be used for smaller amounts, but stirring by hand is so quick and easy I usually don't use the mixer for small batches.

- Rolled fondant can be purchased already made, which is practical for large volume baking. An excellent product is available under the name Masa Ticino (page 428).

UNDERSTANDING

Rolled fondant is traditionally made with glucose. As corn syrup is merely a lower concentration of corn sugar (it contains more water) it will yield close to the same results if the water balance in the recipe is maintained. Technically, 9 tablespoons corn syrup contain the same corn sugar (glucose) as ½ cup glucose, but the amounts given here are more convenient to measure and work as well.

Although the outside of the fondant will form a thin hard crust, the glycerine keeps the inside soft and chewy. Glycerine is available at candy supply stores (page 429).

$\mathcal{T}$his fondant is my proudest creation! When draped around a cake, at first glance it looks like "plastic chocolate" (a traditional combination of chocolate and corn syrup), but the differences are soon apparent. Instead of a high shine, it has a soft glow that seems lit from within, strongly reminiscent of the warm sensuality of fine Italian leather. And the taste! It can best be compared to an upscale Tootsie Roll: intensely chocolaty and fudgy. The cocoa keeps the fondant from being too sweet. It also allows it to be more malleable than "plastic chocolate" because there is only 3.5 percent cocoa butter compared to the 20 percent in the chocolate used to make plastic chocolate. This makes Chocolate Rolled Fondant a treat even for those on a low-saturated-fat diet.

$\mathcal{C}$hocolate Rolled Fondant

MAKES
2¾ POUNDS /
1 KILOGRAM
250 GRAMS
(enough to cover a 9-inch by
3-inch cake and a 6-inch by
3-inch cake)

INGREDIENTS	MEASURE	WEIGHT	
	volume	pounds/ounces	kilograms/grams
gelatin	1 tablespoon	•	10 grams
water	⅓ liquid cup	2.75 ounces	80 grams
corn syrup	⅔ liquid cup	7.5 ounces	215 grams
glycerine	1 tablespoon	•	18 grams
solid white vegetable shortening	¼ cup	1.75 ounces	48 grams
vanilla	1 teaspoon	•	4 grams
powdered sugar	6¼ cups (lightly spooned into cup)	1 pound 9 ounces	720 grams
unsweetened cocoa (Dutch-processed) or 2½ cups nonalkalized cocoa such as Hershey's	2 cups + 2 tablespoons (lightly spooned into cup)	7 ounces	200 grams

Sprinkle the gelatin over the water in a 2-cup heatproof glass measure or bowl and allow to sit for 5 minutes. Set in a small pan of simmering water and stir until the gelatin is dissolved. (This can also be done in a few seconds in a microwave on high power, stirring once or twice.) Blend in the corn syrup and glycerine, then add the shortening and stir until melted. Remove from the heat and stir in vanilla.

Mix the sugar and cocoa in a large bowl and make a

STORE:
1 week room tempereature, 1 month refrigerated, 6 months frozen. Although refrigerated fondant does not lose its texture, the flavor becomes unpleasant after 1 month.

well in the center. Add the gelatin mixture and stir with a wooden spoon until blended. Mix with your hands and knead vigorously in the bowl until it forms a ball. Turn out onto a smooth, lightly greased surface such as Formica or marble, clean your hands, and knead until smooth and satiny. If the fondant seems dry or brittle, add several drops of water and knead well. The water will make it very sticky and messy at first. When the mixture holds together, scrape the counter clean, lightly grease it, and knead the fondant until smooth.

Chocolate Rolled Fondant may be used at once but is easier to work with if made 1 day ahead to give the moisture a chance to distribute evenly. It is important to cover the fondant to prevent drying out. Wrap tightly with plastic wrap and place in an airtight container.

When ready to roll out, spray the work surface and rolling pin with nonstick vegetable spray. Don't be alarmed if tiny cracks appear in the surface of the fondant; the warmth from kneading or pressure from the rolling pin will make it smooth and satiny. For covering a cake or making ribbons and appliqués, see page 360.

TIPS:
- If the cocoa is lumpy, process it in a food processor for a few seconds until powdery. If lumpy cocoa is used it may not incorporate evenly into the fondant. If this should happen, the chocolate fondant can also be placed in the food processor for a few seconds until completely smooth. Don't try to process the whole batch at one time.
- I use nonstick vegetable spray to grease the counter, rolling pin, cutters—even my hands.
- If stored fondant seems very stiff, a few seconds in the microwave before kneading it will make it pliable.
- Don't be tempted to substitute butter for the solid white shortening. This is one rare instance where there is no perceivable difference in flavor and the shortening actually blends better (without steaking) than the butter.

UNDERSTANDING
Compared to Classic Rolled Fondant, Chocolate Rolled Fondant replaces 7 ounces powdered sugar with cocoa. Because cocoa behaves differently, the fondant now requires double the shortening, a little more glucose or corn syrup, and about double the water.

$\mathcal{P}$astillage

(pahsteeAHJ)

$\mathcal{P}$astillage is rolled fondant without any of the softening ingredients (glycerine, corn syrup, or shortening). It is used mainly for decorative ribbons, three-dimensional shapes, and appliqués because it dries bone-hard and crusts more quickly than fondant.

MAKES
1¼ POUNDS/
600 GRAMS/
1¾ CUPS

INGREDIENTS	MEASURE	WEIGHT	
	volume	pounds/ounces	kilograms/grams
gelatin	1 tablespoon	•	10 grams
water	scant ⅓ liquid cup	2.5 ounces	74 grams
powdered sugar	4 cups (lightly spooned into cup)	1 pound	454 grams
cornstarch	½ cup (lightly spooned into cup)	2.25 ounces	64 grams
optional: pinch cream of tartar	•	•	•

Sprinkle the gelatin over the water in a small heatproof glass cup and allow to sit for 5 minutes. Set in a small pan of simmering water and stir until the gelatin is dissolved. (This can also be done in a few seconds in a microwave on high power.) Remove from the heat.

Combine the sugar, cornstarch, and optional cream of tartar in a large bowl and make a well in the center. Add the gelatin mixture and stir with a wooden spoon until blended. Mix with lightly greased hands and knead vigorously in the bowl until most of the sugar is incorporated. Turn out onto a smooth, lightly greased surface such as Formica or marble and knead until smooth and satiny. If the pastillage seems very dry, add several drops of water and knead well. If it seems too sticky, knead in more powdered sugar. The pastillage will resemble a smooth, well-shaped stone. When dropped, it should not spread.

Pastillage is easiest to work with if it has rested for at least 1 hour. It dries very quickly so it is important to cover it to prevent drying. I wrap it in a cloth rubbed with a bit

STORE:
1 month room temperature.
Can be frozen indefinitely.

of solid white shortening, then tightly in plastic wrap, and place it in an airtight container.

When ready to roll out, spray the work surface and rolling pin with nonstick vegetable spray. For making ribbons and appliqués, see page 363. Pastillage can be rolled out as thinly as 1/16 inch. It dries and holds its shape very quickly.

TIPS:
- If stored pastillage seems very stiff, a few seconds in the microwave make it pliable.
- To give pastillage the look of real marble, dab it with a bit of coffee concentrate or brown food color and knead only until the color streaks.

UNDERSTANDING

The acidity of cream of tartar whitens the pastillage. Because there is no corn syrup or shortening, the pastillage does not have the pearlized quality of rolled fondant.

CARAMEL

TIPS FOR WORKING WITH CARAMEL

- Do not make any form of caramel except caramel sauce in humid weather—it will be sticky.
- When making the sugar syrup, bring it to a boil stirring constantly, then stop stirring so sugar will not crystallize.
- Oil the counter and all utensils to prevent sticking.
- Use a pan that conducts heat well (such as unlined copper, aluminum, or anodized aluminum) so that cooking stops soon after it is removed from the heat. Alternately, have ready a larger pan or sink partly filled with cold water to immerse the bottom of the pan. Do not use a pan with a tin or nonstick lining as the melting point is below that of caramel.
- To determine the color of the caramel, use an accurate thermometer or drop a bit of caramel on a white surface such as a porcelain plate. When making spun sugar, too light a caramel produces a ghostly effect, too dark produces a brassy color when spun.
- To prevent breakage, never put a thermometer used for caramel into water until completely cool.
- Soaking utensils in hot water will remove all hardened caramel.
- When making a caramel cage, allow the caramel to cool until it falls in thick strands. Make extra loops at the base for strength.

- To make large amounts of spun sugar, cut the loops of a wire whisk with a wire cutter or bend the tines of a "cake breaker" (page 464).
- *Most importantly:* When making caramel, be careful to concentrate every moment. Sugar burns are extremely painful.

DO NOT MAKE IN HUMID WEATHER—CARAMEL
WILL BE STICKY

Caramel for a Cage and Gold Dust

*T*his amber, hard-as-glass burnt sugar offers many dramatic ways to enhance cakes. Drizzled on the back of a bowl it becomes a lacy, golden cage with which to encase a cake; spun in the air it metamorphosizes into golden angel's hair; ground into a powder and sprinkled on top of buttercream, it sparkles like gold dust. Combined with ground nuts and melted chocolate the caramel becomes a wonderful confection that can be rolled paper thin and draped over a cake.

INGREDIENTS	MEASURE	WEIGHT	
	volume	*pounds/ounces*	*kilograms/grams*
sugar	1 cup	7 ounces	200 grams
water	⅓ liquid cup	2.75 ounces	80 grams
cream of tartar	⅛ teaspoon	•	•
optional: Crystallized Violets (page 326)	•	•	•

In a small heavy saucepan combine the ingredients and cook over medium-low heat, stirring constantly, to dissolve the sugar. Increase the heat and boil without stirring until pale amber (350°F. to 360°F.). Remove from the heat and set the bottom of the pan in cold water to stop the cooking. Allow to cool for 7 minutes or until no more than 240°F. The caramel will not fall in thick strings when warmer. Reheat if necessary. (I like to pour caramel into a heatproof glass measure. Reheating is then easily accomplished by a few seconds in a microwave on high power.)

TO MAKE CAGE

Invert a Kugelhupf pan (page 447) and cover it, preferably with a nonstick liner or foil. If using nonstick liner, tape it

STORE:
The caramel cage can be returned to the outside of the well-oiled Kugelhupf pan. Stored in an airtight container at room temperature away from humidty, it will keep 2 to 3 weeks. The caramel powder will keep several weeks at room temperature and several months frozen.

to the inside of the pan to keep it in place. If using foil, mold it to the pan and trim it flush with the bottom. Do not curve the foil under the pan or the cage will crack when the foil is removed. The neck of the pan can be held or suspended from a soda bottle. Dip a spoon in the caramel and allow the caramel to fall over the pan in lacy strands. If desired, glue crystallized violets on the cage with dabs of caramel.

When the cage has hardened, remove it from the pan. With the nonstick liner it will slide right off, but with the foil it is necessary to invert onto a soft towel. Carefully remove the pan and the foil by pulling it gradually away from the sides of the cage.

TO MAKE CARAMEL POWDER
Remelt any remaining caramel and pour on a piece of foil to harden. Break into small pieces and process in a food processor until powdery. Store in an airtight jar.

TIPS: A porcelain spoon is perfect for applying caramel because it does not conduct heat.

Candied violets or dragées can be attached to the cage before it has completely hardened or can be attached later using more melted caramel or a dot of Royal Icing (page 294).

INGREDIENTS	MEASURE	WEIGHT	
	volume	*pounds/ounces*	*kilograms/grams*
hazelnuts, peeled	1 cup	5 ounces	142 grams
sugar	⅔ cup	5 ounces	142 grams
water	¼ liquid cup	2 ounces	60 grams

Bake the hazelnuts in a 350°F. oven for 20 minutes or until lightly browned. Place them on a nonstick or lightly oiled baking sheet or a 12-inch square of lightly oiled heavy-duty foil.

In a small heavy saucepan combine the sugar and water and bring to a boil over medium heat, stirring constantly, until the sugar is dissolved. Increase heat to medium-high and boil undisturbed until the sugar beings to caramelize. It will begin to look like dark corn syrup and take on the characteristic smell of burnt sugar. (The temperature should be 370°F.) *Immediately* pour the caramel over the nuts. Allow to harden completely (15 to 20 minutes). Remove from the sheet and break into a few pieces. Grind in a food processor until finely powdered.

UNDERSTANDING

This praline powder has 50 percent hazelnuts, just like the finest quality praline paste, but it has a crunchier texture.

VARIATION

CHOCOLATE PRALINE: Quick-temper 8 ounces chocolate (page 381), preferably extra bittersweet or bittersweet, to 89°F to 91°F. Stir in the praline powder until smooth. Pour the mixture onto six 12-inch long sheets of wax paper, preferably butcher's wax (page 464). Cover with more wax paper and roll into thin oval sheets. Stack on a baking sheet and chill briefly or until firm enough to peel off paper. For shaping, see decorative techniques, page 386. Store airtight. If necessary, chocolate can be retempered even with the praline in it.

STORE:
3 weeks room temperature.

Caramel
for Spun Sugar
(Angel's Hair)

INGREDIENTS	MEASURE	WEIGHT	
	volume	*pounds/ounces*	*kilograms/grams*
sugar	½ cup	3.5 ounces	100 grams
corn syrup	⅓ liquid cup	3.75 ounces	108 grams
optional: grated beeswax	1 teaspoon	•	•

STORE:
In an airtight container at room temperature with low humidity, spun sugar nests will keep 2 to 3 weeks. Frozen they will keep for months. Spun sugar will keep for several hours at room temperature if the weather is very dry. If humid, it becomes sticky and tends to settle or mat instead of maintaining light, separate strands.

Cover the floor near the table or countertop with newspaper. Oil the handles of 2 long wooden spoons or broom sticks and tape them to the countertop 12 inches apart so that the handles extend well beyond the edge of the counter.

Have ready near the range a 2-cup or larger heatproof glass measure.

In a small heavy saucepan stir together the sugar and corn syrup and bring to a boil over medium heat, stirring constantly. Increase the heat and boil until amber and a thermometer registers 360°F. The caramel will continue cooking from the residual heat. If the temperature is below 360°F., the caramel will be pale and the spun sugar white instead of gold; over 370°F. it will have a brassy color. I find 370°F. produces the perfect color.

Transfer the caramel immediately to the heatproof glass measure to stop the cooking. Allow to cool for a few minutes. Add the beeswax and, when the smoking stops, check the caramel by lifting it with a fork to see if it will fall in strings rather than droplets. (Allow to cool a little longer if droplets form.)

Stand on a stool so that your arms are above the wooden handles. Using a cut whisk, bent cake breaker (page 464), or 2 forks held side by side, dip into the caramel and vigorously wave back and forth, allowing sugar to fall in long, fine threads over the handles. Waving must be continuous or small droplets will form. (It is normal to have a few of these droplets, known poetically as angel's tears.) If the caramel starts to get too thick, return briefly to the heat but be careful not to darken or burn it.

Wrap the strands around the base and sides of a cake or oiled form as they will not stay flexible for too long, especially if the beeswax was omitted. Any leftover strands may be shaped into little nests by pressing them into lightly oiled custard cups and freezing them in airtight containers. They can be filled with small colorful ovals of ice cream or sorbet.

UNDERSTANDING

See Sugar Syrups (page 435). The nature of sugar syrup, which is prone to recrystallization when agitated, makes it necessary to use "interfering agents" such as cream of tartar, lemon juice, or corn syrup to inhibit recrystallization when the caramel is to be used for dipping or agitated in any way. If, for example, when making praline you were to add the hazelnuts to caramel which does not have an interfering agent, the caramel would harden and crystallize and the texture would not be as fine as when the caramel is poured over the nuts and allowed to harden into a transparent sheet. Corn syrup is an invert sugar which inhibits crystallization. It is added with beeswax to caramel for spun sugar because it keeps the strands flexible. Beeswax is preferable to paraffin because it has a higher smoking point.

Caramel can be made with no water by constantly stirring the sugar to prevent uneven browning. Just a few drops of lemon juice can be added to prevent crystallization if the caramel will be used for dipping.

I find it far easier to add a little water to dissolve the sugar before allowing it to caramelize. The resulting caramel seems just as hard. Adding a large quantity of water, on the other hand, slows down caramelization which results in a softer, stickier caramel.

Nougatine

(NEW gateen)

In France nougatine, or nut brittle, is used for a number of decorative effects. When cool and hardened, it becomes strong enough to support considerable weight. It is often shaped into tiny cornucopias and filled with buttercream or into tart and barquette forms to replace conventional pastry shells. Leftover pieces can be coarsely crumbled in a food processor or with a mortar and pestle and sprinkled on ice cream or pressed into the sides of a frosted cake.

The color of finished nougatine, the shape and size of the nuts, and the proportion of nuts to sugar vary according to use. For decorative work, the nougatine is more attractive when paler in color, with fewer nuts. Untoasted nuts make a more attractive contrast. For tiny pieces, sliced nuts are more difficult to mold, so coarsely chopped nuts are preferable. For nougatine that is prepared primarily for eating, allowing the syrup to reach a darker color results in a stronger, richer flavor, and a higher proportion of nuts is desirable.

INGREDIENTS	MEASURE	WEIGHT	
	volume	*pounds/ounces*	*kilograms/grams*
sugar	⅔ cup	4.5 ounces	132 grams
corn syrup	⅓ liquid cup	3.75 ounces	108 grams
butter	1 tablespoon	0.5 ounce	14 grams
toasted sliced almonds, coarsely chopped *	1 cup	3 ounces	85 grams

* For large decorative pieces, use ¾ cup (2.25 ounces/64 grams) untoasted almond slices.

In a small heavy pan combine the sugar and corn syrup and bring to a boil, stirring constantly. Stop stirring and allow to boil undisturbed until pale amber to deep brown. Remove from the heat, add the butter, and stir in the almonds.

Scrape the mixture onto a lightly oiled marble surface or baking sheet. Using oiled spatulas or triangular scrapers, turn the nougatine, folding in the corners to ensure even cooling. When cool enough to handle, cut off a small amount and keep the rest warm and flexible in a 300°F. oven with the door ajar, under a hot lamp, or on a warming tray lined with lightly greased foil.

Use a lightly oiled heavy rolling pin and heavy pressure to roll the nougatine as thin as possible. In France a *laminoir* ("hollow iron rod") is used. For rolling nougatine, I prize my solid stainless steel rod (a gift from my cabinet-making father). The heavy weight makes rapid rolling easier, but an ordinary oiled wooden rolling pin will also work when pressure is applied. (For a heavy metal rolling pin, see J. B. Prince, page 465.)

Work quickly: If the nougatine hardens you will have to return it briefly to the heat until flexible again. When cutting shapes, be sure to oil all cutters or knives. To mold nougatine, press into or over a lightly oiled mold. Cut any uneven edges with a serrated knife while still warm. A pizza cutter or scissors work well if the nougatine is warm enough; if too cold the nougatine will shatter. For instructions on shaping barquettes, see page 368.

UNDERSTANDING

Nougatine, which is opaque, differs from transparent caramel by the controlled crystallization of the sugar. Butter is added as the interfering agent to keep the addition of nuts from prematurely crystallizing the sugar. The mixture is then turned and folded to promote the formation of fine, even sugar crystals, giving the nougatine its characteristic golden-brown opaque color.

VARIATION

NOUGATINE HONEY CRUNCH: I developed this honeyed version of nougatine especially for Queen Bee cake (page 185). The honey makes the nougatine delightfully sticky (as I imagine a beehive to be). For ease in application, it is best prepared the same day as the cake. For 2 cups of Nougatine Crunch, make ½ recipe nougatine, replacing the corn syrup with ¼ cup honey and cooking the syrup to 360°F. Roll into a thin sheet and, when cool, chop coarsely.

Quintessential Marzipan

MAKES
¾ POUND / 340
GRAMS
1 cup + 2 tablespoons
(enough to cover a 9-inch by
2-inch cake)

I am really excited about this newly developed marzipan. It has the silkiest texture and most aromatic almond flavor of any marzipan I have ever tasted. Poured fondant, easily made in the food processor, is the secret for its marvelous texture. Powdered sugar is added to make the marzipan stiff enough for rolling into a thin sheet.

INGREDIENTS	MEASURE	WEIGHT	
	volume	*pounds/ounces*	*kilograms/grams*
almond paste	scant ¾ cup	7 ounces	200 grams
Food Processor Poured Fondant (page 305), flavored with almond extract	scant ⅓ cup	3.5 ounces	100 grams
powdered sugar	½ cup − 1 tablespoon (lightly spooned into cup)	1.75 ounces	50 grams

STORE:
6 months refrigerated, 1 year frozen. Allow to come to room temperature before kneading to prevent oil separation.

This marzipan is very easy to make in a food processor. It can also be made in a heavy-duty mixer such as a KitchenAid or kneaded by hand.

In a food processor fitted with a steel blade, combine all the ingredients and process for a few seconds until blended. The marzipan should still be in pieces. Dump onto a counter (preferably wood to absorb excess oil) and knead until smooth.

Wrap tightly in plastic wrap and place in an airtight container. Allow to rest for at least 1 hour before using.

Keep the marzipan well covered to avoid drying out while working with it. If the marzipan does become slightly dry and cracky, rub your fingers lightly with shortening and knead lightly.

TO ROLL OUT MARZIPAN

Roll out ¹⁄₁₆-inch thick between 2 sheets of plastic wrap or on a smooth counter lightly dusted with cornstarch. See "How to Cover a Cake with Marzipan" (page 363).

TIP: Any impurities, such as flecks of almond skin, can be removed using the tip of a sharp knife.

UNDERSTANDING

This marzipan has 62 percent sugar and 38 percent nuts. This is based on an almond paste which contains 33 percent sugar (page 430). Marzipan normally has between 30 and 50 percent nuts. The higher the percentage of sugar, the whiter the color but the stiffer and more difficult it is to roll.

Classic marzipan is almond paste with extra sugar and glucose (or corn syrup) added to make it stiff enough for rolling. Most of the sugar/glucose is normally added in the form of a 250°F. syrup. Since poured fondant is also a sugar syrup, made with the same ratio of sugar to glucose but with controlled crystallization, it produces marzipan with a smoother texture.

Almond paste is a mixture of almonds, bitter almonds, sugar, and glucose. Bitter almonds have a distinctive, aromatic flavor. As bitter almonds are very difficult, if not impossible, to obtain, it is best to use commercial almond paste.

VARIATION

ORANGE MARZIPAN: Roland Mesnier, the White House pastry chef, shared this marvelous way of flavoring and delicately coloring marzipan. The orange zest also lends a slightly tart, refreshing quality to the marzipan. Knead 3 tablespoons very finely grated orange zest into 1 cup of marzipan.

GREEEN TEA MARZIPAN: Powdered Japanese green tea added to almond paste makes a speedy marzipan with a lovely, pale green color. Although there is not really any perceivable flavor of green tea, the marzipan is far less sweet since no additional sugar is added. The marzipan is also compatible in spirit for decorating a Green Tea Biscuit filled with Green Tea Mousse Cream (page 261). Elizabeth Andoh, a food writer and specialist in Japanese cuisine, and I created this recipe as a joint effort.

To make Green Tea Marzipan: Knead 6 tablespoons almond paste with 1 teaspoon powdered green tea. Roll out between 2 sheets of plastic wrap and cut into decorative shapes with a cookie cutter or sharp knife.

Marzipan for Modeling

MAKES
¾ POUND /
340 GRAMS
(1¼ cups)

This is a quick and easy marzipan with an ideal texture for sculpting figures or roses. Use food color very sparingly. For the most realistic effect, vary the hues of the petals, using the lightest for the outer ones.

While the marzipan works wonderfully for shaping, it is not as delicious to eat as Quintessential Marzipan (page 320), so it is best reserved for decorations.

INGREDIENTS	MEASURE	WEIGHT	
	volume	*pounds/ounces*	*kilograms/grams*
almond paste	½ cup	5 ounces	142 grams
cornstarch	½ cup (lightly spooned into cup)	2 ounces	60 grams
powdered sugar	½ cup (lightly spooned into cup)	2 ounces	60 grams
corn syrup	3 tablespoons	2 ounces	62 grams
optional: paste food color	•	•	•

STORE:
6 months refrigerated, indefinitely frozen. Allow to come to room temperature before kneading to prevent oil separation.

This marzipan is very easy to make in a food processor. It can also be made in a heavy-duty mixer such as a KitchenAid or kneaded by hand.

Mix together the almond paste, cornstarch, and powdered sugar until it falls in fine crumbs. Add the corn syrup mixed with a tiny speck of optional food color and process until well incorporated. (The mixture should not look greasy. If you do overmix, the marzipan will be usable if allowed to rest until the oil is reabsorbed.) Pinch a small amount to see if it holds together. If still too dry, add a few drops of corn syrup.

Dump onto a smooth counter or work surface and knead until very smooth and uniform in color. Wrap tightly with plastic wrap and place in an airtight container. Allow to rest for at least 1 hour before using.

Keep the marzipan well covered to avoid drying out while working with it. If the marzipan does become slightly dry and cracky, rub your fingers lightly with shortening and knead lightly. Cover tightly with plastic wrap and place in an airtight container.*

* For instructions on working with marzipan, see page 363.

People who don't like marzipan usually change their minds when they encounter this pistachio version. I created it as a surprise layer inside each tier of my brother's wedding cake (page 219). The thin line of pale green between layers of pale yellow buttercream and Crème Ivoire is an enchanting contrast, especially with the pale pink petals and green stems of the roses above. Pistachio Marzipan also makes marvelous ivy leaves to entwine around a Cordon Rose Chocolate Christmas Log (page 197).

$\mathcal{P}$istachio Marzipan

MAKES
5 OUNCES /
142 GRAMS
(enough for a 9-inch disc)

INGREDIENTS	MEASURE	WEIGHT	
	volume	*pounds/ounces*	*kilograms/grams*
shelled unsalted pistachio nuts	¼ cup	1.25 ounces	38 grams
powdered sugar	¾ cup (lightly spooned into cup)	3 ounces	86 grams
corn syrup	1 tablespoon + 1 teaspoon	1 ounce	27 grams
glycerine or unflavored oil	½ teaspoon	•	3 grams
optional: 2 drops green food color			

Bake the nuts in a 350°F. oven for 5 to 10 minutes or until the skins separate from the nuts when scratched lightly with a fingernail. Remove as much skin as possible.

Process the nuts in a food processor until a smooth paste is obtained. Add the sugar and process until well mixed. Add the corn syrup and glycerine and process until well blended, about 20 seconds. The mixture will appear dry, but a small amount pressed between your fingers should hold together. If it seems too dry, add more corn syrup, ¼ teaspoon at a time. If you wish to deepen the color, add the optional food coloring. For ivy leaves, a dark green is desirable, so paste food color (which is more intense) should be used. Process until the marzipan has a smooth, dough-like consistency. Knead briefly by hand until uniform in color.

Marzipan may be used at once but is easier to work

STORE:
6 months refrigerated, 1 year frozen.

with if allowed to rest 1 hour. Wrap tightly with plastic wrap and place in an airtight container.*

NOTE: My imaginative friend Lora Brody, of *Growing Up on the Chocolate Diet* and *Indulgences* fame, came up with a splendid idea for this marzipan. She doubled the recipe and rolled it out into a large rectangle about 17 inches by 12 inches. She then prepared a Biscuit Roulade (page 142), spread it with 2 cups of Neoclassic Buttercream (page 230), and topped it with the Pistachio Marzipan sheet before rolling it. The combination of colors, textures, and flavors is exquisite.

The roll can be served unadorned or frosted with Crème Ivoire (page 248) and decorated with chopped pistachios and a long-stemmed pink rose. For an even more intense pistachio flavor, make the optional syrup for the Biscuit Roulade (page 142) and flavor it with Pistasha liqueur.

* For instructions on rolling out discs and ivy leaves see page 363.

Chopped Nuts

*N*uts surrounding a cake provide an elegant decorative effect. Almonds, macadamias, hazelnuts, pecans, and walnuts all make wonderful coatings. Lightly toasting them brings out the flavor.

Some nut skins, such as hazelnut, are very bitter and should be removed by toasting or blanching. An easy system for skinning the recalcitrant hazelnut is to place ⅔ cup nuts (3 ounces/85 grams) in a saucepan containing 1½ cups boiling water. Add 2 tablespoons baking soda and boil 3 minutes. Test a nut by running it under cold water to see if the skin slips off easily. If not, boil a few minutes longer. Rinse the nuts well under cold running water and toast in a 350°F. oven for 20 minutes or until golden brown.

Cool and coarsely chop. If using a food processor with the metal blade, pulse until uniform in size; then finish by hand using a large chef's knife for best texture.

You will need ¾ cup chopped nuts (3 ounces/85 grams) for a 9-inch by 3-inch cake; 1 cup (4 ounces/114 grams) for a 12-inch by 3-inch cake; and 1⅓ cups (5.25 ounces/152 grams) for an 18-inch by 12-inch cake. I always make extra because leftover nuts keep for months in the freezer and may be used as they are or recrisped in a 400°F. oven for 5 minutes. For greater uniformity, I like to shake nuts in a fine strainer to rid them of smaller fragments and powder.

TO APPLY NUTS TO CAKE

The frosted cake should be attached to a cardboard round no larger than the cake. If the cake is not too heavy, support it on the palm of your hand. Tilt the cake a bit toward the other hand, cupped to hold the nuts, and press the nuts gently into the sides. Alternately, if the cake is heavy, place it on a large sheet of foil and use a bench scraper (page 456) or wide, flat spatula to lift the nuts onto the sides of the cake.

Chocolate Rose Modeling Paste

This combination of corn syrup and chocolate is also known as plastic chocolate. It is not nearly as delicious to eat as Chocolate Rolled Fondant (page 309), but it has the advantage of drying to a very firm, brittle consistency, making it ideal for modeling exquisitely delicate red or dark chocolate roses. Brushing the roses with a thin layer of corn syrup creates a finish as shiny as porcelain.

MAKES 8 ROSES

INGREDIENTS	MEASURE	WEIGHT	
	volume	*pounds/ounces*	*kilograms/grams*
RED ROSES			
red summer coating *	•	6 ounces	170 grams
powdered red food coloring *	1 teaspoon	•	•
optional: powdered blue food coloring	•	•	•
corn syrup	2 tablespoons	1.5 ounces	41 grams

*Summer coating, also known as compound chocolate, and powdered red food coloring are both available at candy supply stores (see pages 424 and 428).

Melt the coating in a double boiler set over very hot tap water (110°F. to 115°F.) on low heat. The top must not touch the water.

Remove from the heat and stir in red food coloring. Mix in a few specks of blue coloring to tone down the brightness if necessary.

Stir in the full amount of corn syrup (push it off spoon with your finger). At this point, the chocolate will begin to harden and form a ball.

STORE:
The mixture will keep for several weeks if placed in airtight container or may be frozen indefinitely. Reknead just until pliable. Dried roses will keep for over 1 year if stored airtight in a cool, dry room or the refrigerator.

Crystallized Flowers

Scrape onto plastic wrap and wrap tightly. Place in an airtight container and allow to rest and firm for at least 6 hours at room temperature.

Knead briefly until soft and supple before shaping. Keep well covered to avoid drying out while working.*

VARIATIONS

WHITE CHOCOLATE ROSES: Use white summer coating or white chocolate and reduce the corn syrup to 1 tablespoon + 1 teaspoon.

DARK CHOCOLATE ROSES: Use bittersweet chocolate and increase the corn syrup to 3 tablespoons + 1 teaspoon.

*C*ommercially candied or crystallized violets are nice to have on hand but only about 1 in 20 actually resembles the flower it once was! Making your own crystalized flowers is time-consuming, but the results are dazzling. By handling each flower separately, the petals stay separate. Most flowers can be crystallized successfully (see page 428 for edible flowers). My favorites are tiny rose buds, cymbidiums (which look like miniature orchids), wild violets, and lilacs. As the colors tend to fade, I add a little powdered food coloring or paste color to the sugar. You will have to judge for yourself on the amount, as food coloring varies from brand to brand. It is best to make the color a little more intense if not planning to use the finished flowers for several months, as it fades slightly. Most flowers will keep for years—with the exception of lilacs, which brown slightly after a few months. Crystallized flowers look spectacular caught up in strands of spun sugar (page 316). Crystallized lilacs have a firm little stub at the bottom which makes them ideal for embroidering the sides and top of a cake, especially one frosted with White Chocolate Buttercream (pages 346 to 348) such as White Lilac Nostalgia (page 167) or Classic Rolled Fondant (page 306). (Use a toothpick to make a small hole in the surface of the fondant in order to insert the lilac.)

*For instructions on modeling roses, see page 390.

TO CRYSTALLIZE FLOWERS YOU WILL NEED

- superfine granulated sugar: 9 dozen lilac blossoms require only 2 tablespoons sugar but make ⅓ cup to have ample for spooning over the blossoms.
- powdered or paste food color: Wilton makes a grape paste color the perfect hue for crystalled lilacs and a violet paste color the perfect hue for crystalled violets.
- lightly beaten egg white: 9 dozen lilac blossoms require ½ egg white (1 tablespoon).
- small edible flowers (page 428).

In a small bowl mix the sugar and food color with your fingers until a uniform color is achieved, adding more color if necessary to deepen the shade. Pass the sugar through a fine sieve if necessary to perfectly distribute the color. It is best not to use the food processor for this as the sugar crystals lose their glitter.

With a small paint brush, paint the egg white over the flower petals on all sides. Holding the flower above the bowl of colored sugar, spoon the sugar lightly over it, coating all sides. Gently shake off the excess and place on a nonstick surface. Allow the flowers to dry thoroughly (about 24 hours) and then store airtight away from direct sunlight to prevent fading.

TIPS: Violets will have the best shape if you allow them to dry upside down. Use a hair clip or clothespin to suspend them by their stems until dry.

Gum arabic, available in candy supply stores, can be used in place of egg white for extra sparkle. Dissolve it in a tiny amount of water.

Fruit Toppings and Purees

*F*ruit, fresh, dried, and conserved, adds much to the flavor and appearance of cakes. It can be used as a topping for cheesecakes, charlottes, or even frosted cakes like Star-Spangled Rhapsody (page 169).

Conserves make tart and colorful glazes which temper the sweetness of buttercreams and layer cakes.

Preserved fruits and concentrated purees make wonderfully flavored buttercreams and whipped creams (which I call cloud creams). Making your own conserves enables you to decrease the sugar and maintain more of the integrity of the fruit. I concentrate the fruit juices so much that neither pectin nor a high proportion of sugar is necessary for gelling. My thick conserves contain whole fruit and very little sugar.

Included in this chapter are recipes for making your own chestnut and pumpkin purees. Although the canned varieties are excellent in flavor and texture and undeniably convenient, during the fall and winter, when these fresh ingredients are available, it's nice to be able to use them. The flavor is always a shade more delicious. This is not always true with fruit. Reconstituted dried apricots, for example, give much more flavor than the fresh fruit. Strawberries, frozen without sugar, are often more delicious than most fresh strawberries—even picked at the height of the season.

This chapter has a new and exciting technique for making fruit purees. It involves concentrating the juices without cooking the fruit itself. The resulting purees will enable you to make buttercreams and whipped creams which have the flavor of the fresh fruit at the peak of its season!

$\mathcal{F}$ruit jellies and preserves, particularly tart ones such as raspberry, apricot, and currant, make easy and beautiful toppings for cakes. Ruby Raspberry Jewel Glaze lends a brilliant glow to Chocolate Flame (page 87). A pale golden glisten of Apple Jewel Glaze keeps the poached pears juicy and fresh atop Ethereal Pear Charlotte (page 175).

Jewel Glaze is also ideal for attaching chocolate bands to a cake (page 387).

A 9-inch cake needs ½ cup glaze, a 12-inch cake ¾ cup plus 2 tablespoons. Leftover glaze keeps for months refrigerated.

MAKES A FULL
½ CUP
(enough to glaze a 9-inch
to 10-inch cake)

INGREDIENTS	MEASURE	WEIGHT	
	volume	*pounds/ounces*	*kilograms/grams*
fruit jelly or preserves	½ cup	5.25 ounces	154 grams
fruit liqueur* or eau-de-vie (see suggestions following recipe)	1 tablespoon	0.50 ounces	14 grams

* *Complementary Liqueurs*
For raspberry jelly: Chambord or eau-de-vie de framboise
For apricot jelly: Barack Palinka or apricot brandy
For currant jelly: Cassis
For apple jelly: Calvados or pear liqueur

STORE:
1 year refrigerated.

POINTERS FOR SUCCESS:
If glazing on top of frosting, be sure the glaze is barely warm and that the buttercream firm to the touch or it will melt.

In a small heavy saucepan melt the jelly over low heat. Stir in the liqueur or hot water to thin slightly and strain.

If you are using a glaze to seal the surface of a porous cake prior to glazing with chocolate, pour the glaze on the cake while still hot and fluid. Use a long metal spatula to spread it evenly.

To glaze a buttercream-frosted cake, chill the frosted cake until the buttercream is firm. Using the back of a long sharp knife, make shallow parallel diagonal slashes evenly across the cake, first in 1 direction and then at a 45° angle to create diamond shapes. Wipe the blade clean after each cut. When the glaze is applied it will sink deeply into these cuts, providing an intensely colored design. The glaze should be barely warm when applied and the buttercream solid to the touch to keep it from melting.

Put any leftover glaze into a container with a tight-fitting lid and refrigerate.

To use preserves or apricot lekvar: Apricot lekvar contains the skin of the apricot as well as the fruit. It is thicker and more intensely flavored than ordinary apricot preserves. It is necessary to strain apricot preserves or lekvar to obtain a clear glaze. Start with 1½ times the amount you need. Use a food processor to soften the preserves and then heat to melt before pressing through a fine sieve. Add the liqueur at the end or use warm water before sieving.

VARIATIONS

SHINY JEWEL GLAZE: A small amount of gelatin will produce a thicker but transparent fluid glaze which holds up for several days. Place 7 tablespoons water in a custard cup. Sprinkle 2 teaspoons gelatin over it and allow to soften for at least 5 minutes. Heat in a microwave on high power, stirring once or twice, or in a pan surrounded by simmering water until the gelatin is dissolved. Add the gelatin to the melted and sieved jelly and liqueur. Refrigerate until thickened slightly or stir over ice water until syrupy. Use at once.

CRAN-RASPBERRY GLAZE: This flavorful, pretty glaze is wonderful to top a creamy cheesecake (page 81) as a holiday dessert.

In a small saucepan dissolve 4 teaspoons cornstarch in ¾ cup cranberry-raspberry juice, preferably made from frozen concentrate. Bring to a boil, stirring constantly. Lower the heat and simmer for 1 minute. Remove from the heat and stir in 1 tablespoon Chambord (black raspberry) or Boggs (cranberry) liqueur. Spoon over the cake, spreading it evenly.

It is worth every bit of the work involved to make this recipe because a conserve of this quality cannot be bought. It would take a jar of commercially made jam 2⅓ times the size to equal the amount of fruit used for this method. This raspberry conserve captures the magical essence of the berry. The side benefits are a kitchen permeated with the scent of raspberry and the sight of bowls filled with velvety, ruby-red berries. There also seems to be an atavistic pleasure in the act of preserving summer's bounty for the cold winter months ahead.

This unique method of preparing jam triples the concentration of the fruit so that it gels without having to add pectin or the accompanying high amount of sugar (in excess of two thirds more). The conserve is tart and intensely flavored, with a deep garnet hue. It is perfect for spreading on cake rolls or adding to buttercream.

Cordon Rose Raspberry Conserve

**MAKES
1 QUART**
4 half-pint jars + ½ cup
(2.5 pounds/1 kilogram 157 grams)

INGREDIENTS	MEASURE	WEIGHT	
	volume	*pounds/ounces*	*kilograms/grams*
sugar	2 cups + 2 tablespoons	15 ounces	425 grams
water	1 liquid cup + 2 tablespoons	9.25 ounces	266 grams
raspberries	3 quarts	3 pounds	1 kilogram 361 grams

In a large-diameter pot combine the sugar and water and bring to a boil, stirring constantly. Boil for 1 minute. Add 3 to 4 cups berries (so that they are in a single layer) and boil 1 minute. Remove with a slotted spoon or skimmer to a colander suspended over a bowl to catch the syrup. Reduce the syrup in the pot to 2 cups and repeat the procedure with more berries. From time to time return the syrup that drains from the cooked berries to the pot. Skim the white foam from the surface.

When the last batch of raspberries is completed, boil the syrup down to 2 cups (the temperature will be 210°F.) and reserve. Sieve the berries to remove most of the seeds. (When condensing raspberries to this degree, leaving all the seeds would be excessive; however some seeds lend a nice texture to the conserve. I use the colander and the sieve

STORE:
I have stored this conserve for as long as 4 years. The flavor does not deteriorate, but after 2 years the color deepens and is less bright.

attachment on my KitchenAid, which has large enough holes to allow a few seeds to pass through. You can also use a food mill fitted with the finest disc.) You should have 2 cups raspberry pulp and ⅔ cup seeds.

Add the sieved berries to the reserved syrup and simmer 10 minutes or until reduced to 4 cups. Fill canning jars which have been rinsed in boiling water, leaving ⅜-inch head space. Screw on the caps and place them in a water bath, covered, for 10 minutes after the water comes to a boil. Remove and allow to cool before checking the seal.

Jars in the water bath must be sitting on a rack to allow the water to flow all around them, and the water must be high enough to cover them by 1 inch. They must be upright to expel any air inside the jars, producing a vacuum which seals the jars. If this process is eliminated, be sure to store the conserve in a cool, dry area away from light as there are no preservatives in it to prevent mold from forming. (If mold does form, scrape it off and reboil the conserve.) The conserve takes 2 days in the jar to thicken.

TIP. The conserve can be prepared using raspberries frozen without sugar. Allow them to defrost in a colander, reserving the juice. Add the juice to the sugar syrup and proceed as with fresh berries. The flavor will be indistinguishable from conserve prepared with fresh berries.

NOTE: Half-pint jars can hold only 7 fluid ounces because of the ⅜-inch head space required on top. You will have a bonus of about ½ cup conserve left. Refrigerated it will keep for 2 weeks.

UNDERSTANDING

Formula: 1 pound berries/5 ounces sugar/3 ounces water
A large unlined copper pot is traditional for jam-making because the faster the berries and syrup cook, the better the flavor and gelling. Be sure to use a pot with a large diameter to speed evaporation of the syrup.

Raspberries are very fragile and washing causes them to break down faster. Raspberry growers have assured me that any sprays are administered at a prescribed time so that their effects have entirely dissipated before harvesting. They do not recommend washing the berries. If washed, berries should be cooked as soon as possible.

This highly concentrated conserve has very little sugar—only about one twelfth the sugar and four times the concentration of most commercial jams made with pectin. It is designed to be added to buttercreams and whipped cream and spread on cake rolls. More sugar can be added if the conserve is to be used as a spread on toast.* Either way, it captures the quality of fresh ripe strawberries. Strawberries during the peak of the season are full of sweet sunny flavor. Out of season frozen berries make a far more delicious conserve.

Cordon Rose Strawberry Conserve

**MAKES
3½ CUPS**
4 half-pint jars
(2 pounds 3 ounces/
988 grams)

INGREDIENTS	MEASURE	WEIGHT	
	volume	*pounds/ounces*	*kilograms/grams*
hulled strawberries	4 quarts	4 pounds	1 kilogram 814 grams
sugar *	1 cup + 2 tablespoons	8 ounces	227 grams
water	1½ liquid cups	12 ounces	354 grams

* To make strawberry conserve for spreading on toast, add 3 ounces (a scant ½ cup) sugar.

If the berries are sandy, wash them before hulling and dry on paper towels.

In a large-diameter pot combine the sugar and water and bring to a boil, stirring constantly. Boil for 1 minute. Add 3 to 4 cups berries (so that they are in a single layer) and boil 1 minute. Remove with a slotted spoon or skimmer to a colander suspended over a bowl to catch the syrup. Reduce the syrup in the pot to 1¾ cups and repeat the procedure with more berries. From time to time return the syrup that drains from the cooked berries to the pot. Skim the white foam from the surface.

When the last batch of berries is completed, boil the syrup down to 1¾ cups (the temperature will be 208°F.)

Return the berries to the syrup and simmer 10 minutes or until reduced to 3½ cups.

Fill canning jars which have been rinsed in boiling water, leaving ⅜-inch head space. Screw on the caps and place them in a water bath, covered, for 10 minutes after the water comes to a boil. Remove and allow to cool before checking the seal.

STORE:
I have stored this conserve for as long as 4 years. The flavor does not deteriorate, but after 2 years the color deepens and is less bright.

Jars in the water bath must be sitting on a rack to allow the water to flow all around them, and the water must be high enough to cover them by 1 inch. They must be upright to expel any air inside the jars, producing a vacuum which seals the jar. If this process is eliminated, be sure to store the conserve in a cool, dry area away from light as there are no preservatives in it to prevent mold from forming. (If mold does form, scrape it off and reboil the conserve.) The conserve takes 2 days in the jar to thicken.

TIPS:

- Recently I discovered an extraordinary essence of wild strawberry imported from France. A few drops perform magic in this or any strawberry conserve (page 427).
- The conserve can be prepared using strawberries frozen without sugar. Allow them to defrost in a colander, reserving the juice. (This will take several hours.) Add the juice to the sugar syrup and proceed as with fresh berries. The flavor will be indistinguishable from conserve prepared with fresh berries.

UNDERSTANDING

Strawberries contain more water than raspberries so it is necessary to start with 4 pounds instead of only 3 pounds to get the same quantity of conserve.

Formula: 1 pound berries/2 ounces sugar/3 ounces water

A large unlined copper pot is traditional for jam because the faster the berries and syrup cook, the better the flavor and gelling. Be sure to use a pot with a large diameter to speed evaporation of the syrup.

Apricot Puree

$\mathcal{D}$ried California apricots make a puree with greater flavor and richer hue than fresh apricots, even at the height of their season. The puree freezes well so I always have some on hand to add to buttercreams or to swirl into cheesecake batter.

MAKES
1½ TO 1¾ CUPS
(unsweetened)

INGREDIENTS	MEASURE	WEIGHT	
	volume	*pounds/ounces*	*kilograms/grams*
dried California apricots	2 cups, packed	12 ounces	340 grams
water	1½ liquid cups	12.5 ounces	354 grams
lemon juice, freshly squeezed	1½ tablespoons	1 ounce	23 grams
optional: superfine sugar	½ cup + 1 tablespoon	4 ounces	113 grams

In a small saucepan place the apricots and water and allow to stand, covered, for 2 hours. Simmer 20 minutes on very low heat, tightly covered, or until the apricots are soft. Puree along with any remaining liquid in a food processor.

Press through a fine strainer (page 457). You should have 1½ to 1¾ cups.* Stir in the lemon juice. (If you have less puree, slightly decrease the lemon juice.)

To make lightly sweetened puree, add sugar to equal ⅓ the volume of the puree (i.e., if there is only 1 cup puree, add ⅓ cup of sugar instead of ½ cup + 1 tablespoon). Store in an airtight container.

TIP: Premium-quality California apricots, found in specialty and health food stores, are brighter orange and have a superior flavor to most packaged varieties.

NOTE: It is essential to use a fine strainer to achieve the best texture.

STORE:
5 days refrigerated, 1 year frozen.

*I get 1¾ cups (1 pound/473 grams) using the Cuisinart power strainer attachment. If using the power strainer, there is no need to process the apricots first.

P each Puree

*P*eaches and cream are a time-honored combination. This puree is the base for my Peach Cloud Cream charlotte filling. When it's a great peach season I use ripe, juicy peaches and make extra to freeze for later in the year. When peaches are lacking in flavor, I buy frozen ones with no sugar added.

INGREDIENTS	MEASURE	WEIGHT	
	volume	*pounds/ounces*	*kilograms/grams*
9 ripe peaches, peeled and pitted	5 cups of slices	2 pounds (without peels and pits)	907 grams
lemon juice, freshly squeezed	1 tablespoon	0.5 ounce	16 grams
almond extract	1 teaspoon	•	4 grams
vanilla	¼ teaspoon	•	•

STORE:
2 days refrigerated, 8 months frozen.

In a food processor process the peaches briefly until broken up and liquidy. Press through a food mill fitted with a fine disc or use a fine strainer (page 457) to obtain a smooth puree. Combine the puree and lemon juice in a heavy non-corrodible saucepan and simmer until reduced to 2¼ cups. Cool and stir in the extracts. Store in an airtight container.

TIP: To peel peaches, place in simmering water for 1 minute or until the skins slip off easily. Do not add this puree to cheesecake batter as it will curdle it.

UNDERSTANDING
Almond has an excellent affinity with peach. Vanilla serves as a flavor enhancer for both.

$\mathcal{R}$aspberries are the crown jewels of the baking world. This tart, intensely flavored puree is ideal to temper the sweetness of buttercreams and to add flavor to whipped creams. Lightly sweetened, it also makes a velvety sauce that is the very essence of fresh raspberry.

The secret is that the juices are concentrated by 4 times their original volume, but the pulp is not cooked at all. Raspberry puree is wonderful with Ethereal Pear Charlotte (page 175), and 1 tablespoon poured into the hollow of a whipped cream dollop is the ideal foil for the richness of Chocolate Oblivion Truffle Torte (page 84). In fact, I wouldn't serve the cake without it. Since the puree stays fresh even after months in the freezer, I always prepare extra for storing.

$\mathcal{R}$aspberry Puree and Sauce

MAKES
1⅓ CUPS PUREE
(10 ounces/290 grams)
1⅔ CUPS
LIGHTLY
SWEETENED
SAUCE
(14.75 ounces/422 grams)

INGREDIENTS	MEASURE	WEIGHT	
	volume	*pounds/ounces*	*kilograms/grams*
raspberries, frozen with no sugar added	2 (12-ounce) bags	24 ounces	680 grams
lemon juice, freshly squeezed	2 teaspoons	•	10 grams
optional: sugar	⅔ cup	4.75 ounces	132 grams

In a strainer suspended over deep bowl thaw the raspberries completely. This will take several hours. (To speed thawing, place in an oven with a pilot light.) Press the berries to force out all the juice. There should be 1 cup.

In a saucepan (or in a microwave* on high power) boil the juice until reduced to ¼ cup. Pour it into a lightly oiled heatproof cup.

Puree the raspberries and sieve them with a food mill fitted with the fine disc. Or use a fine strainer to remove all seeds. You should have 1 liquid cup puree. Stir in the raspberry syrup and lemon juice. To make a lightly sweetened sauce, measure again. There should be 1⅓ liquid cups. If you have less, add less sugar. The correct amount of sugar is ½ the volume of the puree. (To 1 cup puree, add ½ cup sugar.) Stir until sugar dissolves.

*If using a microwave, place the juice in a 4-cup heatproof glass measure or bowl to allow for bubbling.

STORE:
10 days refrigerated, 1 year frozen. The puree can be thawed briefly and refrozen several times with no ill effect.

POINTERS FOR SUCCESS:
Be sure to use unsweetened berries. Berries in syrup cannot be reduced as much because the sugar thickens the mixture before the intense flavor can be obtained.

Raspberry seeds are very small and can pass through most food mills. This sauce used to be tedious and time-consuming to make because the seeds cling to the pulp. Pressing through a fine strainer has taken me as long as 30 minutes. Carl Sontheimer recently designed an attachment to the Cuisinart food processor which is the pureer of my dreams! It removes *all* the tiny raspberry seeds in a matter of minutes and is easy to clean. I am very grateful for the hours of work this saves me (page 457).

TIP: If using fresh berries, you will need 1½ pounds or 1½ quarts. In order to make them exude their juices, they must be frozen and thawed to break down the cell membranes.

UNDERSTANDING

I once gave Robert Linxe of Maison du Chocolat in Paris a taste of my raspberry puree flavored with expensive eau-de-vie de framboise. He told me without hesitation that lemon is the best possible enhancer for raspberry. And he is absolutely right (although there are times when I add both, often replacing the framboise with Chambord, a sweeter black raspberry brandy).

The microwave method of reducing the raspberry juice gives the purest flavor because it does not come into contact with direct heat, preventing any slight browning or caramel flavor.

Strawberry Puree and Sauce

MAKES
1¼ CUPS PUREE
(10.5 ounces/300 grams)
1⅓ CUPS
LIGHTLY
SWEETENED
SAUCE
(12.25 ounces/350 grams)

*I*t is amazing how this puree captures the flavor of sun-warmed strawberries at their peak—more so than the actual strawberries themselves when eaten out of season! This is partly because strawberries for freezing are picked at their prime and also because this method of concentrating the juices without cooking the fruit results in a puree of double the concentration and fresher flavor than conventional ones. (This is a technique I have discovered to make the berries surrender all their flavor while maintaining their brilliant color.)

I use the strawberry puree lightly sweetened as a sauce. Unsweetened, it's great for Strawberry Cloud Cream filling for charlottes (page 264) or with Golden Butter Cream Cake as a glorious Strawberry Shortcake (page 34). It is also delicious with Génoise au Chocolat (page 129) and as a buttercream flavoring.

INGREDIENTS	MEASURE	WEIGHT	
	volume	pounds/ounces	kilograms/grams
whole strawberries, frozen without sugar	20 ounce bag	20 ounces	567 grams
lemon juice, freshly squeezed	2 teaspoons	•	10 grams
optional: sugar	¼ cup	1.75 ounces	50 grams

In a colander suspended over a deep bowl thaw the strawberries completely. This will take several hours. Press them, if necessary, to force out the juice. There should be close to 1¼ cups of juice.

In a small saucepan (or a microwave* on high power) boil the juice until reduced to ¼ cup. Pour it into a lightly oiled heatproof glass measure.

In a food processor puree the strawberries. You should have 1 full liquid cup of puree. Stir in the strawberry syrup and lemon juice. To make a lightly sweetened sauce, measure again. There should be 1¼ liquid cups. If you have less, add less sugar. The correct amount of sugar is ⅕ the volume of the puree. (For 10 tablespoons puree, add 2 tablespoons sugar.) Stir until the sugar dissolves.

TIP: Fresh berries are fine to use only in season when the berries are full of flavor. If using fresh berries, you will need 20 ounces or 5 cups. In order to make them exude their juices, they must be frozen and thawed to break down the cell membranes. A few drops of French essence of wild strawberry (page 427) add flavor intensity.

UNDERSTANDING

The little seeds in strawberries create a lovely textural effect and, together with the pink color of the buttercream or whipped cream, give the unmistakable message of strawberry flavor.

The microwave method of reducing the strawberry juice gives the purest flavor because it does not come into contact with direct heat, preventing any slight browning or caramel flavor.

STORE:
10 days refrigerated, 1 year frozen. The puree can be thawed briefly and refrozen several times with no ill effect.

---

* If using a microwave, place the juice in a 4-cup heatproof glass measure or bowl to allow for bubbling.

Lemon Curd

$\mathcal{I}$f you love lemon (and who doesn't) the sunny lilting freshness of lemon curd will be addictive straight out of the jar. It makes an attractive topping, accentuating the lemon in Cordon Rose Cream Cheesecake (page 81). Blended with Perfect Whipped Cream (page 264) or Italian Meringue (page 266), it also makes a luscious filling for Biscuit Roulade (page 142) or an airy filling for charlottes (page 369). It even makes a fabulous addition to Mousseline Buttercream (page 245). Thank God for lemons. They are available year round and despite domestication are always wonderful.

Lemon curd was brought over by the colonists from England, where it is known as lemon cheese or lemon butter. The first time I tasted it I was ready to go to extremes to get the recipe. According to the *Wise Encyclopedia of Cookery* (where I found my first recipe for this English treat), the recipe was a guarded secret for years. Now many versions abound. This is my version—perhaps a little less sweet and more lemony than most. More sugar can be added to taste while the curd is still warm.

INGREDIENTS	MEASURE	WEIGHT	
	volume	*pounds/ounces*	*kilograms/grams*
4 large egg yolks	2 full fluid ounces	2.5 ounces	74 grams
sugar	½ cup + 2 tablespoons	4.5 ounces	125 grams
lemon juice, freshly squeezed (about 2½ large lemons)	3 fluid ounces (use a liquid measuring cup)	3.25 ounces	94 grams
unsalted butter, softened	4 tablespoons	2 ounces	57 grams
pinch of salt	•	•	•
finely shredded lemon zest	2 teaspoons	•	4 grams

STORE:
3 weeks refrigerated. Longer storage dulls the fresh citrus flavor.

POINTERS FOR SUCCESS:
If the citrus fruit is heated (about 10 seconds in a mi-

In a heavy noncorrodible saucepan beat the yolks and sugar until well blended. Stir in the remaining ingredients except the lemon zest. Cook over medium-low heat, stirring constantly, until thickened and resembling a thin hollandaise sauce, which thickly coats a wooden spoon but is still liquid enough to pour. The mixture will change from translucent to opaque and begin to take on a yellow color on the back of a wooden spoon. It must not be allowed to boil or it will curdle. Whenever steam appears, remove briefly from heat, stirring constantly, to keep from boiling. When the curd has thickened, pour at once into a strainer. Press with the back of a spoon until only coarse residue remains. Discard the residue. Stir in the lemon zest and cool. Pour into an airtight container. The curd will continue to thicken while resting and chilling.

TO GLAZE CHEESECAKE
Pour the lemon curd over a chilled cake while the curd is still warm and liquid. Spread quickly with a metal spatula to form a smooth film.

UNDERSTANDING
An aluminum pan should not be used because it reacts with the egg yolks, turning them a chartreuse. Sugar raises the coagulation point of the yolk. It also protects it from premature coagulation during the addition of the citric acid. If the citrus juice were added directly to the unprotected yolk, it would partially coagulate and, when strained, a large percentage would be left behind in the strainer.

When yolks reach the boiling point, they begin to curdle. Commercial establishments sometimes bring the curd to the boiling point and strain immediately. The part that has begun to curdle is discarded. This is done merely for speed (it's one way to take the guesswork out of whether the mixture is hot enough!).

Straining the lemon or lime curd after cooking produces the silkiest texture because it removes any coagulated bits of egg. The zest is therefore added after straining. If desired, it can be added with the juice and removed on straining. This way, it imparts some of its flavor without adding texture. For orange curd, it is important to add the orange zest with the juice to intensify the elusive orange flavor.

VARIATIONS
LIME CURD: Replace the lemon juice and zest with freshly squeezed lime juice and zest. (Limes are smaller than lemons but contain much more juice. Three small limes should suffice.) Decrease the sugar to ½ cup (3.5 ounces/100 grams) as lime is much less tart than lemon. The Lime Curd will be yellow with green flecks from the zest. If desired, add a few drops of green liquid food coloring. Be conservative; only the palest of green hues is attractive.

crowave oven on high power) and rolled around while pressing on it lightly, the fruit will release a significantly greater quantity of juice.

To prevent curdling, be sure to mix the sugar well with the yolks before adding the juice. Use a heavy noncorrodible pan which conducts heat evenly or a double boiler. To further prevent curdling, do not allow the mixture to boil. Remove immediately from the heat when thickened and strain at once as the residual heat in the pot will raise the temperature.

If you are working with an accurate thermometer, the temperature of the thickened curd will be 196°F.

PASSION CURD: This curd has a glorious flavor and deep golden color. Replace the lemon juice and zest with an equal volume (3.5 ounces/100 grams) of fresh or frozen passion fruit juice (page 431). Decrease the sugar to ½ cup (3.5 ounces/100 grams).

ORANGE CURD: Orange juice is much sweeter than lime juice and most varieties do not have enough acidity to thicken the curd as well as lemon or lime does. Orange curd has a delicious flavor and beautiful color but will still be slightly liquid even when chilled. This curd makes delicious Grand Marnier Orange Mousseline Buttercream (page 245) or lovely orange-flavored whipped cream (page 264).

To make Orange Curd: Reduce 1 cup freshly squeezed orange juice to 2 tablespoons (preferably in a microwave on high power). Use only ½ cup sugar and add 4 teaspoons orange zest to the yolk mixture before heating. Do not strain. (If you can obtain blood oranges, reduce to only ¼ cup as they have higher acidity and will thicken the curd substantially.)

Candied Zest

MAKES I CUP
(5.25 ounces/150 grams)

*C*itrus peel makes a flavorful and attractive decorative touch when cut into fine strips and sweetened in a sugar syrup. This candied zest is particularly suited to decorating a cake containing citrus fruit.

INGREDIENTS	MEASURE	WEIGHT	
	volume	*ounces*	*grams*
3 large thick-skinned oranges	•	•	•
sugar	1 cup	7 ounces	200 grams
water	1 liquid cup	8.25 ounces	236 grams
corn syrup	1 tablespoon	•	21 grams
optional: grenadine syrup	1 teaspoon	•	•

With a small sharp knife remove strips of peel, avoiding the bitter white pith beneath. If any pith remains on the zest, scrape it away. Cut the peel into fine julienne strips.

Place in a saucepan of boiling water and simmer 15 minutes to soften and remove bitterness. Drain and rinse under cold water.

In the same saucepan combine the sugar, water, and corn syrup and bring to a boil, stirring constantly. Stop stirring, add the zest, and cover tightly. Simmer over low heat for 15 minutes without stirring or uncovering. Remove from the heat and cool, covered. To brighten the color, add the grenadine.

Refrigerate the candied zest in the syrup in an airtight container up to 1 month. When ready to use, drain the zest. If you wish to use the syrup for cakes, add water to equal 1½ times the volume of the syrup to dilute the sweetness and add an orange-based liqueur to taste.

UNDERSTANDING
The corn syrup prevents crystallization of the sugar when the zest is added.

STORE:
1 month refrigerated.

Fresh Cherry Topping

MAKES
ENOUGH FOR
A 9-INCH
CAKE

For me, summer begins with cherry picking. As a New Yorker, it is always a treat to become reacquainted with how fruit grows. One of the neighborhood farms where we have our weekend house has four sour cherry trees and a "pick your own" policy. I love the sight of the bright green leaves against a clear blue sky and hundreds of tiny luminous red globes suspended from the branches. I'm often the only one picking (which is heaven). Last year there was a family (grandmother, mother, and granddaughter) at the tree next to mine. I overheard exultations of the pie to come and the merits of different shortenings in the crust. I felt an immediate and pleasant connection to these fellow bakers. They asked me if I worked for the farm because I was using small shears to cut the stems. Actually, I've found that leaving the stem on keeps the cherries from deteriorating so quickly before processing.

I love fresh cherry pie but at least half of the cherries I pick go for toppings for my cheesecakes. Tart red cherries, bursting with juice and cooked only until thickened, blend perfectly with lemon-scented cream cheese.

INGREDIENTS	MEASURE	WEIGHT	
	volume	pounds/ounces	kilograms/grams
tart pitted cherries and juice from pitting	1¾ cups	10 ounces	280 grams
sugar	½ cup	3.5 ounces	100 grams
cornstarch	1½ tablespoons	•	12 grams
pinch of salt	•	•	•
almond extract	⅛ teaspoon	•	•

STORE:
If stems are left on, fresh cherries will keep refrigerated 3 days. Cover lightly with a clean towel. Cherries keep their shape best when freezing if sprinkled first with 2 tablespoons sugar per 10 ounces pitted cherries. The sugar holds the juices when the cell walls break. If your freezer stays

In a 1½-quart saucepan toss the cherries, juice, sugar, cornstarch, and salt. Allow to sit for at least 30 minutes until the sugar draws out more cherry juice.

Cook over moderate heat, stirring constantly, until thickened and boiling. Simmer 1 minute. The mixture should just barely drop from a spoon. Remove from the heat and stir in the almond extract. Cool slightly and spoon over cold cheesecake.

TIP: I find that commercial cherry pitters don't work very well. Either they allow a smaller pit to pass through, which can break a tooth if it makes its way into the topping, or the cherries become squashed and misshapen. I once asked the proverbial little old lady sitting on the porch selling cherries how *she* pitted them. She pointed to the gray bun perched on top of her head. When I looked mystified, she plucked out a large heavy metal hairpin. She explained that she inserts the looped end into the stem end of the cherry and uses the loop to pull out the pit.

Since that day I have tried a crochet hook, a new elaborate German cherry pitter, and an antique model—and still find the hairpin the fastest and best preserver of the cherry's plump shape.

around 0°F. or below, the cherries will keep 2 years without losing their bright red color or flavor. If necessary, ⅛ teaspoon red food coloring added before cooking will perk up any color lost during freezing.

POINTERS FOR SUCCESS: Stir constantly to prevent lumping of the cornstarch. The mixture must reach a full boil for the cornstarch to swell and thicken.

Winter Cherry Topping

MAKES ENOUGH FOR A 9-INCH CAKE

*F*resh sour-cherry season is all too short (only about 2 weeks) so if it should escape you one year, this recipe is a great way to brighten the flavor of canned cherries. Cherry Kijafa (cherry wine from Denmark) gives the fruit a gorgeous dark red color and luscious flavor.

INGREDIENTS	MEASURE	WEIGHT	
	volume	*pounds/ounces*	*kilograms/grams*
tart pitted water-packed cherries	1 pound can	1 pound	454 grams
sugar	¼ cup + 2 tablespoons	2.75 ounces	75 grams
Cherry Kijafa	3 fluid ounces (use glass measure)	3.5 ounces	96 grams
cornstarch	1 tablespoon	•	8 grams
pinch of salt	•	•	•
almond extract	⅛ teaspoon	•	•

Stir constantly to prevent
lumping of the cornstarch.
The mixture must reach a
full boil for the cornstarch
to swell and thicken.

DAY BEFORE

In a colander suspended over a deep bowl drain the cherries for 30 minutes or until they lose ¾ cup juice. (Press lightly if necessary.) Reserve only 2 tablespoons juice. There will be almost 1 cup of cherries.

In a 1½-quart saucepan combine the 2 tablespoons juice, sugar, and Cherry Kijafa, stirring until the sugar is dissolved. Add the cherries and bring to a boil. Cover and cool. Refrigerate until the following day.

Drain the cherries again for 30 minutes or until 7 fluid ounces (14 tablespoons) are obtained. Reduce the liquid to ½ cup. Pour into a bowl and cool completely.

In the same saucepan place the cornstarch and salt and gradually stir in the cooled liquid, then the cherries. Bring to a full boil and simmer 1 minute. The mixture should just barely drop from a spoon. Remove from the heat and stir in the almond extract. Cool slightly and spoon over cold cheesecake.

TIP: Bottled Morello sour cherries from Hungary or Poland, available in specialty food stores, offer exceptionally full flavor.

Brandied Burgundy Cherries

MAKES
I PINT

*I*n addition to combining with Vanilla Ice Cream (page 285) and Hot Fudge (page 88) for a deliriously good sundae, Brandied Burgundy Cherries are a traditional part of Swiss Black Forest Cake (page 190). The brandy keeps the cherries from freezing rock hard when making the ice-cream version of the Black Forest Cake.

Brandied cherries are flavorful after only 12 hours but the longer they stand, the more mellow they become.

INGREDIENTS	MEASURE	WEIGHT	
	volume	*pounds/ounces*	*kilograms/grams*
pitted bing cherries in heavy syrup	1 pound can	1 pound	454 grams
sugar	2 tablespoons	1 ounce	25 grams
kirsch or Cognac	¼ cup	2 ounces	56 grams

In a colander suspended over a deep bowl drain the cherries for 30 minutes. Reserve ½ cup syrup. There will be about 1½ cups cherries.

In a medium saucepan combine the syrup and sugar and bring to a boil, stirring constantly. Add the cherries and simmer, covered, 1 minute. Remove from the heat. Transfer the cherries with a slotted spoon to a pint jar and add the kirsch or Cognac.

Boil the syrup until reduced to ¼ cup and pour over the cherries. Cover tightly and swirl to mix. If planning to store longer than 3 months, add enough liqueur to reach almost to the top of the jar. Cool, cover tightly, and refrigerate.

VARIATIONS

MORELLO CHERRIES: From Hungary or Poland, these are a tart and delicious alternative. They are packed in 2-pound 1-ounce jars (Dean & DeLuca, page 445) so double the recipe, using a total of ½ cup sugar (tart cherries need more sugar), 1 cup cherry liquid, and ½ cup kirsch or brandy.

FROZEN CHERRIES: Available in supermarkets, these are more delicious than canned and just about as good as fresh! To use frozen cherries, empty two 12-ounce bags cherries frozen without sugar into a colander suspended over a bowl and allow to defrost. This will take several hours. Add enough water to the juice to equal 1 cup. Add ½ cup sugar and proceed as for canned cherries.

FRESH CHERRIES: When I have a windfall of fresh dark cherries, I use this method adapted from Helen Witty and Elizabeth Schneider Colchie's invaluable book *Better Than Store-Bought*. For 1 pint cherries, simmer 1 cup pitted cherries with ¾ cup water in a covered saucepan for 10 minutes or until easily pierced with a cake tester. Remove the cherries with a slotted spoon to a pint jar and add the kirsch or brandy. Add ½ cup sugar to the liquid in the pan and bring to a boil, stirring constantly. Reduce to ¼ to ⅓ cup and pour over the cherries. Cover tightly and swirl to mix. Add enough liqueur to reach almost to the top of the jar. (The recipe can be increased if desired.)

STORE:
At least 1 month in the refrigerator or a cool, dark closet. The cherries will keep almost indefinitely.

Fresh Blueberry Topping

*Q*uickly tossing uncooked blueberries in this hot glaze turns them a dark, bright blue without softening them. The berries remain tart and juicy with a fine sparkle. This makes a lovely topping for Star-Spangled Rhapsody (page 169) or Cordon Rose Cream Cheesecake (page 81).

INGREDIENTS	MEASURE	WEIGHT	
	volume	*pounds/ounces*	*kilograms/grams*
fresh blueberries	2¾ cups	12 ounces	340 grams
arrowroot or cornstarch	1 tablespoon	•	8 grams
sugar	¼ cup	1.75 ounces	50 grams
water	½ liquid cup	4 ounces	118 grams
lemon juice, freshly squeezed	1½ teaspoons	•	8 grams

Rinse the berries and dry well with paper towels. Place in a bowl.

Have ready a colander or strainer large enough to hold the berries.

In a small saucepan mix the arrowroot and sugar. Stir in the water and lemon juice and heat, stirring constantly, until clear and thickened. Remove from the heat and add the blueberries, tossing until coated. Remove to the colander, drain, and discard any glaze not clinging to the berries. Use as soon as possible.

UNDERSTANDING

Arrowroot is preferable to cornstarch because it adds sparkle and because it starts to swell and thicken the liquid before reaching the boiling point, lessening the chance of overheating the berries. Cornstarch must be brought to a full boil in order to completely thicken the liquid.

NOTE: If the liquid does not thicken, then the arrowroot is too old. Arrowroot sometimes sits on the shelf for years as not many recipes require it.

*F*rozen blueberries have excellent flavor but slightly lose their shape when defrosted. This potential disadvantage turned out to be a desirable quality in the creation of this glistening, dark blue topping. It can be used in the same way as Fresh Blueberry Topping (page 348), but also provides a smoother "lake" on which to float the swans for the Blueberry Swan Lake (page 165).

Winter Blueberry Topping

MAKES ENOUGH FOR A 10-INCH CAKE

INGREDIENTS	MEASURE	WEIGHT	
	volume	*pounds/ounces*	*kilograms/grams*
frozen blueberries	12-ounce bag	12 ounces	340 grams
arrowroot or cornstarch	1 tablespoon	•	8 grams
sugar	¼ cup	1.75 ounces	50 grams
finely grated lemon zest	1 teaspoon	•	2 grams

In a colander suspended over a bowl thaw the blueberries completely. This will take several hours. Reserve the juice.

In a small saucepan stir together the arrowroot and sugar and whisk in the reserved juice. Cook over medium heat, stirring constantly until thickened. Remove from the heat and fold in the blueberries and lemon zest. Put in a bowl and cool to room temperature before using on the cake.

UNDERSTANDING

Arrowroot is preferable to cornstarch because it adds sparkle. It starts to swell and thickens the liquid before reaching the boiling point so it should not be allowed to boil or it will thin. Cornstarch must be brought to a full boil in order to completely thicken the liquid.

NOTE: If the liquid does not thicken, then the arrowroot is too old. Arrowroot sometimes sits on the shelf for years as not many recipes require it.

STORE:
6 hours room temperature.

Poached Pears

**MAKES
4 HALVES**

*T*hese lovely, translucent pears, enhanced by William's pear liqueur or eau-de-vie, are thinly sliced and provide an elegant topping for Ethereal Pear Charlotte (page 175). Of course they are delicious alone or with a thin lacing of Chocolate Cream Glaze (page 271) for the renowned dessert Poires Belle Hélène.

INGREDIENTS	MEASURE	WEIGHT	
	volume	*pounds/ounces*	*kilograms/grams*
2 large ripe but firm pears, such as Bartlett or Bosc*	4 inches long	1 pound	454 grams
water	1½ liquid cups	12.5 ounces	354 grams
lemon juice	2 teaspoons	•	10 grams
William's pear liqueur or eau-de-vie	2 tablespoons	1 ounce	28 grams
sugar	¼ cup	1.75 ounces	50 grams
vanilla bean, split lengthwise	1 inch	•	•

STORE:
3 days refrigerated.

* Select pears that measure 4 inches in length because they just fit when fanned inside the charlotte *biscuit*.

Peel, halve, and core the pears just before poaching so that they do not darken.

In a saucepan just large enough to hold the pears in a single layer combine the water, lemon juice, eau-de-vie, sugar, and vanilla bean and stir to dissolve the sugar. Add the pears and bring to a boil. Simmer over low heat, tightly covered, for 8 to 10 minutes or until a cake tester inserted in thickest part of a pear enters easily. The pears should still be slightly firm.

Remove from the heat and cool, covered. Refrigerate the pears in their liquid until ready to use.

When ready to use for the charlotte, drain the pears, reserving the liquid. Remove the vanilla bean and scrape the seeds into the liquid. Reduce the liquid to 1½ cups and use for preparing the Pear Bavarian Cream (page 290).

Use a sharp thin knife to slice the pears lengthwise for the top of the charlotte.

UNDERSTANDING

Sugar has been kept to a minimum so that the sweetened pear syrup, in addition to the Italian meringue, will not oversweeten the charlotte. If you are planning to eat the pears separately and will not use the poaching liquid for another dessert, it is fine to add up to ⅔ cup sugar to the poaching liquid. This liquid can be refrigerated and reused many times for poaching more pears.

Fresh Preserved Pineapple

*M*aking preserved pineapple is quite simple and well worth the effort. Ripe Hawaiian pineapple is superb but even the often underripened more local fruit comes to life when given this treatment. There is simply no comparison between fresh preserved pineapple and the canned variety! This puree makes a sensational ice cream (page 286) and buttercream (page 234).

MAKES 3 CUPS PUREE
(10.5 ounces/300 grams)

INGREDIENTS	MEASURE	WEIGHT	
	volume	*ounces*	*grams*
sugar *	2 cups	14 ounces	400 grams
water	1 liquid cup	8.25 ounces	236 grams
1 pineapple, peeled, cored, and cut into chunks	4 cups	23 ounces	652 grams

* This amount of sugar is for a puree to be added to ice cream. If planning to use for buttercream, use only 1 cup of sugar.

In a medium noncorrodible saucepan combine the sugar and water and bring to a boil, stirring constantly. Add the pineapple and, without stirring, return to a boil. Cover and cool overnight at room temperature.

Drain the pineapple, reserving the syrup. You will have about 3 liquid cups syrup.

Puree the pineapple in a food processor or a food mill fitted with fine disc.

STORE:
Syrup: 3 weeks refrigerated.
Puree: 3 days refrigerated, 6 months frozen.

Freshly Grated Coconut

*F*reshly grated coconut is a fabulous topping for cakes, worlds apart from the sweetened canned or packaged varieties. A medium coconut, weighing about 1½ pounds, will yield about 3¾ cups (10.5 ounces/300 grams) of grated coconut.

To open the coconut, *preheat oven to 400°F.* With an icepick or nail and hammer, pierce the three holes at one end of the coconut. Drain liquid and reserve, if desired, for another use. Bake coconut until shell cracks (about 20 minutes). Wrap it with a towel to keep the shell from flying about and use a hammer to crack open the shell. Separate the coconut meat from the shell and use a vegetable parer to remove the brown skin. With the fine shredding disc of a food processor or grater, grate the coconut meat.

For toasted coconut, spread grated meat on a baking sheet in a single layer and bake at 350°F. for about 10 minutes or until light brown.

LAGNIAPPE: To make a delectable *Piña Colada Cake,* make Génoise Classique (page 120) and cut it into two layers. Sprinkle it on all sides with piña colada syrup. To make syrup, stir together ½ cup reconstituted frozen unsweetened pineapple juice, ¼ cup canned cream of coconut, and 3 tablespoons light rum. Make whipped cream, using 1½ cups heavy cream, 2½ tablespoons sugar, and ¾ teaspoon vanilla.

Use 1 cup of whipped cream to fill the cake and sprinkle it with ½ cup grated coconut. Frost the cake with the remaining whipped cream and sprinkle the sides and top with about 1 cup of the grated coconut.

*C*hestnuts are, of course, a starchy vegetable not a fruit, but when pureed and sweetened, the faintly spicy, earthy flavor is an unusual addition to buttercreams and whipped cream. The creams are wonderful for frosting chestnut butter cake, chestnut *génoise*, or chocolate cake. Canned chestnuts from France are fine to use (page 420), but the fresh chestnut puree is even more delicious.

*C*hestnut Puree

INGREDIENTS	MEASURE	WEIGHT	
	volume	*pounds/ounces*	*kilograms/grams*
about 36 chestnuts	•	1 pound 2 ounces	510 grams
milk	1 liquid cup	8.5 ounces	242 grams

Using a chestnut cutter or a sharp paring knife, cut an X through the skin on the flat side of each chestnut.

In a medium saucepan place the chestnuts and cold water to cover and bring to a boil. Simmer for a few minutes. Turn off the heat and remove a few nuts at a time to peel. Remove both the outer shell and as much of the inner skin as possible.

In a medium saucepan combine the chestnuts and milk and simmer covered until easily pierced with a cake tester, 20–40 minutes, depending on how dry the chestnuts are. Add more milk if necessary to keep them covered. Cool and then drain, reserving milk, and process in a food processor. To obtain a silky smooth puree and remove any bits of skin, pass through a food mill fitted with the fine disc. Or use a fine strainer (page 451). If puree is very stiff, stir in some of the reserved milk. Store in an airtight container.

NOTE: Crème de Marrons contains pieces of candied chestnut and is almost 50 percent sugar and glucose.

Purée de Marrons has water added which makes it too soft for certain preparations.

To use canned chestnuts, simply drain them and process in a food processor as you would fresh chestnuts.

VARIATIONS
LIGHTLY SWEETENED CHESTNUT PUREE FOR BUTTER-CREAM: Place 1 cup (8.5 ounces/244 grams) chestnut puree in a food processor. Add ⅓ cup powdered sugar, lightly

STORE:
Sweetened or unsweetened chestnut puree will keep for 1 week refrigerated, 1 year frozen.

spooned into cup (1.25 ounces/37 grams), and 1 table-spoon dark rum. Process briefly until smooth.

NOTE: The puree for adding to whipped cream has double the powdered sugar (page 262).

EASY CHESTNUT BUTTERCREAM: This buttercream is less airy but smoother and more chestnutty than either Classic or Silk Meringue Chestnut Buttercreams. It is even strong and elastic enough for piping string work! As it contains no egg it has a longer shelf life as well. To make 3 cups buttercream, blend together 1 cup chestnut puree (9.25 ounces/264 grams), ⅔ cup powdered sugar, lightly spooned into cup (2.5 ounces/75 grams), 1 cup softened, unsalted butter (8 ounces/213 grams), and 1 scant tablespoon dark rum.

Pumpkin Puree

STORE:
Airtight: 6 months

*I*f the mood strikes you to make a Pumpkin-Walnut Ring (page 71) around Halloween time, chances are you may be tempted to use fresh pumpkin for the puree. It is simple to make, especially if you own an electric power strainer attachment to your food processor (page 457).

The smallest pumpkin will make a lot more puree than the 1 cup needed for the recipe, but it's a perfect cake for holiday gift-giving as it stores well, so you can make several cakes. Alternately, the puree can be frozen for at least 6 months.

Bake the pumpkin whole in a 375°F. oven until soft, about 2 hours. If you have a microwave, cut the pumpkin in half and microwave cut side down. Start with 5 minutes per pound on high power and rotate the halves partway through to promote even cooking. In either case, cut off the stem to avoid an unpleasant odor and cook until the pumpkin feels soft when pressed.

Allow the pumpkin to cool. Scrape out the seeds.* Remove the skin and puree the pumpkin in a food processor. Press the puree through a food mill fitted with a fine disc or a fine strainer to remove any fibers.

*Baked pumpkin seeds are a bonus my husband adores. Place them in a single layer on a baking sheet and return to the oven until dry.

aking a cake look as wonderful as it tastes can be as enjoyable as baking it. Decorations serve two important purposes: They lend a festive touch while masking imperfections in the icing.

Actually, a frosted cake does not have to look perfect. In fact, it is less inviting to eat if the frosting is so smooth and free of air bubbles or spatula marks that it looks almost plastic. Cake is food. Have fun with it. (When I was a food stylist for magazines, my colleagues and I would gloat about how we were brought up "not to play with our food" but now we were having our revenge and being paid for it!) Cakes offer the opportunity to execute one's most creative fantasies. To make a cake with a simple, elegant look, however, requires a great deal more skill than it takes to cover a cake with lots of piped festoons.

Piping fine decorations takes practice but there are many "tricks of the trade" which make it possible to produce magnificent cakes without ever picking up a pastry bag.

This chapter is devoted to making the cake look terrific. Some of the decorative touches are delightfully easy, others are for the craftsperson who enjoys painstaking, detailed handwork.

Special Effects and Decorative Techniques

PREPARING THE CAKE

LEVELING

If a cake is not level before icing, it is unlikely that the iced cake will look even. Icing can be used to fill in small imperfections, but the top of the cake should be leveled with a serrated blade. If you don't have a cake leveler (page 461), an easy method is to place the cake in the pan in which it was baked and use the rim of the pan as a guide for a long serrated knife. If cake is too low in the pan, raise it slightly by placing cardboard rounds beneath it.

If the cake is to be covered with rolled fondant, the sharp edges around the top should be beveled slightly to keep the fondant from cracking.

My favorite ways of cutting a cake into layers all involve using a serrated blade at least the length of the diameter of the cake.

For one method, I also use a set of metal bars called retainer bars. They are used in the candy industry to mold melted sugar, retaining the flow. (They are available at candy-making supply stores such as Maid of Scandinavia, page 465.) The bars come in a set of four and each is ¾-inch high. I use the bars as tracks, placing the cake between two of them and allowing the knife blade to rest on their surface while cutting through the cake. The result is 2 perfectly even ¾-inch-high layers. (When I want to trim a cake to 1½ inches high, I stack the bars so that they are that height.) This system works so well I went to a metal supply shop and found beautiful brass bars of varying heights. Wood strips also work but are much lighter, so they need to be taped to the work surface (Fig. 1).

1

A second method is to use an adjustable cake slicer (page 461).

A third method, requiring the least equipment and the most self-assurance, is known as the eyeballing method. The cake is placed on a turntable and a long serrated knife is held against the side where you estimate (by eye) the middle to be. The turntable is revolved as the knife cuts a shallow groove all around the cake. This provides a track for the knife to "ride" in when cutting through the cake. Be sure to use a firm forward and side-to-side motion when cutting, checking occasionally to ensure that the knife is still in the groove. It is easiest to hold one hand palm downward on top of the cake while slicing. This keeps your fingers safe when the knife slices through to the other side (Fig. 2).

2

For ease in separating the layers, slide a cardboard round or removable pan bottom between them.

FILLING A long metal spatula and turntable help to create a smooth, even layer of buttercream. A filling between two cake layers is usually ¼-inch thick. Heap frosting on top of the cake layer. Use a long spatula, pressing firmly with a back and forth motion without lifting up spatula; this may cause the crust to lift away from the cake. When entire surface is covered, hold the long spatula halfway across the cake with the blade almost flat against the surface of the frosting and, pressing lightly, smoothly rotate turntable in one full circle.

Chill the cake for 5 minutes in the freezer or about 20 minutes in the refrigerator to set the frosting before placing the second layer on top. This prevents the filling from becoming uneven and also enables you to move the top layer if the placement is not exact.

I use the removable metal bottom of a quiche pan or loose

bottom pan to support the second layer while placing it on top of the filling.

A serrated knife is also the ideal tool to cut cakes into different shapes. To cut an octagon shape, for example, for Rose Trellis Cake (page 207), make a cardboard template to place on top of the cake as a cutting guide. As the baked cake will measure 8½ inches in diameter, first cut a circle of that size. (Plain cardboard is easier to cut than corrugated.) Then make eight 3¼-inch connecting lines. Each line should begin and end at the edge of the circle. Cut exactly on the lines and the octagon template is complete. Place on top of the cake and cut 8 sides, cutting straight down through the cake.

CUTTING DECORATIVELY SHAPED CAKES

Sponge-type cakes absorb syrup most easily if the bottom and top crusts are removed. If left on, the crusts would become pasty.

REMOVING THE CRUST

It is only necessary to remove the thinnest possible layer. To remove the bottom crust, scrape gently with a serrated knife. The top crust tends to separate easily from the cake with the help of a long serrated knife.

The best technique for applying a syrup to *génoise* or *biscuit* is to sprinkle it rather than brush it because brushing picks up crumbs. The best implement is a large medical syringe. (Use your imagination; syringes are made for other, usually medical, uses and they will work well for cakes if reserved only for this use.)

SYRUPING

To support the cake while frosting, it should be on a rigid surface such as a serving plate or cardboard round. If using a serving plate, slide a few strips of wax paper under the edges. These keep the platter clean and can be pulled out after the cake is frosted.

SUPPORTING THE CAKE FOR DECORATING

Cardboard rounds have the advantage of providing a guide for the amount of frosting used on the sides of the cake since they are cut the size of the cake pan and the cake normally shrinks ½ inch in diameter. When smoothing the sides, keep the spatula pressed to the side of the cardboard, not allowing it to tilt toward the cake, to get a ¼-inch layer of frosting (the distance between the cake and edge of the cardboard).

Whatever surface is used to support the cake, a small dab of frosting or melted chocolate in the center helps keep the cake in place.

If the sides have a lot of loose crumbs, it is helpful to apply a crumb coating to seal them in and keep them from getting into the frosting. A thin layer of warmed fruit Jewel Glaze (page 329) or piping gel (page 431) can be brushed over the cake to seal in

CRUMB COATING

the crumbs. It is best to allow the glaze to dry until it feels tacky before frosting. It is also possible to use a very thin coat of frosting as a crumb coating.

COVERING THE CAKE

The six basic methods of covering a cake are:

1. Dusting it with cocoa or powdered sugar, placing a stencil on top before dusting, if desired, to create a pattern.
2. Glazing with or without buttercream underneath (page 271).
3. Frosting and encrusting with nuts (page 234).
4. Frosting and making designs in the frosting with a spatula, serrated knife, or other items (page 359).
5. Frosting and decorating with a pastry tube (page 398).
6. Covering the cake with rolled fondant (page 360).

To frost a cake smoothly and evenly with buttercream takes practice. It is deceptive to look at cake decorating books where you will see pictures of cakes with sides smooth as plaster. Actually they are as close to plaster as you can get—they are covered with royal icing (sometimes referred to as cake decorator's cement) that has been allowed to dry until very hard and is then sanded down to a smooth finish, an impossibility with buttercream.

There is a baker's trick to frost a cake smoothly and evenly which requires special equipment but little practice. The results are always picture perfect. The equipment consists of a flan ring or loose-bottom pan and a butane torch or electric hair dryer.

The cake is molded with the frosting right in the pan, using the top of the pan to level the frosting. Just enough heat is applied to the outside to melt the thinnest layer of frosting so that the cake can be slid out with perfectly frosted sides and top.

To frost a cake using this method, place a cardboard round the exact size of the mold's diameter in the bottom. If necessary, use a few pieces of tape to hold it in place. The sides of the mold should not be more than ¼-inch higher than the cake or the frosting will be too thick. Extra cardboard rounds can be used to raise the cake to the proper height.

With a metal spatula, coat the sides of the mold with ¼-inch buttercream or frosting and slide the cake into the mold. Scoop buttercream on top (repeat if using more layers), filling the entire mold, and use a long metal spatula, ruler, or knife to level it. To make a wavy line, use a serated knife, moving it from left to right as you pull it forward (Fig. 1). Chill the cake to set the frosting for at least 1 hour or freeze for 10 minutes.

To unmold: Set a heavy canister on top of a turntable. The diameter of the canister must be smaller than the removable section

1

of the mold. Remove any tape holding the mold to the cardboard bottom and using a butane torch or hair drier, rotate the turntable so the sides of the cake are heated evenly. Not much heat is required, especially if using the torch. One steady turn around is usually sufficient to release the cake.

Firmly press down the sides of the mold until it slides away from the cake. A perfectly frosted cake will be perched atop the canister (Fig. 2).

To frost a cake in the traditional way, use a metal spatula to cover the sides and top with a thin frosting. A stiff frosting will not go on smoothly, so, if necessary, warm the frosting to soften it. Heaping on large gobs will help to keep the crust from coming up and excess frosting is easy to remove.

I like to start with the sides of the cake. If the cake is 9 inches or smaller, I frost the sides by holding the cake in the palm of one hand, smoothing the frosting with a small metal spatula. (The cake is supported by a cardboard round.) [Fig. 1] Cakes larger than 9 inches are too heavy for me so I use a turntable. To smooth the frosting, the spatula should be held parallel to the sides of the cake and the blade angled slightly outward so that the edge can remove excess frosting. Hold the spatula steady and rotate the turntable with the other hand. (Fig. 2).

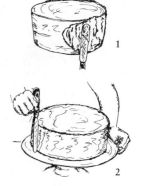

When frosting the sides, bring the frosting up ¼-inch higher than the top of cake to make a foundation for the top frosting. When the sides are reasonably smooth (you can go back to them after finishing the top), heap frosting on top of the cake. Use a long spatula, pressing firmly with a back-and-forth motion without lifting up the spatula because that might lift the crust away. When the entire surface is covered, hold the spatula halfway across the cake with the blade almost flat against the frosting. Pressing lightly, rotate the turntable in 1 full circle (Fig. 3). Remove the excess frosting from the sides by holding a small spatula parallel to the sides and rotating again. If the cake needs further smoothing, dip a spatula in hot water, shake off the water, and repeat the smoothing process, pressing lightly as there will be little excess frosting to remove.

EMBOSSED FROSTING

The frosted sides of a tall cake tier sometimes look a bit plain. One solution is piping a design in frosting such as a scroll border (page 403). Another solution is creating a pattern in the icing itself. Larry Rosenberg, in *Cake Decorating Simplified: The Roth Method,* came up with a most original and creative way to accomplish this. He uses the rough pattern embossed on paper towels to pattern the frosting. The basic technique is to press 3 thicknesses of paper towels against the side of the frosted layer. Spray the paper towels liberally with a water mister so they won't stick to the frosting. Press the paper towels against the sides of the cake using a metal spatula (as if you were smoothing the frosting). It is fine to do a small area at a time. Remove the towels, spraying with more water if necessary.

SWIRLED FROSTING

1

One of the most appealing decorations, especially for chocolate cake, is a luxurious series of swirls covering the sides and top. No other decoration is needed to tell the eye that this cake is going to be delicious. If making swirls, the cake should be frosted with the same basic technique but great care needn't be taken to ensure evenness. Simply use a small metal spatula to make circular swirls in the icing (Fig. 1).

SPIKES

2

Perky little peaks of frosting are easy to make and add a whimsical touch. They can be used only for the sides or for the top as well. To make the spikes, do not smooth the frosting too thinly or evenly as there must be enough frosting to pull out into peaks. Use a small metal spatula to lift the frosting away from the cake. The icing should be fairly stiff (Fig. 2).

RIBBON

Attractive ribbon is an easy decoration for the sides of a cake. Of course it must be removed before serving.

Choose a waterproof ribbon for soft frostings; any ribbon is fine for Classic Rolled Fondant (page 306) or a firm frosting such as Crème Ivoire (page 248). Gold lamé and grosgrain are two of my favorites. Most ribbon can be taped to hold it in place. Tape does not work on the lamé so I use a spot of royal icing, a paper clip hidden by a chocolate rose leaf, or a hat pin with a large head (so that it cannot accidentally be left in the cake when serving).

CUTTING A FROSTED CAKE

Use a thin, sharp blade. When the blade reaches the bottom of cake, wiggle it slightly to be sure that the slice is free and slide it out. Never lift the blade straight up through the top of the cake as it will lift crumbs into the frosting and mar the appearance.

HOW TO COVER A CAKE WITH ROLLED FONDANT (PAGE 306)

Working with rolled fondant is a real pleasure. It feels like silk and looks like alabaster. It's a lot easier to make a cake look wonderful with rolled fondant than with buttercream, providing that it is rolled no less than ¼-inch thick. Thinner fondant will show all the imperfections of the cake it is covering.

To practice handling the fondant, try applying it to the back of a cake pan before committing it to a cake. This way it can be gathered up, rekneaded, and rerolled without being full of crumbs.

The first step before applying the fondant is to place the cake on a rigid cardboard base. If this step is omitted, the cake cannot be moved until the fondant becomes very firm, which takes about 24 hours. If the cake base is flexible and the fondant only partially dry, it will wrinkle.

The next step is to bevel the edge (page 355) and to coat the cake with a very thin layer of buttercream or melted jelly to adhere to the fondant. (A little beaten egg white will also work.)

Fondant should be rolled on a lightly greased surface until large enough to cover the entire cake layer. If a layer is 9 inches by 3 inches, for example, it will require rolling the fondant to 15 inches in diameter. Don't worry if it is a little small as fondant can be stretched at least ¾ inch and smoothed into place. Never pull the fondant, however, because it will tear. Rotate fondant after every 2 or 3 rolls to ensure that it is not sticking. If necessary, apply more nonstick vegetable spray or shortening to the work surface. In cool, dry weather, or if rolling a large piece of fondant, I cover the fondant with plastic wrap to keep the surface from drying and cracking. When covering cakes 12 inches and larger, it helps to use a rolling pin to lift fondant. Lightly spray surface of fondant with nonstick vegetable spray so it doesn't stick when rolled around the pin.

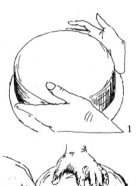

Use your hands palms down to lift the rolled fondant over the cake. Quickly smooth over the top, using a circular motion and starting from the center to prevent air bubbles. (Bubbles can be pierced with a needle and smoothed out if necessary.) Use your palms to smooth and ease the fondant against the sides, working from the top down in a semicircular motion (Fig. 1). Oil from your hands will give the fondant a lustrous glow.

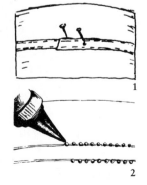

Use a pizza cutter or small sharp knife to trim the fondant at the base (Fig. 2). If necessary, it is fine to continue to smooth the fondant as it dries during the first 30 minutes or so. (Actually, it's hard to resist.)*

Small vertical slits can be made at even intervals around the sides with a Detecto knife or scalpel so short pieces of ribbon can be inserted. This gives the illusion that the ribbon is weaving in and out of the fondant.

To attach a narrow band of satin ribbon around the cake, pin one end to the cake. Wrap it around the circumference, overlap the ends, and secure with a second pin (Fig. 1). Pipe tiny beads of royal icing with a number 1 or 2 round decorating tube along both edges of ribbon (Fig. 2). When the cake has been completely encircled, the pins can be removed.

* Candy supply stores such as Maid of Scandinavia carry differently shaped crimpers for decorating rolled fondant. Fondant must be crimped soon after applying, while still soft and malleable.

For the base, use a number 8 round decorating tube. If points form, flatten and smooth them with a damp artist's paint brush.

For a pale golden luminescence, use an artist's brush to dust on hardened fondant with edible gold petal dust (Maid of Scandinavia, page 445).

CHOCOLATE ROLLED FONDANT (PAGE 309): Chocolate Rolled Fondant can be used to cover a cake in the same way as white fondant, but, since it is a little trickier to work with, I have developed a slightly different design for it which is easier to execute. It consists of a top disc and band.

Roll out a disc ⅛ inch thick on top of a piece of smooth plastic wrap. Transfer the plastic wrap and disc to a baking sheet and cut into a circle slightly larger than the diameter of the cake, using an inverted cake pan or lid as a guide and a pizza wheel or the tip of sharp knife to cut. Freeze for 10 minutes or until very firm. Invert onto another sheet of plastic wrap, peel off the plastic wrap from the bottom, and reinvert onto the cake while still firm enough to handle easily. Smooth the edge to follow the contour of the cake.

For the band, measure the circumference of the cake and cut a piece of heavy-duty plastic sheeting (it comes in rolls in 5 & 10 or hardware stores) a few inches longer than the circumference and a few inches wider than the desired height. A good height is 1 to 2 inches higher than the sides. A 9-inch cake will need a band that is 28¼ inches long. Place the plastic on a flat surface and roll the fondant into a long rope. Lay it on the middle of the plastic and roll into a thin band ⅛-inch thick. Using a long plastic ruler and a pizza cutting wheel, even the edges, cutting the bottom edge flush with the bottom of the plastic. Use your finger to smooth the upper edge so that it thins slightly. Allow the band to sit for 30 minutes or until firm but still flexible. Use the plastic to lift the fondant and curve it around the sides of the cake—which have been brushed with a thin coating of melted Jewel Glaze (page 329). If the fondant is very soft and floppy, refrigerate for a few minutes to firm. Peel away the plastic and curve the top edge gently toward the top of the cake to create a graceful free-form design.

Do not store for a long period of time in a covered container as fondant will absorb moisture from the cake or frosting and become sticky.

Chocolate Fondant is also perfect for making butterflies. Roll it out on plastic wrap 1/16-inch thick and cut with a lightly greased butterfly cutter. Make a V support form from heavy-duty foil or use the recesses of an egg crate to prop up the wings until the fondant dries.

Marzipan is best rolled out between sheets of plastic wrap to prevent sticking. Although marzipan can be used to cover a cake, because it develops a hard crust I prefer to use it only as a component inside the cake—such as the leaf-thin pistachio marzipan inside Pistachio and Rose Wedding Cake (page 219). When asked to use marzipan for the top of a cake, I am always careful to keep it covered with plastic wrap until shortly before serving time.

As marzipan tends to be too sweet in large doses, I roll it only 1/16-inch thick. A lightly greased cake pan or vol-au-vent cutter works well as a cutting guide. Because I roll marzipan so thin, discs are easiest to handle when frozen. Slip marzipan, still on plastic wrap, onto a lightly greased rimless baking sheet and freeze a few minutes until firm. Flip marzipan over so that the plastic wrap is on top. Position over the cake and carefully slide off the sheet onto the cake. It cannot be moved once in place. Marzipan sheets can be rolled out on a surface lightly dusted with cornstarch and then draped or rolled loosely over the rolling pin to transfer to the cake.

Both rolled fondant and marzipan lend themselves to hand-modeling and appliques. Rolled fondant is the more flexible of the two, so it is easier to use for long cutouts such as ribbons.

When rolling fondant for appliques and ribbon, I use a sheet of plastic wrap under it to ensure that it will release in 1 piece and roll it out 1/16-inch thick. Use the straight edge of a lightly greased plastic ruler to cut strips of ribbon. It is best to place the ribbons on the cake while the fondant is still flexible enough to curve the bow and drape the streamers in a natural manner. Small lightly greased cookie cutters can be used to stamp out decorative shapes which can be dried and stored airtight at room temperature just about indefinitely. When ready to place them on a fondant-covered cake, first paint the bottoms with a little egg white. Oriental vegetable cutters found in your city's Chinatown come in shapes from dragons to exquisitely simple ginkgo leaves.

I cut Pistachio Marzipan (page 323) in ivy-shaped leaves using a plastic gum paste cutter from Wilton (page 466) (Fig. 1). Veins can be simulated with slight pressure from the back edge of a knife blade.

To make a stem for a rose (complete with thorns), roll a piece of tinted fondant or marzipan into a long thin stem (Fig. 2). With the tip of a knife, make tiny slashes in the stem, opening them out slightly to form thorns (Fig. 3). The leaves can be cut free-hand and veined with the back of a knife. To scallop the edges, make tiny slashes in the sides.

To make curved flowers such as forget-me-nots, stamp out the shape with a flower cutter (Maid of Scandinavia, Wilton, and

HOW TO COVER A CAKE WITH MARZIPAN (PAGE 320)

HAND-MODELED AND CUTOUT DECORATIONS

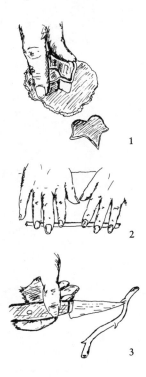

1

2

3

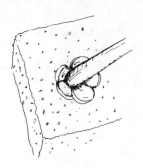

ceramic supply stores carry these). To make it curve, place the flower in the palm of your hand (dusted with cornstarch or lightly greased) or on a small piece of foam rubber and, using a little wooden stick with a rounded end (also available at above stores) or a cotton swab, press into the center of the flower, causing the petals to curve upward. Allow the flowers to dry until firm enough to hold their shape.

MARZIPAN ROSES

No icing squeezed from a tube can ever equal the exquisite delicacy and detail of a rose hand-sculpted from marzipan or chocolate paste. It is, in fact, so life-like, that it's my favorite flower to use on cakes. (I was once described by Jim Gaynor in *Cuisine* magazine as "Marzipan Rose"!)

Brides sometimes give these marzipan flowers as souvenirs to their bridesmaids. Marzipan is easier to work with than chocolate paste, so the technique for making roses can be slightly more elaborate and the flower can support more petals. Ceramic and cake decorating supply stores carry rose petal cutters in varying sizes, but the large end of a pastry tube (such as a 2D which is almost 1 inch in diameter) also works if you roll the marzipan slightly thicker for the larger petals. Grease the cutting edge if the marzipan sticks.

I like to tint marzipan for roses the palest possible shade of pink. To achieve this shade, use only the point of a needle's worth of paste food color. Or tint only a small batch a stronger pink and knead bits of it into untinted marzipan. You'll be surprised at how easily the color can turn to bubble gum pink if too much is used.

Another realistic touch is to tint the marzipan for the inner petals a slightly deeper shade. I like to work with a real rose in front of me for inspiration.

TIP: After rolling out and cutting the petals, use a fingertip to thin the edges of the petals. If the marzipan seems slightly soft and the petals droop, allow them to dry for a few minutes before applying them.

NOTE: Marzipan roses can be purchased through Albert Uster Imports (page 445).

To shape roses: Begin by forming the center cone and base. Use the natural contours of your hand to form a pointed cone and pedestal base which will be removed after the rose is completed (Fig. 1).

Have ready a little bowl of water or lightly beaten egg white and a small artist's paint brush.

Roll out thin sheets of marzipan between 2 pieces of plastic wrap—but not too thinly because each piece will be rolled and shaped a second time. Keep the marzipan covered at all times to prevent drying.

Cut out a free-form rounded rectangle 2 inches long. Lift it from the plastic sheet and roll it a second time between plastic wrap to thin it (Fig. 2). Wrap it around the cone, overlapping to form a point and then folding it back. This is the closed bud of the flower (Fig. 3).

Cut three 1-inch rounds for petals. Remove each, 1 at a time, to a second set of plastic sheets and roll the upper section to thin tip and form oval shape (Fig. 4). Place around the bud, overlapping slightly and curving one side realistically back (Fig. 5). Paint tiny dabs of water or egg white toward base to attach the petals. A small metal cuticle pusher is ideal for molding the petals and pushing them slightly away from the center bud.

For the second row of 3 petals, the rounds must be rolled slightly more elliptically because they have a wider circumference to cover. Cut three 1¼-inch rounds, again making the edges thinner than the base (Fig. 6). When the petals are in place, use a fingertip to form a center point and curve the sides slightly back (Fig. 7).

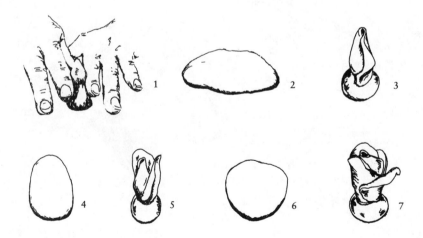

For a full-blown rose do one final row of 4 petals. These will be the widest—almost oval in shape as they have the greatest distance to cover (Fig. 8). Use a slightly larger cutter (1½ inches) to cut three initial circles, because, if they are thinned too much to achieve the correct size, they will not be sturdy enough. Use fingertips to create 3 points on each petal, encouraging the edges in between to roll back slightly (Fig. 9). You may need to prop up this final row of petals using little balls of fondant dipped in cornstarch to keep the petals in place until they dry enough to hold by themselves.

The completed rose will hold its shape well if placed in a bed of cornstarch to support the petals. When the marzipan sets and is firm enough to hold its shape, cut off the base with a small sharp knife. When the rose is thoroughly dry, use a small paintbrush or dust atomizer to dust off the cornstarch.

ROLLED FONDANT CALLA LILIES

These flowers are very easy to form and make lovely decorations for an Art Deco-inspired cake. All that is required is white rolled fondant, beaten egg white, and yellow sugar crystals (available in supermarkets or at candy-making supply stores such as Maid of Scandinavia). If you like, you can tint a small amount of fondant pale green to make sepals at the base.

Start with the centers by rolling thin ¼-inch-diameter ropes of fondant. Cut off sections slightly shorter than the projected length of the finished flower. Round 1 end. Brush the entire piece with lightly beaten egg white and roll in the yellow sugar crystals. Allow to dry until firm enough to handle (Fig. 1).

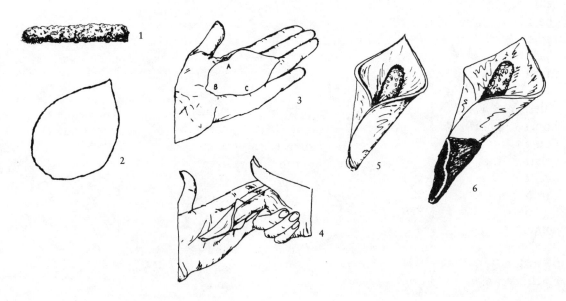

For flowers, roll the fondant thin and cut out ovals 3 inches long, with 1 end rounded and the other pointed (Fig. 2).* Bring together the rounded ends, overlapping slightly, and use a tiny bit of egg white to hold them in place (Fig. 3). Slip the center in place so that it comes to 1 inch from point. Cut out a 1½-inch circle of rolled green fondant for the sepal. Roll to elongate it slightly and wrap it around the base. (Fig. 6). Allow the flowers to dry until very firm before placing them on the cake. For a realistic effect, brush centers of flowers with powdered yellow food coloring.

FRESH FLOWERS

A much speedier method than hand-modeling flowers is to use real flowers! (See list of appropriate and edible flowers on page 428.) The stems of sweetheart roses can be inserted into the cake by making a small hole with a skewer or they can be strewn around each tier. They will remain fresh-looking for hours. If they must be placed the day before, little flower sinkers (page 463) can be inserted into the cake to keep the flowers watered and fresh.

Real roses are sometimes too tightly closed to look their best. If time does not allow them to be placed in warm water, a florist's trick is to blow on them to force them open. Imperfect outer petals can be removed.

DRIED FLOWERS

One of my friends and former students, Jan Kish of La Petite Fleur in Columbus, Ohio, flies special-order cakes all over the country. Because shipping cakes by plane does not lend itself to the use of fresh flowers, she sometimes uses dried flowers and herbs to decorate the cakes. The exquisite pastel shades and ethereal textures provide a slightly faded, dreamlike quality. Some of the flowers and herbs she uses are: tiny pink sweetheart roses, larkspur, globe amaranth, lavender, thyme, myrtle, and rosemary. Each has its own symbolic meaning: rosemary for remembrance, myrtle for virginity, lavender for love.

MARZIPAN BEES

I designed these bees for Queen Bee cake (page 185) and, quite honestly, they can be more time-consuming than the cake. But if you are a craftsperson you will love making them. The gossamer gelatin wings look almost real. Sheet gelatin and icing pens are available through Maid of Scandinavia (page 445). Thin plastic can be used in place of the gelatin but, of course, is inedible.

Shape the bee's body from marzipan tinted bright yellow (a combination of Wilton's golden yellow and lemon yellow food color produces just the right shade). Use the tip of a sharp knife to make 2 tiny slashes at the neck to receive the wings. Use a black icing pen or pipe black-tinted royal icing to form eyes and

---

* Wilton, page 466, makes a gum paste calla lily cutter which offers a subtle curve to the flower's edge.

stripes. Cut free-form oval wings with sharp pointed ends from sheet gelatin. To make the wings more visible, tint them with an artist's brush very lightly moistened with water tinted with golden food color.

Insert the wing tips into the slashes and allow them to dry until very firm.

If you are planning to suspend the bees above the cake before drying, make a small hole in front of the neck with a sharp needle and insert a 6-inch piece of dried angel hair pasta. Insert the other end of the pasta into a piece of styrofoam and allow the bee to dry for 24 hours before placing in the cake. (If there is a slight breeze, the bees will sway above the cake.)

NOUGATINE BARQUETTES AND CUTOUTS

Nougatine (page 318) is easy to work with because it can be re-warmed any number of times to maintain the proper consistency. Professionals usually work with a heat lamp to keep the nougatine soft but a hot tray or oven works well too.

Nougatine must be warm when cut or it will shatter. If it hardens while working with it, return it briefly to a 300°F. oven or foil-covered hot tray.

Nougatine can be cut with a knife, heavy-duty round or oval nougatine cutters, a pizza cutter, or sharp kitchen shears. The cutters should be oiled so that they don't stick to the nougatine.

To cut out ovals of nougatine for barquettes, fashion a foil template by pressing foil into the barquette mold, then flattening it and cutting out the shape. When the nougatine is cool enough to handle, cut it into 4 equal parts and roll 1 of them into an 8-inch by 6-inch rectangle ⅛-inch thick. Keep the other 3 pieces warm in the oven with the door ajar. If the nougatine has cooled and hardened, warm it again until soft enough to mark easily.

1

Using a pizza cutter and the template as guide, mark the oval on the nougatine. When cool enough to handle, cut out the oval with scissors (Fig. 1). Each rectangle will make 3 barquettes.

2

Press the nougatine oval into a lightly greased barquette mold (Fig. 2). The nougatine must be hot enough to remain flexible. If necessary, return briefly to heat source just until flexible (not too long or it will lose its shape). When cool, remove the hardened nougatine barquette from the mold and proceed with the remainder. The barquettes will keep for several weeks if stored airtight at room temperature away from direct sunlight, heat, and humidity.

Another interesting use for nougatine is to cut it in triangles and spread one side of each triangle with tempered dark chocolate. This can be used to make a pinwheel around the top of a cake (similar to the traditional décor for a Dobos Torte). Small triangles or irregular pieces make elegant and delicious petits fours to serve with coffee at the end of a formal dinner.

A charlotte consists of a cream filling encased in a thin layer of a sponge-type cake such as a *biscuit*. The filling is stabilized with gelatin to make it firm enough to hold its shape for slicing. Charlottes are formed in a mold which will support their shape until the gelatin sets.

There are many delightful cake shapes and designs for lining a mold, flan, or springform. The completed charlotte often looks like a feat of wizardry, but actually the various shapes are easy to accomplish by cutting rectangles of thin cake and sandwiching them together with jam. Biscuit Roulade (page 142) is an ideal cake to use for this purpose because it is baked in large thin layers and is springy enough to compress and mold into complex shapes without sacrificing delicacy of texture. *Génoise* works well for cutting and overlapping long strips to form a dome shape. And, of course, Biscuit à la Cuillière (or ladyfingers) encircling the filling is the classic Charlotte Russe. Before filling the lined mold with cloud creams, Bavarian creams, or whipped cream, the cake can be brushed lightly with syrup or sprinkled with liqueur. If filling the cake with a fruit cloud cream such as strawberry or raspberry, a nice addition is to brush the base of the cake with a thin coating of the fruit sauce. Piping free-form loops or swirls with the cloud cream, after smoothing the surface, and spooning some of the fruit sauce into the depressions also makes an attractive design.

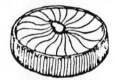

A 6-cup (1.5 liter) bowl is a good size for domed charlottes. When lined with a thin layer of cake it will hold 5 cups of filling. Loose-bottom 8-inch or 9-inch pans or springforms are good sizes for other shapes. (Flan rings are fine, but will not be exactly 8 or 9 inches.) The exact height of the sides is unimportant, but should be at least 2¼ inches high to offer adequate support. An 8-inch ring needs 5 to 6 cups filling; a 9-inch ring 6 to 7 cups. The inner circumference of an 8-inch ring is 25 inches and a 9-inch ring is 28 inches. This means you will need about seventeen 1½-inch-wide ladyfingers (or a 25-inch-long cake strip) to line an 8-inch ring and nineteen 1½-inch-wide ladyfingers (or a 28-inch-long cake strip) to line a 9-inch ring. A 7½-inch to 8½-inch round of cake is trimmed to fit just inside the circle of the cake to serve as the base. This can be cut from a sheet of *biscuit* or piped from Biscuit à la Cuillière batter (page 148).

A single layer of Biscuit Roulade is easiest to cut using scissors. A serrated knife works best for layers or sandwiches of *biscuit*, which cut most precisely when frozen.

SPIRALED DOME: Lining the bowl with plastic wrap makes it easy to unmold a dome-shaped charlotte. Lightly oil a 6-cup bowl and line it as smoothly as possible with plastic wrap, leaving a small overhang. Measure the diameter of the bowl. You will need a round *biscuit* base slightly smaller.

When the *biscuit* has finished baking, use the lining to slip it out of the pan onto the counter and cut off a strip from one of the short ends just large enough to serve as the base. While still hot, roll the *biscuit* as indicated in the recipe and allow it to cool. When the cut strip has cooled, cut with shears into a circle for the base. Wrap with plastic and set aside.

The jelly-roll slices used to line this charlotte must be tightly rolled for the most attractive appearance. To accomplish this, un-roll the cooled *biscuit*, leaving it on the nonstick liner or towel, and spread with a very thin layer of Cordon Rose Raspberry Conserve (page 331) or commercial jam (about ½ cup). For height-ened flavor, stir 2 teaspoons Chambord (black raspberry liqueur) into the conserve.

Roll up the *biscuit* tightly ⅓ of the way and turn so that the unrolled portion is facing you. Lap over the lining or towel to cover the rolled section and a little of the flat section. Hold the edge of a straight-sided baking sheet at an angle on top of the towel just at the point where the rolled section ends. Press firmly against the roll and tug the bottom of the towel toward you. Lift away the overlap. Continue rolling ⅓ of the way and repeat the process. Finish rolling and repeat 1 more time, again angling the sheet just at the base of the completed roll. The roll will be 1¾ inches in diameter. Wrap snugly with plastic wrap, then foil, and freeze until firm enough to slice.

With a small serrated knife, cut into ¼-inch-thick slices. To line the mold, start by placing 1 slice in the center and place slices around it as tightly as possible to avoid gaps. It is sometimes nec-essary to cut slices in half or smaller to fit the last row. Cover the *biscuit*-lined bowl tightly to keep it from drying out until the fill-ing is ready. Fill the mold and place the round *biscuit* base in place. Cover tightly and refrigerate until set (at least 4 hours).

To unmold: Invert onto a serving plate and lift away the bowl, tugging gently on the plastic wrap to release it. To prevent drying out, glaze with melted jelly or Shiny Jewel Glaze (page 330) or simply leave the plastic wrap in place until serving time.

VERTICAL STRIPES: For this elegant design, thin layers of *biscuit* are sandwiched with raspberry conserve and cut into small rectangles to line the sides of a loose bottom or springform pan. A disc of Biscuit à la Cuillière, cut to fit inside, serves as the base.

Bake the Biscuit Roulade (page 142) and allow it to cool flat.

To cut the *biscuit,* use a pizza wheel or a sharp knife and a ruler to score where the cuts should be. Use sharp shears to do the actual cutting.

Trim the edges so that the *biscuit* measures exactly 10 inches by 16 inches. Cut the *biscuit* lengthwise into 4 equal rectangles. Each will be 2½ inches wide by 16 inches long. Spread 3 of them with a smooth layer of Cordon Rose Raspberry Conserve or seedless commercial raspberry jam. You will need about ¾ cup to complete the cake. For extra flavor intensity, thin the conserve with 1 tablespoon Chambord (black raspberry liqueur). If using commercial jam, heat and sieve it and use it warm.

Stack the rectangles carefully on top of each other, ending with the layer without jam. The flat side of a long metal ruler set against the side helps to even the layers. Cut the finished stack in half, to form 2 shorter stacks (each 7½ inches long).

You now have two 4-layer rectangles 2½ inches wide and 2 inches high (Fig. 1). (The only important measurement is the width because when sliced and positioned in the pan, it will determine the height of the striped border.) Wrap the rectangles in wax paper and slip it into a large heavy-duty plastic freezer bag. Place on a flat surface such as a baking sheet to maintain the shape and freeze until firm.

Use a small serrated knife to cut the rectangles into ⅜-inch-thick slices (Fig. 2). Trim tops and bottoms so that each slice is even and the same height.

If molding the charlotte in a springform, you may remove the inner disc and place the outer ring directly on a serving plate. If using a loose-bottom pan, leave the inner disc in place but line with a parchment round if planning to remove the disc before serving.

Lightly butter the inside of the ring. Place *biscuit* slices around the ring so that the stripes are straight up and down. Brush 1 side of each slice with a light coating of conserve before placing the next rectangle firmly against it.

Measure the inside diameter of the *biscuit*-lined ring for making the *biscuit* disc. Cover tightly with plastic wrap and set aside while preparing the disc and filling.

Pipe and bake a spiral of Biscuit à la Cuillière (page 148) the desired size of the charlotte base. When cool, trim if necessary and fit snugly into the bottom of the lined ring (Fig. 3). Scoop in the filling, cover tightly, and refrigerate until set (at least 4 hours). *To unmold:* For a springform, release the sides and lift away. For a loose-bottom pan, place on top of a sturdy canister smaller than

the pan bottom opening and press firmly downward. The sides will slip down to the counter and the charlotte can be lifted off the canister because it is supported by the pan base.

STRIPED DOME: Until it is cut into, this dramatic design defies analysis. The striped motif is achieved by cutting and overlapping thin rectangles from a square *génoise*. The chocolate-frosted bottom crust determines the striping effect. No cake base is necessary for this charlotte.

Bake the Génoise Classique (page 120) using an 8-inch-long by 2-inch-high metal pan. Unmold onto a lightly greased rack. When cool, wrap well with plastic wrap and allow to sit overnight to firm for cutting. Prepare ½ the syrup recipe on page 120.

When ready to mold the cake, use a soft tape measure to measure the inside of a 6-cup bowl. Measure from center point to edge, making sure that the tape follows the curve of the bowl. It should measure 5½ inches. Using a long serrated knife, remove the top crust and trim the *génoise* so that it is perfectly square. Cut off 1 edge so that 1 side measures exactly 6 inches (1 inch more than the curve of the bowl for safety margin).

Make ½ cup Ganache Frosting (page 267). Spread 2 tablespoons hot ganache over bottom of *génoise*. Chill for 15 minutes to set the ganache before slicing. Set aside the remaining ganache at room temperature to use for piping decorations on top after unmolding.

Invert the cake, ganache side down, onto lightly greased foil and cut into ¼-inch by 6-inch strips with a thin sharp knife, wiping the blade between each slice. Cut 1 end of the unfrosted side of each strip on a diagonal so it comes to a point (Fig. 1). This will prevent too much cake from building up in the center. Prepare Chocolate Chip Whipped Cream (page 258) and set aside briefly while lining the mold.

Lightly oil the 6-cup glass bowl and line smoothly with buttered plastic wrap, buttered side up, allowing a slight overhang. Starting at the bottom center of the bowl, place a strip of *génoise* from center to edge, placing the pointed edge at the center, the cut edge facing right, and the frosted edge facing left (Fig. 2).

Brush the strip with syrup and a thin coating of whipped cream reserved from the filling. Place a second strip, starting at the center and slightly overlapping the first strip at the rim. Brush with syrup and thin coating of whipped cream and continue to work clockwise from right to left, always having the frosted edge facing left so that it will show on the outside in a striped motif when unmolded. When you come to the last strip, tuck the side under the first strip.

Trim the excess *biscuit* flush with the edge of the bowl using shears (Fig. 3). Cover tightly with plastic wrap while preparing the filling.

Fill the cake-lined dome, chill until set (at least 2 hours if using Chocolate Chip Whipped Cream, 4 hours if Bavarian or cloud cream), and unmold onto a serving plate, tugging gently on the plastic wrap overhang to release the cake. Use the reserved ganache to pipe a fluted design on top with a number 103 rose tube to cover any imperfections.

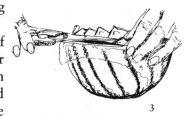

3

Nonstick liner, parchment, or foil can be used to line pans for piping Biscuit à la Cuillière batter (page 148). It is also possible to grease and flour the pan and create guidelines in the surface of the flour.

If using parchment, guidelines can be drawn directly on it with pen or pencil. The parchment is inverted before piping so that the lines show through, but the ink or pencil marks don't come into direct contact with the batter. Guidelines for foil can be marked with a skewer. A nonstick liner, however, is my favorite surface because the baked *biscuit* slides off it without any problem. I use a bright felt-tip marker to make guidelines on a brown paper bag and cover it with the nonstick liner.

For piping ladyfingers, make parallel lines 3 inches apart. For discs, use a round cake pan to mark circles.

PIPING TECHNIQUES

Biscuit batter flows easily so it is unnecessary to squeeze the pastry bag. (If the piped designs do not hold their shape it means that the egg whites were not beaten stiffly enough.) To stop the flow of batter, tilt the tube up just before you think it will be necessary. Work steadily so that the batter can be baked soon after preparing it. This will enable it to retain as much air and lightness as possible.

PIPED LADYFINGERS: Using a number 9 large round tube (¾-inch diameter), pipe ladyfingers, leaving a ¼-inch space in between each as the batter will spread sideways while piping the next finger. (After baking, the ladyfingers will be attached to each other in continuous strips. Each finger will be about 1½ inches wide.) Start piping just inside the top guideline and stop shortly before reaching the bottom one, moving the tip slightly forward and up to control the batter flow.

PIPED SPIRAL BASE: Using a number 9 large round tube, hold the pastry bag in a vertical (straight up-and-down) position with the tube at least 1½ inches above the pan. To achieve full height and a rounded shape, the batter must be allowed to fall from the tube and not be pressed against the pan. Start in the center, moving the tip with your entire arm in smooth circles. To prevent gaps, allow spirals of batter to fall against the sides of—almost on top

1

2

of—previous spirals. The weight of the batter will cause them to fall exactly in place.

PIPED DAISY TOP: Making this fancy design to top a charlotte involves piping a tear-drop shape or shell design without ridges. Review piped shell borders (page 399). Start each tear drop at the outer edge, ending with a point or "tail" at the center (Fig. 1). Use a number 9 large round tube. When the petals of the daisy are complete, finish the center with a round dot (Fig. 2).

To bake piped biscuit: *Bake in a preheated 400°F. oven* for 8 to 10 minutes or until *biscuit* is light golden brown and springy to the touch (page 186).

To assemble: If molding the Charlotte Russe in a springform pan, you may remove the inner disc and place the outer ring directly on a serving plate. If using a loose-bottom pan, leave the inner disc in place but line with a parchment round if planning to remove the disc before serving.

Lightly oil the inside of the ring. If the ladyfingers have not been freshly baked, sprinkle them with a little liqueur. Use the ladyfinger strips to line the inside of the ring. Place the *biscuit* base in the bottom, trimming it if necessary for a snug fit. Scoop filling into the lined mold. Level with a small angled spatula. If using the daisy top, trim the tops of the ladyfingers encircling the mold so that they are flush with the filling and cover with the daisy top, sprinkled with liqueur. Refrigerate until set (at least 4 hours).

To unmold: For a springform, release the sides and lift away. For a loose-bottom pan, place on top of a sturdy canister smaller than the pan bottom opening and press firmly downward. The sides will slip down to the counter and the charlotte can be lifted off the canister because it is supported by the pan base.

SPECIAL MERINGUE PIPING TECHNIQUES

COCOA MERINGUE STICKS: Great for munching by themselves, these sticks are also used to create The Enchanted Forest (see color photograph).

Piping fine lines demands a great deal of control if you want them to be perfectly straight. Fortuitously, however, I discovered that irregularly piped sticks look even more interesting. Line three 17-inch x 12-inch baking sheets with a nonstick liner or parchment. Fit a pastry bag with a number 12 round decorating tube and fill the bag with Cocoa Meringue (page 298). Hold the bag at a slight angle away from you with the tube several inches above the pan. Starting at the top of the pan, squeeze the meringue with steady pressure, allowing it to drop from the tube. Leave ⅜-inch between the lines of meringue. To obtain the irregular, nubbly appearance in the color photograph, lower the tube while piping, allowing it to touch the surface so extra meringue will build up around edges.

Bake at 200°F. for 50 minutes or until dry. If a tiny bit of stickiness remains in center, it will dry out after removal from the oven. Remove carefully from the baking sheet and cut or break into uneven lengths ranging from 2 to 4 inches.

PINE NEEDLES: Delicious to eat by themselves or with ice cream, they make a delightful garnish for the Cordon Rose Chocolate Christmas Log (see color photograph).

Line a baking sheet with a nonstick liner or parchment. Fit a pastry bag with a number 3 decorating tube and fill the bag with Pine Needle Meringue (page 298). Hold the bag at a 45° angle with the tube slightly above the pan. Each pine needle consists of 2 sticks joined at the top, but the shapes can vary. Pipe some straight in an upside-down V and others crossing 1 stick over the other. Bake at 200°F. for 30 minutes or until dry but not starting to color. Remove carefully from the baking sheet with a small angled spatula. These pine needles are quite fragile. For a realistic effect, dip the joined end into melted dark chocolate.

MERINGUE OR DACQUOISE DISCS AND HEARTS: A nonstick liner, parchment, or foil can be used to line the baking sheets for piping meringue or *dacquoise*. They must be totally grease free. If using parchment, guidelines can be drawn directly on it with a pen or pencil. The parchment is inverted before piping so that the lines show through but the ink or pencil marks don't come into direct contact with the meringue. Guidelines for foil can be marked with a skewer. A nonstick liner, however, is my favorite surface because the baked meringue slides off without a problem. I use a bright felt-tip marker to make guidelines on a brown paper bag and cover it with the nonstick liner.

To pipe a spiral disc, fit a nylon pastry bag with a number 6 large, round tube (½-inch diameter) and fill with meringue or *dacquoise*.

Hold the bag in a vertical position (straight up-and-down) with the tube at least 1½ inches above the pan. To achieve full height and a rounded shape, the batter must be allowed to fall from the tube and not be pressed against the pan. Start either in the center or at the outer edge, moving the tip with your entire arm in smooth circles. To prevent gaps, allow the spirals of batter to fall against the sides of—almost on top of—previous spirals. The weight of the mixture will cause them to fall exactly in place.

To form hearts, use a heart-shaped pan as a guide to draw the shape. To pipe the mixture, begin by outlining the outside edge, starting and ending at the indentation. Continue piping 1 row at a time, ending in the center. Use a small brush dipped in water to correct mistakes.

If time allows and the oven has a pilot light, meringue or *dacquoise* can be baked for 1 hour at 200°F. and then left to dry overnight in a turned-off oven.

Alternately, bake meringue at 200°F. for 2 to 2½ hours or until dry but not beginning to color. *Dacquoise* can also be baked at 200°F. for 1 to 1½ hours or until dry.

MERINGUE MUSHROOMS: These little mushrooms look astonishingly real when dusted lightly with cocoa to simulate earth. They are perfect for decorating the Cordon Rose Chocolate Christmas Log (see color photograph).

Make ½ recipe Figure Piping Meringue (page 297). This will make about thirty 1½-inch-diameter mushrooms. Line a baking sheet with a nonstick liner, parchment, or foil. Fit a pastry bag with a number 3 round decorating tube and a second bag with a number 6 round pastry tube (½-inch in diameter). Fill the bags with meringue mixture, placing about ¼ cup in bag with smaller tube. Set aside. Use the larger tube to pipe the caps and stems.

To pipe the caps: Hold the bag upright with the tube slightly above the baking sheet. Squeeze with a steady, even pressure, gradually raising the tube as the meringue begins to build up but keeping tip buried in the meringue. When you have achieved a well-rounded shape, stop the pressure as you bring the tip to the surface. Use the edge of the tip to shave off any point, moving it clockwise (Fig. 1). Points can also be removed by pressing gently with a moistened fingertip.

To pipe the stems: Hold the bag perpendicular to baking sheet with the tube touching it. Squeeze with heavy pressure, keeping the tip buried in the meringue until you build a ¾-inch-high cone wide enough at the base not to topple over (Fig. 2).

Bake at 200°F. for 45 minutes or until firm enough to lift from the baking sheet. With a sharp knife point, make a small hole in the underside of each cap. Use the smaller tube to pipe a tiny dab of meringue in the hole and attach the stem by inserting the pointed end (Fig. 3). Place the mushrooms, caps down, on the baking sheet and return to the oven for 20 minutes or until thoroughly dry.

Speed Production Method: For less perfect but faster mushrooms, bake the stems until very firm, about 1 hour. To pipe the caps, wet the baking sheet and cover with parchment. Pipe the caps and bake 10 to 15 minutes or until firm enough to lift off the sheet but still soft. Push the caps down gently on top of the stems and return the finished mushrooms to oven. Lower the temperature to 150°F. and bake for 45 minutes or until completely dry.

MERINGUE SWANS: One recipe Figure Piping Meringue (page 297) will make 4 swans and lots of extra parts in case of breakage.

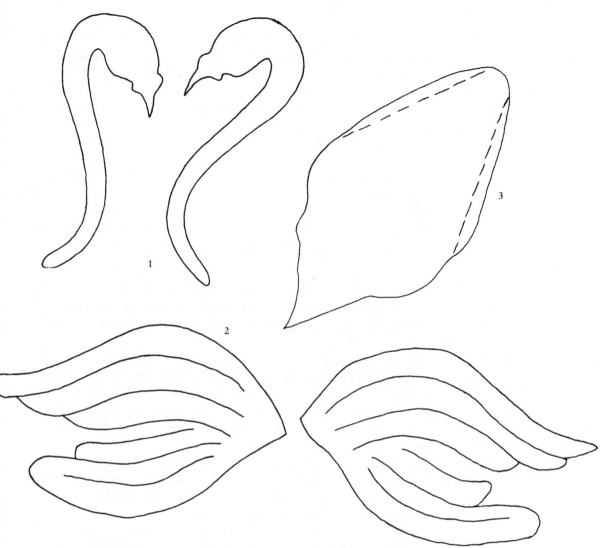

1

2

3

Make templates for the head, wings, and body by drawing on parchment (Figs. 1, 2, and 3). Turn over and attach to a baking sheet with a small dab of meringue.

Fit a pastry bag with a number 9 round pastry tube (¾-inch diameter) and a second bag with a number 8 round decorating tube (³⁄₁₆-inch diameter). Fill the bags with meringue.

Use the larger tube to pipe the bodies. Use a side-to-side motion as you move from the rounded front to the pointed back. Use a small wet spatula to create sharply angled, straight sides.

Use the smaller tube to pipe the wings, head, and necks. For eyes, use tiny black sesame seeds (available in Japanese markets) or toast sesame seeds in a lightly oiled frying pan until dark. Reserve leftover meringue for attaching the parts.

Bake the meringue parts at 200°F. until they are dry but not beginning to brown, about 2 hours. Cool and gently peel off paper. Use a drinking straw to create a hole ¼-inch deep near the front of the bodies. (Necks will be fitted into these holes.)

Attach the wings to the sides using some of the leftover meringue. Return the bodies to the 200°F oven for 30 minutes. Remove carefully and cool. The swans will keep in a dry room for weeks.

At the last minute, when ready to position the swans on the finished cake, prepare stiffly beaten whipped cream (page 253). Place the whipped cream in a small pastry bag fitted with a large closed star tube (number 2D). Position the bodies on the cake. Pipe the whipped cream into the bodies to create ruffled backs. Place heads and necks in the holes in the bodies using a dab of leftover meringue or whipped cream to secure. Let rest against the whipped cream for support. With a number 8 small round tube, pipe an upside-down tear-drop shape between the front of the wings for breast.

NOTE: For swans the easy way, purchase plastic swans at a party supply store or mail-order from Wilton (page 466) and paint them with a thin coat of royal icing. Icing works best if not too stiff.

CHOCOLATE

All chocolate that we buy has been tempered during production to perfect its consistency and glossy appearance. Tempering controls the crystalline structure of the cocoa butter. It also inhibits the formation of large crystals with lower melting points, which result in "bloom" (gray streaks on the surface) and a coarse crumbly texture.

Chocolate that does not contain cocoa butter, such as compound chocolate or summer coating (page 423), can be melted and used for decorations without tempering. Real chocolate, however, which contains cocoa butter, must be retempered if it is melted for decorations or if it loses its temper and grays due to improper temperature during storage.

Tempering chocolate consists of controlling the temperature at which the chocolate melts and sets. The classic method of tempering involves using a marble slab and an accurate thermometer. This produces the glossiest sheen for the longest period of time. Quicker methods which don't require any special equipment will still tame the chocolate into submission for any of the decorative techniques offered in this chapter. If you prefer not to temper chocolate, use compound chocolate as real chocolate melted without tempering will be an unending source of frustration.

Tempering is unnecessary when the chocolate will not be used in its pure state, for example when it is mixed with heavy cream for a ganache glaze.

Two important rules for melting chocolate:

1. Chocolate must never exceed 120°F. or there will be a loss of flavor.
2. Water—even a drop in the form of steam—must never touch the chocolate.

When a droplet of water enters melted chocolate, the chocolate becomes lumpy (a process called seizing). Shirley Corriher's "sugar bowl theory" explains this process. If you place a wet spoon in a sugar bowl, hard, irregular crystals form. If you pour a cup of water in the bowl, the sugar would merely dissolve. Chocolate behaves the same way because it also contains sugar crystals (even unsweetened, "bitter" chocolate has natural sugar). There must be a minimum of 1 tablespoon water per ounce of chocolate to keep this from happening.

If seizing does occur, the addition of fat such as vegetable shortening, clarified butter, or cocoa butter will somewhat restore the chocolate to a workable condition.

For melting chocolate, unlined copper is the traditional "chocolate pot" because it is so responsive to changes in temperature. Aluminum, preferably lined with a nonstick surface, or heatproof glass also work well. Enameled cast iron, however, is unsuitable because the residual heat will overheat the chocolate. Ideally, chocolate should be heated to 120°F., the point at which all the different fat fractions in the cocoa butter are melted.

When melting chocolate or cocoa butter, temperatures exceeding 120°F. adversely affect the flavor. There are many acceptable methods for melting dark chocolate (or cocoa butter). If the heat source does not exceed 120°F. (pilot light of oven, lowest setting on an electric griddle, or hot tray, page 459), it is fine to add the dark chocolate in large pieces and leave it to melt unmonitored. When the heat source is capable of bringing the chocolate over 120°F., however, the chocolate should be finely chopped or grated to ensure uniformity of melting. The chocolate must be carefully watched and stirred to avoid overheating. If using a microwave oven on high power, for example, the chocolate must be stirred every 15 seconds without fail. If using a double boiler, water in the lower container should not exceed 140°F. and the upper container should not touch the water. The chocolate should be stirred constantly.

Milk and white chocolate must always be stirred frequently while melting because they contain milk solids which seed (lump) if left undisturbed.

Remove chocolate from the heat source when it reaches 115°F. as the temperature may continue to rise and stir vigorously to prevent overheating and to distribute the cocoa butter evenly.

Always melt chocolate uncovered as moisture could condense on the lid, drop back in the chocolate, and cause seizing.

If chocolate has been stored in a cool area (not refrigerated, where it could absorb moisture), it grates more finely and evenly. The grating disc on a food processor works well for large chunks. Thin bars can be broken up and grated in the container of the food processor fitted with the stainless steel blade.

The ideal situation for working with chocolate is a cool, *dry,* draft-free area at 65°F. to 70°F. At temperatures above 74°F. the chocolate will not behave properly. For all methods of tempering, chocolate should be heated initially to 120°F. and the final temperature of the specific kind should be:

Dark chocolate	88°F. to 91°F.
Milk chocolate	84°F. to 87°F.
White chocolate	84°F. to 87°F.
Compound chocolate (summer coating)	100°F.

Compound chocolate does not contain cocoa butter so tempering is not required. Compound chocolate should be heated over hot tap water (about 115°F.) only to a temperature of 100°F. and used at this temperature. A dab placed just below your lower lip will feel barely warm.

To hold chocolate at its ideal temperature during use, place the container with the chocolate on a foil-covered heating pad turned to its lowest setting. Or return the container to the heat source very briefly, stirring constantly.

Because the formation of cocoa butter crystals continues as long as the chocolate is in a melted state, tempered chocolate will eventually thicken too much to produce a smooth coating. When this happens, melted untempered chocolate may be stirred in until the chocolate reaches the proper consistency without exceeding its ideal temperature. (This is known as drip feeding.)

If chocolate is allowed to exceed its ideal temperature, fat crystals will start to melt, allowing cocoa particles to drop and leaving cocoa butter crystals on the surface as unattractive streaks and spots.

If chocolate gets too cold, it will be thick and dull.

Chocolate-covered sweets are sometimes refrigerated for a few minutes after dipping in tempered chocolate. This produces a crisper coating, referred to as "snap." Chocolate can also be allowed to harden at cool room temperature. Any leftover chocolate can be spread thin on foil, allowed to harden, and retempered many times as long as a small percentage of new chocolate is added.

CLASSIC METHOD: This method results in the most glossy, crisp chocolate which will set with the most reliability. Use it for the most demanding chocolate techniques such as dipping, bands, and sheets.

The main difference between the classic method and other methods is that here the melted chocolate is cooled to 80°F., which is below the final dipping temperature. When heating it to the ideal temperature, all large and unstable cocoa butter crystals (which have a low melting point) dissolve, leaving only the stable crystals on which to complete crystallization or hardening of the chocolate.

Chop or grate the chocolate and bring it to 115° F. to 120°F (Fig. 1). Remove from the heat, stirring vigorously for a few seconds to cool. (If using a double boiler, be careful to wipe off moisture clinging to the bottom of the upper container insert so that it won't drip onto the chocolate.)

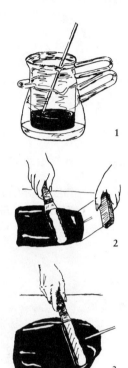

1

2

3

Pour ⅔ of the melted chocolate onto a smooth, cool, dry surface (ideally marble). Spread with an angled spatula and bench scraper (Fig. 2). Move the chocolate towards the center, clean the scraper with the spatula, and spread continuously until the chocolate begins to thicken (80°F. to 82°F.). Scoop it immediately into the container with the remaining melted chocolate (do not allow it to harden on counter) and return it to heat, stirring continuously. It will require very little heat to reach proper working temperature (page 380). (Fig. 3.)

QUICK-TEMPERING METHOD: There are several comparable methods for quick-tempering chocolate. All involve reserving some already tempered unmelted chocolate to serve as the pattern of cocoa butter crystal formation for the melted chocolate. (All chocolate you buy has already been tempered.) The unmelted chocolate is added to the melted chocolate and stirred until the temperature descends to the ideal temperature. This can be tested either with an accurate thermometer (page 451) or by placing a dab of chocolate just below your lower lip. At the point when it just begins to feel cool, it is about 91°F. (the ideal temperature for dark chocolate). Use one of these methods for simple techniques and small decorative shapes such as pine cone petals, cigars, or leaves.

1. The simplest of all methods is to remove the melting chocolate from the heat source before it has fully melted and stir until fully melted and cool.

2. It is equally simple to add clarified butter, vegetable shortening, or oil to the chocolate, preferably before melting. This serves two purposes. It produces a thinner coating of chocolate and the addition of extra fat also keeps the existing cocoa butter in suspension. Because it is a different type of fat it retards formation of large cocoa butter crystals. For dark chocolate use 1 tablespoon fat for every 3 ounces chocolate. For milk

and white chocolate use only 1 teaspoon fat for 3 ounces of chocolate. (Note: The chocolate will be softer so do not use for cigarettes or petals.)

3. When melting chocolate, reserve a large 2- to 3-inch piece. Melt the chocolate to 115°F. to 120°F., remove from the heat, and add the reserved chocolate. Stir until the correct temperature has been reached and remove any unmelted chocolate. (Wrap this in plastic wrap. It can be used for future tempering or melting.)

4. Chop or grate chocolate, reserving about ⅓. Heat the larger amount to 115°F. to 120°F. and remove from the heat. Stir in the reserved chocolate, 1 tablespoon at a time, stirring until it is cooled to proper temperature.

DECORATIVE TECHNIQUES

CHOCOLATE SNOWFLAKES: I call these snowflakes because they should be so thin that they melt instantly on the tongue. This is an easy garnish to make as there is no need to melt or temper the chocolate. Use white chocolate for white snowflakes. Dark chocolate makes pale brown flakes.

The chocolate needs to be as hard as possible to make thin flakes, so don't leave it in a warm kitchen. A large piece of chocolate is easiest to work with, but a flat bar will also work.

Use a melon-baller to scrape the chocolate, making short, light strokes that do not cut too deeply into the chocolate. A good-quality melon-baller, produced by knife manufacturers such as Wüsthof, has sharpened edges and works best to cut thin flurries of chocolate.

Allow the flakes to fall onto a small cool baking sheet. Place the sheet inside a large plastic bag and shake the flakes into the bag. Avoid touching them because they melt very easily. Store refrigerated or at cool room temperature. Use a large spoon to lift chocolate flakes onto the cake.

CHOCOLATE CURLS: Another simple decorative technique that doesn't require tempering, curls are easy to make providing the correct chocolate is used and that it is at the right temperature and has not absorbed moisture from humidity. (I tried these once during a New Orleans summer, and, although the room was air-conditioned, I could not get the chocolate to curl.)

Couverture chocolate (page 423), which comes in large blocks, makes the most attractive, shiny curls. I have had the best luck with any of the three Lindt bittersweet couvertures (Courante, Excellence, or Surfin).

If the chocolate is left in an 80°F. room for several hours it is usually a good working temperature. Alternately, a small block of chocolate can be softened to perfect consistency by placing it under a lamp (from the heat of the light bulb) or in a microwave oven using 3-second bursts of high power. It takes a few tries to get the chocolate soft enough without oversoftening it, but once this point is reached it will stay for at least 10 minutes during which time many curls can be formed.

Chocolate can be curled with a melon-baller, but my favorite utensil is a sharp potato peeler.

Hold the chocolate block in one hand, against a wad of paper toweling so that heat of your hand doesn't melt the chocolate. Hold the peeler against the upper edge and, digging in one edge of the cutter, bring the blade toward you. Greater pressure forms thicker, more open curls. Lighter pressure makes tighter curls. If the chocolate is not warm enough it will splinter. If too warm, it will come off in soft strips that will not curl. If not too soft, strips can be rolled into curls with cool fingertips.

CHOCOLATE CIGARETTES: These are actually long curls. To make cigarettes, it is necessary to quick-temper the chocolate using any method on page 381. Spread the tempered chocolate into a long band ⅛-inch-thick on a smooth marble or Formica counter and allow it to set. Don't wait too long or the chocolate will harden too much and will not curl. Test small sections at the edges to see when the consistency is perfect.

Using a knife or pizza wheel, score the chocolate to determine the desired length of the cigarette. Using a triangular scraper held at a 45-degree angle to the chocolate, push firmly against the counter, starting at the bottom of the chocolate band and pushing away from you. The higher the angle and the thinner the chocolate, the tighter the curl.

Use a pancake turner to lift the cigarettes and store airtight, refrigerated, or at cool room temperature.

CHOCOLATE PINE CONE PETALS: Quick-temper 6 ounces milk or bittersweet chocolate (page 381). This will make two 24-inch by 18-inch sheet cake pans of petals—enough for Chocolate Pine Cone (page 196). Tape a sheet of parchment or foil on a flat surface. Dip the tip of a small metal spatula in the chocolate and dab it onto the parchment, pressing lightly down to form a tapered petal shape while drawing the spatula toward you. The petals should be ¾-inch wide and 1-inch long. When the petals have set and are easy to remove from the parchment, store airtight refrigerated or at cool room temperature. (Use a flexible spatula to remove them from the parchment).

Use tweezers to place the petals on the cake.

SUCCESSFUL CHOCOLATE RUFFLES: This can be the most painstaking and frustrating of any decorative technique I know—even for a professional chocolatier—because, if working with real chocolate, the precise temperature is more critical than for any other technique. Too cold and the chocolate splinters; too warm and it melts in your fingers. This is a technique worth mastering simply because chocolate ruffles are the most spectacular of all chocolate decorations.

It has taken me years to come up with a reliable method for ruffling chocolate. Frankly, I almost gave it up as a lost cause. Especially after having traded notes from LeNôtre's professional class in France for a lesson from a French chocolatier—who gave up after claiming that he required refrigerated marble.

Only recently, through a more intimate understanding of chocolate's varied peculiarities, I have at last worked out a method that is, perhaps, as idiosyncratic as the chocolate. It does not involve changing the chocolate's ingredients, only its texture. It is accomplished by precise control of temperature but does not involve any special equipment. With great pleasure I share the secret.

The chocolate must be melted in a special way I refer to as quick-tempering method. If tempered according to the classic method, the crisp "snap" desirable for other uses makes the chocolate too brittle to ruffle. If fully melted and not tempered at all the chocolate will still ruffle but the surface will have a crumbly, unattractive appearance.

Room temperature should be between 70°F. to 75°F. Have a small bowl of ice water nearby so you can dip in the fingers of your left hand if their heat starts to melt the chocolate. (Be sure to dry your fingers before touching the chocolate.)

To quick-temper the chocolate, see page 379. While the chocolate is melting, warm a baking sheet either by placing it in the oven with a pilot light or running it under hot water and wiping it totally dry. It should feel warm not hot. You will need 5 ounces bittersweet chocolate to cover a 17-inch by 12-inch pan. Ten ounces of chocolate ruffles will be enough to cover an 8-inch or 9-inch cake.

Using a long angled spatula, spread the chocolate in a thin even layer on the back of the warm baking sheet. Place it in the refrigerator for exactly 5 minutes. Remove from the refrigerator and place on a counter so that one edge is against the wall for stability. The top will be slightly dull which means it has set, but the underneath will be soft. The chocolate will continue to firm at room temperature. Allow it to sit at room temperature for 15 to 25 minutes. Test a small area with a triangular scraper. When the chocolate is firm enough to ruffle, it will maintain this ideal texture for at least 20 minutes. If room temperature is below 70°F., however, it may harden before this time.

For ruffling, the angle of the triangular scraper has to be less than for making chocolate curls—about 20 degrees. If you are right-handed, start at the bottom left side of the baking sheet, pushing firmly against the chocolate in the direction of the wall. The right edge of the spatula should move in a straight line, but to help ruffle the chocolate it should at the same time be angled slightly to the left. About 2 inches is an attractive width. As you push chocolate with the scraper in your right hand, use the thumb and forefinger of your left hand to lightly pleat the chocolate (Fig. 1). If the chocolate is too tightly pleated, gently stretch the ruffle slightly apart.

1

Set the finished ruffles on the counter where they will continue to firm. When no longer flexible, they can be transferred by hand or with a thin flexible pancake turner. Either place directly on the frosted cake or on a cool baking sheet for storage. To store, keep ruffles airtight, either refrigerated or at cool room temperature.

To place on the frosted cake, start at an outside edge and place a single, continuous row of ruffles. The next row should overlap the first. Use the smallest ruffles for the center (Fig. 2). Do feel free to experiment with chocolate ruffling to your heart's content. Imperfect ruffles are still attractive or can be remelted and tempered or used for ganache.

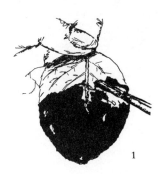

2

CHOCOLATE LEAVES: This is an impressive, easy, but somewhat tedious technique. When my assistant Hiroko Ogawa returned to Japan, she left me with a dowry of over one hundred white chocolate leaves—a much-appreciated gift. If only a few chocolate leaves are needed, summer coating is the best choice because it doesn't require tempering. When surrounding a cake with an embrace of chocolate rose leaves, I like to use the best possible real chocolate. Couverture (page 423) makes the most glossy, elegant leaves.

Rose, lemon, maple, and geranium leaves are some of my favorite shapes. Select well-shaped leaves with no holes. Wash leaves and dry thoroughly. Each leaf can be used several times until it tears.

1

Holding a leaf by its stem and supporting it underneath with a finger or the palm of your hand, use a small metal spatula or artist's brush to smooth an even layer of chocolate on the underside of the leaf (Fig. 1). (Be sure to use the veiny underside as all the delicate lines will be imprinted on the chocolate.) Don't allow chocolate to get on the other side of the leaf or it may break when peeling off the leaf.

Carefully place the chocolate leaf on a baking sheet lined with foil, parchment, or wax paper and refrigerate or freeze for 3 minutes, until set and no longer shiny. If using large leaves, add a second coat of chocolate for stability. White chocolate and couverture also require second coats as the chocolate is thinner when melted and the light shines through in spots when placed on the cake.

To remove the chocolate from the leaf, peel back the stem end, touching the chocolate as little as possible (Fig. 2) If chocolate adheres to the leaf, it has not set long enough.

To apply the leaf to the cake, brush a small dab of melted chocolate (cool to the touch) on the back and gently press it against the side of the cake, angling it slightly so that the tip is at the 1:00 position.

CHOCOLATE FOSSILING: I developed this technique quite accidentally in an amusing way. I was giving a demonstration at the Miami Hilton and time was running short, so I was forced to sprinkle a layer of powdered sugar and place the prepared chocolate leaf on a still-warm chocolate cake. The effect was sensational. The chocolate melted slightly, flattening into the cake, while maintaining the shape of the leaf. It exactly resembled a fossil.

CHOCOLATE DISCS AND CUTOUTS: Sheets of chocolate can be cut into many shapes to decorate cakes. Quick-temper the chocolate (page 381) and with an angled spatula spread it ⅛-inch thick on wax paper, preferably butcher's wax (page 464), which will give it a high sheen. Or cover with a second sheet of wax paper and spread with a rolling pin. When the chocolate is firm enough to cut but not so firm that it will break, use either a cookie cutter or template and the sharp point of a knife to create shapes.

To make a round disc, such as the one used for Queen Bee cake (see color photograph), use an inverted lid or a cake ring as a guide. To cut round holes in the disc, use the back of a large pastry tube or round cookie cutter 1-inch in diameter and the tip of a knife if necessary to lift out the chocolate rounds.

Freeze for a few minutes or allow to set at cool room temperature. When chocolate has set completely and will separate cleanly from the paper, invert onto a flat surface and peel off the paper. Use a pancake turner to lift or transfer the disc.

CHOCOLATE AND CHOCOLATE PRALINE SHEETS: Large thin sheets of chocolate or chocolate praline look magnificent draped around a cake, transforming it into a modern soft sculpture that never turns out looking exactly the same way twice. Praline sheets adhere to the frosting on the cake.

A trick I have worked out over the years is that, since chocolate is very sensitive to changing temperatures, I use this to my advantage by switching rooms for different stages. The oval sheets of chocolate are fairly rigid at cool room temperature but become perfectly flexible in a warmer (75°F. to 80°F) room.

Make the chocolate praline sheets on pages 315 and 386. Only 4 large sheets are needed to encase a 9-inch cake so the 2 extra are in case of breakage. Any leftovers can be remelted, re-tempered, and cut into decorative shapes. Begin by laying each sheet on the counter and peeling off the top layer of paper. Lift up 1 sheet using the bottom paper to support it and press the long side against the cake, curving it gently. Carefully peel away the wax paper. Place a dab of frosting near the edge and attach a second sheet, overlapping the first.

Continue with the remaining chocolate sheets until the cake is surrounded. If room temperature is warm enough, the sheets of chocolate will begin to curve toward the center of the cake. Coax them gently into graceful, undulating shapes, allowing their natural inclination to be your guide. If the chocolate remains resolutely rigid, wave a hair drier briefly and evenly over the chocolate sheets. Stop before they appear to have softened and wait a few moments as it is easy to overdo the heat and melt the chocolate. To this day, this process feels slightly scary, slightly risky, and delightfully creative! A word of reassurance: Whatever happens and however it winds up looking, the chocolate praline sheets are always delicious. A former student and good friend, Judi Elkins, once encased a cake in praline sheets that were not softened enough and shattered on top of and around the cake. She left the cake in the kitchen and served another dessert in its place. But in a moment of somewhat wacky postprandial inspiration, her husband, Paul, dubbed the abandoned cake "The Polish Apple Torte" in deference to his Polish origins and invited the guests into the kitchen to try what Judi had thought of as a kitchen disaster. Everyone adored the cake. Not a soul questioned the fact that there were no apparent apples in it. And many ordered the cake from Judi for their own parties.

CHOCOLATE BANDS: A dark, gleaming chocolate band, surrounding the cake and 1 or more inches taller, provides a smooth finish for the cake's sides. The hollow at the top can be filled with whipped cream, piped into opulent swirls, brandied cherries, or lots of fat chocolate curls. The top of the band can be cut straight or in graceful or even wildly irregular waves.

To make a chocolate band, measure the circumference of the cake and cut a piece of wax paper a few inches longer. Fold the wax paper the desired height of the band. It should be at least 1 inch higher than the finished height of the cake. If planning to scallop the band add an extra inch or two. Brush the sides of the cake with melted Jewel Glaze (page 329) to attach the band.

For a band long enough to encircle a 9-inch cake, classic-temper or quick-temper 4 to 8 ounces dark chocolate, preferably couverture. Eight ounces will be sufficient to make a band 5 inches high. (If you don't temper the chocolate when melting it or if the room is too warm, the band will not be firm enough to wrap around the cake.)

Using an angled spatula, spread the chocolate evenly over the wax paper strip, making it a little longer than the desired length. Lift the strip by the ends and transfer to a clean section of the counter to set. When firm but still malleable, use a small sharp knife to cut a free-form scalloped design along one side if desired. Attach the strip, scalloped side up, to the side of the cake. Gently pull away the wax paper and use a bit of melted chocolate or jelly to attach where the ends overlap. If the chocolate sticks to the paper, allow it to set longer or refrigerate for a few minutes until firm enough to release cleanly. The scalloped edge will break away easily on slight pressure to reveal the scalloped border.

CHOCOLATE LATTICE BAND: This is pretty much the same technique as the solid chocolate band but the chocolate is piped in a free-form filigree before wrapping it around the cake. As the sides of the cake will show through the openings of the filigree, they should be smoothly frosted with chocolate frosting, preferably lighter than the filigree to show off the design.

You will need 2 ounces chocolate for a lattice band to encircle a 9-inch cake, so melt 3 ounces chocolate to have enough extra to squeeze in the parchment cone. The piping chocolate must be thickened slightly so that it will fall smoothly from the parchment cone like a spider's web. Although a drop of water will cause the chocolate to seize or lump, a fraction of a drop will thicken it in a more controlled way. Glycerine (page 429) is the ideal liquid to use because it contains a very minute proportion of liquid. Stock syrup will also work. (Bring an equal volume of water and sugar to a full rolling boil, cover, and cool.) Add only 1 drop glycerine or stock syrup at a time, stirring and testing thickness by allowing the chocolate to drop from a height of 4 inches. If it falls in a smooth string, the thickness is right.

If using real chocolate as opposed to compound chocolate, it should be quick-tempered (page 381) before adding glycerine or syrup.

Chocolate is traditionally piped from a parchment cone because a metal tube would make the chocolate too firm. To make a parchment piping cone (page 394), cut off only a tiny bit from the end and try piping a few swirls to test the thickness of the line. If too thin and chocolate does not flow evenly, cut a tiny bit more from the tip. Allow the chocolate to fall in a thin fluid line, using the motion of your entire arm to form curves.

If the chocolate hardens in the tip, press with your fingers to soften it and squeeze out any hard lumps blocking the opening.

Pipe a free-form filigree on wax paper and allow to set until dull. Wrap around the cake, peeling back one end of wax paper slightly to overlap ends. Chill until very firm and carefully peel off the paper.

CHOCOLATE WRITING: The fluid flow of melted chocolate produces a very elegant script even without perfect penmanship. Some of the most beautiful chocolate writing I have ever seen on a cake was piped by my Oriental students in exquisite Chinese calligraphy.

Chocolate writing looks most elegant on top of a chocolate-glazed cake. Prepare the chocolate and parchment cone as for the above filigree lattice. If you prefer not to risk free-form writing, make a template by tracing letters (page 412) or designing your own letters. Tape a piece of nonstick liner (page 458) or parchment over the template and trace the design in chocolate. Chill the chocolate until very firm before removing from the liner. Remove with a very thin knife blade or spatula. Or set the design near the edge of a table and, pressing the back edge of the liner to the table, slowly pull the liner from the chocolate design until almost completely released. Lift the design with a small angled spatula.

If writing directly on the cake, *Cocoa Piping Gel* is slightly softer and much shinier than chocolate. *To make ⅓ cup:* In a small saucepan stir together 3 tablespoons piping gel, 1 tablespoon hot water, 3 tablespoons unsweetened cocoa, and 6 tablespoons powdered sugar. Cook over low heat, stirring constantly, until just smooth. Cool completely to obtain piping consistency.

CHOCOLATE DOILIES: I pipe this directly on the serving plate as it is for visual effect only and does not get eaten. Summer coating (page 423) or the above cocoa piping gel are appropriate choices as they require no tempering. If using summer coating, thicken the chocolate as for filigree lattice (page 388) and fill a parchment cone.

Pipe free-form swirls or flowers directly on the serving plate, surrounding the cake. If you wish to follow a precise pattern, use a flat glass serving plate and tape a template underneath it. Remove the template after piping the design.

CHOCOLATE GLAZING WITH WEBBING: Dark, shiny Chocolate Cream Glaze (or Chocolate Butter Glaze) is one of the most stunning adornments for a cake. The sides of a glazed cake are always, however, slightly lumpy or less perfect than the top, so I usually surround the sides with chocolate rose leaves, a chocolate band, or cutouts.

Webbing the top of the cake with lines of contrasting white chocolate makes an interesting variation.

Glaze the cake (page 271 or 273) and prepare a white chocolate decorating glaze. Quick-temper 2 ounces white chocolate by removing it from the heat before fully melted and stirring until melted. Stir in either 1 tablespoon flavorless oil or 1 tablespoon + 1 teaspoon Armagnac or Cognac. Fill a parchment cone or plastic squeeze bottle* with the white chocolate, and before the glaze sets, pipe either evenly spaced straight lines across a square cake or concentric circles on a round cake.

For straight lines, start at 1 edge of the cake and lightly drag a small knife blade at even intervals in a straight line toward you— at right angles to the piped white lines. To reverse the direction of the lines, turn the cake around and repeat, making lines between the first set of lines.

For circles, start at the center of the cake, dragging the knife blade to the edge at 8 evenly spaced intervals. Then reverse the direction, starting at the edge and going toward the center for 8 more lines between the first 8 lines.

CHOCOLATE ROSE MODELING: Knead Chocolate Rose Modeling Paste (page 325) until pliable and roll between sheets of plastic wrap until 1/16-inch thick. Cut small circles for petals using the back of a pastry tube or lightly greased rose petal cutters (page 461) (Fig. 1). (Use a 1-inch cutter for the first row, a 1¼-inch cutter for the second row, and a 1½-inch cutter for the third row.) Roll the circles to elongate them slightly, leaving the base thick for support and thinning the upper section only.

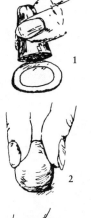

If chocolate becomes too soft, allow it to sit briefly and it will get firm.

Form the base of the rose by shaping a small ball and then pinching it to form a cone shape (Fig. 2).

Wrap chocolate petals around the base, overlapping them as you go (Fig. 3). The first set of 3 petals should curve inward to hide the core. The second row of 3 petals should be straight up, and the third row should curve out and open up slightly. Push petals away from each other and the core with a blunt instrument such as a metal cuticle pusher (Fig. 4). For a natural look, use your fingertips to softly curl back the edges of each petal except for the first row of inner petals (Fig. 5).

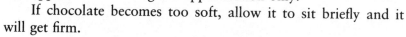

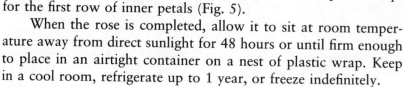

When the rose is completed, allow it to sit at room temperature away from direct sunlight for 48 hours or until firm enough to place in an airtight container on a nest of plastic wrap. Keep in a cool room, refrigerate up to 1 year, or freeze indefinitely.

* Available in drugstores by asking for a squeeze bottle for hair coloring.

PORCELAINIZING CHOCOLATE ROSES: For a glaze that dries as hard and shiny as porcelain, brush a well-dried chocolate rose* with unflavored oil. Before the oil has a chance to be absorbed and appear dry, coat the petals with light corn syrup. Allow to dry for several hours or until the glaze is hard to the touch.

I learned both string figures and the intricate art of origami (Japanese paper folding) from books. It was not easy but it was possible. Piped cake decorations, however, were another matter. I carefully followed the printed instructions that came with the pastry bag and tube set, but the blobs emerging from my pastry tip bore no semblance to the fine ridged swirls in the pictures. I did not realize that the main problem was the consistency of the icing. Too soft and the shapes will not be articulated; too stiff and the icing will break sharply instead of curving into smooth designs.

It was a two-week intensive course at Wilton Enterprises in Chicago that turned me into a cake decorator. I am also indebted to Wilton for writing piping directions that explain the angle of the pastry bag in terms of both degrees of elevation and clock position. This concept, together with the *proper icing consistency,* makes it indeed possible to learn from the printed page.

Piped decorations take practice but are a lot of fun. It is a great project to do with children because they are so delighted with whatever design they manage, even if it does not resemble the "model." To keep icing from coming out of the top of the bag and making a mess, I use a twist-tie to secure the opening.

At Wilton the first decoration we learned was the star. It is easy to pipe and even when imperfectly executed looks attractive.

Top Border: A continuous decoration piped around the top of a cake.

Bottom Border: A continuous decoration piped around the base of a cake (which has the added function of sealing in freshness).

Side Decoration: Piped decorations used around the sides of a cake.

Decorating or Pastry Bag: The container that holds the decorating tube, coupler, and icing or buttercream.

Coupler: A grooved insert and retainer ring that allows tube changes without changing bags.

Decorating Tubes: Open end tubes in various shapes used to form icing decorations.

Flower Nail: A round, flat nail head used as a turntable surface for making icing flowers.

---

* Rose must dry for at least 3 days or the glaze does not take evenly.

There are 6 basic tubes that produce most of the popular cake decorations. Each tube is available in a variety of sizes, but the decorations they produce are the same.

Star Tube: For making stars, shells, rosettes, ropes, zigzags, puffs, fleurs-de-lis, and scrolls.

Drop Flower Tube: For making two different flower varieties.

Round Tube: For writing, dots, pearls, strings, outlines, and beads.

Rose Tube: For making roses, rosebuds, sweet peas, and ruffles.

Leaf Tube: For making leaves.

Basket Weave Tube: For making plain and ribbed stripes and basket weave design.

PREPARING
A POLYESTER
DECORATING BAG

One of the major advantages of the polyester bag, aside from being reusable and comfortable to hold, is that it can be used with a coupler so you can change tubes without emptying or changing bags.

To cut a bag to accommodate the coupler, separate the coupler and drop the base, narrow end down, into the bag. Force down the coupler as far as it will go. With a pen or pencil, mark the spot on the outside of the bag where the bottom thread is outlined against the material (Fig.1).

Push the base of the coupler back up into the bag and cut across where the mark was made, cutting in a slight curve rather than sharply across it. The beginning and end of the cut should be slightly higher than the middle so that when end is open, it will be round (Fig. 2).

Push the coupler base back through the bag opening. Two threads should be showing (Fig. 3). To secure a tube in place, slip

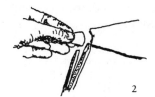

1   2   3   4

it onto the coupler base and twist the ring over it, threading it onto the base (Fig. 4).

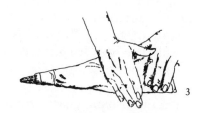

1   2   3

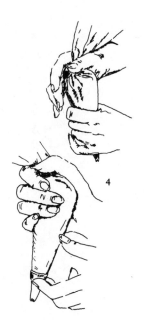

4

To fill bag: Fold down the top to form a generous cuff and hold it beneath the cuff. Use a long spatula to fill the bag ½ full. Filling it more risks melting and softening the icing from the heat of your hand (Fig. 1).

To remove the icing from the spatula, hold the bag on the outside between your thumb and fingers and pull the spatula out of the bag, pinching the icing (Fig. 2). Unfold the cuff and using the side of your hand, force icing toward the tip (Fig. 3). Twist the bag closed. To be sure that no air is trapped in the bag, squeeze a small amount of icing into a bowl. It is a good idea to do this when refilling the bag or the little explosion of air when old icing meets new can disrupt the piped decoration.

To hold bag: Place the twisted part of the bag in the V between your thumb and forefinger. Lock your thumb over your forefinger to keep the icing in the lower part of the bag (Fig. 4). Press your remaining fingers against the side of the bag so that when you squeeze out the icing, you squeeze from the side while your thumb presses from the top.

Steady the front end of the bag with the fingers of the other hand to support the weight of the bag and to establish the direction of the tip.

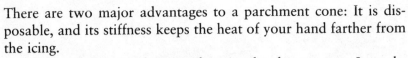

There are two major advantages to a parchment cone: It is disposable, and its stiffness keeps the heat of your hand farther from the icing.

In an emergency I have used a triangle of wax paper. It works well but does not hold up quite as long.

In these illustrations, the points of the triangle have been labeled A, B, and C.

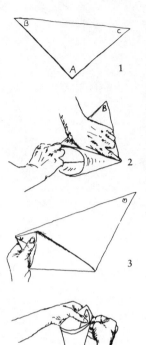

Place the triangle on a flat surface with A pointing toward you (Fig. 1). Curl C up and under, bringing it toward you until points A and C meet. The curled edge from C should lie on top of the edge between A and B. The parchment will curve more easily if you extend your right elbow while doing this (Fig. 2). Hold points C and A together with your left hand while picking up B with your right (Fig. 3). Wrap B around to meet points A and C in the back, forming a cone (Fig. 4). Hold the bag with both hands, thumbs inside, and slide B and C in opposite directions to make a W formation (Fig. 5). Tugging point B slightly upward will help to form a sharp, closed point (Fig. 6).

Turn down the top and secure with a staple. Tape the outside seam of the bag (Fig. 7). Use a small strip of tape near the pointed end. This will keep the cone from unfolding and the icing from coming out the side (Fig. 8).

If piping chocolate, cut off the tiniest amount possible from the tip. If piping icing, make an opening for the tube by clipping off ¾-inch from the tip (Fig. 9). Too large a hole will allow the tube to fall through, too small and the parchment will cut off part of the frosting's design. Make the cut slightly curved, as for the polyester bag, so the opening will be round and icing will not creep out around the edges.

Drop the tube into the cone, narrow end first, and push forward to make sure the tip is exposed. The weight of the icing will hold it securely in place.

  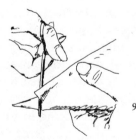

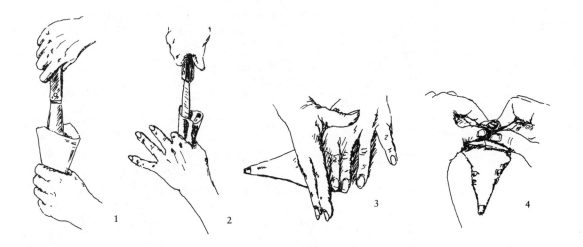

1   2   3   4

To fill cone: Hold near the bottom and use a long spatula to fill with icing, forcing it down (Fig. 1). Fill ½ full, removing the icing from the spatula by pinching it between thumb and fingers from outside of bag, while withdrawing spatula (Fig. 2).

Closing the cone: Parchment cones must be closed tightly to keep icing from escaping through the top. First, smooth the top flat, using the side of your hand to force the icing toward the tip (Fig. 3). Then fold in each side and roll down the top until it is close to the icing (Fig. 4). Lock your thumb over the top with your remaining fingers curled around the side.

STIFF   MEDIUM   THIN

Different shapes and types of decoration require different consistencies of icing or buttercream. For example, flowers with upright petals such as roses require a stiff icing; most borders such as the shell and star require a medium icing; and string work, leaves, and writing require a thin icing.

    Royal icing can be thinned by adding glycerine or corn syrup or stiffened by adding extra powdered sugar. Buttercreams can be softened by heat or firmed up by refrigeration.

CONSISTENCY
OF ICING AND
BUTTERCREAM

To determine the consistency of an icing or buttercream, take a small dollop and dab it on the work surface. With a small spatula, lift it to form a peak.

Stiff icing will hold a ¾-inch peak.

Medium icing will hold a ½-inch peak.

Soft icing will hold a ¼-inch peak.

COLOR SHADING
This technique gives a subtle two-tone effect to each decoration piped from the tube. It is particularly suitable for piped roses.

Mix two or more batches of icing so that the colors are in the same tone but vary slightly in intensity of hue. Starting from close to the tip and continuing to the top of the bag, make a long crease. With a metal spatula place a long strip of icing against the crease. Carefully place a second shade of icing up against the first strip and continue until the bag is full. Strips should only be as long as ½ the bag so that it is not overfilled.

STORING PIPED DECORATIONS
Decorations made from royal icing can be air-dried and stored indefinitely at room temperature.

Buttercream decorations which are not piped directly on the cake should be chilled or frozen until firm enough to transfer to the cake. If time is short, a buttercream rose can be transferred directly to the cake with scissors: Hold them slightly open to lift the rose from the flower nail; set down on the cake with the scissors still slightly open; then close the scissors and slide away from the rose.

Practice "Buttercream"

MAKES 3 CUPS

This buttercream is for practicing piping techniques. Vegetable shortening stays firmer at warm temperatures than does butter because it has a higher melting point. While this quality makes it suitable for playing with decorating techniques it makes it undesirable for eating because its slow melting point makes it feel like an oily skin against the palate.

Practice buttercream may be reused almost indefinitely. Rebeat occasionally using a flat beater at slow-medium speed to keep it smooth. It may be chilled to speed up firming if it softens during use.

INGREDIENTS	MEASURE	WEIGHT	
room temperature	*volume*	*pounds/ounces*	*kilograms/grams*
solid vegetable shortening	1½ cups	10 ounces	287 grams
powdered sugar	4 cups (lightly spooned into cup)	1 pound	452 grams
water	2 tablespoons *	0.5 ounce	15 grams
light corn syrup	1 tablespoon †	0.75 ounce	20 grams

*For *thin* consistency used for writing, stems, and leaves use 3 tablespoons water and 2 tablespoons light corn syrup. The corn syrup adds a slight shine, moistness, and stretchy quality to the icing.
†For *stiff* consistency used for flowers with upright petals such as roses, omit the corn syrup.

STORE:
1 year room temperature, indefinitely refrigerated.

In a large mixing bowl place shortening. Gradually beat in remaining ingredients on low speed, alternating dry and liquid. Increase speed to medium and beat until smooth and creamy. Scrape the sides occasionally. Store in an airtight container.

The two most important criteria for piping decorations with a pastry tube (in addition to icing consistency) are the position of the bag and the amount and type of pressure applied.

Position of bag: The position in which the bag is held must be precise to produce a specific design. Position refers both to the *angle* of the bag relative to the work surface and the *direction* in which it points. The two basic angles at which the bag is positioned are:

90 degree (perpendicular)
45 degree (halfway between vertical and horizontal)

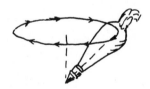

When decorating, one hand is used to squeeze the bag and the other to help establish and steady the angle. If drop flowers or stars come out asymmetrical, chances are the bag is not being held at a 90° angle (perpendicular to the decorating surface).

Most tubes have symmetrical openings, however, there are some tubes, such as the rose tube, which are broader at the base than at the tip. When this is the case, the position of the tube must also be considered. The rose tube is almost always used with the broad end down.

Direction of the bag: This refers to the direction in which the end of the bag, farthest from the tip, is pointing. It is most easily described by using the position of numbers on a clock face. To

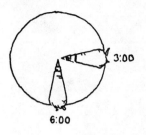

3:00

6:00

better visualize this, try holding the bag at an angle to the surface and keeping the tip in place, make a circle with the back end of the bag by rolling your wrist. Imagine that the circle is a clock face.

Direction of movement when piping: A right-handed person should always decorate from left to right; a left-handed person from right to left except when writing.

Pressure control: The size and uniformity of icing decorations are determined by the amount and type of pressure exerted on the bag. Some decorations require a steady, even pressure, others require a gradual tapering off. The more rhythmic and controlled the pressure, the more exact the decoration.

It is also particularly important to release all the pressure before lifting off the tube to prevent little "tails" of icing from forming. Try wiggling your fingers slightly to be sure they are not inadvertently exerting pressure before lifting off the tube.

PIPED BORDERS AND SIDE DECORATIONS

STAR: This makes a very attractive outline to border a cake or can be used to fill in sections or even the entire surface of a cake. Place the stars close enough together so that the points interlock and fill in all gaps.

Icing Consistency: Medium

Tube: Any star tube (18 or 22 is a good size for most borders)

Position of Bag: 90-degree upright angle, tube ¼-inch above surface

Method: Squeeze bag firmly without moving it until the icing star is as wide as you desire. Push tube down slightly and stop squeezing. Slowly and precisely lift the tube straight up and away.

NOTE: You can change the size of the star by increasing the length of time you squeeze or by the amount of pressure. If too much icing is squeezed, the lines will start to waver.

Two of the most common problems in piping show up when piping stars:

1. continuing to squeeze while lifting off the tube.

2. not holding the tube upright for a symmetrical decoration.

ROSETTE: Rosettes are often used as continuous borders or, when piped with a large tube and widely spaced, as a decorative demarcation for portion size.

Icing Consistency: Medium

Tube: Any star tube

Position of Bag: 90-degree upright angle, tube ¼-inch above surface

Method: As you squeeze out the icing, move the tube in a tight arc from the 9:00 position around to the 6:00 position (Fig. 1). Release the pressure but do not lift the tube until you have followed the circular motion all the way around to the 9:00 position from which you started (Fig. 2). This will give the rosette a wrap-around look.

SHELL: If there were only one border to be used in cake decorating, the graceful shell would be my first choice. In fact, the shell or one of its many variations is almost always present on some part of a decorated cake.

Icing Consistency: Medium

Tube: Any star tube (18 and 22 are the most commonly used)

Position of Bag: 45- to 90-degree angle at 6:00, tube slightly above surface. (I prefer the flatter, wider shell you get from the higher angle.)

Method: Squeeze firmly, allowing the icing to fan out generously as you lift up the tube slightly. (Do not move the tube forward; the force of the icing will push the shell slightly forward on its own.) (Fig. 1)

Gradually relax the pressure as you lower the tube to the surface. This gradual tapering off forms a graceful tail. Stop the pressure and pull away the tube without lifting it off the surface to draw the tail to a point (Fig. 2).

To make a second shell for a border, line up the tube at the tip of the first shell's tail. The slight forward thrust of the icing will just cover the tail of the preceding shell. When viewed from the side, the shells should be gently rounded, not humped. If humped, you are lifting the tube too high above the work surface (Fig. 3).

2

3

REVERSE SHELL: For an interesting variation, the reverse shell border produces shells which alternate in direction.
Icing Consistency: Medium
Tube: Any star tube (18 and 22 are the most commonly used)
Method: Squeeze firmly, allowing the icing to fan out as for a regular shell. Then move the tube to the left, up and around, in a question mark shape (Fig. 1). Gradually relax the pressure as you pull the tube down to the center, forming a straight tail. Repeat the procedure—only this time swing the tube around to the right in a backward question mark. Continue alternating shells around the border (Fig. 2).

1

2

FLEUR-DE-LIS: Yet another variation of the shell, a fleur-de-lis is composed of 3 shells—a regular shell and 2 reverse shells. It is most often used for the sides of a cake.
Icing Consistency: Medium
Tube: Any star tube (18 and 22 are the most commonly used)
Method: Pipe an elongated shell (Fig. 1). To its left, pipe a reverse shell, shaped like a regular question mark (Fig. 2). To its right, pipe another reverse shell shaped like a backward question mark.

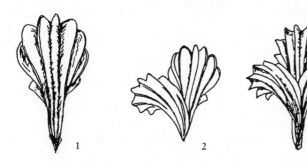

Allow the tails of the reverse shells to come up on top of the center shell, being careful to have all tails meet to form a point (Fig. 3).

SHELL WITH FLUTE: Combining 2 different piping techniques, the shell and the stand-up petal used for a sweet pea (page 406), results in an unusual and elegant decorative effect.

Icing Consistency: Medium

Method: Make a shell border, allowing a little extra room between each shell to accommodate the flute (Fig. 1). To make a flute, use the rose tube 104. Allow the wide end of the tube to rest between the 2 shells. Squeeze the bag while raising the tube slightly to allow the flute to rise between the 2 shells (Fig. 2). Stop the pressure, lower the tube, and pull away. Repeat this procedure between every shell or every other shell.

RUFFLE: Ruffles are used on the sides of a cake.

Icing Consistency: Medium

Tube: Any rose tube (104 is often used)

Position of Bag: 45-degree angle at 3:00, tube with wide end down and narrow end slightly raised from the surface

Method: Squeeze firmly using a back-and-forth motion to produce zigzag ruffles

DOTS AND PEARLS: One or two staggered rows of balls create a lovely, graceful border. Dots are subtle and delicate on the sides of a cake as well.

Icing Consistency: Soft

Tube: Any round tube (3 is a nice size for the sides, 8 for a 12-inch base, 6 for a 9-inch base, 4 for a 6-inch base)

Position of Bag: 90-degree upright to surface, tube slightly above surface

Method: Squeeze with steady, even pressure. As the icing begins to build up, raise the tube with it keeping the tip buried in the icing. When a well-rounded shape is achieved, stop the pressure as you bring the tip to the surface. Use the edge of the tip to shave off any point, moving the tip in a clockwise direction. Points are more apt to form with stiffer icing. Points can also be removed by waiting until the icing crusts slightly and pressing gently with a fingertip. If the icing is still soft, dip the fingertip in water first.

ROPE: This border consists of a chain of S shapes intertwined to create the illusion of a twisted rope. It is quite easy to accomplish.

Icing Consistency: Medium

Tube: Any star tube (18 and 22 are usually used)

Position of Bag: 45-degree angle at 4:30, tube lightly touching surface

Method: Squeeze with steady, even pressure. Move the tube up, around, and down to the right to create a sideways S curve. Stop squeezing and lift the bag away. Insert the tube under the left side of the S and repeat the same procedure, lifting the tube as you go up and around.

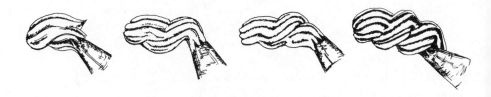

BASKET WEAVE: When the basket weave is used to decorate the sides of a cake and flowers are used on top, it creates the illusion of a basket filled with flowers.

The basket weave is an easy but somewhat time-consuming technique. Since the entire sides of the cake will be covered with icing to form the basket weave, only the thinnest coating of icing should be used to frost the cake.

Icing Consistency: Medium

Tube: 3 and 47

Position of Bag: 45-degree angle at 6:00 for vertical lines, 3:00 for horizontal lines

Method: Basket weave goes more quickly if two bags are used. For vertical stripes, use tube 3. Starting at the top of the cake, touch the tip to the surface to attach the icing and then raise the tube slightly to allow the icing to fall freely against the side of the cake. (This will produce a more even line.) Squeeze evenly and firmly, drawing the tube down the side to the bottom and touch the tip at the bottom.

For horizontal basket weave, use tube 47 with serrated side facing up. Use the round line as the center guide for the stripes. With the tip touching the surface, start squeezing, lifting slightly to ride over the vertical line. Stop squeezing and pull very slightly to straighten the stripe. Touch down to the surface to attach. Space the second stripe one stripe width away from the first. Repeat until to the bottom of the cake.

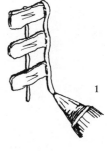

Starting from the top, drop a second vertical line down the side of the cake to cover the right edges of stripes. (If a little stripe sticks out, don't worry, it will be covered by the next alternating row of stripes.) (Fig. 1).

For the second row of stripes, pipe between the first row, again using the vertical line as a center guide. To create the illusion of wicker weaving in and out, be sure to tuck the tip slightly under the vertical line before you begin squeezing. Don't worry about small gaps, "real" baskets have them too! (Fig. 2.)

NOTE: For a different variety of basket weave, use tube 47 for vertical and horizontal lines.

SCROLLWORK: Albeit a bit baroque, scrollwork lends a charmingly antique quality to the sides of a cake.

Icing Consistency: Medium

Tube: 3 and 16 (a round tube and a star tube)

Position of Bag: 45-degree angle

Method: Use tube 3, touching the surface lightly, to draw an inverted C shape with a long tail pointing to the left. Starting at the top of the C, draw a second C with a long tail upside down. Continue around the cake, reversing C shapes as you go. Add

curved lines to the tails of the C (Fig. 1).

With tube 16, trace over the design, making a series of feathery reverse shells (page 400), all facing the same direction (Fig. 2).

Note: For a softer effect, use a round 5 tube in place of the star tube (Fig. 3).

STRING WORK: String work is unquestionably the most refined and elegant of all borders. It does not appear often, even on wedding cakes, because it is exacting and time-consuming. All it really requires is patience and an icing of proper consistency. Royal icing made with liquid egg white is ideal because it is strong and elastic enough for the finest string work. Buttercream, however, also works if the strings are kept relatively short.

Icing which is too thick will not flow easily from the tube and will break. If too thin, it will lack elasticity and snap. To test consistency, drop a loop of icing from your finger and adjust as necessary.

Icing Consistency: Thin

Tube: Any small round tube (3 is often used)

Position of Bag: The height of the bag should be shoulder level and at 4:30, the tube lightly touching the surface only to attach. For maximum control, keep the height of the tip constant. Do not allow the tube to follow the drop of the string. (This is a very common error in piping strings. Not allowing the tip to drop goes against all instincts!)

Method: With dots of icing, mark a row of equally spaced points around the perimeter of the cake. Touch the tip of the tube to attach the icing at first dot. While squeezing, pull the bag away from the surface toward you. Continue squeezing to allow the icing to droop naturally. Resist the temptation to follow the droop of the icing with the tip. The tip should be the same distance from the surface as the distance from point to point. Stop squeezing and touch the tip to the next dot to attach the loop. Continue around the entire cake. To form a double row of string work,

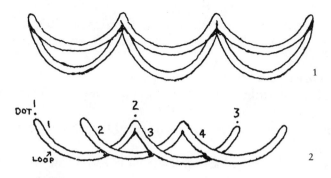

complete the first row and then pipe a second row of shallow loops inside the first (Fig. 1). For an even more striking effect, overlap the string work to create an interwoven look. This is much less complicated than it appears. First make a standard size loop, starting at the first dot and ending at the second. Starting at the center top of that loop, attach the icing and drop another loop, attaching it between the second and third dots. The third loop starts where the first loop ended and finishes at the third dot. The fourth loop starts where the second loop ended. Believe me, this is easier done than said! (Fig. 2.)

The size of the loop and the distance between loops should be in proportion to the size of the cake. A small loop looks insignificant on a large cake; a large loop looks disproportionate on a small cake.

DROP FLOWERS: These are the simplest flowers to make. They can be piped directly onto a cake or onto wax paper to be air-dried or frozen and then lifted onto the cake.

PIPED FLOWERS

Icing Consistency: Stiff
Tube: Any star tube or drop flower tube (closed star)
Position of Bag: 90-degree upright angle, tube ¼-inch above surface
Method: For a straight flower, squeeze the bag firmly without moving it until the icing flower is as wide as you desire. Push the tube down slightly and stop squeezing. Slowly and precisely lift the tube up and away.

For a swirled flower, turn the hand holding the bag as far to the left as possible. As you squeeze, turn your hand to the right as far as possible and stop the pressure. This should be a gradual motion. It helps to use the surface as a pivot by pressing the tip lightly to the surface. Dot the centers if desired, using a round number 3 tube and contrasting color.

SWEET PEA: This simple flower can be piped in sprays directly onto a cake or made ahead. If made from royal icing, the sharp stem can be poked into the side of a cake to suspend the flower firmly in place.

Icing Consistency: Stiff

Tube: Any rose tube (104 is often used); a number 3 round tube for the stem

Position of Bag: 45-degree angle at 11:00 for the base and 6:00 for the petals

Method: To make the base, rest the wide end of the rose tube on the surface with the narrow end very slightly elevated. As you start squeezing, swing the tube gradually from 11:00 to 1:00, forming a flat arc (Figs. 1 and 2).

For the petals, rest the tube on the surface at the bottom center of the base with the narrow end pointing straight up. As you squeeze, raise the tube slightly, then lower and stop the pressure. Rock your hand slightly forward to break off the icing (Fig. 3–5). Repeat this procedure to make 2 side petals, angling the tube first slightly to the left, then to the right (Figs. 6 to 8).

For the stem, use a number 3 round tube to touch the base of the flower, and as you squeeze to build up icing, gradually draw the tube away, relaxing the pressure to form stem (Fig. 9).

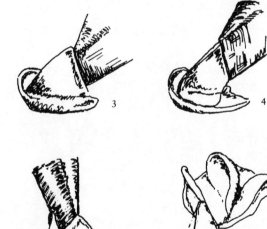

LILY OF THE VALLEY: There is a special tube and technique that makes it possible to capture this charming bell shape.

Icing Consistency: Stiff

Tube: 1 and 80

Position of Bag: 45-degree angle

Method: Pipe a narrow curved stem with a number 1 tube. Use a wet, fine paint brush to smooth out any bumps and bubbles (Fig. 1). Pipe the outline of a leaf and several tiny stems off the main stem. Each small stem will hold an individual blossom (Fig. 2).

Change to a number 80 tube. Hold the tube slightly above the surface, curved end toward you. Squeeze out a small amount of icing until it curves upwards. Then touch the bottom of the curve to the cake and continue squeezing while moving up and over toward you in a slightly circular movement (Fig. 3). Stop the pressure completely and pull away the tube. To keep the bell shape from opening up, pull the tube away in a slightly downward motion.

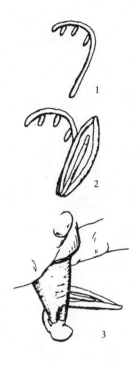

ROSEBUDS AND HALF ROSE: These flowers are exquisitely realistic. They can be formed directly on the cake or made ahead.

Icing Consistency: Stiff

Tube: Any rose tube (104 is often used); number 3 round tube for the stem and sepals

Position of Bag: 45-degree angle at 3:00, tube with wide end down and narrow end straight up. Careful positioning is critical to achieve this shape.

Method: With the wide end of the tube touching the surface, start squeezing, moving the tip sharply back and forth to create a cupped base. Release the pressure and twist your hand slightly to the right to open up the right side of the cup and keep it from curving over. Slide the tip down and away from the side to release the icing and create a sharp edge (Fig. 1).

Line up the tube so that the entire opening touches the entire right edge of the base. Leaving the tube still and in place, squeeze the bag firmly. Icing will catch the edge and roll itself into an interlocking center bud (Fig. 2).

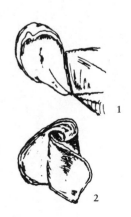

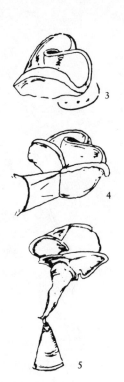

Attach the stem or go on to create a half rose.

For a half rose, hold the tube wide end down and narrow end straight up to the left of the base. Squeeze, raising the tube slightly, then lower and stop the pressure to form a side petal (Fig. 3). This is the same basic motion as for the base only it stops midway at the center of the flower. Follow the same procedure to make a second side petal, going from right to left and slightly overlapping the first petal (Fig. 4). To form stem and sepals, use round tube number 3. Touch the base, allowing icing to build up while gradually drawing the tube away (Fig. 5). Bury the tip in the base and gradually relax the pressure as you move the tip up the petal and slightly away to form 3 sepals.

PIPED ROSE: There is something about a rose piped from a pastry tube that is pure magic. People are always spellbound when watching a demonstration of piped roses—even I, after all these years of decorating cakes, find myself in awe, forgetting that I can do them too!

Piped roses make a time-honored decoration for any cake. For a new twist, make royal icing rose candleholders by inserting a candle in the center of each rose before the icing dries. When the icing has dried completely, lay the rose on its side and pipe a 1½-inch stem from its base. When thoroughly dry, poke the stem directly into the cake by first making a small hole with a metal skewer.

Icing Consistency: As stiff as possible while still squeezable

Tube: 12 round tube for the base; any rose tube (104 is most often used) for the petals

Position of Bag: For base: rose nail is held in left hand, bag at 90-degree upright angle, tube slightly above nail.

For petals: 45-degree angle at 4:30, tube with wide end touching base and narrow end turned slightly inward and then gradually outward for each row of petals.

Base: Attach a wax paper square to the rose nail with a dot of icing. Hold the bag perpendicular to nail, with the number 12 round tube touching the center. Squeeze with heavy pressure, keeping the tip buried in the icing until you build up a good size base (Fig. 1). Ease pressure as you gradually raise the tube to form a bottom-heavy conical shape (Fig. 2). This base should be 1½ times as high as the opening of the rose tube used to make the petals (Fig. 3).

Bud: Hold the bag at a 45-degree angle to the nail, with the back over to the right so your fingertips face you. Touch the wide end of rose tube 104 to the top of icing base, with the narrow end turned slightly inward (Fig. 4).

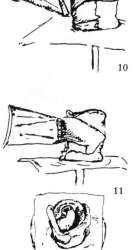

As you start to squeeze, pull the tube up and away from the top of the base, stretching the icing into a ribbon band (Fig. 5). At the same time, turn the nail counterclockwise and swing the band of icing around the tip and back down to where you first started, overlapping starting point and continuing down to the bottom of the base for stability (Fig. 6).

First Row of 3 Petals: Touch the wide end of the rose tube to the icing bud close to the bottom, with the narrow tube end pointing straight (Fig. 7). Turn the nail counterclockwise and move the tube up, around, and down toward you in a half-circle motion to form a petal (Fig. 8). Turn the nail a ⅓ turn for each petal.

Following the same procedure, start at the base of the first petal, overlapping it slightly, and squeeze out icing as you move the tube up, around, and down toward you to form a second petal (Fig. 9).

Again, following same procedure, start at the base of the second petal and squeeze out icing as you turn the nail to form a third petal, slightly overlapping the first petal (Figs. 10 and 11).

Second Row of 4 Petals: Touch the wide end of the rose tip to just under the first row of petals in the center of one of them, with the narrow end of the tube pointing slightly outward. As you

squeeze, turn the nail a ¼ turn and move the tube up, around, and down to form a petal. Starting at base of this petal, follow the same procedure to make 3 more petals. The petals should be same height as those in the first row (Figs. 12 and 13).

Third Row of 5 to 7 Petals: Touch the wide end of the rose tube to the base under the second row of petals in the center of one of them, with the narrow end of the tube pointing slightly farther out than the previous row. Again turn the nail slightly and squeeze out the first petal. Follow the same procedure until the last row of petals has been completed (Fig. 14).

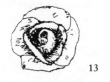

TIP: If you wish to curve the edges of the petals, dip a fingertip in cornstarch and gently mold them.

Remove the rose from the nail by lifting the wax paper square from the nail. If you haven't used wax paper, remove the rose with scissors held in a slightly open position (Fig. 15). Do not close the scissors until the rose is positioned on the cake or other surface.

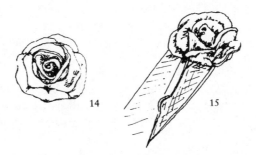
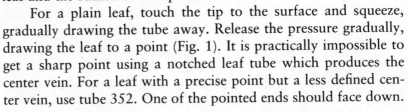

PIPED LEAVES: Pale green tinted icing leaves, piped around and between the roses, add a nice touch.

Icing Consistency: Thin
Tube: 67 or 352
Position of Bag: 45-degree angle
Method: There are 2 basic types of piped leaves: the plain or flat-leaf and the ruffled stand-up leaf.

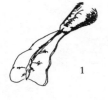

For a plain leaf, touch the tip to the surface and squeeze, gradually drawing the tube away. Release the pressure gradually, drawing the leaf to a point (Fig. 1). It is practically impossible to get a sharp point using a notched leaf tube which produces the center vein. For a leaf with a precise point but a less defined center vein, use tube 352. One of the pointed ends should face down.

For a stand-up leaf, squeeze with heavier pressure to build up a base to support the leaf. Then pull the tube straight up and away as you relax the pressure and draw to a point (Fig. 2). If you have built up an adequate base and the leaf will not stand up, the icing is too thin or soft.

Writing requires thin icing which flows smoothly from the tube and lots of penmanship practice. I personally do not like to see writing on a cake, but sometimes the occasion calls for it, so I try to make it as integral a part of the design as possible.

Practice on an inverted cake pan or the counter before piping the writing directly onto the cake. Unless you have a lot of experience writing on cakes, it is easy to become rusty. Printing is a lot easier than script.

Icing Consistency: Thin

Tube: Any small round tube (3 is the most often used)

Position of Bag: 45-degree angle at 6:00 for printing, 3:00 for script

Method: For printing, touch the tip to the surface. As you start squeezing, raise the tip slightly to keep the lines even. Stop squeezing a little before the end of the line and tug ever so slightly to straighten the line before touching the tip down to attach. Release the pressure, remove the tip, and start the next line.

For script, the tip should always be touching the surface lightly.

For both printing and script, be sure to move your entire arm, not just your hand. This results in a smoother design.

ROYAL ICING CALLIGRAPHY: Because I, like most people, do not write on cakes every day of the week, it is risky business indeed to find myself with a pastry bag poised above an up-to-that-point perfect cake—wondering how I'm going to fit in the letters and how they will look and what I will do if I ruin the cake.

To avoid this anxiety, I have worked out the following risk-free system for getting the letters on the cake, plus a choice of capital letter calligraphy.

Wherever I have traveled, I have searched for attractive letters to use for cakes. My search finally ended one day on a flight between San Francisco and New York. I found the unusual type style on page 412 in a stunning in-flight magazine called *Vis à Vis*. It took months to track it down, but I finally found their headquarters and received official permission to use the letters for this book. They are courtesy of *Vis à Vis* (East-West Network) and were designed by the talented L.A.-based artist and logo designer Michael Manoogian.

A decorative monogram can be fun to create and makes an attractive design. Make a template by photocopying or tracing the letters, reducing or increasing the size as desired. Tape the tracing securely to rigid cardboard or a baking sheet and lay a nonstick liner on top. Use a few pieces of tape to hold it in place. Pipe,

following the design. Use a number 3 tube for the letters and a number 1 for the optional "illumination" (free-form lines and swirls decorating the letter).

Remember to hold the tube above the surface so the icing falls freely. The icing should be soft enough to flow smoothly but stiff enough for control.

Allow the icing to dry thoroughly before removing the panel from the template. A small angled spatula is perfect for lifting the letters and placing them on the cake. A lightly held tweezer is also handy.

GOLD LEAF: For the most elegant and stunning effect, gold leaf can be applied to the letters. Real 22-karat gold leaf, sometimes referred to as patent gold, is available in sign-painting supply stores. It comes in thin sheets which seem to dissolve on touch. The gold is not absorbed into the system so it offers no nutritive value, although some fancifully say that it is good for the heart. In India, gold leaf is used to decorate desserts or to float in a magical liquid pool on soup. Goldwasser, a German liqueur, also contains flecks of gold. My friend Bob Miller, an artist, even gilds his Thanksgiving turkey, managing to partially gild himself as well in the joyful process!

Using gold on letters is tricky but thrilling because it is so very beautiful. When I asked the salesman how to make the gold stick he suggested "sizing" until I told him it was for eating. Egg white, however, works very well.

To apply gold, use a fine artist's brush to brush a thin coating of lightly beaten egg white on a small section of the letter. Lift a small piece of gold leaf with a sharp pointed tweezer and lay it on top. It will tend to curve around and cling to the egg white. Use the same brush to smooth it in place. If the letters are used on rolled fondant, the gold can be applied after the letters are in place as it will not stick to the fondant. Use a bit of egg white to attach letters to the fondant.

Icing Consistency: Thin
Tube: Round number 2
Position of Bag: 45-degree angle
Method: Trace or photocopy the drawing onto paper with dark ink.

The ideal surface for piping these delicate panels is a nonstick liner (page 458) because it is easy to remove the delicate filigree work without risking breakage. Parchment can also be used but removal is more risky. In any event, minor breakage can be repaired even after the panels are attached to the cake, but it is always safer to make one or two extra.

Tape the tracing securely to rigid cardboard or a baking sheet and lay the nonstick liner on top. Use a few pieces of tape to hold it in place. Pipe, following the design. If desired, use pink royal icing for contrast, to pipe roses. It is unimportant if you deviate from the design because after removing the template it will always look breathtakingly beautiful.

Remember to hold the tube above the surface so the icing falls freely. The icing should be soft enough to flow smoothly but stiff enough for control. Pipe a second line on top of the first around the outside edge for extra stability. Carefully slide out the template and use it as the guide for all of the panels.

Allow the icing to dry for at least 30 minutes before removing the panels from the liner. It helps to hold the panels on a flat counter, allowing small sections to extend over the edge. Support the panel with a broad spatula while pulling the liner down and away from the extended section. Small breaks can be filled in and repaired even when on the cake.

PAINTED ROYAL ICING FLOWERS

Using a damp artist's brush to shape the piped icing creates subtle effects. Use only enough water to keep the brush marks from showing.

LILIES OF THE VALLEY: Piping and then painting the tiny flowers onto a fondant-covered cake gives the illusion of fine embroidery.
Icing Consistency: Thin
Tube: Round number 1
Position of Bag: 45-degree angle
Method: Pipe a narrow curved stem, using a number 1 tube (Fig. 1). Use a wet, fine paint brush to smooth out any bumps and bubbles. Pipe the outline of a leaf and several tiny stems off the main stem (Fig. 2). Each small stem will hold an individual blossom. For the blossoms, pipe small oval dots of icing on the ends of each stem (Fig. 3). Using the brush, pull down points from each oval to form bell-shaped blossoms (Fig. 4). Dilute green food coloring with water to produce the palest possible shade. Use the brush to highlight the flowers with touches of color.

1

2

3

4

BLEEDING HEART FLOWERS:
Icing Consistency: Thin for leaves, medium for blossoms
Tube: Round numbers 2 and 5; star number 14
Method: The heart-shaped flowers are piped entirely with a decorating tube, but the leaves are outlined and filled in with the aid of an artist's brush. For the leaves, use paste food color to tint the royal icing a deep shade of green. Mix in a little blue if the color is too bright. Keep in mind that the color will darken so make it a little lighter than the color you want. The leaves should be outlined free-form following the sketch and using a number 2

tube (Fig. 1). The same tube can be used to pipe the stems. To fill in the leaves, switch to a number 5 tube and squeeze out the icing with a back-and-forth motion (Fig. 2). Work on one leaf at a time so that the icing does not start to crust. Smooth squiggles of icing with a wet brush (Fig. 3). Tint some of the icing bright pink for the flowers. The heart shape is piped like a shell design (page 399) but with a plain round number 5 tube so that it looks like a tear drop. For closed buds, pipe only one teardrop shape. For blossoms, pipe two side-by-side teardrops, first angling the tube slightly to the left, then slightly to the right (Fig. 4). Change to a number 1 round tube to add curved strings to the point (Fig. 5). Pipe a tiny upside-down shell with white icing and use a number 14 star tube for the tip of the blossom (Fig. 6).

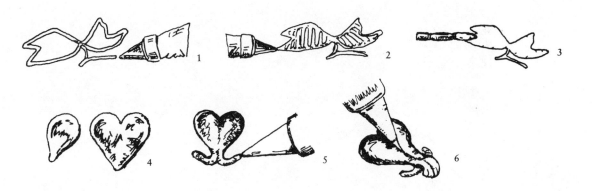

PART III

INGREDIENTS AND EQUIPMENT

$\mathcal{M}$y interest in the science of ingredients began when I was a freshman at the University of Vermont. I had just learned to make lemon meringue pie in a foods class and wanted to share the marvelous eating experience with some friends. We were all very poor so everyone contributed money for the ingredients. It was, therefore, especially humiliating, when, after using three quarters of a box of cornstarch, the filling still would not thicken. Determined to get to the bottom of this mystery, I analyzed each ingredient and finally settled on the water as the only possible culprit. We submitted the water for a mineral test and, sure enough, it had the highest possible level. This made me aware that there was more to cooking—and especially baking—than met the eye. It was many years before I made lemon meringue pie again.

It seems like forever ago that baking seemed such an utter and thrilling mystery.

It was about a decade later that I became seriously interested in cake baking and wrote my master's thesis on yellow cake. I remember making the cake one day when a neighbor stopped by to visit. Bob was from rural Georgia where, in those days, people raised most of what they ate. His mother had a pig killed every year, turning the entire animal into the best home-smoked sausage I have ever encountered. (Bob had endeared himself to me for life by sharing his precious supply.)

That day, as he watched me transfer the batter to the cake pan, he said: "You must be a good cook." "Why?" I asked. His answer: "Because you cook the way my mother cooks; nothing goes to waste. It's an attitude. People who cook that way seem to care about it more, so it comes out better."

That, in a nut shell, is my philosophy about ingredients. When you love what you do, no ingredient goes to waste so only the very best need be chosen in the first place. And, of course, it is not the quality of the ingredients alone that makes the difference between the extraordinary and the mediocre—it is the reverence with which one approaches baking and the desire to offer the best of what many consider to be the best part of the meal, dessert.

Ingredients

BAKER'S JOY: This is a combination of flour and oil for spraying on cake pans. It is faster and neater than greasing and flouring and produces a beautifully sealed, crumb-free crust. If you can't find it in your local supermarket, get in touch with the manufacturer for the nearest distributor (page 445). This is a fabulous product.

BAKING POWDER: Baking powders are mixtures of dry acid or acid salts and baking soda with starch or flour added to standardize and help stabilize the mixtures. Double-acting means that they will react, or liberate carbon dioxide, partially from moisture during the mixing stage and partially when exposed to heat during the baking stage. It is, therefore, important to store the baking powder in an airtight container to avoid humidity. There is also a substantial loss of strength in baking powder after one year. Date the bottom of the can when you first buy it, or write the expiration date on the lid with a felt-tip marker.

I use Rumford baking powder, an all-phosphate product containing calcium acid phosphate. It lacks the bitter aftertaste associated with SAS baking powders, which also contain sodium aluminum sulfate. (The supposed advantage of SAS powders is that they release a little more carbon dioxide during the baking stage than during the mixing stage, but I find I can interchange equal volume and weight of either type of baking powder.)

Rumford baking powder is usually available in health food stores (probably because aluminum compounds are considered dangerous by many health-conscious people).

BAKING SODA: Sodium bicarbonate has an indefinite shelf life if not exposed to humidity. In Canada I once discovered a wonderful variety called Cow Brand (goodness knows why). It contained a tiny amount of a harmless chemical ingredient which prevented it from clumping. Unless you can obtain this type of baking soda, it is best to sift it before measuring.

BEESWAX: Used for making spun sugar because of its high melting point, it helps keep the strands flexible. Bee's wax is available at sculptor's supply stores, some sewing supply stores, and, of course, through apiaries.

CHESTNUTS: Most of the canned chestnuts I have seen come from France. Different types of puree vary widely in sugar content so pay close attention to the label. **Marrons entiers au naturel:** These are whole peeled chestnuts in water. **Crème de marrons:** This cream, made up of candied pieces of chestnut, has a total of 48 percent sugar and glucose. This is not to be confused with chestnut puree, for it is far too sweet for any of the uses in this book. **Purée de marrons au naturel:** The label reads that only glucose is added, so this product is virtually unsweetened. It does, however, contain water, making it too soft for some uses. To find this puree, try specialty food stores such as Dean & DeLuca (page 445).

Albert Uster Imports carries Carma's chestnut puree and an excellent, firm, lightly sweetened puree, also called Purée de Marrons, which contains 20 to 22 percent sugar. **Marrons glacés:** These whole candied chestnuts are suitable for garnishing.

CHESTNUT FLOUR: This flour, which is mainly starch, is made from milled dried chestnuts. It is available from France in health food stores. Georgio DeLuca of Dean & DeLuca has produced wonderfully flavored chestnut flour from the magnificent chestnuts of Italy.

To retain the distinctive flavor, chestnut flour should be refrigerated. It will keep for at least one year.

Chocolate is a very important ingredient in cakes and butter-creams. Working with it over the past ten years, I have found there is an enormous difference in both texture and flavor among brands and have developed my own personal preferences. I highly recommend that you do a blind tasting to determine your own.

One of my favorite dark chocolates is Lindt's Courante, a couverture that can be used in place of bittersweet chocolate for the recipes in this book (see page 442 for exact sugar content equivalencies). I also love Tobler's Extra Bittersweet and Tradition and Lindt's Excellence. (Lindt also has a couverture called Excellence, so be careful not to confuse the two.) Another favorite is French Valrhôna's Extra Bittersweet, which has a delicious, winy undertone (available through Gourmand, page 445). An excellent American Chocolate is Nestlé's Chocolat d'Or (available through International Leisure Activities, page 445). When it comes to milk chocolate I adore Lindt for its creamy smoothness and lovely caramel flavor notes, and I absolutely cannot stay away from Hershey's Golden Almond bar. For white chocolate, the only one I find acceptable is Tobler's Narcisse. Others are sweeter and sometimes almost chalky.

Fortunately, Tobler chocolate is carried in many supermarkets. In New York a great discount place to buy chocolate is called Economy Candy on Essex Street. Lindt Courante is available through Hauser Chocolatier, Inc. (page 445).

Many fine chocolates, such as Tobler, are produced under Kashruth supervision. Write to the manufacturer or distributor for a letter of certification if you want to use a chocolate in kosher cooking.

Brands of chocolate differ partly because of special formulas unique to each company, which determine the blend of the beans, the type and amount of flavorings, and the proportions of chocolate liquor and cocoa butter. Taste and texture are also greatly affected by the length of roasting, grinding, and conching. Grinding reduces particle size and conching—a wavelike motion—releases volatile oils, develops flavor, and coats the sugar and cocoa particles with cocoa butter, which reduces the feeling of gritty abrasiveness. Too much conching can result in an oily texture. European, particularly Swiss, chocolate is usually conched for up to 96 hours, which produces the characteristic velvety-smooth texture Europeans favor and which some Americans find too rich. (At least that used to be the case. Since the recent chocolate craze hit this country, I doubt if many people find anything chocolate too rich.) American chocolate may be conched for only 4 to 5 hours if at all, though some brands claim as many as 74 hours of conching.

Lecithin, an emulsifier found in soy beans, is used to stabilize chocolate. Its presence reduces the amount of cocoa butter required to cover the cocoa particles. It frees the cocoa butter to act as a floating medium for the particles. It also reduces viscosity, making it less thick. Only a very small quantity is necessary, for example 1 gram lecithin per kilogram for white chocolate, slightly more for dark chocolate. Lecithin is used in even the finest quality chocolate. As it is not "Kosher for Passover," a Swiss company, Maestrani, exports an excellent chocolate containing no lecithin. The dark chocolate is pareve (contains no dairy products). See Taam-Tov Food, Inc. (page 445).

The U.S. government provides restrictions and classifications for chocolate that dictate the type of fat and percentage of chocolate liquor. To be classified as real chocolate, it must contain no fat other than cocoa butter (with the exception of 5 percent dairy butter to aid emulsification, which does not have to appear on the label).

PURE CHOCOLATE: Pure chocolate, also referred to as bitter, baking, or unsweetened chocolate, contains only chocolate liquor (cocoa solids and cocoa butter) and flavorings. Depending on the variety of the cocoa bean used, 50 to 58 percent of the chocolate liquor is cocoa butter, averaging 53 percent. The bulk of the remainder, the cocoa solids, contains 10.7 percent protein and 28.9 percent starch. (This is the same amount present in the nibs—the term for the cocoa bean after removal of the pod—before processing.) No lecithin may be added, but a great variety of flavorings is permissible, such as vanilla or vanillin (synthesized vanilla), ground nuts, coffee, salt and various extracts.

COCOA: Cocoa is the pure chocolate liquor with three-quarters of the cocoa butter removed. The remaining cocoa is then pulverized. Most European cocoa is Dutch-processed, which means that the cocoa has been treated with a mild alkali to mellow the flavor and make it more soluble. There is no need to sift cocoa for a recipe when it will be dissolved in water. In recipes such as Chocolate Rolled Fondant or Chocolate Meringue, it is advisable to process or sift the cocoa if it is lumpy so that it will incorporate more evenly.

My favorite Dutch-processed cocoa is Lindt's from Switzerland, which recently has become available in this country. It comes in dark and light (I prefer the dark) and is carried by Hauser Chocolatier, Inc. Poulain, Valrhôna, and Van Houten are also excellent Dutch-processed cocoas. My favorite nonalkalized cocoa is Hershey's. It offers the characteristic chocolate flavor most Americans grew up adoring. Smelling the cocoa will tell you a lot about its flavor potential but the best test is baking a cake with it.

COCOA BUTTER: The quality of cocoa butter is related to the quality of the bean from which it came and the process of separating it from the chocolate liquor. Many chocolatiers prefer Swiss cocoa butter, which is produced by cold pressing and is lighter in color and finer in flavor. Swiss cocoa butter is carried by Albert Uster Imports (page 445).

When working with cocoa butter, it is helpful to know that it is solid at room temperature and that it has a low melting point (just below body temperature) that is called "sharp," meaning it changes quickly from solid to liquid, unlike butter which is more gradual. Adding cocoa butter to mixtures will make them firmer but will also offer more of a melt-in-the mouth experience.

Store cocoa butter in an airtight container so that it doesn't pick up other flavors. Refrigerated, it will keep for several years.

Cocoa butter is a vegetable fat and contains no cholesterol. It is, unfortunately, high in saturated fat.

BITTERSWEET OR SEMISWEET AND EXTRA BITTERSWEET: Bittersweet or semisweet and extra bittersweet (for which there is no U.S. government standard) are pure chocolate liquor with sugar, vanilla or vanillin, and extra cocoa butter added. Semisweet morsels have to be more viscous to maintain their chip shape during baking. Every manufacturer has his own terminology or formula for this category of chocolate. They can be used interchangeably in recipes, but their sweetness levels will vary. (For more precise sweetness equivalencies, see page 444.)

COUVERTURE: Used for candy dipping and some decorative work, this is often referred to as compound chocolate in the United States. In Europe, however, it is made from the highest quality real chocolate, which has a high percentage of cocoa butter, resulting in low viscosity and subsequently a thin coating and a glossy sheen when used for dipping or decorations such as chocolate bands. There is no U.S. standard for the European couverture either, but in Europe couverture must have a minimum of 36 percent cocoa butter and may have as much as 40 percent. Japanese couverture may have as much as 42 percent.

MILK CHOCOLATE: Milk chocolate contains pure chocolate liquor, milk solids, butter, vanilla or vanillin, and extra cocoa butter.

Milk chocolate does not have as long a shelf life as dark chocolate because the milk solids become rancid (though not as quickly as in white chocolate due to the protective presence of cocoa solids).

WHITE CHOCOLATE: White chocolate is not considered to be "real chocolate" in the United States because it contains no cocoa solids. Better-quality white chocolates are, however, made with cocoa butter and have a delicious flavor. White chocolate contains about 30 percent fat, 30 percent milk solids, and 30 percent sugar. It also contains vanilla or vanillin and lecithin. When melted, it sets faster than dark chocolate but is softer at room temperature. Its shelf life is much shorter than dark chocolate because of the milk solids.

In addition to making delicious buttercreams and cakes, a small amount of melted white chocolate is great in an emergency to thicken buttercream or pastry cream. This small amount of white chocolate adds firmness without significantly altering the character of the mixture.

COMPOUND CHOCOLATE: Compound chocolate is classified as chocolate "flavor" because, instead of cocoa butter, it contains vegetable shortening such as soya, palm kernel, or coconut oil. This type of fat is more stable than cocoa butter and does not require tempering (page 380) to prevent bloom (discoloration). It also affords the chocolate a higher melting point, which means it will remain unmelted at warmer temperatures. For this reason, it is sometimes referred to as "summer coating." Its taste is acceptable and some people find it delicious (they can't have tasted the real thing), but it lacks the complexity and fullness of fine-quality chocolate. Still, for small decorative touches when you don't have time to temper chocolate, it is a joy to have on hand.

Compound chocolate is produced in many colors. It is available at candy supply houses and by mail through Maid of Scandinavia. Albert Uster Imports makes my favorite dark compound chocolate called Carma Glaze. It is very dark and lustrous and comes in a 13.25 pound block suitable for large-scale use.

AVERAGE CHOCOLATE MASS AND COCOA BUTTER CONTENT: Chocolate mass refers to the total amount of cocoa solids and cocoa butter.

cocoa (breakfast cocoa—usually Dutch-processed): 22 to 25 percent cocoa butter

cocoa (regular—usually nonalkalized): 10 to 21 percent cocoa butter

bitter or unsweetened baking chocolate (pure chocolate liquor): 50 to 58 percent cocoa butter, averaging 53 percent

couverture chocolate: 60 to 78 percent chocolate mass of which 36 to 40 percent is cocoa butter

extra bittersweet chocolate: 60 percent chocolate mass of which 30 percent is cocoa butter

semisweet or bittersweet chocolate: 49.5 to 53 percent chocolate mass of which 27 percent is cocoa butter. U.S. government standards requires a minimum of 35 percent chocolate liquor.

semisweet bits: 42.5 percent chocolate mass of which 29 percent is cocoa butter

sweet chocolate: 34 percent chocolate mass of which 27 percent is cocoa butter. U.S. government standards requires a minimum of 29 percent chocolate liquor.

milk chocolate: 34 to 38 percent chocolate mass of which 29 to 33 percent is cocoa butter, plus 12 percent whole milk solids. U.S. government standards requires a minimum of 10 percent chocolate liquor.

STORING CHOCOLATE: The best way to store chocolate or cocoa is to keep it well wrapped in an airtight container (chocolate is quick to absorb other odors and must not be exposed to dampness) at a temperature of 60°F. to 75°F. with less than 50 percent relative humidity. Under these conditions dark chocolate should keep well for at least two years. I have experienced chocolate stored at ideal conditions for several years and it seems to age like a fine wine, becoming more mellow and subtle. Milk chocolate keeps, even at optimum conditions, for only a little over one year and white chocolate, about one year.

CITRON, ANGELIQUE, AND MIXED CANDIED FRUITS: Used primarily for fruit cake and decorative work, they are available through Albert Uster Imports and specialty food stores. Stored airtight at room temperature, they last for years. Do not refrigerate as they become rock hard.

COBASAN: This is a wonderful product from Germany for stabilizing whipped cream and buttercreams. It consists of sorbitol and glucose. A minute quantity added before whipping the cream, or before adding the butter to the buttercream, emulsifies the fat, enabling the whipped cream to hold up for as long as 6 hours at room temperature and making it easier to pipe buttercream without it softening as quickly. It does not work, however, with ultrapasteurized cream because the fat molecules are altered due to the higher heat at which this cream is pasteurized.

Cobasan is available from Albert Uster Imports. The plastic bottle contains 1 quart which will probably last a lifetime unless you open a bake shop!

CORNSTARCH AND ARROWROOT: These two starches have twice the thickening power of flour and produce more translucent glazes. Arrowroot also adds a slight sparkle. Thickening is accomplished by absorption of liquid. As the starch granules absorb the liquid, they swell and become fragile. It is, therefore, very important not to stir vigorously after thickening has occurred because it will break down these fragile, swollen granules and the glaze will be thin.

Cornstarch does not thicken until it has reached a full boil (212°F.), while arrowroot requires only 158°F. to 176°F. Prolonged cooking past the thickening point will also break down the starch and thin the glaze.
NOTE: Starches have limited shelf life. If they are stored for several years they will eventually lose their thickening power.

CREAM OF TARTAR: Potassium acid tartrate is a by-product of the wine industry. Its shelf life is indefinite. I have found that by adding 1 teaspoon cream of tartar per 1 cup egg whites, it stabilizes them so that it becomes virtually impossible to dry them out by overbeating. Cream of tartar is also used as an interfering agent in sugar syrups to inhibit crystallization and to lower the pH of certain batters, such as angel food cake, to produce a whiter crumb.

BUTTER: Butter is one of my favorite flavors. The best fresh, un-salted butter has the flowery, grassy smell of a summer meadow. It seems downright unfair that this indispensable ingredient should not be equally wonderful for one's health. But it isn't. So the only solution is to eat smaller portions—but never to substitute any other solid fat.

DAIRY

Salted butter does not have the glorious flavor of fresh un-salted butter. If only salted butter is available, remove 1 teaspoon salt from the recipe per pound of butter used. It is also possible to make your own butter from cream, but if only ultra-pasteurized cream is available it may not be worth the trouble. Commercial butter is made from cream with a very high butterfat content and is churned immediately after flash pasteurization. This ensures the best flavor and longest shelf life. If you make your own butter, it will stay fresh for only one week.
To make butter: Place heavy cream in a food processor and process until it begins to thicken. For every cup of cream, add 2 tablespoons cold water. Process until the cream separates into solids. Strain out the liquid (this unsoured buttermilk is delicious to drink) and dry the resulting butter thoroughly with paper towels. One cup of cream yields about 3 ounces butter.

When buying commercial butter, grade A or AA contains about 81 percent fat, 15.5 percent water, and 6 percent protein. Lower grades will contain more water. Two ways to determine the water content are if the refrigerated butter remains fairly soft and if, when the butter is cut, small droplets of water appear. Excess water can be removed by kneading the butter in ice water for several minutes and then drying it thoroughly with paper towels.

Store butter airtight as it absorbs odors very readily. Avoid wrapping directly in foil as the butter may absorb a metallic odor. Butter freezes well for several months. Be sure to let it defrost completely before clarifying or it may burn instead of brown.

CLARIFIED BUTTER: Several recipes in this book call for clarified *beurre noisette*. This refers to clarified butter which has browned to the color of *noisettes* (French for "hazelnuts"). *Beurre noisette* offers a richer, more delicious flavor.

When butter is clarified, the water evaporates and the milk solids drop to the bottom. The milk solids cannot begin to brown until all the water has evaporated. When adding clarified butter to chocolate, it is important that no water remain, so milk solids in the butter should have started to turn golden brown before the liquid butter is strained.

To clarify butter: Melt butter in a heavy saucepan over medium heat, partially covered to prevent spattering. Do not stir. When the butter looks clear, cook, uncovered, watching carefully until the solids drop and begin to brown. When the bubbling noise quiets, all the water has evaporated and the butter can burn easily. To make *beurre noisette,* allow the solids to turn dark brown. Strain immediately through a fine strainer or cheesecloth-lined strainer. Clarified butter will keep for months refrigerated or just about indefinitely frozen, as it is the milk solids that cause the butter to become rancid quickly. I always make extra to have on hand. (The browned solids are excellent for adding flavor to bread dough.) Clarified butter will only be 75 percent the volume of whole butter. For example, if you need 3 tablespoons clarified butter, start with 4 tablespoons butter.

MILK: Milk contains 87.4 percent water, 3.5 percent protein, and 3.5 to 3.7 percent fat.

Nature's most perfect milk, in my opinion, is goat's milk. Goat's milk is lower in cholesterol with more finely emulsified butterfat, and the flavor is slightly sweeter and seems purer than cow's milk. If you are lucky enough to have access to goat's milk, feel free to use it in any recipe calling for milk.

CULTURED BUTTERMILK: Buttermilk contains 90.5 percent water, 3.6 protein, and 1.5 to 2 percent butterfat. It is a soured product, obtained by treating skim or part-skim milk with a culture of lactic acid bacteria.

HALF AND HALF: Half and half is ½ light cream and ½ milk. It contains 79.7 percent water, 3.2 percent protein, and 11.7 percent fat. If you ever run out of milk and have half and half, it's easy to substitute for milk required in a recipe (page 443).

LIGHT CREAM: Light cream contains 71.5 percent water, 3 percent protein, and 20.6 percent fat. It is increasingly difficult to find.

HEAVY CREAM: Heavy cream contains 56.6 percent water, 2.2 percent protein, and 36 to 40 percent fat (averaging 36 percent). If the heavy cream in your area seems low in butterfat (is difficult to beat and separates easily), it is easy to increase the butterfat content (page 254).

Heavy cream can be frozen for several months, defrosted, and used for making either ganache or butter cake. Freezing, however, alters the fat structure, making cream impossible to whip and unsuitable for making emulsifications such as *crème anglaise* or ice cream. (The texture will not be smooth.)

SOUR CREAM: Sour cream contains 71.5 percent water, 3 percent protein, and 18 to 20 percent fat. It is made from light cream, soured by the addition of lactic acid culture.

EGGS: All my recipes use USDA grade large eggs. As a rule of thumb, 5 extra-large eggs equal about 6 large eggs. Values for recipes in this book are given for weight and volume so it's fine to use any size egg if you weigh or measure them. As the weight of the eggs and thickness of the shell can vary a great deal even within a given grade (from 1.75 ounces to 2.5 ounces for large eggs), I find it safer to weigh or measure even when using large eggs.

Egg white contains: 87.6 percent water and 10.9 percent protein
Egg yolk contains: 51.1 percent water, 16 percent protein, and 30.6 percent fat

Egg whites freeze perfectly for at least one year. It is also possible to freeze yolks. Stir in ½ teaspoon sugar per yolk to keep them from becoming sticky after they are defrosted. (Remember to subtract this amount of sugar from the recipe.)

DRAGÉES (drahZJAYS): These little balls of silver or gold consist mainly of sugar. The USDA considers them nontoxic and acceptable for decorative use. Of course, they are not intended to be consumed by the handful. Dragées are carried by cake-decorating supply stores such as Maid of Scandinavia (page 445). When asking for them, it is safer to refer to them as silver or gold balls as no two people pronounce this item the same way!

ESSENCES: Exquisite steam-distilled French fruit essences such as wild strawberry, passion fruit, and apricot are available in tiny bottles from La Cuisine (page 445). A few drops go a long way. They are quite inexpensive.

The protein content of flour is listed on the bag and refers to the **FLOUR** number of grams of protein per 4 ounces/113 grams flour.

SWAN'S DOWN OR SOFTASILK CAKE FLOUR: 8 grams of protein per 4 ounces/113 grams flour. Caterers have told me that when they get 100-pound sacks of cake flour of a different brand than these, they do not get as fine a texture in their cakes.

Self-rising cake flour contains 1½ teaspoons baking powder and ½ teaspoon salt per cup of flour. It is fine to use this flour for recipes requiring the same proportion of baking powder if you eliminate the baking powder and salt from the recipe. The cakes preceding the All-Occasion Downy Yellow Cake, for example, use less baking powder per cup of flour, so self-rising flour will cause the cake to collapse.

A case of Swan's Down cake flour, containing twelve 2-pound boxes, can be purchased for about $16 by calling their toll-free number (page 445).

BREAD FLOUR: 14 grams of protein per 4 ounces/113 grams flour.

ALL-PURPOSE FLOUR: 8 to 14 grams of protein per 4 ounces/113 grams flour.*
Storage: Flour should be stored away from the heat so that it doesn't dry out. I find that cake flour can be stored for several years, but after 2 years, bread flour seems to lose some of its strength. Bread flour, which I purchase from a mill, becomes rancid after 8 months. Flour with the bran removed, such as cake flour and supermarket bread flour, does not become rancid or attract bugs readily.

FLOWERS: Fresh flowers make beautiful and even flavorful additions to cakes but great care must be taken to ensure that they are not a poisonous variety. Some edible flowers are apple blossoms, borage flowers, cimbidiums, citrus blossoms (orange and lemon), day lilies (not tiger lilies, which have spots), English daisies, hibiscus, hollyhocks, honeysuckle, lilacs, pansies, petunias, nasturtiums, roses, tulips, and violets. Nonedible flowers such as lilies of the valley are fine to use as part of an arrangement or corsage for the top of the cake which will be lifted off before serving.

Marzipan roses can be purchased through Albert Uster Imports (page 445).

FONDANT: Masa Ticino is a ready-made rolled fondant product that comes in 15.5-pound boxes for the commercial baker. It has a slightly lustrous surface and needs only to be kneaded lightly and rolled. It is available from Albert Uster Imports (page 445).

FOOD COLOR: Liquid food color, available in grocery stores, is fine when just a little color is needed. For stronger colors, paste food colors are preferable because they do not alter the consistency of the frosting as much. Powdered food color is even more intense than paste but can be very messy. Both paste and powder are suitable for adding to chocolate. Liquid food color will cause the chocolate to seize and become unworkable.

Colors are available in a great variety; there is even one that makes an off-white frosting whiter. In general, food color intensifies as it sits so it is best to mix colors with ingredients a few hours before using them.

---

*To calculate the percentage of protein in flour, multiply the number of grams of protein contained in 113 grams of flour (this information is found in the nutritional information listed on the package) by 100 and divide the resulting number by 113.
Example: For cake flour: $\frac{8 \times 100}{113} = 7$ percent

Use glycerine, not water, to thin paste color or it will become brittle. Another caveat: Frostings containing lemon juice will turn an off-color if blue food color is added.

Paste and powder food color are available at candy supply stores and by mail-order through Maid of Scandinavia (page 445) and Wilton (page 445). The former even has food color pens.

GELATIN: According to Knox, their gelatin, which comes in 7-gram/¼-ounce packages, is equal to 5 sheets of leaf gelatin measuring 2⅞ inches by 8½ inches. It will gel 2 cups liquid. I find that 1 package of gelatin measures 2¼ teaspoons. Leaf gelatin should be soaked 30 minutes in cold water until it becomes soft like plastic wrap. Water is then squeezed out and gelatin soaked in hot liquid until dissolved. Some people prefer leaf gelatin to powder because it imparts less flavor. I do not find the difference significant.

Powdered gelatin should be softened in cool water for at least 5 minutes before being heated to dissolve it. According to the Lipton Research Department, "While it is true that extensive boiling will de-nature unflavored gelatin . . . normal use in recipes, including boiling, will not adversely affect the product."

Gelatin will continue to thicken a mixture over a 24-hour period. Once it has reached its maximum thickness, it will not thicken any further (even on freezing—another myth dispelled). Freezing also does not affect thickening power. The gelatin mixture can be frozen, thawed, remelted, and refrozen several times before losing its strength.

GLYCERINE: Glycerine is a clear, heavy liquid made from fats and oils. It is used in rolled fondant to add sheen and keep the texture soft. It is ideal to thicken chocolate to the consistency for decorative piped work. It also works to thin paste food colors. Glycerine is available in candy or winemaking supply stores and from Maid of Scandinavia (page 445) and Wilton (page 445).

GOLD: 22-karat gold leaf and silver leaf are available in sign-painting supply stores. "Gold" and "silver" powders are available through the Chocolate Gallery (page 445).

GREEN TEA (POWDERED): Japanese powdered green tea, which I use to flavor whipped cream, *biscuit,* and marzipan, is available in Eastern food supply stores and by mail-order from Katagiri (page 445).

LEKVAR: Apricot lekvar is apricot preserves which contain the skin of the apricot as well as the fruit. The flavor is more intense and delicious than ordinary apricot preserves. Available through Paprikas Weiss (page 445) and Maid of Scandinavia (page 445).

NUTS: Freshly shelled nuts have the best flavor but the shelled canned varieties are excellent and are a lot more convenient.

The skin on hazelnuts is very bitter and difficult to remove. An easy method, taught to me by Carl Sontheimer (father of the food processor), uses baking soda. For ½ cup of nuts, have 1½ cups boiling water in a large saucepan and add 2 tablespoons baking soda. Boil the nuts for 3 minutes. The water will turn black from the color in the skins. Test a nut by running it under cold water. The skin should slip off easily. If not, boil a few minutes longer. Rinse nuts well under cold running water and crisp or brown them in a 350°F. oven for 20 minutes, watching carefully so that they don't burn. Hazelnuts, also called filberts, are available from Hazy Grove Nuts (page 445).

Pistachio nuts will lose flavor if boiled. Their skin is not bitter but if added to mixtures will spoil the lovely, pale green color. To remove this skin, toast the nuts for 10 minutes in a 350°F. oven and use your fingers or fingernails to remove the skin. Salted pistachio nuts should not be used for dessert recipes. If your supermarket does not carry unsalted pistachio nuts, they can be ordered shelled and unsalted from Marcel Akselrod (page 445) or Keenan Farms (page 445).

Lightly toasting all nuts greatly enhances their flavor.

Nuts keep well over one year if stored airtight in the freezer. I use either freezer bags, expelling all the excess air, or glass canning jars, filling the empty head space with wadded-up plastic wrap.

Nuts should always be at room temperature before grinding to prevent them from exuding too much oil. When grating or grinding nuts such as almonds, starting with sliced nuts results in more even and drier ground nuts. For every cup of ground almonds needed, start with 1¼ cups sliced almonds.

If only whole nuts are available, start using the grating disc of the food processor. Then switch to the metal blade and pulse until the nuts are finely chopped. A tablespoon or so of cornstarch, flour, or powdered sugar—borrowed from the rest of the recipe—will help absorb oil and prevent the ground nuts from clumping.

A small food processor seem to work best for evenly grinding nuts. The Mouli hand-grater also does a fine job.

NUT PASTES: Nut paste terminology is among the most confusing in the baking industry. Diamond brand almond paste, for example, claims to be 100 percent pure almond. This actually means that it contains no other nut substance and not that it doesn't contain any sugar! (In the industry, peach kernel pits are sometimes substituted for almonds to make a less expensive "almond" paste.) Imported almond pastes may contain as much as 50 percent sugar. Distributors such as Marcel Akselrod and Albert Uster have this information about the products they carry.

Almond paste manufactured in America usually consists of 25 to 35 percent sugar (some of which is invert) and sweet and bitter almonds. (The bitter almonds are much more intense in flavor than the sweet.) Almond paste is used to make marzipan by adding additional sugar.

The recipes in this book calling for almond paste require the domestic, or 25 to 35 percent sugar, variety.

Diamond brand almond paste is available at some supermarkets and through Maid of Scandinavia (page 445). Marcel Akselrod (page 445) and Albert Uster (page 445) also carry almond paste in larger quantities.

Pure 100 percent pistachio paste with no sugar added is also available in a small container from Marcel Akselrod. This is an excellent product made from the most flavorful pistachio nuts. The skins have not been removed, however, so a small amount of food color will be necessary to restore the characteristic green color.

Pure 100 percent hazelnut paste with no sugar added is available in a small container from Albert Uster. This is a fabulous addition to white chocolate when adding extra sugar is undesirable, as with Crème Ivoire Praliné (page 249). It is impossible to make a hazelnut paste of this smoothness without highly specialized equipment.

Praline paste consists of hazelnuts or a combination of almonds, hazelnuts, and 50 percent sugar. (Lesser qualities have a higher percentage of sugar.) I prefer the 100 percent hazelnut and caramelized sugar variety. This can be purchased in small, expensive quantities through Maison Glass (page 445). A small amount goes a long way and it is worth every penny. I have experimented endlessly only to find that homemade praline paste always has a slightly gritty consistency.

Praline paste keeps 1 year refrigerated and indefinitely frozen. On storage, some of the oil separates and floats to the top. This can be stirred back into the praline paste or poured off to use in Guilt-Free Chocolate Chiffon Cake (page 158) or White Chocolate Buttercream (page 248) in place of some of the neutral oil called for in the recipe.

OIL: Mineral oil, available in drugstores and winemaking supply stores, is excellent for adding to chocolate because it never becomes rancid. Safflower or other flavorless oils are fine but become rancid quickly and cannot be stored without refrigeration for more than a few weeks. When using walnut oil, smell it first to ensure that it has not become rancid. Walnut oil is carried by specialty food stores such as Dean & DeLuca (page 445). When using oil to make cakes, it is important that it contain no silicates because they act to prevent the foaming necessary for aerating the cake. Most oils are made without the addition of silicates; a glance at the label will tell you if it has been added.

PAM: I prefer Pam to other nonstick vegetable spray products because it has virtually no odor. It is composed of lecithin, a natural emulsifying agent derived from soybeans, and a tiny amount of soybean oil. Nonstick spray is particularly useful when working with rolled fondant. It prevents the fondant from sticking without having to add cornstarch or powdered sugar which could mar its surface.

PASSION FRUIT: An excellent frozen puree is carried by Marcel Akselrod (page 445)

PIPING GEL: Clear piping gel consists mainly of corn syrup, agar agar, and tartaric acid (cream of tartar). It is available at cake-decorating supply stores such as Maid of Scandinavia and Wilton. I find it useful for attaching chocolate bands to a cake when I don't want to use a flavored jelly. Piping gel can also be lightly tinted with food color or mixed with cocoa, powdered sugar, and water to make a brilliantly glossy chocolate decorating medium (page 389).

SUGAR   **HOW SUGAR IS MADE:** Sucrose, the primary sugar used in cake-making, is a sugar obtained from sugar beets or sugar cane. There is absolutely no difference between these two sources in the final product if the sugar is refined to 99.9 percent sucrose. A molecule of sucrose is composed of one fructose and one glucose molecule joined together to form a simple carbohydrate, easy to digest and full of energy. Other plants are capable of making sugar, but both cane and beet make it in quantities large enough to support refining. Sugar from the plants is dissolved in water and the resulting syrup is boiled in large steam evaporators. The substance that remains is crystallized in heated vacuum pans and the liquid, now called molasses, is separated from the crystals by spinning it in a centrifuge. At this stage the sugar is known as raw sugar and contains 3 percent impurities or extraneous matter. The raw sugar crystals are washed with steam and are called turbinado sugar, which is 99 percent pure sucrose. Although it closely resembles refined white sugar in sweetening ability and composition, it cannot always be substituted in recipes. Its moisture content varies considerably, which, coupled with its molasses flavor and coarse granulation, can affect a recipe without careful adjustment.

Refined white sugar is processed from turbinado sugar. The turbinado sugar is heated again to a liquid state, centrifuged, clarified with lime or phosphoric acid, and then percolated through a column of beef-bone char or mixed in a solution of activated carbon. This last process whitens the sugar and removes all calcium and magnesium salts. Finally, the sugar is pumped back into vacuum pans where it is heated until it crystallizes. The resulting sugar is 99.9 percent sucrose. Sugar that is less refined may be somewhat gray in color and the protein impurities may cause foaming when the sugar is added to the liquid in a given recipe.

BROWN SUGAR: Most brown sugar is ordinary refined sucrose with some of the molasses returned to it (3.5 percent for light brown sugar, 6.5 percent for dark brown). I like to use dark Muscovado sugar from Malawi (available at Dean & DeLuca, page 445). Muscovado natural raw sugar doesn't have its natural molasses removed, so its flavor seems more pure and subtle. When a recipe calls for brown sugar, it is light brown sugar unless otherwise specified.

Equal volume of either type of brown sugar compared to white sugar has the same sweetening power, but brown sugar must be measured by packing it into the cup. Dark brown sugar weighs the most because of the added molasses. Molasses also adds moisture to the sugar. Brown sugar contains 2.1 percent water while plain white sucrose only contains .5 percent.

If you run out of brown sugar and have white sugar and molasses on hand, it's easy to make your own (see substitutions, page 442).

MOLASSES: Containing 24 percent water, unsulfured molasses such as Grandma's has the best flavor because it is refined from the concentrated juice of sugar cane. The sulfured variety is usually a byproduct of sugarmaking and tastes of the residues of sulfur dioxide introduced during the sugarmaking process.

REFINER'S SYRUP: Containing 15 to 18 percent water, this is a delicious by-product of sugar refining. When syrup, after many boilings, ceases to yield crystals it is filtered and concentrated into this golden-colored syrup. Lyle's, a British company, packages it as Lyle's Golden Syrup. It can be used interchangeably with light corn syrup. Refiner's syrup is carried by specialty stores such as Dean & DeLuca (page 445).

GLUCOSE: Containing 15 to 19.7 percent water, glucose is an invert sugar found in many plants and in great abundance in corn. It is manufactured in syrup form in varying concentrations. Hospitals use it at very low concentrations. Glucose with suitable concentration for baking is thicker than corn syrup. It is subject to fermentation and will develop small bubbles and a sour taste, so once the container is opened it should be refrigerated. If kept airtight and not contaminated by a wet spoon, for example, it will last indefinitely. The 19.7 percent water (42° to 43° Baumé) glucose is available through candymaking supply houses and by mail-order through Maid of Scandinavia (page 445) and Wilton (page 445).

CORN SYRUP: Containing about 24 percent water, corn syrup consists of glucose (from corn sugar) with fructose added to prevent crystallization. It is susceptible to fermentation if contaminated, so care should be taken not to return any unused portion to the bottle. Fermented corn syrup has a sour taste and should be discarded. If used in low concentration, corn syrup has, by volume, half the sweetening power of sucrose but in high concentration is about equal. Since the major difference between glucose and corn syrup is the water content, if some of the water in the corn syrup is evaporated, it can be used interchangeably with glucose (see Approximate Equivalencies and Substitutions, page 442).

GRANULATIONS AND FORMS OF SUGAR: All 99.9 percent refined sucrose has equal sweetening power despite the degree of granulation. Powdered sugar has 3 percent cornstarch added to prevent lumping, but aside from this small percentage 1 pound of sugar equals 1 pound of sugar. (This may seem obvious, but I have read strange things to the contrary.)

Regular granulated or fine granulated: This is the all-purpose sugar found in most sugar bowls and available in all supermarkets. This granulation is suitable for making syrups, but for most other baking a finer granulation is preferable. Using a food processor it is possible to make a more finely granulated sugar, but the crystals will not be as uniform in size as in commercially produced finer grain sugars. Don't confuse the term fine granulated with superfine which is much finer.

Extra-fine: Available commercially, this sugar is also known as fruit sugar because it is used in the preservation of fruits. Most professional bakers use this granulation as their all-purpose sugar if they can't find *baker's special.* When used in cakes, it results in a fine crumb and lighter texture because, with the smaller crystals, more surface area is available to trap air. In the creaming process, the sharp or angular surfaces of the sugar crystals catch air. If the surface were smooth, as with powdered sugar, the grains would just clump together and not allow air in between. The more crystals there are, the more air will be incorporated. Finer sugar also dissolves more easily and makes lighter, more delicate meringues.

Baker's special: Available commercially, this sugar is slightly finer than extra-fine and almost as fine as superfine. This is the perfect granulation for all cake baking. I buy it in 100-pound sacks. A close approximation can easily be made in the food processor using a coarser granulation and processing for a few minutes.

Castor sugar: This is a term that appears in British cookbooks. The sugar, commonplace in England, is slightly finer than baker's special. If you are converting a British recipe, substitute *baker's special* or the more widely available superfine sugar.

Bar sugar, superfine, or ultrafine: This is the finest granulation of sugar and comes only in 1-pound boxes. It is sometimes called bar sugar because it is used in bars to make drinks that require fast-dissolving sugar. For the same reason, it is ideal for making meringues and cakes.

Loaf or cube sugar: This is merely granulated sugar that has been pressed into molds when moist and then allowed to dry so it maintains the shape. Some recipes, particularly in the confectionery area, specify loaf sugar because at one time it was more refined. Today, this is not the case. In fact, due to modern methods of manufacturing, the cubes have traces of oil from the molds, which makes them less desirable for sugar boiling.

Medium coarse and coarse pearl sugar: Known as "strong' sugar because it resists color changes and inversion at high temperatures, this type of sugar is ideal for confections and cordials. The large granules are sometimes used to sprinkle on cookies and pastries.

Powdered, confectioner's, or icing sugar: While it is possible to achieve a very fine granulation in a food processor, it is not possible to make true powdered sugar. This can only be done commercially. At one time, powdered sugar was stone-ground, but now it is ground in a steel magnesium rotary which turns against varying degrees of fine screens, each one determining a different fineness of the grind. The coarser the granulation of the initial sugar, the more even will be the final grind. As might be expected, the finer the granulation, the greater the tendency of the sugar to lump, which explains why 3 percent cornstarch is added to absorb any moisture from the air before the sugar can. The cornstarch adds what is perceived as a raw taste and makes powdered sugar less suitable than granulated sugar for use with ingredients that are not to be cooked.

Powdered sugar comes in 3 degrees of fineness; 10X, the finest (available in supermarkets), 6X, and 4X, both of which are available commercially. Maid of Scandinavia carries what they claim to be even finer than 10X powdered sugar, suitable for the finest string work in royal icing. 10X works well for fine designs with royal icing, and I have sometimes even used 6X with excellent results.

In general it is preferable to avoid sifting powdered sugar for royal icing because of the possibility of lint or other impurities causing discoloration or blocking the tiny openings of the smaller decorating tubes. But, if the powdered sugar is lumpy, sifting becomes necessary. Great care should be taken that all utensils and work surfaces are sparkling clean.

SUGAR SYRUPS: When making a sugar syrup for Italian meringue or classic buttercream, for example, the sugar is concentrated to produce a supersaturated solution from a saturated one. A saturated sugar solution contains the maximum amount of sugar possible at room temperature without precipitating out into crystals. A supersaturated sugar solution contains more sugar than the water can dissolve at room temperature. Heating the solution enables the sugar to dissolve. Cold water is capable of holding double its weight in sugar, but by heating it more sugar can dissolve in the same amount of water. A sugar solution begins with sugar, partially dissolved in at least one-third its weight of cold water. It is stirred continuously until boiling, at which time all the sugar is dissolved. If sugar crystals remain on the sides of the pan they should be washed down with a wet pastry brush. The solution is now considered supersaturated and, to avoid crystallization, must no longer be stirred.

As the water evaporates, the temperature of the solution rises and the density increases. Concentration of the syrup is dependent upon the amount of water left after evaporation. The temperature of the syrup indicates the concentration. As long as there is a lot of water in the syrup, the temperature does not rise much above the boiling point of water. But when most of the water has boiled away, the temperature can now rise dramatically, passing through various stages (page 436) and eventually rising to the temperature of melted sugar (320°F.) when all the water is gone.

Concentration can also be measured by density using a saccharometer or Baumé sugar weight-scale. A Baumé scale is graduated from 0 to 44° and corresponds in a direct relationship to the degrees Fahrenheit or Centigrade. The degree of evaporation can also be measured by consistency by dropping a small amount of the syrup into ice water.

Supersaturated solutions are highly unstable and recrystallization can occur from agitation or even just by standing unless the solution was properly heated in the first place. The use of an "interfering agent" such as invert sugar (a little more than one-fourth the weight of the granulated sugar), butter, cream of tartar, or citric acid helps keep the solution stable by interfering with the crystalline structure formation. This is useful when the solution will be used in a way that will involve repeatedly dipping into it, such as for making spun sugar.

As melted sugar reaches higher temperatures, many chemical changes begin to occur. The sugar cannot start to caramelize until all the water is evaporated. As it starts to caramelize, its sweetening power decreases. At this point, when all the water has evaporated, stirring will not cause the sugar to crystallize. The addition of a significant amount of an ingredient, such as nuts, can lower the temperature considerably and this will cause crystallization to occur instantly if no interfering agent was used.

Caramel is extremely difficult to make in humid weather because sugar is highly hygroscopic (attracts water). The moisture in the air will make the caramel sticky.

When sugar syrup has been prepared in advance, it is sometimes necessary to check the exact quantity of sugar and water it contains. It is important to know that the Baumé reading in a cold solution measures slightly higher than the same solution when hot.

Another variant that affects density reading is altitude. Because water boils at a lower temperature as altitude increases (there is less air pressure weighing on top of the water to prevent it from changing from liquid into vapor), there will be a different temperature for the same concentration of sugar syrup at different altitudes. For each increase of 500 feet in elevation, syrup should be cooked to a temperature 1°F. lower than the temperature called for at sea level. If readings are taken in Celsius, for each 900 feet of elevation cook the syrup to a temperature 1°C. lower than called for at sea level. These adjustments should be made up to 320°F., the melting point of sugar. Altitude does not change this.

TEMPERATURES AND TESTS FOR SUGAR SYRUP

215°F.   *Thread:* The liquid sugar may be pulled into brittle threads between the fingers. This is used for candy, fruit liqueur making, and some icings.

220 to 222°F.   *Pearl:* The thread formed by pulling the liquid sugar may be stretched. When a cool metal spoon is dipped into the syrup and then raised, the syrup runs off in drops which merge to form a sheet. This is used for the above and also for jelly.

220 to 234°F.   *Blow or Soufflé:* The bubbles in the boiling sugar resemble snowflakes. The syrup spins a 2-inch thread when dropped from a spoon. This is used for making sugar candy and syrup.

234 to 240°F.   *Soft ball:* Syrup dropped into ice water may be formed into a ball which flattens on removal from the water. This is used for fondant, fudge, peppermint creams, and classic buttercream.

244 to 248°F.   *Firm ball:* Syrup dropped into ice water may be formed into a firm ball which does not flatten on removal from the water. This is used for caramels, nougats, and soft toffees.

250 to 266°F.   *Hard ball:* Syrup dropped into ice water may be formed into a hard ball which holds its shape on removal but is still plastic. This is used for toffee, divinity, marshmallows, and popcorn balls.

270 to 290°F.   *Soft crack:* Syrup dropped into ice water separates into threads which are hard but not brittle. This is used for butterscotch and taffy.

300 to 310°F.   *Hard crack:* Syrup dropped into ice water separates into hard, brittle threads. This is used for brittle and for glacéed fruits.

320°F.   *Clear liquid:* The sugar liquefies. This is used for making barley sugar (a candy).

338°F.   *Brown liquid:* The liquefied sugar turns brown. This is used for light caramel.

356°F.   *Medium brown liquid:* The liquefied sugar darkens. This is used for praline, spun sugar, caramel cages, and nougatine.

374°F.   *Dark brown liquid:* The liquefied sugar darkens further. This is used as a coloring agent for sauces.

410°F.   *Black Jack:* The liquefied sugar turns black and then decomposes.

VANILLA: When Marcel Akselrod sent me a sample vanilla bean, I knew when it had arrived because, when I went to pick up my mail, the entire letter box was perfumed with the heavenly smell of Tahitian vanilla. The bean was fatter and more moist than any I had ever seen. Vanilla beans vary enormously in quality. The best beans come from Tahiti, Madagascar, and Mexico. The Tahitian beans are larger than the others and all three are about twice the size and more highly perfumed than other beans. This makes it difficult to give equivalencies for distilled vanilla (extract), which also varies enormously in concentration (referred to commercially as "folds"). The Tahitian beans are so aromatic, I use one-half a bean in a recipe specifying one bean.

Sometimes you will notice a white substance coating the vanilla beans. This is not mold; it is flavorful vanilla crystals.

Vanilla accentuates other flavors. The bean adds a subtle depth of flavor and unique sweet quality. The extract, though easier to use, lacks that sweet roundness and in excess will even impart a bitter edge.

My favorite vanilla extract is produced by Méro and comes from Grasse, the perfume region of France. It is available from La Cuisine (page 445). I like to transfer it to a plastic squeeze-bottle dispenser with a pointed tip and add a Tahitian vanilla bean. (This is a great use for used vanilla beans, which still have lots of flavor even after the seeds have been removed. Be sure to rinse the bean if it has been used to flavor another liquid and dry it in a low oven or with the heat of the oven's pilot light.)

The recipes in this book which call for vanilla extract refer to the supermarket variety for purposes of standardization. When I use Méro vanilla extract, I use a little less than one-half the amount specified in these recipes.

My next choice after Méro vanilla is Nielsen-Massey vanilla, which is carried by many specialty stores such as Dean & DeLuca (page 445) and Williams-Sonoma (page 445). Recently, Nielsen-Massey has introduced an excellent Tahitian vanilla extract.

YEAST: I prefer using fresh yeast to dry, just on general principle. I like its lively reaction and forthright, earthy smell. But if the yeast isn't absolutely fresh, the final baked product will have a slightly sour taste. The best way to determine freshness is by smell, as the color may not have changed even when slightly past its prime. Fresh yeast freezes indefinitely, but certain precautions must be taken in defrosting. Yeast is a live organism and must be "awakened" gradually from the frozen state. To defrost, place in the refrigerator for a minimum of 48 hours. Since a few yeast cells will have been destroyed in the process, use ¼ more than specified in the recipe.

It's fine to use dry yeast (see substitutions, page 443), but the quick- or rapid-rise yeasts need a different procedure. For one thing, they cannot be proofed. In the 10 minutes of proofing time, they will have thoroughly exhausted all their energy and leavening power.

ZEST: Zest refers to the colored portion of the citrus peel. The white portion, or pith, should be avoided as it is quite bitter. The fruit is easier to zest before squeezing.

A zester is the ideal piece of equipment to remove only the outer peel (see page 458). The fine strips should then be chopped with a knife or food processor. I like to add some of the sugar from the recipe and process it with the zest. This keeps the zest from clumping and disperses it more evenly when added to the larger mixture. A vegetable peeler will also work to remove wider strips which can then be cut or chopped fine.

WEIGHTS The weight of all ingredients for recipes in this book is given in both the metric and avoirdupoir systems. The grams have been rounded off to the nearest whole number without decimal points (except for leavening which needs to be more precise), the ounces to the nearest quarter ounce. Either system works, but do not expect the mathematics to correlate exactly.

There is no doubt about it; weighing is faster, easier, and more accurate than measuring. Most bakers, including myself, prefer the metric system for its precision in small quantities. There isn't any adjustment necessary if you have a metric scale and the recipe gives metric amounts! If you do not have a scale with a digital readout, round off the grams to the nearest convenient number. The amount will still be quite accurate as, after all, one gram is only about one twenty-eighth of an ounce.

The way I have presented the volume measures is the way in which I would measure them. Instead of writing 6 tablespoons sugar, I express it as ¼ cup + 2 tablespoons because that is the more convenient approach. Also, the fewer measures used, the less room for error.

I am offering a chart of weights for your convenience in converting other recipes. The weights were determined by innumerable trials over a three-year period at seven stories above sea level with a Mettler scale (which is used in scientific laboratories). I spent my entire first paycheck as a chocolate consultant on this scale, with no regrets. People ask me the point in having such accurate equipment when most people will not. My feeling is that if I am to set the standard, I want it to be as close to the absolute as possible. That way, when others deviate, it will still work because there is always a range of acceptable error.

For those who measure instead of weigh, the *dip and sweep* method of measuring refers to dipping the measuring cup into a bin containing the ingredient and sweeping off the excess with a long, flat spatula or knife.

Lightly spooned into cup refers to spooning the ingredient into the cup and then sweeping off the excess with a long, flat spatula or blade. This method yields less of the ingredient than the dip and sweep method.

Sifted means that the ingredient is sifted into a cup that is sitting on a counter. The cup is never touched or (perish the thought) shaken. Only the handle is held when the excess is swept off with a spatula or knife.

Dry ingredients should be measured in a cup designed for solids. I prefer the Foley stainless-steel set of measuring cups and spoons. The 2-tablespoon cup, however, measures less than it should. Other measuring cups may vary in size and are generally less reliable.

Liquid ingredients, including honey and other syrups, should be measured in a liquid measure with a spout. There is a difference in volume between liquid and solid measuring cups. The most accurate liquid measure at the present time is made by Oven Basics. I happened to find it when I was teaching in Florida and to my delight, 1 cup of water weighed exactly 8.337 ounces/236.35 grams, which is the dictionary definition of an 8-ounce cup of water. This is not true of many other brands. Some are off by quite a bit, and the marks are not level.

FOOD SUBSTANCE	METHOD OF MEASURE	WEIGHT OF I CUP	
		ounces	*grams*
FATS butter		8	227
clarified butter (*beurre noisette*)		6.8	195
cocoa butter		9	256
vegetable shortening		6.75	191
mineral oil		6.86	196
safflower oil		7.5	215
walnut oil		7.5	215
FLOURS			
cake	sifted lightly spooned dip and sweep	3.5 4 4.5	100 114 130
all-purpose	sifted lightly spooned dip and sweep	4 4.25 5	114 121 145
bread	sifted lightly spooned dip and sweep	4.25 4.5 5.5	121 130 157
buckwheat	lightly spooned dip and sweep	4 4.5	115 125
whole wheat	sifted	4.5	125

FOOD SUBSTANCE	METHOD OF MEASURE	WEIGHT OF 1 CUP	
		ounces	grams
chestnut	sifted	3.8	109
cornstarch	lightly spooned or sifted	4.2	120
Dutch-processed cocoa	sifted lightly spooned dip and sweep	2.6 3.25 3.33	75 92 95
nonalkalized cocoa such as Hershey's: same as Dutch-processed except for LIQUIDS	lightly spooned	2.9	82
heavy cream		8.12	232
milk, buttermilk, sour cream, and half and half		8.5	242
molasses		11.25	322
corn syrup		11.5	328
glucose		11.75	336
honey		11.75	336
refiner's syrup		12	340
apple jelly		10.75	308
water		8.337	236
lemon juice, strained		8.75	250
orange juice, strained		8.5	242
amaretto		8.75	250
Barack Palinka (apricot eau-de-vie)		7.7	222
Chambord (black raspberry liqueur)		9.1	260
Cherry Kijafa (cherry wine)		8.9	255
Cognac		7.9	225
Cointreau		8.5	244
Kahlúa (coffee liqueur)		9.6	267
kirsch (cherry eau-de-vie)		7.8	224
light rum		7.8	224

FOOD SUBSTANCE	METHOD OF MEASURE	WEIGHT OF 1 CUP	
		ounces	*grams*
Mandarine Napoléon		8.5	243
Myers's Rum (dark rum)		7.7	220
Pistasha		7	200
Vodka		8	230
William's pear liqueur or eau-de-vie		7.7	222
NUTS			
almonds	slivered	4.2	120
	sliced or coarsely chopped	3	85
	finely ground	3.75	107
	powder fine	3.12	89
walnuts, pecans, and hazelnuts	coarsely chopped	4	114
	whole	5	142
pistachios	whole	5.32	152
almond paste		10	284
hazelnut praline paste		10.88	308
CHESTNUT			
Purée de Marrons (unsweetened)		8.8	252
homemade Purée de Marrons (unsweetened)		8.5	244
Carma Purée de Marrons (25 to 30 percent sugar)		9.5	272
SUGAR			
granulated and superfine	dip and sweep	7	200
powdered	lightly spooned	4	115
light brown	packed	7.66	217
dark brown	packed	8.4	239

FOOD SUBSTANCE	QUANTITY	WEIGHT	
		ounces	*grams*
EGGS			
in shell	1 large egg	2	56.7

FOOD SUBSTANCE	QUANTITY	WEIGHT	
		ounces	*grams*
without shells (3 tablespoons + ½ teaspoon)	1 large egg	1.75	50
2 tablespoons	1 large egg white	1.05	30
3½ teaspoons	1 large egg yolk	0.65	18.6
OTHER			
baking powder	1 teaspoon		4.9
baking soda	1 teaspoon		5
cream of tartar	1 teaspoon		3.1
gelatin	1 teaspoon		3.1
glycerine	1 teaspoon		6
poppy seeds	¼ cup	1.25	36
salt	1 teaspoon		6.7
vanilla or almond extract	1 teaspoon		4
grated citrus zest	1 teaspoon		2

APPROXIMATE EQUIVALENCIES AND SUBSTITUTIONS

Making one thing into another is never 100 percent, but in a pinch it's nice to know how to come close to the original.

Most substitution charts tell you how to sour milk with vinegar to replace buttermilk. While the acidity level seems the same, the sour flavor is nowhere near the rich, full tanginess of buttermilk. Of course, substituting an item such as granulated sugar and molasses for brown sugar is another story, because adding molasses to granulated sugar is the way brown sugar is made in the industry as well.

FOR	SUBSTITUTE
glucose	Bring 1 cup light corn syrup to a full boil and remove from the heat. Cool completely and stir in ½ cup unheated corn syrup.
1 pound unsalted butter	1 pound lightly salted butter but remove 1 teaspoon salt from the recipe
1 cup milk	1 cup minus 1 tablespoon half and half, remove 1 tablespoon butter from the recipe, and add 2 tablespoons water
1 cup sifted cake flour	¾ cup sifted, *bleached* all-purpose flour plus 2 tablespoons cornstarch (this is 15% cornstarch)
1 cup light brown sugar	1 cup granulated sugar plus ¼ cup unsulfured light molasses
1 cup dark brown sugar	1 cup granulated sugar plus ½ cup unsulfured light molasses
0.25-ounce package (2¼ teaspoons) active dry yeast	1 packed tablespoon (0.75 ounce) compressed fresh yeast
1 packed tablespoon (.75 ounce) compressed fresh yeast	1 packed tablespoon plus 1 packed teaspoon (1 ounce) thawed frozen compressed fresh yeast

NOTE: The yeast equivalency is approximate and works well. If you have a scale accurate for small amounts, you may want the more precise conversion:

1 package active dry yeast = 2¼ teaspoons = .25 ounce = 7 grams

1 package compressed fresh yeast = .6 ounce = 17 grams

If recipe calls for dry yeast, × 2.42 is amount of fresh needed.

If recipe calls for fresh yeast, × .41 is amount of dry yeast needed.

Using volume, you need 1.4 times the volume of packed fresh yeast to replace dry.

CHOCOLATE

Exchanging one type of semisweet or bittersweet chocolate for another will work but will often give surprisingly different flavor results. Even if the percentages of cocoa solids, cocoa butter, and sugar are the same, the type of bean and degree of roasting is responsible for significant variations. If may also result in different texture. The best way to determine which bittersweet or semisweet chocolate to use is to taste it.

Chocolatiers are given the exact contents of the chocolate they use by the manufacturers. For the consumer to get this information is next to impossible. For me, it took two trips to Switzerland. I am greatly indebted to Dr. Buser and Markus Gerber of Tobler and Rüdi Sprüngli of Lindt for entrusting me with this valuable information. (I flew home from Switzerland feeling as though I had the crown jewels tucked into my notebook.)

The main factor to consider in exchanging bittersweet or semisweet chocolate is the sugar content, so the following is a list of approximate sugar content for 1 ounce chocolate.

Lindt Courante: 2 teaspoons sugar
Tobler extra bittersweet: 2¾ teaspoons sugar
Tobler Tradition, Lindt Excellence: 3¼ teaspoons sugar
Tobler Bittersweet, Lindt Surfin, and most American semisweet chocolate: 3½ teaspoons sugar

I find the quality of bitter (unsweetened) chocolate available to the consumer in this country lacking, so I always substitute a fine-quality bittersweet or semisweet. If you have a favorite chocolate recipe calling for bitter (unsweetened) chocolate and wish to improve the flavor: For every ounce of bitter chocolate called for, substitute 2 ounces bittersweet or semisweet. For every 2 ounces of bittersweet or semisweet used, remove 2 tablespoons sugar and ⅔ teaspoon butter from the recipe.

Cocoa offers a richer, stronger chocolate flavor to cakes than does chocolate. Fewer cocoa solids than contained in the chocolate are necessary to achieve the same flavor intensity (see Understanding Cakes, page 474), but it is necessary to dissolve the cocoa in liquid to unlock the full flavor.

To convert a cake recipe using bittersweet or semisweet chocolate to a more chocolaty cocoa cake: For every ounce of bittersweet or semisweet chocolate, substitute 1 tablespoon plus 1¾ teaspoons (.33 ounce/9.5 grams) cocoa, 1 tablespoon plus ½ teaspoon sugar (.5 ounce/14.5 grams), 1½ teaspoons unsalted butter (.25 ounce/7 grams). For full flavor, be sure to dissolve the cocoa in at least ¼ cup liquid in the recipe.

To convert a cake recipe using unsweetened chocolate to a more chocolaty cake: For every ounce of bitter or unsweetened chocolate, substitute 3 tablespoons cocoa plus 1 tablespoon cocoa butter or unsalted butter. For full flavor, be sure to dissolve the cocoa in at least 2 tablespoons liquid in recipe.

Other useful chocolate information: To approximate 1 ounce couverture when you need a chocolate that will coat thinly, use 1 ounce fine-quality bittersweet or semisweet chocolate plus ½ teaspoon (.19 ounce/5.4 grams) cocoa butter.

Alberto-Culver Company (Baker's Joy): 2525 Armitage Avenue, Melrose Park, Illinois 60160. 312/450-3000

Albert Uster Imports Inc.: 9211 Gaither Road, Gaithersburg, Maryland 20877. 800/231-8154

Beatrice Dairy Products, Inc. (Keller's Butter): Subsidiary of Beatrice U.S. Food Corp., Harleysville, Pennsylvania 19438. 215/256-8871

Chocolate Gallery: 135 West 50th Street, New York, New York 10020. 212/582-3510

Dean & DeLuca: 121 Prince Street, New York, New York 10012. 212/431-1691; outside New York: 800/227-7714, Monday–Friday, 9 A.M.–5 P.M.

Gourmand: 636 South Pickett Street, Alexandria, Virginia 23304. 703/461-0600

Hauser Chocolatier, Inc.: 18 Taylor Avenue, Bethel, Connecticut 06801. 203/794-1861

Hazy Grove Nuts (hazelnuts or filberts): P.O. Box 25753, Portland, Oregon 97225. 503/244-0593.

International Leisure Activities (Nestlé's chocolate): 107 Tremont City Road, Springfield, Ohio 45503. 513/399-0783

Katagiri and Company, Inc.: 224 East 59th Street, New York, New York 10022. 212/755-3566

Keenan Farms, Inc. (unsalted pistachio nuts): P.O. Box 248, Avenal, California 93204. 209/386-9516

La Cuisine: 323 Cameron Street, Alexandria, Virginia 22314. 800/521-1176

Maid of Scandinavia: 32–44 Raleigh Avenue, Minneapolis, Minnesota 55416. 800/328-6722

Maison Glass: 52 East 58th Street, New York, New York 10022. 212/755-3316

Marcel Akselrod: 530 West 25th Street, New York, New York 10001. 212/675-7777

Nielsen Massey Vanillas: 28392 North Ballard Drive, Lake Forest, Illinois 60045. 312/362-2207

Paprikas Weiss Importer: 1546 Second Avenue, New York, New York 10028. 212/288-6003

Swan's Down Cake Flour: Luzianne Blue Plate Foods, 640 Magazine Street, New Orleans, Louisiana 70130. 800/692-7895, Monday–Friday, 9 A.M.–2:30 P.M.

Taam-Tov Food, Inc.: 188 28th Street, Brooklyn, New York, 11232. 718/788-8880

Wilton Enterprises: 22440 West 75th Street, Woodridge, Illinois 60517. 312/963-7100

MAJOR
INGREDIENT
DISTRIBUTORS
AND
MANUFACTURERS

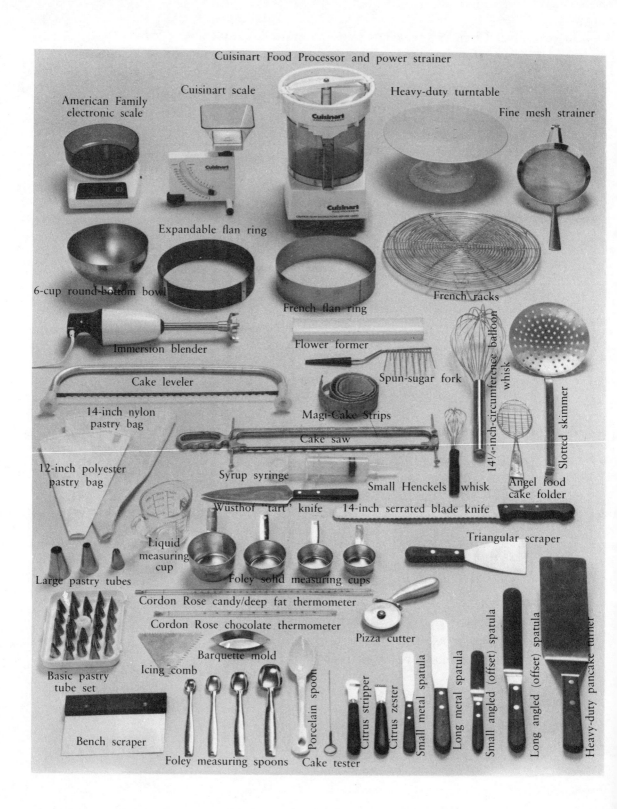

Cuisinart Food Processor and power strainer

American Family electronic scale

Cuisinart scale

Heavy-duty turntable

Fine mesh strainer

Expandable flan ring

6-cup round-bottom bowl

French flan ring

French racks

Immersion blender

Flower former

Spun-sugar fork

14¼-inch-circumference balloon whisk

Cake leveler

14-inch nylon pastry bag

Magi-Cake Strips

Slotted skimmer

Cake saw

12-inch polyester pastry bag

Syrup syringe

Small Henckels whisk

Angel food cake folder

Wusthof "tart" knife

14-inch serrated blade knife

Liquid measuring cup

Triangular scraper

Large pastry tubes

Foley solid measuring cups

Cordon Rose candy/deep fat thermometer

Cordon Rose chocolate thermometer

Pizza cutter

Basic pastry tube set

Icing comb

Barquette mold

Citrus stripper

Citrus zester

Small metal spatula

Long metal spatula

Small angled (offset) spatula

Long angled (offset) spatula

Heavy-duty pancake turner

Bench scraper

Porcelain spoon

Foley measuring spoons

Cake tester

17-inch by 12-inch sheet cake pan

Set of 2-inch-high cake pans

Magic Line 2-inch-high rectangular pans

10-inch tube pan

Heating core

12-cup Bundt pan

Bundt-style muffin pans

6-cup fluted tube pan

9-cup Kugelhupf pan

3-inch-high loose-bottom pan

9-inch brioche pan

5-cup savarin ring mold

Checkerboard pan set

9-inch heart pan

4-cup loaf pan

9¼-inch oval pan

9-inch by 2-inch springform pan

3½-cup Turk's-head pan

Equipment

*M*any people assume that fine cake baking requires not only a wealth of technical knowledge but also a labyrinth of specialized equipment. In reality, apart from basics such as mixing bowls, rubber scrapers or spatulas, and noncorrodible saucepans, the equipment for successful baking can be boiled down to ten items. Of course there are many delightful gadgets designed to make work more efficient, but the following items are indispensable:

OVEN   Accurate oven temperature is extremely important for cake baking. As ovens can lose their calibration, they should be checked every few months. Most oven thermometers are quite inaccurate, so I usually use the Cordon Rose sugar syrup thermometer, wiring it to the rack to hold it in position. The thermostat in most ovens fluctuates at least 10°F. above and below ideal temperature. The new Wolf commercial ranges, however, have minimal fluctuation. Another test for oven temperature is to make All-Occasion Downy Layer Cake (page 39). If it takes longer than the recommended time, you know that your oven is too low at the setting used.

The ideal oven for cake baking is one which has little distance from top to bottom and a rotating turntable. Home models which come closest to this ideal are countertop convection/microwave models. The turntable is actually designed for the microwave option, but it happens to be ideal for even baking as well. I do not like commercial convection ovens because the fans are too powerful for fragile items. (I'll always remember the class with White House pastry chef Roland Messnier when his *langue du chat* butterflies actually flew off the baking parchment and crashed into the gusty fan of the Blodgett convection oven!)

Countertop models with fans blowing directly down on the cake are equally undesirable.

Zephyr (source 27) produces a beautifully engineered device (resembling a UFO) that will convert most electric ovens to convection.

Although manufacturers say to lower the temperature 25°F. when using countertop convection ovens, I find that using the same temperature as a normal oven results in the same baking time.

ELECTRIC MIXER   An electric hand-held mixer can be used for any cake or buttercream but is not powerful enough to handle a very stiff mixture such as royal icing or fondant. It also does not do quite as good a job as a large heavy-duty mixer in aerating *génoise* and other foam cakes. My favorite electric hand mixer, more powerful than most, is manufactured by Krups. With an optional attachment it doubles as an immersion blender (page 457).

People who do a lot of baking sooner or later end up with a heavy-duty stand mixer. The two best mixers of this sort are the KitchenAid K5 series and the Kenwood Major from England, currently distributed under the name General Slicing (sources 10 and 19). They are both excellent mixers. The Kenwood has a larger capacity (7 quarts compared to 5 quarts) but works well with small amounts. It also has a stronger motor with a device which protects it from burning out if overheated. The conical shape of the bowl and the ability to adjust the beaters to come as close as possible to the bottom make for thorough and even mixing. The K5 beater cannot be adjusted, but the whisk beater will reach the bottom of the bowl if it is not fully engaged. Push it on its holder but do not lock it into position. Lower the beater to hold it in place. It will just reach the bottom of bowl. (Thank you, Carole Walter.)

The only problem with the Kenwood mixer is that the motor is so loud I use ear plugs to preserve my hearing.

Heavy-duty mixers offer the choice of a flat "spade" beater and a whisk beater. The flat beater is intended for general mixing and the whisk beater to beat as much air as possible into the mixture, such as when beating egg whites, or sponge-type cakes.

I find pouring shields more cumbersome than helpful. When adding flour or powdered sugar, which tends to fly out of the bowl, I drape a large piece of plastic wrap over the top of the mixer, including the top of the bowl. Any powdery substance which leaps up does not cling to the plastic as it would to a cloth towel, and the plastic enables you to see what is happening to the mixture.

It is useful to have a second bowl and even a second whisk beater as many cake and buttercream recipes are made in two parts.

The K5 can handle up to 2 cups egg whites (16 large whites), a 7-egg *génoise,* an 8-egg butter cake, or any mixture that will not exceed 4 quarts. The Kenwood can handle any mixture that will not exceed 6 quarts.

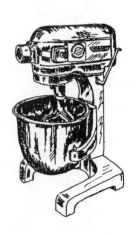

For larger-scale baking the 20-quart Hobart is an ideal size. It can also be used with a 10-quart bowl. These two bowls can handle any recipe in the master cake section of this book in one batch. I chose the model Hobart makes for hospitals, which is stainless steel with stainless steel beaters. The salesman tried to talk me out of it because it was so much more expensive than the enameled steel model, but I explained to him it was like investing in art—it is as beautiful to me as a piece of sculpture.

It is sometimes difficult to find a repair service for a mixer, especially for the Kenwood, so I am listing a repair service licensed to repair both the Kenwood and the KitchenAid (source 1).

CAKE PANS　The cake pans used most in this book are 9 inches by 1½ inches because they are the most readily available. Aluminum pans with a dull finish are ideal and straight sides are preferable as cakes baked in straight-sided pans are easier to frost. Avoid shiny pans, black pans, or glass pans (see Baking and Storing Cakes, page 20).

RACKS　Any rack can be used to allow air circulation for quick cooling of a cake. The best racks I have found are from France (sources 6 and 13). The wire is closer together, offering more support. To prevent cakes from sticking to the racks, I occasionally spray them with nonstick vegetable spray. I never use soap on the racks, just a spray of water or a wet brush when necessary to remove crumbs.

METAL SPATULAS　A small metal spatula with a narrow 4-inch blade and a wooden handle is the best implement for frosting a cake. It is also helpful to have one with a longer blade for smoothing the top (sources 14, 16, and 24).

LIQUID MEASURES　The most accurate and well-marked heatproof measuring cups I have found are made by Oven Basics. When shopping for measuring cups, look for ones with level markings. A cup of water read below the meniscus (the curved upper surface of the water) should be close to 8 ounces. In addition to measuring liquids, these cups are ideal for pouring hot sugar syrup into an egg mixture. They also help to maintain the temperature of the syrup which keeps it fluid enough to pour. The handles remain cool to the touch and the spouts control the way the liquid pours. If heated first with boiling water, the cup will be even more effective in retaining heat.

SOLID MEASURES　Foley stainless-steel cups are the most attractive and most accurate. Tupperware's cups are also excellent and include a practical ⅔ cup and ¾ cup. Solid measures must have unbroken, smooth rims, making it possible to level off any excess.

Foley stainless-steel measuring spoons and Tupperware heavy-duty plastic are my favorites. I especially like the Tupperware spoons because they include unusual sizes such as ⅛ teaspoon, 4 teaspoons, and ½ tablespoon. I have found other brands of measuring spoons to be somewhat smaller than these two brands.

MEASURING SPOONS

This item can sieve fruit purees with seeds, clarify butter, and sift flour. The stainless-steel extra-fine mesh strainers from Italy are my favorite (available in gourmet kitchen shops).

FINE STRAINER

This is the item I miss most when I teach in other places. It is difficult to take with me because planes do not allow passengers to board with knives in their hand luggage (and I never trust vital equipment to the baggage compartment). In order to level a cake or slice it horizontally, it is essential to have a serrated blade longer than the diameter of the cake. This is a difficult knife to find but fortunately Albert Uster Imports (source 4) carries an excellent 14-inch blade version called "wavy edge slicer 14-inch round tip." The serrated blade also can be used to make wavy lines on an iced cake's surface (page 358).

LONG SERRATED KNIFE

NICE TO HAVE

SCALE: An accurate scale makes baking much faster and more reliable. My favorite noncommercial battery-operated model, which travels with me when I teach, is the American Family Electronic Scale (model 3500 Tanita, page 465, source 3). My favorite non-electric scale is produced by Cuisinarts. It weighs only up to 10 ounces/300 grams but is designed on the pendulum principle rather than spring and thus is accurate to plus or minus 2 grams. At home I use the Mettler PE 16 electronic scale, a top-quality, very expensive laboratory scale from Switzerland, accurate to within .2 gram. It weighs up to 35 pounds/16,000 grams, which makes it convenient for large-scale baking such as wedding cakes (source 15). All three scales can be used to weigh in avoirdupoir or metric systems.

THERMOMETERS: Thermometers are used in cooking when precise temperatures must be obtained, as when working with chocolate, sugar syrups, and yeast. Even a few degrees of inaccuracy are enough to put chocolate out of temper so that it won't set correctly, produce Italian meringue that will never thicken, or kill yeast so that brioche won't rise. For a thermometer to be reliable, it must be accurate to within 1°. I used to assume that a thermometer was an absolute measure of temperature. Then I discovered that the instrument, used to measure variables, could itself be a

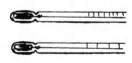

variable by as much as 20°F.! And worse yet, it may vary in its inaccuracy at different degrees of its range. Driven by a personal need for reliable thermometers, I decided to have them manufactured to my own criteria.

Once having made the commitment to produce highly accurate thermometers for the food industry, I approached a manufacturer specializing in laboratory thermometers, where precision is an imperative. The thermometers they produce are made to industrial specifications and are calibrated to standards traceable to the National Bureau of Standards in Washington, D.C.

The Cordon Rose chocolate thermometer has a range of 40°F. to 130°F. in widely spaced 1-degree increments (sources 8, 11, 14, and 18).

The Cordon Rose candy/deep fat thermometer has a range of 20°F. to 500°F. in 2-degree increments (sources 8, 14, and 18).

Two key points in producing an accurate thermometer: It must be glass with the calibration (scale) etched directly on it, and it must be mercury if it has a high range. Mercury exceeds the accuracy of any other material including that used for electronics. It is the only substance which will continuously repeat the identical reading of a given temperature.

Problems with other materials:

1. Thermometers with metal stems and dials are made using two different kinds of metal coils which expand and contract at different rates. When one metal expands more than the other, the dial turns. After continued use, the coils tend to wear, decreasing accuracy.

2. Thermometers with calibration or degree reading on a wooden or metal plaque attached to the glass thermometer and not directly on it may not be lined up to precisely the right point.

3. Digital thermometers are battery-operated. As the battery wears, accuracy decreases.

But no matter how accurate the thermometer, or any other instrument of measure, it is still prone to human error. It becomes necessary to understand how to use and care for a thermometer— a simple matter but one that must be learned.

How to read a thermometer: Since many people hold a thermometer with the left hand while stirring with the right, I designed the Cordon Rose thermometers with two opposing scales so that they can be read left- or right-handed.

A thermometer should be read at eye level, slanted slightly to one side. The immersion level, indicated by an etched ring toward the base, is the point at which a thermometer is calibrated to read most accurately. Thermometers should be immersed up to this level when read, although one that is well made will still read with a fair degree of accuracy despite the degree of immersion. If working with a small amount of liquid, tilt the pan slightly to increase the depth of the liquid when reading the thermometer.

The highest accuracy of a thermometer is not at either extreme of its scale.

How to care for a thermometer: It is best to hang a thermometer out of harm's way as rattling around in a drawer may cause mercury separation.

This can also occur if the thermometer was handled roughly during shipping or if it has been dropped. To reunite mercury into one solid column, the mercury must either descend to its lowest point or rise to its highest. If the highest temperature is below the boiling point, this can be done by slowly immersing the bulb in boiling water and removing it as soon as the mercury is reunited. If the scale is higher but not above 450°F., it can be placed in an oven set at a temperature slightly above its highest point. Never place the bulb of the thermometer directly over an open flame.

To prevent breakage, avoid extremes in temperature. When removing the thermometer from a hot liquid, for example, do not place it on a cold drain board. Also, do not allow the thermometer to rest on a pan's bottom, because when it lies on its side the uneven heat distribution could cause it to crack. Clips to attach thermometers to the side of a pan are prone to slipping because they do not conform to a universal pan size or shape. I prefer to hold the thermometer, which is possible as the glass does not conduct the heat.

WHISKS: I find two sizes of whisks particularly useful for baking: a small one which will reach into the corners of a saucepan or bowl and an enormous balloon whisk for folding one mixture into another in place of a spatula. My large whisk measures 14¼ inches in circumference (source 8).

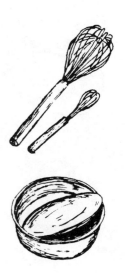

CAKE PANS: In addition to the standard 9-inch by 1½-inch pans, there are several other sizes and shapes required for the recipes in this book. Two of my favorite manufacturers of sturdy straight-sided 2-inch-high cake pans are Chicago Metallic (source 19) and Magic Line (source 16).

The Magic Line includes 2-inch and 3-inch-high loose-bottom pans, which I prefer to springforms for their heavier weight. (I like to use the removable bottom discs to transfer cake layers.) The line also includes sturdy square and rectangular pans with perfectly squared corners and a hard to find 6-inch (4-cup) tube pan with a removable bottom. This size is perfect for one-fourth the recipe used in the standard 10-inch (16-cup) tube pan.

The following is a list of harder to find pans and their sources:
2-inch-high wedding cake pans from 6 to 18 inches: Sources 14, 16 and 18 (Maid of Scandinavia has promised to carry all sizes including odd numbers such as 13 and 15).

17-inch by 12-inch sheet cake pan: My favorite is by Wearever (source 18) or Magic Line (source 16) because it is heavy enough not to warp.

Bundt, Baby Bundt, Bundt-lette and Bundt-style muffin pans: Cast aluminum is the best but not available for the muffin pans (source 14).

9-inch wide by 2-inch-high Wilton heart-shaped pan: Sources 14, 18, and 24.

9¼-inch by 6⅝-inch Wilton oval cake pan: Sources 14 and 24.

Heating core: Parrish (source 16) makes a "heating core" which can be placed in the center of any cake pan, turning it into a tube pan. A 9-inch (10-cup) tube pan with a removable bottom is ideal for baking half-size chiffon and angel food cakes but is very difficult to find. A 9-inch springform with a heating core works perfectly!

3½-cup Turk's head pan: Perfect for fruitcake (source 21).
2-inch-high expandable flan ring: I enjoy using flan rings to mold cakes, but the standard French flan rings do not conform to the American cardboard rounds used for the base of the cake. A French

black steel expandable flan ring, however, adjusts to fit cake rounds from 7 to 14 inches in diameter (source 13).

9-inch-wide by 3-inch-high brioche pan: Sources 8, 13, and 14.

Making your own pan: If you ever need a pan of a certain size and cannot order it in time, it is possible to make a pan from foil. I learned this technique when I worked at Reynolds Aluminum Company many years ago. An advantage to a foil pan is that the sides can be taken apart after baking, making it function as a springform.

To make a foil pan: Wrap a cardboard cake round with a layer of foil, securing it on the bottom with tape. Multiply the diameter by 4 (this will be the circumference) and tear off a length of heavy-duty foil to correspond. Fold this foil in half lengthwise and in half again to make a band 4½ inches wide. If the pan only needs to be 2 inches high, fold in half one more time. Cut short ½-inch snips on a long side at 1-inch intervals. Place the foil-covered circle on a can or other object to elevate it. Fold the foil band around it, attaching it by bending the snipped ends flat against the bottom of the circle. Attach with tape. Allow the band to overlap and secure with tape. Stand the pan upright and place it on a baking sheet for extra support.

Round-bottom bowl: A perfectly round-bottom bowl for molded charlottes is next to impossible to find. Dean & DeLuca (source 8) carries a magnificently designed stainless-steel model from Germany in the useful 6-cup and other sizes. (Corning makes a 6-cup glass bowl with a relatively small flat area at the bottom.)

VOLUME OF STANDARD PAN SIZES

5 inches x 2 inches	2⅔ cups
6 inches x 2 inches	3¾ cups
7 inches x 2 inches	5¼ cups
8 inches x 2 inches	7 cups
9 inches x 2 inches	8⅔ cups
10 inches x 2 inches	10¾ cups
11 inches x 2 inches	13 cups
12 inches x 2 inches	15½ cups
13 inches x 2 inches	18 cups
14 inches x 2 inches	21 cups
15 inches x 2 inches	24 cups
16 inches x 2 inches	27½ cups
17 inches x 2 inches	31⅓ cups
18 inches x 2 inches	34¾ cups
13 inches x 9 inches x 2 inches	15 cups
18 inches x 12 inches x 2 inches	29 cups

A round cake pan is ¾ the volume of a square cake pan of the same size. So to determine the volume of a square cake pan, multiply the volume of a round cake pan of the same diameter by 1.33.

Loaf pans (measured from the top):

8 inches x 4 inches x 2½ inches	4 cups
8½ inches x 4½ inches x 2½ inches	6 cups
9 inches x 5 inches x 3 inches	8 cups

Heart-shape pan:

| (9 inches at its widest point, 8 inches from center to point, 2 inches high) | 8 cups |

Oval pan (9¼ inches x 6⅝ inches)	6 cups
Angel cake tube pan (6 inches x 3 inches)	4 cups
Angel cake tube pan (9 inches x 3 inches)	10 cups
Angel cake tube pan (10 inches x 4 inches)	16 cups

To determine the volume of an odd-shaped pan, use a liquid measure to pour water into the pan until it reaches the brim.

Rule of thumb for odd-size pans: For Génoise Classique (page 120), use half the number of eggs as the cup capacity of the pan. For butter cake, use one quarter as many eggs as the cup capacity. Example: An 8-cup capacity pan uses a 4-egg formula for Génoise Classique and a 2-egg formula for a butter cake (1 whole egg = 2 yolks or 1½ whites.)

MAGI-CAKE STRIPS: These metallic fabric strips (page 20) help to produce a level cake ideal for icing and decorating (source 14).

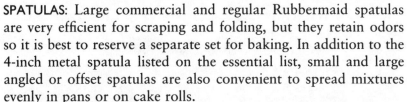

SPATULAS: Large commercial and regular Rubbermaid spatulas are very efficient for scraping and folding, but they retain odors so it is best to reserve a separate set for baking. In addition to the 4-inch metal spatula listed on the essential list, small and large angled or offset spatulas are also convenient to spread mixtures evenly in pans or on cake rolls.

A broad inflexible spatula or pancake turner is useful for lifting iced cake layers (sources 14, 16, 18, and 24).

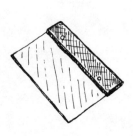

BENCH SCRAPER: Metal bench scrapers are excellent for cleaning counters without scratching. Plastic scrapers (*cornes* in French, probably because they were originally made from horns) are also useful for other purposes because of their flexibility. At LeNôtre's school in France, the professor always had a *corne* tucked in his toque for leveling a cake, tasting batter, or folding ingredients together. The phrase I heard the most often during my week of study was *"Où est ma corne?"* ("Where is my scraper?")—like the proverbial absentminded professor looking for his glasses. Immediately following this request, twenty cornes were enthusiastically brought forth before he remembered that his was in its usual location—his hat.

IMMERSION BLENDER: A powerful, portable blender that enables you to mix in any suitable container, it is particularly useful for smoothing chocolate or buttercream mixtures. (The Krups portable mixer has an immersion blender attachment.)

SAUCEPAN WITH NONSTICK COATING: A medium-size heavy saucepan such as Wearever with a nonstick lining is ideal for *crème anglaise,* sugar syrups, and reducing liquids because very little of the liquid sticks to the pan. Do not use for caramel as very high temperatures will eventually damage the lining. (Available at housewares stores and the Broadway Panhandler, source 18.)

CUISINART POWER STRAINER: This beautifully designed attachment to the food processor juicer pays for itself by extracting more puree than any other device I have used. Unlike a food mill, it does not allow even the tiniest raspberry seed to pass through. It is also very easy to clean. See source 7 for the number to call for the closest distributor.

SIFTER: The primary reason flour is sifted is to separate and aerate the flour particles, enabling them to mix more uniformly with the liquid. It does not do an adequate job of mixing dry ingredients; this is better accomplished in the mixer or even by stirring with a fork.

I am not an advocate of the triple sifter because, if I have already weighed the flour, I am never certain how much gets lost in the labyrinth of the sifter. When making *génoise,* for example, I sift the flour before mixing the batter so that it will be ready to add at the right moment. Then I sift a second time onto the batter. I prefer an electric sifter (at the present time only battery-powered ones are available) because it only has one mesh strainer and is very fast (source 14). A strainer works well too with a tablespoon to press the flour through it.

CARDBOARD ROUNDS: Corrugated cardboard rounds (also referred to as cake circles) are invaluable for supporting cake layers. They are available in large quantities from paper supply houses and in small packages from cake-decorating supply stores (sources 14, 16, 18, and 24).

The best ones have a waxy waterproof surface called glassine. Doilies can be attached to the cardboard with double-sided tape or a loop of regular tape.

I also have a lifetime supply of elegant, golden cardboard

rounds embossed with my logo, which I ordered from France. It was, unfortunately, necessary to order an enormous quantity to fulfill the minimum requirement so most of my closets are stacked with these rounds. I sometimes use the 6-inch ones as postcards!

GLASSINE DOILIES: These doilies are treated with glassine to make them greaseproof so that they do not show stains or disintegrate from moisture. They are available at paper supply houses and some cake-decorating supply stores such as Maid of Scandinavia (source 14).

PARCHMENT: Parchment is available at cake-decorating supply stores and specialty stores in rounds and rolls for lining the bottoms of cake pans and triangles to make piping bags. I use parchment cones instead of pastry bags when working with food coloring, which usually stains the bags, and also when working with a particularly heat-sensitive frosting. The stiffness of the parchment prevents your hand from coming as close to the frosting as a cloth bag would allow, so the frosting remains firmer for a longer time. Lining pan bottoms with parchment enables the cake to release perfectly when unmolding.

REUSABLE NONSTICK PAN LINERS: This is one of my favorite products because absolutely nothing sticks to it, making it ideal for caramel, meringues, and ladyfingers. It has been around for many years but is sometimes difficult to find. Buckeye Kitchen in Connecticut (page 465) carries it under the name sanStick (source 5).

SLOTTED SKIMMER: A medium or large skimmer makes a much better folding instrument than does a rubber spatula, because the small holes provide just the right resistance to blend ingredients without deflating the batter. It helps to bend back the handle slightly to decrease the angle.

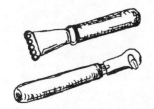

ANGEL FOOD CAKE FOLDER: This inexpensive device is almost extinct. It was designed specifically for folding flour into very stiff meringue for angel food cake and it is perfectly suited to the task. I found this item in the Vermont Country Store Catalog (source 20). They refer to it as an "old-time wire kitchen beater." It doesn't always appear in the catalog, but they assure me that they have a large supply.

ZESTER AND STRIPPER: I will always remember the look on James Beard's face when he described these utensils to our class many years ago. He held a small object in either hand and said: "This is the zester and *this* is the stripper." He had a definite gleam in his eye.

A zester has a small metal head with tiny rough holes in it.

When scraped across a citrus fruit, it penetrates just deeply enough to remove the peel without touching the bitter pith beneath. The stripper, on the other hand, removes wider strips of the same peel.

PORCELAIN SPOONS: These spoons, made of French porcelain, are designed to be tasting spoons because they do not conduct heat or absorb odors. This also makes them perfect for stirring hot liquids, and they can be used in the microwave. I especially like porcelain spoons for making caramel cages. It's easier to see the true color of the caramel against the white of the porcelain (source 6, 8, and 18).

CAKE TESTER: Cake-decorating supply stores carry thin metal wires with loops at the end which make only a small hole in a cake when testing for doneness. Wooden toothpicks are fine to use also.

MARKING PEN: Stationery stores carry a marking pen called El Marko which writes on plastic containers and foil and is not obliterated by moisture, perfect for items to be stored in the freezer.

MARBLE: The Kitchen Bazaar in Washington, D.C., (source 12) carries an 18-inch square of marble for a very reasonable price. This is a good size for everything from pastry to chocolate and nougatine. Do not allow citrus juice or alcohol to touch the marble as it will stain it and spoil the finish.

HOT TRAY OR GRIDDLE: If your oven does not have a pilot light, hot trays with temperature controls or electric griddles work well for melting chocolate, providing they do not exceed 120°F. To check the temperature, set the control at the lowest possible mark, place a cup of water with a thermometer in it on the tray or griddle and take a reading over a period of 2 hours or until you feel sure that the temperature will not exceed 110°F. (to be on the safe side). The Farberware griddle, on its lowest setting, is engineered to maintain a stable temperature of 90 to 110°F. If the heat is below 120°F., you should be able to rest the palm of your hand on its surface without discomfort for 3 seconds. Another good heat source is the area above some refrigerators. Every dwelling has different sources of natural heating or cooling areas.

CUISINART GRIDDLE: This beautifully designed griddle is perfect for pancakes. A 13-inch stainless-steel surface encases a 2½ pound solid copper disc, providing exceptionally even heat for so large a size.

HEART-SHAPED ELECTRIC WAFFLE IRON: An electric waffle iron produces the most uniformly golden, crisp waffles with the least effort (always a plus first thing in the morning). I prefer the non-stick version (source 22).

SPECIAL PANCAKE PANS: The Danish Ebleskiver pan produces rounded pancakes puffs (sources 8, 13, and 18). The Swedish "Plett" pan is ideal for making perfectly shaped 2½-inch pancakes or blini (sources 13 and 18).

SYRUP SYRINGE: A large plastic syringe without needle is more efficient for sprinkling cakes with syrup than a pastry brush. It is even calibrated to measure the amount used for each side of the cake. If you can't coax one from your doctor, they are available at medical supply stores. Although intended to be disposable, they can be reused indefinitely for syrup. I use a 70 cc syringe (about 2.25-ounce capacity) and shake out the liquid rather than use the plunger. After washing, do not reinsert the plunger until ready to use or it will stick. Before using, spray the inside lightly with non-stick vegetable spray.

ICE-WATER BATH: When a recipe says to "cool to room temperature" and you want to do this quickly, an ice-water bath works well, providing the mixture can be stirred to equalize the temperature. To make an ice-water bath, place ice cubes in a large container and add enough cold water just to float them. Sprinkle a handful of salt on top to lower the temperature (as in making ice cream). If the mixture to be cooled is in a glass bowl, which holds the temperature, and it should not be chilled beyond a specific point, have ready some hot water to take the chill off the bowl when it has reached the proper temperature. Mixtures that should not be stirred, such as ganache, can be placed in a large heat-conductive pan such as copper. Setting the pan on a marble counter will further draw out the heat.

HOT-WATER BATH (BAIN MARIE): There are many times when you need to heat something very gently rather than over direct heat. If you do not own a double boiler, or if it is too small, use a saucepan or pot whose opening is slightly smaller than the diameter of the mixing bowl. Fill it with a few inches of hot or simmering water and place the bowl on top. In most cases you will not want the bottom of the bowl to touch the water. Stir or fold the mixture continuously while heating.

When using a hot water bath for custard-type cakes, it is best to place a piece of parchment in the bottom of the pan containing the water so that the pan with the batter does not come into direct contact with the metal of the larger pan.

CAKE SERVING KNIFE: My favorite serving knife is a thin-bladed triangular "tart" knife made by Wüsthof (source 26). They also make a small deeply serrated knife ideal for beveling cake edges or for cutting airy sponge-type cakes.

CHERRY PITTER: In the Fruit Topping chapter I described how to use a hairpin to pit cherries. Large hairpins are sometimes difficult to find. "Jumbo metal hairpins" are available through the Vermont Country Store (source 20).

GLASS CAKE DOME: This attractive and useful serving piece allows you to show off the cake while keeping it moist and fresh. It is difficult to find cake domes in large sizes so it's great to know that a company called ACC manufactures them in 8-inch, 10-inch, and 11-inch diameters. If you contact them (source 2) they will tell you the store closest to you which carries their products.

Some of my best cake-decorating supplies were never manufactured with cakes in mind. Orthodontic pliers, a tiny agate spatula, a set of scalpels, and a magnificent scalloped serving plate were all once used in my mother's dental office. Rose petal cutters, a tiny wooden roller I use for marzipan, and a handsome stainless steel flour scoop came from a pottery and ceramic supply store. Windsor-Newton paintbrushes, an 18-inch metal ruler for smoothing cake tops, a clear plastic ruler, and an assortment of flexible and unusually shaped spatulas came from an art supply store. And small quantities of ingredients are stored in stainless-steel dressing jars from a surgical supply house.

TURNTABLE: An inexpensive plastic turntable such as a lazy Susan, sold in supermarkets, works as well as a heavyweight footed variety. Either can be elevated by placing it on a large inverted cake pan. The commercial heavyweight turntable is necessary when frosting and decorating large tiered cakes. Mine doubles as a sturdy but elegant cake server by placing a large serving plate or marble round on top. It is available at cake-decorating supply stores and by mail order (sources 14, 16, and 24).

CAKE LEVELER: This 16-inch serrated blade has three adjustable heights: 1½ inches, 1¾ inches, and 2 inches. As most wedding cake layers fall between these sizes, it is very practical for obtaining perfectly level layers (source 14).

A cake saw, with multiple adjustments using two thumb screws rather than fixed notches, is also practical (source 16).

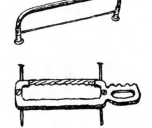

Basic decorating tube set: Wilton and Ateco produce sturdy tubes which are nickel coated and have welded, almost invisible seams. (Ateco also has a less expensive line in which the seams are visible, resulting in less precise piping.) When the tubes flatten and become deformed through much use, an inexpensive plastic tube corrector is all that is needed to put them back into shape. Plastic couplers make it possible to change tubes without emptying the pastry bag.

Bekanol tubes, the Rolls-Royce of decorating tubes, are manufactured in England, but the only address I have for ordering them (and it was hard to come by) is in South Africa (source 25). These tubes are made of shiny, sturdy cast metal. They are long and elegant, with precisely cut openings, making them ideal for the finest string and lace work. Their numbers do not correspond in any way to the American tubes, so it is easiest to order the whole set of 21 tubes. A metal coupler can be ordered for them also. Expect to wait several months for shipment. It is worth it, though. These pastry tubes will last a lifetime.

I keep a separate set of tubes for working with royal icing as even a trace of grease will break it down. Only hot water is needed to wash tubes encrusted with royal icing. Alternately, tubes can be well washed and soaked in a little vinegar to ensure removal of grease.

A basic set of tubes includes:

 small round tubes: Numbers 2, 3, 4, 12
large round tube: Number 6 (½-inch diameter)
large round tube: Number 9 (¾-inch diameter)

 star tubes: Numbers 18, 22

 drop flower: Numbers 30, 131

 leaf tubes: Numbers 67, 70

 rose tubes: Numbers 102, 103, 104

 lily of the valley tube: Number 181

 Number 7 flower nail for piping roses

(Sources: 14, 16 and 24)

PASTRY BAGS: In addition to small parchment bags, I use two sizes and types of pastry bags. The 12-inch polyester bag is made by Wilton and the 14-inch nylon bag comes from France and is also available at most cake-decorating supply stores. The soft nylon bag is ideal for piping whipped cream mixtures. It is not as effective for fat-based mixtures because the grease seeps through the material. For this purpose, I prefer the polyester bag, which is also soft enough for comfort in the hand but firm enough to prevent too much transfer of heat from your hand to the frosting. Bags larger than 12 inches are not as suitable for buttercreams because the heat of the your hand softens large quantities of buttercream. It is also more difficult to squeeze unless your hand is very large.

To remove all traces of buttercream from pastry bags, it helps to soak them in hot water and vinegar.

Just as I have a separate set of tubes for royal icing, I also reserve one pastry bag to use only for royal icing to avoid the possibility of grease contamination. Alternately, polyester bags can be soaked in vinegar and detergent to remove any traces of grease or odor. To dry bags, invert them over tall, narrow soda or wine bottles.

Nylon bags are so soft and floppy that the easiest way to fill them is to place them in a blender container, cuffing the top of the bag over the opening for support. (Seal off the opening first by twisting the bag directly above the tube and pushing it into the tube to keep the filling from leaking out.)

Disposable plastic bags, which can be used one time and thrown out, are also available through cake-decorating supply stores (sources: 14, 16, and 24).

FLOWER FORMERS: This set of long plastic tubes, cut in half lengthwise, provides concave and convex surfaces for drying icing flowers and chocolate leaves to a more natural, lifelike shape. They are available at cake-decorating supply stores.

FLOWER SINKERS: If using real flowers a day ahead to decorate a cake, these plastic vials, equipped with tiny sponges to hold water, will keep the flowers fresh. The smallest ones are available either from a florist or flower supply shop.

RIBBON: The most beautiful ribbon I have found comes from Ets G. Bonnet-J. Mazaud and Cie, in Paris (source 9). That is where I get my gold lamé ribbon. They also carry a ribbon line called *dégradé,* which has a rainbow of color, each one gradually bleeding into the next. Any ribbon can be used around a cake covered with rolled fondant or white chocolate buttercream, but ribbon should be waterproof or grease resistant if the cake is frosted with a softer buttercream.

CAKE BASES: Heavy cardboard serving boards covered with decorative foil are available at cake-decorating supply stores such as Maid of Scandinavia (source 14). Rolls of decorative foil are also available should you choose to cover your own wood base. It is also possible to use a mirror as a cake base, providing it is at least ⅛-inch thick.

BUTCHER'S WAX: Available in paper goods supply stores, this shiny heavy-duty wax paper is wonderful for chocolate work. The surface of the chocolate set against the wax paper takes on a high shine.

TRIANGULAR SCRAPER: Cake-decorating supply stores often carry this tool for making chocolate ruffles. It is actually a hardware store item.

PIZZA CUTTER: The heavy-duty commercial variety offers steady, even pressure for cutting rolled fondant, marzipan, and nougatine (sources 8 and 14).

SPUN SUGAR FORK: Oddly enough, this is the one item that does not have its own official design. In France pastry chefs traditionally use wire whisks, whose curved loops have been cut with snips to form straight wires. Another way to make a device for spun sugar is to use a cake breaker designed for cutting angel food cakes. Bend every other tine in opposing directions (source 14).

NOTE ABOUT SHOPPING FOR EQUIPMENT

Many of the places listed on pages 465 and 466 have catalogs which they will send if you call or write requesting them. Maid of Scandinavia offers the most extensive catalog.

The Bridge Company is a New York institution—where I timidly bought my first cake pan over 20 years ago. (Fred Bridge has a reputation both for quality equipment and for utter impatience with anything vaguely resembling frivolity. His lovely wife, Carolyn, who used to be a top food photography cake stylist, used to give me valued advice on cake baking.)

Bridge carries a variety of quality pans and cake-decorating equipment from France.

Charles Lamalle, a charming Frenchman, has another New York shop catering to lovers of French baking equipment. He is primarily a wholesaler but will also sell to consumers.

Dean & DeLuca in New York's SoHo is known for carrying unique items of fine quality.

The Broadway Panhandler, also in SoHo, has some of the best equipment and prices in town.

La Cuisine in Alexandria, Virginia, is an excellent source for French baking equipment.

The Kitchen Bazaar in Washington, D.C., has several stores and a newsletter that keeps you informed of special sales and new developments in equipment.

Williams-Sonoma has many stores and an elegant mail-order catalog which reflects the quality of equipment they carry. They are the exclusive U.S. distributor of the Ugolini Minigel—my favorite ice-cream machine.

1. **Acme American Repairs:** 99 Scott Avenue, Brooklyn, New York 11237. 718/456-6544
2. **ACC:** P.O. Box 118, Hewlett, New York 11557. 516/569-1300
3. **American Family Scale Company, Inc.:** 3718 South Ashland Avenue, Chicago, Illinois 60609. 312/376-6811
4. **Albert Uster Imports, Inc.:** 9211 Gaither Road, Gaithersburg, Maryland. 800/231-8154
5. **Buckeye Kitchen:** P.O. Box 102, Darien, Connecticut 06820
6. **Charles Lamalle:** 36 West 25th Street, New York, New York 10010. 212/242-0750
7. **Cuisinarts, Inc.:** 5 Wisconsin Avenue, Norwich, Connecticut 06360. 800/243-8540
8. **Dean & DeLuca:** 121 Prince Street, New York, New York 10012. 212/431-1691; outside New York: 800/227-7714, Monday–Friday, 9 A.M.–5 P.M.
9. **Ets G. Bonnet-J. Mazaud and Cie:** 325, rue Saint-Martin, Paris 3ième 75003 France. 33-1-4272-3582
10. **General Slicing:** 1152 Park Avenue, Murfreesboro, Tennessee 37130. 615/893-4820
11. **J. B. Prince Company, Inc.:** 29 West 38th Street, New York, New York 10018. 212/302-8611. (Professional culinary equipment only)
12. **Kitchen Bazaar:** 1098 Taft Street, Rockville, Maryland 20850. 301/424-7501
13. **La Cuisine:** 323 Cameron Street, Alexandria, Virginia 22314. 800/521-1176
14. **Maid of Scandinavia:** 32–44 Raleigh Avenue, Minneapolis, Minnesota 55416. 800/328-6722
15. **Mettler Instrument Corporation:** Box 71, Hightstown, New Jersey 08520. 609/448-3000
16. **Parrish Decorating Supplies, Inc.:** 314 West 58th Street, Los Angeles, California 90037. 213/750-7650
17. **The Bridge Company:** 214 East 52nd Street, New York, New York 10022. 212/688-4220
18. **The Broadway Panhandler:** 520 Broadway, New York, New York 10012. 212/966-3434

19. **The Hobart Corporation:** Troy, Ohio 45374. 513/335-7171
20. **The Vermont Country Store:** Route 100, Weston, Vermont 05161. 802/824-3184
21. **Turkart:** P.O. Box 2737, Paterson, New Jersey. 800/526-5209
22. **Vitantonio:** 34355 Vokes Drive, East Lake, Ohio 44094.
23. **Williams-Sonoma:** Mail Order Department, P.O. Box 7456, San Francisco, California 94120-7456. 415/421-4242
24. **Wilton Enterprises:** 22440 West 75th Street, Woodridge, Illinois 60517. 312/963-7100
25. **Wool Craft and Hobby Shop:** P.O. Box 1660, 212A Longmarket Street, Pietermaritzburg, South Africa 3201. 27-331-54051
26. **Wüsthof-Trident of America, Inc.:** 2 Westchester Plaza, P.O. Box 546, Elmsford, New York 10523. 914/347-2185
27. **Zephyr Convection Cooking Systems:** 841 Latour Court, Suite C, Napa, California 94558. 800/635-7774.

PART IV

SPECIAL SECTION FOR PROFESSIONALS AND PASSIONATE AMATEURS

*C*hefs de cuisine often boast about having worked in some of the great kitchens of France. As a baker, I am equally proud to say that I have spent time as a consultant in the research and development laboratories of one of our nation's largest baked goods corporations.

My taste has been honed by years of eating all over the world and my techniques by years of experience as a student and teacher. But to have had the oppportunity of working with scientific experts, of tasting and seeing the results of countless experiments, is an experience that I treasure. I have, in fact, spent so much time analyzing and thinking about cakes that I sometimes feel as though I've entered the microcosmic structure of the cake itself!

I am also grateful to my wonderful friend Shirley Corriher, a research biochemist and inspired cooking teacher, who over the years has unearthed many valuable articles from scientific journals and spent innumerable hours discussing and illuminating cake theory. It is this understanding which enables me to be both creative and successful.

Say, for example, that you want to convert your favorite cheesecake recipe to a white chocolate cheesecake. Adding white chocolate without taking into account that it contains 30 percent sugar and then removing this amount from the sugar in the recipe will oversweeten the cake.

Baking without an understanding of the ingredients and how they work is like baking blindfold. Sometimes everything works. But when it doesn't you have to guess at how to change it.

Cakes made with flour fall into 3 basic categories:
• Butter cake, containing solid butter or other shortening.
• Sponge-type cake, containing a high proportion of eggs to flour and melted butter or oil.
• Sponge-type cake, containing a high proportion of eggs to flour but no butter, oil, or other fat.

The easiest way to compare the cakes in these 3 categories is with a chart showing the percentage of liquid, egg, flour, sugar, and fat. The chart takes into account that unclarified butter is not 100 percent fat. Butter actually contains about 81 percent fat and 15.5 percent liquid. (Clarifying removes the liquid and milk solids.)

Under-standing Cakes

Looking at this chart, I see for the first time that, although I thought my pound cake formula had equal weights of eggs/flour/ sugar with slightly more butter, when taking into account the amount of liquid contained in the butter, the formula, in fact, has the exact same percentage of butter fat as other ingredients! The chiffon cake has almost the same proportions as the *génoise* with syrup except that the liquid and sugar are added to the chiffon cake before baking.

Analyzing this chart tells you to some degree what the cake will be like. The *génoise*, when moistened with syrup, has a sugar and liquid content similar to that of butter cake. Since the *génoise* has a much higher percentage of egg, which also contributes moisture, it will seem moister than the butter cake as well as lighter in texture. The angel food cake at 34 percent sugar and with only egg whites and no fat to weigh it down, is a lot sweeter and lighter than pound cake—which has only 22 percent sugar, whole eggs, and a lot of butter.

PERCENTAGES OF MAJOR INGREDIENTS IN BASIC CAKE TYPES					
Type of cake	*liquid*	*egg*	*flour*	*sugar*	*fat* *
Pound Cake	12%	22%	22%	22%	22%
Pancake	52%	20%	23%	0%	5%
Basic Butter Cake	24%	10%	27%	27%	12%
Génoise Classique with Syrup	0% 22%	46% 31%	23% 16%	23% 25%	8% 6%
Biscuit Roulade with Syrup	0% 15%	59% 47%	14% 11%	27% 27%	0% 0%
Biscuit de Savoie with Syrup	0% 32%	51% 28%	23% 13%	26% 27%	0% 0%
Biscuit à la Cuillière	0%	50%	25%	25%	0%
Sponge Cake	4%	45%	20%	31%	0%
Angel Food Cake	6%	47%	13%	34%	0%
Chiffon Cake	14%	35%	18%	24%	9%

* Total fat content exclusive of the milk solids and water contained in the butter

Basic American butter cake is one of the world's best. It is flavorful yet not overly sweet, soft and light in texture, and moist enough
to stand on its own or to accommodate a variety of fillings and
frostings.

The ingredients fall into two main categories: Those that form
and strengthen the cake structure and those that weaken it.

In the first category are flour and eggs, both of which contain
proteins that coagulate when baked to form the framework or
supporting structure of the cake. The flour also contains starch
which gelatinizes (absorbs water) and stabilizes the structure.

In the second category are fat, sugar, and leavening, which
in varying ways tenderize the structure by weakening it.

Liquid bridges both categories because it combines with the
gluten forming proteins of flour to form gluten, one of the structural networks of the cake. But excessive liquid causes a cake to
collapse. Usually a cake with weak structure resembles an M
(straight sides but sinking center). A cake containing too much
liquid, however, resembles an X (level top but sides caved in toward
the middle). A butter cake batter with too much liquid will be
thin and the baked cake will be heavy. A batter with less liquid
will be thicker and the resulting cake lighter with a more open
crumb. The perfect balance of liquid offers both structural support and moistness that is also perceived as tenderness.

CAKE FLOUR: Cake flour contains 2 gluten-forming proteins, glia-
din and glutenin. When liquid is added, they connect to form the
resilient strands that provide a small part of the cake's structure.
The most important structural component, however, is starch,
which absorbs water and swells (gelatinizes) to set the structure.

Cake flour is made from finely milled soft winter wheat which
is high in starch and low in gluten-forming proteins. Because of
its finer granulation, it absorbs fat and moisture more quickly
than hard spring wheat which contains more protein.

The size of the gas cells in a cake determines the quality of
the grain of the finished cake and is directly dependent upon how
much the batter expands during baking before the cells rupture.
This is influenced partly by the size of the flour particles, partly
by the batter's pH, and partly by the type of shortening used.
Cake flour, due to bleaching by cholorination, has a lower pH
(more acid) than other flours. This produces a sweeter flavor and
a finer, more velvety crumb because the greater acidity lowers the
temperature at which the proteins coagulate. This also makes it
possible for the cake structure to support more sugar, butter, and
heavier particles such as chopped nuts or chocolate.

The chlorination process offers other advantages. It attacks

INGREDIENTS

the starch granules, enabling water to enter more easily. In industry, cake flour is often milled with sugar so that the sugar particles become imbedded in the flour granules, providing an avenue for the water to enter and hydrate the starch. Chlorination also serves to inhibit gluten formation. Recent research has revealed that fat adheres to the surface of chlorinated starch particles, resulting in better aeration (more even, uniform distribution of air).

It is possible to substitute equal weights of *bleached* all-purpose flour for cake flour by adding a small percentge of cornstarch. But the result will not be the same because the flour is coarser and the pH higher. Self-rising cake flour cannot be used interchangeably with cake flour because it contains approximately 1½ teaspoons baking powder and ½ teaspoon salt per cup of flour. This will coarsen and weaken the texture of cakes requiring only 1¼ teaspoons or less baking powder per cup.

EGGS: Eggs contribute structure and serve as a means for incorporating air into the batter. They also supply some of the cake's liquid. The yolk of an egg is a rich source of natural emulsifying agents, which help suspend the fat evenly throughout the batter. Cakes prepared with egg whites only are slightly softer than those with either whole egg or all yolk because the yolk becomes firmer after coagulating (baking) than does the white. In a layer cake recipe 1 egg can be replaced by 2 yolks or 1½ whites. If using all yolks, the structure will be slightly weaker, so the baking powder needs to be decreased by ¼ teaspoon for every 3 yolks used. (Yolks tenderize by coating some of the gluten-forming proteins in the flour, preventing excessive gluten formation.)

The advantage of using only yolks is superior flavor and a more golden color. The crust also browns more because the yolk is higher in protein and contains fat.

BUTTER: Butter, or solid fat, tenderizes and aerates the cake. It tenderizes by coating some of the gluten-forming proteins in the flour, preventing excessive gluten formation. Cells created by air beaten into the fat provide focal points for the collection of the steam formed in baking and for the carbon dioxide liberated from sodium bicarbonate by the acid in baking powder. Unsalted butter produces the best flavor, not only because of its own incomparable flavor but also because it releases the flavors of other ingredients more fully. A cake with less butter, for example, will seem less sweet. Margarine or other fats do not release flavor as well.

Butter will hold the maximum amount of air if its temperature is 65°F. to 75°F. when beaten. During baking, the melting fat makes the batter more mobile because fat is insoluble (does not dissolve) in water. It disperses into tiny particles throughout the batter. Some people use up to 50 percent hydrogenated shortening instead of pure butter because it contains emulsifiers that disperse the fat more evenly, increasing the elasticity on the film of protein around the air bubbles for better volume and texture. I find, however, that using 100 percent butter at the correct temperature yields perfect texture in addition to superior flavor.

SUGAR: Sugar contributes flavor (sweetness) and facilitates the incorporation of air into the fat. Superfine sugar is preferable because the finer the crystals, the more numerous the air cells. Powdered sugar is not suitable because it lacks the sharp crystal edges which help incorporate the air. In a batter containing a large amount of sugar, the gas cells expand more before the batter sets because the sugar elevates the temperature at which the egg protein coagulates and the starch granules gelatinize. This creates a more open texture, weakening the cake's structure and making it melt faster in the mouth. It should be noted that tenderness and softness are two different qualities. A cake high in sugar will fall apart easily (is more "tender") but it also has a harder "mouth feel."

Sugar "tenderizes" cake in two significant ways. It competes with the starch to absorb the liquid, preventing the structure from becoming too rigid. It also combines with the 2 gluten-forming proteins in the flour to prevent them from forming gluten. Interestingly, even if the gluten is already formed when the sugar is added, the sugar still combines with the proteins to break up the gluten. In a baked cake sugar also serves to retain moisture.

SALT: The only function of salt in a cake is to accentuate or heighten flavor. Without salt, the cake would have a decidedly flat taste.

LEAVENING: Baking powders are mixtures of dry acid or acid salt and baking soda with starch or flour added to standardize and stabilize the mixtures. They are formulated so that there is no excess of either baking soda or acid left in the product after the desired reaction is accomplished. The product of their reaction is carbon dioxide, which aerates and lightens the batter by enlarging the already existing air cells creamed into the fat. (It does not create new air cells.) Double-acting means that part of the reaction takes place when the baking powder comes into contact with liquid and the remainder is activated by heat during baking.

Too little baking powder results in a tough cake with a humped top, compact crumb, and poor volume. Too much baking powder results in a coarse, open, fragile crumb and often a fallen center.

Baking soda may be used in a cake formula to neutralize an acid ingredient such as molasses, sour cream, or cocoa which has not been "dutched" (treated with alkali). A half teaspoon of baking soda is required to neutralize the acid of 1 cup of sour milk. This process (the lactic acid of the sour milk reacting with the baking soda) provides leavening equal to that of approximately 4 times its volume of baking powder. So if a formula calls for ½ cup milk and 1½ teaspoons baking powder, it is possible to substitute ½ cup sour milk and the ¼ teaspoon baking soda necessary for neutralization. This equals the leavening power of 1 teaspoon baking powder so only ½ teaspooon of baking powder needs to be added. Molasses needs ½ to 1 teaspoon baking soda per cup for neutralization.

Because the acidity of these products varies, there is the risk of adding more baking soda than can be dissipated by the amount of acid present. This excessive alkalinity will slow down coagulation of the proteins and result in a coarse, open crumb and bitter, steely flavor. It is preferable to use too little baking soda rather than too much.

In working with buttermilk formulas for layer cake, I find that ½ cup buttermilk + ¼ teaspoon baking soda equals 1⅛ teaspoons baking powder rather than the 1 teaspoon suggested by the U.S.D.A. This indicates that these figures are not exact and substitutions have to be taken with a grain of salt, so to speak. In any event, I prefer not to neutralize the flavor of buttermilk with baking soda, as I find the taste fuller and the texture finer using baking powder alone.

COCOA: Cocoa is superior to chocolate for cake baking because it provides more intense chocolate flavor. To get equal intensity using chocolate, it is necessary to use the equivalent of more cocoa solids, cocoa butter, and dairy butter unless the chocolate is cooked with water as in Moist Chocolate Génoise (page 132). This is because the flavor components in chocolate are locked in by the cocoa butter. Cooking the chocolate in water dissolves the surrounding barrier of cocoa butter and swells the cocoa particles until they rupture, unlocking the flavor components.

Cocoa has a toughening effect on cake structure so cakes containing cocoa have a higher amount of baking powder to compensate.

Baking soda is traditionally used for chocolate cakes because it neutralizes its mild acidity. The color of a devil's food cake is due to the pigments supplied by the cocoa or chocolate. They change color with a change in hydrogen ion concentration. At a pH of 5.0 they are yellow. Baking soda, which increases the alkalinity, turns the hue to mahogany red at 7.5 pH. The increase in pH also results in the coarser texture and bitter flavor usually associated with devil's food cake. If using "dutched chocolate," it is unnecessary, in fact undesirable, to add baking soda to neutralize acidity because the dutching process is an alkali treatment of the cocoa beans during roasting which eliminates acetic acid, giving the cocoa smoother flavor, richer color, and improved solubility. (Some people perceive undutched cocoa as stronger, others as more bitter rather than more intense in chocolate flavor.)

Sometimes a process called "instantizing" is used to roughen and fluff up the grains of cocoa and make them dissolve more easily.

LIQUID: Milk products are the preferred liquid for yellow or white butter cakes and water is usually the preferred liquid for chocolate butter cakes. Milk products offer a richer flavor, but the proteins in milk solids cause chocolate to have a bitter taste. (Taste a chocolate cake made with milk alongside one made with water to note the remarkable difference in flavor.) Fruit juices are not recommended because they alter the acid balance of the batter, which affects the texture and causes it to become gummy.

In addition to taste, the function of liquid in a cake batter is to dissolve the salt and sugar and make possible the reaction of the soda and acid in the baking powder to form carbon dioxide. Liquid also disperses the fat and flour, hydrates the protein and starch in the flour, and provides steam to leaven the cake.

MIXING THE BATTER   I have adapted the two-stage method of mixing batter, used commercially with high-ratio shortening (which makes it possible to use a higher ratio of sugar), for use with butter. (I do not consider it an advantage to have more sugar and unequivocally prefer the flavor of butter to other shortenings.) Shortening is capable of aeration at a wider range of temperatures than butter. But if the butter is 65°F. to 75°F. and the other ingredients are at room temperature,* this mixing method is my preferred one. It is much faster and easier than the creaming method, and the results are more consistent. The grain is finer and more velvety and the crumb more tender than with the creaming method.

The two-stage method produces a more tender cake because the butter is added to the flour with a minimum of liquid (just enough to disperse the fat) at the beginning of the mixing process. The butter coats some of the gluten-forming proteins in the flour, preventing excessive gluten formation. This protects the cake from toughening due to overmixing. A significant amount of air still gets incorporated into the batter with this method. Proof of this is that, although the pan is filled only ½ full instead of the usual ⅔, the batter still rises to the top.

Another advantage of the two-stage method is that since all the dry ingredients are added together, at the beginning, it is possible to disperse them evenly with the mixer. As sifting does not uniformly disperse dry ingredients unless repeated many times, using the mixer instead is a great time and energy saver. (Flour should be sifted once to aerate and separate the particles which enable it to hydrate more evenly.)

The single most critical factor to successfully baking a cake is oven temperature. No matter how carefully ingredients are weighed, measured, and mixed, an oven that is too cool or too hot will ruin a cake's texture. Since most oven thermometers are less than adequate, the best test is to bake All-Occasion Downy Yellow Cake (page 39). This basic butter cake will give you a clue as to how your oven is callibrated.

BAKING THE CAKE

There is a lot you can tell from the outside appearance of a baked cake. If the top crust is evenly golden brown and flat or gently rounded, the cake within will be fine-grained, soft, and tender. If the cake is peaked and tests done before 20 minutes, your oven is too hot. If it sinks slightly in the middle, takes more than 30 minutes to bake, and has a coarse texture, your oven is not hot enough.

When a cake bakes, expanding gas from steam and leavening enlarges the air bubbles trapped in the fat during the mixing process. The bubbles expand until the surrounding cell walls rupture, the flour and egg proteins coagulate, and the flour's starch gela-

---

* Ideally, the butter should be 70°F., the liquid and eggs 60°F., and the finished batter 70°F. to 75°F.

tinizes to set the structure. At too low a temperature heat penetration is slow and the cells overexpand and collide, forming larger cells before coagulation and gelatinization can set the structure. This explains why the grain is coarser in a cake that has been baked too slowly and why a 12-inch cake is somewhat coarser than a 6-inch cake.

WHAT CAN GO WRONG

Assuming you are working with a well-balanced formula, when a butter cake falls, peaks and cracks, or has poor texture, the first thing to consider is the oven temperature. The next is the proportion of ingredients (how they were weighed or measured). Incorrect substitutions without adjustments are often the problem; jumbo eggs instead of large, all-purpose flour instead of cake flour without making the necessary adjustments, or old baking powder.

The next thing to consider is the method of mixing the batter. If using the two-stage method, this is rarely a problem. It is hard to toughen the batter by overbeating because the early addition of the butter serves as protection. With the creaming method, overmixing develops the gluten, especially if all-purpose flour has been used, and results in a tight grain with a peaked top. The leavening has to force its way through the tough cell walls, creating long tunnels and erupting and cracking the surface of the cake.

Undermixing does not form enough gluten, which results in a crumbly, coarse grain and a very flat top crust with a slightly fallen center.

Assuming you are making one of the cake recipes in this book, and you have accurately weighed or measured the ingredients, the most common problems and their causes are:

PROBLEM	CAUSE
cracked or peaked surface and or large tunnels	oven too hot or batter overmixed
coarse grain and sunken center	oven too cold, batter undermixed, or too much baking powder
poor volume, compact texture	old or too little baking powder or cold eggs and/or butter
dry cake, tough crust	overbaking or pan too big
burnt bottom and undercooked batter	inadequate air circulation in oven

UNDER-STANDING GÉNOISE AND SPONGE (FOAM)-TYPE CAKES

Sponge-type cakes are characteristically lighter and springier than butter cakes. When comparing the percentage of ingredients in a *génoise* to that of a basic butter cake (page 470), it's easy to see why this is the case. *Génoise* sprinkled with syrup (which is the way it is usually consumed) has about 3 times the amount of egg as butter cake and only about ½ the flour and butter.

I cut the flour for my *génoise* recipe with 50 percent cornstarch, thereby lowering the overall percentage of protein. It is possible to decrease the cake flour in this way because one of the major differences between sponge-type cakes and butter cakes is that the sponge cake structure comes primarily from egg protein reinforced by starch from the flour. A *génoise* actually can be made without any flour protein by using all starch, but the texture will not be quite as light or resilient.

The main goal in making a sponge-type cake is to achieve as much volume in the baked cake as possible. Since the eggs are the most important ingredient for volume, the way in which they are beaten, their temperature, and the manner of adding other ingredients to them are all important considerations. *Génoise,* for example, contains butter, which weighs down the egg foam, so to counteract this the eggs are warmed before beating to help them attain their greatest possible volume. The butter is also added warm to keep it from solidifying and resting too heavily on the egg foam.

Too much volume is not desirable either because if there is more volume than the structure can support the *génoise* will collapse.

Again referring to the chart (page 470), comparing Biscuit de Savoie without syrup to *génoise* without syrup shows why the *biscuit* will be lighter than the *génoise.* It has no fat to weigh it down plus it has more sugar and egg for aeration. For this reason, it is not necessary to heat the eggs for a *biscuit* in order to increase the amount of volume during beating. It is desirable, however, to bake the *biscuit* in an ungreased pan because the absence of fat (except for the small amount in the yolk) and the high proportion of egg would cause the *biscuit* to shrink away from the sides of the pan and collapse.

A *génoise* or Biscuit de Savoie would be dry and somewhat tough without a moistening syrup. The perfect amount softens the texture. If too much is added, however, the cake becomes almost mushy. Biscuit de Savoie can hold a lot more syrup than *génoise* because it has a stronger structure.

A sponge-type cake without fat requires either a moistening syrup or a high proportion of sugar to tenderize it. American sponge cake, for example, traditionally uses no syrup but it has 31 percent sugar and angel food cake has 34 percent sugar. Chiffon cake, which has the moist richness of butter cake with the lightness of sponge-type cake, uses oil to tenderize it so it can get by with only 24 percent sugar, less than a butter cake. (It has 9 percent oil compared to the 12 percent butter in the butter cake but oil, which is liquid, coats the protein more effectively, so less is needed to achieve a similar degree of tenderness). A small amount of baking powder adds just enough extra volume without endangering the fragile structure. Superfine sugar is preferable, as in butter cakes, because the finer the crystals, the more numerous the air cells.

Sponge, chiffon, and angel food cakes are all so light and spongy they require the added support of a tube pan for maximum volume and must hang upside down to stretch and keep from collapsing until cool enough for the structure to set. Angel food is the lightest cake because it has all egg whites for the largest and most stable foam (requiring less flour for structure) and the highest proportion of sugar. Since coagulated egg whites are rubbery in the absence of fat, the extra amount of sugar is necessary to "tenderize" the cake. There is a limit as to how much sugar can be added to a cake. Beyond a certain point, the sugar will actually prevent the batter from setting by raising the coagulation temperature of the egg and limiting starch gelatinization.

Cake flour produces better sponge-type cakes than does all-purpose because of its finer granulation, lower protein content, and lower pH. Cream of tartar, which is an acidic salt, is also added to stabilize the egg whites and lower the pH, creating a finer grain, making the cake more tender, and keeping it from shrinking. It is thought that the acid enables the films of protein in the air cells of the foam to last until the heat can set the structure. In a white angel food cake, the lower pH will make the crumb whiter.

As with butter cakes, a high baking temperature for sponge-type cakes promotes a more rapid setting of the batter and absorption of less water by the starch of the flour. This results in a greater volume and a moister, more tender cake. Higher temperatures also improve texture but are not equally beneficial to the external appearance of the cake. Above 350°F. the crust of sponge-type cakes becomes overbrowned.

Foolproof Formulas and Techniques for Making Large Wedding and Special Occasion Cakes

This chapter, devoted to the large special occasion cake, is for the master cake baker or dedicated home baker. It contains all the information needed to make *any* size white, yellow, or chocolate butter cake from 6 to 18 inches and any yellow or chocolate *génoise* from 6 to 12 inches. It also tells you how much buttercream and syrup are required for each. There are recipes for other favorite cakes in large proportions, such as cheesecake and pound cake, and detailed instructions for assembling and storing tiered cakes.

The Showcase Cakes chapter, beginning on page 163, contains 5 completed examples of tiered wedding cakes. But the information in this chapter will enable you to make endless variations of just about any cake your heart desires.

While it is possible to produce large cakes without any special equipment other than large pans and a sufficient number of racks, certain pieces of equipment make the job much easier and more efficient. A 10- or 20-quart Hobart mixer, for example, makes it possible to mix the batter for a 3-Tiered Wedding Cake for 150 people in one batch. With the KitchenAid K5 (5-quart mixer), it is necessary to divide the batter into 2 batches for a butter cake and 4 batches for *génoise*. A highly motivated person could even use an electric hand-held mixer by preparing the batter in 4 batches (2 for the 12-inch layers, 1 for the 9-inch layers, and 1 for the 6-inch layers).

Another major consideration when making large cakes is oven size. I once made a 4-tiered wedding cake in my apartment kitchen. The two 15-inch bottom layers and two 6-inch top layers were baking in my Wolf oven while the two 12-inch layers baked in the Sharp countertop convection oven and the two 9-inch layers in the Cusinart Air Surge. Since I like to turn each layer 90 degrees halfway through its specific baking time to promote even baking, timers were going off at mad intervals. I decided that, henceforth, 3 tiers at a time would be my limit.

Refrigeration space is not usually a problem, because most cakes put together the day before the event can sit at cool room temperature overnight.

A large wedding or special occasion cake somehow manages to require an extraordinary number of bowls, pans, and utensils and usually takes at least 12 hours of solid work to complete. I don't know how the following tradition ever got started, but somehow, when the cake is frosted and ready for the piped decorations, that is my moment of glory, of supreme joy and celebration, because now the best part can begin: the artwork. I fill the pastry bag, pour a tiny glass of my best Napoleon cognac (which I find far too strong at any other time), and am transported to another world.

When the mess is cleared away and the cake sitting on its pedestal, ready to be photographed for my album, it always amazes me how this pristine and exquisite cake could have created such havoc. And I wonder idly how many non-bakers ever realize the work that goes into its preparation. It really doesn't matter though; there is the pleasure of coming into contact with people who are at their happiest, either about to be married or celebrating some other joyous event. Then there is the unparalleled joy of creation, making the cake.

A beginner's greatest fear when embarking on a first wedding cake is that it won't look even. When I used to give week-long baking classes, I would take the students to visit New York bakeries. They were surprised, when encouraged to scrutinize the cakes and decorations close up (as ruthlessly as they would their own), that, although scarcely a cake was perfectly level or the decorations very precise, the overall effect was still impressive.

I'll always remember the night my husband came into the room to look at my latest creation before going to bed. I had been baking wedding cakes for about two years, and one had even been photographed for *Bon Appétit* magazine. He appraised the newest cake and then said evenly: "You're getting really good; they're beginning to look level."

Actually, it was *Bon Appétit* that started my wedding cake business when they asked me to make a special occasion cake for an article featuring my cooking school. It was the first time they had ever presented a wedding cake. It was also the first time that I had ever made one. My concept was to offer a cake that the bride could bake for her own wedding and which could be prepared in advance to give her time to attend to last-minute details. The cake, covered with rolled fondant and decorated with pale pink marizpan roses and tiny dots reminiscent of pearls cascading from the top, is included in this book. It was my first experience in having an inner vision materialize with such fidelity, and it is still my favorite wedding cake.

While over the years many people have made the cake, if not for their own wedding then for a sister's or daughter's, an inordinate number of them wanted me to make the cake myself. I never considered this possibility when I wrote the article. The first person to call was planning her daughter's wedding 18 months away. She was planning the décor to match the cake—even the bridesmaids' dresses were to be dotted Swiss! One baker from Long Island called to berate me jokingly for designing dots. She said: "Everyone wants dots now and you know what a pain . . . they are to make!" Since that time seven years ago, I have made over 100 wedding or special occasion cakes. At first my husband and I often attended the weddings because I had gotten to know the bride so well while designing her cake. Eventually, to Elliott's relief, the novelty wore off.

SPECIAL THINGS TO CONSIDER WHEN EMBARKING ON A TIERED CAKE

- *Oven space:* Assess how many layers can be baked at one time and coordinate this with the refrigeration space available for holding unbaked batter. Alternately, decide how many batches of batter you will mix. Remember: Cake pans *must* have air circulation all around them while baking. Do not overcrowd them.
- *Refrigeration space:* Check available space if the completed cake needs to be refrigerated. Refrigerator racks can be removed to give more height.
- *Equipment:* Beyond the basics, such as pans and spatulas, there will be special pieces of equipment necessary to complete some of the tiered cakes.
  Review the Equipment chapter (page 446) or see the list of special equipment and structural supports needed for each recipe in the Showcase Cakes chapter (pages 163 to 224).
- *Cooling racks:* Keep in mind that you will need a rack for each cake layer.
- *Magi-Cake Strips:* Highly recommended for more even layers, an important factor in having the finished cake look attractive and professional (pages 20 and 456).
- *Mixer Capacity*
  Cake layers: Indication of mixer size and number of batches necessary is given at the top of each recipe in this chapter.
  Buttercreams: The buttercreams in this chapter can be made in 1 batch in a 5-quart mixer. With a hand-held mixer you will need to make 2 or 3 batches.

SUGGESTED CAKE SIZE OPTIONS

The average-size wedding cake consists of 3 tiers—12 inches, 9 inches, and 6 inches—and feeds about 150 people. A 3-tier cake is the largest convenient size to cut and serve, so, if extra cake is desired, a sheet cake can be baked, frosted, and portioned in the kitchen. Since it will be behind the scenes, there is no need for time-consuming decoration.

In Canada and Japan there is another interesting approach to the problem of serving a tiered wedding cake. The Hotel Okura in Tokyo, the most fashionable location for modern Japanese weddings, devotes an entire storeroom to elaborate, artificial cake constructions. These wedding cakes are fairy tale monuments of royal icing, entirely inedible save for a small hollow section into which is inserted and frosted a wedge of fruitcake for the bride to cut and serve to the groom. Meanwhile, the rest of the fruitcake, baked in large rectangles, is conveniently being cut back-stage in the kitchen. This way the guests don't have to wait nearly as long for their pieces of cake and all can be served more or less at the same time!

This chapter contains recipes for the standard 3-tier butter cake in white, yellow, and chocolate, the same size cake in classic or chocolate *génoise,* and cheesecake.

For those who prefer a towering presentation of 4 or more tiers, I am also offering a chart which will enable you to bake any size butter cake from 6 inches to 18 inches and a second chart with frosting amounts. These charts are the soul of this book and took years to perfect. It will save you the hours of planning, calculation, and trepidation I went through each time someone requested a different amount of cake (which seemed to be each time).

Wedding cake portions are traditionally small because they are usually served after a large dinner which often includes other desserts as well. People are surprised by how little cake is actually needed in relation to the number of guests, partly because these days many people forgo dessert entirely. There are always some who leave before the cake-cutting ceremony, which comes at the very end.

When I calculate the number of servings necessary for a butter cake, I estimate that my base formula of 1 cup flour (or flour/cocoa) serves 11. This works out to be about 1.5 tablespoons flour per serving. The size of the serving is either a square 2 inches high by 2 inches deep by 1⅝ inches wide or a slim rectangle 4 inches high by 2 inches deep by ¾ inch wide.

The only time I ran out of cake was when I made Golden Glory Wedding Cheesecake (page 217) for my niece Joan Beranbaum Stackhouse's wedding. The wedding was in Westport, Connecticut, and just prior to the event the cake was being photographed nearby for Martha Stewart's book *Weddings.* All of our relatives and Joan's friends knew about this and were eagerly saving their appetites. Some people, alas, lined up for seconds before everyone else had received a first serving. I could have used two wedding cakes that day! I encouraged Joan to serve the top tier too, as this cheesecake doesn't freeze well anyway, and promised to bake her one exactly like it for her first anniversary.

NUMBER OF SERVINGS	PAN SIZE (all pans are round and 2 inches high)
40	one 12-inch pan *
50	two 10-inch pans
75	two 10-inch and two 7-inch pans
80†	one 18-inch x 12-inch sheet pan
100	one 15-inch and one 12-inch pan
110	two 12-inch and two 8-inch pans
150	two 12-inch, two 9-inch, and two 6-inch pans
175	two 13-inch, two 10-inch, and two 7-inch pans
200	two 15-inch, two 10-inch, and two 6-inch pans
225	two 15-inch, two 11-inch, and two 7-inch pans
250	two 15-inch, two 12-inch, and two 9-inch pans
275	two 15-inch, two 12-inch, two 9-inch, and two 6-inch pans
300	two 16-inch, two 13-inch, and two 10-inch pans
350	two 18-inch, two 14-inch, and two 10-inch pans
450	two 18-inch, two 15-inch, two 12-inch, two 9-inch, and two 6-inch pans

* For butter cakes use 4 times the base formula, for yellow *génoise* 7 times the base formula, for chocolate *génoise* 8.75 times the base formula.
†Sheet cake servings are 2 inches by 2 inches by 1⅝ inches. If cut into 2-inch squares, it would make 54 servings.

NOTE: For aesthetics, the relationship of tiers to each other must be taken into account. If you wish to combine different sizes not on the chart, try stacking the cake pans to see the effect.

BUTTER WEDDING CAKES

Wedding cakes are usually prepared with white, yellow, or even chocolate butter cake. The firm yet tender texture makes it ideal for constructing multitiered layers.

To keep a butter cake fresh and moist when preparing more than twenty-four hours ahead, sprinkle the layers with Syrup (page 505). Use 3 cups of Syrup for every 6½ cups of sugar used to prepare the cake batter.

3-Tier White or Yellow Butter Wedding Cake to Serve 150*

INGREDIENTS	MEASURE	WEIGHT	
room temperature	*volume*	*pounds/ounces*	*kilograms/grams*
FOR TWO 6-INCH BY 2-INCH LAYERS AND TWO 9-INCH BY 2-INCH LAYERS			
9 large egg whites *or*	1 liquid cup † + 2 tablespoons	9.5 ounces	270 grams
12 large egg yolks	7 fluid ounces †	7.75 ounces	223 grams
milk	2 cups †	17 ounces	484 grams
vanilla	1 tablespoon + 1½ teaspoons	•	18 grams
sifted cake flour	6 cups	1 pound 5 ounces	600 grams
sugar	3 cups	1 pound 5 ounces	600 grams
baking powder	2 tablespoons + 2 teaspoons	•	39 grams
salt	1½ teaspoons	•	10 grams
unsalted butter (must be softened)	1½ cups	12 ounces	340 grams
FOR TWO 12-INCH BY 2-INCH LAYERS			
10½ large egg whites *or*	1⅓ liquid cups †	11 ounces	315 grams
14 large egg yolks	1 liquid cup †	9 ounces	260 grams
milk	2⅓ liquid cups †	1 pound 3.75 ounces	564 grams
vanilla	1 tablespoon + 2¼ teaspoons	•	21 grams

* Requires a 5-quart mixer.

INGREDIENTS	MEASURE	WEIGHT	
room temperature	*volume*	*pounds/ounces*	*kilograms/grams*
sifted cake flour	7 cups	1 pound 8.5 ounces	700 grams
sugar	3½ cups	1 pound 8.5 ounces	700 grams
baking powder	2 tablespoons + 1¾ teaspoons	•	38 grams
salt	1¾ teaspoons	•	12 grams
unsalted butter (must be softened)	1¾ cups	14 ounces	400 grams

†Use a glass measuring cup.

Grease the pans, line the bottoms with parchment or wax paper, and then grease again and flour. For very even cakes use Magi-Cake Strips (pages 20 and 456).

INSTRUCTIONS FOR MIXING BATTER FOR ALL SIZES OF WHITE AND YELLOW BUTTER CAKES

Arrange 2 oven racks as close to the center of the oven as possible with at least 3 inches between them.

Preheat the oven to 350°F.

In a medium bowl, lightly combine the whites or yolks, ¼ of the milk, and the vanilla.

In a large mixing bowl combine all the dry ingredients and mix on low speed for 1 minute to blend. Add the butter and remaining milk. Mix on low speed until the dry ingredients are moistened. Beat at medium speed (high speed if using a hand mixer) for 1½ minutes to aerate and develop the cake's structure. Scrape down the sides.

Gradually beat in the egg mixture in 3 batches, beating for 20 seconds after each addition to incorporate the ingredients and strengthen the structure. Scrape down the sides.

Scrape the batter into the prepared pans, filling about halfway, and smooth with a spatula. (For exact batter weight in each pan, refer to the chart on page 483.) Arrange the pans in the oven so that air can circulate around them. Do not allow them to touch each other or the oven walls. Bake 25 to 35 minutes for 6-inch layers, 35 to 45 minutes for 9-inch layers, and 40 to 50 minutes for 12-inch layers or until a tester inserted near the center comes out clean and the cake springs back when pressed lightly in the center. In the

FINISHED HEIGHT:
Each layer is about 1½ inches.

STORE:
Airtight: 2 days room temperature, 5 days refrigerated, 2 months frozen.

SERVE:
Room temperature.

6-inch and 9-inch pans, the cakes should start to shrink from the sides only after removal from the oven. The 12-inch layers should bake until they just start to shrink from the sides. To promote more even baking, turn the 12-inch layers 180° (halfway around) halfway through the baking time. Do this quickly so the oven temperature does not drop.

Allow the cakes to cool in the pans on racks for 10 minutes (20 minutes for 12-inch layers). Loosen the sides with a spatula and invert onto greased wire racks. To prevent splitting, reinvert and cool completely before wrapping airtight with plastic wrap and foil.

NOTE: Do not underbake the 12-inch layers.

When preparing the cake more than 24 hours ahead of serving or if extra moistness is desired, sprinkle layers with 3 cups of Syrup (page 505).

3-Tier Chocolate Butter Wedding Cake to Serve 150*

INGREDIENTS	MEASURE	WEIGHT	
room temperature	*volume*	*pounds/ounces*	*kilograms/grams*
FOR TWO 6-INCH BY 2-INCH LAYERS AND TWO 9-INCH BY 2-INCH LAYERS			
6 large eggs	10 scant fluid ounces†	10.5 ounces (weighed without shells)	300 grams
water (boiling)	2 liquid cups†	1 pound 0.75 ounce	473 grams
vanilla	1 tablespoon + 1½ teaspoons	•	18 grams
sifted cake flour	4¾ cups	1 pound 0.5 ounce	475 grams
unsweetened cocoa (Dutch-processed)	1¼ cups + 2 tablespoons (lightly spooned into cup)	4.5 ounces	125 grams

* Requires a 5-quart mixer.

INGREDIENTS	MEASURE	WEIGHT	
room temperature	*volume*	*pounds/ounces*	*kilograms/grams*
sugar	3 cups	1 pound 5 ounces	600 grams
baking powder	3 tablespoons	1.5 ounces	44 grams
salt	1½ teaspoons	•	10 grams
unsalted butter	1½ cups	12 ounces	340 grams
FOR TWO 12-INCH BY 2-INCH LAYERS			
7 large eggs	11 fluid ounces †	12.25 ounces (weighed without shells)	350 grams
water (boiling)	2⅓ liquid cups †	1 pound 3.5 ounces	550 grams
vanilla	1 tablespoon + 2¼ teaspoons	•	21 grams
sifted cake flour	5½ cups	1 pound 3.5 ounces	553 grams
unsweetened cocoa (Dutch-processed)	1½ cups + 2 tablespoons (lightly spooned into cup)	5 ounces	147 grams
sugar	3½ cups	1 pound 8.5 ounces	700 grams
baking powder	2 tablespoons + 2¾ teaspoons	•	43 grams
salt	1¾ teaspoons	•	12 grams
unsalted butter	1¾ cups	14 ounces	400 grams

†Use a glass measuring cup.

Grease the pans, line the bottoms with parchment or wax paper, and then grease again and flour. For very even cakes use Magi-Cake Strips (pages 20 and 456).

INSTRUCTIONS FOR MIXING BATTER FOR ALL SIZES OF CHOCOLATE BUTTER CAKES

Arrange 2 oven racks as close to the center of the oven as possible with at least 3 inches between them.

Preheat the oven to 350°F.

FINISHED HEIGHT:
Each layer is about 1½ inches.

STORE:
Airtight: 2 days room temperature, 5 days refrigerated, 2 months frozen.

SERVE:
At room temperature.

In a medium bowl whisk together the cocoa and boiling water until smooth and cool to room temperature.

In another medium bowl lightly combine the eggs, ¼ of the cocoa mixture, and the vanilla.

In a large mixing bowl combine all the remaining dry ingredients and mix on low speed for 1 minute to blend. Add the butter and remaining cocoa mixture. Mix on low speed until the dry ingredients are moistened. Beat at medium speed (high speed if using a hand mixer) for 1½ minutes to aerate and develop the cake's structure. Scrape down the sides.

Gradually beat in the egg mixture in 3 batches, beating for 20 seconds after each addition to incorporate the ingredients and strengthen the structure. Scrape down the sides.

Scrape the batter into the prepared pans, filling about halfway, and smooth with a spatula. (For exact batter weight in each pan, refer to the chart on page 483.) Arrange the pans in the oven so that air can circulate around them. Do not allow them to touch each other or the oven walls. Bake 25 to 35 minutes for 6-inch layers, 35 to 45 minutes for 9-inch layers, 40 to 50 minutes for 12-inch layers or until a tester inserted near the center comes out clean and the cake springs back when pressed lightly in the center. In the 6-inch and 9-inch pans, the cakes should start to shrink from the sides only after removal from the oven. The 12-inch layers should bake until they just start to shrink from the sides. To promote more even baking, turn the 12-inch layers 180° (halfway around) halfway through the baking time. Do this quickly so the oven temperature does not drop.

Allow the cakes to cool in the pans on racks for 10 minutes (20 minutes for 12-inch layers). Loosen the sides with a small metal spatula and invert onto greased wire racks. To prevent splitting, reinvert and cool completely before wrapping airtight with plastic wrap and heavy-duty foil.

NOTE: Do not underbake the 12-inch layers. If you cut the tops of the cake layers to make them more level, you will notice many small holes. Do not be alarmed because they do not show up when cake is sliced. The crumb will be fine and even.

When preparing the cake more than 24 hours ahead of serving or if extra moistness is desired, sprinkle layers with 3 cups of Syrup (page 505).

The chart that follows will show you how to make any size cake and how many people each layer will serve. There is often confusion regarding layers and tiers. A wedding cake is made up of tiers, each tier consisting of 2 equal layers sandwiched with filling.

To use the chart, you will need a calculator, a piece of paper, and a pencil. Refer to the size cake you want and mark down the Rose factor which applies to 2 layers. For example, let's say you want to make a 2-tier yellow cake consisting of an 8-inch tier and a 12-inch tier. The Rose factor for two 8-inch layers is 3.5; the Rose factor for two 12-inch layers is 7.

The 8-inch size falls in baking powder level 1; the 12-inch size, in baking powder level 3. Because each size requires a different amount of baking powder in proportion to the other ingredients, 2 separate batters are needed.

To make the batter for the 8-inch layers, multiply each ingredient in the base formula by Rose factor 3.5. For the baking powder, refer to level 1 for yellow cake. The number will be 1½ teaspoons. Multiply this by 3.5.

To make the batter for the 12-inch layers, multiply each ingredient in the base formula by Rose factor 7. For the baking powder, refer to level 3 for yellow cake. The number will be 1⅛ teaspoons. Multiply this by Rose factor 7. That's all there is to it. Refer to page 494 if you need a review of mixing techniques. If you bake often, you will not need this because the simple technique is the same for all the butter cakes in this book.

For irregularly shaped pans, refer to page 456 in the Ingredients and Equipment chapter.

HOW TO MAKE
ANY SIZE ROUND
BUTTER CAKE
FROM 6-INCHES
TO 18-INCHES

MASTER CHART FOR BUTTER CAKES

	pan size (2 layers each 2 inches high)	number of servings (2 layers)	Rose factor (number of times to multiply base)	batter weight for each pan	baking time at 350°F.
BAKING POWDER LEVELS					
Level 1	6 inches	20	2	12.5 ounces/356 grams	25–35 minutes
	7 inches	25	2.5	1 pound/460 grams	25–35 minutes
	8 inches	35	3.5	1 pound 6.75 ounces/650 grams	30–40 minutes
Level 2	9 inches	45	4	26.25 ounces/750 grams	30–40 minutes
	10 inches	55	5	2 pounds/930 grams	30–40 minutes
Level 3	11 inches	65	6	2.5 pounds/1 kilogram 140 grams	35–45 minutes
	12 inches	75	7	2 pounds 13.5 ounces/1 kilogram 330 grams	40–50 minutes
	13 inches	100	9	3 pounds 12.5 ounces/1 kilogram 725 grams	40–50 minutes
	14 inches	110	10	4 pounds 3.5 ounces/1 kilogram 920 grams	40–50 minutes
Level 4	15 inches	130	12	5 pounds/2 kilograms 280 grams	40–50 minutes
	16 inches	150	14	6 pounds/2 kilograms 700 grams	45–55 minutes
	17 inches	175	16	6 pounds 12.5 ounces/3 kilograms 90 grams	45–55 minutes
Level 5	18 inches	185	17	7 pounds 3.5 ounces/3 kilograms 280 grams	45–55 minutes
Level 6	13-inch x 9-inch rectangle	40	3.5–4	1 kilogram 300 grams–1 kilogram 500 grams	40–50 minutes
	18-inch x 12-inch rectangle	80	7–8	2 kilogram 670 grams–3 kilograms 50 grams	35–45 minutes

TIPS: Large layers are more prone to underbaking than overbaking. The cake should just start to shrink from the sides of the pan when done. Be sure to use Magi-Cake Strips (pages 20 and 456) for very even layers.

A 12-inch by 2-inch pan (Rose factor 4) serves 40 to 50 people and is a good size for large parties. The single layer will be 1¾ inches high.

NOTE: Batter weight takes into account the amount clinging to the bowl and beater (about the same regardless of the batter size). Larger sizes will therefore have proportionately more batter; for example, 4 times the Rose factor will yield slightly more than double 2 times the Rose factor.

Base Formula for Butter Cakes

SERVES 11
WEDDING
CAKE
PORTIONS

INGREDIENTS	MEASURE	WEIGHT	
room temperature	*volume*	*ounces*	*grams*
WHITE BASE CAKE 1½ large egg whites	3 tablespoons	1.5 ounces	45 grams
milk	⅓ liquid cup	2.75 ounces	80 grams
vanilla	¾ teaspoon	0.11 ounce	3 grams
sifted cake flour	1 cup	3.5 ounces	100 grams
sugar	½ cup	3.5 ounces	100 grams
baking powder	see amount for each individual cake size (page 490)		
salt	¼ teaspoon	0.05 ounce	1.67 grams
unsalted butter (must be softened)	4 tablespoons	2 ounces	56.75 grams
Total Batter Weight: 13.5 ounces/387 grams (+ baking powder)			

INGREDIENTS	MEASURE	WEIGHT	
room temperature	*volume*	*ounces*	*grams*
YELLOW BASE CAKE 2 large egg yolks	2 tablespoons + 1 teaspoon	1.25 ounces	37 grams
milk	⅓ liquid cup	2.75 ounces	80 grams
vanilla	¾ teaspoon	0.11 ounce	3 grams
sifted cake flour	1 cup	3.5 ounces	100 grams
sugar	½ cup	3.5 ounces	100 grams
baking powder	see amount for each individual cake size (page 490)		
salt	¼ teaspoon	0.05 ounce	1.67 grams
unsalted butter (must be softened)	4 tablespoons	2 ounces	56.75 grams
Total Batter Weight: 13.2 ounces/379 grams (+ baking powder)			

BAKING POWDER AMOUNTS FOR YELLOW AND WHITE BASE CAKES				
Level 1	6-inch to 8-inch cakes	1½ teaspoons per base	0.26 ounce	7.35 grams
Level 2	9-inch to 10-inch cakes	1⅓ teaspoons per base	0.23 ounce	6.52 grams
Level 3	11-inch to 14-inch cakes	1⅛ teaspoons per base	0.19 ounce	5.51 grams
Level 4	15-inch to 17-inch cakes	1 teaspoon per base	0.17 ounce	4.90 grams
Level 5	18-inch cakes	⅞ teaspoon per base	0.15 ounce	4.25 grams
Level 6	sheet cakes	1¼ teaspoons per base	0.21 ounce	6.13 grams

NOTE: The weights are in more precise units than most scales are capable of registering. When making just a few tiers, I use measuring spoons. I have given these weights for large-scale baking. When they are multiplied, the amounts are more practical to weigh and more accurate.

UNDERSTANDING

The larger the pan size, the less baking powder is used in proportion to the other ingredients. This is because of surface tension. The larger the diameter of the pan, the slower the heat penetration and the less support the rising cake receives because the sides are farther from the center. Baking powder weakens the cake's structure by enlarging the air spaces, so decreasing the baking powder strengthens the structure and compensates for retarded gelatinization and the decrease in support.

SERVES 11
WEDDING CAKE PORTIONS

INGREDIENTS	MEASURE	WEIGHT	
room temperature	*volume*	*ounces*	*grams*
CHOCOLATE BASE CAKE unsweetened cocoa (Dutch-processed)	3 tablespoons + 1½ teaspoons (dip and sweep method)	0.75 ounce	21 grams
water	⅓ liquid cup (use glass measuring cup)	2.75 ounces	78 grams
1 large egg	3 tablespoons + ½ teaspoon	1.75 ounces (weighed without shells)	50 grams
vanilla	¾ teaspoon	0.11 ounce	3 grams
sifted cake flour	¾ cup + 2 teaspoons	2.75 ounces	79 grams
sugar	½ cup	3.5 ounces	100 grams
baking powder	see amount for each individual cake size (below)		
salt	¼ teaspoon	0.05 ounce	1.67 grams
unsalted butter (must be softened)	4 tablespoons	2 ounces	56.75 grams
Total Batter Weight: 13.65 ounces/390 grams (+ baking powder)			

BAKING POWDER AMOUNTS FOR CHOCOLATE BASE CAKES				
Level 1	6-inch to 8-inch cakes	1⅝ teaspoons per base	0.28 ounce	7.96 grams
Level 2	9-inch to 10-inch cakes	1½ teaspoons per base	0.26 ounce	7.35 grams
Level 3	11-inch to 14-inch cakes	1¼ teaspoons per base	0.21 ounce	6.13 grams
Level 4	15-inch to 17-inch cakes	1⅛ teaspoons per base	0.19 ounce	5.51 grams
Level 5	18-inch cakes	1 teaspoon per base	0.17 ounce	4.9 grams
Level 6	sheet cakes	1⅓ teaspoons per base	0.23 ounce	6.52 grams

SPECIAL
INSTRUCTIONS
FOR MIXING A
SINGLE BATTER
FOR VARYING
SIZES OF BUTTER
CAKE LAYERS

Despite the different amounts of baking powder required for different size layers, there is a way to save time and mix all the batter at once. If you bake tiered cakes often, this is a very efficient and useful technique to possess. It requires a 10-quart Hobart mixer and enough oven space to bake all the layers at once or a refrigerator to hold some of the layers while the others are baking. Describing this method is rather like tying a shoelace— once you learn, it's easy to do but awkward to put into words. I assure you that once you try it you will find it easier than mixing separate batches, yet each cake will come out level and with perfect texture. It's best to calculate all the amounts before starting to mix the batter. Once you have these formulas worked out for your most common size cakes, you won't need to refer to the chart. Don't be put off by the figures; it's simple grade school mathematics. Double-check your multiplication and the system is infallible.

1. First choose the sizes of the cake layers. Refer to the Master Chart for Layer Cakes (page 483) and write down the Rose factor for each pan size. Add these numbers and the sum will be the *total Rose factor* by which to multiply everything in the base except for the baking powder.

2. To determine the baking powder, choose the level for the largest pans you are using and multiply it by the *total Rose factor* (for all the tiers).

3. Mix the batter, and scale out (pour into pans and weigh) only the pans in the largest level, referring to the chart for the weight of the batter in each pan. (Be sure to subtract the weight of the pans!)

4. Now go back to the chart and find the Rose factors for the remaining layers. Add and the total will be the new Rose factor.

5. Multiply this new factor by the original level of baking powder. That is how much baking powder is now remaining in the batter.

6. Now choose the level of baking powder for the next largest pans and multiply it by the new Rose factor. This is how much baking powder must now be in the batter.

   To determine the amount to add, calculate the difference (subtract the amount needed in the batter from the amount already in the batter). This is how much baking powder it is necessary to add.

7. To add baking powder: Dissolve it in the smallest possible amount of ice water and stir it thoroughly into the remaining batter.

8. Scale this batter into all pans in the same level and proceed with remaining batter in the same way.

Here is an example to help you double-check the system. (I am using only the metric system for the example as too many figures would be confusing, but of course the avoirdupoir system or volume works in the same way.)

EXAMPLE: *Batter for a 3-tier yellow cake using 6-inch, 9-inch, and 12-inch pans.*

1. The total Rose factor for these layers is *13.*
2. *5.51 grams* (1⅛ teaspoons) baking powder (the level for the largest pan size, 12 inches) times the total Rose factor *13* = *71.63 grams.*
3. Put *1 kilogram + 330 grams* of batter in each 12-inch pan.
4. The Rose factor for the remaining 9-inch and 6-inch layers is 6 (the new Rose factor).
5. Multiply the original level of baking powder (*5.51 grams*) by 6. This equals *33 grams* (the amount of baking powder now in the batter).
6. The baking powder level for the next largest pans (9 inches) is *6.52 grams* (1⅓ teaspoons). Multiply by 6 to get *39 grams.* This is how much baking powder must now be in the batter. To determine the amount to add, calculate the difference between what must now be in the batter (*39 grams*) and the amount already in the batter (*33 grams*). The difference is 6 *grams* (about 1¼ teaspoons).
7. Dissolve the *6 grams* of baking powder in the smallest possible amount of ice water and stir it thoroughly into the remaining batter.
8. Put *750 grams* of batter in each 9-inch pan.
9. The Rose factor for the 6-inch layers is 2 (the new Rose factor).
10. Multiply 2 by the original level of baking powder used (*5.51 grams*). This equals *11 grams* (the amount of baking powder now in the batter).
11. The baking powder level for the 6-inch pans is *7.35 grams* (1½ teaspoons). Multiply by 2 to get *14.7 grams.* This is how much baking powder must now be in the batter.

    To determine the amount to add, calculate the difference between what must now be in the batter (*14.7 grams*) and the amount already in the batter (*11 grams*). The difference is *3.7 grams* (¾ teaspoon).
12. Dissolve the *3.7 grams* of baking powder in the smallest possible amount of ice water and stir it thoroughly into the remaining batter.
13. Put *356 grams* of batter in each 6-inch pan. All the batter will have been used.

NOTE: The idea of adding baking powder to the already prepared batter may seem controversial, but here's why it works: The baking powder must be double acting and it must be evenly dispersed. This is best accomplished by dissolving it. Ice water is used to dissolve the baking powder because double-acting baking powder is activated partly by liquid and partly by heat. The cold water retards this reaction.

For the same reason, cake batter, once poured into the pan, can be refrigerated for several hours before baking and will lose no discernible volume.

GÉNOISE WEDDING CAKES

It is a delightful surprise to find airy, moist *génoise* inside a large wedding cake. Despite its delicate texture, it is possible to tier a *génoise* using supporting structures (page 534). The problem is that without a 10-quart Hobart mixer the *génoise* has to be made in 4 batches. Even with a 20-quart Hobart, it should be made in 2 batches because there is too much loss of volume during the time it takes to divide a single batch into 6 pans and then place them in the oven.

If you only have a KitchenAid K5 (and I remember the days when I used to say: "If only I *had* a K5!") and you want to make a 3-tiered *génoise* wedding cake for 150 people, refer to the chart on page 497 for quantities. The two 6-inch layers can be prepared as one batch, the two 9-inch as a second batch, and each 12-inch layer as a separate batch. (Need I add, this is a true labor of love.)

When folding the flour into the egg and sugar mixture, be sure to incorporate all the flour particles completely or they will become encapsulated in the batter and fall to the bottom of the cake. If this should happen, wait until the cake is cool and with the tip of a sharp knife pick out the particles. (Because they are heavier than the rest of the batter, they fall to the bottom.) Once, years ago, I was lazy and left them in the cake. Everyone admired the "unusual little nuts!"

3-Tier Génoise Classique Wedding Cake to Serve 150*

INGREDIENTS	MEASURE	WEIGHT	
room temperature	volume	pounds/ounces	kilgrams/grams
FOR TWO 6-INCH BY 2-INCH LAYERS AND TWO 9-INCH BY 2-INCH LAYERS			
clarified *buerre noisette* (clarified browned butter, page 426)	½ liquid cup† plus 1 tablespoon	4 ounces	110 grams
vanilla	1 tablespoon	•	12 grams
12 large eggs	19 fluid ounces (2 liquid cups +3 fluid ounces)†	1 pound 5 ounces (weighed without shells)	600 grams
sugar	1½ cups	10.5 ounces	300 grams
sifted cake flour	1½ cups	5.25 ounces	150 grams
cornstarch	1¼ cups (lightly spooned into cup)	5.25 ounces	150 grams
FOR TWO 12-INCH BY 2-INCH LAYERS			
clarified *beurre noisette* (clarified browned butter, page 426)	⅔ liquid cup†	4.5 ounces	130 grams
vanilla	1 tablespoon + 1 teaspoon	•	16 grams
14 large eggs	22 fluid ounces (2¾ liquid cups)†	24.5 ounces (weighed without shells)	700 grams
sugar	1¾ cup	12 ounces	350 grams
sifted cake flour	1¾ cups	6 ounces	175 grams
cornstarch	1⅓ cups + 2 tablespoons (lightly spooned into cup)	6 ounces	175 grams
SYRUP: 5 cups (page 505). Refer to the chart on page 502 for how much to apply to each layer.			

* Requires a 10-quart Hobart mixer.
† Use glass measuring cups.

After trimming the bottom and top crusts, each layer is about 1½ inches.

STORE:
Without syrup, 2 days room temperature, 5 days refrigerated, 2 months frozen. After completing the cake, the flavors ripen and the moisture is more evenly distributed 1 day later.

SERVE:
Room temperature or lightly chilled.

Grease the pans, line the bottoms with parchment or wax paper, and then grease again and flour. For very even cakes use Magi-Cake Strips (pages 20 and 456).

INSTRUCTIONS FOR MIXING BATTER FOR ALL SIZES OF GÉNOISE CLASSIQUE

Arrange 2 oven racks as close to the center of the oven as possible with at least 3 inches between them.

Preheat oven to 350°F.

Warm the *beurre noisette* until almost hot (110°F. to 120°F). Add the vanilla and keep warm.

In a large mixing bowl set over a pan of simmering water place the eggs and sugar and heat until just lukewarm, stirring constantly. (The eggs may also be heated by placing them *still in their shells* in a large mixing bowl in an oven with a pilot light for 3 hours or overnight.)

Using the whisk beater, beat on high speed for 5 minutes or until triple in volume.

Meanwhile, sift together the flour and cornstarch.

Transfer the egg mixture to a bowl large enough to fold in the other ingredients. Remove 3 cups of the egg mixture and thoroughly whisk it into the *beurre noisette*. (If making the batter in several batches, decrease amount of egg mixture removed accordingly. For example, if making batter for only two 9-inch layers, reserve only 2 scant cups.)

Sift ½ flour mixture over the remaining egg mixture, folding gently but rapidly with a large balloon whisk or slotted skimmer until the flour has almost disappeared. Repeat with remaining flour mixture until all the flour has entirely disappeared. Fold in the butter mixture only until incorporated.

Pour immediately into the pans (they will be at least two thirds full) and bake immediately 20 to 35 minutes for 6-inch and 9-inch layers and 30 to 40 minutes for 12-inch layers or until the cake is golden brown and starts to shrink slightly from the sides of the pan. Avoid opening the oven door before the minimum time is over or the cake may fall. Test towards the end of baking by opening the oven door slightly and, if at a quick glance it does not appear done, close the door at once and check again in 5 minutes.

Loosen the sides with a small metal spatula and unmold at once onto lightly greased racks. Reinvert to cool. Remove the crust when ready to complete the cake and sprinkle the syrup evenly on all layers (page 357).

NOTE: 12-inches is the largest round *génoise* that can be made without loss in quality of texture. A larger pan does not offer enough support.

3-Tier Génoise au Chocolat Wedding Cake to Serve 150*

INGREDIENTS	MEASURE	WEIGHT	
room temperature	*volume*	*ounces*	*grams*
FOR TWO 6-INCH BY 2-INCH LAYERS AND TWO 9-INCH BY 2-INCH LAYERS			
clarified *beurre noisette* (clarified browned butter, page 426)	½ liquid cup† + 1 tablespoon	4 ounces	110 grams
unsweetened cocoa (Dutch-processed)	¾ cup + 3 tablespoons (lightly spooned into cup)	3 ounces	87 grams
water (boiling)	¾ liquid cup†	6.25 ounces	177 grams
vanilla	1 tablespoon	•	12 grams
15 large eggs	3 liquid cups†	1 pound 10.25 ounces (weighed without shells)	750 grams
sugar	1½ cups	10.5 ounces	300 grams
sifted cake flour	2 cups + 2 tablespoons	7.5 ounces	213 grams
FOR TWO 12-INCH BY 2-INCH LAYERS			
clarified *beurre noisette* (clarified browned butter, page 426)	⅔ liquid cup†	4.5 ounces	130 grams
unsweetened cocoa (Dutch-processed)	1 cup + 1 tablespoon (lightly spooned into cup)	3.5 ounces	100 grams
water	1 liquid cup†	8.25 ounces	236 grams
vanilla	1 tablespoon + 1 teaspoon	•	16 grams

* Requires a 10-quart Hobart mixer.
† Use glass measuring cups.

INGREDIENTS	MEASURE	WEIGHT	
room temperature	*volume*	*ounces*	*grams*
18 large eggs	3½ liquid cups†	2 pounds (weighed without shells)	900 grams
sugar	1¾ cup	12.25 ounces	350 grams
sifted cake flour	2½ cups	8.75 ounces	250 grams
SYRUP 5 cups (page 505). Refer to the chart on page 503 for how much to brush on each layer.			

† Use glass measuring cups.

FINISHED HEIGHT:
After trimming the bottom and top crusts, each layer is about 1½ inches.

STORE:
Without syrup, 2 days room temperature, 5 days refrigerated, 2 months frozen. After completing the cake, the flavors ripen and the moisture is more evenly distributed 1 day later.

SERVE:
Room temperature or lightly chilled.

Grease the pans, line the bottoms with parchment or wax paper, and then grease again and flour. For very even layers use Magi-Cake Strips (pages 20 and 456).

INSTRUCTIONS FOR MIXING BATTER FOR ALL SIZES OF GÉNOISE AU CHOCOLAT

Arrange 2 oven racks as close to the center of the oven as possible with at least 3 inches between them.

Preheat the oven to 350°F.

Warm the *beurre noisette* until almost hot (110°F. to 120°F.). Keep warm.

In a medium bowl place the cocoa and boiling water and whisk together until the cocoa is completely dissolved. Stir in the vanilla and set aside, leaving the whisk in the bowl. Cover with plastic wrap to prevent drying.

In a large mixing bowl set over a pan of simmering water place the eggs and sugar and heat until just lukewarm, stirring constantly. (The eggs may also be heated by placing them *still in their shells* in a large mixing bowl in an oven with a pilot light for 3 hours or overnight.)

Using the whisk beater, beat on high speed for 5 minutes or until triple in volume. Transfer the egg mixture to a bowl large enough to fold in the other ingredients.

Remove 3 cups of the egg mixture and whisk it into the cocoa mixture until smooth. (If making batter in several batches, decrease the amount of egg mixture removed accordingly. For example, if making batter for only two 9-inch layers, reserve only 2 cups.)

Sift the flour over the remaining egg mixture, folding gently but rapidly with a slotted skimmer or spatula until all flour has entirely disappeared. Fold in the cocoa mixture until almost evenly incorporated. Add the *beurre noisette* in 2 batches, folding with a large balloon whisk or rubber spatula* just until evenly incorporated. Pour immediately

* Fingers work well to feel for lumps of flour. They can be dissolved by pressing between thumb and forefinger.

into the pans (they will be at least three-quarters full) and bake 25 to 35 minutes for 6-inch and 9-inch layers and 35 to 45 minutes for 12-inch layers or until the cake starts to shrink from the sides of the pan. Avoid opening the oven door before the minimum time is over or the cake may fall. Test toward the end of baking by opening the oven door slightly and, if at a quick glance it does not appear done, close the door at once and check again in 5 minutes.

Loosen the sides with a spatula and unmold at once onto lightly greased racks. Reinvert to cool. Remove the crust when ready to complete the cake and sprinkle the syrup evenly on all layers (page 357).

NOTE: 12 inches is the largest *génoise* that can be made without loss in quality of texture. A larger pan does not offer enough support.

Syrup for 3-Tier Génoise to Serve 150

MAKES 5 CUPS
(2 pounds 15 ounces/
1 kilogram 340 grams)

INGREDIENTS	MEASURE	WEIGHT	
room temperature	*volume*	*pounds/ounces*	*kilograms/grams*
sugar	1¾ cups + 2 tablespoons	13 ounces	375 grams
water	3⅓ liquid cups *	1 pound 11.75 ounces	787 grams
liqueur	1 liquid cup*	8.5 ounces	240 grams

* Use glass measuring cups.

In a 2-quart saucepan with a tight-fitting lid combine the sugar and water and bring to a rolling boil, stirring constantly. Cover immediately, remove from the heat, and cool completely. Transfer to a liquid measuring cup and stir in the liqueur. If syrup has evaporated slightly, add enough water to equal 5 cups syrup.

STORE:
1 month refrigerated in an airtight container.

HOW TO MAKE 6-INCH TO 12-INCH ROUND GÉNOISE

The chart that follows will show you how to make any size *génoise* from 6 inches to 12 inches plus an 18-inch sheet cake. I find that in a round *génoise* 12 inches is the largest size possible without loss of quality in texture. Larger pans do not offer adequate support. This chart will also tell you how many people each layer will serve and how much syrup is needed for each layer.

To use the chart, you will need a calculator, a piece of paper, and a pencil. Refer to the size cake you want and mark down the Rose factor which applies to 2 layers. Turn to the Classique Base or Chocolat Base on page 504 and multiply each ingredient by the Rose factor.* The figures on the base chart may appear awkward (such as 1.8 teaspoons) but, when multiplied by the Rose factor, will yield more reasonable amounts. If, for example, after multiplying, you end up with 4.8 teaspoons, simply round off to the nearest convenient unit of measure, 4¾ teaspoons. These tables are precise to enable you to have more leeway in rounding off the figures. Charts sometimes have a way of looking ominous and restricting, but there is a range of acceptable deviation and a few grams more or less will not be discernible.

MASTER CHART FOR GÉNOISE CLASSIQUE

pan size (2 layers each 2 inches high)	number of servings (2 layers)	Rose factor (number of times to multiply base)	baking time at 350°F.	syrup needed for 2 layers
6 inches	20	4	20–25 minutes	⅔ cup
7 inches	25	5	20–25 minutes	1 cup
8 inches	35	7	25–35 minutes	1⅓ cups
9 inches	45	8	25–35 minutes	1½ cups
10 inches	55	11	25–30 minutes	2 cups
11 inches	65	13	25–30 minutes	2½ cups
12 inches	75	14	30–35 minutes	2¾ cups
13-inch by 9-inch rectangle	45	8	20–30 minutes	1½ cups
18-inch by 12-inch rectangle	75	14–16	30–40 minutes	2¾ to 3 cups

*If using volume instead of weight, keep in mind that 3 teaspoons = 1 tablespoon and 16 tablespoons = 1 cup.

TIPS: Large layers are more prone to underbaking than overbaking. The cake should just start to shrink from the sides of the pan when done. Be sure to use Magi-Cake Strips (pages 20 and 456) for even layers.

Pans can be filled up to ½ inch from top.

One 12-inch by 2-inch layer (Rose factor 7) serves 40 to 50 people and is a good size for large parties. (Please check above table for two 12-inch layers and divide in half to make 1 layer).

MASTER CHART FOR GÉNOISE AU CHOCOLAT				
pan size (2 layers each 2 inches high)	number of servings (2 layers)	Rose factor (number of times to multiply base)	baking time at 350°F.	syrup needed for 2 layers
6 inches	20	5	30–35 minutes	⅔ cup
7 inches	25	7	30–35 minutes	1 cup
8 inches	35	9	30–35 minutes	1⅓ cups
9 inches	45	10	30–35 minutes	1½ cups
10 inches	55	14	35–40 minutes	2 cups
11 inches	65	16	35–40 minutes	2½ cups
12 inches	76	18	40–45 minutes	2¾ cups
13-inch by 9-inch rectangle	45	10	30–40 minutes	1½ cups
18-inch by 12-inch rectangle	75	18–20	40–50 minutes	2¾ to 3 cups

TIPS: Chocolate *génoise* layers are more prone to underbaking than overbaking and will fall slightly if not baked long enough. The cake should start to shrink from the sides of the pan when done. Be sure to use Magi-Cake Strips for even layers (pages 20 and 456).

Pans can be filled up to ½ inch from top.

A 12-inch by 2-inch layer (Rose factor 8.75) serves 40 to 50 people and is a good size for large parties. Multiply everything in the base by 8.75, but it's fine to use 9 large eggs.

Base Formulas for Génoise

INGREDIENTS	MEASURE	WEIGHT	
room temperature	*volume*	*ounces*	*grams*
GÉNOISE CLASSIQUE BASE			
clarified *beurre noisette* (clarified browned butter, page 426)	0.75 tablespoon	0.32 ounce	9 grams
vanilla	0.25 teaspoon	•	1 gram
1 large egg	3 tablespoons + ½ teaspoon	1.75 ounces (weighed without shell)	50 grams
sugar	2 tablespoons	0.88 ounce	25 grams
sifted cake flour	2 tablespoons	0.44 ounce	12.5 grams
cornstarch	1 tablespoon + 2 teaspoons	0.44 ounce	12.5 grams
GÉNOISE AU CHOCOLAT BASE			
clarified *beurre noisette* (clarified browned butter, page 426)	1.8 teaspoons	0.25 ounce	7 grams
unsweetened cocoa (Dutch-processed)	1 tablespoon (lightly spooned into cup)	0.2 ounce	5.8 grams
water	2.4 teaspoons	0.42 ounce	12 grams
vanilla	0.2 teaspoon	•	0.8 gram
1 large egg	3 tablespoons + ½ teaspoon	1.75 ounces (weighed without shells)	50 grams
sugar	1.6 tablespoons	0.7 ounce	20 grams
sifted cake flour	2.3 tablespoons	0.5 ounce	14.2 grams

Base Formula for 1 Cup Syrup

M A K E S 1 C U P
(9.25 ounces/264 grams)

INGREDIENTS	MEASURE	WEIGHT	
room temperature	*volume*	*ounces*	*grams*
sugar	6 tablespoons	2.5 ounces	75 grams
water	⅔ liquid cup (use glass measuring cup)	5.5 ounces	156 grams
liqueur of your choice	3 tablespoons	1.5 ounces	40 grams

In a saucepan with a tight-fitting lid combine the sugar and water and bring to a rolling boil, stirring constantly. Cover immediately, remove from the heat, and cool completely. Transfer to a liquid measuring cup and stir in the liqueur. If the syrup has evaporated slightly, add enough water to equal 1 cup syrup. (If multiplying this base for a larger quantity, add water to equal the appropriate amount).

STORE:
1 month refrigerated in an airtight container.

WEDDING CHEESECAKES

Isn't it almost unbelievable that a creamy 12-inch cheesecake will support 2 tiers of cake on top of it? Actually, I wasn't sure that it would, so the first time I tried it involved a certain amount of risk. I remember my husband saying (as he drove the cake over bumpy roads to Connecticut, trying not to hear my panicked gasps): "What are you worried about; you've never had a cake collapse!" And my answer: "This could be the first time! To my knowledge no one has ever tiered a cheesecake before, and it may be for a good reason."

Completed the night before, the bottom of the 12-inch tier looked like it had widened ever so slightly and tiny cracks had developed under the surrounding ribbon. Nonetheless the cake stayed in perfect shape throughout the 2-hour drive, and 2-hour outdoor photo session, and then an additional 2-hour wait at room temperature before serving.

Part of what supports the creamy custard filling are plastic straws and cardboard rounds between the tiers. Delicious White Chocolate Cream Cheese Buttercream (page 525) encases each tier and offers additional support.

If you like, you can bake 2 sheets of Biscuit Roulade (page 142), preferably the almond version, and cut circles to serve as bases for each tier. (The 12-inch round needs to be patched a bit as the pan is only 18 inches by 11 inches). If using the *biscuit,* you can eliminate the cornstarch in the cheesecake batter because the *biscuit* will absorb any excess moisture. Attach the *biscuit* to the cardboard rounds with a little buttercream. It is also fine to unmold the cheesecake layers directly onto cardboard rounds without using any base as long as the rounds are waterproofed with a thin layer of buttercream.

The wedding cheesecake consists of a single 3-inch-deep layer per tier. I am giving the formula for 12-inch, 9-inch, and 6-inch layers as well as a slightly smaller formula suitable for an 18-inch by 12-inch by 2-inch sheet cake, which is a very convenient size for a large party. I once covered an 18-inch sheet cheesecake in alabaster rolled fondant for a bar mitzvah and wrote the Ten Commandments in 14-karat gold Hebrew calligraphy on top. The border consisted of bright blue forget-me-nots with tiny silver dragées in the centers and entwined with white royal icing scroll-work (the colors of the flag of Israel). It was the most beautiful cake I ever made.

I was so happy decorating it that I started to sing long-forgotten Hebrew songs from my childhood. I had pleasant thoughts of my great-grandfather, who was a rabbi in Russia, and of his wife after whom I was named. I even found a complete miniature replica of a Torah and located the particular section appropriate for the day of the year that the bar mitzvah boy would read. I painted the plastic posts with gold paint and set the torah between the two illuminated tabloids of the Ten Commandments. (The owner of the paint store refused payment because it was for a Torah, even though I told him it was going on a cake. He said he wanted to support Judaism in whatever form he found it. I was very touched.)

I still remember my surprise and bewilderment when the bar mitzvah mother told me hesitatingly that she had expected something—well—a little more fancy. Plumes I suppose.

NOTE: Don't forget to arrange for refrigeration space!

3-Tier Wedding Cheesecake to Serve 150*

INGREDIENTS	MEASURE	WEIGHT	
room temperature	*volume*	*pounds/ounces*	*kilograms/grams*
cream cheese	10 (8-ounce) packages	5 pounds	2 kilograms 268 grams
sugar	5 cups	2 pounds 3 ounces	1 kilogram
cornstarch	⅓ cup	1.5 ounces	40 grams
15 large eggs	3 liquid cups†	26.25 ounces (weighed without shells)	750 grams
lemon juice, freshly squeezed	¾ liquid cup†	6.5 ounces	188 grams
vanilla	2½ tablespoons	1 ounce	30 grams
salt	1¼ teaspoon	•	8 grams
sour cream	15 cups (3 quarts + 3 cups)	8 pounds	3 kilograms 630 grams
optional: Apricot Swirl Filling (page 510)	4 cups	2 pounds 15 ounces	1 kilogram 328 grams

* Requires 5-quart mixer large enough to handle the batter in 2 batches. It can also be prepared in several batches in a food processor (page 82).
† Use glass measuring cups.

12-inch, 9-inch, and 6-inch cake pans, each 3 inches deep, plus 3 larger pans to serve as water baths. (The sides of the water bath pans must be 3 inches or under or baking will be slowed.) Grease the baking pans and line the bottoms with parchment or wax paper.

Party
Cheesecake
to Serve 100*

INGREDIENTS	MEASURE	WEIGHT	
room temperature	*volume*	*pounds/ounces*	*kilograms/grams*
cream cheese	8 (8-ounce) packages	4 pounds	1 kilogram 814 grams
sugar	4 cups	1 pound 12 ounces	800 grams
cornstarch	¼ cup	1 ounce	30 grams
12 large eggs	2 liquid cups + 3 fluid ounces*	1 pound 5 ounces	600 grams
lemon juice, freshly squeezed	½ liquid cup†	4.5 ounces	125 grams
vanilla	2 tablespoons	•	24 grams
salt	1 teaspoon	•	7 grams
sour cream	12 cups (3 quarts)	6 pounds 6 ounces	2 kilograms 904 grams
optional: Apricot Swirl Filling (page 510)	3¼ cups	2 pounds 6 ounces	1 kilogram 79 grams

* Requires a 5-quart mixer large enough to handle to batter in 2 batches. It can also be prepared in several batches in a food processor (page 82).
† Use glass measuring cups.

18-inch by 12-inch by 2-inch cake pan greased and bottom lined with parchment or wax paper. If possible, have ready a larger pan, such as a full size sheet pan, to serve as water bath. (The sides of the water bath pan must be 2 inches or less.)

TO UNMOLD:
Have ready sturdy corrugated glassine-coated cardboards the size of the cake layers or ½ inch larger if planning to frost (waterproofed with a thin layer of

INSTRUCTIONS FOR MIXING BATTER FOR ALL SIZES OF CHEESECAKE
Arrange oven racks as close to the center of the oven as possible with at least 4 inches between them.

Preheat the oven to 350°F.

In a mixing bowl beat the cream cheese and sugar, preferably with flat beater, until very smooth (about 3 minutes). Beat in the cornstarch. Beat in the eggs, 1 at a time, beating after each addition until smooth and scraping down the sides of the bowl. Add the lemon juice, vanilla, and salt and beat until incorporated. Beat in the sour cream just until blended.

Pour the filling into the prepared pan(s). (If adding apricot filling, see page 510.) It will come close to the top(s). Set the pan(s) in the larger pan(s) and fill each surrounding pan with at least 1 inch hot water. Bake in the preheated oven for 50 minutes. Turn off the oven and allow the cakes to cool in the oven without opening the door for 1 hour. Remove to rack(s) and cool to room temperature (1 hour for the smaller layers, longer for the 12-inch layer and sheet cake). Cover with plastic wrap and refrigerate overnight.

buttercream), to serve as a base for each layer.

Run a thin metal spatula between the sides of each cake and the pan, making sure to press well against the sides of the pan, and place the pan on heated burner for 10 to 20 seconds, moving it back and forth. Invert onto a cardboard prepared round and remove the parchment. If the cake does not release, return to the hot burner for a few more seconds.

Refrigerate until ready to frost (see White Chocolate Cream Cheese Buttercream, page 525).

STORE:
3 days refrigerated before frosting or decorating; 24 hours refrigerated after decorating. Texture suffers on freezing.

SERVE:
Lightly chilled.

Apricot Swirl Filling for Cheesecake

MAKES ABOUT 4 CUPS

INGREDIENTS	MEASURE	WEIGHT	
room temperature	*volume*	*pounds/ounces*	*kilograms/grams*
dried California apricots	2½ cups, packed	1.75 pounds	794 grams
water	1 quart	2 pounds	945 grams
lemon juice, freshly squeezed	3 tablespoons	1.5 ounces	47 grams
sugar	1 cup	7 ounces	200 grams

STORE:
5 days refrigerated, 1 year frozen.

In a small saucepan place the apricots and water and allow to stand, covered, for 2 hours. Simmer 20 minutes over very low heat, tightly covered, or until the apricots are soft. Puree along with any remaining liquid in a food processor or blender. Press through a food mill or fine strainer (page 457). You should have 3 to 4 cups puree. Use only up to 3¼ cups and store the remainder. Stir in the lemon juice and sugar. Store in an airtight container until ready to make the cheesecake batter.

To use the filling, fill each of the prepared pans ⅓ full with batter. Drizzle the filling over the batter and swirl with a small metal spatula. Pour in more batter to a capacity of ⅔ and repeat with more filling. Top with the remaining batter and filling and swirl again. Use a total of 3¼ cups for sheet cake, 2½ cups filling for the 12-inch pan, 1 cup for the 9-inch pan, and ½ for the 6-inch pan. (To bake, see page 509.)

TIP: Premium-quality California apricots, found in specialty and health food stores, are brighter orange and have a superior flavor to most packaged varieties.

This is the large-scale version of Perfect Pound Cake (page 25). Baked in a large Bundt pan, it has a beautiful golden crust and impressive shape. Although firmer than the small version, it is still meltingly tender and buttery. The plain pound cake is excellent but, if you like, try one of the variations on pages 26 and 27. (You will need to multiply any variation ingredients by 3.5.)

Party-Perfect Pound Cake

SERVES 25 to 30

INGREDIENTS	MEASURE	WEIGHT	
room temperature	*volume*	*ounces*	*grams*
milk	3 fluid ounces	3 ounces	90 grams
6 large eggs	9½ fluid ounces	10.5 ounces	300 grams (weighed without shells)
vanilla	1 tablespoon	•	12 grams
sifted cake flour	3 cups	10.5 ounces	300 grams
sugar	1½ cups	10.5 ounces	300 grams
baking powder	1 teaspoon	•	5 grams
salt	¾ teaspoon	•	5 grams
unsalted butter (must be softened)	27 tablespoons (about 1⅔ cups)	13.5 ounces	383 grams

Preheat the oven to 350°F.

In a medium bowl combine milk, eggs, and vanilla and beat lightly.

In a large mixing bowl combine the dry ingredients and mix on low speed for 1 minute to blend.

Add the butter and ½ the egg mixture. Mix on low speed until dry ingredients are moistened. Beat at medium speed (high speed if using a hand mixer) for 1 minute to aerate and develop the cake's structure.

Scrape down the sides. Gradually beat in the remaining egg mixture in 2 batches, beating for 20 seconds after each addition to incorporate the ingredients and strengthen the structure. Scrape down the sides.

Scrape the batter into the prepared pan and smooth with a spatula. The batter will be 1½ inches from the top.

Bake 45 to 50 minutes or until a wire cake tester inserted in the center comes out clean and the cake springs back when pressed lightly in the center and is just starting to shrink from the sides of the pan. Cool completely before wrapping airtight.

One 12-cup Bundt pan or 9-cup Kugelhupf, greased and floured.

FINISHED HEIGHT: 3 inches.

STORE: Airtight: 3 days room temperature, 1 week refrigerated, 2 months frozen.

SERVE: Room temperature.

NOTE: Although a 12-cup Bundt pan could accommodate an 8-egg formula (1⅓ times the size of the 6-egg formula), I find that the texture is not as tender.

If you are lucky enough to possess a cast-aluminum unlined Bundt pan, your pound cake will have the most beautiful crust. Nordicware currently produces only the cast-aluminum Bundt pan with a nonstick liner which darkens the crust. Avoid lighter weight Bundt pans as they do not bake as evenly and darken the crust.

As a point of interest, while developing this large-scale recipe, I discovered that contrary to a layer cake, extra baking powder makes a pound cake more chewy rather than more tender.

LARGE-SCALE BUTTER-CREAMS FOR WEDDING CAKES

The biggest dilemma when making a wedding or special occasion cake is how much frosting and filling will be necessary. In a bakery this is never a problem because any excess frosting from one cake can easily be used for the next. A small caterer or home baker does not usually know when the next cake will be, particularly one which will require that particular frosting.

I have kept records over the years as to how much of which kind of frosting I use for different size cakes. The chart on the following page reflects the results. I have given slightly generous amounts because it is better to have too much frosting than to have to make a new batch at the last minute. And it is difficult to gauge exactly how much frosting each person will use.

The amounts on the chart assume that the filling and frosting will be applied no less than ⅛ inch thick and no more than ¼ inch thick. A layer cake usually shrinks so that it is ½ inch smaller in diameter than the pan. Cardboard cake rounds are made the same size as standard cake pans. This means that there is ¼ inch between the sides of the cardboard and the sides of the cake. It is easy to use the side of the board as a guide, applying ¼ inch of frosting all around. It isn't necessary to use this method or as much frosting around the sides of a square or rectangular cake, because it is simpler to make frosting level when working with a straight line instead of a curve.

The chart also suggests amounts of buttercream for decorating. I prefer piped buttercream decorations that are small and elegant for both esthetic and gustatory reasons, but, if your preference is for a more opulent style be sure to make some extra buttercream.

The *génoise* in the master cake section are all 1½ inches high and the layer cakes are 1¾ inches to 2 inches high. This means that each tier of 2 layers will be about 3¾ inches to 4¾ inches high when frosted (the height of the layers plus the cardboard, filling, and frosting).

This depends, of course, on the amount of frosting used.

Following the chart are 6 buttercream recipes suitable for wedding or special occasion cakes, in quantities sufficient to fill, frost, and decorate a 3-tiered cake for 150 people.

MASTER CHART FOR FROSTING QUANTITIES				
cake size (2 layers)	amount needed between the layers	amount needed for top	amount needed for sides	total amount needed
6 inches	⅓ cup	⅓ cup	1 cup	2 cups
7 inches	⅔ cup	⅔ cup	1¼ cups	2½ cups
8 inches	¾ cup	¾ cup	1½ cups	3 cups
9 inches	1 cup	1 cup	1⅔ cups	3⅔ cups
10 inches	1¼ cups	1¼ cups	1¾ cups	4¼ cups
11 inches	1½ cups	1½ cups	2 cups	5 cups
12 inches	1¾ cups	1¾ cups	2 cups	5½ cups
13 inches	2 cups	2 cups	2⅓ cups	6⅓ cups
14 inches	2½ cups	2½ cups	2½ cups	7½ cups
15 inches	2¾ cups	2¾ cups	2⅔ cups	8 cups
16 inches	3¼ cups	3¼ cups	3 cups	9½ cups
17 inches	3⅔ cups	3⅔ cups	3⅓ cups	10⅔ cups
18 inches	4 cups	4 cups	4 cups	12 cups
1 layer 13 inches by 9 inches by 1¾ inches	1¼ cups	2 cups	1¼ cups	4½ cups
18 inches by 12 inches by 1¾ inches	•	4 cups	2 cups	6 cups

EXTRA BUTTERCREAM FOR DECORATING

For 3 graduated tiers with the bottom tier no larger than 12 inches, add 1 to 2 cups buttercream.

For 3 graduated tiers with the bottom tier larger than 15 inches, add 3 cups buttercream.

NOTE: A 5-quart mixer can handle up to 16 cups buttercream.

Mousseline Buttercream for a 3-Tier Cake to Serve 150

MAKES 11 CUPS
(without optional additions)
(4¾ pounds/2 kilograms
144 grams)

*T*his buttercream is very light, smooth, and incredibly easy to use for piped decorations. It is soft enough for beautiful shell borders yet strong enough to pipe roses. Liqueur gently perfumes the buttercream, and, if it's tinted, it also enhances the color. Mandarine, for example, lends the palest aura of apricot. If the wedding cake requires a whiter look, use a clear liqueur.

This is a thrilling buttercream to prepare because it starts off looking thin and lumpy and, about three quarters of the way through, starts to emulsify into a luxurious cream.

A word of caution: If the butter is too soft or the room too hot, what could have been a satin-smooth cream breaks down into a grainy hopeless puddle. Once this buttercream is made, however, it holds up better than any other.

INGREDIENTS	MEASURE	WEIGHT	
room temperature	*volume*	*pounds/ounces*	*kilograms/grams*
unsalted butter, softened but cool (65°F.)	5 cups	2.5 pounds	1 kilogram 134 grams
sugar	2½ cups	17.5 ounces	500 grams
water	¾ cup	6.25 ounces	177 grams
12 large egg whites	1½ liquid cups (use glass measuring cup)	12.5 ounces	360 grams
cream of tartar	1½ teaspoons	•	12 grams
liqueur such as Grand Marnier or an eau-de-vie	1 liquid cup (use glass measuring cup)	8.5 ounces	240 grams
optional additions: see below			

STORE:
2 days room temperature, 10 days refrigerated, 8 months frozen. Allow buttercream to come to room temperature before rebeating

In a mixing bowl beat the butter until smooth and creamy and set aside in a cool place.

Have ready a 2-cup heatproof glass measure near the range.

In a medium size heavy saucepan (preferably with a nonstick lining) stir together 2 cups sugar and the water.

Heat, stirring constantly, until the sugar dissolves and the syrup is bubbling. Stop stirring and turn down the heat to the lowest setting. (If using an electric range remove from the heat.)

In another mixing bowl beat the egg whites until foamy, add the cream of tartar, and beat until soft peaks form when the beater is raised. Gradually beat in the remaining ½ cup sugar until stiff peaks form when the beater is raised slowly.

Increase the heat and boil the syrup until a thermometer registers 248°F. to 250°F. (firm-ball stage). Immediately pour into the glass measure to stop the cooking.

Beat the syrup into the whites in a steady stream. Do not allow the syrup to fall on the beaters or it will spin onto the sides of the bowl. Start by pouring a small amount of the syrup onto the whites with the mixer turned off. Beat at high speed for 5 seconds. Stop mixer and add a larger amount of syrup. Beat for 5 seconds. Continue with remaining syrup. For the last addition, use a rubber scraper to remove the syrup clinging to the glass measure. Beat at low speed for 2 minutes or until cool.

Beat in the butter at medium speed, 1 tablespoon at a time. At first the mixture will seem thin but will thicken beautifully by the time all the butter is added. If at any time it looks curdled, raise the speed slightly and beat until smooth before continuing to add more butter.

Lower the speed slightly and gradually drizzle in the liqueur.

Rebeat lightly from time to time to maintain silky texture. Buttercream becomes spongy on standing.

OPTIONAL ADDITIONS

These flavorful additions (except for the white chocolate) will also tint the buttercream. If you want the outside of the cake to be white, consider using one of these variations for the filling such as the Lemon Curd Mousseline in the Dotted Swiss Dream (page 222).

CHOCOLATE MOUSSELINE: Beat in 12 ounces melted and cooled extra bittersweet or bittersweet chocolate.

WHITE CHOCOLATE MOUSSELINE: Beat in 12 ounces melted white chocolate, preferably Tobler Narcisse.

FRUIT MOUSSELINE: Add up to 2 cups of lightly sweetened Raspberry or Strawberry Puree (page 338) or Orange, Passion, Lemon, or Lime curd (pages 340 to 342).

it or it will break down irretrievably.

POINTERS FOR SUCCESS: Correct butter temperature is crucial. If you suspect that the butter was too warm (or the kitchen is very hot) and the buttercream starts thinning out and curdling, check the temperature. If the mixture does not feel cool, refrigerate it until it reaches 65°F. to 70°F. or until cool to the touch. If by chance you have used butter straight from the refrigerator and the mixture feels ice-cold, suspend the bowl over a pan of simmering water (don't let it touch the water) and heat very briefly, stirring vigorously when the mixture starts to melt slightly at the edges. Dip the bottom of the bowl in a larger bowl of ice water for a few seconds to cool it. Remove and beat by hand until smooth.

Neoclassic Buttercream for a 3-Tier Cake to Serve 150

*T*his pale yellow buttercream is perfect both as a creamy filling and as a silky undercoat for Crème Ivoire Deluxe in Pistachio and Rose Wedding Cake (see color photograph). If you would like to flavor the buttercream, see additions to buttercream (pages 518 to 521).

MAKES 8 CUPS
(without optional additions)
(3½ pounds/1 kilogram
600 grams)

INGREDIENTS	MEASURE	WEIGHT	
room temperature	*volume*	*pounds/ounces*	*kilograms/grams*
12 large egg yolks	7 fluid ounces	7.75 ounces	223 grams
sugar	1½ cups	10.5 ounces	300 grams
corn syrup	1 liquid cup (use glass measuring cup)	11.5 ounces	328 grams
unsalted butter (must be softened)	4 cups	2 pounds	907 grams
optional: liqueur or eau-de-vie of your choice	¼ to ½ cup (use glass measuring cup)	2 to 4 ounces	60 to 120 grams

STORE:
6 hours room temperature, 1 week refrigerated, 8 months frozen.

POINTERS FOR SUCCESS:
The syrup must come to a rolling boil or the buttercream will be too thin.

Have ready near the range a lightly greased 2-cup heat-proof glass measure.

In the bowl of an electric mixer, beat the yolks until light in color. Meanwhile, combine the sugar and corn syrup in a medium size saucepan (preferably with a nonstick lining) and heat, stirring constantly, until the sugar dissolves and the syrup comes to a rolling boil. (The entire surface will be covered by large bubbles.) *Immediately transfer to the glass measure to stop the cooking.*

Beat the syrup into the yolks in a steady stream. Do not allow the syrup to fall on the beaters or the syrup will spin onto the sides of the bowl. Start by pouring a small amount of syrup over the yolks with the mixer turned off. Immediately beat at high speed for 5 seconds. Stop the mixer and add a larger amount of syrup. Beat for 5 seconds. Continue with the remaining syrup. For the last addition, use a rubber scraper to remove the syrup clinging to the glass measure.

Beat until completely cool. Gradually beat in the butter, then any of the optional flavorings (pages 518 to 521). Place in an airtight bowl. Bring to room temperature before using. Rebeat if necessary to restore the texture.*

Classic Buttercream for a 3-Tier Cake to Serve 150

*T*his recipe produces the same buttercream as the Neoclassic version. If you would like to flavor the buttercream, see the additions to buttercream (pages 518 to 521).

MAKES 8 CUPS
(without optional additions)
(3 pounds 2.5 ounces/
1 kilograms 440 grams)

INGREDIENTS	MEASURE	WEIGHT	
room temperature	*volume*	*pounds/ounces*	*kilograms/grams*
12 large egg yolks	7 fluid ounces	7.75 ounces	223 grams
sugar	2 cups	14 ounces	400 grams
water	1 liquid cup	8.25 ounces	236 grams
unsalted butter (must be softened)	4 cups	2 pounds	907 grams
optional: liqueur or eau-de-vie of your choice	¼ to ½ liquid cup (use glass measuring cup)	2 to 4 ounces	60 to 120 grams

Have ready near the range a greased 2-cup heatproof glass measure.

In the bowl of an electric mixer, beat the yolks until light in color. Meanwhile, combine the sugar and water in a medium saucepan (preferably with a nonstick lining) and heat, stirring constantly, until the sugar dissolves and the syrup is boiling. Stop stirring and boil to the soft-ball stage (238°F.). *Immediately transfer to the glass measure to stop the cooking.*

* Do not rebeat chilled buttercream until it has reached room temperature or it may curdle.

STORE:
6 hours room temperature, 1 week refrigerated, 8 months frozen.

POINTERS FOR SUCCESS:
See Sugar Syrups (page 435). To prevent crystallization, do not stir after the syrup comes to a boil. To keep temperature from rising, remove the syrup from the pan as soon as it has reached 238°F.

Beat the syrup into the yolks in a steady stream. Do not allow the syrup to fall on the beaters or the syrup will spin onto the sides of the bowl. Start by pouring a small amount of syrup over the yolks with the mixer turned off. Immediately beat at high speed for 5 seconds. Stop the mixer and add a larger amount of syrup. Beat for 5 seconds. Continue with the remaining syrup. With the last addition, use a rubber scraper to remove the syrup clinging to the glass measure. Beat until completely cool.

Gradually beat in the butter, then any of the optional flavorings (pages 518 to 521). Place in an airtight bowl. Bring to room temperature before using. Rebeat if necessary to restore texture.*

Variations For One Recipe of Classic or Neoclassic Buttercream

*C*lassic or Neoclassic Buttercream can be used plain or as a base for any number of flavors. One recipe can accommodate as much as 1 cup liquid without becoming too soft. Spirits heighten the flavor of a buttercream but do not add them to buttercreams already containing fruit purees as they will become too liquid. Spirits are best kept in the background, so start with ¼ cup and then add to taste.

Fresh fruit purees such as raspberry and strawberry blend beautifully with classic buttercreams and maintain their lovely hues. Apricot puree tends to curdle buttercream slightly, so heated and strained apricot preserves or lekvar (page 429), cooled to room temperature, are preferable.

The sweetness level of the base buttercream is balanced so whatever is added must be neither too sweet nor too tart or adjustments to the base need to be made as indicated.

CLASSIC CHOCOLATE: Classic buttercreams can incorporate 12 ounces melted chocolate without becoming too stiff. This results in a light chocolate color and flavor which does not overpower yellow or white cake layers.
To make chocolate buttercream: Beat 12 ounces melted and cooled chocolate, preferably extra bittersweet or bittersweet, into the buttercream.

---

* Do not rebeat chilled buttercream until it has reached room temperature or it may curdle.

CLASSIC CHOCOLATE CARAMEL CRUNCH: The flavors of caramel and chocolate blend beautifully and the powdered caramel adds a slightly crunchy texture. Because caramel is sweet it is best to use extra bittersweet chocolate in the base.

To make chocolate caramel crunch buttercream: Beat ½ cup powdered caramel (page 313) into Classic Chocolate.

CLASSIC COFFEE: This method of making coffee extract yields a buttercream with the rich taste of good strong coffee.

To make coffee buttercream: Beat ¼ cup Medaglia d'Oro instant espresso powder dissolved in 2 teaspoons boiling water into the buttercream. For a more aromatic flavor, add ¼ to ½ cup Kahlúa.

CLASSIC MOCHA ESPRESSO: Chocolate and coffee always make a lovely combination.

To make mocha espresso buttercream: To Classic Chocolate, add ¼ cup Medaglia d'Oro instant espresso powder dissolved in 2 teaspoons boiling water. For more intense coffee flavor, add ¼ to ½ cup Kahlúa.

CLASSIC PRALINE: The best praline paste (page 430), a smooth combination of hazelnuts and caramelized sugar, makes a fabulous addition to any buttercream. Because the paste contains about 50 percent sugar it is necessary to remove some of the sugar from the base.

To make praline buttercream: When making buttercream, decrease the sugar by 3 tablespoons. Beat ½ cup praline paste into the finished buttercream.

CLASSIC CHOCOLATE PRALINE: Praline intensifies the delicious flavor of chocolate.

To make chocolate praline buttercream: Beat 12 ounces melted and cooled bittersweet chocolate into Classic Praline Buttercream. Alternately, beat ½ cup praline paste into Classic Chocolate Buttercream if it was prepared with extra bittersweet chocolate. (Either method will be the same level of sweetness.)

CLASSIC PRALINE CRUNCH: Praline powder (page 315) is made of ground hazelnuts and caramel but is not turned into a paste. This gives a crunchy texture to the buttercream.

To make praline crunch buttercream: When making the buttercream, decrease the sugar by 3 tablespoons. Beat ⅔ cup praline powder (page 315) into the finished buttercream.

CLASSIC CHOCOLATE PRALINE CRUNCH: This buttercream is like Classic Chocolate Praline except for the crunchy texture provided by the praline powder.

To make chocolate praline crunch buttercream: Beat 12 ounces melted and cooled bittersweet chocolate into Classic Praline Crunch Buttercream. Alternately, beat ⅔ cup praline powder into Classic Chocolate Buttercream if it was prepared with extra bittersweet chocolate. (Either method will be the same level of sweetness.)

CLASSIC CHESTNUT: This buttercream is excellent with chocolate cake.

To make chestnut buttercream: To make 6 cups of buttercream, start with ½ recipe buttercream and add 2 times the quantity of recipe for lightly sweetened rum-flavored chestnut puree (page 353).

CLASSIC RASPBERRY: My Raspberry Sauce is so concentrated it scarcely affects the consistency of the buttercream base. This is the purest raspberry flavor of any frosting I have ever experienced.

To make raspberry buttercream: Beat 1 cup lightly sweetened Raspberry Sauce (page 337) into the finished buttercream. If not planning to use the same day, add a few drops of red food color to prevent fading.

CLASSIC STRAWBERRY: The strawberry flavor is surprisingly fresh and intense. It is, of course, silky and creamy but has the added interest of the tiny strawberry seeds. I find that strawberries frozen without sugar have more flavor than most commercially available fresh-picked strawberries—even at the height of season.

To make strawberry buttercream: Beat 1 cup unsweetened Strawberry Puree (page 338) into the finished buttercream with a few optional drops of essence of wild strawberry (page 427) for further intensity. If not planning to use the same day, add a few drops of red food color to prevent fading.

CLASSIC APRICOT: This buttercream has a tart, honeyed flavor and a very pale golden color.

To make apricot buttercream: Beat 1 cup heated, strained, and cooled apricot preserves or lekvar (page 429) into the finished buttercream with a few optional drops of essence of apricot (page 427) for further intensity.

CLASSIC PINEAPPLE: Home-preserved pineapple is a delicious, slightly tart addition to buttercream.

To make pineapple buttercream: Beat 2 cups pureed pineapple (page 351) into the finished buttercream and add 2 to 4 tablespoons kirsch or rum.

CLASSIC LEMON: To achieve a truly lemon flavor it is necessary to use both fresh lemon juice and lemon extract (actually the pure oil of lemon). Lemon juice alone is not intense enough and the extract alone is too bitter.
To make lemon buttercream: When making the buttercream, replace ½ cup water with ½ cup freshly squeezed lemon juice. After adding the butter, beat in ½ teaspoon lemon extract.

CLASSIC ORANGE: An intense orange flavor is difficult to achieve using orange extract because it is quite bitter. Finely grated orange zest and an aromatic French orange essence (page 427), which includes the pulp, do produce an excellent orange flavor.
To make orange buttercream: Add 4 teaspoons orange essence and 2 tablespoons orange zest to the finished buttercream.

CLASSIC ORANGE BLOSSOM: Orange flower water gives this buttercream the perfume of orange blossoms. Be sure to add the Tang. It consists mainly of orange oil. The small amount adds the lilting zip associated with fresh orange flavor.
To make orange blossom buttercream: Add 2 teaspoons (27 grams) Tang dissolved in ⅔ cup orange flower water, 2 tablespoons (36 grams) orange zest, and ¼ cup Grand Marnier to the finished buttercream.

CLASSIC PASSION: This buttercream captures the slightly tart, utterly distinctive taste of fresh passion fruit.
To make passion buttercream: Beat up to 1½ cups passion curd (page 342) into finished buttercream and add 2 teaspoons of essence of passion fruit (page 427) for further intensity.

Crème Ivoire Deluxe for a 3-Tier Cake to Serve 150

Luxury White Chocolate Buttercream

MAKES
5¼ CUPS

*C*rème Ivoire is like a bonbon or chocolate truffle. On first bite it seems firm, only to dissolve immediately in the mouth, releasing the buttery and faintly chocolaty flavors.

The color of this glorious buttercream is pale ivory, reminiscent of an antique satin wedding gown. It is excellent as a frosting for a wedding cake and ideal when someone requests a chocolate wedding cake with a traditional ivory-colored exterior.

The contrast of the bittersweet dark chocolate cake against the silky sweet white chocolate buttercream is spectacular. Because of its richness and firm consistency, I like to fill and lightly frost the cake with Neoclassic (page 516) or Classic Buttercream (page 517). Because I then frost and pipe decorations with the Crème Ivoire, I am giving a smaller recipe than for the other buttercreams.

INGREDIENTS	MEASURE	WEIGHT	
room temperature	*volume*	*pounds/ounces*	*kilograms/grams*
white chocolate (preferably Tobler Narcisse)	16 (3-ounce) bars	3 pounds	1 kilogram 360 grams
cocoa butter, melted *	½ liquid cup†	4.5 ounces	128 grams
clarified unsalted butter‡	½ liquid cup†	3.5 ounces	98 grams
flavorless oil such as mineral or safflower	½ liquid cup†	3.5 ounces	100 grams

STORE:
Mineral oil has an indefinite shelf life, but safflower oil will become rancid in a matter of weeks. Therefore, if prepared with mineral oil, buttercream will keep at room temperature for 1 month. (The clarified butter shortens its shelf life at room temperature.) If prepared with another oil, store at room temperature 1 week, refrigerate 3 months, or freeze 1 year.

POINTERS FOR SUCCESS:
Follow directions on how to clarify butter. When melting the chocolate, stir often and

* Melt the cocoa butter in a double boiler, under the heat from the pilot light of an oven, or in a microwave the same way as for dark chocolate (page 379).
† Use a glass measuring cup.
‡ If you do not have clarified butter on hand, you will need to clarify 11 tablespoons (5.5 ounces/156 grams) unsalted butter. In a heavy saucepan melt the butter over medium heat, partially covered to prevent splattering. When the butter looks clear, cook, uncovered, watching carefully until the solids drop and just begin to brown. Pour immediately through a fine strainer or a strainer lined with cheesecloth.

Break the chocolate into individual squares and place in a bowl set over a pot of hot water (no hotter than 160°F.) on low heat. The water must not touch the bottom of the bowl. Add the cocoa butter, clarified butter, and oil.

Remove from the heat and stir until the chocolate begins to melt. Return to the heat if the water cools, but be careful not to let it get too hot. Stir until smooth. (The chocolate may be melted with the oil and butters in a microwave oven *if stirred every 15 seconds*. Remove before fully melted and stir, using the residual heat to complete melting.)

Because of the milk solids in the white chocolate, the buttercream must be chilled and stirred to prevent seeding (the formation of tiny lumps). Fill a large bowl with ice cubes and water and sprinkle with 1 or 2 tablespoons salt. Fill a second bowl or the sink with very hot water. Set the bowl of buttercream in the ice water. Stir constantly with whisk until you just see whisk marks on the surface. Immediately place the bowl over the bowl of hot water to take off the chill. This will only take seconds. Feel the bottom of the bowl. It should feel cool not cold.

Allow the buttercream to sit for a few minutes, stirring occasionally with whisk. If it does not form peaks when the whisk is raised, chill again for a short time.

be sure that not even a drop of water gets into the melted chocolate. If seeding should occur, try beating with an immersion blender (page 427) or remelt the buttercream, pass through a fine strainer, and chill again, stirring constantly. Be sure to use a fine-quality white chocolate which contains cocoa butter. I find Tobler Narcisse to have the best flavor and the least sweetness.

Frosting the cake first with a thin layer of Classic Buttercream offers an interesting textural contrast and gives the Crème Ivoire an ideal surface for adherence. Otherwise it will have a tendency to separate from the cake when cut. (I also use the Classic Buttercream plain or flavored as a filling.)

Keep piped decorations simple, such as a shell border (page 399). This buttercream pipes with more exquisite detail than any other, but the heat of your hand will make piping more than a few designs at a time difficult. To counteract this problem, use several parchment bags, placing just a small amount of buttercream in each, and switch bags at first sign of softening. Cooling your hand in ice water also helps.

Crème Ivoire for a 3-Tier Cake to Serve 150

White Chocolate Buttercream

MAKES 14 CUPS

*T*he delicious creamy flavor of this buttercream is similar to the deluxe version but is simpler and less expensive to make. It consists of pure white chocolate softened to frosting consistency by a neutral oil. It has that wonderful melt-in-the mouth quality offered by the cocoa butter in the white chocolate. (That is the only "butter" in the buttercream.)

This buttercream has a perfect frosting consistency so it does not require an undercoat of Classic Buttercream, but it is too soft to hold its shape for decorative piping. If you wish to make decorative borders on your cake, prepare 1 or 2 cups Crème Ivoire Deluxe (page 246).

INGREDIENTS	MEASURE	WEIGHT	
room temperature	*volume*	*pounds/ounces*	*kilograms/grams*
white chocolate (preferably Tobler Narcisse)	37⅓ (3-ounce) bars	7 pounds	3 kilograms 175 grams
flavorless oil such as mineral or safflower	3 liquid cups (use a glass measuring cup)	1 pound 5 ounces	600 grams

STORE:
Mineral oil has an indefinite shelf like, but safflower oil will become rancid in a matter of weeks. Therefore, if prepared with mineral oil, buttercream will keep at room temperature for 6 months. If prepared with another oil, store at room temperature 1 week, refrigerate 3 months, or freeze 1 year.

POINTERS FOR SUCCESS:
Carefully follow directions for melting chocolate. Be sure that not even a drop of water gets into the melted chocolate. If seeding should occur, try beating with an immersion blender (page 427) or remelt the buttercream, pass through a fine

Break the chocolate into individual squares and place in a bowl set over a pot of hot water (no hotter than 160°F.) on low heat. The water must not touch bottom of bowl. Add the oil.

Remove the pot from the heat and stir until the chocolate begins to melt. Return to the heat if the water cools, but be careful it does not get too hot. Stir until smooth. (The chocolate may be melted with the oil in a microwave oven *if stirred every 15 seconds*. Remove before fully melted and stir, using the residual heat to complete melting.)

Because of the milk solids in the white chocolate, the buttercream must be chilled and stirred to prevent seeding (the formation of tiny lumps). Fill a large bowl with ice cubes and water and sprinkle with 1 or 2 tablespoons salt. Fill a second bowl or the sink with very hot water. Set the bowl of buttercream in the ice water and stir constantly with whisk, until you just see whisk marks on the surface. Immediately place the bowl over the bowl of hot water to take off the chill. This will only take seconds. Feel the bottom of the bowl. It should feel cool not cold.

Allow the buttercream to sit for a few minutes, stirring occasionally with whisk. If it does not form peaks when the whisk is raised, chill again for a short time.

strainer, and chill again, stirring constantly. If the weather is 80°F. or above, reduce the oil to 6 tablespoons (3 liquid ounces).

White Chocolate Cream Cheese Frosting For a 3-Tier Cake to Serve 150

MAKES 13 CUPS

*T*his ivory-colored buttercream is mellow and creamy—a perfect complement for cheesecake. It makes an unusual and spectacular presentation because it pipes wonderfully and is the identical color of the cheesecake within. White chocolate adds firmness of texture, sweetness, and an undefinable flavor.

INGREDIENTS	MEASURE	WEIGHT	
room temperature	*volume*	*pounds/ounces*	*kilograms/grams*
white chocolate (preferably Tobler Narcisse)	8 (3-ounce) bars	1½ pounds	680 grams
cream cheese (must be softened)	4 (8-ounce) packages	2 pounds	907 grams
unsalted butter (must be softened)	2 cups	1 pound	454 grams
lemon juice, freshly squeezed	¼ cup	2 ounces	62 grams

Break the chocolate into individual squares and place in a bowl set over a pot of hot water (no hotter than 160°F.) on low heat. The water must not touch the bottom of the bowl.

Remove the pot from the heat and stir until the chocolate begins to melt. Return to the heat if the water cools, but be careful it does not get too hot. Stir until smooth. (The chocolate may be melted in a microwave on high power *if stirred every 15 seconds.* Remove before fully melted and stir, using the residual heat to complete melting.)

STORE:
1 day room temperature, 2 weeks refrigerated, 2 months frozen. Allow to come to room temperature before rebeating.

POINTERS FOR SUCCESS:
Do not overheat the chocolate and stir constantly while melting. Be sure no

moisture gets into the melted chocolate (see Melting White Chocolate, page 379). Beat constantly while adding the chocolate to prevent lumping. If lumping should occur, it can be remedied by pressing the buttercream through a fine strainer.

Buttercream may separate slightly if room temperature is very warm. This can be corrected by setting the bowl in ice water and whisking mixture. The buttercream becomes spongy on standing. Rebeat to restore smooth creamy texture. Use ice to chill your hand during piping to maintain firm texture.

Allow the chocolate to cool to room temperature, stirring occasionally.

In a mixing bowl beat the cream cheese (preferably with a flat beater) until smooth and creamy. Gradually beat in the cooled chocolate until smoothly incorporated. Beat in the butter and lemon juice. Use at once or to ensure smoothness rebeat at room temperature before frosting.*

NOTE: My friend Shirley Corriher reports that when using this frosting for a wedding cake in the heat of an Atlanta summer, she tried decreasing the butter to 4 ounces and it held up quite well.

Silk Meringue Praline Buttercream for a 3-Tier Cake

MAKES 13 CUPS

*T*his is one of my very favorite buttercreams. It is smooth and delicious, airy yet stable. It is resistant to warm temperatures and is a dream for piping decorations. Because the buttercream takes on the pale golden color of the praline paste (see the color photograph of the Chocolate Praline Wedding Cake) it is suitable for a wedding cake only when the traditional white look is not required. It goes well with any type of butter cake or *génoise*.

---

* Do not rebeat chilled buttercream until it has reached room temperature or it may curdle.

INGREDIENTS	MEASURE	WEIGHT	
room temperature	*volume*	*pounds/ounces*	*kilograms/grams*
CRÈME ANGLAISE			
sugar	¾ cup	5.25 ounces	150 grams
15 large egg yolks	9 fluid ounces *	9.75 ounces	279 grams
3 large vanilla beans, split lengthwise †	•	•	•
milk	1½ liquid cups	12.75 ounces	363 grams
ITALIAN MERINGUE			
sugar	1 cup + 5 tablespoons	9.25 ounces	262 grams
water	⅓ liquid cup *	2.75 ounces	80 grams
6 large egg whites	¾ liquid cup *	6.25 ounces	180 grams
cream of tartar	¾ teaspoon	•	•
unsalted butter (must be softened), beaten until creamy	6 cups	3 pounds	1 kilogram 360 grams
praline paste	1½ cups	1 pound	454 grams

*Use a glass measuring cup.
†Vanilla bean offers the most delicious flavor, but, if you wish to avoid the little black specks, replace the beans with 1 tablespoon vanilla extract, added to the cooled *crème anglaise*. If using Tahitian beans, use only 1½ beans.

TO MAKE CRÈME ANGLAISE

Have ready near the range a sieve set over a bowl. In a medium, heavy noncorrodible saucepan combine the sugar, yolks, and vanilla bean.

In a small saucepan bring the milk to the boiling point. Add ⅓ cup to the yolk mixture, stirring constantly. Gradually add the remaining milk, stirring, and cook over medium-low heat, stirring constantly, until just before the boiling point. The mixture will start to steam slightly and an accurate thermometer will register 170°F. (The temperature must not exceed 180°F. or the mixture will curdle.)

Immediately pour into the strainer, scraping up any clinging to the pan.

Scrape the small black seeds from the vanilla bean into the custard and cool to room temperature. (To speed the cooling, place the bowl in another bowl or sink partially filled with ice water.) Cover and refrigerate up to 5 days or until ready to complete buttercream.

STORE:
6 hours room temperature, 1 week refrigerated, 8 months frozen. If frozen or refrigerated, be sure to allow the buttercream to come to room temperature before rebeating it or it will break down. The buttercream may look almost soupy when it has reached room temperature, but rebeating will make it as firm as new!

POINTERS FOR SUCCESS:
Crème Anglaise: The temperature must reach at least 160°F. and must not exceed 180°F. or it will curdle.
Italian Meringue: For maximum stability, the syrup must reach 248°F. and not exceed 250°F. as higher temperatures will break

down the whites. The whites must be free of any grease or trace of yolk. Do not overbeat.

Buttercream: Rebeat when it becomes spongy.

TO MAKE ITALIAN MERINGUE

Have ready near the range a 2-cup heatproof glass measure.

In a small heavy saucepan (preferably with a nonstick lining) stir together 1 cup sugar and the water. Heat, stirring constantly, until the sugar dissolves and the syrup is bubbling. Stop stirring and turn down the heat to the lowest setting. (If using an electric range, remove from the heat.)

In a mixing bowl beat the egg whites on low speed until foamy, add the cream of tartar, and beat on high speed until soft peaks form when the beater is raised. Gradually beat in the remaining 5 tablespoons of sugar until stiff peaks form when the beater is raised slowly.

Increase the heat and boil the syrup until a thermometer registers 248°F. to 250°F. (firm-ball stage). Immediately pour into the glass measure to stop the cooking.

With the mixer on high speed, beat the syrup into the whites in a steady stream. Do not allow the syrup to fall on the beaters or the syrup will spin onto the sides of the bowl. Use a rubber scraper to remove the syrup clinging to the glass measure. Beat at low speed until cool. (Italian Meringue keeps for 2 days refrigerated. Rebeat briefly before using.)

TO COMPLETE BUTTERCREAM

In a large mixing bowl (at least 5 quarts) place the butter and beat on medium speed for 30 seconds. Gradually beat in the *crème anglaise* and praline paste until smooth. Add the Italian meringue in 4 batches, beating briefly until just incorporated. If the mixture looks curdled instead of silken smooth, it is too cold. Allow it to sit at room temperature to warm to 70°F. before continuing to beat or place the bowl in a hot water bath very briefly until the buttercream against the sides of the bowl just starts to melt. Remove at once and beat until smooth. This buttercream becomes slightly spongy on standing. Rebeat before using.

NOTE: To make plain Silk Meringue Buttercream, increase the sugar to 1½ cups (10.5 ounces/300 grams) and omit the praline paste. You may also make any of the variations on pages 241 to 243 by using the plain Silk Meringue Buttercream and tripling the optional additions.

A large single-layer round or rectangular cake looks stunning glazed with a dark, shiny Chocolate Cream Glaze. It also is the most delicious of all chocolate glazes. Cognac heightens the flavor, but if a fine-quality chocolate is used the Cognac is optional.

This recipe makes enough to glaze a 12-inch by 2-inch by 1¾-inch cake. For an 18-inch by 12-inch by 2-inch cake, double the recipe.

INGREDIENTS	MEASURE		WEIGHT
	volume	*pounds/ounces*	*kilograms/grams*
bittersweet chocolate	6 (3-ounce) bars	1 pound 2 ounces	510 grams
heavy cream	2 cups	1 pound	464 grams
optional: Cognac	2 tablespoons	1 ounce	28 grams

TO PREPARE CAKE FOR GLAZING

Brush all crumbs from the surface and place on a cardboard round the same size as the cake. Suspend the cake on a rack set on a baking sheet to catch excess glaze.

It is best to have enough glaze to cover the cake with one application as touch-ups don't usually produce as flawless a finish. Excess glaze can be frozen and reheated at a later date.

TO PREPARE GLAZE

In a food processor with the metal blade, break the chocolate into pieces and process until very fine (or finely grate the chocolate). Place in a medium-size heavy saucepan.

Heat the cream to the boiling point and pour three quarters of it over the chocolate. Cover for 5 minutes to allow the chocolate to melt. Gently mix until smooth, trying not to create air bubbles. Pass through a fine strainer, stir in the optional Cognac, and allow to cool just until tepid.

CHECK FOR CONSISTENCY

At a tepid temperature, a small amount of glaze should mound a bit when dropped from a spoon before smoothly disappearing. If the glaze is too thick and the mound remains on the surface or the glaze seems curdled, add some of the warm remaining cream by the teaspoon. If the glaze should happen to be too thin, gently stir in a small amount of melted chocolate.

STORE:
3 days room temperature, 2 weeks refrigerated, 6 months frozen.

POINTERS FOR SUCCESS:
Your favorite semisweet or bittersweet eating chocolate will result in the best chocolate glaze. If the chocolate is not smooth-textured in the bar it will not be smooth in the ganache either.

The butterfat content of cream varies, which will affect the consistency of the glaze. Always check for consistency at a tepid temperature. If it is the correct consistency when tepid, even if it is too cool when applied and lumps, the cake can be placed in a warm oven for a few seconds and glaze will smooth. If glaze had been tested when hot and was the right consistency, but was poured when too cool and lumped, the extra heat would not help. On the other hand, if glaze had been the correct consistency when cool, it would never firm adequately on the cake.

To reheat, use a double boiler, stirring gently, or a microwave on high power, stirring and folding every 7 seconds.

Pistachio Marzipan for a 3-Tier Cake

MAKES
1¼ POUNDS /
567 GRAMS
(enough for 12-inch, 9-inch, and 6-inch discs)

When the consistency is correct, use at once or store and reheat. The glaze should be poured onto the center of the cake, allowing the excess to flow down the sides. Smooth quickly and evenly with a large metal spatula, moving it lightly back and forth across the top until smooth. If any spots on the sides remain unglazed, use a small metal spatula to lift up some glaze which has fallen onto the baking sheet and apply to uncovered area.

Lift rack and tap lightly to settle glaze. Lift cake from rack using a broad spatula or pancake turner and set on a serving plate or on a clean rack if planning to apply a second coat of glaze.

If you want to cover the cake more thickly and evenly, 2 coats can be applied by the following technique: Pour the glaze over cake and smooth quickly with a spatula to create a thin, even coat. Refrigerate for 20 minutes or until firm. Apply a second coat of tepid glaze. (You will need about 1½ times the glaze for a double coat.)

Allow to set for at least 2 hours at room temperature. Refrigerating will dull the glaze slightly.

*P*eople who don't like marzipan usually change their minds when they encounter this pistachio version. I created it as a surprise inside each tier of my brother's wedding cake (page 219).

INGREDIENTS	MEASURE	WEIGHT	
	volume	*pounds/ounces*	*kilograms/grams*
shelled unsalted pistachio nuts	1 cup	5.25 ounces	152 grams
powdered sugar	3 cups (lightly spooned into cup)	12 ounces	340 grams
corn syrup	⅓ liquid cup (use a glass measure)	4 ounces	108 grams
glycerine or unflavored oil	2 teaspoons	•	•
optional: 8 drops green food color	•	•	•

Bake the nuts in a 350°F. oven for 5 to 10 minutes or until the skins separate from the nuts when scratched lightly with a fingernail. Remove as much of the skin as possible.

In food processor process the nuts until a smooth paste is obtained. Add the powdered sugar and process until well mixed. Add the corn syrup and glycerine and process until blended, about 20 seconds. The mixture will appear dry, but a small amount pressed between your fingers should hold together. If it seems too dry, add more corn syrup, ¼ teaspoon at a time. If you wish to deepen the color, add the optional food coloring. Continue processing until the marzipan has a smooth, doughlike consistency. Knead briefly by hand until uniform in color.

The marzipan may be used at once, but is easier to work with if allowed to rest 1 hour. Wrap tightly with plastic wrap and place in an airtight container.

To roll discs, divide the marzipan in half. Roll ½ between 2 sheets of plastic wrap into a thin circle 13 inches in diameter. Peel off the top layer of plastic. Using a lightly greased 12-inch cake pan bottom as a guide, cut out a 12-inch circle with a sharp knife or pizza cutter. Knead the leftover marzipan into the remaining marzipan. Roll this portion between plastic wrap into a thin circle 10 inches in diameter. Using a lightly greased 9-inch cake pan bottom as guide, cut out a 9-inch circle. Knead the leftover marzipan together and again roll it out between plastic wrap into a thin circle 7 inches in diameter. Using a lightly greased 6-inch cake pan, cut out a 6-inch circle.

It is easiest to apply marzipan if it has been frozen for a few minutes to make it less flexible. Place the 12-inch circle, still covered with plastic wrap, on a baking sheet and freeze. The marzipan will adhere to the plastic wrap. Position it over the 12-inch tier of a frosted cake, supporting the marzipan with your palm if necessary, and lay it on the cake. It should not be moved once it is positioned. Peel off the plastic. Repeat with remaining circles.

STORE:
6 months refrigerated, 1 year frozen.

Classic Rolled Fondant for a 3-Tier Cake to Serve 150

MAKES
ABOUT 7½
POUNDS/
3 KILOGRAMS
402 GRAMS
(enough to cover 12-inch, 9-inch, and 6-inch tiers)

The alabaster perfection of rolled fondant makes an exquisite background for decorating a wedding cake. It seals in the freshness of the cake for several days, giving time for the most ethereal and elaborate of piped decorations.

In England, where this fondant originated, it is traditional even for home cooks to wear only white when preparing it, as even a fleck of lint can cause an off color in the pristine white.

These days rolled fondant is used more in Australia than in any other country—no doubt why a cake covered in rolled fondant and decorated with royal icing is often referred to as the fabled Australian method of cake decorating.

INGREDIENTS	MEASURE	WEIGHT	
room temperature	*volume*	*pounds/ounces*	*kilograms/grams*
gelatin	3 tablespoons	1 ounce	28 grams
water *	¾ liquid cup	6.25 ounces	177 grams
glucose †	1½ cups (use a glass measure)	17.5 ounces	504 grams
glycerine	3 tablespoons	2 ounces	54 grams
solid white shortening	¼ cup + 2 tablespoons	2.5 ounces	72 grams
powdered sugar	24 cups (lightly spooned into cup)	6 pounds	2 kilograms 722 grams

STORE:
1 month room temperature. Can be frozen indefinitely.

* For a flavor variation, replace ½ the water with rosewater or orange flower water.
† 1½ cups (17.25 ounces/492 grams) corn syrup will give equal results if you use only ½ cup + 1 tablespoon water instead of ¾ cup.

Sprinkle the gelatin over the water in a 4-cup heatproof measuring cup or bowl and allow it to sit for 5 minutes. Set the cup in a small pan of simmering water and stir until the gelatin is dissolved. (This can also be done in a few seconds in a microwave on high power.) Blend in the glucose and glycerine, then add the shortening and stir until melted. Remove from the heat.

Place sugar in a very large bowl and make a well in

the center. Add the gelatin mixture and stir with a wooden spoon until blended. Mix with lightly greased hands and vigorously knead in the bowl until most of the sugar is incorporated. Turn out onto a smooth lightly greased surface such as Formica or marble and knead until smooth and satiny.

If the fondant seems very dry, add several drops of water and knead well. If it seems too sticky, knead in more powdered sugar. The fondant will resemble a smooth, well-shaped stone. When dropped, it should spread very slightly but retain its shape. It should be malleable like clay, soft but not sticky.

Rolled fondant may be used at once but seems to work much more easily when allowed to rest for several hours. It is important to cover the fondant to prevent drying. Wrap tightly with plastic wrap and place in an airtight container.* It will firm slightly on standing.

When ready to roll out, spray the work surface and rolling pin with nonstick vegetable spray. For covering a cake, see page 360.

TIPS: A 20-quart Hobart with a spade beater can be used to do the initial mixing. Kneading must be done by hand or the texture suffers. For small hands, divide the mixture into two batches. Be sure to keep each batch covered to prevent drying.

FROSTING, TIERING, AND STORING WEDDING CAKES

PREPARING THE CAKE FOR FROSTING

OUTSIDE CRUST: In order to frost a cake evenly and smoothly, it must be as level as possible and have a crumb-free crust. There are two baker's tricks that make this easy to accomplish. The first is to spray Baker's Joy on the cake pans. This combination of flour and oil results in a beautifully sealed crust. The second trick is to wrap the cake pans with Magi-Cake Strips (pages 20 and 456). Together with well-balanced formulas and varying the amount of baking powder for different cake sizes, these tips result in very level cake layers.

If a cake should come out domed, use a serrated knife with a blade longer than the diameter of the cake to level it. Or use a cake leveler or cake saw (page 461).

If the sides are uneven and there seem to be many loose crumbs, a crumb coating such as Jewel Glaze (page 329) or a very thin layer of frosting keeps the crumbs from marring the surface of the frosting.

*If stored fondant seems very stiff, a few seconds in the microwave before kneading will work wonders to make it pliable.

When covering a cake with rolled fondant, it is necessary to bevel the top edge to soften the angle, preventing the fondant from cracking. A small serrated knife is perfect for this.

It is also necessary to apply a thin layer of jelly or frosting to all surfaces of the cake so that the fondant will adhere well. (See piping jell, page 431, or Jewel Glaze, page 329.) A pastry feather or brush works well.

CAKE SERVING BASE: It is usually difficult to find large, perfectly flat cake plates for wedding cakes. A few possible solutions are: ¼-inch-thick plywood covered with florist foil, ¼-inch to ½-inch-thick sandblasted glass (see color photograph), or ⅛-inch Plexiglass or a mirror. All must be custom made. Wooden boards can be painted with gold leaf, but this must be done at least 2 days ahead so that the odors have disappeared before the cake is placed on the base. Cake decorating supply stores also carry decorative silver or gold foil in rolls and large round serving boards covered with foil. Aesthetically, the serving base should be about 3 inches to 5 inches larger in diameter than the bottom tier of the cake.

SUPPORTING THE CAKE

Making a tiered wedding cake is like constructing an edifice out of improbable elements. Certain supports are vital to keep one tier from sinking into another and to prevent the entire cake from collapsing. When making a wedding cake, I often feel like an architect.

BOTTOM SUPPORT: To start with, each tier must be supported by a rigid but lightweight base. Disposable cardboard is the easiest solution.

Corrugated cardboard cake rounds the size of standard cake pans are available at cake-decorating supply stores (page 457) or can be cut from cardboard. I prefer the precut rounds because their edges are smooth, making it easier to use them as a guide for smoothing the frosting on the sides. Those waterproofed with a glassine surface are ideal.

To keep the cake from slipping off the cardboard spread a few dabs of frosting on the cardboard before placing the layer on it.

Frost the cake layers (see page 359 if you need to review frosting techniques) and attach the bottom tier to the serving board before inserting any inner supports. To attach to serving board, use several strips of strong double-sided adhesive tape or make loops of tape (known as Mobius loops) on the serving board.

INTERNAL SUPPORT: To enable the bottom layers to support the weight of additional tiers, wooden dowels are traditionally inserted into each tier to distribute the weight. Wooden dowels are difficult to cut, so one day, as my husband was watching me struggle with wire cutters and shooting stumps of dowels, he came up with the brilliant solution of using plastic non-flexible straws instead. My immediate response was "impossible," but he assured me that plastic can support a great deal of weight and the hollow centers offer more support by displacing less cake. He added that, unlike wood, the plastic would not interface with the surrounding cake, causing an off flavor. I tried a test cake, piling many brass weights on top and, after three days had elapsed, found that this technique really does work. I published the plastic straw technique as part of a wedding cake article for a national food magazine and received one indignant, bordering on outraged, letter insisting that the cake in question would certainly collapse. But since that time I have noticed the straw technique appearing in other books on cake decorating and regret that it couldn't have been patented!

To insert plastic straw supports, first mark an outline on the frosted cake tier where the next tier will go. Use the pan that the layer was baked in as a guide. If the cake was frosted with a soft buttercream invert the pan, center it, and press lightly to leave an imprint (Fig. 1). If the topping is a firm one, such as the Crème Ivoire Deluxe or Rolled Fondant, center the pan and allow the bottom to rest on the buttercream. Use a toothpick to make little holes in the frosting all around the base of pan (Fig. 2).

Insert a plastic straw into the center of the cake until it touches the base and mark the straw with a pencil at the cake surface (Fig. 3). Remove the straw and cut off at the pencil mark. Use this straw as a guide to cut other straw supports the same length.

Insert 1 straw in the center of the cake and the other straws equidistant in a circle just inside the guide marks. A 12-inch layer needs 8 straws and 1 for the center. A 9-inch layer needs 6 straws and 1 for the center. The top tier does not need supports because nothing heavy will be resting on it.

An *inflexible* heavy-duty pancake turner is the best device for lifting and placing the tiers. A small angled spatula helps to support the edge while removing the pancake turner and displaces less frosting. Lift each tier with the pancake turner, using your other hand to support the other side and center it over the tier below, using the outline as your guide. Allow the side of the cake by your hand to touch down and gently lower the other side. Leave enough space so that the pancake turner does not touch any frosting. Gradually slide away the pancake turner (Fig. 1). When you al-

PLACING THE TIERS

most reach the edge, transfer the weight to the small angled spatula and carefully slide it out (Fig. 2).

Pipe a border of buttercream around the base of each tier to seal in the freshness and give the edge a finished appearance.

NOTE: If cake is to be transported a great distance over rough terrain, you can stake the tiers as extra security to keep them from sliding. Sharpen one end of a wooden dowel, 1 inch lower than the height of the finished cake, and using a hammer, drive it through to the bottom. Frost or place ornament on top of cake to hide the small hole.

STORING THE WEDDING CAKE

A cake frosted and decorated with buttercream can be made 1 day ahead and left at cool room temperature (except for cheesecake, which requires refrigeration). If made with butter cake, it will keep refrigerated for 3 days. It is essential that a butter cake be removed from the refrigerator 6 hours before serving or the texture will not be soft and light. If the wedding cake is made with *génoise* it will keep refrigerated for 5 days. Remove from the refrigerator at least two hours ahead to allow the buttercream to soften. A wedding cheesecake must be refrigerated until serving day and keeps for 24 hours refrigerated.

TRANS- PORTING AND SERVING WEDDING CAKES

TRANSPORTING THE WEDDING CAKE

William Greenberg, a famous New York baker, gave me some important advice at the beginning of my cake baking career: "There are only two people trustworthy enough to deliver a wedding cake—the person who baked it and the person who paid for it." As a consequence, I have never had a single disaster befall one of my cakes (except, of course, for my brother's wedding cake, which suffered the fate of a major blizzard and a hungry airline crew).

Usually I have the customer pick up the cake, but if I am going to the wedding I always deliver it personally. At first I would bring a pastry bag filled with icing in case of repair, but as I never once needed it, I abandoned the practice.

The ideal protection for a tiered cake is a corrugated cardboard box just slightly larger than the base. It is also safer for the box to be higher than the top tier so that the top flaps can be taped closed. The rigid sides of the box cannot touch the sides of the cake because the frosted cake sides are smaller than the bottom cake base on which they are resting.

If the weather is cool, the trunk of a car offers the most level area for the cake. A damp terry towel under the cake box helps to keep it from sliding. Try to avoid major bumps in the road when driving.

Wedding cake portions are traditionally small because they usually are served after a large dinner that often includes other desserts. The size of the serving is either a square 2 inches high by 2 inches deep and 1⅝ inches wide (the tier divided into 2 layers) or a slim rectangle 4 inches high by 2 inches deep by ¾ inch wide (the full height of the tier).

After the bride cuts the traditional first slice from the bottom tier, the top tier is removed if she is planning to save it for her first anniversary. This is a tradition that probably started when wedding cakes were made of fruitcake and could survive one year in the freezer. Treating butter cake or *génoise* in this manner is a tradition that I heartily hope will be forgotten. (Let's not even discuss the tradition of the bride's sleeping with a piece of the cake under her pillow!)

The most practical way to cut 8-inch or larger tiers of wedding cake is in concentric circles until the small 4-inch to 6-inch center round remains. That should be cut into narrow wedges. It is easiest to start with the top tier and remove each tier before cutting, but it is also possible to cut each tier while it is still resting on the tier below.

Bibliography

BOOKS

Alikonis, Justin J. *Candy Technology*. Westport, Conn.: AVI Publishing Company, Inc., 1979.

Amendola, Joseph. *The Bakers' Manual*. Rochelle Park, N.J.: Hayden Book Company, 1972.

————, Donald E. Lundberg. *Understanding Baking*. Boston: CBI Publishing Company, Inc., 1970.

Charley, Helen. *Food Science*. 2nd ed. New York: John Wiley & Sons, 1982.

Child, Julia, Louisette Bertholle, and Simone Beck. *Mastering the Art of French Cooking*. New York: Alfred A. Knopf, 1961.

Cook, Russell, L. *Chocolate Production and Use*. New York: Harcourt Brace Jovanovich, Inc., 1982.

Clifton, Claire. *Edible Flowers*. New York: McGraw-Hill Book Company, 1984.

Frohne, Dietrich, and Hans Jurgen Pfänder. *A Color Atlas of Poisonous Plants*. London: Wolfe Publishing Company, 1983.

Griswold, Ruth M. *The Experimental Study of Foods*. Boston: Houghton Mifflin Company, 1962.

Handbook of Food Preparation. Washington, D.C.: The American Home Economics Association, 1975.

Hanle, Zack, and Donald Hendricks. *Cooking with Flowers*. Los Angeles: Price/Stern/Sloan Publishers, Inc., 1971.

Healy, Bruce, and Paul Bugat. *Mastering the Art of French Pastry*. New York: Barrons, 1984.

Heatter, Maida. *Maida Heatter's Book of Great Desserts*. New York: Alfred A. Knopf, 1974.

Kraus, Barbara. *The Dictionary of Sodium, Fats, and Cholesterol*. New York: Grosset & Dunlap, 1976.

Lang, Jennifer Harvey. *Tastings*. New York: Crown Publishers, Inc., 1986.

Lees, R., and E. B. Jackson. *Sugar Confectionery and Chocolate Manufacture*. New York: Chemical Publishing Co., Inc., 1975. New York: Grosset & Dunlap, 1974.

Mattle, Von Josef. *Praline Passe-Partout*. Zürich: Schweizerischer Bäckerei-und Konditorei-Personal-Verband, 1980.

McGee, Harold. *On Food and Cooking*. New York: Charles Scribner's Sons, 1984.

Minifie, Bernard W. *Chocolate, Cocoa and Confectionery: Science and Technology Second Edition*. Westport, Conn.: AVI Publishing Company, Inc., 1980.

Montagné, Prosper. *The New Larousse Gastronomique*. New York: Crown Publishers, Inc., 1977.

The New International Confectioner. London: Virtue & Company Limited, 1981.

Paul, Pauline C., and Helen H. Palmer. *Food Theory and Applications*. New York: John Wiley & Sons, 1972.

Peckham, Gladys C. *Foundations of Food Preparation*. 2nd ed. London: The Macmillan Company, 1969.

Sultan, William J. *Practical Baking*. Westport, Conn.: AVI Publishing Company, 1976.

Thuries, Yves. *Le Livre de Recettes d'un Compagnon du Tour de France: Pâtisserie Francaise*. Paris: Société Editar, 81170 Cordes-Sur-Ciel, 1980.

Watt, Bernice K., and Annabel L. Merrill. *Composition of Foods*. Agriculture Handbook No 8. Agricultural Research Service, United States Department of Agriculture. Revised December 1963. Approved for reprinting October 1975.

The Wilton Way of Cake Decorating. Vol. I. Woodridge, Ill.: Wilton Enterprises, Inc., 1974.

Wirz-Fischer, Johann-Heinrich. *Manual Illustré Suisse de la Confiserie-pâtisserie*. Switzerland: Herausgeber, 1963.

Witty, Helen, and Elizabeth Schneider Colchie. *Better Than Store-Bought*. New York: Harper & Row, 1979.

ARTICLES

Ash, David J., and John C. Colmey. "The Role of pH in Cake Baking." *The Bakers Digest,* February 1973, pp. 36–42, 68.

Carlin, George T. "A Microscopic Study of the Behavior of Fats in Cake Batters." *Cereal Chemistry,* Vol. 21 (May 1944), pp. 189–199.

Handleman, Avrom R., James F. Conn, and John W. Lyons. "Bubble Mechanics in Thick Foams and Their Effects on Cake Quality." *Cereal Chemistry,* Vol. 38 (May 1961), pp. 294–305.

Howard, N. B., D. H. Hughes, and R.G.K. Strobel. "Function of the Starch Granule in the Formation of Layer Cake Structure." *Cereal Chemistry,* Vol. 45 (July 1968), pp. 329–338.

Miller, Byron S., and Henry B. Trimbo. "Gelatinization of Starch and White Layer Cake Quality." *Food Technology,* April 1965, pp. 208–216.

Miller, L. L., and C. Setser. "Xanthan Gum in a Reduced-Egg-White Angel Food Cake." *Cereal Chemistry,* Vol. 60, No. 1 (1983), pp. 62–64.

Mizukoshi, M. "Model Studies of Cake Baking. III. Effects of Silicone on Foam Stability of Cake Batter." *Cereal Chemistry,* Vol. 60, No. 5 (1983), pp. 396–402.

Seguchi, M. "Oil-Binding Capacity of Prime Starch from Chlorinated Wheat Flour." *Cereal Chemistry,* Vol. 61, No. 3 (1984), pp. 241–247.

Thompson, S. W., and J. E. Gannon. "Observations on the Influence of Texturation, Occluded Gas Content, and Emulsifier Content on Shortening Performance in Cake Making." *Cereal Chemistry,* Vol. 33 (May 1956), pp. 181–189.

Wilson, J. T., and D. H. Donelson. "Studies on the Dynamics of Cake-Baking." *Cereal Chemistry,* Vol. 40 (Sept. 1963), pp. 466–481.

Wolfert, Paula. "Brioche and Its Many Uses: A New Approach." *The Pleasures of Cooking,* Vol. II, No. 4 (1979), pp. 2–13.

Wootton, J. C., N. B. Howard, J. B. Martin, D. E. McOsker, and J. Holme, "The Role of Emulsifiers in the Incorporation of Air into Layer Cake Batter Systems. *Cereal Chemistry,* Vol. 44 (May 1967), pp. 333–343.

Index

When a recipe has more than one reference, the first page number, in **boldface,** refers to the recipe itself; page numbers which follow refer to other recipes in which the main recipe is used.

chocolate cream glaze, **271–272**, 44–46, 52–53, 198–199

dark chocolate filling, frosting, and sauce, **269–270**, 179–180, 196, 197

light whipped filling and frosting, **268–269**, 136–137, 138–141, 144, 181–183, 195, 201–202

praline, 270

quick light whipped, 268–269

raspberry, **276**, 199–201

sour cream, **275**, 35–36, 37–38, 69–70

white, **278**, 84–87

gel, piping, 431

cocoa, 389

gelatin, 429, 442

génoise, 118, 119–137

biscuit vs., 477

bittersweet cocoa almond, 134–135

chestnut, **122–124**, 189–190

au chocolat, **129–131**, 184

base formula for, 504

master chart for, 503

mixing batter for all sizes of, 500–501

3-tier wedding cake to serve 150, 499–501

classique, **120–122**, 166–167, 169–170, 179–180, 264

base formula for, 504

master chart for, 502–503

mixing batter for all sizes of, 498

3-tier wedding cake to serve 150, 497–498

golden, **125–126**, 172–173

highlights for successful, 119

Jeffrey, fudgy, 136–137

moist chocolate, **132–133**, 190–192, 201–202

nut-flavored chocolate, 131

riche, 122

syruping, 357

understanding, 476–478

unmolding, 22

wedding cakes, 496–504

white, **127–128**, 202–204

ginger biscuit, 144

glass cake domes, 461

glassine:

cardboard rounds, 457

doilies, 458

glaze, glazing:

chocolate butter, 273–274

chocolate cream, **271–272**, 44–46, 52–53, 192, 198–199

for large cakes, 529–530

chocolate walnut drizzle, **249–250**, 71–72, 158–160

cran-raspberry, **330**, 81–84

crème ivoire, **248–249**, 48–49, 50–51, 84–87

crème ivoire deluxe, **246–247**, 48–49, 50–51, 84–87, 167

jewel, **329–330**, 81–87, 175–177, 217–219

shiny apricot, 178

shiny jewel, **330**, 175–177

webbing with, 389–390

glucose, 433, 440

substituting for, in recipes, 443

glycerine, 429, 442

gold dust, caramel, **313–314**, 172–173

golden:

almond cake, 37–38

butter cream cake, **34–35**, 207–209, 264

cage, 172–173

génoise, **125–126**, 172–173

glory wedding cheesecake, 217–219

Grand Marnier cake, 44–46

luxury butter cake, 48–49

wheat carrot ring, 75–76

gold leaf, 429

on royal icing letters, 412

Grand Marnier:

cake, golden, 44–46

crêpes Suzette, 112–113

strawberry Maria, 184

grating chocolate, 380

greasing and flouring pans, 20–21

green tea, 429

biscuit, 144

marzipan, **321**, 261

mousse cream, **261**, 144

griddles, 59

guilt-free chocolate chiffon cake, 158–160

half and half, 427, 440

hand-modeled and cutout decorations, 363–373

barquettes and cutouts, nougatine, 368–369

bees, marzipan, **367–368**, 185–186

butterflies, 362

calla lilies, rolled fondant, **366–367**, 204–206

charlotte shapes, 369–374

curved flowers, 363–364

ivy leaves, pistachio marzipan, **363**, 197

pinwheels, 369

ribbon, 363

roses, marzipan, **364–365**, 222–224

stems and leaves, marzipan, **363**, 216–217

hazelnut(s):

caramel for praline powder and chocolate praline, 315

chocolate indulgence, 86

dacquoise, **302–303**, 166–167, 262–263

paste, 430–431, 441

removing skin on, 429–430

weighing, 441

see also praline

heart(s):

meringue or dacquoise, 375–376

-shaped electric waffle irons, 459

high altitude adjustments, 21–22

holiday hallelujah streusel brioche, **94–97**, 98–100

honey:

buttercream, royal, **235**, 34–35, 185–186

nougatine crunch, **319**, 185–186

queen bee, 185–186

weighing, 440

hot fudge, **88**, 87

hot trays, 459

hot-water baths (bains marie), 460

ice cream:

fire and ice, 286

pineapple, **286**, 168–169

roll, Black Forest, 193–194

torte, Black Forest, 192–193

vanilla, **285–286**, 87, 116–118, 192–194

ice-water baths, 460

icing:

royal, **294–296**, 202–206, 207–209, 214–216, 222–224

calligraphy, 411–412

chocolate, 296

flowers, painted, 414–415

rose lattice panels, 413–415

see also buttercream frostings and fillings; piped icing decorations

immersion blenders, 457

ingredients, 419–445

angelique, 424

arrowroot, 424–425

Baker's Joy, 419–420

baking powder, 420, 442, 473

in tiered cakes, 494–496

baking soda, 420, 442, 473

beeswax, 420

butter, 425, 472

beurre noisette, 426, 439

clarified, 426, 439

greasing pan with, 20

making, 425–426

mixing batter and, 474–475

substituting type of, in recipes, 443

weighing, 439

buttermilk, 473

leavening and, 473

replacing, in recipes, 442

weighing, 440

candied fruit, 424

chestnut(s), 420

ABOUT THE AUTHOR

*R*ose Levy Beranbaum has her B.S. and M.A. in food science and culinary arts. In addition to continuing her studies at many of the world's leading cooking schools, she has also studied art and design at the Fashion Institute of Technology in New York City.

Rose is a member of many professional food organizations such as Les Dames d'Escoffier and the International Association of Cooking Professionals, where she has received accreditation as a food writer and teacher.

Rose is a frequent contributor to all the major food magazines and *The New York Times*. She is also consultant to the baking and chocolate industries.

For ten years Rose was owner and director of the Cordon Rose Cooking School in New York City.

Both Rose and her husband, Elliott, work in New York City.